SOFTWARE AND HARDWARE ENGINEERING
MOTOROLA M68HC12

Fredrick M. Cady

Department of Electrical and Computer Engineering

Montana State University

James M. Sibigtroth

Transportation Systems Group

Motorola, Inc.

New York   Oxford

OXFORD UNIVERSITY PRESS

2000

Oxford University Press

Oxford   New York
Athens   Auckland   Bangkok   Bogotá   Buenos Aires   Calcutta
Cape Town   Chennai   Dar es Salaam   Delhi   Florence   Hong Kong   Istanbul
Karachi   Kuala Lumpur   Madrid   Melbourne   Mexico City   Mumbai
Nairobi   Paris   São Paulo   Singapore   Taipei   Tokyo   Toronto   Warsaw

and associated companies in
Berlin   Ibadan

Published by Oxford University Press, Inc.,
198 Madison Avenue, New York, New York, 10016
http://www.oup-usa.org

Oxford is a registered trademark of Oxford University Press

Library of Congress Cataloging-in-Publication Data

Cady, Fredrick M., 1942-
    Software and hardware engineering. Motorola M68HC12 / Fredrick
M. Cady, James M. Sibigtroth.
      p.   cm.
    Includes bibliographical references.
    ISBN 0-19-512469-3 (pbk.)
    1. Software engineering.   2. Computer engineering.   3. Programmable
controllers.   I. Sibigtroth, James M.   II. Title.
    QA76.758 .C32 2000
    005.1—dc21
                                                    99-35430
                                                    CIP

Printing (last digit): 9 8 7

Printed in the United States of America
on acid-free paper

This textbook is Y2K compliant.

CONTENTS

Chapter 3   An Assembler Program   *27*

Chapter 4   The M68HC12 Instruction Set   *51*

Chapter 5   D-Bug12 Monitor and Debugger   *109*

Chapter 6   Programs for the M68HC12   *135*

Chapter 7   M68HC12 Parallel I/O   *163*

Chapter 8   M68HC12 Interrupts   *188*

Chapter *9*   M68HC12 Memories   *225*

Chapter 10   M68HC12 Timer   *291*

Chapter *11*   M68HC12 Serial I/O   *353*

Chapter *12*   M68HC12 Analog Input   *399*

Chapter 13 Fuzzy Logic   *421*

Chapter 14 Debugging Systems   *451*

Chapter 15   Advanced M68HC12 Hardware   *506*

PREFACE

Software and Hardware Engineering: Motorola M68HC12, together with *Microcontrollers and Microcomputers: Principles of Software and Hardware Engineering*, is designed to give the student a fundamental understanding of microcontroller-based systems. The material is aimed at the sophomore, junior, or senior level electrical engineering, electrical engineering technology, computer engineering, or computer science student taking a first course in microcomputers. Prerequisites are a digital logic course and a first course in a programming language.

This text is a successor to *Software and Hardware Engineering: Motorola M68HC11* and, like that text, its overall objective is to provide an introduction to the architecture and design of hardware and software for the Motorola M68HC12. Although *Software and Hardware Engineering: Motorola M68HC12* is designed to accompany a text explaining the general principles of software and hardware engineering, it can stand alone as a reference for M68HC12 users. It gives many programming and hardware interfacing examples that will enable students to become accomplished software and hardware designers. Of course, no one should expect to become an expert in using the M68HC12 in a single course.

The following study plan, summarized in Table I, will help the reader become familiar with the principles of microcomputer systems and to learn about the M68HC12 microcontroller as an example. A well-designed course should have the student learn general design principles illustrated by examples of a specific processor. Table I shows how this text could be combined with *Microcontrollers and Microcomputers: Principles of Hardware and Software Engineering* to give the student fundamental knowledge that can be used when applying other processors later in a successful engineering career.

Two major members of M68HC12 family, the MC68HC812A4 and the MC68HC912B32, are described in detail. We also compare features of the M68HC12 with the M68HC11 for those students and engineers familiar with that microcontroller.

In addition to covering the features common to all members of the M68HC12 family of microcontrollers, advanced features are discussed. These include the memory expansion capabilities of the MC68HC812A4 in Chapter 9 and the pulse-width modulator of the MC68HC912B32 in Chapter 10. The enhanced Serial Communications Interface (SCI) and Serial Peripheral Interface (SPI) are discussed in Chapter 11 and the analog-to-digital converter in Chapter 12. The fuzzy logic instruction set is covered in Chapter 13 with an example program showing a general-purpose inference engine. Chapter 14 describes the Background Debug™ module and other debugging features of the M68HC12 family. Chapter 15 describes advanced architectures of the M68HC12.

	TABLE I Study Plan	
Study Goals	**Microcontrollers and Microcomputers: Principles of Hardware and Software Engineering**	**Software and Hardware Engineering: Motorola M68HC12**
Overview	Chapter 1. Introduction	Chapter 1. Introduction
Learn about the architecture of stored program computer	Chapter 2. The Picoprocessor: An Introduction to Computer Architecture	
Learn about different registers in a CPU and how the codes used for various information affect how we interpret the Condition Code Register	Chapter 3. Introduction to the CPU: Registers and Condition Codes	Chapter 2. Introduction to the M68HC12 Hardware
Learn about the various ways a CPU can address memory	Chapter 4. Addressing Modes	
Learn how an assembler works and some of the techniques of programming in assembly language; learn how to operate your laboratory assembler	Chapter 5. Assembly Language Programming and Debugging	Chapter 3. An Assembler Program
See how instructions can be grouped into categories that help make your beginning programming tasks easier; become familiar with the instruction set		Chapter 4. The M68HC12 Instruction Set
Learn how to debug assembly language programs		Chapter 5. D-Bug12 Monitor and Debugger
Learn how to properly design more complex software	Chapter 6. Top Down Software Design	
Develop an effective assembly language programming style		Chapter 6. Programs for the M68HC12
Learn about parallel data transfer, timing, addressing, and I/O interfaces	Chapter 7. Computer Buses and Parallel Input/Output	Chapter 7. M68HC12 Parallel I/O
Learn about interrupts and interrupt service routines	Chapter 8. Interrupts and Real-Time Events	Chapter 8. M68HC12 Interrupts
Learn about the different types of memory and how the organization of the memory is affected by the type of computer system being designed	Chapter 9. Computer Memories	Chapter 9. M68HC12 Memories
Learn about the timer in the M68HC12		Chapter 10. M68HC12 Timer
Become familiar with the elements of serial I/O; learn how to deal with the problems of serial interfacing	Chapter 10. Serial Input/Output	Chapter 11. M68HC12 Serial I/O
Learn how various A/D and D/A devices work and how to specify either in a system	Chapter 11. Analog Input and Output	Chapter 12. M68HC12 Analog Input

	TABLE I (continued)	
Study Goals	**Microcontrollers and Microcomputers: Principles of Hardware and Software Engineering**	**Software and Hardware Engineering: Motorola M68HC12**
Learn how a fuzzy logic inference engine works by studying the fuzzy logic instruction set		Chapter 13. Fuzzy Logic
Learn more advanced debugging techniques using background debugging		Chapter 14. Debugging Systems

Chapter 1

Introduction

1.1 Introduction

This text gives specific information and examples for the Motorola M68HC12 microcontroller. Our goal is not simply to repeat the information that is in Motorola's *68HC12 CPU12 Reference Manual* or the *Technical Summaries* for any of the various versions of the M68HC12. Instead, we want to give you the extra information needed to become proficient at using the M68HC12 by providing examples that explain the many details found in the *Reference Manual* and *Technical Summaries*. Although the M68HC12 is based on the M68HC11, you do not need to know and understand the M68HC11 to use this book. However, those already familiar with the M68HC11 can easily see the differences between the two microcontrollers in tables we include in the following material. With this information you can quickly upgrade your knowledge of the M68HC11 to the M68HC12. If you have not studied the general principles of microcomputer software and hardware design, you may want purchase a copy of *Microcontrollers and Microcomputers: Principles of Software and Hardware Engineering*, also published by Oxford University Press.

1.2 Computers, Microprocessors, Microcomputers, Microcontrollers

A computer system is shown in Figure 1–1. We see a *CPU* or *central processor unit, memory,* containing the program and data, an *I/O interface* with associated *input and output devices,* and three *buses* connecting the elements of the system together. The organization of the program and data into a single memory block is called a *von Neumann* architecture, after John von Neumann who described this general-purpose, stored-program computer in 1945. This is a classical computer system block diagram, and the M68HC12 has this basic architecture.

Until the Intel Corporation introduced the first microprocessor, the 4004, in 1971, the CPU was constructed of many components. Indeed, in 1958 the Air Force SAGE computer required 40,000 ft², 3 MW of power, and had 30,000 tubes with a 4K×32-bit word magnetic core memory.[1] The Digital Equipment Company's PDP-8 was the first mass-produced minicomputer and appeared in 1964. This was the start of a trend toward

> A *microcomputer* is a microprocessor with added memory and I/O.

---

[1] *The History of Electronic Computing*, Association for Computing Machinery.

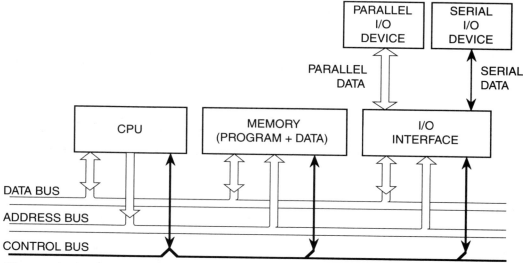

Figure 1−1   Basic computer system.

less expensive, smaller computers suitable for use in nontraditional, non-data-processing applications. Intel's great contribution was to integrate the functions of the many element CPU into one (or at most a few) integrated circuits. The term *microprocessor* first came into use at Intel in 1972[2] and, generally, refers to the implementation of the central processor unit functions of a computer in a single, large-scale integrated (LSI) circuit. A *microcomputer*, then, is a computer built using a microprocessor and a few other components for the memory and I/O. The Intel 4004 allowed a four-chip microcomputer consisting of a CPU, a read-only memory (ROM) for program, read/write (random-access) memory (RAM) for data, and a shift register chip for output expansion.

The Intel 4004 was a four-bit microprocessor and led the way to the development of the 8008, the first 8-bit microprocessor, introduced in 1972. This processor had 45 instructions, a 30-μsec average instruction time, and could address 16 Kbytes of memory. Today, of course, we have advanced far beyond these first microcomputers.

The M68HC12 is primarily used in applications where the system is dedicated to performing a single task or a single group of tasks. Examples of dedicated applications are found almost everywhere in products such as microwave ovens, toasters, and automobiles. These are often *control* applications and make use of microcontrollers. A *microcontroller* is a microcomputer with its memory and I/O integrated into a single chip. The number of microcontrollers used in products is mind-boggling. In 1991, over 750 million 8-bit microcontrollers were delivered by the chip manufacturers[3] and by 1997 Motorola had delivered over two billion M6805 microcontrollers.

> A *microcontroller* is a computer with *CPU, memory,* and *I/O* in one integrated circuit chip.

---

[2]   Noyce, R. N., and M. E. Hoff, Jr., *A History of Microprocessor Development at Intel,* IEEE MICRO, February 1981.
[3]   *EDN,* January 21, 1993.

1.3 Some Basic Definitions

Throughout this text we use the following digital logic terminology:

Logic High: The higher of the two voltages defining logic true and logic false. The value of a logic high depends on the logic family. For example, in the TTL family, logic high (at the input of a gate) is signified by a voltage greater than 2.0 V. This voltage is known as V_{IHMIN}.

Logic Low: The lower of the two voltages defining logic true and false. In TTL, a logic low (at the input of a gate, V_{ILMAX}) is signified by a voltage less than 0.8 V.

Tristate™ or Three-State: A logic signal that can neither source nor sink current. It presents a high impedance load to any other logic device to which it is connected.

Assert: Logic signals, particularly signals that control a part of the system, are *asserted* when the control, or action named by the signal, is being done. A signal may be low or high when it is asserted. For example, the signal WRITE means that it is asserted when the signal is logic high.

Active Low: This term defines a signal whose assertion level is logic low. For example, the signal $\overline{READ}$ is asserted low and is stated "read-bar."

Active High: Used to define a signal whose assertion level is logic high.

Mixed Polarity Notation: The notation used by most manufacturers of microcomputer components defines a signal by using a name, such as WRITE, to indicate an *action*, and a polarity indicator to show the *assertion level* for the signal. It is common practice to use the complement "bar" for active low signals and the lack of the complement for active high. Thus, the signal WRITE indicates that the CPU is doing a write operation when the signal is high. $\overline{READ}$ denotes a read operation is going on when the signal is low.

CPU: Central processor unit. The CPU contains the logic hardware to execute all instructions.

MCU: Microcontroller unit. A microcontroller is a CPU with memory and I/O devices all on one integrated circuit chip.

1.4 Notation

Throughout this text, the following notation is used:

- Hexadecimal numbers are denoted by a leading $; e.g., $FFFF is the hexadecimal number FFFF. When two memory locations are to be identified, the starting and ending addresses are given as $FFFE:FFFF.

- A # indicates immediate addressing mode. Be *very* careful about this because it is *very* easy to forget this symbol when writing assembly language programs.

1.5 Bibliography and Further Reading

Motorola provides a reference manual for the 68HC12[1] commonly called the "purple book," and each variation of the basic CPU12 processor, for example the MC68HC812A4, has its own technical summary.[2,3] A CD-ROM with many of the technical specifications and documents is available from Motorola.

1.6 References

1. *68HC12 CPU12 Reference Manual,* Motorola, 1996.
2. *MC68HC812A4 Technical Summary,* MC68HC812A4TS/D, Motorola, 1996.
3. *MC68HC912B32 Technical Summary,* MC68HC912B32TS/D, Motorola, 1997.

Chapter 2

Introduction to the M68HC12 Hardware

OBJECTIVES

This chapter introduces the register resources of the M68HC12 CPU, including the condition code register, and its addressing modes, and we specify where the M68HC12 differs from the M68HC11. We also briefly describe the differences between two version of the M68HC12, the MC68HC812A4 and MC68HC912B32. Our goal is to have you understand enough about the system to be able to start programming exercises. More advanced features of the CPU will be tackled after you have started programming.

2.1 Chapter Prestudy Material

Before starting this chapter, you should be introduced to the basic architecture of a stored program computer. You should understand how registers, especially the condition code register, are used in the M68HC12. You will need to know addressing terminology and memory addressing modes used by the M68HC12.[1]

2.2 Introduction

The stored program computer shown in Figure 1–1 serves as a model for the basic operation and architecture of the Motorola M68HC12 microcontroller. The M68HC12 is a high-density complementary metal-oxide semiconductor (HCMOS) integrated circuit,[2] which contains the CPU with its registers and ALU, memory (RAM, EEPROM, and Flash), a powerful timer section, and a variety of input and output features.

Figure 2–1 shows the block diagram of the MC68HC812A4 single-chip microcontroller. When you first learn about a new microcontroller, look at its block diagram. Our first overview of the M68HC12 shows many (more than the M68HC11) I/O ports. We will have to learn more about

---

[1] Chapters 2, 3, and 4 in *Microcontrollers and Microcomputers: Principles of Software and Hardware Engineering* cover this material.

[2] This is the HC in the part designator 68HC12.

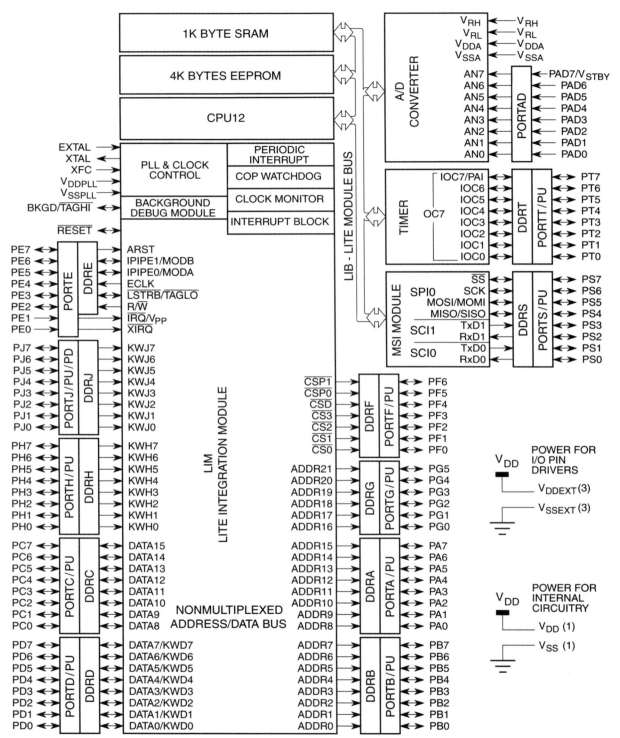

Figure 2-1 MC68HC812A4 block diagram.

the details of these, but at this point it is important to see, in general, what features may be available. Starting in the upper right corner, we see an A/D converter block. There are eight input channels, accessed by Port AD7-AD0. We will see in Chapter 12 that these can be digital as well as analog inputs, and we will learn that it is an 8-bit A/D. The next block, labeled *TIM*, is the timer I/O port. It has eight channels, each of which can be selected to provide the *input capture* or *output compare* functions. These pins can also be general purpose, bidirectional, digital I/O. Chapter 10 will cover the timer functions. Next is Port S, the serial I/O port. There are two, asynchronous serial ports (SCIs) and one serial peripheral interface (SPI). When not in use as serial I/O functions, any of these port bits can be digital input or output pins. Chapter 11 discusses the serial I/O of the M68HC12. Continuing down the right side, Port F can be a general-purpose 7-bit I/O port, or any of these bits can be used as programmable chip select pins for expanded memory or I/O. Ports G, A, B, C, and D are used either as general-purpose I/O in single-chip mode or for address and data buses in expanded modes. These modes are described more fully in Chapter 7. Ports H and J can be general-purpose I/O pins or *key wakeup* pins. Each of these can generate an interrupt and are useful for interrupt driven I/O. The M68HC12 interrupt capabilities are discussed in Chapter 8. Port E can be general-purpose I/O and is also used for special control signals in expanded mode operation and for interrupts.

The top left side of Figure 2–1 shows that the M68HC12 has 1 Kbytes of static RAM (up from 256 bytes in the M68HC11) and 4 Kbytes of EEPROM (up from 512 bytes in the M68HC11). It also has a single-wire background debug module that will prove to be extremely useful for debugging products using the M68HC12. The operation of this feature will be covered in Chapter 14.

Two Versions of the M68HC12

Motorola makes different versions of its microcontrollers with different features in each, and we will concentrate on two of them. The block diagram of the MC68HC912B32 is shown in Figure 2–2. It has some differences in its I/O capabilities when compared to the MC68HC812A4, but its main distinguishing feature is that it has 32 Kbytes of FLASH EEPROM program memory on the chip. This makes it ideal for single-chip applications. On the other hand, the MC68HC812A4 is more suited to applications needing more memory because it can address over 5 Mbytes for both program and data storage. Table 2–1 summarizes the major differences between these M68HC12s; the details will be given in following chapters.

TABLE 2–1 MC68HC812A4 and MC68HC912B32 Differences		
	MC68HC812A4	**MC68HC912B32**
Serial I/O	Two asynchronous serial ports (SCIs), one synchronous serial port (SPI)	One asynchronous serial port (SCI), one synchronous serial port (SPI), one SAE J1850 byte data link controller (BDLC)
Pulse width modulator	None	Four 8-bit channels
External address and data busses	Nonmultiplexed 8- or 16-bit data, 16-bit address	Multiplexed 8- or 16-bit data, 16-bit address
Memory expansion	Up to 5 Mbytes	None
Single-chip vs expanded mode	Most applicable for expanded memory applications	Ideal for single-chip applications
On-chip memory	1 Kbyte RAM, 4 Kbytes EEPROM	1 Kbyte RAM, 768 bytes EEPROM, 32 Kbytes FLASH EEPROM

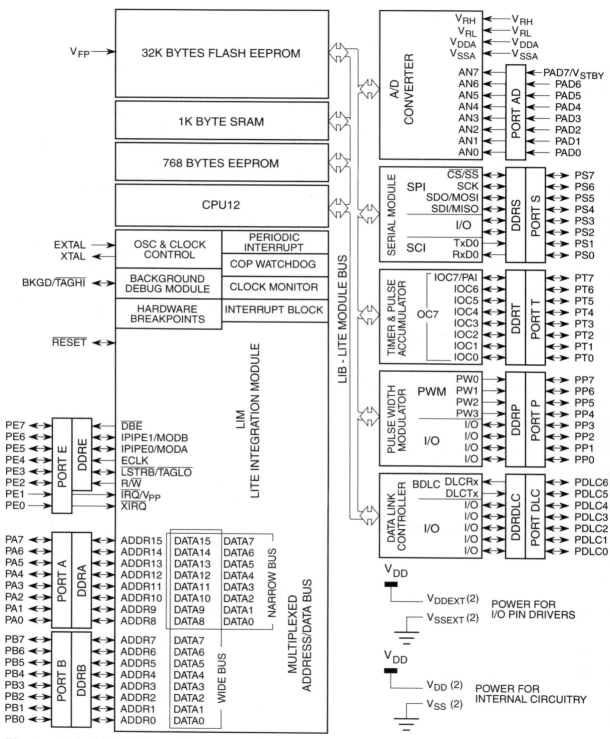

Figure 2-2 MC68HC912B32 block diagram.

2.3 The CPU, Registers and Operating Modes

M68HC12 and M68HC11 Architecture Summary	
M68HC12	**M68HC11**
True 16-bit architecture with the ability to work with the mostly 8-bit M68HC11 instruction set	8-bit architecture
16-bit data and address buses	8-bit data and 16-bit address buses
The M68HC12 includes additional ports and is able to address external memory with nonmultiplexed, 16-bit address and data buses in *expanded-wide* mode or a nonmultiplexed, 8-bit data bus in *expanded-narrow* mode for less expensive external memory systems	Has single-chip and expanded modes of operation; uses a multiplexed address/ data bus for expanded mode operation

The M68HC12 can operate in a number of modes depending on the size of the system to be built.

The M68HC12 is a 16-bit microcontroller. It has 16-bit data and address buses allowing a memory space of 64 Kbytes. A built-in memory management system, which will be discussed in Chapter 9, allows the MC68HC812A4 to address more than 5 Mbytes of memory. Depending on the size of the system to be built, one may choose a M68HC12 operation mode with an 8-bit data bus that can thus use a low-cost, 8-bit memory.

The Programmer's CPU Model

M68HC12 and M68HC11 Programmer's Model
The M68HC12 programmer's model (the register set) is identical to the M68HC11

The *programmer's model* includes two 8-bit accumulators, two 16-bit index registers, a 16-bit stack pointer, and a condition code register.

The programmer's model of the CPU, i.e., the set of registers that may be manipulated using the instruction set, is shown in Figure 2–3.

Accumulators A, B, and D: There are two 8-bit accumulators, *A* and *B*. Each may be a source or destination operand for 8-bit instructions. Some instructions have 16-bit operands and treat the two 8-bit accumulators as a single, 16-bit accumulator, with A being the most significant byte. When used in these instructions, the concatenation of A and B is called accumulator *D*. D is not a register in addition to A and B. Instructions that modify D also modify A and B.

Index Registers X and Y: The two 16-bit index registers are used primarily for indexed addressing, although there are some arithmetic instructions involving the index registers.

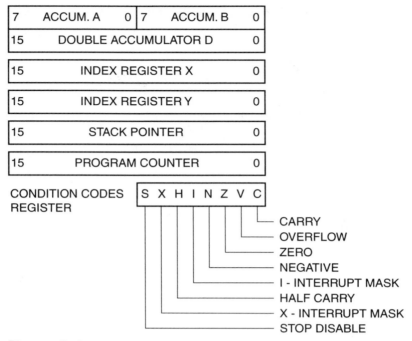

Figure 2-3   Programmer's model.

Stack Pointer: The stack pointer maintains a program stack in RAM and must be initialized to point to RAM before use. The stack pointer always points to the last used memory location for a push operation.[3] It is automatically decremented when pushing data onto the stack and incremented when data are removed.

Program Counter: Although the program counter is usually shown in the programmer's model, the programmer does not have direct control over it like the other registers. Its size is usually given to show the amount of memory that can be directly addressed. In the M68HC12 the PC can be used as the base register for certain indexed addressing modes.

Condition Code Register: The M68HC12 has 4 bits that are set or reset during arithmetic or other operations. These are the *carry* (C), *two's-complement overflow* (V), *zero* (Z), and sign or *negative* (N) bits. A fifth bit, the *half-carry* (H), is set if there is a carry out of bit 3 in an arithmetic operation. There are no conditional branching instructions that test this bit, but it is used by the Decimal Adjust for Addition (DAA) instruction. Figure 2-3 and Table 2-2 show other bits to control the M68HC12. The I bit (Interrupt Request Mask) may be used to globally mask and unmask the interrupt features of the processor. Bit 6, the X bit, is a mask bit for the $\overline{\text{XIRO}}$ interrupt input. These bits are described in more detail in Chapter 8. Finally, bit 7, the S or STOP disable bit, allows or disallows the STOP in-

> The M68HC12 has *carry, two's complement overflow, zero,* and *sign* condition code register bits.

---

[3] In comparison, the stack pointer in the M68HC11 points to the next available memory byte location.

TABLE 2–2 M68HC12 Condition Code Register Bits

Bits Modified by Various Instructions

Bit	Flag	Conditions for Setting
0	C	If a carry or borrow occurs
1	V	If two's-complement overflow occurs
2	Z	If the result is zero
3	N	If the most significant bit of the result is set
5	H	This is the half-carry bit and is set if a carry or borrow out of bit 3 of the result occurs

Bits Associated with M68HC12 Control

Bit	Flag	Use
4	I	Interrupt mask
6	X	X interrupt mask
7	S	Stop disable

struction. The STOP instruction is important in applications in which low-power consumption is a design goal. We will talk more about this instruction in Chapter 15.

Data Types

Table 2–3 shows data types that may be used in the M68HC12. In addition to data types used in the M68HC11, 5- and 9-bit signed integers may be used as offsets in indexed addressing and 32-bit integers are used in extended arithmetic instructions.

Control Registers

512 registers are used to control how the CPU uses its I/O resources.

Another important part of the programmer's responsibility is the set of 512 memory locations (initially located at $0000–$01FF) called the control registers. These registers contain bits to control various aspects of the microcontroller in addition to being used in input and output data. The specific details of these registers, and examples showing their use, will be covered in other chapters.

TABLE 2–3 M68HC12 and M68HC11 Data Types Comparison

Data Type	M68HC12	M68HC11
Bit	Yes	Yes
5-bit signed integers	Used only as offsets for indexed addressing	No
8-bit signed and unsigned integers	Yes	Yes
9-bit signed integers	Used only as offsets for indexed addressing	No
16-bit signed and unsigned integers	Yes	Yes
16-bit effective addresses	Yes	Yes
32-bit signed and unsigned integers	Used for extended division, extended multiply, and extended multiply-and-accumulate instructions	No

Operating Modes

The operating mode of the M68HC12 is determined by the states of three signals when the microcontroller is reset. Table 2–4 compares the M68HC12 and M68HC11 operating modes. There are two basic modes in the M68HC12 processor. *Special* modes allow greater access to protected control registers and bits for special testing and system development. *Normal* modes protect some registers and bits from accidental change. The normal modes for the M68HC12 include *Normal Single-Chip*, where Ports A–D are used for general purpose I/O, *Normal Expanded-Narrow*, where an 8-bit data bus and 16-bit address bus may be implemented, and *Normal Expanded-Wide*, which provides 16-bit address and data buses. We will discuss these modes in more detail in Chapters 7 and 15.

2.4 Background Debug Mode

Background debug mode (BDM) is a special mode that can be used for system development. As you develop systems for special applications, there may not be a standard user interface, such as a keyboard and display, that you find in your computer laboratories. The BDM uses special hardware and firmware built into the M68HC12. You can interact with (debug) the M68HC12 system by connecting a debugging POD to the *BKGD* pin. Chapter 14 will discuss this important feature in more detail.

2.5 Memory Map

Each derivative of the M68HC12 contains RAM and EEPROM internally. You can add more than 5 Mbytes of memory externally in expanded modes in the MC68HC812A4. The memory map, which shows what kind of memory is at what addresses, depends on the operation mode, single-chip or expanded. Figure 2–4 shows single-chip and expanded mode memory maps.

TABLE 2–4 Comparison of M68HC12 and M68HC11 Operating Modes						
M68HC12 Mode	**BKGD**	**MODB**	**MODA**	**M68HC11 Mode**	**MODB**	**MODA**
Special Single-Chip	0	0	0	Special Bootstrap	0	0
Special Expanded-Narrow	0	0	1			
Special Peripheral	0	1	0			
Special Expanded-Wide	0	1	1	Special Test	0	1
Normal Single-Chip	1	0	0	Normal Single-Chip	1	0
Normal Expanded-Narrow	1	0	1	Normal Expanded	1	1
Reserved	1	1	0			
Normal Expanded-Wide	1	1	1			

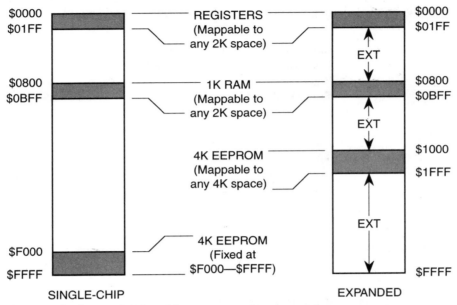

Figure 2-4　MC68HC812A4 memory maps.

2.6 Addressing Modes

Comparison of M68HC12 and M68HC11 Addressing Modes		
Addressing Mode	**M68HC12**	**M68HC11**
Immediate	8- and 16-bit operands	8- and 16-bit operands
Direct	8-bit addresses	8-bit addresses
Extended	16-bit addresses	16-bit addresses
Indexed	5-, 9-, and 16-bit signed offset	8-bit unsigned offset
	A, B, and D register offset	No
	Pre- and postincrementing and decrementing	No
Indexed-Indirect	16-bit or D register offset	No
Inherent	Yes	Yes
Relative	8- and 16-bit signed offset	8-bit signed offset

There are seven addressing modes for memory and I/O locations: (1) immediate, (2) direct, (3) extended, (4) indexed, (5) indexed-indirect, (6) inherent, and (7) relative. The indexed addressing modes include pre- and postincrement and decrement instructions, and you may also use the A, B, or D registers as the indexed addressing offset. There are also indexed-indirect addressing instructions. These latter, enhanced addressing modes are not available in the M68HC11.

We use the following notation to describe addressing modes and other operations in the next several chapters:

Register Name	Indicates a register and its contents.
	Example: A refers to accumulator A and its contents.
→	Right arrow indicates a data transfer operation.
	Example: A → B indicates the contents of A are transferred to B.
(...)	Contents of a memory location.
	Example: ($1234) → B indicates the contents of memory location $1234 are transferred to B.
((...))	This is for indirect addressing modes. The inner parentheses specify a memory address whose contents are the address of the data.
	Example: A → (($1234)) indicates that the contents of A are transferred to a memory location whose address is in $1234:1235.

Immediate Addressing

Comparison of M68HC12 and M68HC11 Immediate Addressing
The immediate addressing modes are identical to the M68HC11

Immediate addressing is used when an operand is a *constant* known at the time the program is written. If this is the case, the data can *immediately* follow the instruction in the memory. A memory map of the immediate addressing mode is shown in Figure 2–5 where the data may be 8 or 16 bits.

Immediate addressing is used to initialize registers with constants known at the time the program is written. Several examples of immediate addressing are given in Example 2–1.

> *Immediate addressing requires a # prefix for the immediate data operand.*

In Example 2–1 note that a # sign appears before each of the numerical operands. **It is *VERY* important to remember to include this when using immediate addressing. It is also *VERY* easy to forget it.** The # sign is a symbol that tells the assembler to use immediate addressing and not another addressing mode. For example, if you write LDAA 64, the assembler will generate an instruction that loads A from *memory location 64*, not with the *value 64*. **Beware of this problem in your programs.** We will discuss more of the assembler's syntax in Chapter 3.

The data immediately follows the opcode.

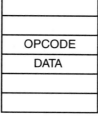

OPCODE
DATA

F i g u r e   2 – 5   Immediate addressing.

EXAMPLE 2–1   Immediate Addressing Examples

```
adrimmc.asm          Assembled with CASM 04/11/1998 13:03 PAGE 1

0000 8640        1    ldaa     #!64      ; Decimal 64 → A
0002 8664        2    ldaa     #$64      ; Hexadecimal 64 → A
0004 CE1234      3    ldx      #$1234    ; Hexadecimal 1234 → X
```

Direct and Extended Addressing

Comparison of M68HC12 and M68HC11 Direct and Extended Addressing
Direct and extended addressing modes in the M68HC12 are identical to the M68HC11

Although these are listed as two separate modes by Motorola, both are commonly called direct memory addressing.

Direct addressing in the M68HC12 can address an operand in the first 256 bytes of memory.

Direct addressing, in the terminology used by Motorola, is known also as base page, reduced direct, or zero-page addressing. In the Motorola version of direct addressing, the instruction contains an 8-bit memory address from or to which data are read or written. The instruction supplies the least significant byte of the address and the CPU sets the high byte equal to $00. Thus, direct addressing can access the first 256 bytes of memory (addresses $0000–$00FF).

Extended addressing can address the full 64-Kbyte address space.

Extended addressing uses a 16-bit address to specify a location in the entire 64-Kbyte address space. These are 3-byte instructions. Figure 2–6 shows a memory map for an extended addressing instruction.

Example 2–2 and Example 2–3 show the direct and extended addressing modes. Note the absence of the # that was used in immediate addressing and that an address can be specified either in decimal or in hexadecimal, although hexadecimal is much more commonly used.

Indexed Addressing

The M68HC12 has redefined the M68HC11 indexed addressing modes and added several new indexed modes. These reduce execution time and eliminate code size penalties for using the Y index register. In addition to indexed addressing using an offset, new indexed addressing modes offer pre- and postincrement and decrement of the index register. The A, B, or D registers may be used to provide the offset, and there are two new indexed-indirect addressing modes. Further, indexed addressing may be used with the stack pointer (SP) register and, for some instructions, the program counter (PC). Table 2–5 summarizes the M68HC12 indexed instruction operations.

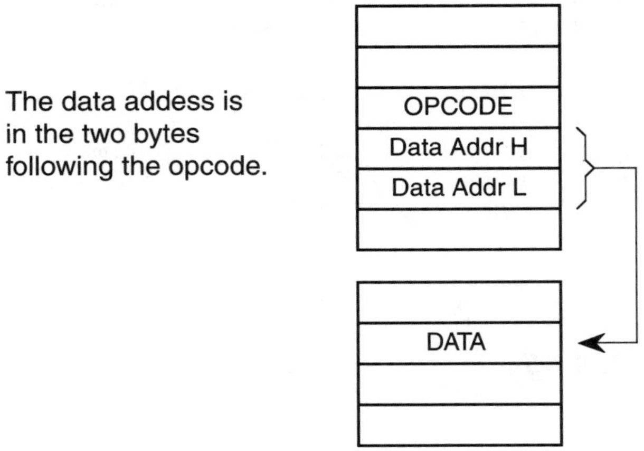

The data addess is
in the two bytes
following the opcode.

OPCODE
Data Addr H
Data Addr L

DATA

Figure 2-6   Extended memory addressing.

There are two index registers, X and Y, that are used primarily in the indexed addressing modes. In the M68HC12, the SP register and, for some instructions, the PC can be also used. The form of the indexed addressing instruction is

Operation   Offset,Index_Register

where *Index_Register* is either *X, Y, SP,* or *PC,* and *Offset* is an *signed 5-, 9-,* or *16-bit* value added to the contents of the index register. This addition specifies the effective address but does not change the contents of the index register. The addition is modulo 65,536.[4]

EXAMPLE 2-2   Direct Addressing

adrdirc.asm   Assembled with CASM 04/11/1998 13:09 PAGE 1

```
0000 9664        1        ldaa      $64        ;  ($0064) → A
0002 5BFF        2        stab      !255       ;  B → ($00FF)
0004 DE0A        3        ldx       !10        ;  ($000A:000B) → X
```

EXAMPLE 2-3   Extended Addressing

adrextc.asm   Assembled with CASM 04/11/1998 21:47 PAGE 1

```
0000 B61234      1        ldaa      $1234      ;  ($1234) → A
0003 FC1234      2        ldd       $1234      ;  ($1234:1235) → D
0006 7EC000      3        stx       $c000      ;  X → ($C000:C001)
```

---

[4] Modulo *N* addition means that if the sum, say *M,* is greater than *N,* the result returned is *M − N.* For example, for indexed addressing where the contents of the X register is $FFFE and the offset is $10, the effective address is $000E.

TABLE 2-5 Summary of M68HC12 Indexed Operations

Operand Syntax		Comments
ldaa	,r	**5-, 9-, or 16-bit signed, constant offset**
ldaa	n,r	n = −16 to +15 for 5 bit
		n = −256 to +255 for 9 bit
		n = −32,768 to 32,767 for 16 bit[a]
		r can be X, Y, SP, or PC; r is not changed by the instruction
ldaa	n,−r	**Automatic predecrement**
		n = 1 to 8 and is substracted from the contents of register r before the data value is fetched
		r can be X, Y, or SP (not PC); r is modified by the instruction
ldaa	n,+r	**Automatic preincrement**
		n = 1 to 8 and is added to the contents of register r before the data value is fetched
		r can be X, Y, or SP (not PC); r is modified by the instruction
ldaa	n,r−	**Automatic postdecrement**
		n = 1 to 8 and is substracted from register r after the data value is fetched
		r can be X, Y, or SP (not PC); r is modified by the instruction
ldaa	n,r+	**Automatic postincrement**
		n = 1 to 8 and is added to register r after the data value is fetched
		r can be X, Y or SP (not PC); r is modified by the instruction
ldaa	A,r	**Accumulator offset**
ldaa	B,r	The contents of A, B, or D are used as a 16-bit, *unsigned* offset
ldaa	D,r	r can be X, Y, SP, or PC; r is not changed by the instruction
ldaa	[n,r]	**16-bit offset indexed-indirect**
		r can be X, Y, SP, or PC; r is not changed by the instruction
ldaa	[D,r]	**Accumulator D offset indexed-indirect**
		r can be X, Y, SP, or PC; r is not changed by the instruction

[a]*Note that in modulo-2^{16} arithmetic, −1 is equivalent to +65,535 so the 16-bit offsets can be thought of as unsigned.*

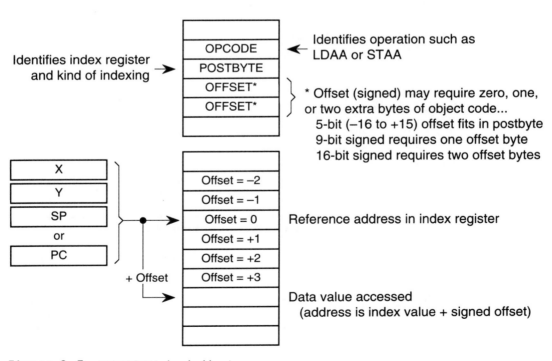

Figure 2-7 M68HC12 indexed addressing.

Figure 2–7 shows how indexed addressing works in the M68HC12. This addressing mode is called *based addressing* in some other systems.

Indexed Addressing Using a Constant Offset

M68HC12 and M68HC11 Indexed with Constant Offset	
M68HC12	**M68HC11**
5-, 9-, or 16-bit signed offset from X, Y, SP or PC	8-bit unsigned offset from X or Y only

> The *effective address* in *indexed addressing* is the sum of a 5-, 9-, or 16-bit signed constant and the contents of the X, Y, SP, or PC register.

The first two instructions in Example 2–4 use an offset value of zero. This effectively provides a *register indirect addressing* mode.

Indexed Addressing with Automatic Incrementing and Decrementing

Comparison of M68HC12 and M68HC11 Automatic Incrementing and Decrementing	
M68HC12	**M68HC11**
Automatic pre- and postincrementing and decrementing of the X, Y or SP	None

The M68HC12 has added automatic incrementing and decrementing of the index register. The instruction format is

Operation	Value,-Index_Register	to predecrement
Operation	Value,Index_Register-	to postdecrement
Operation	Value,+Index_Register	to preincrement
Operation	Value,Index_Register+	to postincrement

EXAMPLE 2–4   M68HC11 Indexed Addressing

```
adindx1c.asm          Assembled with CASM 04/11/1998 18:42 PAGE 1

0000 A600        1  ldaa   ,x       ; (X+0)  5-bit offset → A
0002 A600        2  ldaa   0,x      ; (X+0)  5-bit offset → A
0004 A6E040      3  ldaa   !64,x    ; (X+64) 9-bit offset → A
0007 A6E9C0      4  ldaa   -!64,y   ; (X-64) 9-bit offset → A
000A 6A9F        5  staa   -1,SP    ; A → (SP-1) 5-bit offset
000C A6FA1388    6  ldaa   !5000,PC ; (PC+5000) 16-bit offset → A
```

---

where *Value* is an integer from 1 to 8 and *Index_Register* is *X, Y,* or *SP. Value* is added or subtracted from the *Index_Register* either before (*pre*) or after (*post*) the data value is transferred. Unlike the constant offset-type instructions, the contents of the index register *are changed* by instruction. See Example 2–5.

Accumulator Offset Indexed Addressing

M68HC12 and M68HC11 Accumulator Offset Indexed Addressing	
M68HC12	**M68HC11**
Offset from the X, Y, SP, or PC registers using the A, B, or D registers	None

A limitation of the indexed addressing in the M68HC11 is that only a constant offset may be used to find the effective address. In the M68HC12, a register, whose contents obviously can be a variable, can be used. The instruction format is

Operation   Register,Index_Register

where *Register* is *A, B,* or *D* and *Index_Register* is *X, Y, SP,* or *PC*. The instruction calculates the effective address by adding the 8- or 16-bit value to the Index_Register. Like the other constant offset instructions, this *does not change* the actual contents of the registers. See Example 2–6.

EXAMPLE 2–5   Index Addressing with Post- and Preincrementing and Decrementing

```
adindx2c.asm          Assembled with CASM 11/15/1998  14:04  PAGE 1
                   1 ; Pre-decrement
0000  A629         2    ldaa    !7,-X   ; X-7 → X, (X) → A
                   3 ; Post-decrement
0002  A63E         4    ldaa    !2,X-   ; (X) → A, X-2 → X
                   5 ; Pre-increment
0004  A620         6    ldaa    !1,+X   ; X+1 → X, (X) → A
                   7 ; Post-increment
0006  A630         8    ldaa    !1,X+   ; (X) → A, X+1 → X
```

EXAMPLE 2–6   Accumulator Offset Indexed Addressing

```
adindx3c.asm          Assembled with CASM 11/15/1998  14:06  PAGE 1

0000  A6E5       1  ldaa    B,X   ;  (X+B) → A
0002  E6EC       2  ldab    A,Y   ;  (Y+A) → B
0004  EDE6       3  ldy     D,X   ;  (X+D:X+D+1) → Y
```

Indexed-Indirect Addressing

Comparison of M68HC12 and M68HC11 Indexed-Indirect Addressing	
M68HC12	**M68HC11**
16-bit offset from the X, Y, SP, or PC using a 16-bit constant or the D register	None

There are two indirect addressing modes in the M68HC12 and these are shown in Figure 2–8. The address of the data to be manipulated is held in a memory location. The address of this memory location, then, is generated by the instruction. This mode is called *indexed-indirect* because indexed addressing is used first to find the address of the data. That address is then used to find the data.

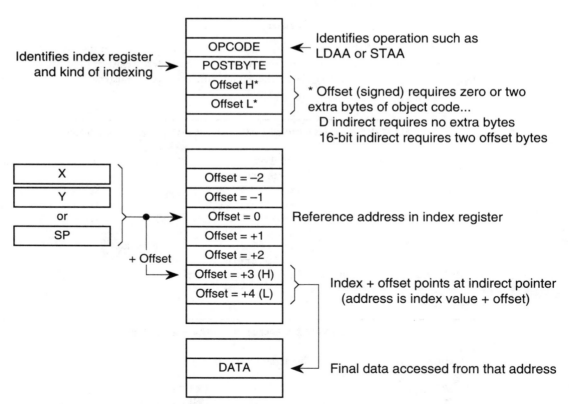

F i g u r e 2 – 8   M68HC12 indexed-indirect addressing.

The instruction format for indexed-indirect addressing is

| Operation | [**Offset,Index_Register**] | for constant, 16-bit offset or |
| Operation | [**D,Index_Register**] | to use the D register for the offset |

where *Offset* is a 16-bit value, *D* is accumulator D, and *Index_Register* is *X*, *Y*, *SP*, or *PC*. The square brackets distinguish this addressing mode from the other constant offset addressing modes. See Examples 2–7 and 2–8.

Inherent Addressing

Inherent addressing means that all data for the instruction are within the CPU. Inherent addressing is the same in the M68HC12 and M68HC11. See Example 2–9.

EXAMPLE 2–7   16-Bit Constant Indexed-Indirect Addressing

```
adindx4c.asm           Assembled with CASM  04/11/1998  18:53  PAGE  1

0000  CE5000      1    ldx     #$5000      ; $5000 → X, Initialize X
0003  A6E30064    2    ldaa    [$64,X]     ; (($5064)) → A
0007  6AE3FFFF    3    staa    [-1,X]      ; A → (($4fff))
```

EXAMPLE 2–8   Indexed-Indirect Addressing Using Accumulator D

```
adindx5c.asm           Assembled with CASM  04/11/1998  18:55  PAGE  1

0000  CE5000      1    ldx     #$5000      ; $5000 → X, initialize X
0003  CC0064      2    ldd     #$064       ; $0064 → D, initialize D
0006  EFE7        3    lds     [D,X]       ; (($5064)) → SP
```

EXAMPLE 2–9   Inherent Addressing

```
adrinhc.asm            Assembled with CASM  04/11/1998  21:31  PAGE  1

0000  1806        1    aba               ; A + B → A
0002  08          2    inx               ; X+1 → X
0003  B781        3    exg     a,b       ; A ↔ B
```

Relative Addressing

Comparison of M68HC12 and M68HC11 Relative Addressing	
M68HC12	**M68HC11**
Both 8- and 16-bit signed (two's-complement) offsets	Only 8-bit signed offset

Relative addressing is used for branch instructions.

Branch instructions use relative addressing because they often do not jump very far from the current program location. If this is the case, and the new address is within an 8-bit displacement from the program counter, relative addressing may be used. These are called *short branches*. If the address to which to program is branching is more than +127 or −128 bytes from the current PC location, a *long branch* with a 16-bit offset can be used. In the M68HC12 instruction set, branch instructions use relative addressing whereas jump instructions use extended or indexed addressing. The assembler correctly calculates the branch instruction offset based on the label to which you are branching. Both short (8-bit, two's-complement with an allowable range of −128 to +127) and long (16-bit, −32,768 to +32,767) relative branches may be used in the M68HC12. Loop primitive instructions, including DBEQ, DBNE, IBEQ, IBNE, TBEQ, and TBNE use 9-bit offsets allowing a range of −256 to +255. See Example 2–10.

2.7 Reset

Comparison of MC68HC812A4 and M68HC11 Reset Action	
M68HC12	**M68HC11**
I, X, and STOP bits are set to mask interrupts and disable the STOP mode	The same
512-byte I/O control register is mapped initially at $0000–$01FF	64-byte I/O control register is mapped initially to $1000–$103F
1 Kbyte of RAM located initially at $0800–$0BFF	256 bytes of RAM located initially at $0000–$00FF
4 Kbytes of EEPROM located initially at $1000–$1FFF for expanded modes and $F000–$FFFF for single-chip modes.	512 bytes fixed location at $B600–$B7FF

The M68HC12 reset is an active low signal applied to the $\overline{\text{RESET}}$ pin. Figure 2–9 shows a typical reset circuit in which the MC34064 is a low-voltage inhibit device that holds the $\overline{\text{RESET}}$ signal low when V_{DD} is below the proper operating voltage for the M68HC12. This circuit is required for safe operation of the processor and provides a *power on reset* (*POR*). An optional manual reset switch is also shown.

EXAMPLE 2-10 Relative Addressing

```
adrrelc.asm          Assembled with CASM 04/11/1998 21:36 PAGE 1

0000 2002     1  THERE:      bra    WHERE    ; Forward branch
0002 A7       2              nop
0003 A7       3              nop
0004 22FA     4  WHERE:      bhi    THERE    ; Conditional branch back
0006 18260256 5              lbne   LONG_BRANCH
000A          6              DS     256      ; Simulate instructions
              7  LONG_BRANCH:
0260 A7       8              nop
```

The Reset Action

> The system *power on reset vector* is retrieved from $FFFE:FFFF.

When $\overline{\text{RESET}}$ is asserted, some internal registers and control bits are forced to an initial state, but the stack pointer and other CPU registers are indeterminant. This means they must be initialized before they are used. The condition code register I and X bits are set to mask interrupts (interrupts cannot occur until you unmask them) and the S bit is set to disable the STOP mode. After the reset initialization is done, and assuming a system clock is present, the CPU fetches a *vector* from memory locations $FFFE:FFFF. This vector is the

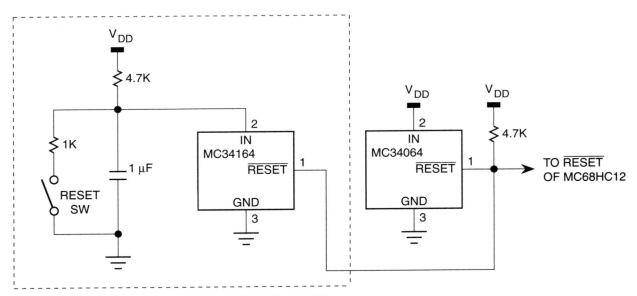

OPTIONAL POR DELAY AND MANUAL RESET SWITCH

Figure 2-9 Typical external reset circuit.

address of the first instruction to be executed. Thus, to turn on and run the M68HC12, these memory locations must contain the location of the program to be executed after reset.

There are other consequences of the $\overline{\text{RESET}}$ signal. The M68HC12 can configure its internal memory space. On reset, the M68HC12 allocates the first 512 bytes to the Control Register Block and assigns 1 Kbyte of RAM to locations $0800–$0BFF. RAM and the I/O control registers can be relocated to any 2-Kbyte boundary in the memory map if certain instructions are executed after the reset. In the M68HC12 the EEPROM can be relocated as well, but at power-up the EEPROM in the MC68HC812A4 initially occupies the 4 Kbytes from $1000–$1FFF. Chapter 9 shows us how to change these memory map locations.

The parallel I/O system is also affected by $\overline{\text{RESET}}$. Details are given in Chapter 7, but for now it is sufficient to know that bidirectional I/O lines are configured as high impedance inputs. This is a configuration that is safe, i.e., two outputs will not be connected.

Also associated with the I/O system and $\overline{\text{RESET}}$ is the operating mode. During the reset process, the BKGD, MODA, and MODB pins are read to select the operating mode for the MPU. Operating modes are discussed in Chapters 7 and 15.

The timer system is also reset. Some registers are set to initial values and some are indeterminant. Details of the timer section are covered in Chapter 10.

All interrupt flags are cleared and the interrupt system is disabled because the interrupt handling capabilities must be programmed before they can be used. M68HC12 interrupts are covered in detail in Chapter 8.

The serial I/O and the analog-to-digital converter capabilities are disabled on reset also. Serial I/O is discussed in detail in Chapter 11. The analog-to-digital converter is described in Chapter 12.

Causes of Reset

In addition to the $\overline{\text{RESET}}$ signal applied to the microcontroller by an external manual reset or low-voltage sensing circuit, there is an active-high reset signal *ARST*. This uses the same vector as $\overline{\text{RESET}}$. There are two other on-chip systems that can sense failures and reset other parts of the system. If the clock oscillator stops or is running too slowly, the CPU is reset as described in the above section with the exception that the reset vector address is at $FFFC:FFFD. If this failure occurs, the processor can execute code written especially for this event.

> A *watchdog timer* generates a reset if your program runs away or goes into some error condition.

Another interesting reset is from the *COP watchdog timer*. COP stands for *CPU Operating Properly* and a watchdog timer is a device that generates a reset if the program does not keep the timer from timing out. This allows us to regain control of the processor if something happens to the program. Memory locations $FFFA:FFFB contain the vector to the code to be executed if the watchdog timer times out.

Reset Summary

As we start to program the M68HC12, it is sufficient to know that on reset all registers in the programmer's model are indeterminant, except the I, X, and S bits in the condition code register. The address of the first instruction to be executed is fetched from $FFFE:FFFF.

2.8 Conclusion and Chapter Summary Points

These are enough hardware details to understand before learning the instruction set. There is, of course, an enormous amount of information and details to be learned before becoming proficient at programming and applying the microcontroller in a variety of applications. After you have learned the instruction set and how to write simple assembly language programs, we will return to more hardware topics in Chapters 7–15.

- The M68HC12 is a 16-bit microcontroller with a 16-bit address bus.

- The M68HC12 is source code (but not machine code) compatible with the M68HC11.

- There are two 8-bit accumulators, A and B, two 16-bit index registers, X and Y, and a 16-bit stack pointer register.

- The condition code register contains the carry, two's-complement overflow, zero, and sign bits used by the conditional branching instructions.

- There are 512 I/O control registers starting at memory location $0000. The control registers can be relocated to any 2-Kbyte boundary.

- Internal RAM memory can be relocated to any 2-Kbyte boundary.

- Internal EEPROM memory can be relocated to any 4-Kbyte boundary.

- The M68HC12 supports the immediate, direct, extended, indexed, indexed-indirect, inherent, and relative addressing modes.

- The A, B, and D registers can be used to provide a variable offset for indexed and indexed-indirect addressing.

- A # must be used with the operand in immediate addressing instructions.

- Direct addressing is limited to the first 256 bytes of memory.

- Extended addressing can address the entire 64-Kbyte address space.

- The effective address in indexed addressing is the sum of an 5-, 9-, or 16-bit signed offset and the contents of either the X, Y, SP, or PC registers.

- When the M68HC12 receives a power-on reset signal, it fetches the address of the first instruction to be executed from the vector location $FFFE:FFFF.

2.9 Bibliography and Further Reading

AN1057: Selecting the Right Microcontroller Unit, Motorola Semiconductor Application Note, Phoenix, AZ, 1990.

Cady, F. M., *Microcontrollers and Microcomputers,* Oxford University Press, New York, 1997.

68HC12 CPU12 Reference Manual, CPU12RM/AD, Motorola, 1996.

MC68HC812A4 Technical Summary, MC68HC812A4TS/D, Motorola, 1997.

MC68HC912B32 Technical Summary, MC68HC912B32T/D, Motorola, 1997.

2.10 Problems

2.1   Which of the M68HC12 ports is used for the A/D converter inputs?

2.2   Which of the M68HC12 ports is used with serial I/O?

2.3   Draw the programmer's model for the M68HC12.

2.4   Which bits in the M68HC12 condition code register may be tested with conditional branching instructions?

2.5   Calculate the effective address for each of the following examples of indexed addressing.
    a. X = $5000
       LDAA   0,X   EA = ?
    b. Y = $5000
       STAA $10,Y   EA = ?
    c. X = $500D
       LDAA $25,X   EA = ?

2.6   Describe the following M68HC12 addressing modes:
    Immediate, Direct, Extended, Indexed, Indexed-Indirect, Inherent, Relative.

2.7   Discuss the relative advantages and disadvantages of direct and extended addressing.

2.8   Discuss the relative advantages and disadvantages of extended and indexed addressing.

2.9   What is in the following CPU registers after a system reset?
    A, B, CCR, Stack Pointer.

2.10   Discuss how the CPU fetches the first operation code of the first instruction to be executed following a system reset.

Chapter *3*

An Assembler Program

O B J E C T I V E S

This chapter discusses the operation of a typical assembler.[1] We will learn the assembler syntax now to be able to more easily understand examples showing the instruction set in the next chapter.

3.1 Assembly Language Example

In this chapter we learn about some of the features of a typical assembler, at least enough to be able to understand the syntax of the examples in the next chapter. We only discuss the operation of an *absolute* assembler, which is simplest, at least for beginning assembly language programmers. When we start to develop more complex and longer assembly language programs, we will need to learn about *relocatable* assemblers and *linkers*.

An assembler converts source files to machine code, but before we look at how CASM12 operates, let us consider a short example.[2] At this stage you probably will not know what the instructions mean or what they do, nor will you understand all that the assembler does. Our goal is to give an overview of the process before we show the component parts of an assembly language program and how the assembler works.

Probably the most famous of all beginning programs, at least for C language programmers, is one that prints "Hello World!" Example 3–1 is a simple program doing just that.

The sample program in Example 3–1 has several parts. The listing you see is called the *.LST* file and is produced by the CASM12 assembler to use when debugging and documenting your work. It shows, from left to right in columns, (1) *Loc*, the address in memory where the assembled code is

---

1   The assembler described in this chapter is CASM12, a component of an integrated assembly language development system including an editor, cross-assembler, and communications environment. CASM12 is provided by Motorola with their evaluation boards (EVBs). CASM12 and other products for the M68HC12 can be purchased from P&E Microcomputer Systems ⟨http://www.pemicro.com/⟩.

2   Chapter 5 in *Microcontrollers and Microcomputers: Principles of Software and Hardware Engineering*, Oxford University Press, New York, 1997, describes how an assembler converts source files to machine code. It also has information to help with debugging and hints for writing assembly language programs.

EXAMPLE 3–1   Hello World! Example Program

helloc.asm   Assembled with CASM 03/29/1998 22:52 PAGE 1

Loc   Obj Code   Line   Source Line

```
                     1   ; Example program to print "Hello World"
                     2   ; Source File: hello.asm
                     3   ; Author: F. M. Cady
                     4   ; Created: 4/97
                     5   ; Constant equates
0000                 6   EOS:    EQU    0      ; End of string
                     7   ; Debug-12 Monitor equates
0000                 8   printf: EQU    $FE06 ; Print a string
                     9   ; Memory map equates
0000                10   PROG:   EQU    $0800 ; RAM in the EVB
0000                11   DATA:   EQU    $0900 ; Middle of RAM
0000                12   STACK:  EQU    $0a00 ; Stack pointer
0800                13           ORG    PROG  ; Locate the program
                    14   ; Initialize stack pointer
0800  CF0A00        15           lds    #STACK
                    16   ; Print Hello World! string
0803  CC080C        17           ldd    #HELLO ; Pass the adr of the string
0806  FEFE06        18           ldx    printf ; The adr of the printf routine
0809  1500          19           jsr    0,x
                    20   ; Return to the monitor
080B  3F            21           swi
                    22   ; Define the string to print
080C  48656C6C      23   HELLO:  DB     'Hello World!',EOS
      6F20576F
      726C6421
      00
```

---

found, (2) *Obj Code*, the assembled code bytes, (3) *Line*, the source code line number, and finally (4) *Source line*, the source code with label, opcode, operand, and comment fields. In this program *lines 1–4* are comments that introduce the program. *Line 6* uses an *assembler pseudooperation*, called an *equate* or *EQU*, to define the value used for the *symbol EOS*. This defines the code-byte that signifies the end of the message to be printed on the terminal (like the null byte at the end of a string in a C program). *Line 8* defines the location of a subroutine in the D-Bug12 monitor that will print the message. *Lines 10–12* define memory areas to be used by the program and *line 13 locates* the program in the RAM memory for the Motorola evaluation board. The actual program code appears in *lines 15–21*. The stack pointer register is initialized (*line 15*), the message is printed (*lines 17–19*), and the program terminates by returning to the EVB debugging monitor in *line 21*. At the bottom of the program (*line 23*), an assembler pseudooperation, define byte (DB), defines the message *Hello World!*

This is a complete assembly language program for the M68HC12, and you will be producing programs that look very much like this. In the following sections we will examine each component part of a program and describe the operation of the CASM12 assembler.

3.2 M68HC12 CASM12 Assembler

> The CASM12 assembler converts M68HC12 assembly language source files into S19 files that can be loaded into the microcontroller's memory.

The CASM12 assembler runs on an IBM-compatible personal computer and *cross-assembles* code for the M68HC12 microcontroller. It produces an *S-Record* file that is loaded into the M68HC12 memory.

The assembler converts the program's operation mnemonics to opcodes and its operands to operand codes. Your primary task at this time is to learn the syntax of this assembler to be able to specify operations and operands. You will also learn about assembler pseudooperations and directives that help the assembler do its job and make programs easier for us to read.

> CASM12 is an *absolute* assembler.

When you are using an *absolute assembler*, all source code for the program must be in one file or group of files assembled together. This is the easiest way to operate and we will use it to begin your programming chores. As your programs grow, however, you will probably change to a more powerful assembler with relocatable features.

3.3 Assembler Source Code Fields

Each source code line has four fields—label, operation mnemonic, operand, and comment, as shown in Table 3–1. The fields are separated by a white space (usually one or more tab characters, shown as ⟨tab⟩ so the fields line up) and there are specific rules for each field.

Label Field

> The *label field* starts in the first column of the source code line.

The *label field* is the first field of a source statement. A label is a symbol followed (optionally) by a colon. The label is optional but when used can provide a symbolic memory reference, such as a branch instruction address, or a symbol for a constant. A valid label has the following characteristics:

- A label has 1 to 16 characters, which may be of the following:

  Upper or lower case letters a–z.

  Digits 0–9.

  The dollar sign ($), underscore (_), or dash (-).

- A label must start with an alphabetic character.

- A label must start in the first column of the source code line.

TABLE 3–1 Source Code Fields

Label field		Opcode field		Operand field		Comment field
EXAMPLE:	⟨tab⟩	ldaa	⟨tab⟩	#64	⟨tab⟩	;Initialize A reg

- Upper and lower case characters are not distinct; the assembler treats lower case the same as upper case.

- A label may end with a colon (:).

- A label may appear on a line by itself.

- Long labels are truncated to 16 characters.

> A *whitespace* is a space or ⟨Tab⟩ character.

A whitespace character (blank or ⟨tab⟩) must be in the first character position in the line when there is no label, and there must be a white space between the label and the following opcode. See Example 3–2 for different kinds of labels.

A label may not occur more than once in your program. If it does, the assembler will give an error message noting that the symbol has been redefined. Remember also that a label must start with an alphabetic character and must start in the first column.

Opcode or Operation Field

> The *opcode field* begins after the first whitespace character.

The *opcode* field contains either a *mnemonic* for the operation, an *assembler directive* or *pseudooperation*, or a *macro name*. It must be preceded by at least one white space. The assembler is insensitive to the case of the mnemonic; all upper case letters are converted to lower case. See Example 3–3.

Operand Field

> The *operand field* follows the opcode with at least one whitespace character between.

The assembler uses the *operand* field to produce the binary code for the operand, and the interpretation of this field depends to a certain extent on the opcode. The operand must follow the opcode and be preceded by at least one white space. Operands can be the *symbols*, *constants*, or *expressions* that are evaluated by the assembler. The operand field also specifies the addressing mode for the instruction as shown in Table 3–2.

EXAMPLE 3–2 Labels

```
labelc.asm              Assembled with CASM   03/30/1998   03:34  PAGE 1

             1    TEST:                  ; Legal label
             2    _TEST:                 ; Legal label
             3    TEST$:                 ; Legal
             4    TEST$DATA:             ; Legal. Sometimes the $ is used as a
             5                           ; separator to make the label more
             6                           ; readable
             7    TestData:              ; Legal, more readable
             8    Test_Data:             ; Legal, more readable yet
             9    Label                  ; Legal. A label does not need a colon
```

EXAMPLE 3–3   Operation Field

```
opfieldc.asm          Assembled with CASM   03/30/1998 03:40 PAGE 1

0000 87     1    CLRA          ; Legal mnemonic
0001 A7     2    nop
0002 A7     3    NoP           ; Equivalent to nop, NOP.
            4  CLRA            ; Not legal. There must be at
            5                  ; least one white space in front
            6                  ; of the mnemonic.
0003 08     7    DB    $08     ; Legal assembler directive
```

Symbols: A symbol represents an 8- or 16-bit integer value that *replaces* the symbol during the assembler's evaluation of the operand. For example, if the symbol CRLF is defined as $0D0A, the assembler replaces each occurrence of CRLF in your program with $0D0A. Special symbols are the asterisk (*) and dollar sign ($), which represents the current 16-bit value of the location (program) counter.

> The default base for numbers is hexadecimal.

Constants: Constants are numerical values that do not change during the program. Constants may be specified in one of four formats—decimal, hexadecimal, binary, or ASCII. The format indicators shown in Table 3–3 can be given as a prefix or a suffix. The default base is normally hexadecimal and is chosen if no other format specifier is given. The default base for the assembler can be changed by the BASE directive.

Decimal Constants: *Decimal constants* must fall between 0 and $+2^{16} - 1$ but depend on the size of constant being defined. The decimal constant is specified with a (!) prefix or (T) suffix. In each line shown in Example 3–4 the data value to be loaded into the register is a decimal value. Example 3–14 shows how to use the *define byte (DB)* directive to define decimal constants that can be stored in memory.

TABLE 3–2   Operand Formats and Addressing Modes

Operand Format	Addressing Mode/Instruction Type
No operand	Inherent
Expression	Direct, extended, or relative
#Expression	Immediate[a]
Expression,R	Indexed offset with X, Y, SP, or PC
Expression,−R	Indexed automatic predecrement
Expression,+R	Indexed automatic preincrement
Expression,R−	Indexed automatic postdecrement
Expression,R+	Indexed automatic postincrement
Accumulator,R	Indexed accumulator
[Expression,R]	Indexed indirect
[D,R]	Indexed indirect D accumulator
Expression,Expression	Bit set or clear
Expression,R,Expression	Bit set or clear
Expression,Expression,Expression	Bit test and branch
Expression,R,Expression, Expression	Bit test and branch

[a] *It is excruciatingly important that you remember to include the # when you want immediate addressing mode.*

TABLE 3-3 Base Designators for Constants		
Base	**Prefix**	**Suffix**
Binary (2)	%	Q
Decimal (10)	!	T
Hexadecimal (16)	$	H

Hexadecimal Constants: Although hexadecimal is the default base, we choose to identify hexadecimal numbers with the prefix $ to be consistent with many other assemblers for Motorola microcomputers. You may also use the suffix H. Hexadecimal values are a string of digits from the hexadecimal symbol set (0–9, A–F). See Example 3–5. Hexadecimal constants are used more frequently in assembly language programs than decimal constants, particularly when specifying addresses. However, if it makes sense to write a decimal constant, do not convert the decimal value to the hexadecimal value. Write it as a decimal constant and let the assembler convert it. Inspect the *Obj Code* in Examples 3–4 and 3–5 to see that a constant, such as 100_{10} can be specified as either a decimal or a hexadecimal value. You should chose the one that makes the most sense to you when you read the program.

EXAMPLE 3–4   Decimal Constants

```
decimalc.asm            Assembled with CASM    03/30/1998   04:00   PAGE  1

  0000  8664          1     ldaa    #!100    ;  100 → A
  0002  8664          2     ldaa    #100T    ;  100 → A
  0004  CE04D2        3     ldx     #!1234   ;  1234 → X
```

EXAMPLE 3–5   Hexadecimal Constants

```
hexc.asm                Assembled with CASM    03/30/1998   04:02   PAGE  1

  0000  8664          1     ldaa    #$64     ;  $64 = 100 → A
  0002  869C          2     ldaa    #$9c     ;  $9c = -100 → A
  0004  CE1234        3     ldx     #$1234   ;  $1234 → X
```

EXAMPLE 3–6   Binary Constants

```
binaryc.asm             Assembled with CASM    04/02/1998   20:58   PAGE  1

  0000  8664          1     ldaa    #%01100100          ;  100 → A
  0002  8664          2     ldaa    #01100100q          ;  100 → A
  0004  8664          3     ldaa    #01100100Q          ;  100 → A
  0006  869C          4     ldaa    #%10011100          ;  -100 → A
  0008  CE091A        5     ldx     #%0001001000110100  ;  $1234 → X
  000B  86F0          6     ldaa    #%11110000          ;  MS nibble mask
```

EXAMPLE 3–7

Show four ways to specify the code for the ASCII code for the character **C** and choose the best way to load the ASCII code into the A register in a program.

Solutions:
>ASCII—"C"
>Hexadecimal—$43
>Decimal—!67
>Binary—%01000011

The best way to load the A register with the ASCII code for the character C is

```
ldaa    #"C"
```

Binary Constants: Binary constants are specified by the percent sign (%) prefix or (Q) suffix and are comprised of 1s and 0s. See Example 3–6. Use binary constants to make programs more readable. Suppose you wanted to define a mask for the four least significant bits of a byte; using %00001111 is more readable than using hexadecimal $0F and is far better than decimal 15.

ASCII Constants: Single *ASCII constants* or *strings* of one or more ASCII characters are enclosed in single (' ') or double quotation marks (" "). The assembler can assign the ASCII code for any printable character. Use this feature to specify ASCII characters instead of writing the hexadecimal code. The assembler will always make the conversion from the character to the code correctly. It is better to specify 'A' than $41, although they are equivalent. See Examples 3–7 and 3–15.

> *Expressions* make programs more readable and easier to use in other applications.

Expressions: An expression is a combination of symbols, constants, and algebraic operators. The assembler evaluates the expression to produce a value for the operand. CASM12 algebraic operators are shown in Table 3–4.

Expressions are evaluated with a normal algebraic operator precedence, which can be altered by using parentheses. Because expressions are evaluated by the assembler, they may be used for constants only. Nevertheless, the use of expressions is very powerful and can make a program more readable. It can also make it more portable and useful in other applications. See Examples 3–8 and 3–9.

Comment Field

The last field in the source statement is the *comment*. Comments start with a semicolon (;) and can be a complete line. Any line starting with a (;) or an (*) in column 1 is a comment line. The source program may have blank lines also.

TABLE 3–4 Assembler Expressions

+	Addition	−	Subtraction
*	Multiplication		
/	Division produces truncated result	\	Special division (divide by zero = zero)
>	Shift right	<	Shift left
&	Bitwise AND	|	Bitwise OR
^	Bitwise Exclusive OR		

EXAMPLE 3–8   Expressions

```
expr2c.asm                 Assembled with CASM   11/15/1998  18:52  PAGE 1

                        1   ; Test of all expression operators
      0000              2   ONE:      EQU     1
      0000              3   TWO:      EQU     2
      0000              4   SMALL:    EQU     $FF
                        5   ;
      0000  03          6   ADD:      DB      {ONE+TWO}       ; Addition
      0001  01          7   SUB:      DB      {TWO-one)       ; Subtraction
      0002  02          8   ASL:      DB      {ONE<1}         ; Arith shift left
      0003  7F          9   LSR:      DB      {SMALL>1}       ; Logical shift right
      0004  3F         10             DB      {SMALL>2}       ; Logical shift right
      0005  00         11   AND:      DB      {ONE&TWO}       ; Bitwise AND
      0006  03         12   OR:       DB      {ONE|TWO}       ; Bitwise OR
      0007  03         13   XOR:      DB      {ONE^TWO}       ; Bitwise Exclusive OR
      0008  04         14   MULT:     DB      {TWO*TWO}       ; Multiplication
      0009  01         15   DIV:      DB      {TWO/TWO}       ; Division
      000A  01         16   DIV1:     DB      {TWO\TWO}       ; Special Division
      000B  00         17   DIV2:     DB      {TWO\0}         ; Special Division
```

EXAMPLE 3–9   Using an Assembler Expression

Assume an assembler program with two data buffers with the start of each signified by the labels DATA_1 and DATA_2. The two buffers are sequential in memory and the amount of data in each buffer changes in programs for different applications. Assume that somewhere in your program you want to load the B register with the number of bytes in the DATA_1 buffer. Use an expression to do that.

Solution:

```
expr1c.asm                 Assembled with CASM   11/15/1998  18:54  PAGE 1

    0000  C664          1       ldab    #{DATA_2-DATA_1}; Immediate addressing;
                        2                               ; The assembler computes the
                        3                               ; difference between the
                        4                               ; address of DATA_2 and
                        5                               ; DATA_1
                        6   ;
    0002                7   DATA_1:   DS      !100            ; Allocate 100 bytes
    0066                8   DATA_2:   DS      2*!100          ; Allocate 200 bytes
```

3.4 Assembler Pseudooperations and Directives

Assembler *pseudooperations* and *directives* instruct the assembler how to do its job.

Assembler pseudooperations and directives are an important and vital part of an assembler program. Assembler pseudooperations are like opcode mnemonics because they appear in the opcode field, but they are not part of the microcontroller's instruction set. Pseudooperations can *define* the program's *location* in memory so all memory addresses are correct. They allow *symbols* and the *contents of memory* locations to be de-

TABLE 3–5 CASM12 Assembler Pseudooperations and Directives

Pseudooperations	
Code Location	
ORG	Set program counter to the origin of the program
Defining Symbols	
EQU	Equate symbol to a value
Reserving or Allocating Memory Locations	
DS	Define Storage
RMB	Reserve Memory Byte
Defining Constants in Memory	
DB	Define Byte constants
FCB	Form Constant Byte constants
DW	Define Word (16-bit) constants
FDB	Form Double Byte constants
Directives	
Source Control	
BASE	Change the default input base to 2, 8, 10 or 16
INCLUDE	Include a file in the source input stream for assembly
Conditional Assembly	
IF	Conditional assembly start if a condition is true
IFNOT	Conditional assembly start if a condition is false
ELSEIF	Start of the ELSE code for a conditional assembly
ENDIF	End of a conditional assembly section
SET	Set a condition to be true for conditional assembly
SETNOT	Set a condition to be false for conditional assembly
Macro Definition	
MACRO	Create a macro
MACROEND	End of a macro definition
Listing Control	
CYCLE_ADDER_ON	Start counting instruction cycles
CYCLE_ADDER_OFF	Stop counting instruction cycles
EJECT	Begin a new page for the listing
HEADER	Define a string for a header on all listing pages
LIST	Turn on the assembler listing file output
NOLIST	Turn off the assembler listing
PAGE	Begin a new page for the listing
PAGELENGTH	Set the length of a listing page
PAGEWIDTH	Set the width of a listing page
SUBHEADER	Define a string for a subheader on all listing pages

fined. Assembler pseudooperations also allocate memory locations for variable data storage. In short, pseudooperations help the assembler generate code for the program. Assembler directives control how the assembler creates its output files, especially the list file. Table 3–5 shows pseudooperations and directives available in the CASM12 absolute assembler.[3]

Assembler Pseudooperations

Code Location

> *ORG* is used to *locate* sections of the program in the correct type of memory.

ORG (Set Program Counter to Origin): The ORG pseudooperation changes the assembler's location counter to the value in the expression. An ORG defines where your program is to be located in the various sections of ROM and RAM memory. See Example 3–10.

```
ORG    〈Expression〉 [; Comment]
```

Defining Symbols

> An *EQU* is the most frequently used assembler pseudooperation.

EQU (Equate a Symbol to a Value): EQU is used more than any other pseudooperation in assembly language programming because it is good programming practice to use symbols where constants are required. Then, if the constant needs to be changed, only the equate is changed. When the program is reassembled, all occurrences of constants are changed.

```
〈Label:〉    EQU    〈Expression〉 [; Comment]
```

EXAMPLE 3–10   ORG—Set Program Counter to Origin

```
orgc.asm              Assembled with CASM   04/04/1998  13:56  PAGE 1

 0000            1  ROM:      EQU    $F000   ; Location of ROM
 0000            2  RAM:      EQU    $0800   ; Location of RAM
 0000            3  STACK:    EQU    $0a00   ; Location of stack
                 4  ;
 F000            5            ORG    ROM     ; Set program counter to ROM
                 6                            ; for the program
                 7  ; The following code is located at memory address ROM
 F000 CF0A00     8            lds    #STACK  ; Initialize SP
 F003 B60800     9            ldaa   DATA_1  ; Load from memory address RAM
                10  ;         - - -
 0800           11            ORG    RAM     ; Set program counter to RAM
                12                            ; for the data
 0800 20        13  DATA_1:   DB     $20     ; Set aside $20 bytes
```

---

[3] In the syntax discussion for each of the assembler pseudooperations and directives, the following notation is used:

[ ]   Brackets denote an optional element.

〈 〉   Angle brackets enclose a syntactic variable to be replaced by a user-entered value.

Any constant value can be defined for the assembler using the EQU. The EQU directive must have a label and an expression. It is a useful documentation technique to have a comment with each EQU to tell other programmers reading your program what the symbol is to be used for. An EQU does not generate any code that is placed into memory. See Example 3–11. The default base used to evaluate expressions and other data is hexadecimal, but you can change the default with the BASE directive.

Reserving Memory Locations

> The *Define Storage* or *Reserve Memory Byte* pseudooperation is used to allocate memory for variable data storage.

DS (Define Storage) or RMB (Reserve Memory Byte): The DS and RMB sets aside memory locations by incrementing the assembler's location counter by the number of bytes specified in the expression. The block of memory reserved is NOT initialized with any value.

```
[Label:]    DS    〈n〉    [; Comment]

[Label:]    RMB   〈n〉    [; Comment]
```

Use this directive to allocate storage for variable data areas in RAM and then initialize the variables, if required, in the program at run time. See Examples 3–12 and 3–13.

Defining Constants in Memory

The following pseudooperations define constants for ROM. We highly recommend that you do not use them to initialize variable data areas in RAM. RAM data areas should be *allocated* with the DS and then *initialized* at run time as shown in Example 3–13.

EXAMPLE 3–11   EQU—Equate Symbol

```
equc.asm              Assembled with CASM   11/15/1998  18:59   PAGE 1

0000            1   CRLF:    EQU    $0D0A      ; For each occurrence of
                2                              ; CRLF, the assembler will
                3                              ; substitute the value $0D0A
0000            4   COUNT:   EQU    5          ; Loop counters often need to
                5                              ; be initialized
0000            6   COUNT1:  EQU    COUNT*5    ; The assembler can evaluate
                7                              ; an expression to provide
                8                              ; a value of 25 for COUNT1
0000            9   LSMASK:  EQU    $0F        ; A mask that picks off the
                10                             ; least significant nibble
                11                             ; in a byte
0000            12  ls_mask: EQU    %00001111  ; A binary mask equate is
                13                             ; more readable and
                14                             ; informative than one
                15                             ; given in hexadecimal
```

EXAMPLE 3–12   DS—Define Storage

```
dsc.asm              Assembled with CASM  04/09/1998  01:34  PAGE 1

     0000        1  COUNT_3:   EQU    $10
     0000 10     2  BUFFER:    DB     COUNT_3   ; Allocates $10 bytes
     0001 20     3  BUFFER1:   DB     2*COUNT_3 ; Allocates $10 words
```

DB (Define Byte) or FCB (Form Constant Byte): The DB and FCB pseudooperations allocate memory locations and assign values to each.

[⟨Label:⟩]   DB   ⟨Expression⟩, [⟨expression⟩]

[⟨Label:⟩]   FCB   ⟨Expression⟩, [⟨expression⟩]

DB and FCB can define byte-sized constants. If the expression evaluates to greater than 8 bits, an error message is generated and you should use the DW or FDB pseudooperations. See Example 3–14.

EXAMPLE 3–13

Show how to use the DS directive to reserve 10 bytes for data. Initialize each byte to zero in a small program segment.

Solution:

```
dsex1c.asm           Assembled with CASM    04/09/1998  01:35  PAGE 1

     0000          1  NUMBER:  EQU    !10      ; Number of bytes allocated
     0000          2  PROG:    EQU    $0800    ; Program location
     0000          3  RAM:     EQU    $0900    ; Location of RAM
     0800          4           ORG    PROG
                   5  ;        - - -
     0800 C60A     6           ldab   #NUMBER  ; Initialize B with a loop
                   7                            ; counter
     0802 CE0900   8           ldx    #BUF     ; X points to the start of the
                   9                            ; buffer
     0805 6930    10  loop:    clr    1,x+     ; clear each location and
                  11                            ; point to the next location
     0807 0431FB  12           dbne   b,loop   ; Decrement the loop counter
                  13                            ; and branch if the loop
                  14                            ; counter is not zero
                  15  ;        - - -
     0900         16           ORG    RAM      ; Locate the data area
     0900         17  BUF:     Ds     NUMBER   ; Allocate the data area
```

EXAMPLE 3–14 Define Constant

```
dcc.asm                 Assembled with CASM   04/04/1998  16:55  PAGE  1

                   1  ; Decimal constants examples
0000 64            2          DB     !100      ; Define a byte
0001 0064          3          DW     !100      ; Define a word
                   4  ; Hexadecimal constant examples
0003 23            5          DB     $23       ; Valid
0004 1234          6          DW     $1234     ; Valid
0006 ABCD          7          DW     $abcd     ; Valid
0008 ABCD          8          DW     $ABCD     ; Upper case same as lower
                   9  ; Binary constant examples
000A 05           10          DB     %0101     ; Valid
000B 11           11          DB     0011      ; Invalid, missing %. CASM
                  12                           ; thinks this is hex 11
000C AF           13          DB     %10101111 ; Valid
                  14
                  15  ; Initializes four memory locations with the data
                  16  ; 01, 02, $10, and $ff
000D             17  MAX:     EQU    !255
000D 010210FF    18  DATA:    DB     01,02,$10,MAX
                  19  ;
                  20  ; The assembler can evaluate an expression
0011             21  NUM:     EQU    4
0011             22  MAX_CNT: EQU    5
0011 14          23  TOTAL:   DB     NUM*MAX_CNT
```

DW (Define Word) or FDB (Form Double Byte): The DW and FDB pseudooperations allocate memory locations and assign values to each.

    [⟨Label:⟩]   DW   ⟨Expression⟩,[⟨expression⟩]

    [⟨Label:⟩]   FDB   ⟨Expression⟩,[⟨expression⟩]

> Strings of ASCII characters may be defined with the *DB* directive.

DW and FDB can define word-sized (2-byte) constants. Do not put any spaces between the expressions.

You will frequently use strings of characters in programs that have a user interface. Example 3–15 shows how to do this using the DB directive.

Assembler Directives

Assembler directives are similar to pseudooperations in that they can affect how code is generated. Directives also control the look of the listing file. Directives are invoked by placing a /, #, or $ as the first character of a line followed by the directive and any parameters. Table 3–5 shows the directives in CASM12.

EXAMPLE 3–15   ASCII Strings

```
asciic.asm                Assembled with CASM   04/09/1998  01:39   PAGE 1

0000 416162        1            DB     'A','a','b'
0003 54686973      2            DB     'This is a string'
     20697320
     61207374
     72696E67
0013 54686973      3            DB     "This is a string too"
     20697320
     61207374
     72696E67
     20746F6F
0027              4     CR:      EQU    $0d ; ASCII code for carriage ret
0027              5     LF:      EQU    $0a ; ASCII code for line feed
0027 48657265     6            DB     'Here is a string with',CR,LF
     20697320
     61207374
     72696E67
     20776974
     680D0A
003E 63617272     7            DB     'carriage return and line feed',CR,LF
     69616765
     20726574
     75726E20
     616E6420
     6C696E65
     20666565
     640D0A
005D 63686172     8            DB     "characters inserted"
     61637465
     72732069
     6E736572
     746564
```

Source Control

The default base when specifying constants is hexadecimal. This can be changed with the BASE directive.

        $BASE   [⟨n⟩]

where *n* is 2, 8, 10, and 16. The parameter specified must be in the current base or must have a base qualifier on it. See Example 3–16.

INCLUDE: This directive will include a specified file in the stream to be assembled. You can maintain a common file for equates, for example, to be included in each assembly language program.

        $INCLUDE   "⟨file specification⟩"

EXAMPLE 3–16   Setting the Default Base

```
basec.asm           Assembled with CASM 04/09/1998  01:41  PAGE  1

0000 8610      1    ldaa  #10      ; Hexadecimal default
0002           2    #BASE !10      ; Change to decimal
0002 860A      3    ldaa  #10      ; Loads decimal 10
0004           4    $BASE 16       ; Change base back to 16
0004 8610      5    ldaa  #$10     ; This loads $10 also
0006 860A      6    ldaa  #0a      ; This loads decimal 10
```

The file specification is given in double (") or single (') quotes. If the file is not in the current working directory, you must include a path in the file specification. See Example 3–17.

You may choose to have the include file contents in the list file by assembling the program with the optional parameter *I* in the command line as shown in Sections 3.6 and 3.7.

Conditional Assembly

You may have seen the IF-THEN-ELSE structure in a high-level language. We know the code for the THEN part is executed if the conditional is true, and the ELSE part if the conditional is false. A conditional assembly is very similar but only the appropriate segment of code is included in the assembled program. Note that this *does not* produce code that is an executable IF-THEN-ELSE structure. We will see how to write structured code in Chapter 6.

The conditional assembly feature allows you to write code that can be customized at assembly time. Example 3–18 shows how to choose a set of equates for one of two different versions of the D-Bug12 monitor. Conditional assembly may be invoked with the following directives:

$SET	Expression	Set Expression to a "true" value.
$SETNOT	Expression	Set Expression to a "false" value.
$IF	Expression	Start of code to be assembled if Expression is true.
$IFNOT	Expression	Start of code to be assembled if Expression is false.
$ELSEIF		Start of code to be assembled if the code after IF or IFNOT is not assembled.
$ENDIF		The end of the conditional assembly code.

Listing Control

The listing control directives allow you to control the format of the listing file. These directives can be put in the source file with a $, /, or # like the other directives, or they may be embedded (and

---

EXAMPLE 3–17   INCLUDE Directive

```
$INCLUDE  "registers.h"
$INCLUDE  '..\equates\ioregs.inc'
```

EXAMPLE 3–18   Conditional Assembly

```
ifelsec.asm               Assembled with CASM    11/15/1998  19:12  PAGE 1

                  1  ; Set the version number for this software
0000              2  PARAM1:  EQU     $76      ; Parameter to use for vers 1
0000              3  PARAM2:  EQU     $77      ; Parameter to use for vers 2
0000              4  $SET     Ver1
                  5  ;  . . .
                  6  ; The conditional assembly follows.
0000              7  $IF      Ver1
                  8  ; This code is assembled if Ver1 has been SET.
0000 8676         9           ldaa    #PARAM1
0002             10  $ELSEIF
                 11  ; This code will be assembled if Ver1 has been SETNOT.
                 12           ldaa    #PARAM2
0002             13  $ENDIF
```

---

thus do not appear in the list file) by placing a period (.) in column one immediately followed by the directive. The following directives are available:

.CYCLE_ADDER_ON	Turns on a counter that counts the number of clock cycles used in each program step. The cycle counter parameter (C) must be included in the command line when you assemble the program for this directive to work. See Section 3.6.
.CYCLE_ADDER_OFF	Turns off the cycle counter and displays the total number of cycles since the counter was turned on. See Example 3–19 where the cycle counter is turned on to count the number of clock cycles in part of the program.
.PAGE or .EJECT	Inserts a page break in the listing file.
.HEADER 'String'	The string enclosed in quotes will be printed as a header on the listing pages.
.SUBHEADER 'String'	The string enclosed in quotes will be printed as a subheader starting on the next page of the listing.
.LIST and .NOLIST	.LIST and .NOLIST enable and disable the inclusion of source code in the listing file. When you are working on a long file, it is useful to print only those sections that you need. You can eliminate the listing of an include file by bracketing the $INCLUDE directive with .NOLIST and .LIST. Placing .NOLIST at the end of the source file will suppress the listing of the symbol table.
.PAGELENGTH ⟨n⟩	This sets the length of the source code line to be included in the listing file. The default is 64 lines.
.PAGEWIDTH ⟨n⟩	This sets the width of the page. The default is 80.

EXAMPLE 3–19   Cycle Counting

```
cyclec.asm                    Assembled with CASM    04/09/1998  20:37  PAGE  1

                        1  ; Example program to print "Hello World"
                        2  ; Source File: hello.asm
                        3  ; Author: F. M. Cady
                        4  ; Created: 4/97
                        5  ; Constant equates
0000                    6  EOS:  EQU   0          ; End of string
                        7  ; Debug-12 Monitor equates
0000                    8  printf:    EQU   $FE06   ; Print a string
                        9  ; Memory map equates
0000                   10  PROG:      EQU   $0800   ; RAM in the EVB
0000                   11  DATA:      EQU   $0900   ; Middle of RAM
0000                   12  STACK:     EQU   $0a00   ; Stack pointer
0800                   13             ORG   PROG    ; Locate the program
                       14  ; Initialize stack pointer
0800                   15  $CYCLE_ADDER_ON
0800 [02] CF0A00       16             lds   #STACK
                       17  ; Print Hello World! string
0803 [02] CC080C       18             ldd   #HELLO  ; Adr of the string
0806 [03] FEFE06       19             ldx   printf  ; Adr of printf routine
TOTAL CYCLES = 7 decimal
0809                   20  $CYCLE_ADDER_OFF
0809 [04] 1500         21             jsr   0,x
                       22  ; Return to the monitor
080B [09] 3F           23             swi
                       24  ; Define the string to print
080C      48656C6C     25  HELLO:     DB    'Hello World!',EOS
          6F20576F
          726C6421
          00
```

Macros

A macro assembler is one in which frequently used assembly instructions can be collected into a single statement. It makes the assembler more like a high-level language. For example, the problem might require a short code sequence to divide A by four

```
asra    ; Divide A by 2
asra    ; Divide by 2 again
```

in many parts of your program. This code is too short to be written as a subroutine so a macro is appropriate. Macros are often used for short segments of code, say less than 10 assembler statements. There are three stages of using a macro. The first is the *macro definition*, and a typical definition is shown in Example 3–20. The assembler directives MACRO and MACROEND encap-

---

EXAMPLE 3–20   MACRO Definition

```
MU100:        EQU    !199    ; Delay loop counter
$MACRO        Delay_100
; Macro to delay 100 microseconds for the A/D start up
              psha           ; save the A reg
              ldaa    #MU100
loop: deca
              bne     loop
              pula           ; restore the A reg
$MACROEND
```

---

sulate the code to be substituted when the macro is invoked. The label *Delay_100* is used in the second stage—the *macro invocation*. It is written in the source program where the lines of code would normally be placed. The third stage, *macro expansion*, occurs when the assembler encounters the macro name in the source code. The macro name is expanded into the full code that was defined in the definition stage. See Examples 3–21 and 3–22.

The syntax for the macro invocation in the source file where you want to use it is

[⟨label⟩:]   ⟨macro_name⟩   [⟨argument list⟩]

This is *calling* a macro, much like calling a subroutine, except for each instance of the call the code is expanded. Example 3–22 shows both the macro definition and its subsequent call. In this example, the expanded macro code is included in the listing by assembling the program with the optional command line parameter (*M*). See Section 3.6.

Macro Parameters

Substitutable parameters can be used in the source statement when the macro is called. These allow you to use a macro in different applications. Parameters are specified in the macro definition by a percent character ($\%n$) where n is the nth parameter. When the macro is called, arguments from the argument list are substituted into the body of the macro as literal string substitutions. Example 3–23 shows a macro definition and call using a parameter to control how many times the A register is shifted left. The parameter, num, appears in the macro definition to remind you how it is used and to be helpful in documentation.

EXAMPLE 3–21   MACRO Invocation

```
; macrocal.asm
;
;
; Invoke the delay macro
     Delay_100
;
```

EXAMPLE 3–22   MACRO Expansion

```
        1      ; Here is the macro definition
 0000          2  MU100:    EQU      !199      ; Delay loop counter
 0000          3  $MACRO    Delay_100
               4  ; Macro to delay 100 microseconds for the A/D start up
               5            psha              ; save the A reg
               6            ldaa     #MU100
               7  loop:     deca
               8            bne      loop
               9            pula              ; restore the A reg
 0000         10  $MACROEND
              11  ;
              12  ;        - - -
              13  ; Invoke the delay macro
 0000 macro   14            Delay_100
 0000 36      15  PSHA
 0001 86C7    16  LDAA #MU100
 0003 43      17  LOOP: DECA
 0004 26FD    18  BNE LOOP
 0006 32      19  PULA
```

EXAMPLE 3–23   MACRO Parameters

```
               1  ; Macro definition for a variable arithmetic
               2  ; shift left of the A register
 0000          3  $MACRO    alsa_n    num
               4  ; Shift the A register left num bits
               5  ; where n is a parameter in the macro call.
               6  ; Save B to set up a loop counter
               7            pshb              ; Save B on the stack
               8            ldab     #%1
               9  loop:     asla              ; Shift the A reg
              10            dbne     b,loop   ; Decr and branch if
              11                              ; not zero
              12            pulb              ; restore the B reg
 0000         13  $MACROEND
              14  ;
              15  ;
              16  ; The macro call is with a parameter
 0000 macro   17            alsa_n   !3
 0000 37      18  PSHB
 0001 C603    19  LDAB #%1
 0003 48      20  LOOP: ASLA
 0004 0431FC  21  DBNE B,LOOP
 0007 33      22  PULB
```

Labels in Macros

Multiple occurrences of a label in a program are normally not allowed, and for this reason the labels in a macro are changed automatically each time they are used. Macro labels may not be longer than 10 characters, and when the macro is expanded the assembler appends :nnnn to make each label unique.

Macros and Subroutines

Macros and subroutines have similar properties.

- Both allow the programmer to reuse segments of code. However, each time a macro is invoked, the assembler expands the macro and the code appears "in line." A subroutine code is included only once. Thus, macro expansions make the program larger.

- The subroutine requires a call or jump-to-subroutine and the macro does not. This means that the subroutine is a little slower to execute than the macro and the subroutine call uses stack space temporarily.

- Both macros and subroutines allow changes to be made in one place (the macro definition or the subroutine).

- Macros and subroutines make the program easier to read by hiding details of the program. Usually, when reading a program, you do not need the details of how it is doing something, just an indication of what it is doing.

3.5 Assembler Output Files

The assembler produces the *assembler listing*, which includes a *symbol table*, and an *S-Record* file that is loaded into the microcontroller's memory to be executed.

Assembler Listing: This is one of your main debugging tools and you should have an up-to-date copy when testing your code. Always work from the listing file rather than a source file because the listing gives much more information. The file has the format shown in Table 3–6.

The *Loc* column gives the address in memory where the object bytes, indicated by *Obj Code*, are located. Often errors in the program can be spotted by looking at these bytes. For example, if a decimal constant for an operand is written without the !, a glance at the assembled code will show this error. If the cycle counter is enabled, *Cycles* give the number of machine cycles used. *Line* is the source code line number. *Source Line* is reprinted exactly from the source program, including labels and comments.

Symbol Table: The symbol table is appended to the bottom of the list file. It may be eliminated from the listing by including the assembler directive .NOLIST at the end of the source code.

TABLE 3–6 Assembler List File Output

Loc	[Cycles]	Obj Code	Line	Source Line

It lists all symbols you have used in your program alphabetically and their values. Example 3–24 shows the symbol table from the Hello, World! program we saw in Section 3.1.

Cross-Reference Table: Some assemblers can produce another useful file called the *cross-reference table*. The cross-reference table also lists your symbols alphabetically and shows the line number in which the symbol is defined as well as each line in your program in which the symbol is referenced. Both the symbol table and the cross-reference table are useful listings for debugging.

EXAMPLE 3–24   Symbol Table

```
hellosym.asm              Assembled with CASM    04/05/1998    16:33    PAGE  1

                      1   ; Example program to print "Hello World"
                      2   ; Source File: hello.asm
                      3   ; Author: F. M. Cady
                      4   ; Created: 4/97
                      5   ; Constant equates
     0000             6   EOS:    EQU  0         ; End of string
                      7   ; Debug-12 Monitor equates
     0000             8   printf: EQU  $FE06     ; Print a string
                      9   ; Memory map equates
     0000            10   PROG:   EQU  $0800     ; RAM in the EVB
     0000            11   DATA:   EQU  $0900     ; Middle of RAM
     0000            12   STACK:  EQU  $0a00     ; Stack pointer
     0800            13           ORG  PROG      ; Locate the program
                     14   ; Initialize stack pointer
     0800 CF0A00     15           lds  #STACK
                     16   ; Print Hello World! string
     0803 CC080C     17           ldd  #HELLO  ; Pass the adr of the string
     0806 FEFE06     18           ldx  printf  ; The adr of the printf routine
     0809 1500       19           jsr  0,x
                     20   ; Return to the monitor
     080B 3F         21           swi
                     22   ; Define the string to print
     080C 48656C6C   23   HELLO:  DB   'Hello World!',EOS
          6F20576F
          726C6421
          00

   Symbol Table
DATA            0900
EOS             0000
HELLO           080C
PRINTF          FE06
PROG            0800
STACK           0A00
```

3.6 Assembler Invocation

CASM12 is a DOS command-line program. You can be in a DOS window and enter the following command line:

```
CASM12 filename.asm [param1 param2 param3 ...]
```

The command line can contain optional parameters to control the operation of the assembler. The parameters can be any of the following, in any order, separated by at least one space:

L	Turns on the listing (.LST) file. The assembly time is increased when the listing file is turned on.
S or H	Enables either a HEX or S19 format for the object file. If H or S is absent, an object file is not produced.
C	Include cycle counts in the list file. This must be on to enable the CYCLE_ADDER_ON directive.
M	Enables the listing of macro expansion.
I	Source code within INCLUDE files will be printed.

If you are operating in a Windows environment, you can execute a small batch file that runs the assembler and then pauses to let you inspect any error messages. See Example 3–25.

3.7 Assembler Errors

If the assembler encounters errors, an error message appears on the console screen and further processing of the source file halts. You must fix each error before going on with the assembly. CASM12 errors are shown in Table 3–7.

3.8 Chapter Summary Points

- CASM12 is an absolute assembler.

- There must be a white space between each of the four fields in a source code line.

EXAMPLE 3–25   Batch File to Run CASM12

```
echo off
rem This batch file runs the CASM12 assembler to
rem assemble the file given as parameter %1.
rem It generates a list file (L), an S19 object file (S)
rem and expands macros (M) as the default output choices.
rem You may include parameters %2 and %3 to turn on other
rem features such as the cycle counter (C) and include file
rem listing (I).
c:\(path)\casm12 %1.asm l s m %2 %3
pause
```

TABLE 3-7 CASM12 Errors

Number	Error	Explanation
1	Parameter invalid, too large, missing or out of range	There is an error in the operand field; it may be an invalid number or representation of a number, or it may be that the parameter evaluates to a number that is larger than allowed
2	Too many conditional assembly variables	You may have up to 25 conditional variables
3	Conditional assembly variable not found	The variable in the IF or IFNOT statement has not been declared with a SET or SETNOT
4	Include directives nested too deep	Includes may be nested only 10 levels
5	Invalid base value	The base parameter for the BASE directive may be set to 2, 8, 10, or 16
6	Undefined label	The label has not been declared
7	Too many labels	See error 16
8	MACRO parameter too long	The macro is expecting a different number of parameters than it received
9	MACRO label too long	Macro labels may be only 10 characters
10	INCLUDE file not found	The file specified has not been found; specify the full path if necessary; there is no default extension; it must be specified is it exists; be sure the file name is enclosed in quotes
11	Unrecognized operation	The opcode is unknown
12	Duplicate label	The label is already in use
13	Invalid opcode	The opcode is wrong
14	Error writing .LST file	Check the available disk space
15	Error writing object file	Check the available disk space
16	Out of memory	The assemble ran out of system memory; try creating a file that is an INCLUDE directive only; assembling this file will leave the maximum amount of memory available for the assembler
17	'}' found	An expression started with '}' did not end in '}'

- Labels are not case sensitive; ABCD is the same as AbCd.

- You must not have duplication of labels.

- Labels may optionally end with a colon (:).

- The opcode field contains operation mnemonics, assembler pseudooperations or directives, or macro names.

- The opcodes, pseudooperations, and directives are not case sensitive.

- The operand field may have symbols, constants, or expressions.

- The default base for constants is hexadecimal.

- Decimal constants are signified by a !.

- Hexadecimal constants are signified by a $.

- Binary constants are signified by a %.

- ASCII constants are signified by enclosing the character in single (' ') or double (" ") quotes.

- Assembler pseudooperations and directives allow you to direct the assembler how to do its job.

- Program code and other constant data should be located in ROM memory using the ORG pseudooperation.

- Data variables should be located in RAM memory using the ORG pseudooperation.

- Memory space for data variables should be allocated using the DS or RMB pseudooperation.

- An EQU directive allows us to define symbols and constants.

- Byte constants to be in ROM memory may be defined using the DB.

- ASCII string constants in ROM memory may be defined using the DB or FCB pseudooperation.

- Sixteen-bit constants in ROM memory are defined using the DW or FDB pseudooperation.

- The assembler may produce a listing with a symbol table and object files.

- A current listing file should be printed to help with debugging.

3.9 Problems

3.1   Give four ways to specify each of the following constants.
    a. The ASCII character X
    b. The ASCII character x
    c. 100_{10}
    d. 64_{16}

3.2   Give the symbol used when specifying a constant in the following bases: hexadecimal, decimal, binary, ASCII.

3.3   What assembler pseudooperation is used to allocate memory for data variables?

3.4   What assembler pseudooperation is used to define strings of ASCII characters?

3.5   What assembler pseudooperation is used to define byte constants in ROM memory?

3.6   What assembler pseudooperation is used to set the assembler's location counter?

3.7   How are data storage areas located when using the CASM12 assembler?
    a. By using ORG pseudooperations
    b. By using DB pseudooperations
    c. By using DS pseudooperations
    d. All of the above

3.8   Your hardware designer tells you that the microcontroller will have ROM located at addresses $E000 to $FFFF and RAM at $0800 to $0FFF. Show how to inform the assembler so that it locates its code and data areas properly.

3.9   Give the addressing mode and the effective address for each of the following instructions:
    a. LDAA   #5
    b. LDAA $5
    c. LDAA $5,X
    d. STAA $081A

Chapter 4

The M68HC12 Instruction Set

OBJECTIVES

This chapter describes and gives examples of how to use the instructions in the M68HC12 instruction set. The instructions are grouped into functional categories. When you learn these categories, you will be able to find a particular instruction to give you the function you need in your program.

4.1 Introduction

Learning a new instruction set is easier if you *first learn the categories of instructions* to be found and then *learn what instructions are in each category.*

You are about to start on what seems like a difficult and frustrating task—learning the instruction set of a computer. The M68HC12 has over 1000 instructions. Remembering all of these is a daunting task. If the number of different operations is counted, there are 188, still a considerable number. However, there are only a few (17) different *categories* of instructions. Our strategy for learning the instruction set is first to learn the different instruction categories, which are based on the function or service supplied by the instruction, and then to see what operations are in each category. Programming then becomes much simpler. We *know* what has to be done, for example, temporarily saving a variable for later use; we then *look* in the *instruction category* for the correct operation and *choose* an *addressing mode* to complete the instruction. Of course it is not quite as simple as this. Simultaneously we have to manage the resources in the programmer's model and plan what will be happening to those resources a few instructions later.

The following sections describe the operation of instructions in the various instruction categories, giving examples. A Motorola publication, *CPU Reference Manual*, CPU12RM/AD, contains complete descriptions, including cycle-by-cycle details, of all M68HC12 instructions.

4.2 M68HC12 Instruction Set Categories

In this chapter we cover all of the instructions in 17 different categories. At each step in your program, you will pick the operation and the appropriate addressing mode. A summary of all instructions in their respective categories is given in Table 4–1. Keep a copy of this list in your programming notebook because it will allow you to easily look up the correct mnemonic for an instruction.

TABLE 4–1 M68HC12 Instruction Set Categories[a]

Mnemonic	Operation	Mnemonic	Operation
Load Registers (see Section 4.4)			
LDAA	$(M) \rightarrow A$	LDAB	$(M) \rightarrow B$
LDD	$(M:M+1) \rightarrow D$	LDS	$(M:M+1) \rightarrow SP$
LDX	$(M:M+1) \rightarrow X$	LDY	$(M:M+1) \rightarrow Y$
LEAS[b]	**EA $\rightarrow$ SP**	**LEAX**	**EA $\rightarrow$ X**
LEAY	**EA $\rightarrow$ Y**		
PULA	$(SP) \rightarrow A$	PULB	$(SP) \rightarrow B$
PULD	**(SP:SP+1) $\rightarrow$ D**	**PULC**	**(SP) $\rightarrow$ CCR**
PULX	$(SP:SP+1) \rightarrow X$	PULY	$(SP:SP+1) \rightarrow Y$
Store Registers (see Section 4.4)			
STAA	$A \rightarrow (M)$	STAB	$B \rightarrow (M)$
STD	$D \rightarrow (M:M+1)$	STS	$SP \rightarrow (M:M+1)$
STX	$X \rightarrow (M:M+1)$	STY	$Y \rightarrow (M:M+1)$
PSHA	$A \rightarrow (SP)$	PSHB	$B \rightarrow (SP)$
PSHD	**D $\rightarrow$ (SP:SP+1)**	**PSHC**	**CCR $\rightarrow$ (SP)**
PSHY	$Y \rightarrow (SP:SP+1)$	PSHX	$X \rightarrow (SP:SP+1)$
Transfer/Exchange Registers (see Section 4.5)			
TFR	**Any Reg $\rightarrow$ Any Reg**	**EXG**	**Any Reg $\leftarrow \rightarrow$ Any Reg**
Move Memory Contents (see Section 4.6)			
MOVB	**(M1) $\rightarrow$ (M2)**	**MOVW**	**(M1:M1+1) $\rightarrow$ (M2:M2+1)**
Decrement/Increment (see Section 4.7)			
DEC	$(M)-1 \rightarrow (M)$	DECA	$A-1 \rightarrow A$
DECB	$B-1 \rightarrow B$	DES	$SP-1 \rightarrow SP$
DEX	$X-1 \rightarrow X$	DEY	$Y-1 \rightarrow Y$
INC	$(M)+1 \rightarrow (M)$	INCA	$A+1 \rightarrow A$
INCB	$B+1 \rightarrow B$	INS	$SP+1 \rightarrow SP$
INX	$X+1 \rightarrow X$	INY	$Y+1 \rightarrow Y$
Clear/Set (see Section 4.8)			
CLR	$0 \rightarrow (M)$	CLRA	$0 \rightarrow A$
CLRB	$0 \rightarrow B$		
BSET	$1 \rightarrow (M\ bits)$	BCLR	$0 \rightarrow (M\ bits)$
Arithmetic (see Section 4.10)			
ABA	$A+B \rightarrow A$	ABX	$B+X \rightarrow X$ (see LEAX)
ABY	$B+Y \rightarrow Y$ (See LEAY)	ADDA	$A+(M) \rightarrow A$
ADDB	$B+(M) \rightarrow B$	ADDD	$D+(M:M+1) \rightarrow D$
ADCA	$A+(M)+C \rightarrow A$	ADCB	$B+(M)+C \rightarrow B$
DAA	Decimal adjust		
SUBA	$A-(M) \rightarrow A$	SBA	$A-B \rightarrow A$
SUBD	$D-(M:M+1) \rightarrow D$	SUBB	$B-(M) \rightarrow B$
SBCB	$B-(M)-C \rightarrow B$	SBCA	$A-(M)-C \rightarrow A$
NEG	2's Complement (M)	NEGA	2's Complement A
NEGB	2's Complement B	**SEX**	**Sign Extend A,B,CCR**
MUL	Unsigned $A*B \rightarrow D$	**EMUL**	**Unsigned D*Y $\rightarrow$ Y:D**
EMULS	**Signed D*Y $\rightarrow$ Y:D**		

TABLE 4-1 (continued)

Mnemonic	Operation	Mnemonic	Operation
IDIV	Unsigned D/X → X,D	**EDIV**	**Unsigned Y:D/X → Y,D**
EDIVS	**Signed Y:D/X → Y,D**	**IDIVS**	**Signed D/X → X,D**
FDIV	Fractional D/X → X,D		

Logic (see Section 4.11)

ANDA	A·(M) → A	ANDB	B·(M) → B
ANDCC	**CCR·(M) → CCR**		
EORB	B EOR (M) → B	EORA	A EOR (M) → A
ORAB	B OR (M) → B	ORAA	A OR (M) → A
ORCC	**CCR OR (M) → CCR**		
COM	1's Complement (M)	COMA	1's Complement A
COMB	1's Complement B		

Rotates/Shifts (see Section 4.9)

ROL	Rotate Left (M)	ROLA	Rotate Left A
ROLB	Rotate Left B	ROR	Rotate Right (M)
RORA	Rotate Right A	RORB	Rotate Right B
ASL	Arith Shift Left (M)	ASLA	Arith Shift Left A
ASLB	Arith Shift Left B	ASLD	Arith Shift Left D
ASR	Arith Shift Right (M)	ASRA	Arith Shift Right A
ASRB	Arith Shift Right B		
LSLA	Logic Shift Left A	LSL	Logic Shift Left (M)
LSLD	Logic Shift Left D	LSLB	Logic Shift Left B
LSRA	Logic Shift Right A	LSR	Logic Shift Right (M)
LSRD	Logic Shift Right D	LSRB	Logic Shift Right B

Data Test (see Section 4.12)

BITA	Test bits in A	BITB	Test bits in B
CBA	A-B	CMPA	A-(M)
CMPB	B-(M)	CPD	D-(M:M+1)
CPX	X-(M:M+1)	CPY	Y-(M:M+1)
CPS	**SP-(M:M+1)**		
TST	Test (M)=0 or negative	TSTA	Test A=0 or negative
TSTB	Test B=0 or negative		

Fuzzy Logic and Specialized Math (see Section 4.18 and Chapter 13)

MEM	**Membership Function**	**REV**	**MIN-MAX Rule Eval**
REVW	**Weighted Rule Eval**	**WAV**	**Weighted Average**
EMINM	**MIN(D,(M:M+1)) → (M:M+1)**	**EMIND**	**MIN(D,(M:M+1)) → D**
MINM	**MIN(A,(M)) → (M)**	**MINA**	**MIN(A,(M)) → A**
EMAXM	**MAX(D,(M:M+1)) → (M:M+1)**	**EMAXD**	**MAX(D,(M:M+1)) → D**
MAXM	**MAX(A,(M)) → (M)**	**MAXA**	**MAX(A,(M)) → A**
ETBL	**16-bit Table Interpolate**	**EMACS**	**Mult and Accumulate**
TBL	**8-bit Table Interpolate**		

Conditional Branch (see Section 4.13)

BMI	Short branch minus	**LBMI**	**Long branch minus**
BPL	Short branch plus	**LBPL**	**Long branch plus**
BVS	Short branch 2's compl overflow set	**LBVS**	**Long branch 2's compl overflow set**

TABLE 4–1 (continued)

Mnemonic	Operation	Mnemonic	Operation
BVC	Short branch 2's compl overflow clear	**LBVC**	**Long branch 2's compl overflow clear**
BLT	Short branch 2's compl less than	**LBLT**	**Long branch 2's compl less than**
BGE	Short branch 2's compl greater than or equal	**LBGE**	**Long branch 2's compl greater than or equal**
BLE	Short branch 2's compl less than or equal	**LBLE**	**Long branch 2's compl less than or equal**
BGT	Short Branch 2's compl greater than	**LBGT**	**Long branch 2's compl greater than**
BEQ	Short branch equal	**LBEQ**	**Long branch equal**
BNE	Short branch not equal	**LBNE**	**Long branch not equal**
BHI	Short branch higher	**LBHI**	**Long branch higher**
BLS	Short branch lower or same	**LBLS**	**Long branch lower or same**
BHS	Short branch higher or same	**LBHS**	**Long branch higher or same**
BLO	Short branch lower	**LBLO**	**Long branch lower**
BCC	Short branch carry clear	**LBCC**	**Long branch carry clear**
BCS	Short branch carry set	**LBCS**	**Long branch carry set**

Loop Primitive (see Section 4.14)

Mnemonic	Operation	Mnemonic	Operation
DBEQ	**Decr and branch = 0**	**DBNE**	**Decr and branch <> 0**
IBEQ	**Incr and branch = 0**	**IBNE**	**Incr and branch <> 0**
TBEQ	**Test and branch = 0**	**TBNE**	**Test and branch <> 0**

Jump and Branch (see Section 4.15)

Mnemonic	Operation	Mnemonic	Operation
JMP	Jump to address		
JSR	Jump to subroutine	**CALL**	**Call subroutine**
RTS	Return from subroutine	**RTC**	**Return from CALL**
BSR	Branch to subroutine		
BRN	Short branch never	**LBRN**	**Long branch never**
BRA	Short branch always	**LBRA**	**Long branch always**
BRSET	Branch bits set		
BRCLR	Branch bits clear		

Condition Code (see Section 4.16)

Mnemonic	Operation	Mnemonic	Operation
ANDCC	**Clear CCR Bits**	ORCC	Set CCR Bits

Interrupt (see Section 4.17)

Mnemonic	Operation	Mnemonic	Operation
CLI	Clear interrupt mask	SEI	**Set interrupt mask**
SWI	S/W interrupt	RTI	Return from interrupt
WAI	Wait for interrupt	**TRAP**	**S/W interrupt**

Miscellaneous (see Section 4.19)

Mnemonic	Operation	Mnemonic	Operation
NOP	No Operation	STOP	Stop clocks
BGND	**Background debug mode**		

[a]*(M) indicates the instruction addresses memory using immediate, direct, extended, or indexed addressing. Register Name (A, B, D, X, Y, SP, PC) indicates the contents of that register. (SP) means on the stack. C denotes the contents of carry flag. CCR denotes the contents of the condition code register.*
[b]*New instructions for the M68HC12 (compared with the M68HC11) are marked in* **bold**.

4.3 M68HC12 Instruction and Operand Syntax

The following sections show all of the M68HC12 instructions grouped into instruction categories. For each instruction we also show its syntax and how to specify an instruction's operands for the various addressing modes.

As we learned in Chapter 3, an assembly language program step is an *operation*, signified by the instruction *mnemonic*, followed by one or more *operands*. Table 4–2 shows a short-hand notation to describe the operands. Starting in Section 4.4, we will describe all of the M68HC12 instructions using tables and examples. Look at Table 4–3, which shows the instructions in the load register category, and Table 4–4, which shows the operand syntax for these instructions. For example, to load the A register with 8-bit data using immediate addressing we see the instruction syntax is

```
LDAA      #data8i
```

which means "load accumulator A with 8-bit immediate data." A typical instruction would be

```
LDAA #$28
```

Table 4–4 shows two forms for indexed addressing:

```
LDAA const,xysp
LDAA data3,-xys+
```

The first means "load accumulator A with an 8-bit value using indexed addressing." The offset is given by *const*, which may be 0 or any 5-, 9-, or 16-bit value. The index register may be X, Y, the stack pointer, or the program counter (*xysp*). A typical indexed addressing instruction is

```
LDAA 3,X.
```

The second form means "load accumulator A with an 8-bit value using automatic pre- or post-decrement or increment, indexed addressing." The increment or decrement value is given by *data3*, which must be in the range of 1 to 8, and the index register that may be used is X, Y, or the stack pointer (*xsp*). A typical instruction of this type is

```
LDAA 1,X+
```

4.4 Load and Store Register Instructions

Eight-Bit Load and Store Instructions

The main decision you make when choosing the load and store instructions is the type of addressing. As a review, remember the following:

- *Immediate* addressing gets the data from the next byte(s) in memory and is used only for constant data known when the program is written or assembled.

- *Direct* addressing and *extended* addressing access other memory locations. Direct addressing is limited to the first 256 locations whereas extended addressing can address the entire 64-Kbyte memory space.

- There are a variety of *indexed addressing* modes in the M68HC12. The *effective address* is calculated by adding an offset to either the X, Y, SP, or, sometimes, the PC register. You may use any of the offsets shown in Table 4–7. There are 8- and 16-bit load and store instructions as shown in Examples 4–1 to 4–5.

TABLE 4-2 M68HC12 Operand Syntax

data8i	8-bit immediate data
data16i	16-bit immediate data
adr8a	8-bit direct memory address
adr16a	16-bit extended memory address
constx	Indexed addressing constant: 0 or any 5-, 9-, or 16-bit value
xysp	Either of the X, Y, SP, or PC registers
xys	Either of the X, Y, or SP registers
abd	Either of the A, B, or D registers
const16	16-bit indexed addressing constant
data3	3-bit, pre- or postincrement or decrement value in the range 1–8
−xys+	Pre- or postincrement or decrement of register X, Y, or SP
re19	Label of a branch destination −512 to +511 locations

TABLE 4-3 Load Register Instructions

NEW M68HC12 LOAD INSTRUCTIONS		
Function	**Opcode**	**Operation**
Load Effective Address	LEAX	Load effective address into X, Y, and SP
	LEAY	
	LEAS	
Pull Condition Code Register	PULC	Pull condition code register from stack
Pull D Register	PULD	Pull D register from stack

Function	Opcode	Symbolic Operation	IMM	DIR	EXT	IDX	IDR	INH	N	Z	V	C
Load Accumulator A	LDAA	(M) → A	x	x	x	x	x		⇕	⇕	0	—
Load Accumulator B	LDAB	(M) → B	x	x	x	x	x		⇕	⇕	0	—
Load Accumulator D	LDD	(M:M+1) → D	x	x	x	x	x		⇕	⇕	0	—
Load Stack Pointer	LDS	(M:M+1) → SP	x	x	x	x	x		⇕	⇕	0	—
Load Index Register X	LDX	(M:M+1) → X	x	x	x	x	x		⇕	⇕	0	—
Load Index Register Y	LDY	(M:M+1) → Y	x	x	x	x	x		⇕	⇕	0	—
Load SP Effective Address	LEAS	EA → SP				x			—	—	—	—
Load X Effective Address	LEAX	EA → X				x			—	—	—	—
Load Y Effective Address	LEAY	EA → Y				x			—	—	—	—
Pull A from Stack	PULA	(SP) → A						x	—	—	—	—
Pull B from Stack	PULB	(SP) → B						x	—	—	—	—
Pull CCR from Stack	PULC	(SP) → CR						x	⇕	⇕	⇕	⇕
Pull D from Stack	PULD	(SP:SP+1) → D						x	—	—	—	—
Pull X from Stack	PULX	(SP:SP+1) → X						x	—	—	—	—
Pull Y from Stack	PULY	(SP:SP+1) → Y						x	—	—	—	—

Addressing Mode[a]; *Condition Codes[b]*

[a]IDX, indexed addressing; IDR, indexed-indirect addressing.
[b]Only the condition register bits of interest to the programmer are shown in these tables. The S, X, and I bits are related to the STOP and interrupt group instructions, and, although the H bit is modified by many instructions, it is of no concern to us. The following notation is used to show changes in the condition code register:

—	no change	⇑	May be set or remain cleared
0	reset to zero	⇓	May be cleared or remain set
1	set to one	?	May be changed but final state unknown
⇕	changed to one or zero		

TABLE 4-4 Load Instruction Operand Syntax

Mnemonic	Immediate	Direct	Extended	Indexed	Indexed-Indirect	D Indexed-Indirect
LDAA,LDAB	#data8i	adr8a	adr16a	constx,xysp data3,−xys+	[const16,xysp]	[abd,xysp]
LDD,LDX,LDY,LDS	#data8i	adr8a	adr16a	constx,xysp data3,−xys+	[const16,xysp]	[abd,xysp]
LEAS,LEAX,LEAY				constx,xysp data3,−xys+		

TABLE 4-5 Store Register Instructions

NEW M68HC12 STORE INSTRUCTIONS		
Function	**Opcode**	**Operation**
Push CCR	PSHC	Push condition code register on stack
Push D Register	PSHD	Push D register on stack

			Addressing Mode						Condition Codes			
Function	Opcode	Symbolic Operation	IMM	DIR	EXT	IDX	IDR	INH	N	Z	V	C
Store Accumulator A	STAA	A → (M)		x	x	x	x		$\updownarrow$	$\updownarrow$	0	—
Store Accumulator B	STAB	B → (M)		x	x	x	x		$\updownarrow$	$\updownarrow$	0	—
Store Accumulator D	STD	D → (M:M+1)		x	x	x	x		$\updownarrow$	$\updownarrow$	0	—
Store Stack Pointer	STS	SP → (M:M+1)		x	x	x	x		$\updownarrow$	$\updownarrow$	0	—
Store Index Register X	STX	X → (M:M+1)		x	x	x	x		$\updownarrow$	$\updownarrow$	0	—
Store Index Register Y	STY	Y → (M:M+1)		x	x	x	x		$\updownarrow$	$\updownarrow$	0	—
Push A to Stack	PSHA	A → (SP)						x	—	—	—	—
Push B to Stack	PSHB	B → (SP)						x	—	—	—	—
Push CCR to Stack	PSHC	CCR → (SP)						x	—	—	—	—
Push X to Stack	PSHX	X → (SP:SP+1)						x	—	—	—	—
Push Y to Stack	PSHY	Y → (SP:SP+1)						x	—	—	—	—

TABLE 4-6 Store Instruction Operand Syntax

Mnemonic	Immediate	Direct	Extended	Indexed	Indexed-Indirect	D Indexed-Indirect
STAA,STAB,STD STS,STX,STY		adr8a	adr16a	constx,xysp data3,−xys+	[const16,xysp]	[abd,xysp]

TABLE 4-7 Indexed Addressing Summary

Offset	Registers Used	Instruction Format	
5-, 9-, and 16-bit signed integer,	X, Y, SP, or PC	opcode	offset,register
A, B, or D register	X, Y, SP, or PC	opcode	A,register
		opcode	B,register
		opcode	D,register
+1 to +8 automatic increment or decrement	X, Y, SP	opcode	decrement,−register
		opcode	increment,+register
		opcode	decrement,register−
		opcode	increment,register+
16-bit or D register indexed-indirect	X, Y, SP, or PC	opcode	[offset,register]
		opcode	[D,register]

> Most load and store instructions modify the condition code register.

Notice in Tables 4–3 and 4–5 that load and store instructions modify the condition code register. This could adversely affect your program as shown in Example 4–3 where the BNE LOOP instruction is supposed to branch until the DECB instruction decrements the B accumulator to zero, setting the Z bit to one. By putting the LDAA #$64 instruction between the DECB and the BNE LOOP, the Z bit will never be one and the program will stay in the loop forever. Example 4–4 shows how to fix the problem.

Sixteen-Bit Load and Store Instructions

The 16-bit load and store instructions move data to and from memory. In Motorola systems, the most significant byte is stored at the effective memory address and the least significant byte is stored in the next location. Figure 4–1 shows how the store and load instructions access memory.

Most programs use a variety of load and store instructions. Example 4–6 shows a program that uses the M68HC12 A/D converter to sense a temperature from a nonlinear transducer, like the thermocouple shown in Figure 4–2. A *look-up table* is used to convert the analog-to-digital (A/D) value to its temperature value. Indexed addressing using the B register is used to access the table values based on the input A/D value.

Stack Instructions

Comparison of M68HC12 and M68HC11 Stack Instructions	
M68HC12	**M68HC11**
Stack pointer points to the last used location	Stack pointer points to the next available byte location

> The stack pointer register must point to RAM and stack operations must be balanced.

The stack is an area of RAM used to *temporarily* save data. The 16-bit *stack pointer (SP) register* points to the last byte placed on the stack. The stack pointer must be initialized, with an LDS #address instruction, where address is a valid RAM memory address, or at least no more than one higher than the highest address of the RAM to be used for the stack.

EXAMPLE 4-1   Load and Store Register Instructions

```
ldstc.asm                Assembled with  CASM  11/15/1998  20:33  PAGE  1

                  1   ; Immediate addressing
0000 8640         2        ldaa   #!64      ; Decimal  64 → A
0002 CF0C00       3        lds    #$0c00    ; $0c00 → SP
                  4   ; Direct addressing
0005 D664         5        ldab   $64       ; ($0064) → B
0007 5A65         6        staa   $65       ; A → ($0065)
                  7   ; Extended addressing
0009 B61234       8        ldaa   $1234     ; ($1234) → A
000C FE1234       9        ldx    $1234     ; ($1234:1235) → X
000F 7E0800      10        stx    $0800     ; X → ($0800:0801)
                 11   ; Indexed addressing
0012 E6E017      12        ldab   !23,x     ; (X+23) → A
0015 6B40        13        stab   ,y        ; B → (Y)
0017 A63E        14        ldaa   !2,x-     ; (X) → A
                 15                         ; X-2 → X  (Auto decrement)
                 16   ; Indexed-indirect addressing
0019 EEEF        17        ldx    [d,y]     ; ((D+Y)) → X
001B A6E30064    18        ldaa   [!100,x]  ; ((X+100)) → A
```

EXAMPLE 4-2

A. What is in A and the N, Z, V, and C CCR bits after an LDAA #$70 instruction is executed?
    Solution:
    A = $70, NZVC = 000-. The - means that the carry bit is not changed.
B. What does the LDAA #$64 instruction do?
    Solution:
    It loads A with the value $64 and sets the NZVC bits to 000-.
C. What does the instruction LDAA #!64 do?
    Solution:
    It loads A with the value 64_{10} and sets the NZVC bits to 000-.
D. What does the instruction LDAA $64 do?
    Solution:
    It loads A from memory location $0064 and sets the NZVC bits according to the data value.
E. The X register contains $4000. What does the instruction STAA $10,X do?
    Solution:
    It stores the contents of A into memory location $4010.
F. What does the instruction STAB DATA do?
    Solution:
    It Stores B into the memory location at the label DATA. It also modifies the N and Z bits according to the data and resets the V bit to 0. The carry bit is unchanged.

EXAMPLE 4–3   Load and Store Instructions Modify the CCR

```
ldex1c.asm        Assembled with CASM   04/12/1998   20:49    PAGE 1

0000             1  COUNT: EQU    !8      ;Loop counter
                 2  ;         - - -
0000 C608        3         ldab  #COUNT;Initialize loop counter
                 4  ;   - - -
                 5  LOOP:
                 6  ; Here is the code for whatever has to be
                 7  ; done in a loop. At the end of the loop,
                 8  ; we decrement the loop counter and branch
                 9  ; back if it hasn't been decremented to zero.
                10  ;   - - -
0002 53         11         decb         ; Decrement the B register and
                12                       ; branch to LOOP if
                13                       ; the B register is not zero
0003 8664       14         ldaa  #$64   ; But first load the A register
                15                       ; with some data
0005 26FB       16         bne   LOOP
```

EXAMPLE 4–4

How could you reorganize the code in the previous example to ensure the branch is taken properly?

Solution:

```
ldex2c.asm       Assembled with CASM 04/12/1998 20:55 PAGE 1

0000             1  COUNT2: EQU    !8       ; Loop counter
                 2  ;        - - -
0000 C608        3          ldab  #COUNT2 ; Initialize loop counter
                 4  ;        - - -
                 5  LOOP:
                 6  ; Here is the code for whatever has to be
                 7  ; done in a loop. At the end of the loop,
                 8  ; we must decrement the loop counter and
                 9  ; branch back if it has not been decremented
                10  ; to zero.
                11  ;        - - -
0002 8664       12          ldaa   #$64    ; Load the A register with
                13                          ; some data BEFORE the
                14                          ; decrement
0004 53         15          decb           ; Decrement the B register
                16                          ; and branch to LOOP if
                17                          ; the B register is not zero
0005 26FB       18          bne    LOOP
```

EXAMPLE 4–5

A. What does the instruction LDX #DATA do?
    Solution:
    It loads the X register with the 16-bit value of DATA. DATA may be a label on a
    memory location or may be defined by an assembler EQU directive. The N and Z
    bits are modified, the V bit is reset to 0, and the C bit is unchanged.
B. What does the instruction LDX #$1234 do?
    Solution:
    It loads the X register with the value $1234 and sets the NZVC bits to 000-.
C. What does the instruction LDX $1234 do?
    Solution:
    It loads the X register from memory locations $1234 and $1235 and modifies the
    NZVC bits according to the data.
D. What does the instruction LDX DATA do?
    Solution:
    It loads the X register from the memory locations starting at the label DATA. Two lo-
    cations are used, DATA and DATA+1.

There are three main uses for the stack:

● Temporarily saving a few bytes of data from a register; this is commonly done when entering a subroutine where you do not want to disturb the contents of a register.

● Saving the return address when the program jumps to or calls a subroutine.

● Allocating data space for temporary variables such as "automatic" variables in C.

The push (PSH) and pull (PUL) instructions store to and load data from the stack. Figure 4–3
shows push and pull operations. Figure 4–3a shows the stack pointer pointing to the last data byte
pushed onto the stack. The result of pushing 2 bytes is shown in Figure 4–3b and c. New Data 1
and New Data 2 are now in memory and the stack pointer has been decremented twice. The result of a pull is shown in Figure 4–3d and a subsequent push in Figure 4–3e.

Normally stack operations must be balanced, i.e., when retrieving data from the stack, say
when restoring the contents of registers at the end of a subroutine, there must be the same

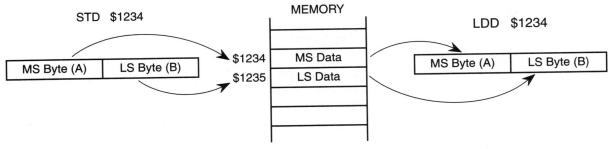

Figure 4–1   16-bit load and store instructions.

EXAMPLE 4–6   Indexed Addressing Instruction Example

Figure 4–2 shows the transfer function of a nonlinear temperature transducer being read by an analog-to-digital converter. Instead of calculating the temperature using a nonlinear equation to convert the A/D readings, a look-up table can be used. Each position (address) in the table will contain the value of the temperature for each reading. The A/D value is used to calculate an *index* into the table to retrieve the temperature. Here is a code example to do this.

```
linrex1c.asm              Assembled with CASM 04/12/1998 21:19 PAGE 1

0000                1 ADR1H:    EQU    $72     ; A/D result register 1
                    2 ;         - - -
                    3 ; Now get an A/D value and linearize it
0000 D672           4         ldab    ADR1H  ; Get the A/D value
0002 CD0007         5         ldy     #TBLE  ; Init Y to start of TABLE
0005 E6ED           6         ldab    b,y    ; B now has linearized value
                    7 ;         - - -
0007 01020204       8 TBLE: DB       01,02,02,04,05,06,06
     050606
                    9
                   10 ; (256 values for an 8-bit A/D input. Each
                   11 ; location in the table has the "corrected"
                   12 ; value for what was input into the B
                   13 ;     accumulator.)
```

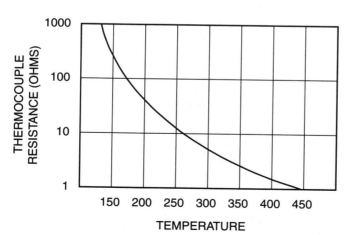

F i g u r e 4 – 2   Nonlinear thermocouple temperature transducer transfer characteristic.

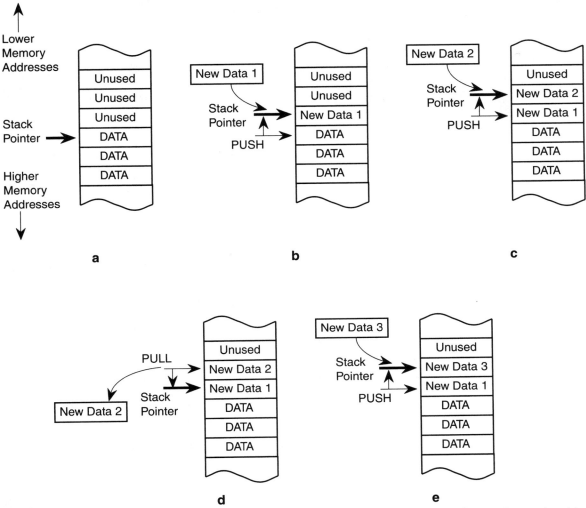

Figure 4–3 Stack operations. (a) Stack pointer before stack operations. (b) Stack pointer after a push operation. (c) Stack pointer after a second push operation. (d) Stack pointer after a pull operation. (e) Stack pointer after a third push operation.

number of PSHes as PULs. Also, PULs must be in the reverse order of the PSHes. See Examples 4–7 to 4–11.

The jump and call instructions for transferring to a subroutine also use the stack. When a JSR SUB instruction is executed, the address of the instruction immediately following the JSR is called the return address. This is the location to which the program must return after the subroutine is over, and it is pushed onto the stack. Thus, a JSR is like a push of the program counter followed by a jump to the subroutine. The return from subroutine instruction, RTS, pulls the return address from the stack.

EXAMPLE 4-7

What is wrong with the following code in a subroutine?

```
push2c.asm       Assembled with CASM 04/16/1998 19:27 PAGE 1

0000 34     1 SUB:     pshx        ; Save the registers
0001 36     2          psha
            3 ;        - - -
            4 ;        - - -
0002 37     5          pshb        ; Temp save some data
            6 ;        - - -
            7 ;        - - -
0003 32     8          pula        ; Restore the registers
0004 30     9          pulx
0005 3D    10          rts
```

Solution:
The stack operations are unbalanced. There is one more push than pull. The subroutine will not return to the proper place in the calling program.

EXAMPLE 4-8

What is wrong with the following code segment?

```
push3c.asm       Assembled with CASM 04/16/1998 19:30 PAGE 1

0000        1 COUNT:   EQU      8
            2 ;
0000 C608   3          ldab     #COUNT    ; Initialize counter
            4 LOOP:
            5 ;        - - -
            6 ;        - - -
0002 36     7          psha               ; Temp save A reg
            8 ;        - - -
            9 ;        - - -
0003 53    10          decb               ; Decr and branch
0004 26FC  11          bne      LOOP
0006 32    12          pula
```

Solution:
This is also an unbalanced stack operation. There is a push with no corresponding pull inside the loop.

EXAMPLE 4–9

What is wrong with the following sequence of code in a subroutine?

```
push1c.asm        Assembled with CASM  04/16/1998  19:24  PAGE 1

0000 34           1 SUB:       pshx        ; Save the registers
0001 36           2            psha
0002 37           3            pshb
                  4 ;          - - -
                  5 ;          - - -
0003 30           6            pulx        ; Restore the registers
0004 32           7            pula
0005 33           8            pulb
0006 3D           9            rts
```

Solution:
The pull operations must be in the reverse order to properly restore the registers.

EXAMPLE 4–10   Using the Stack to Save Data

```
stack1c.asm       Assembled with CASM  04/16/1998  19:13  PAGE 1

0000              1 STACK: EQU  $0a00    ; Equate the stack pointer
                  2                      ; initialization value.
0000 CF0A00       3            lds  #STACK ; Init the stack pointer.
                  4 ;          - - -
0003 36           5            psha        ; Put the A register on stack
0004 34           6            pshx        ; Put the X register on stack
                  7 ;          - - -
0005 30           8            pulx        ; Must pull the data in the
0006 32           9            pula        ; reverse order
```

EXAMPLE 4–11

What does the following program sequence do?

```
      PSHX
      PULY
```

Solution:

Copies the contents of the X register into the Y register. The condition code register is not modified. An equivalent instruction is TFR X,Y.

High level languages such as C use the stack to temporarily store data. The M68HC12 supports a clean, practical way to allocate and deallocate stack space. The *load effective address* instructions covered in the next section provide this capability.

Load Effective Address Instructions

New M68HC12 Load Effective Address Instructions
LEAX, LEAY, and LEAS are new in the M68HC12 instruction set

An *effective address* (*EA*) is the memory address from or to which data are transferred. Indexed addressing instructions form the effective address by combining an *offset* with a *register*. The M68HC12 has three new instructions that allow the programmer to load the effective address into the stack pointer (LEAS), the X register (LEAX), or the Y register (LEAY). For example, the instruction

```
ldaa    $10,x
```

loads the A register from memory location ($10 + the contents of the X register). Thus, the effective address is ($10 + the contents of the X register). The instruction

```
leay    $10,x
```

will load this effective address into the Y register. The load effective address instructions allow us to calculate memory addresses at run time without modifying the contents of the condition code register.

Shortly we will see some instructions that allow us to increment or decrement the contents of a register. This is useful in stepping through a table of data. For example, the INX instruction increments the X register by one. If we want to change the X, Y, or SP register by more than one, the LEA_ can be used. See Example 4–12.

In Example 4–12 we see an example of an instruction that modifies the stack pointer. This seems to contradict the advice given in the last section to keep stack operations balanced by keeping the

---

EXAMPLE 4–12   Load Effective Address Instructions

Assume X = $1234, Y = $1000, and SP = $0A00. Give the contents of each affected register after the following instructions are executed:

Instruction	*Result*
LEAX !10,X	X = X + 10_{10} = $1234 + $000A = $123E
LEAX $10,Y	X = Y + $10 = $1000 + $0010 = $1010
LEAS -!10,SP	SP = SP − 10_{10} = $0A00 − $000A = $09F6

EXAMPLE 4–13   Transferring Many Bytes to a Subroutine

leasex1c.asm   Assembled with CASM 04/16/1998 20:19 PAGE 1

```
              1 ; Demonstration of LEAS instruction
              2 ; Adds 10 bytes passed on the stack and
              3 ; returns the sum on the A register
0000          4 NUM:     EQU      !10            ; Number of bytes to add
0000          5 PROG:    EQU      $0800          ; Program location
0000          6 DATA:    EQU      $0900
0000          7 STACK:   EQU      $0a00          ; Top of the stack
              8 ;
0800          9          ORG      PROG
0800 CF0A00  10          lds      #STACK
             11 ; Push NUM bytes on the stack from an
             12 ; arbitrary data buffer
0803 C60A    13          ldab     #NUM           ; Initialize counter
0805 CE0900  14          ldx      #BUF           ; Initialize X pointer
             15 ; DO get the data
0808 A600    16 LoadLoop: ldaa    0,x
             17 ; and put it on the stack
080A 36      18          psha
080B 08      19          inx      ; Increment the pointer
             20 ; WHILE the counter is not equal to zero
080C 0431F9  21          dbne     b,LoadLoop
             22 ; Calculate the sum
080F C60A    23          ldab     #NUM
0811 160817  24          jsr      CalcSum
             25 ; After returning from the subroutine, you can check
             26 ; the carry bit for an overflow and you
             27 ; can restore the stack pointer
0814 1B8A    28          leas     NUM,SP
0816 3F      29          swi
             30 ; Subroutine to calculate a sum of NUM bytes
             31 ; on the stack.
             32 ; Input:  B register contains the number to add
             33 ; Output: A register contains the sum
             34 ; Registers Modified: A, B, and CCR
             35 CalcSum:
             36 ; When the subroutine is entered, the SP is pointing
             37 ; at the return address. Move it to point to the data.
0817 1B82    38          leas     2,SP           ; SP+2 → SP
             39 ; Now get the data and add it all up
0819 32      40          pula                    ; Get first byte
081A 53      41          decb                    ; Adjust the counter
             42 add_loop:
             43 ; DO add the byte the SP is pointing to, and
             44 ; then increment the SP to point to the next byte
```

EXAMPLE 4–13 Continued

```
081B  ABB0        45              adda    1,SP+
                  46  ; WHILE the counter is not equal to zero
081D  0431FB      47              dbne    b,add_loop
                  48  ; A register has the sum, restore the SP to pointing
                  49  ; to the return address.
0820  1B94        50              leas    {0-NUM-2},SP
0822  3D          51              rts     ; Return to the program
                  52  ; Set up the data buffer area and put some data in it
0900              53              ORG     DATA
0900  01020304    54  BUF:        DB          1,2,3,4,5,6,7,8,9,!10
      05060708
      090A
```

---

number of pushes and pulls equal. Clearly the LEAS −!10,SP instruction will change the stack pointer in some way. This technique is often used when variables are temporarily stored on the stack as in a C program or when transferring many bytes of data to a subroutine. Example 4–13 shows how to do this.

Explanation of Example 4–13

This program passes a number of bytes to a subroutine, which adds them together and returns the sum to the calling program. For this example, the number of bytes to be added is defined by the EQU on *line 4*. The program is located by the ORG on *line 9* and the data bytes are located in RAM at *line 53* and then defined by the DB at *line 54*. After the stack pointer, the X register, and a counter are initialized in *lines 10–14*, the data are loaded from BUF and pushed onto the stack (*lines 15–21*). The B register is initialized at *line 23* with the number of bytes to be added and the program jumps to the subroutine in *line 24*. We will learn more about the jump to subroutine (JSR) instruction in *line 24* in Section 4.15, but for now it is sufficient to understand that the JSR pushes the return address (2 bytes) onto the stack before jumping to the subroutine.

The subroutine starts on *line 38*. The LEAS 2,SP adds two to the stack pointer so that it now points to the *last* byte of data pushed onto the stack. We now want to sum this byte with the remaining NUM−1 bytes. We decrement the B register counter, *line 41*, and then, using postincrement, indexed addressing we add the next byte (*line 45*). ADDA 1,SP+ means the following:

> Add the data pointed to by the SP register to the A register (leaving the addition in the A register) and then increment the SP register.

At *line 47* we see a DBNE B,ADD_LOOP. This instruction decrements the B register counter, and if it is not zero, branches back to *line 42* to add the next byte into the summation. When we are done with this loop, *line 50* adjusts the stack pointer so that it points to the return address. LEAS {0−NUM−2},SP decrements the stack pointer by 12. The RTS instruction at *line 51* returns the calling program at *line 28* where the stack pointer is adjusted to account for its movement when putting data on the stack in the first place. This *restores* the stack pointer to the value it had at *line 14* and we see that we have not violated our principle of keeping a balanced stack.

4.5 Transfer Register Instructions

Transfer register instructions (Table 4–8) transfer data only within the CPU. When saving data temporarily, use one of these if the destination register is not otherwise in use. Transfer instructions copy the source data to the destination register and exchange instructions swap the contents of the two. The TAB, TBA, TFR ⟨reg⟩,C, and EXG ⟨reg⟩,C instructions affect the condition code register but the rest of the transfer and exchange instructions do not. The M68HC11 had a limited set of transfer and exchange instructions and the M68HC12 allows any register to be transferred or exchanged. The rules for transferring or exchanging between 8- and 16-bit registers are shown in Table 4–9. See Examples 4–14 and 4–15.

> *Transfer register* instructions are useful for temporarily saving data.

TABLE 4–8 Transfer Register Instructions

NEW M68HC12 TRANSFER INSTRUCTIONS		
Function	**Opcode**	**Operation**
Transfer Registers	TFR	Transfer any register to any register
Exchange Register	EXG	Exchange any two registers

Function	Opcode	Symbolic Operation	Addressing Mode Inherent	N	Z	V	C
Transfer A to B	TAB	A → B	x	↕	↕	0	—
Transfer B to A	TBA	B → A	x	↕	↕	0	—
Transfer Registers	TFR	Reg → Reg	x	—	—	—	—[a]
Exchange Registers	EXG	Reg ← → Reg	x	—	—	—	—

M68HC11 Instructions	Opcode	Symbolic Operation	Equivalent M68HC12 Instructions
Transfer (S)+1 to X	TSX	SP+1 → X	TFR S,X
Transfer (S)+1 to Y	TSY	SP+1 → Y	TFR S,Y
Transfer X-1 to Stack Pointer	TXS	X-1 → SP	TFR X,S
Transfer Y-1 to Stack Pointer	TYS	Y-1 → SP	TFR Y,X
Exchange D and X	XGDX	X ← → D	EXG D,X
Exchange D and Y	XGDY	Y ← → D	EXG D,Y

[a]*When the CCR is the destination register, all condition code bits take on the value of the source register bits, except the X mask bit, which cannot be changed from zero to one.*

TABLE 4–9 8-Bit and 16-Bit Transfer and Exchange Instructions

Transfer	8-bit → 16-bit	The 8-bit source is transferred to the low byte of the destination; the sign of the source is extended into the high byte of the destination; see the SEX instruction
	16-bit → 8-bit	The low byte of the 16-bit source is transferred to the 8-bit destination
Exchange	8-bit ← → 16-bit	The low bytes of the registers are exchanged and the high byte of the 16-bit register is set to $00

EXAMPLE 4–14

What is in the A, B, and the NZVC bits after the following sequence of instructions is executed?

```
LDAA        #$AA
TAB
```

Solution:

A = $AA, B = $AA, NZVC = 100–

EXAMPLE 4–15

What is in the stack pointer and the Y registers after the following sequence is executed?

```
LDX        #$1234
TXS
TSY
```

Solution:
        S = $1233, Y = $1234

4.6 Move Instructions

Move instructions (Tables 4–10 and 4–11) allow you to transfer data from one memory location to another without using any CPU registers. This is an important feature in a processor with only a few registers. For these instructions, indexed addressing with 9- and 16-bit constant offsets and indexed-indirect addressing are not allowed. Five-bit constant, accumulator, and automatic increment and decrement indexing are allowed. See Examples 4–16 and 4–17.

4.7 Decrement and Increment Instructions

Decrement and *increment* instructions subtract or add one to the operand.

Decrement and increment instructions (Tables 4–12 and 4–13) are used in many assembler language programs. All of these, except the DES and INS instructions (LEAS −1,S and LEAS 1,S), modify one or more CCR bits. Example 4–18 shows how to use decrement and increment instructions in a loop that transfers data from one table to another. Examples 4–19 to 4–21 show how to decrement 8- and 16-bit counters. See also Examples 4–22 and 4–23.

TABLE 4–10 Move Instructions

		NEW M68HC12 MOVE INSTRUCTIONS									
Function	**Opcode**	**Function**									
Move registers	MOVB	Move a byte from one memory location to another									
	MOVW	Move a word from one memory location to another									

			Addressing Mode						**Condition Codes**			
Function	**Opcode**	**Symbolic Operation**	**IMM**	**DIR**	**EXT**	**IDX**	**IDR**	**INH**	**N**	**Z**	**V**	**C**
Move Byte	MOVB	(M1) → (M2)	x		x	x			—	—	—	—
Move Word	MOVW	(M1:M1+1) → (M2:M2+1)	x		x	x			—	—	—	—

4.8 Clear and Set Instructions

These instructions clear and set bits; CLR, CLRA, and CLRB are self-explanatory. BSET and BCLR are bit addressing instructions. Any bit in an operand can be modified without affecting the others. The bit clear (BCLR) and bit set (BSET) instructions clear or set individual bits in the selected memory location. The format of these instructions is

```
BCLR      Operand,Mask
BCLR      Operand,Mask
```

Operand is a memory location specified using direct addressing in the first 256 memory locations and extended or indexed addressing for the rest of memory. The bits to be cleared or set are specified by 1s in the *Mask* byte. Any bits in the mask that are zero indicate bits in the operand that are NOT affected by the instruction.

BCLR and BSET are useful when controlling external devices one bit at a time. Figure 4–4 shows eight light-emitting diodes (LEDs) connected to Port H of the M68HC12. As we will see in Chapter 7, data may be output to Port H by writing to memory location $0024. Writing a 1

TABLE 4–11 Move Instruction Operand Syntax

Mnemonic	Immediate → Extended	Immediate → Indexed	Extended → Extended	Extended → Indexed	Indexed → Extended	Indexed → Indexed
MOVB	#data8i, adr16a	#data8i, constx,xyxp #data8i, data3,−xys+	adr16a, adr16a	adr16a, constx,xysp adr16a, data3,−xys+	constx,xysp, adr16a data3,−xys+, adr16a	constx,xysp, constx,xysp data3,−xys+, data3,−xys+
MOVW	#data16i, adr16a	#data16i, constx,xyxp #data16i, data3,−xys+	adr16a, adr16a	adr16a, constx,xysp adr16a, data3,−xys+	constx,xysp, adr16a data3,−xys+, adr16a	constx,xysp, constx,xysp data3,−xys+, data3,−xys+

EXAMPLE 4–16

```
movex0c.asm            Assembled with CASM 04/18/1998 02:23 PAGE 1

                   1  ; Examples of move instructions and
                   2  ; their M68HC11 equivalents
                   3  ; Initialize 8-bit memory
0000 180B6400     4          movb     #$64,DATA1
     1A
                   5  ; Equivalent M68HC11 instructions
0005 36            6          psha      ; If you don't want to lose
                   7                    ; the data in A reg
0006 8664          8          ldaa     #$64
0008 7A001A        9          staa     DATA1
000B 32           10          pula
                  11  ;        - - -
                  12  ; Initialize 16-bit memory
000C 1804001B     13          movw     DATA2,DATA3
     001D
                  14  ; Equivalent M68HC11 instructions
0012 3B           15          pshd
0013 FC001B       16          ldd      DATA2
0016 7C001D       17          std      DATA3
0019 3A           18          puld
                  19  ;        - - -
001A              20  DATA1:   DS       1
001B              21  DATA2:   DS       2
001D              22  DATA3:   DS       2
```

---

to a bit in Port H turns the LED off and writing a 0 turns it on. Example 4–24 shows a program segment to succesively turn on LEDs zero to seven in a loop. See also Example 4–25 and 4–29.

4.9 Shift and Rotate Instructions

There are 34 shift and rotate instructions (Tables 4–16 and 4–17). Each shifts or rotates the operand only one bit position each time the instruction is executed. Let us look at the shift instructions first. There are two kinds of shifts—arithmetic and logical—and each shifts left and right. Inspect Figures 4–5 to 4–8.

> The arithmetic shift right instruction *preserves the sign* of the number.

The logical shift instructions shift a zero into either the least significant or most significant bit position. The arithmetic instructions are used for numbers. As shown in Figures 4–5 and 4–7, the logical and arithmetic shift left instructions are identical. Shifting numerical data to the left one bit is equivalent to multiplying the number by 2. The arithmetic and logical shift right instructions are different, as can be seen by comparing Figures 4–6 and 4–8. Shifting a number right is equivalent to dividing by 2 and shifting the most significant bit to the right *preserves the sign.* The two rotate instructions can be seen in Figures 4–9

EXAMPLE 4–17

Write a program segment to reverse the order of data in a 100-byte table.

Solution:

```
movex1c.asm        Assembled with CASM  04/18/1998  02:32  PAGE 1

0000               1  COUNT:  EQU   !100            ; Length of the table
                   2  ;        - - -
                   3  ; Reverse the data in the table
0000 CE0013        4          ldx   #TABLE          ; Point to start of the table
0003 CD0076        5          ldy   #TABLE+COUNT-1  ; Point to the end byte
0006 C632          6          ldab  #{COUNT/2}      ; Init counter
0008 A600          7  LOOP:   ldaa  0,x             ; Get a byte out
                   8                                ; of the way
000A 180A4030      9          movb  0,y,1,x+        ; Get from bottom,
                  10                                ; put in top and
                  11                                ; increment
                  12                                ; the top pointer
000E 6A7F         13          staa  1,y-            ; Put top in bottom and
                  14                                ; decrement the bottom
                  15                                ; pointer
0010 0431F5       16          dbne  b,LOOP          ; Decrement counter and
                  17                                ; branch if not done
                  18  ;        - - -
0013             19  TABLE:  DS    COUNT
```

TABLE 4–12 Decrement and Increment Instructions

Function	Opcode	Symbolic Operation	IMM	DIR	EXT	IDX	IDR	INH	N	Z	V	C
Decrement memory	DEC	(M)-1 → (M)			x	x	x		⇕	⇕	⇕	—
Decrement A	DECA	A-1 → A						x	⇕	⇕	⇕	—
Decrement B	DECB	B-1 → B						x	⇕	⇕	⇕	—
Decrement X	DEX	X-1 → X						x	—	⇕	—	—
Decrement Y	DEY	Y-1 → Y						x	—	⇕	—	—
Decrement SP	DES[a]	S-1 → S						x	—	—	—	—
Increment Memory	INC	(M)+1 → (M)			x	x	x		⇕	⇕	⇕	—
Increment A	INCA	A+1 → A						x	⇕	⇕	⇕	—
Increment B	INCB	B+1 → B						x	⇕	⇕	⇕	—
Increment X	INX	X+1 → X						x	—	⇕	—	—
Increment Y	INY	Y+1 → Y						x	—	⇕	—	—
Increment Stack	INS	S+1 → S						x	—	—	—	—

[a]DES and INS are equivalent to LEAS -1,S and LEAS 1,s.

TABLE 4–13 Decrement and Increment Instruction Operand Syntax

Mnemonic	Immediate	Direct	Extended	Indexed	Indexed-Indirect	D Indexed-Indirect
DEC,INC			adr16a	constx,xysp data3,−xys+	[const16,xysp]	[abd,xysp]

EXHIBIT 4–18   Transferring Data from One Buffer to Another

```
dec1c.asm              Assembled with CASM 11/15/1998 23:37  PAGE 1

0000                1  COUNT:    EQU     !100
                    2  ;         - - -
0000 CE000F         3            ldx     #TABLE1 ; "Point" X to start of the
                    4                            ; table of data
0003 CD0073         5            ldy     #TABLE2 ; Point Y to TABLE2
0006 C664           6            ldab    #COUNT  ; Initialize the counter
                    7  ;         - - -
                    8  ; Move data from TABLE1 to TABLE2 and increment the
                    9  ; pointers using auto-increment indexed addressing
0008 180A3070      10  LOOP2:    movb    1,x+,1,y+
000C 0431F9        11            dbne    b,LOOP2 ; Decrement loop counter
                   12  ;         - - -
                   13  ;         - - -
000F              14  TABLE1:   DS      COUNT   ; Reserve COUNT bytes
0073              15  TABLE2:   DS      COUNT   ; for each table
```

EXAMPLE 4–19

Counters are often used in assembly language programs. If there is no free register, you can use a memory location. Show a segment of code that will create and use a counter in memory.

Solution:

```
count1c.asm           Assembled with CASM 04/19/1998 02:33  PAGE 1

0000                1  COUNT:    EQU     !26
                    2  ; Initialize the counter in memory
0000 180B1A00       3            movb    #COUNT,Cnter
     0A
                    4  LOOP:
                    5  ;         - - -
                    6  ;         - - -
0005 73000A         7            dec     Cnter
0008 26FB           8            bne     LOOP
                    9  ;         - - -
000A              10  Cnter:    DS      1          ; 8-bit counter
```

EXHIBIT 4–20

Sometimes a counter is needed that is bigger than 255, or 8 bits. A 16-bit counter can be kept in memory like the 8-bit counter shown in Example 4–19. What is wrong with the code sequence shown below?

```
count2c.asm          Assembled with CASM 04/19/1998  02:36  PAGE 1

0000                 1 BIG:    EQU       !1000
                     2 ; Initialize the counter in memory
0000 180303E8        3         movw      #BIG,Cnter
000B
                     4 LOOP:
                     5 ;       - - -
                     6 ;       - - -
0006 73000B          7         dec       Cnter
0009 26FB            8         bne       LOOP
                     9 ;       - - -
000B                10 Cnter:  DS        2          ; 16-bit counter
```

Solution:
The DEC instruction decrements an 8-bit operand. Thus DEC Cnter will decrement only the most significant byte of the 2-byte counter. In this case, the loop code will be executed only three times, not 1000.

---

and 4–10. These rotate bits around in the operand, including the carry bit, instead of just shifting them.Shifts and rotates maneuver bits around in an operand. Arithmetic shifts can multiply and divide by powers of two sometimes faster than multiply and divide instructions. Example 4–26 shows how to multiply a number by 10 using shift instructions. This demonstrates a use of the ASLD instruction as an alternative to the EMUL multiply instruction. Most programming problems have several ways to achieve the desired result. Examples 4–27 to 4–29 show other uses of the shift and rotate instructions. Example 4–24 shows how to turn LEDs on and off using the BSET and BCLR instructions. A more compact program, shown in Example 4–29, could use a rotate instruction.

4.10 Arithmetic Instructions

Add and Subtract

The M68HC12 *arithmetic instructions* can add, subtract, decimal adjust, negate, multiply, and divide.

Table 4–18 shows the arithmetic instructions and Table 4–19 shows the operand syntax for these instructions. All, except SEX, modify bits in the condition code register. The ADCA, ADCB, SBCA, SBCB instructions add or subtract the carry bit to the operands. This allows multiple byte arithmetic because the carry bit acts as a *link* between one 8-bit addition (or subtraction) and another. See Example 4–30.

EXAMPLE 4–21

Show how to fix the problem illustrated in Example 4–20.

Solution:

Instead of decrementing the memory location with the DEC Cnter instruction, you must do something like the following:

```
count3c.asm           Assembled with CASM  04/19/1998  02:40  PAGE 1

0000                1  BIG:      EQU      !1000
                    2  ; Initialize the counter in memory
0000  180303E8      3            movw     #BIG,Cnter
      0011
                    4  LOOP:
                    5  ;         - - -
                    6  ;         - - -
0006  34            7            pshx               ; Save X register
0007  FE0011        8            ldx      Cnter     ; Get the counter and
000A  09            9            dex                ; decrement it
000B  7E0011       10            stx      Cnter
000E  30           11            pulx               ; Restore X register
000F  26F5         12            bne      LOOP
                   13  ;         - - -
0011               14  Cnter:    DS       2         ; 16-bit counter
```

The ADDD adds 16-bit data from memory to the D accumulator. Remember that the D accumulator is the concatenation of the A and B accumulators. See Example 4–31.

The load effective address instructions, LEAX, LEAY, and LEAS, discussed in Section 4.4, can be considered to be 16-bit arithmetic instructions because they add 16-bit values to the X, Y, and SP registers.

EXAMPLE 4–22

What affect do the STX Cnter and PULX instructions have on the condition code register in Example 4–21?

Solution:

The PULX does not modify the condition code register but the STX instruction does. However, the state of the Z bit, which was set when the DEX instruction was executed, will not be changed by the STX and so the BNE LOOP instruction will work properly.

EXAMPLE 4-23

The program segment shown in Example 4–21 pushes and pulls the X register and re-loads the counter each time through the loop. You would have to do that if the X register were being used somewhere else in the loop. However, if it is not, a shorter, faster program can be written. Show how this can be done.

Solution:

```
count4c.asm          Assembled with CASM  04/21/1998  01:55  PAGE 1

0000              1 BIG:     EQU      !1000
                  2 ; Initialize the counter in the X register
0000 34           3          pshx                ; Save X register
0001 CE03E8       4          ldx      #BIG
                  5 LOOP:
                  6 ;        - - -
                  7 ;        - - -
0004 0435FD       8          dbne     x,LOOP
0007 30           9          pulx                ; Restore X register
                 10 ;        - - -
```

TABLE 4-14 Clear and Set Instructions

Function	Opcode	Symbolic Operation	IMM	DIR	EXT	IDX	IDR	INH	N	Z	V	C
Clear memory	CLR	$0 \to (M)$			x	x	x	x	0	1	0	0
Clear A	CLRA	$0 \to A$						x	0	1	0	0
Clear B	CLRB	$0 \to B$						x	0	1	0	0
Clear Bits in Memory	BCLR			x	x	x			⇕	⇕	0	—
Set Bits in Memory	BSET			x	x	x			⇕	⇕	0	—

TABLE 4-15 Clear and Set Instruction Operand Syntax

Mnemonic	Immediate	Direct	Extended	Indexed	Indexed-Indirect	D Indexed-Indirect
CLR			adr16a	constx,xysp data3,−xys+	[const16,xysp]	[abd,xysp]
BSET,BCLR		adr8a	adr16a	constx,xysp data3,−xys+		

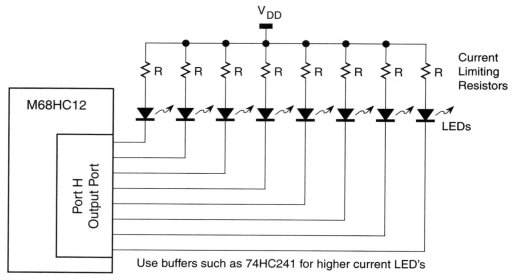

Figure 4-4 BCLR and BSET used for turning on and off LEDs.

EXAMPLE 4-24 LED Program Using BCLR and BSET

```
bset3c.asm          Assembled with CASM  11/15/1998  23:52  PAGE  1

                 1  ; Equates for all the bits
0000             2  BIT0:   EQU    %00000001
0000             3  BIT1:   EQU    %00000010
0000             4  BIT2:   EQU    %00000100
0000             5  BIT3:   EQU    %00001000
0000             6  BIT4:   EQU    %00010000
0000             7  BIT5:   EQU    %00100000
0000             8  BIT6:   EQU    %01000000
0000             9  BIT7:   EQU    %10000000
0000            10  ALL:    EQU    %11111111
0000            11  REGS:   EQU    $0000      ; Start of the I/O regs
0000            12  PORTH:  EQU    REGS+$24   ; Offset for Port H
0000            13  DDRH:   EQU    REGS+$25   ; Data dir register
                14  ;        - - -
0000  4C25FF    15          bset   DDRH,ALL   ; Make all bits outputs
0003  4C24FF    16  LOOP:   bset   PORTH,ALL  ; Turn out all LEDs
0006  4D2401    17          bclr   PORTH,BIT0 ; Turn on bit 0
0009  4D2402    18          bclr   PORTH,BIT1 ; Turn on bit 1
000C  4D2404    19          bclr   PORTH,BIT2 ; Turn on bit 2
000F  4D2408    20          bclr   PORTH,BIT3 ; Turn on bit 3
0012  4D2410    21          bclr   PORTH,BIT4 ; Turn on bit 4
0015  4D2420    22          bclr   PORTH,BIT5 ; Turn on bit 5
0018  4D2440    23          bclr   PORTH,BIT6 ; Turn on bit 6
001B  4D2480    24          bclr   PORTH,BIT7 ; Turn on bit 7
001E  20E3      25          bra    LOOP       ; Do it forever
```

EXAMPLE 4–25

What do you expect to see on the LEDs as the program in Example 4–24 runs?

Solution:

We expect to see the LEDs go out and then come on one at a time, starting from the right, until all are on and then to repeat for eight times.

What do we actually see?

Solution:

All lights will appear to be on because the BCLR and BSET instructions take only 0.5 μsec to execute, much to fast for our eyes to respond. If you traced the program one step at a time, you would see the expected behavior. (The number of clock cycles, and thus the time, required to execute can be found in the *CPU12 Reference Guide*, CPU12RG/AD available from Motorola.)

TABLE 4–16 Shift and Rotate Instructions

Function	Opcode	Memory Addressing Mode						Condition Codes			
		IMM	DIR	EXT	IDX	IDR	INH	N	Z	V	C
Arithmetic Shift Left Memory	ASL			x	x	x		↕	↕	↕	↕
Arithmetic Shift Left A	ASLA						x	↕	↕	↕	↕
Arithmetic Shift Left B	ASLB						x	↕	↕	↕	↕
Arithmetic Shift Left D (16-bit)	ASLD						x	↕	↕	↕	↕
Arithmetic Shift Right Memory	ASR			x	x	x		↕	↕	↕	↕
Arithmetic Shift Right A	ASRA						x	↕	↕	↕	↕
Arithmetic Shift Right B	ASRB						x	↕	↕	↕	↕
Arithmetic Shift Right D (16-bit)	ASRD						x	↕	↕	↕	↕
Logical Shift Left Memory	LSL			x	x	x		↕	↕	↕	↕
Logical Shift Left A	LSLA						x	↕	↕	↕	↕
Logical Shift Left B	LSLB						x	↕	↕	↕	↕
Logical Shift Left D (16-bit)	LSLD						x	↕	↕	↕	↕
Logical Shift Right Memory	LSR			x	x	x		0	↕	↕	↕
Logical Shift Right A	LSRA						x	0	↕	↕	↕
Logical Shift Right B	LSRB						x	0	↕	↕	↕
Logical Shift Right D (16-bit)	LSRD						x	0	↕	↕	↕
Rotate Left Memory	ROL			x	x	x		↕	↕	↕	↕
Rotate Left A	ROLA						x	↕	↕	↕	↕
Rotate Left B	ROLB						x	↕	↕	↕	↕
Rotate Right Memory	ROR			x	x	x		↕	↕	↕	↕
Rotate Right A	RORA						x	↕	↕	↕	↕
Rotate Right B	RORB						x	↕	↕	↕	↕

TABLE 4–17 Shift and Rotate Instruction Operand Syntax

Mnemonic	Immediate	Direct	Extended	Indexed	Indexed-Indirect	D Indexed-Indirect
ASL,ASR,LSR,LSR ROL,ROR			adr16a	constx,xysp data3,−xys+	[const16,xysp]	[abd,xysp]

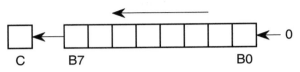

Figure 4–5 Logical shift left (LSL) instructions.

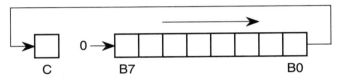

Figure 4–6 Logical shift right (LSR) instruction.

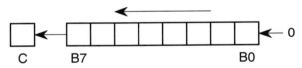

Figure 4–7 Arithmetic shift left (ASL) instructions.

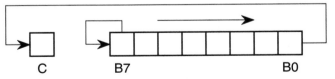

Figure 4–8 Arithmetic shift right (ASR) instructions.

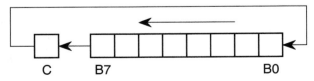

Figure 4–9 Rotate left (ROL) instructions.

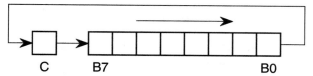

Figure 4–10   Rotate right (ROR) instructions.

EXAMPLE 4–26

Write M68HC12 code to multiply a 16-bit number in the D register by 10 using arithmetic left shift instructions instead of the EMUL instruction.

```
shift1c.asm     Assembled with CASM 04/25/1998 15:31 PAGE 1

0000 7C0009  1         std    TEMP  ; Save in location TEMP
0003 59      2         asld         ; X2
0004 59      3         asld         ; X2 again = X4
0005 F30009  4         addd   TEMP  ; Add the original. Now X5
0008 59      5         asld         ; X2 = X10
             6
0009         7  TEMP:  DS     2     ; Temp storage
```

EXAMPLE 4–27

Assume the A value is $A9. What is the result of each of the following instructions? ASLA, ASRA, LSLA, LSRA, ROLA, RORA.

Solution:
The easiest way to look at these instructions is to show the values in binary. Before each instruction is executed, A contains %10101001. After each instruction, then, we find the following:

Before	*After*	*C*	*A Register*	*Comments*
10101001	ASLA	1	01010010	Zero shifted into bit 0.
10101001	ASRA	1	11010100	Sign bit is preserved.
10101001	LSLA	1	01010010	Same result as ASLA.
10101001	LSRA	1	01010100	Different than the ASRA.
10101001	ROLA	1	0101001C	Carry bit is rotated into bit 0.
10101001	RORA	1	C1010100	Carry bit is rotated into bit 7.

EXAMPLE 4–28

Show how to load the ASCII code for the number 4 into accumulator B and then shift the least significant nibble into the most significant.

Solution:

```
shift2c.asm        Assembled with CASM  04/25/1998  15:39  PAGE 1

0000 C634     1    ldab    #'4'    ; ASCII code for 4
0002 58       2    lslb            ; Shift four bit positions
0003 58       3    lslb
0004 58       4    lslb
0005 58       5    lslb
```

What is in B after these instructions have been executed?

Solution:
B = $40

Decimal Arithmetic

Packed BCD addition must be corrected with the DAA instruction.

The *decimal adjust A* (DAA) instruction is useful when performing arithmetic on packed binary-coded decimal (BCD) numbers which contain the codes for two decimal digits in one byte. When packed BCD numbers are added, the result can be incorrect. For example, the addition of 34_{10} and 29_{10} gives an incorrect result if BCD codes are being used.

Decimal	*BCD Code*
34	0 0 1 1 0 1 0 0
29	0 0 1 0 1 0 0 1
63	0 1 0 1 1 1 0 1

The binary result, 01011101, is incorrect, both as a binary code and a BCD code. The DAA instruction, if executed immediately after the addition of the two BCD numbers, adds a correction factor to the binary result. In this case, $06 is added.

Decimal	*BCD Code*	
34	0 0 1 1 0 1 0 0	
29	0 0 1 0 1 0 0 1	
	0 1 0 1 1 1 0 1	
	0 0 0 0 0 1 1 0	Correction added by DAA
63	0 1 1 0 0 0 1 1	Correct BCD result.

EXAMPLE 4–29

Use a rotate instruction in a loop to successively turn on LEDs zero to seven as in Example 4–24.

Solution:

A zero must be shifted through the bits in a pattern such as 11111110, 11111100, 11111000, . . . A program sequence to do this follows:

```
rotate1c.asm    Assembled with CASM 04/25/1998  15:49  PAGE 1

0000            1  COUNT:  EQU  8          ; Going to do 8 bits
0000            2  ALLBITS: EQU %11111111  ; Spec all bits
0000            3  FIRST:  EQU  %11111110  ; Turn on bit 0
0000            4  PORTH:  EQU  $24        ; Address of Port H
                5  ;            - - -
                6  ; Turn off all bits
                7  OUTER:
0000 4C24FF     8          bset  PORTH,ALLBITS
0003 86FE       9          ldaa  #FIRST     ; Initialize for bit-0
0005 C608      10          ldab  #COUNT
0007 5A24      11  LOOP:   staa  PORTH      ; Turn on a bit
0009 160014    12          jsr   Delay      ; Delay for a while
000C 10FE      13          clc              ; clear carry bit to rotate
               14  ;                        ; into LSB
000E 45        15          rola             ; Shift the ACCA left
000F 0431F5    16          dbne  b,LOOP     ; Do it for 8 bits
0012 20EC      17          bra   OUTER      ; Do it forever
               18  ;            - - -
               19  ; Dummy subroutine
0014 3D        20  Delay:  rts
```

The DAA instruction automatically determines the correction factor to add, depending, in part, on the half-carry bit (H) in the condition code register. Example 4–32 shows packed BCD arithmetic.

Negating and Sign Extension Instructions

Instructions to negate (two's-complement) numeric information are included in the arithmetic group. See Example 4–33.

The sign extend instruction, SEX, is another mnemonic for any 8-bit to 16-bit register transfer, such as TFR B,D. In this case, the sign bit of the B register is *extended* into the most significant byte of the D register (i.e., the A register). SEX may have the A, B, or CCR registers as the source and D, X, Y, or SP as the destination. The instruction would be useful if, when doing 8-bit, signed arithmetic, you wanted to multiply two 8-bit signed numbers. See Example 4–35.

TABLE 4-18 Arithmetic Instructions

New M68HC12 Arithmetic Instructions		
Function	**Opcode**	**Operation**
Sign Extend	SEX	Transfer an 8-bit signed number into a 16-bit register and extend the sign
16-bit Multiplication	EMUL EMULS	Unsigned and signed 16-bit * 16-bit multiplication with 32-bit result
16-bit Signed Division	IDIVS	16-bit/16-bit division producing 16-bit quotient and 16-bit remainder
32-bit Signed and Unsigned division	EDIVS EDIV	32-bit/16-bit division producing 16-bit quotient and 16-bit remainder

Function	Opcode	Symbolic Operation	IMM	DIR	EXT	IDX	IDR	INH	N	Z	V	C
Add B to A	ABA	A+B → A						x	↕	↕	↕	↕
Add Memory to A	ADDA	A+(M) → A	x	x	x	x	x		↕	↕	↕	↕
Add Memory to B	ADDB	B+(M) → B	x	x	x	x	x		↕	↕	↕	↕
Add Memory to D (16-bit)	ADDD	D+(M:M+1) → D	x	x	x	x	x		↕	↕	↕	↕
Add with Carry to A	ADCA	A+(M)+C → A	x	x	x	x	x		↕	↕	↕	↕
Add with Carry to B	ADCB	B+(M)+C → B	x	x	x	x	x		↕	↕	↕	↕
Decimal Adjust	DAA							x	↕	↕	↕	↕
Subtract B from A	SBA	A-B → A						x	↕	↕	↕	↕
Subtract Memory from A	SUBA	A-(M) → A	x	x	x	x	x		↕	↕	↕	↕
Subtract Memory from B	SUBB	B-(M) → B	x	x	x	x	x		↕	↕	↕	↕
Subtract with Carry from A	SBCA	A-(M)-C → A	x	x	x	x	x		↕	↕	↕	↕
Subtract with Carry from B	SBCB	B-(M)-C → B	x	x	x	x	x		↕	↕	↕	↕
Subtract Memory from D (16-bit)	SUBD	D-(M:M+1) → D	x	x	x	x	x		↕	↕	↕	↕
Sign Extend A, B, CCR	SEX							x	—	—	—	—
2s-Complement Memory	NEG	-(M) → (M)			x	x	x		↕	↕	↕	↕
2s-Complement A	NEGA	-A → A						x	↕	↕	↕	↕
2s-Complement B	NEGB	-B → B						x	↕	↕	↕	↕
Unsigned 8-bit Multiply A*B	MUL	A*B → D						x	—	—	—	↕
Unsigned 16-bit Multiply	EMUL	D*Y → Y:D						x	↕	↕	—	↕
Signed 16-bit Multiply	EMULS	D*Y → Y:D						x	↕	↕	—	↕
Unsigned 32/16-bit Division	EDIV	Y:D/X → Y,D						x	↕	↕	↕	↕
Signed 32/16-bit Division	EDIVS	Y:D/X → Y,D						x	↕	↕	↕	↕
Unsigned 16/16-bit Division	IDIV	D/X → (X,D)						x	—	↕	0	↕
Signed 16/16-bit Division	IDIVS	D/X → (X,D)						x	↕	↕	↕	↕
Fractional Division	FDIV	D/X → (X,D)						x	—	↕	↕	↕

TABLE 4-19 Arithmetic Instruction Operand Syntax

Mnemonic	Immediate	Direct	Extended	Indexed	Indexed-Indirect	D Indexed-Indirect
ADCA,ADCB,ADDA, ADDB,SBCA,SBCB, SUBA,SUBD	#data8i	adr8a	adr16a	constx,xysp data3,−xys+	[const16,xysp]	[abd,xysp]
ADDD,SUBD	#data8i	adr8a	adr16a	constx,xysp data3,−xys+	[const16,xysp]	[abd,xysp]
NEG			adr16a	constx,xysp data3,−xys+	[const16,xysp]	[abd,xysp]

EXAMPLE 4–30

Add two 16-bit numbers stored in DATA1:DATA1+1 and DATA2:DATA2+1 using the 8-bit addition instructions. The result is to be stored in DATA3:DATA3+1. Do this using add-with-carry to demonstrate the algorithm used for multiple-byte arithmetic.

Solution:

```
add1c.asm          Assembled with CASM  04/25/1998  16:54  PAGE 1

                1 ; Add the least significant bytes first
0000 B60013     2        ldaa    DATA1+1 ; Get least sig byte of
                3                        ; 16-bit DATA1
0003 BB0015     4        adda    DATA2+1 ; Add in the least sig byte
                5                        ; of 16-bit DATA2
0006 7A0017     6        staa    DATA3+1 ; Save it
                7 ; The carry bit now has a carry out of the least
                8 ; significant byte that must be
                9 ; added into the most significant byte addition.
               10 ; Note that STAA does not change the carry bit.
0009 B60012    11        ldaa    DATA1     ; ldaa does not affect
               12                          ; the carry bit
000C B90014    13        adca    DATA2     ; Add the most significant
               14                          ; byte plus the carry
000F 7A0016    15        staa    DATA3
               16
0012           17 DATA1:  DS      2         ; 16-bit Storage areas
0014           18 DATA2:  DS      2
0016           19 DATA3:  DS      2
```

EXAMPLE 4–31

Add two 16-bit numbers stored in DATA1:DATA1+1 and DATA2:DATA2+1 using a 16-bit add instruction. The result is to be stored in DATA3:DATA3+1.

Solution:

```
add2c.asm          Assembled with CASM  04/25/1998  16:59  PAGE 1

0000 FC0009     1        ldd     DATA1   ; Load 16 bits from
                2                        ; DATA1:DATA1+1
0003 F3000B     3        addd    DATA2   ; Adds 16 bits
0006 7C000D     4        std     DATA3   ; Stores 16 bits
                5 ;      - - -
0009            6 DATA1:  DS      2       ; 16 bit storage locations
000B            7 DATA2:  DS      2
000D            8 DATA3:  DS      2
```

EXAMPLE 4–32   Packed BCD Arithmetic

Assume memory locations DATA4 and DATA5 each contains two decimal digit numbers encoded using packed BCD. Write a small program segment that adds the two numbers, placing the result in DATA6. Show by a numerical example (assume DATA4 = 66_{10}, DATA5 = 26_{10}) what is in the registers at each program step.

Solution:

```
bcd1c.asm              Assembled with CASM  04/25/1998  17:15  PAGE 1

0000  B6000B      1              ldaa    DATA4   ;  01100110 → A
0003  BB000C      2              adda    DATA5   ;  01100110 + 00100110 → A
            3                            ;          = 10001100
0006  1807        4              daa             ;  10001100 + 00000110 → A
            5                            ;                = 10010010
0008  7A000D      6              staa    DATA6   ;  10010010 → DATA6
            7   ;              - - -
000B        8   DATA4:   DS      1
000C        9   DATA5:   DS      1
000D       10   DATA6:   DS      1
```

Explanation:
66_{10} is encoded 01100110 and 26_{10} is 00100110. When these binary numbers are added, the result, 10001100, is incorrect. The computer adds the numbers as if they were two's-complement or unsigned-binary numbers. To correct the result to packed BCD code, the DAA instruction uses the information in the condition code register, including the half-carry bit (H), to add a correction factor.

EXAMPLE 4–33

Assume A contains the following data before the M68HC12 executes the NEGA instruction. What is the result in A and the N, Z, V, and C bits for the negation of each byte?

A = $00, $7F, $01, $FF, $80

Solution:

Before	A Register	N	Z	C	V	Comment
		After				
$00	$00	0	1	0	0	Negating zero gives us zero
$7F	$81	1	0	0	0	Negating +127 gives −127
$01	$FF	1	0	0	0	Negating +1 gives −1
$FF	$01	0	0	0	0	Negating −1 gives +1
$80	$80	1	0	0	1	Negating −128 gives overflow

Multiplication

Signed and unsigned numbers can be multiplied or divided.

Multiply instructions for 16- and 32-bit signed numbers have been included in the M68HC12 instruction set. Table 4–20 summarizes the multiply instructions and Examples 4–34 and 4–35 show short code examples.

The MUL instruction multiplies *8-bit, unsigned numbers* in the A and B accumulators. The 16-bit product resides in the D accumulator.

Sixteen-bit signed and unsigned multiply instructions are EMULS and EMUL, respectively. The algorithms, and thus the hardware required, are different for signed and unsigned multiplication; thus, different instructions are needed. See Example 4–35.

Fractional Number Arithmetic

Signed and unsigned fractional numbers may be multiplied and divided

The add, subtract, and multiply arithmetic instructions can be used also for fractional numbers. A fractional number is one in which the binary point is somewhere other than to the right of the least significant bit. Example 4–36 shows unsigned fractional arithmetic.

TABLE 4–20 M68HC12 Multiply Instructions

Opcode	Data Type	Operation	Comment
MUL	8-bit unsigned	A × B	16-bit product → D; C = 1 if bit 7 of the product = 1 to allow rounding for fractional numbers; see Example 4–34
EMUL	16-bit unsigned	D × Y	32-bit product → D:Y; C = 1 if bit 15 of result = 1
EMULS	16-bit signed	D × Y	32-bit product → Y:D; C = 1 if bit 15 of result = 1

EXAMPLE 4–34

Write a small program to multiply the contents of DATA1 and DATA2. Store the result in DATA3:DATA3+1.

Solution:

```
mul1c.asm        Assembled with CASM  11/16/1998  00:20  PAGE  1

 0000  B6000A    1              ldaa    DATA1    ; Get the multiplier
 0003  F6000B    2              ldab    DATA2    ; Get the multiplicand
 0006  12        3              mul              ; The product is in D
 0007  7C000C    4              std     DATA3
                 5    ;         - - -
 000A            6    DATA1:    DS      1        ; 8-bit multiplier
 000B            7    DATA2:    DS      1        ; 8-bit multiplicand
 000C            8    DATA3:    DS      2        ; 16-bit product
```

EXAMPLE 4–35   8-Bit Signed Multiply

```
sexexc.asm              Assembled with CASM  11/16/1998  00:19  PAGE 1

                    1  ;        - - -
                    2  ; 8-bit * 8-bit signed multiply
0000 B6000F         3          ldaa    DATA1   ; Get the multiplicand
0003 B706           4          SEX     a,y     ; Sign extend into Y
0005 B60010         5          ldaa    DATA2   ; Get the multiplier
0008 B704           6          TFR     a,d     ; Same as SEX a,d
000A 1813           7          emuls           ; Extended multiply Y*D
                    8  ; 32-bit product is in Y:D
                    9  ; The 16 bits we need are in D
000C 7C0011        10          std     DATA3
                   11  ;        - - -
000F               12  DATA1:  DS      1       ; 8-bit multiplicand
0010               13  DATA2:  DS      1       ; 8-bit multiplier
0011               14  DATA3:  DS      2       ; 16-bit product
```

EXAMPLE 4–36   Unsigned Fractional Arithmetic

```
  0.50      .1000       0.75      .1100
+ 0.25    + .0100     - 0.25    - .0100
  0.75      .1100       0.50      .1000

  0.50      .1000
× 0.25    × .0100          0.375/0.5=0.75
  0.125     0000
            0000         .0100=
            1000         .1000                      .1100
            0000                            1000 )0100.0000
          .00100000
```

The 4-bit by 4-bit multiplication in Example 4–36 gives an 8-bit result. When multiplying in the M68HC12 using the MUL instruction, an 8-bit fractional multiply gives a 16-bit fractional result. At times it may be convenient to discard the least significant 8 bits and round-up the result to the most significant 8 bits. The MUL instruction provides a convenient way to do this by automatically setting the carry if bit 7 in accumulator B is one. See Example 4–37. The EMUL instructions operate the same for 16-bit fractional multiplications.

EXAMPLE 4–37   Fractional Multiplication with Rounding

```
mul2c.asm              Assembled with CASM  04/25/1998  17:43  PAGE 1

                   1  ; Multiply fractional numbers
0000 B6000C        2           ldaa    DATA1   ; 8-bit fraction
0003 F6000D        3           ldab    DATA2   ; 8-bit fraction
0006 12            4           mul             ; 16-bit fraction result
0007 8900          5           adca    #0      ; Increment A if B
                   6                           ; is 0.5 or greater
0009 7A000E        7           staa    DATA3   ; 8-bit rounded result
                   8  ;        - - -
000C               9  DATA1:   DS      1
000D              10  DATA2:   DS      1
000E              11  DATA3:   DS      1
```

Division

Division instructions for 16- and 32-bit signed numbers have been included in the M68HC12 instruction set. IDIVS and EDIVS are 16- and 32-bit signed division instructions. Table 4–21 gives a summary of the division instructions and Examples 4–38 to 4–40 show small sample programs.

IDIV, FDIV, and EDIV are for unsigned operands only. IDIV divides the 16-bit integer in the D accumulator by the 16-bit integer in the X register. The 16-bit quotient is placed into the X register and a 16-bit remainder in the D accumulator. If the denominator is zero (divide by 0) the

TABLE 4–21   M68HC12 Division Instructions

Opcode	Data Type	Operation	Comment
IDIV	16-bit, integer, unsigned	D/X	Quotient $\rightarrow$ X, Remainder $\rightarrow$ D. The radix point is the same for both numerator and denominator and is to the right of the LSB. If X = 0 (divide by zero) \$FFFF $\rightarrow$ X and C is set
IDIVS	16-bit, integer, signed	D/X	Quotient $\rightarrow$ X, Remainder $\rightarrow$ D. If divide by zero, D and X are unchanged and C is set; if overflow occurs, V is set
FDIV	16-bit, fractional, unsigned	D/X	Quotient $\rightarrow$ X, Remainder $\rightarrow$ D. Numerator assumed < denominator; radix point for each operand assumed to be the same; overflow (V) bit is set if denominator <= numerator. If divide by zero, \$FFFF $\rightarrow$ X and C is set
EDIV	32-bit, integer, unsigned	Y:D/X	Quotient $\rightarrow$ X, Remainder $\rightarrow$ D. If divide by zero, C is set; if result is > \$FFFF, V is set
EDIVS	32-bit, integer, unsigned	Y:D/X	Quotient $\rightarrow$ X, Remainder $\rightarrow$ D. If divide by zero, C is set

carry bit is set and the quotient X is set to $FFFF. The radix point is the same for both numerator and denominator and is to the right of the least significant bit (bit 0) of the quotient. See Example 4–38.

FDIV performs a 16-bit unsigned fractional divide. The numerator is in the D accumulator and is assumed to be less than the denominator. The denominator is in the X register and the radix point for each of the operands is assumed to be the same; the result is a binary-weighted fraction. As in the IDIV instruction, the carry bit is set to indicate a divide by zero. The overflow bit (V) is set if the denominator is less than or equal to the numerator. The binary fraction quotient is in X and the remainder in D. See Example 4–39.

EDIV and EDIVS are 32-bit divide-by-16-bit unsigned and signed division instructions. The 32-bit dividend in each case is the Y:D register combination and the 16-bit divisor is the X register. A 16-bit quotient is produced in the Y register with a 16-bit remainder in the D. See Example 4–40.

EXAMPLE 4–38

Assume D contains 176_{10} and $X = 10_{10}$. What is in A, B, and X before and after an IDIV instruction?

Solution:

Before the IDIV instruction:
  $D = 176_{10} = \$00B0$, therefore A = $00, B = $B0
  $X = 10_{10} = \$000A$
After the IDIV instruction:
  $176_{10}/10_{10} = 17_{10}$ with a remainder of 6_{10}, therefore
  $X = 17_{10} = \$0011$, $D = 6_{10} = \$0006$, A = $00, B = $06.

EXAMPLE 4–39

Assume D contains 100_{10} and $X = 400_{10}$. What is in A, B, and X before and after an FDIV instruction?

Solution:

Before the FDIV instruction:
  $D = 100_{10} = \$0064$, therefore A = $00, B = $64
  $X = 400_{10} = \$0190$
After the FDIV instruction:
  $100_{10}/400_{10} = 0.25_{10}$ with a remainder of 0, therefore
  $X = 0.25_{10} = \$4000$, $D = 0 = \$0000$, A = $00, B = $00.

EXAMPLE 4–40   Extended, Unsigned Multiply and Divide Instructions

Write a small program to produce DATA1*DATA2/100 where DATA1 and DATA2 are both 16-bit unsigned numbers.

Solution:

```
edivlc.asm              Assembled with CASM 04/25/1998 17:56 PAGE 1

                1 ;                 - - -
                2 ; DATA1*DATA2/100
0000 FC0011      3          ldd     DATA1
0003 FD0013      4          ldy     DATA2
0006 13          5          emul            ; 32-bit prod in Y:D
0007 CE0064      6          ldx     #!100
000A 11          7          ediv            ; Do the division
000B 7D0015      8          sty     DATA3   ; Save quotient
000E 7C0017      9          std     DATA4   ; Save remainder
               10 ;                 - - -
0011           11 DATA1:    DS      2       ; Unsigned multiplier
0013           12 DATA2:    DS      2       ; Unsigned multiplicand
0015           13 DATA3:    DS      2       ; Unsigned quotient
0017           14 DATA4:    DS      2       ; Unsigned remainder
```

4.11 Logic Instructions

The M68HC12 *logic instructions* can AND, OR, Exclusive-OR, and complement.

The logic instructions perform bit-wise logic operations with the two operands (Tables 4–22 and 4–23). The one's-complement instructions are included here because one's-complementing is typically a logic rather than numeric operation. Example 4–41 gives some sample logic operations.

ANDing is sometimes called *masking*. You can mask off certain bits in an operand to use them in some way. Example 4–42 shows a masking operation used to convert packed BCD numbers to ASCII for printing.

4.12 Data Test Instructions

Data test instructions modify the condition code register without changing the operands.

The previous sections have shown that many instructions modify the condition code register bits. All of the test and compare instructions given in Table 4–24 modify only the condition code register bits. The operands themselves are not changed (Table 4–25).

The BITA and BITB instructions AND the contents of the specified accumulator with the contents of the addressed memory location. These instructions are useful for determining if a particular bit in the memory operand is one or zero. Consider an example in which Port H is an input port attached to a set of switches. Our program is to test the state of switch 1

TABLE 4–22 Logic Instructions

NEW M68HC12 LOGIC INSTRUCTIONS		
Function	**Opcode**	**Operation**
AND condition code register	ANDCC	This allows individual bits in the CCR to be reset
OR condition code register	ORCC	This allows individual bits in the CCR to be set

Function	Opcode	Symbolic Operation	IMM	DIR	EXT	IDX	IDR	INH	N	Z	V	C
AND A with Memory	ANDA	A·(M) → A	x	x	x	x	x		↕	↕	0	—
AND B with Memory	ANDB	B·(M) → B	x	x	x	x	x		↕	↕	0	—
AND CCR with Constant	ANDCC	CCR·#data	x						⇓	⇓	⇓	⇓
Exclusive OR A with Memory	EORA	A EOR (M) → A	x	x	x	x	x		↕	↕	0	—
Exclusive OR B with Memory	EORB	B EOR (M) → B	x	x	x	x	x		↕	↕	0	—
Inclusive OR A with Memory	ORAA	A OR (M) → A	x	x	x	x	x		↕	↕	0	—
Inclusive OR B with Memory	ORAB	B OR (M) → B	x	x	x	x	x		↕	↕	0	—
Inclusive OR CCR with constant	ORCC	CCR OR #data	x						⇑	⇑	⇑	⇑
1's-Complement Memory	COM	$\overline{M}$ → (M)			x	x	x		↕	↕	0	1
1's-Complement A	COMA	$\overline{A}$ → A						x	↕	↕	0	1
1's-Complement B	COMB	$\overline{B}$ → B						x	↕	↕	0	1

(attached to bit 1 on Port H) and to do one thing if the switch is zero and another if it is one. Example 4–43 shows a code segment that checks bit 1 of Port H.

The compare instructions subtract one operand from the other, without modifying either, and set the condition code bits. Example 4–43 in the next section shows how conditional branch instructions work after a compare instruction.

TST, TSTA, and TSTB simply test if the operand is zero or negative.

TABLE 4–23 Logic Instruction Operand Syntax

Mnemonic	Immediate	Direct	Extended	Indexed	Indexed-Indirect	D Indexed-Indirect
ANDA,ANDB,EORA, EORB,ORAA,ORAB	#data8i	adr8a	adr16a	constx,xysp data3,−xys+	[const16,xysp]	[adb,xysp]
ANDCC,ORCC	#data8i	adr8a	adr16a	constx,xysp data3,−xys+	[const16,xysp]	[abd,xysp]
COM			adr16a	constx,xysp data3,−xys+	[const16,xysp]	[abd,xysp]

EXAMPLE 4–41

If memory location $0010 contains $B3 and A contains $64, what is the result of the following instructions:

ANDA $10, ANDA #$10, ORAA $10, ORAA #$10, EORA $10, COMA, COM $10

Solution:

ANDA $10	A	0 1 1 0 0 1 0 0	
	(0010)	<u>1 0 1 1 0 0 1 1</u>	
		0 0 1 0 0 0 0 0	

ANDA #$10	A	0 1 1 0 0 1 0 0	Immediate
	$10	<u>0 0 0 1 0 0 0 0</u>	addressing
		0 0 0 0 0 0 0 0	

ORAA $10	A	0 1 1 0 0 1 0 0	
	(0010)	<u>1 0 1 1 0 0 1 1</u>	
		1 1 1 1 0 1 1 1	

ORAA #$10	A	0 1 1 0 0 1 0 0	Immediate
	$10	<u>0 0 0 1 0 0 0 0</u>	addressing
		0 1 1 1 0 1 0 0	

EORA $10	A	0 1 1 0 0 1 0 0	
	(0010)	<u>1 0 1 1 0 0 1 1</u>	
		1 1 0 1 0 1 1 1	

| COMA | A | <u>0 1 1 0 0 1 0 0</u> | |
| | | 1 0 0 1 1 0 1 1 | |

| COM $10 | (0010) | <u>1 0 1 1 0 0 1 1</u> | |
| | (0010) | 0 1 0 0 1 1 0 0 | |

4.13 Conditional Branch Instructions

Comparison of M68HC12 and M68HC11 Conditional Branches	
M68HC12	**M68HC11**
Short (PC relative, 8-bit displacement) Long (PC relative 16-bit displacement)	Short (PC relative, 8-bit displacement only)

The *conditional branch* instructions allow us to test the condition code register bits.

We have seen that many instructions modify the condition code register, and the conditional branch instructions (Table 4–26) test these bits for us. Conditional branch instructions make our machine a computer instead of just a calculator because programs can make decisions based on data that are available when the computer is running. Be

---

EXAMPLE 4–42   Masking Operations

Assume the A accumulator has a packed BCD number to be converted to ASCII and printed (using a subroutine called PRINT). Write a small segment of code using logic instructions to do this.

Solution:

```
mask1c.asm        Assembled with CASM 12/06/1998 14:57 PAGE 1

0000          1 LS_MASK:  EQU   %00001111 ; Least sig nibble mask
              2 ;
0000 B701     3            tfr   a,b    ; Save the BCD number in B
              4 ; Need to print the most significant nibble first
0002 44       5            lsra         ; Shift 4 bits to right
0003 44       6            lsra
0004 44       7            lsra
0005 44       8            lsra
0006 8A30     9            oraa  #$30   ; Convert to ASCII
0008 160014  10            jsr   PRINT  ; Go print it
000B B710    11            tfr   b,a    ; Get the original back
000D 840F    12            anda  #LS_MASK ; Set most sig bits to 0
000F 8A30    13            oraa  #$30   ; Convert to ASCII
0011 160014  14            jsr   PRINT  ; Print it
             15 ;          - - -
             16 ; Dummy subroutine
0014 3D      17 PRINT:     rts
```

---

careful when using a conditional branch to test for something, say a loop counter equal to zero, that another instruction that modifies the CCR is not inserted before the conditional branch is executed. We saw this problem in Example 4–3.

Signed and Unsigned Conditional Branches

> *Signed* and *unsigned number* comparisons need *different* conditional branch instructions.

Another concern is how to handle signed and unsigned numbers. For example, is $FF bigger than $00? It depends on the code. If the code is for an unsigned number, $FF is larger than $00. If a two's-complement signed number system is in use, $FF is smaller than $00. There are *different* conditional branch instructions for *signed* and *unsigned* data. Table 4–27 shows a tabulation of various instructions used for signed and unsigned data. Notice the terminology used. "Greater than" and "less than" imply numerical data and thus are to be used for signed numbers. "Higher-than" and "lower-than" imply unsigned data.

The mnemonics used for the branch instructions make the most sense if we think of them being executed after a compare instruction. For example, if we CMPA $1234 and then use the branch greater than or equal ((L)BGE), we are comparing signed numbers. We would expect the branch to be taken if the value in A is greater than or equal to the contents of memory location $1234.

TABLE 4-24 Data Test Instructions

NEW M68HC12 DATA TEST INSTRUCTIONS		
Function	**Opcode**	**Operation**
Compare Stack Pointer	CPS	Compare the contents of the stack pointer with the contents of a memory location

			Addressing Mode						Condition Codes			
Function	**Opcode**	**Symbolic Operation**	**IMM**	**DIR**	**EXT**	**IDX**	**IDR**	**INH**	**N**	**Z**	**V**	**C**
Test Bits in A	BITA	A·(M)	x	x	x	x	x		⇕	⇕	0	—
Test Bits in B	BITB	B·(M)	x	x	x	x	x		⇕	⇕	0	—
Compare A to B	CBA	A-B						x	⇕	⇕	⇕	⇕
Compare A to Memory	CMPA	A-(M)	x	x	x	x	x		⇕	⇕	⇕	⇕
Compare B to Memory	CMPB	B-(M)	x	x	x	x	x		⇕	⇕	⇕	⇕
Compare D to Memory (16-bit)	CPD	D-(M:M+1)	x	x	x	x	x		⇕	⇕	⇕	⇕
Compare X to Memory (16-bit)	CPX	X-(M:M+1)	x	x	x	x	x		⇕	⇕	⇕	⇕
Compare Y to Memory (16-bit)	CPY	Y-(M:M+1)	x	x	x	x	x		⇕	⇕	⇕	⇕
Compare S to Memory (16-bit)	CPS	S-(M:M+1)	x	x	x	x	x		⇕	⇕	⇕	⇕
Test Memory for zero or negative	TST	(M)-0			x	x	x		⇕	⇕	0	0
Test A for zero or negative	TSTA	A-0						x	⇕	⇕	0	0
Test B for zero or negative	TSTB	B-0						x	⇕	⇕	0	0

The (L)BNE and (L)BEQ instructions test the Z bit. You may wish to think of the (L)BNE as meaning *branch if not equal to zero* and (L)BEQ as *branch if equal to zero*. Make sure you understand why branches are taken or not as shown in Example 4–44.

The short conditional branch instructions use relative addressing. This means that the branch can be at most +127 or −128 bytes from the instruction following the branch instruction. If you try to branch to a location outside these limits, the assembler program will give an error message "parameter out of Range." If this occurs, use a long branch instruction. See Example 4–45.

4.14 Loop Primitive Instructions

The *loop primitive* instructions (Tables 4–28 and 4–29) provide, in one instruction, an operation that is very common in assembly language programs. We often use counters, decrement or increment them, and then branch if the counter equals (or does not equal) zero. The counter may be

TABLE 4-25 Data Test Instruction Operand Syntax

Mnemonic	Immediate	Direct	Extended	Indexed	Indexed-Indirect	D Indexed-Indirect
BITA,BITB,CMPA CMPB,CPD,CPX,CPY CPS	#data8i	adr8a	adr16a	constx,xysp data3,−xys+	[const16,xysp]	[abd,xysp]
TST,TSTA,TSTB			adr16a	constx,xysp data3,−xys+	[const16,xysp]	[abd,xysp]

EXAMPLE 4–43   Using the BITA Instruction

```
bit1c.asm              Assembled with CASM 04/25/1998   18:21 PAGE  1

0000              1  BIT_1:    EQU       %00000010 ; Mask for Bit-1
0000              2  PORTH:    EQU       $24       ; Offset to Port C
                  3  ;         - - -
                  4  ; IF BIT_1 is zero
0000 8602         5            ldaa      #BIT_1
0002 9524         6            bita      PORTH     ; Test Bit-1, Port H
0004 2602         7            bne       do_if_one ; Do the one part
                  8  ; THEN
                  9  ; This is the code to do if the bit is a zero
                 10  ;         - - -
0006 2000        11            bra       end_if    ; Skip the next part
                 12  do_if_one:
                 13  ; This is the code to do if the bit is a one
                 14  ;                   - - -
                 15  end_if:
```

---

any of the registers A, B, D, X, Y, or SP. Note that in contrast with the more usual decrement-and-branch instruction combination that the condition code register is not changed by these instructions. The conditional branching done by these instructions uses a 9-bit offset with −256 to +255 locations. See Example 4–46.

TABLE 4–26 Conditional Branch Instructions

NEW M68HC12 BRANCH INSTRUCTIONS		
All M68HC12 short branch instructions have a long branch companion		

Function	Opcode	Symbolic Operation
Branch if Equal	BEQ, LBEQ	Branch if Z = 1
Branch if Not Equal	BNE, LBNE	Branch if Z = 0
Branch if Minus	BMI, LBMI	Branch if N = 1
Branch if Plus	BPL, LBPL	Branch if N = 0
Branch if Greater Than or Equal (Signed)	BGE, LBGE	Branch if N EOR V = 0
Branch if Less Than or Equal (Signed)	BLE, LBLE	Branch if Z OR [N EOR V] = 1
Branch if Greater Than (Signed)	BGT, LBGT	Branch if Z OR [N EOR V] = 0
Branch if Less Than (Signed)	BLT, LBLT	Branch if N EOR V = 1
Branch if Overflow (Signed)	BVS, LBVS	Branch if V = 1
Branch if No Overflow (Signed)	BVC, LBVC	Branch if V = 0
Branch if Higher (Unsigned)	BHI, LBHI	Branch if C OR Z = 0
Branch if Higher or Same (Unsigned)	BHS, LBHS	Branch if C = 0
Branch if Lower (Unsigned)	BLO, LBLO	Branch if C = 1
Branch if Lower or Same (Unsigned)	BLS, LBLS	Branch if C OR Z = 1
Branch if Carry Clear	BCC, LBCC	Branch if C = 0
Branch if Carry Set	BCS, LBCS	Branch if C = 1
Branch if Bits Set	BRSET	Branch if M·(PC + 2) = 0
Branch if Bits Clear	BRCLR	Branch if M·(PC + 2) = 0

TABLE 4-27 Conditional Branch Instructions for Signed and Unsigned Data

Signed Data Tests		Unsigned Data Tests		Universal Tests	
(L)BMI	Minus				
(L)BPL	Plus				
(L)BVS	Two's-complement overflow	(L)BCS	Carry set = unsigned overflow	(L)BCS	Carry set
(L)BVC	No two's-complement overflow	(L)BCC	Carry clear = no unsigned overflow	(L)BCC	Carry Clear
(L)BLT	Less than	(L)BLO	Lower than		
(L)BGE	Greater than or equal	(L)BHS	Higher or the same		
(L)BLE	Less than or equal	(L)BLS	Lower or the same		
(L)BGT	Greater than	(L)BHI	Higher than		
(L)BEQ	Equal	(L)BEQ	Equal	(L)BEQ	Equal
(L)BNE	Not equal	(L)BNE	Not equal	(L)BNE	Not equal

4.15 Unconditional Jump and Branch Instructions

Unconditional jump and branch instructions (Tables 4–30 and 4–31) always take the branch. The jump instruction, JMP, and jump to subroutine, JSR, use extended, indexed and indexed-indirect addressing and can thus jump to any address in memory. The branch always, BRA, is an unconditional relative addressing branch. Use the branch instructions when you can because they save memory (2 bytes instead of 3 or more). In some processors relative addressing branch instructions are faster than extended addressing jump instructions. This is not true in the M68HC12.

Branches to Subroutines

Use the JSR instruction to call a subroutine. Never use a JMP.

There are five instructions in this group dealing with subroutines. These are the *jump to subroutine* (JSR), *branch to subroutine* (BSR), *call subroutine in expansion memory*, (CALL), *return from subroutine* (RTS), and *return from call* (*RTC*). As you might ex-

---

EXAMPLE 4–44

Assume the A = $FF and memory location DATA = $00. A CMPA DATA instruction is executed followed by a conditional branch. For each of the conditional branch instructions in the table, indicate by yes or no if you expect the branch to be taken.

BGE	BLE	BGT	BLT	BEQ	BNE
BHS	BLS	BHI	BLO		

Solution:

BGE	BLE	BGT	BLT	BEQ	BNE
no	yes	no	yes	no	yes
BHS	BLS	BHI	BLO		
yes	no	yes	no		

EXAMPLE 4-45   Using a Long Branch

```
branch3c.asm          Assembled with CASM  04/25/1998  19:28  PAGE 1

                 1 ;                 - - -
0000 81FF        2                      cmpa   #$FF   ; Compare and Set CCR
                 3
0002 182600FE    4                      lbne   DO_NOT_EQUAL
                 5 DO_EQUAL:
                 6 ; This is the code for the DO IF EQUAL part. The
                 7 ; DS 250 simulates more than 127 bytes of code.
0006             8                      DS     !250
                 9 ;
0100 182000FA   10                      lbra   OVER_NEXT
                11 DO_NOT_EQUAL:
                12 ; This is the code to be done if A does not equal
                13 ; of code.
0104            14                      DS     !250
                15 OVER_NEXT:
```

TABLE 4-28   Loop Primitive Instructions

NEW M68HC12 INSTRUCTIONS							
All loop primitive instructions decrement, increment, or test, and then branch							

Function	Opcode	Symbolic Operation	Addressing Modes REL	N	Z	V	C
Decr and branch = 0	DBEQ	Reg−1 → Reg, Branch if zero	x	—	—	—	—
Decr and branch <> 0	DBNE	Reg−1 → Reg, Branch if not zero	x	—	—	—	—
Incr and branch = 0	IBEQ	Reg+1 → Reg, Branch if zero	x	—	—	—	—
Incr and branch <> 0	IBNE	Reg+1 → Reg, Branch if not zero	x	—	—	—	—
Test and branch = 0	TBEQ	Test Reg, Branch if zero	x	—	—	—	—
Test and branch <> 0	TBNE	Test Reg, Branch if not zero	x	—	—	—	—

TABLE 4-29   Loop Primitive Instruction Operand Syntax

Mnemonic	Register	Rel
DBEQ,DBNE,IBEQ IBNE,TBEQ,TBNE	abdxys	rel9

EXAMPLE 4–46 Loop Primitive Instructions

```
loop1c.asm        Assembled with CASM 04/25/1998 19:29 PAGE 1

                 1 ; Comparing the loop primitive and "normal"
                 2 ; decrement and branch instructions
                 3 ;
0000             4 COUNT:  EQU  !255    ; Counter value
                 5
0000 C6FF        6         ldab #COUNT ; Initialize counter
                 7 ;       - - -
                 8 LOOP:               ; Here is the repetitive code
                 9 ;       - - -
0002 0431FD     10         dbne b,LOOP ; Using the DBNE instruction
                11 ; The alternative is to do the following:
0005 53         12         decb        ; But this sets the CCR bits
0006 26FA       13         bne  LOOP
```

T A B L E 4 – 3 0 Unconditional Jump and Branch Instructions

NEW M68HC12 JUMP AND BRANCH INSTRUCTIONS		
Function	**Opcode**	**Operation**
Expansion Memory	CALL	Call subroutine in expansion memory
Subroutine[a]	RTS	Return from subroutine in expansion memory
Long Branches	LBRA	Long branch always
	LBRN	Long branch never

			Addressing Mode							Condition Codes			
Function	**Opcode**	**Symbolic Operation**	**IMM**	**DIR**	**EXT**	**IDX**	**IDR**	**REL**	**INH**	**N**	**Z**	**V**	**C**
Jump to Address	JMP	EA → (PC)			x	x	x			—	—	—	—
Jump to Subroutine	JSR	EA → (PC)		x	x	x	x			—	—	—	—
Branch to Subroutine	BSR	EA → (PC)						x		—	—	—	—
Call Subroutine	CALL				x	x	x			—	—	—	—
Return from Subroutine	RTS	EA → (PC)							x	—	—	—	—
Return from Call	RTC								x	—	—	—	—
Branch Always	BRA							x		—	—	—	—
	LBRA							x		—	—	—	—
Branch Never	BRN							x		—	—	—	—
	LBRN							x		—	—	—	—

[a]*Expansion memory refers to memory that extents beyond the CPU's normal 64-Kbyte address space. See Chapter 9.*

TABLE 4−31 Jump and Branch Instruction Operand Syntax

Mnemonic	Relative	Direct	Extended	Indexed	Indexed-Indirect	D Indexed-Indirect
JMP,CALL			adr16a	constx,xysp data3,−xys+	[const16,xysp]	[abd,xysp]
JSR		adr8a	adr16a	constx,xysp data3,−xys+	[const16,xysp]	[abd,xysp]
BSR,BRA,LBRA BRN,LBRN	rel9					

pect, the BSR uses relative addressing whereas the JSR uses all other addressing modes. In any event, the instruction contains the effective address of the subroutine to which the program must branch. The address of the instruction immediately following the jump or branch is called the return address. Before starting the subroutine, the return address is pushed onto the stack.

A *return from subroutine*, RTS, is used at the end of the subroutine. When the microcontroller executes the RTS, the return address is pulled from the stack and placed in the program counter.

Two new instructions have been added to the M68HC12 to allow subroutines to be located in *expansion* memory. Some versions of the M68HC12 allow up to 4 Mbytes of addressable program space and up to 1 Mbyte of data space. This is done with a paged architecture. The CALL and the RTC instructions allow subroutines located in expansion memory to be executed and returned from.

There are three (at least) important rules to obey when using subroutines:

1. Always initialize the stack pointer register to point to an area of RAM memory *before* using BSR or JSR. If you do not, the program may or may not run. If the program is acting strangely, check to see if the stack pointer is initialized correctly.

2. *Never, ever* JMP to a subroutine. *Always* use the JSR, BSR, or CALL when transferring to a subroutine.

3. *Never, ever* JMP out a subroutine. *Always* use the RTS or RTC when returning to the calling program or the stack will be unbalanced. See Example 4–47.

4.16 Condition Code Register Instructions

Comparison of M68HC12 and M68HC11 CCR Instructions	
M68HC12	**M68HC11**
ORCC	SEC and SEV converted to ORCC
ANDCC	CLC and CLV converted to ANDCC

The condition code register instructions (Table 4–32) use OR and AND operations to set and clear the carry and overflow bits. These instructions are useful when transferring Boolean information from a subroutine back to the calling program. EXAMPLE 4–48 shows how to use the carry bit to inform the calling program if a variable is out of range or not. You may also use the V bit and

---

EXAMPLE 4–47

What is wrong with the following code segment?

```
jsr1c.asm          Assembled with CASM  04/25/1998  19:44  PAGE 1

0000 160004   1          jsr     SUB     ; Go to the subroutine
0003 A7       2  BACK:   nop             ; The next op code
             3  ;        - - -
             4  ;        - - -
             5  ;        - - -
0004 A7       6  SUB:    nop             ; This is the subroutine
             7  ;        - - -
0005 060003   8          jmp     BACK    ; Go back to main program
```

Solution:
Never jump out of a subroutine. The JSR instruction places the return address on the stack to be used by the RTS instruction. Jumping back leaves the stack unbalanced while RTS removes the return address from the stack. Replace the JMP BACK with an RTS.

Branch If Overflow Clear (BVC) or Branch If Overflow Set (BVS) instructions. The Z and N bits may be used as well.

4.17 Interrupt Instructions

The interrupt instructions shown in Table 4–33 allow us to control if external events can interrupt the normal program flow. Interrupts will be covered in more detail in Chapter 8.

4.18 Fuzzy Logic Instructions

The M68HC12 has a number of instructions that support writing programs for fuzzy logic systems (Table 4–34). We will investigate these features in Chapter 13.

4.19 Miscellaneous Instructions

The BGND instruction enables a special debugging feature in the M68HC12 (Table 4–35). See Chapter 14 for a complete discussion.

The NOP instruction has two useful functions. Each time the NOP is executed, one clock cycle is expended. This can be useful when making a short software delay. The other use is in debugging, where NOPs inserted into the program let instructions be added during debugging without having to reassemble the entire program.

TABLE 4–32 Condition Code Register Instructions

Function	Opcode	Symbolic Operation	Addressing Mode						Condition Codes			
			IMM	DIR	EXT	IDX	IDR	INH	N	Z	V	C
AND CCR with Constant	ANDCC	CCR·#data	x						⇓	⇓	⇓	⇓
Inclusive OR CCR with Constant	ORCC	CCR+#data	x						⇑	⇑	⇑	⇑

EXAMPLE 4–48   Using the Carry Bit for Boolean Information Transfer

This example shows that a condition code register bit can be used to transfer a Boolean result back to the calling program.

```
carry1c.asm        Assembled with CASM  12/06/1998  16:27  PAGE 1

0000          1  STACK:    EQU   $0c00      ; Stack location
0000          2  CARRY:    EQU   %00000001  ; Bit 0 is carry
0000 CF0C00   3            lds   #STACK     ; Init stack pointer
              4  ;         - - -
0003 0702     5            bsr   check_range ; Branch to subroutine
              6                              ; that checks if a
              7                              ; variable is within a
              8                              ; set range.
0005 2400     9            bcc   IN_RANGE   ; C=0 for variable in
             10                             ; range
             11  OUT_OF_RANGE:
             12  ; Print an error message if out of range
             13  ;         - - -
             14  IN_RANGE:
             15  ; Continue with the process
             16  ;         - - -
             17  ;         - - -
             18  ; Subroutine to check if a variable is in range
             19  ; If it is, clear the carry bit, otherwise
             20  ; set the carry bit and return
             21  check_range:
             22  ;         - - -          ; Imagine the code to do
             23  ;         - - -          ; the checking is here.
0007 10FE    24  OK:       clc            ; Clear carry bit
0009 2002    25            bra   DONE
000B 1401    26  NOT_OK:   sec            ; Set carry bit
000D 3D      27  DONE:     rts            ; Return with the
             28                           ; bit clear or set
```

TABLE 4–33 Interrupt Instructions

NEW M68HC12 INTERRUPT INSTRUCTIONS		
Function	**Opcode**	**Operation**
Opcode Trap	TRAP	Unimplemented op code interrupt

			Memory Addressing Mode	Condition Codes							
Function	**Opcode**	**Symbolic Operation**	**INN**	**S**	**X**	**H**	**I**	**N**	**Z**	**V**	**C**
Clear Interrupt Mask	CLI	$0 \rightarrow I$	x	—	—	—	0	—	—	—	—
Set Interrupt Mask	SEI	$1 \rightarrow I$	x	—	—	—	1	—	—	—	—
Return from Interrupt	RTI	$EA \rightarrow PC$	x	⇕	⇕	⇕	⇕	⇕	⇕	⇕	⇕
S/W Interrupt	SWI	$Vector \rightarrow PC$	x	—	—	—	1	—	—	—	—
Wait for Interrupt	WAI		x	—	—	—	—	—	—	—	—
Opcode Trap	TRAP		x	—	—	—	1	—	—	—	—

TABLE 4–34 Fuzzy Logic and Maximum/Minimum Instructions

NEW M68HC12 INSTRUCTIONS											
All fuzzy logic instructions are new											

			Addressing Mode						Condition Codes			
Function	**Opcode**	**Symbolic Operation**	**IMM**	**DIR**	**EXT**	**INDEX**	**INDIR**	**INH**	**N**	**Z**	**V**	**C**
Membership Function	MEM								?	?	?	?
Rule Evaluation	REV								?	?	⇕	?
Weighted Rule Evaluation	REVW								?	?	⇕	⇕
Weighted Average	WAV								?	1	?	?
Minimum $\rightarrow$ D	EMIND	$MIN(D,(M:M+1)) \rightarrow D$				x	x		⇕	⇕	⇕	⇕
Minimum $\rightarrow$ (M)	EMINM	$MIN(D,(M:M+1)) \rightarrow M$				x	x					
Minimum $\rightarrow$ A	MINA	$MIN(A,(M)) \rightarrow A$				x	x		⇕	⇕	⇕	⇕
Minimum $\rightarrow$ (M)	MINM	$MIN(A,(M)) \rightarrow M$				x	x		⇕	⇕	⇕	⇕
Maximum $\rightarrow$ D	EMAXD	$MAX(D,(M:M+1)) \rightarrow D$				x	x		⇕	⇕	⇕	⇕
Maximum $\rightarrow$ (M)	EMAXM	$MAX(D,(M:M+1)) \rightarrow M$				x	x		⇕	⇕	⇕	⇕
Maximum $\rightarrow$ A	MAXA	$MAX(A,M)) \rightarrow A$				x	x		⇕	⇕	⇕	⇕
Maximum $\rightarrow$ (M)	MAXM	$MAX(A,(M)) \rightarrow M$				x	x		⇕	⇕	⇕	⇕
Ext Mult and accum	EMACS											
Table Look-up	ETBL					x			⇕	⇕	—	?
Table Look-up	TBL					x			⇕	⇕	—	?

TABLE 4–35 Miscellaneous Instructions

Function	Opcode	Symbolic Operation	Addressing Mode						Condition Codes			
			I M M	D I R	E X T	I D X	I D Y	I N H	N	Z	V	C
Background Debug	BGND							x	—	—	—	—
No Operation	NOP							x	—	—	—	—
Stop Clocks	STOP							x	—	—	—	—

The STOP instruction stops all microcontroller clocks and puts the microcontroller in a power saving mode. It can be "awakened" from this mode by using an interrupt.

4.20 Chapter Summary Points

- Learning the instruction set is easier if you first learn the categories of instructions available.
- Table 4–3 is useful for quickly finding an operation in the category you want.
- After finding the operation, you must specify the operand and its addressing mode.
- Load and store instructions modify the condition code register.
- Sixteen-bit load and store instructions require two memory locations for the data.
- Push, pull, and other stack operations must be balanced.
- BSET and BCLR instructions set and clear one or more bits in an operand.
- LEAX and LEAY instructions are useful for calculating effective addresses.
- The DAA instruction produces the correct result when adding packed BCD numbers.
- MUL, FDIV, IDIV, EMUL, and EDIV can be used only with unsigned numbers.
- IDIVS, EMULS, and EDIVS can be used with signed (two's-complement) numbers.
- Logical instructions perform a bit-wise logical operation between two operands.
- Data test instructions set the condition code register bits used in conditional branching.
- A compare instruction subtracts one operand from another but does not change either.
- When comparing signed numbers, the conditional branch instructions with the words "greater" and "less" are to be used.
- When comparing unsigned numbers, the conditional branch instructions with the words "higher" and "lower" are to be used.
- The branch instructions all use relative addressing.
- Always use the JSR, BSR, or CALL instruction to transfer to a subroutine.

- Always use the RTS or RTC instructions to transfer back to the calling program.
- Condition code register bits may be used to transfer binary information between parts of a program.

4.21 Bibliography and Further Reading

There are two Motorola references that will help with your programming. The *CPU12 Reference Guide CPU12RG/D Rev.1* is a small, quick reference guide with all instructions and their symbolic operations, addressing modes, hexadecimal machine codes, the number of bytes, the number of clock cycles, and the effect on the condition code register. The *68HC12 CPU12 Reference Manual* contains details for programming all I/O in the M68HC12 and a complete listing of the instruction set.

4.22 Problems

4.1   You be the assembler. Assemble the following source code just as the CASM12 assembler would do it.

```
COUNT:     EQU      !7
MAX:       EQU      !10
ROM:       EQU      $F000
RAM:       EQU      $0800
           ORG      ROM
           ldaa     #COUNT
           adda     #MAX
           staa     DATA
           swi
           ORG      RAM
DATA       DS       1
```

4.2   In the program above, what addressing mode is used for the LDAA instruction?

4.3   In the program above, what addressing mode is used for the STAA instruction?

4.4   What is in memory location $0800 before the program runs?

4.5   For each of the following questions, assume the memory display of the M68HC12 shows:

```
5000  B0  53  05  2B  36  89  00  FF  FE  80  91  3E  77  AB  8F  7F
```

    Give the results after each of the following instructions are executed.

a. LDAA $5000   A = ?, NZVC = ?

b. Assume X = $5000
    LDAA   0,X   A = ?, NZVC = ?

c. Assume X = $5000
    LDAA   6,X   A = ?, NZVC = ?

4.6   Use the contents of memory shown in Problem 4.5 and give the results of the following instructions.

    a. LDX $5000   X = ?

    b. LDY $5002   Y = ?

    c. LDX $5003

       PSHX

       PULD   X = ?, A = ?, B = ?

    d. LDD $5000

       LDX $5002

       XGDX   D = ?, X = ?

    e. Assume X = $5000

       LDD $0A,X   D = ?

4.7   Use the contents of memory shown in Problem 4.5 and give the results of the following instructions.

    a. SP = $5005

       PULA   A = ?, SP = ?

    b. SP = $5005

       PULA   A = ?

       PULB   B = ?

    c. SP = $5005

       PSHA

       PSHB   SP = ?

    d. SP = $500A

       PULA

       PSHB   A = ?, SP = ?

4.8   Why do store instructions not use the immediate addressing mode?

4.9   Use the contents of memory shown in Problem 4.5 and give the results of the following instructions.

    a. Assume X = $5000

       BSET 0,X,$0F   ($5000) = ?

    b. Assume X = $5000

       BSET 6,X,$AA   EA = ?, (EA) = ?

    c. Assume X = $5007

       BCLR 0,X,$AA   ($5007) = ?

    d. Assume Y = $5000

       BCLR 0,Y,$FF   ($5000) = ?

4.10   Assume A = $C9 and the NZVC bits are 1001. Give the result in A and the NZVC bits for each of the following instructions.

    a. LSLA

    b. LSRA

    c. ASLA

    d. ASRA

    e. ROLA

    f. RORA

4.11   The ASLx instructions have the same operation codes as the LSLx instructions. Why?

4.12   Use the contents of memory shown in Problem 4.5 and give the results of the following instructions.

    a. LDAA $5003

```
        LDAB    $5004
        ABA                     A = ?,  B = ?,  NZVC = ?
    b.  LDX     $5000
        LDAB    $5007
        LEAX    B,X             X = ?,  NZVC = ?
    c.  LDAB    $5009
        ADDB    $500A           B = ?,  NZVC = ?
    d. Assume X = $5000
        LDAA    9,X
        ADDA    $0A,X           A = ?,  NZVC = ?
    e. Assume X = $5000
        LDAA    9,X
        SUBA    $0A,X           A = ?,  NZVC = ?
    f.  LDAA    $5000
        LDAB    $5001
        ABA
        ADCA    $5002           A = ?,  NZVC = ?
```

4.13   Use the contents of memory shown in Problem 4.5 and give the results of the following instructions.

```
    a.  LDAA    $5006
        NEGA                    A = ?,  NZVC = ?
    b.  LDAA    $5007
        NEGA                    A = ?,  NZVC = ?
    c.  NEG     $5009           ($5009) = ?,  NZVC = ?
    d.  LDAA    $5006
        COMA                    A = ?,  NZVC = ?
    e.  LDAA    $5007
        COMA                    A = ?,  NZVC = ?
    f.  COM     $5009           ($5009) = ?,  NZVC = ?
```

4.14   After an addition, the carry bit in a status register indicates that a two's-complement overflow has occurred—true or false?

4.15   The following unsigned binary addition was done in the M68HC12. What is the binary result and what are the N, Z, V, and C flags?

```
    01010111
    01100110
```

4.16   Assume the following M68HC12 code is executed in sequence. Give the hexadecimal result in each of the registers after each instruction is executed.

		A	B	N	Z	V	C
ldaa	#$4A	_____	xxxx	___	___	___	___
ldab	#$D3	_____	_____	___	___	___	___
aba		_____	_____	___	___	___	___
adca	#$70	_____	_____	___	___	___	___

4.17   Use the contents of memory shown in Problem 4.5 and give the results of the following instructions.

```
    LDAA    $5002
```

```
        ADDA    $5004      A = ?
        DAA                A = ?
```

4.18   Use the contents of memory shown in Problem 4.5 and give the results of the following instructions.

    a. LDAA $5002

       ORAA $5003   A = ?, NZVC = ?

    b. LDAA $5002

       EORA $5003   A = ?, NZVC = ?

    c. LDAA $500D

       ANDA $500E   A = ?, NZVC = ?

    d. LDAB $5002

       COMB   B = ?, NZVC = ?

4.19   Use the contents of memory shown in Problem 4.5 and give the results of the following instructions.

    a. LDAA $5000

       CMPA $5001   A = ?, NZVC = ?

    b. TST $5006   NZVC = ?

    c. TST $5007   NZVC = ?

4.20   Assume A = $00 and memory location DATA = $B0. A CMPA DATA instruction is executed followed by a conditional branch. For each of the conditional branch instructions in the table, indicate by yes or no if you expect the branch to be taken.

    BGE   BLE   BGT   BLT   BEQ   BNE

    BHS   BLS   BHI   BLO

4.21   Assume A = $05 and memory location DATA = $22. A CMPA DATA instruction is executed followed by a conditional branch. For each of the conditional branch instructions in the table, indicate by yes or no if you expect the branch to be taken.

    BGE   BLE   BGT   BLT   BEQ   BNE

    BHS   BLS   BHI   BLO

4.22   Assume A = $56 and memory location DATA = $22. A CMPA DATA instruction is executed followed by a conditional branch. For each of the conditional branch instructions in the table, indicate by yes or no if you expect the branch to be taken.

    BGE   BLE   BGT   BLT   BEQ   BNE

    BHS   BLS   BHI   BLO

4.23   Assume A = $22 and memory location DATA = $22. A CMPA DATA instruction is executed followed by a conditional branch. For each of the conditional branch instructions in the table, indicate by yes or no if you expect the branch to be taken.

    BGE   BLE   BGT   BLT   BEQ   BNE

    BHS   BLS   BHI   BLO

4.24   Briefly describe what each of the following instructions does. These are separate instructions, not a program.

    COMA; CBA; CMPB 10,X; TSTB; BRN; SWI; BITA $80; BCC LOOP; XGDX; LSR $5000; NEGB

4.25   Draw a memory map showing the contents of the stack expected after the program in Example 4–13 is executed. What value do you expect in the A register after the subroutine adds all the data?

Chapter 5

D-Bug12 Monitor and Debugger

OBJECTIVES

This chapter describes the resident monitor used on Motorola's M68HC12 evaluation boards (EVBs). The monitor is called *D-Bug12* and it allows you to interact with the EVB from a terminal and to enter and debug programs.

5.1 M68HC12 EVB D-Bug12 Monitor

The D-Bug12 Monitor communicates with a terminal program running on a PC.

This chapter describes the second major software tool (after the assembler) that you will be using in the laboratory. The D-Bug12 monitor allows you to enter programs, inspect and modify memory locations, and run and debug programs. It also has utility subroutines that may be used in your programs. The monitor program communicates with the laboratory PCs using a serial port on the EVB. A modem or terminal program runs on the PC to communicate with the EVB.

D-Bug12 Monitor Versions

There are two distinct versions of the D-Bug12 monitor, depending on which Motorola evaluation board you are using. The M68HC12A4EVB (which uses the MC68HC812A4 version of the microcontroller) uses version 1.xxx of the monitor. The monitor in the M68EVB912B32 (using the MC68HC912B32) is version 2.xxx. In this and the following chapters we will use *Ver_1* and *Ver_2* to distinguish between the two versions. Ver_2 is slightly more powerful than Ver_1 because it can allow the 'EVB912B32' to operate as a probe interface between a target system and the user. When operating in this mode, the EVB makes use of the Background Debugging Mode described in Chapter 14. Another difference between the two monitors is that programmer access to D-Bug12 monitor utility routines use different vectors in each. We will discuss this in more detail and show you how to easily generate code for the two versions of the monitor in Section 5.3.

Entering the Monitor

> The communication port parameters are 9600 Baud, 8 data bits, 1 stop bit (9600, 8N1).

Load and execute the terminal program on the PC and turn on the EVB's power supply. If the D-Bug12 monitor prompt does not occur, press the reset switch on the board. After the sign-on message the D-Bug12 prompt is a ⟩ character in the leftmost column of the display.

Command Line Format

The command line format is

⟩⟨*command*⟩ [⟨*parameters*⟩]⟨*Enter*⟩[1]

where

⟩	EVB monitor prompt
⟨command⟩	Command mnemonic (single letter for most commands); command lines are case insensitive
⟨parameters⟩	Expression or address
⟨Enter⟩	Return or Enter key
⟨...⟩	Enclose syntactical variable
[...]	Enclose optional fields
[...]...	Enclose optional fields repeated

Do not enter the ⟨, ⟩, [, or] characters; enter just what is within these characters. All numerical operand values for D-Bug12 monitor commands are assumed to be hexadecimal, except for the Trace and Baud commands.

5.2 Monitor Commands

> D-Bug12 monitor commands may be typed after the "⟩" prompt. Command entry is terminated by typing the ⟨Enter⟩ key.

This section discusses and gives examples for the monitor commands available in Version 1.xxx monitors and Version 2.xxx operating in EVB mode. Chapter 14 covers D-Bug12 commands that can be used when using background debugging.

Assemble/Disassemble: D-Bug12 offers a small assembler program that lets you enter operations and operands. This assembler does not have many of the features that you will find in the cross-assembler you will be using for most of your assembly language programming, but it does allow you to assemble a program from mnemonics and operands entered from the keyboard.

ASM ⟨address⟩

where address is the starting address for the assembler operation.

---

[1] In the command descriptions and examples that follow, information that you type is given in **BOLD**. Commands are terminated by the ⟨*Enter*⟩ key. Response from D-Bug12 is given in Courier font.

Syntax Rules

All numerical operand values for ASM are in *decimal.* To specify a hexadecimal number, use the $ designator (e.g., $64).

Operands are separated by one or more space or tab characters.

Addressing Modes

Immediate	Precede operand value with #
Indexed	Designated by a comma. The comma must be preceded by the offset and must be followed by an X or Y index register, S for the stack pointer or P for those instructions allowing the program counter.
Indexed-Indirect	Enclose the offset and the register(s) in [ ].
Direct	Specify the address in hex.
Extended	Specify the address in hex.
Relative	Calculated by the assembler; specify the absolute destination address preceded by a "$" symbol.

When you are finished entering your program, type a period (.) as the first nonspace character following the assembler prompt to exit ASM mode. You may check that the program has been assembled by doing *ASM* [⟨*address*⟩] and just hitting ⟨*Enter*⟩ at each line. The assembler will disassemble the code and show the instructions. See Example 5–1.

Baudrate: Change the communication rate for the terminal.

> **BAUD ⟨BAUDRate⟩**

EXAMPLE 5–1   Assemble a Program

Assemble a short program starting at $0800 using the D-Bug12 monitor ASM command.

Solution:
⟩**ASM 800**

0800	8603	LDAA	#$03	⟩**ldaa #$2B**	The assembler shows what instruction is currently in the memory. Enter the new instruction after the ⟩ prompt.
0800	862B	LDAA	#$2B		The assembler verifies the instruction you just entered and shows the next instruction followed by the ⟩ prompt.
0802	00	BGND		⟩**staa $a00**	Enter the next instruction.
0802	7A0A00	STAA	$0A00		
0805	8000	SUBA	#$00	⟩**swi**	Enter the next instruction.
0805	3E	SWI			
0806	00	BGND		⟩.	Type period (.) to exit.
⟩					

BAUDRate is a 16-bit unsigned, decimal number specifying the new terminal Baud rate you want. See Example 5–2.

Block Fill: Fill a block of memory with constant data. See Example 5–3.

BF ⟨address1⟩ ⟨address2⟩ [⟨data⟩]

Breakpoint Set: Set breakpoints for debugging.

BR [⟨address, ...⟩]

> Breakpoints are an important debugging tool.

A maximum of 10 breakpoints may be set in RAM memory. *NOBR* [⟨*address*⟩ . . .] removes all breakpoints currently at *address* . . . and *NOBR* (with no address) removes all breakpoints. *BR* shows the breakpoints currently set. Breakpoints in the version 1.xxx monitor (and the version 2.xxx monitor when it is operating in EVB mode) are set by replacing the instruction at the address you give with the software interrupt instruction, SWI. Therefore, breakpoints may not be set in ROM. The monitor saves the original instruction and restores it after a breakpoint is executed and when breakpoints are removed with the *NOBR* command. See Example 5–4. Version 2.xxx has a POD ("probe") mode that uses the background debugging feature to set breakpoints in ROM.

Bulk Erase: Erase the EEPROM.

BULK   Erase all MCU EEPROM locations.

Call: Call and execute a user program subroutine.

CALL [⟨address⟩]

See Example 5–5.

Go to Program: Run the user's program.

G [⟨address⟩]

Go to the address and start running the program. If ⟨*address*⟩ is not given, the current program counter is used. Program execution continues until a breakpoint is encountered or the reset switch is pressed. When the program stops for any reason other than a reset, the reason it stopped and the contents of the registers are displayed, and the next instruction is disassembled. See Example 5–6.

EXAMPLE 5–2   Change the Baud Rate

```
⟩BAUD 9600
Change Terminal BR, Press Return
⟩
```

EXAMPLE 5–3   Block Fill Memory

BF 4000 402F FF   Fill the memory from $4000 to $402F with $FF.

EXAMPLE 5–4   Set Breakpoints

>**BR 83c 84d**   Set breakpoints at $083C and $084D.
Breakpoints: 083C 084D   The monitor shows you what breakpoints have been set.
>**BR**   Show all current breakpoints.
Breakpoints: 083C 084D
>**NOBR 083c**   Clear the breakpoint at $083C.
Breakpoints: 084D
>**NOBR**   Clear all breakpoints.
Breakpoints:
>

EXAMPLE 5–5

>**CALL 83c**   This executes a subroutine starting at $083C. The subroutine
                        must terminate with an RTS instruction and control returns to the
                        monitor when it is executed and the monitor displays the
                        contents of the registers. This is a good way to debug individual
                        subroutines.

Subroutine Call Returned
  PC   SP   X   Y   D = A:B   CCR = SXHI NZVC
 0820   0A00   09FF   0000   0F:FA   1001 0101
>

EXAMPLE 5–6

>**BR 83c**   Set breakpoint at $083C.
Breakpoints: 083C   The monitor shows you what breakpoints have been set.
>**G 800**   Start executing the program located at $0800.
User Breakpoint Encountered

  PC   SP   X   Y   D = A:B   CCR = SXHI NZVC
 083C   09FE   09FF   0000   0F:FA   1001 0101
 083C   34   PSHX
>

Go Till: Go until an address.

  GT [⟨address⟩]

This is similar to the G command except that a temporary breakpoint is set at ⟨address⟩. Code execution starts at the current program counter location and continues to the temporary breakpoint. It is useful in debugging to be able to go to a breakpoint and then execute a number of program statements to another place where you would like to see what is going on. See Example 5–7.

EXAMPLE 5–7   Go Till an Address

⟩*G 800*   Start executing the program located at $0800.
```
User Breakpoint Encountered

   PC      SP      X        Y        D = A:B     CCR = SXHI  NZVC
  083C    09FE    09FF     0000       0F:FA             1001  0101
  083C    34               PSHX
```
⟩*GT 84d*   Go until location $084D.
```
Temporary Breakpoint Encountered

   PC      SP      X        Y        D = A:B     CCR = SXHI  NZVC
  084D    09FE    09FF     F00D       BE:EF             1001  0101
  084D    30               PULX
⟩
```

Help: Prints a D-Bug12 command summary on the screen.

> *HELP*

Load Program: Load an S-Record (S19) program file into the EVB memory.

> *LOAD* [⟨*OffsetAddress*⟩]

Download a program from the host computer. *OffsetAddress* is optional and, if given, adds an offset to each byte's address. This allows code to be downloaded into memory at a location other than the location for which it was assembled. After typing in *LOAD*, execute the command in the modem program to download the hex file to the EVB. If you have downloaded a program and get an error message "Invalid Command," you probably forgot to first use the command *LOAD*.

EXAMPLE 5–8

⟩*MD 5000*   Display 16 bytes starting at memory location $5000. If the
                        starting address is not on a 16-byte boundary, it is rounded
                        down. Each byte is given in hexadecimal and in the equivalent
                        ASCII if it is a printable character.

```
5000 AA AA AA AA 55 55 55 55 AA AA AA AA 55 55 55 55 ....UUUU....UUUU
```

⟩*MD 5000 5020*   Display bytes starting at memory location $5000 through $502F.
                        The display shows three rows of 16 bytes.

```
5000 AA AA AA AA 55 55 55 55 AA AA AA AA 55 55 55 55 ....UUUU....UUUU
5010 55 55 55 55 AA AA AA AA 55 55 55 55 AA AA AA AA UUUU....UUUU....
5020 54 68 69 73 20 69 73 20 61 20 6D 65 73 73 61 67 This is a messag
⟩
```

Memory Display: Display a block of memory. See Example 5–8.

MD ⟨address1⟩ [⟨address2⟩]

Memory Display Word: Display a block of memory as hexadecimal words and ASCII characters. This is the same as the memory display command except 16-bit data are displayed.

MDW ⟨address1⟩ [⟨address2⟩]

Memory Modify: Display and modify memory.

MM ⟨address⟩ [⟨data⟩]

Examine/modify the contents of user memory contents.

MM ⟨address⟩

You may use an interactive mode to examine and modify memory contents. Interactive mode has the following subcommands:

[⟨data⟩]⟨CR⟩	Optionally update the current location and display the next location.
[⟨data⟩]⟨ / ⟩ or ⟨ = ⟩	Optionally update the current location and redisplay the location.
[⟨data⟩]⟨ ^ ⟩ or ⟨ -⟩	Optionally update the current location and display the previous location.
[⟨data⟩]⟨ .⟩	Optionally update the current location and exit modify memory.

When using any of these subcommands, there must be a ⟨space⟩ between the data and the command. See Example 5–9.

Memory Modify Word: Display and modify 16-bit memory locations.

MMW ⟨address⟩ [⟨data⟩]

Memory modify word works the same as the memory modify command shown in Example 5–9.

EXAMPLE 5–9 Modify Memory Locations

⟩**MM 900 aa** Modify memory at location $0900.

⟩**MM 900**⟨**CR**⟩

0900	AA	**00**⟨**CR**⟩	Change $0900 from $AA to 00 and display the next location.
0901	BB	⟨**CR**⟩	Leave $0901 $BB and display $0902.
0902	CC	**f0 /**	Change $0902 to $F0 and redisplay.
0902	F0	**ff ^**	Change $0902 to $FF and display the previous location.
0901	BB	⟨**CR**⟩	Leave $0901 $BB and display $0902.
0902	FF	⟨**CR**⟩	Leave $0902 $FF and display the next location.
0903	00	**EE**⟨**CR**⟩	Change 0903 to $EE.
0904	00	**.**	Exit Memory Modify.

⟩

Move Memory: Copy a block of memory to a destination.

MOVE ⟨address1⟩ ⟨address2⟩ ⟨dest address⟩

The move memory command is effective only when moving blocks of data. In general, instructions should not be moved if they contain jump addresses.

Remove Breakpoints: Remove any breakpoints.

NOBR [⟨address1⟩ ...]

See Example 5–4.

Register Display: Display the CPU12 registers.

RD

All registers are shown.

Register Modify: Interactively examine and modify MCU registers.

RM

RM will display all registers in turn allowing you to either enter new data, accept the current value, or exit the register modify interactive mode by typing a period (.). See Example 5–10.

An individual register can be modified by entering a register name and then an 8-bit or 16-bit value:

⟨*Register Name*⟩ ⟨*Register Value*⟩

The register names to be used and the range of values allowed are shown in Table 5–1. Also, each of the Condition Code Register bits may be changed individually by typing its name and assigning it a 0 or 1. See Example 5–11.

Trace Program:

T [⟨n⟩]

Trace *n* steps of the program where *n* may be a decimal number 1–255. In the Ver_1 monitor and the Ver_2 monitor in EVB mode, trace uses the software interrupt instruction and thus can

---

EXAMPLE 5–10

```
⟩RM
PC=081A 800          Change the program counter to $0800.
SP=0AFF ⟨CR⟩         Leave the stack pointer $0AFF.
X=FFFF 1000          Change the X register to $1000.
Y=BEEF F00D          Change the Y register to $F00D.
A=33 22              Change the A register to $22.
B=33 ⟨CR⟩            Leave the B register $33.
CCR=D0 ⟨CR⟩          Leave the CCR alone.
PC=0800 .            Leave the PC $0800 and exit register modify.
⟩
```

TABLE 5-1   Modify Register Value

Register	Register Name	Legal Range
Program Counter	PC	$0 to $FFFF
Stack Pointer	SP	$0 to $FFFF
X Index Register	X	$0 to $FFFF
Y Index Register	Y	$0 to $FFFF
A Accumulator	A	$0 to $FF
B Accumulator	B	$0 to $FF
D Accumulator (A:B)	D	$0 to $FFFF
Condition Code Register	CCR	$0 to $FF
CCR Bit		
STOP enable	S	0 or 1
Half Carry	H	0 or 1
Negative Flag	N	0 or 1
Zero Flag	Z	0 or 1
Two's-Complement Overflow Flag	V	0 or 1
Carry Flag	C	0 or 1
IRQ Interrupt Mask	IM	0 or 1
XIRQ Interrupt Mask	XM	0 or 1

be used *ONLY* in programs in RAM memory. A Ver_2 monitor in POD mode can trace through a target system's ROM. See Example 5–12.

Upload: Display a block of memory in S-Record format.

UPLOAD ⟨address1⟩ ⟨address2⟩

This command displays the contents of memory from the EVB to the PC in Motorola S-Record format, including an S9 end-of-file record. The output could be captured to disk and then later reloaded into the EVB using the *LOAD* command.

Verify: Compare memory to terminal port downloaded data.

VERIF [⟨address⟩]

Address is an offset, similar to that used in the *LOAD* command. After entering the *VERIF* command, send the Motorola S-Record to the EVB. This allows you to verify that the contents of memory are the same as those given in the S-Record.

EXAMPLE 5-11   Modify Individual Registers

```
⟩PC 0800                        Change the program counter to $0800.
   PC       SP       X        Y       D = A:B    CCR = SXHI  NZVC
  0800     09FE     09FF     0000       0F:FA           1001  0101
⟩a 66                           Change A to $66.
   PC       SP       X        Y       D = A:B    CCR = SXHI  NZVC
  0800     09FE     09FF     0000       66:FA           1001  0101
⟩
```

EXAMPLE 5–12

⟩**T**   Trace one program instruction. The trace command displays all
               registers and disassembles and displays the next instruction to be
               executed.

PC	SP	X	Y	D = A:B	CCR = SXHI	NZVC
083C	09FE	09FF	0000	0F:FA	1001	0101
083C	34		PSHX			

⟩**T**   Repeats the trace command.

PC	SP	X	Y	D = A:B	CCR = SXHI	NZVC
083D	09FC	09FF	0000	0F:FA	1001	0101
083D	35		PSHY			

⟩**T 5**   Trace through five program steps. When you trace *n* instructions you
               see that many register displays before the next prompt.

⟩

5.3 Monitor Utility Routines

These monitor utility routines give you pre-programmed terminal I/O to use in your programs.

Subroutines in the D-Bug12 Monitor program are available to do I/O tasks. They may be accessed by including a JSR instruction in your program.

The monitor routines are written in C and follow standard C language parameter passing techniques. When a function requires more than one parameter, all but the first are pushed onto the stack in right-to-left order. The first parameter in the calling list is passed in the D register. When there is only one parameter simply pass that in the D register. Char (8-bit) parameters must be converted to int (16-bits) with the char 8 bits occupying the low-order byte; 8- and 16-bit results are returned in the D register. Boolean functions return zero for false and nonzero for true results. It is the responsibility of the calling program to place parameters on the stack and to clean up the stack after the function returns. For example, consider wanting to call the function

```
int function_call( int parameter1, char parameter2, int parameter3).
```

The assembly language code to accomplish this call is shown in Example 5–13.

Explanation of Example 5–13

In *line 1*, VECTOR is the address in the monitor where the address of function_call is stored. Three parameters are to be passed to the function and one is returned. The third parameter, parameter3, is an 16-bit integer stored in the memory allocated in *line 15*. It is pushed onto the stack in *lines 2 and 3*. The second parameter is a byte loaded into the B register in *line 4*, converted to 16 bits in *line 5* and pushed onto the stack in *line 6*. The first parameter is passed to the function by loading it into the D register in *line 7*. The JSR instruction in *line 8* uses a form of indexed-indirect addressing that treats the program counter as an index register. The PCR operand mnemonic

EXAMPLE 5–13   Calling Monitor Routines

```
dbparms.asm        Assembled with CASM 08/08/1998 22:41 PAGE 1

0000 15FBFDF9    1  VECTOR    EQU    $FE0A   ; Address of the routine
0000 FC0016      2            ldd    param3  ; Retrieve param 3 from memory
0003 3B          3            pshd           ; Put it on the stack
0004 F60015      4            ldab   param2  ; Retrieve param 2 from memory
0007 B714        5            sex    b,d     ; Convert to 16-bits
0009 3B          6            pshd           ; Put it on the stack
000A FC0013      7            ldd    param1  ; Retrieve param 1 from memory
000D            8            jsr    [VECTOR,PCR] ; JSR to the subroutine
0011 1B84       9            leas   4,sp    ; Clean up the stack
               10  ; At this point the D register contains the int variable
               11  ; returned by the function.
               12  ;         - - -
0013           13  param1:   DS     2       ; Storage for parameter 1
0015           14  param2:   DS     1       ; Storage for parameter 2
0016           15  param3:   DS     2       ; Storage for parameter 3
```

means *program counter relative* addressing. The M68HC12 does not actually support PC relative addressing so the PCR mnemonic instructs the assembler to calculate an offset for the indexed-indirect jump to the subroutine. When the subroutine returns control to our program, the LEAS 4,SP in *line 9* restores the stack pointer to the value it had before the PSHD in *line 3*. This ensures that the stack is balanced.

A note of caution: The D-Bug12 routines preserve only the SP register. If other register values must be preserved, they must be pushed onto the stack before any parameters.

Calling Monitor Routines

In Example 5–13 we see this code statement:[2]

```
jsr [VECTOR,PCR]
```

The D-Bug12 monitor contains vectors that have been initialized to point to each of the monitor routines. The address of each vector is shown in Table 5–2 for both versions of D-Bug12. You may use either a pc relative jump to subroutine or an indirect jump to the subroutine by first loading

---

2   If your assembler does not handle program counter relative (PCR) addressing, you may use these two instructions:

```
ldx   vector   ; Get the vector for the subroutine
jsr   0,x      ; JSR to the subroutine
```

TABLE 5-2 D-Bug12 Monitor Routines

		Vector Address	
		HC12A4EVB	M68EVB912B32
Subroutine	Function	Version 1.xxx	Version 2.xxx
main()	Start of D-Bug12 $FE00	$F680	
Character Routines			
getchar()	Get a character from serial I/O port	$FE02	$F682
putchar()	Send a character out to the serial I/O port	$FE04	$F684
isalpha()	Check if a character is alphabetic	$FE10	$F690
isxdigit()	Check if a character is a hexadecimal digit	$FE0C	$F68C
toupper()	Convert lower-case to upper-case character	$FE0E	$F68E
out2hex()	Output 8-bit number as 2 ASCII hex characters	$FE16	$F696
out4hex()	Output a 16-bit number as 4 ASCII hex characters	$FE18	$F698
String Routines			
printf()	Formatted string output	$FE06	$F686
GetCmdLine()	Get a line of input from the user	$FE08	$F688
sscanhex()	Convert ASCII hex string to a binary integer	$FE0A	$F68A
strcpy()	Copy a null terminated string	$FE14	$F694
strlen()	Returns the length of a null terminated string	$FE12	$F692
Interrupt routines			
SetUserVector()	Setup a vector to a user's interrupt service routine	$FE1A	$F69A
EEPROM Routines			
EraseEE()	Erase all of the EEPROM memory	$FE1E	$F69E
WriteEEByte()	Write a byte in the EEPROM memory	$FE1C	$F69C

the subroutine's address into the X register (with the ldx VECTOR instruction) and then executing the jump to subroutine.

Table 5–2 shows two addresses for each of the D-Bug12 routines, depending on which version of the monitor is installed in your EVB. Normally you will probably be using only one version in any project, but if you are operating in an environment in which you are developing code on either system, it is a nuisance to have separate source files. Fortunately, many assemblers have a *conditional assembly* feature in which you may choose to assemble one section of code or another depending on the state of a Boolean variable. Chapter 3 shows how to do this in detail and Example 5–14 shows how to use conditional assembly to select the correct equates for the version of the monitor in use. When you need code for the other version, you simply change the Boolean variable from a $SET to $SETNOT and reassemble the program.

Summary of D-Bug12 Routines

int EraseEE(void);
Vector: $FE1E   *Stack use:* 4 bytes
Input: None.
Returns: D = 0 and the Z-bit is set if bytes not erased, otherwise nonzero.

Bulk erase the on-chip EEPROM. If any bytes are not erased properly (the erased state is $FF), D is returned zero and the Z-bit set, otherwise D is nonzero and Z = 0. See Examples 5–15 and 5–16.

int getchar(void);
Vector: $FE02   *Stack use:* 2 bytes
Input: None.
Returns: B contains the character.

Retrieve a single character from the terminal SCI. If a character is not waiting, getchar() waits until one is available. The character is returned in B but is not echoed back to the terminal. See Example 5–17.

EXAMPLE 5–14   Conditional Assembly to Select the Monitor Version

```
condasmc.asm  Assembled with CASM  05/23/1998  15:38  PAGE 1

             1 ; Use conditional assembly to choose the correct
             2 ; D-Bug12 monitor addresses
    0000     3 $SET         Ver_1                 ; D-Bug12 Version
             4 ; To change to Ver_1 use $SETNOT   Ver_1
    0000     5 $IF          Ver_1
             6 ; IF Ver_1, then use the following addresses
    0000     7 getchar:     EQU     $FE02
    0000     8 putchar:     EQU     $FE04
    0000     9 $ELSEIF
            10 ; ELSE use the following addresses for Ver_2
            11 getchar:     EQU     $F682
            12 putchar:     EQU     $F684
    0000    13 $ENDIF
            14 ;            - - -
```

EXAMPLE 5–15   int EraseEE(Void);

```
eraseeec.asm         Assembled with CASM  12/08/1998  01:59   PAGE 1

    0000               1 EraseEE: EQU    $FE1E    ; Define Vector
                       2 ;              - - -
                       3 ; Erase the entire EEPROM memory
    0000 15FBFE1A      4                jsr      [EraseEE,PCR]
                       5 ; IF the Z-bit is set, an error has occurred
    0004 2600          6                bne      All_OK
                       7 ; THEN (process error condition)
                       8 ;              - - -
                       9 All_OK:
                      10 ; ELSE continue
```

EXAMPLE 5–16

Show how to modify the program in Example 5–15 if your assembler does not support program counter relative addressing.

Solution:

Change the `jsr [EraseEE,PCR]` instruction to two instructions:
```
     ldx     EraseEE
     jsr     0,x
```

EXAMPLE 5–17   int getchar(void);

```
getcharc.asm           Assembled with CASM  08/08/1998  22:43  PAGE  1

0000                   1  getchar:    EQU    $FE02    ; Define vector
                       2  ;  - - -
0000  15FBFDFE         3              jsr    [getchar,PCR]
                       4  ; The character is returned in B register
```

---

int GetCmdLine(char *CmdLineStr, int CmdLineLen);
Vector: $FE08   *Stack use:* 11 bytes
Input: CmdLineLen on the stack, D = storage address for the string to be input.
Returns: D = 0 always.

Obtain a line of input from the user. Characters are echoed back; at most *CmdLineLen-1* characters may be entered; the backspace character may be used to edit the line; all characters are converted to upper case; ASCII backspace ($08) may be used to edit the buffer; ASCII carriage return ($0D) terminates the command line input and places the ASCII null character ($00) at the end of the line; the carriage return is not returned. The characters are placed in memory at the address passed in *CmdLineStr*. *CmdLineStr* is passed in D and *CmdLineLen* is passed on the stack. GetCmdLine always returns 0 in the D register. See Example 5–18.

int isalpha(int c);
Vector: $FE10   *Stack use:* 4 bytes
Input: B = ASCII character to be tested.
Returns: D = nonzero if the character is alphabetic, otherwise zero.

Tests if the character *c* (in B) is an upper or lower-case alphabetic ASCII character. Returns D nonzero if it is, otherwise it returns 0. See Example 5–19.

int isxdigit(int c);
Vector: $FE0C   *Stack use:* 4 bytes
Input: B = ASCII character to be tested.
Returns: D = nonzero if the character is an ASCII hexadecimal digit, otherwise zero.

Tests if the character *c* in the B register is a valid ASCII hexadecimal digit. Returns D nonzero if it is, otherwise it returns 0. See Example 5–20.

void main(void);
Vector: $FE00   *Stack use:* None
Input: None.
Returns: None.

EXAMPLE 5–18   int GetCmdLine(char #CmdLineStr, int CmdLineLen);

```
getcmd1c.asm          Assembled with CASM 08/08/1998  22:43  PAGE 1

0000                 1  GetCmdLine: EQU    $FE08
0000                 2  COUNT:      EQU    21        ; Number of chars + NULL
                     3  ;           - - -
                     4  ; Get a 20 character (max) line of text from the user
0000 CC0021          5              ldd    #COUNT    ; Number of characters
0003 3B              6              pshd             ; Put it on the stack
0004 CC000C          7              ldd    #BUF1     ; Get the string's address
0007 15FBFDFD        8              jsr    [GetCmdLine,PCR]
000B 3A              9              puld             ; Clean up the stack
                    10  ;           - - -
000C                11  BUF1:       DS     COUNT     ; Storage for the string
                    12                               ; plus the NULL terminator
```

EXAMPLE 5–19   int isalpha(int c);

```
isalphac.asm          Assembled with CASM 12/08/1998  02:02  PAGE 1

0000                 1  isalpha:    EQU    $FE10     ; Set the vector
0800                 2              org    $800
                     3  ; IF CHAR is an alphabetic character
0800 F6080B          4              ldab   CHAR      ; Load B with the character
                     5  ; Check to see if it is alphabetic
0803 15FBF609        6              jsr    [isalpha,PCR]
                     7  ; The D register returns nonzero if it is alphabetic
0807 2702            8              beq    False_Part
                     9  ; THEN (do whatever)
                    10  ;           - - -
0809 2000           11              bra    Endif
                    12  ; ELSE    (do whatever)
                    13  False_Part:
                    14  ;           - - -
                    15  Endif:
                    16  ;           - - -
080B                17  CHAR:       DS     1
```

EXAMPLE 5–20   int isxdigit(int c);

```
isxdig1c.asm          Assembled with CASM  08/08/1998  22:46  PAGE 1

0000                1 isxdigit:   EQU   $FE0C   ; Set the vector
                    2 ; IF CHAR is a hex character
0000 F6000B         3               ldab   CHAR    ; Load B with the character
                    4 ; Check to see if an ASCII character is a hex digit
0003 15FBFE05       5               jsr    [isxdigit,PCR]
                    6 ; The D register returns nonzero if it is hex
0007 2702           7               beq    False_Part
                    8 ; THEN (do whatever)
                    9 ;          - - -
0009 2000          10               bra    Endif
                   11 ; ELSE      (do whatever)
                   12 False_Part:
                   13 ;          - - -
                   14 Endif:
                   15 ;          - - -
                   16
000B               17 CHAR:        DS     1
```

Restart D-Bug12. This is available for you to do some additional startup initialization before starting the monitor.

void out2hex(unsigned int num);
Vector: $FE16   *Stack use:* 70 bytes
Input: B contains the byte to be output.
Returns: Nothing.

Display the byte in the *B register* as two hexadecimal characters. See Example 5–21.

EXAMPLE 5–21   void out2hex(unsigned int num);

```
out2hexc.asm          Assembled with CASM  08/08/1998  22:50  PAGE 1

0000                1 out2hex:   EQU   $FE16   ; Set the vector
                    2 ;            - - -
                    3 ; Print a byte
0000 87             4               clra            ; 0 -) A
0001 F60008         5               ldab   Data     ; Get the byte to print
0004 15FBFE0E       6               jsr    [out2hex,PCR]
                    7 ;            - - -
0008               8 Data:         DS     1
```

---

void out4hex(unsigned int num);
Vector: $FE18   *Stack use:* 70 bytes
Input: D contains the word to be output.
Returns: Nothing.

Display the two bytes in D as four hexadecimal characters. See Example 5–22.

int printf(char *format);
Vector: $FE06   *Stack use:* Minimum of 64 bytes, not including parameter space.
Input: Integer data to be printed on the stack; D contains the address of the format string. The format string must be terminated with zero.
Returns: D = number of characters printed.

Print a formatted string. This routine is the same as the C language printf except floating point numbers cannot be printed. It uses a format specifier string, pointed to by *format*, with all data to be formatted and printed pushed on the stack. The number of characters that are printed are returned in D.

The format string contains ASCII characters to be printed, conversion specifications to all data parameters on the stack to be formatted and printed, and special characters for carriage-return and line-feed. Each conversion specification begins with a percent (%) sign and ends with one of the conversion characters shown in Table 5–3.

The format specification to convert data to be displayed is

$$\% - [\langle Field\ Width\rangle].[\langle Precision\rangle][h\ or\ l]\langle Conversion\ Character\rangle$$

where

%	Signifies the beginning of the conversion specification string.
—	(minus sign) Left justify the converted argument.
Field Width	Integer number specifying the minimum field width for the converted argument.
Precision	Integer number specifying the minimum number of digits for an integer or the maximum number of characters for a string.

EXAMPLE 5–22   void out4hex(unsigned int num);

```
out4hexc.asm        Assembled with CASM 08/08/1998 22:51  PAGE 1

0000               1 out4hex:  EQU  $FE18   ; Set the vector
                   2 ;         - - -
                   3 ; Print a word
0000 FC0007        4           ldd  Data    ; Get the word to print
0003 15FBFE11      5           jsr  [out4hex,PCR]
                   6 ;         - - -
0007               7 Data:     DS   2
```

TABLE 5–3   printf() Format Conversion Characters

Conversion Character	Argument Type, Displayed as
d,i	int, signed decimal number
o	int, unsigned octal number without a leading 0
x	int, unsigned hexadecimal number using abcdef
X	int, unsigned hexadecimal number using ABCDEF
u	int, unsigned decimal number
c	int, single character
s	char *, null terminated string
p	void *, pointer
%	no argument, print a %

h	Display data as a short integer.
l	(lower case L) Display data as a long integer.

Example 5–23 illustrates how to use printf() in your software. The format strings defined in Example 5–23 contain *CR ($0D)* and *LF ($0A)* to print a carriage-return and line-feed. The strings must be terminated by a *zero*.

int putchar(int);
Vector: $FE04   *Stack use:* 4 bytes
Input: B is the character to be printed.
Returns: B returns the character that was printed.

Send the single character in B to the SCI terminal. If the Transmit Data Register is full when the function is called, putchar() waits until it is empty before sending the character. The function returns the character that was sent in the B register. See Example 5–24.

int SetUserVector(int VectNum, address UserAddress);
Vector: $FE1A   *Stack use:* 8 bytes
Input: The address of the interrupt routine is on the stack and D is the number of the interrupt to be serviced. See Table 5–4.
Returns: D = −1 if the vector number is invalid, otherwise D = 0.

Allow user interrupt service routines. See Example 5–25 and Section 5.4. SetUserVector returns −1 ($FFFF) in D if VectNum is an invalid number; otherwise D = 0 on return. We will talk about interrupts and show more examples in Chapter 8.

char *sscanhex(char *HexStr, unsigned int *BinNum);
Vector: $FE0A   *Stack use:* 6 bytes
Input: The address at which the binary integer is to be stored is on the stack; D contains the address of the string to be converted.
Returns: D is a pointer to the terminating character or is a NULL pointer if an error occurred.

EXAMPLE 5–23   int printf(char *format);

Show how the following program prints its data.

```
printf1c.asm        Assembled with CASM  12/08/1998  02:08  PAGE 1

0000             1  printf:    EQU     $FE06   ; Vector location
0000             2  CR:        EQU     $0D     ; Carriage-return
0000             3  LF:        EQU     $0A     ; Line-feed
                 4  ;          - - -
0000 FC001C      5             ldd     Num1    ; Get some data to print
0003 3B          6             pshd            ; Put it on the stack
0004 3B          7             pshd            ; Going to print it twice
0005 CC0020      8             ldd     #FORMAT1; Address of the format
                                                 string
0008 15FBFDFA    9             jsr     [printf,PCR]
000C 1B84       10             leas    4,sp    ; Clean up stack
                11  ;          - - -
000E FC001E     12             ldd     Num2    ; The data to print
0011 3B         13             pshd            ; Put it on the stack
0012 3B         14             pshd
0013 CC004C     15             ldd     #FORMAT2; The format string
0016 15FBFDEC   16             jsr     [printf,PCR]
001A 1B84       17             leas    4,sp    ; Clean up stack
                18  ;          - - -
001C FFFF       19  Num1:      DW      $FFFF
001E 0080       20  Num2:      DW      $80
0020 5369676E   21  FORMAT1:   DB      "Signed Decimal: %d = Unsigned
                                                         Decimal:"
     65642044
     6563696D
     616C3A20
     2564203D
     20556E73
     69676E65
     64204465
     63696D61
     6C3A
0046 2025750D   22             DB         " %u",CR,LF,0
     0A00
004C 48657820   23  FORMAT2: DB        "Hex Number: $%X = Unsigned Decimal:"
     4E756D62
     65723A20
     24255820
     3D20556E
     7369676E
     65642044
     6563696D
     616C3A
```

Convert the ASCII hexadecimal string (pointed to by *HexStr*) to a binary integer at the memory location pointed to by *BinNum*; the converted string must be no greater than $FFFF and terminated by either an ASCII space ($20) or null ($00). The address of the string, *HexStr*, is passed in D and the address at which the number is stored, *BinNum*, is passed on the stack. The function returns either a pointer to the terminating character or a NULL pointer if an illegal hex character is found or the converted value is greater than $FFFF. See Example 5–26.

EXAMPLE 5–23   Continued

```
006F  2025342E    24  DB         "  %4.4d",CR,LF,0
      34640D0A
      00
Solution:
Signed Decimal:  -1 = Unsigned Decimal:  65535
Hex Number:  $80 = Unsigned Decimal:  0128
```

EXAMPLE 5–24   int putchar(int);

```
putcharc.asm         Assembled with CASM  08/08/1998  22:54  PAGE  1

0000                 1  putchar:    EQU      $FE04      ; Define vector
                     2  ;
                     3  ; Print the character in the B register
0000  C641           4              ldab     #"A"
0002  15FBFDFE       5              jsr      [putchar,PCR]
```

EXAMPLE 5–25   int SetUserVector(int VectNum, Address UserAddress);

```
setvectc.asm         Assembled with CASM  08/08/1998  22:55  PAGE  1

0000                 1  SetUserVector:  EQU           $FE1A ; Set the vector
0000                 2  TimerCh0:       EQU      23    ; Timer int number
                     3  ;               - - -
0000  CC000C         4                  ldd      #ISR  ; Get address of interrupt
                     5                                 ; service routine
0003  3B             6                  pshd
0004  CC0023         7                  ldd      #TimerCh0 ; Interrupt number
0007  15FBFE0F       8                  jsr      [SetUserVector,PCR]
000B  30             9                  pulx          ; Clean up stack
                    10  ;               - - -
                    11  ; Dummy interrupt service routine
000C  0B            12  ISR:            RTI
```

char *strcpy(char *s1, char *s2);
Vector: $FE14   *Stack use:* 8 bytes
Input: The address for the destination string (s2) on the stack and the address of the source string (s1) in D.
Returns: The pointer to the source string.

Copy the null-terminated string (including the $00) pointed to by *s1* to the string pointed to by *s2*; *s1* is passed in D; *s2* is passed on the stack. On return, D contains the pointer to *s2*. See Example 5–27.

unsigned int strlen(const char *cs);
Vector: $FE12   *Stack use:* 4 bytes
Input: D is the address of the null-terminated string to be checked.
Returns: D is the length of the string not including the NULL terminator.

Returns, in D, the length of the string pointed to by *cs*. The string is null terminated (ASCII $00); *cs* is passed to strlen in D. See Example 5–28.

EXAMPLE 5–26   char *sscanhex(char *HexStr, unsigned int *BinNum);

```
sscan1c.asm          Assembled with CASM 12/08/1998  02:11  PAGE 1

0000              1  sscanhex:   EQU    $FE0A    ; Set vector address
                  2  ;            - - -
                  3  ; Convert ASCII-hex string to binary
0000 CC000E       4              ldd    #BinNum ; Get the result address
0003 3B           5              pshd            ; Put it on the stack
0004 CC0010       6              ldd    #String ; Get the string's address
0007 15FBFDFF     7              jsr    [sscanhex,PCR]
000B 30           8              pulx            ; Clean up stack
                  9  ; Check for a NULL pointer in the D register
                 10  ; to see if an error occurred.
                 11  ; IF D = 0
000C 2600        12              bne    OK
                 13  ; THEN (process error condition)
                 14  ;            - - -
                 15  ; ELSE all OK continue
                 16  OK:
                 17  ;            - - -
000E            18  BinNum:     DS     2        ; Binary result
0010 46464646   19  String:     DB     "FFFF "  ; The string to convert
     20
                 20  ; Note: this string is terminated with a space.
                 21  ; It could also be terminated with 0.
```

EXAMPLE 5–27   char *strcpy(char *s1, char *s2);

strcpy1c.asm   Assembled with CASM 08/08/1998 22:58 PAGE 1

```
0000                 1  strcpy:       EQU    $FE14  ; Set vector address
                     2  ;        - - -
                     3  ; Copy NULL terminated string
0000 CC000D          4          ldd    #Source ; Put source adr on stack
0003 3B              5          pshd
0004 CC0027          6          ldd    #Dest ; Get destination address
0007 15FBFE09        7          jsr    [strcpy,PCR]
000B 30              8          pulx        ; Clean up stack
000C 3F              9          swi
                    10  ;        - - -
000D 54686973       11  Source: DB     "This is the source string",0
     20697320
     74686520
     736F7572
     63652073
     7472696E
     6700
                    12  ; Allocate storage for destination string
0027                13  Dest:   DS     *-Source
```

EXAMPLE 5–28   unsigned int strlen(const char *cs);

strlen1c.asm   Assembled with CASM 08/08/1998 22:59 PAGE 1

```
0000                 1  strlen:   EQU    $FE12   ; Define the vector
                     2  ;        - - -
0000 CC000A          3          ldd    #String ; Get the string's address
0003 15FBFE0B        4          jsr    [strlen,PCR]
                     5  ; On return, the D register has the length
0007 7C0028          6          std    Str_Len
                     7  ;        - - -
000A 54686520        8  String:  DB     "The length of the string is: ",0
     6C656E67
     7468206F
     66207468
     65207374
     72696E67
     2069733A
     2000
0028                 9  Str_Len:DS            2
```

int toupper(int c);
Vector: $FE0E   *Stack use:* 4 bytes
Input: B contains the character to be converted.
Returns: B contains the upper-case character.

Convert the character *c* (passed and returned in B) to upper case. See Example 5–29.

Boolean WriteEEByte(Address EEAddress, Byte EEData);
Vector: $FE1C   *Stack use:* 12 bytes
Input: The data to be written are on the stack and the address in D.
Returns: D = 0 if the EEPROM is not programmed properly, otherwise nonzero.

Program a byte in the on-chip EEPROM. *EEAddress* is passed in D and the *EEData* on the stack. After programming, the EEPROM location is verified to be the same as the data byte. If it is not, D is returned with a zero value, otherwise, nonzero. See Example 5–30.

5.4 D-Bug12 Monitor Interrupt Vector Initialization

The *interrupt jump vector table* must be initialized with the address of your interrupt service routine.

The D-Bug12 Monitor provides default interrupt service routines. When developing interrupt driven software you can substitute your own interrupt service routines for these defaults. This is done by executing the *SetUserVector* function as shown in Example 5–25. Each M68HC12 interrupt has a number, as shown in Table 5–4, to be passed to the SetUserVector routine. We will see more examples showing how to use this feature in Chapter 8.

EXAMPLE 5–29   int toupper(int c);

```
toupperc.asm        Assembled with CASM 08/08/1998  23:00   PAGE 1

0000              1 toupper:   EQU    $FE0E   ; Define the vector
                  2 ;          - - -
0000 F6000A       3            ldab   L_CHAR  ; Get the character
0003 15FBFE07     4            jsr    [toupper,PCR]
0007 7B000B       5            stab   U_CHAR  ; Save it
                  6 ;          - - -
000A             7 L_CHAR:     DS     1       ; Lower-case character
000B             8 U_CHAR:     DS     1       ; Upper-case character
```

EXAMPLE 5–30   Boolean WriteEEByte(Address EEAddress, Byte EEData);

```
writeeec.asm          Assembled with CASM  08/08/1998  23:01  PAGE 1

0000                   1  WriteEEByte: EQU     $FE1C    ; Set the vector
                       2  ;           - - -
                       3  ; Write the config byte into EEPROM
0000 F6000E            4              ldab     EEData   ; Get the byte to write
0003 3B                5              pshd              ; Put it on the stack
0004 FC000F            6              ldd      Address  ; The address to write
0007 15FBFE11          7              jsr      [WriteEEByte,PCR]
000B 3A                8              puld              ; Clean up stack
                       9  ; IF the Z flag was set, an error has occurred
000C 2600             10              bne      All_OK
                      11  ; THEN (process error condition)
                      12  ;           - - -
                      13  All_OK:
                      14  ; Continue
                      15  ;           - - -
000E                  16  EEData:     DS       1        ; Data for EEPROM
000F                  17  Address:    DS       2        ; Address for EEPROM
```

TABLE 5–4   D-Bug12 Monitor Interrupts

Number$_{10}$	MC68HC812A4 Interrupt (Ver 1.xxx)	MC68HC912B32 Interrupt (Ver 2.xxx)
7	Port H Key Wake Up	Reserved
8	Port J Key Wake Up	BDLC
9	Analog-to-Digital Converter	Analog-to-Digital Converter
10	Serial Communications Interface 1 (SCI1)	Reserved
11	Serial Communications Interface 0 (SCI0)	Serial Communications Interface 0 (SCI0)
12	Serial Peripheral Interface 0 (SPI0)	Serial Peripheral Interface 0 (SPI0)
23	Timer Channel 0	Timer Channel 0
22	Timer Channel 1	Timer Channel 1
21	Timer Channel 2	Timer Channel 2
20	Timer Channel 3	Timer Channel 3
19	Timer Channel 4	Timer Channel 4
18	Timer Channel 5	Timer Channel 5
17	Timer Channel 6	Timer Channel 6
16	Timer Channel 7	Timer Channel 7
14	Pulse Accumulator Overflow	Pulse Accumulator Overflow
13	Pulse Accumulator Input Edge	Pulse Accumulator Input Edge
15	Timer Overflow	Timer Overflow
24	Real Time Interrupt	Real Time Interrupt
25	IRQ and Key wakeup D	IRQ
26	XIRQ	XIRQ
27	Software Interrupt (SWI)	Software Interrupt (SWI)
28	Unimplemented Opcode Trap	Unimplemented Opcode Trap
−1	Return the starting address of the RAM vector table	Return the starting address of the RAM vector table

5.5 Operating Hints for the D-Bug12 Monitor

Table 5–5 summarizes all D-Bug12 commands and utility routines, and here are several helpful hints for using the monitor.

Getting Help: Type *Help* to display a screen showing all the monitor commands.

Downloading Programs: *LOAD*. Use the terminal program to send the *S-Record* file.

Starting a Program: Type *G address* or just *G* to continue from the current address.

Setting Breakpoints: *BR address* sets a breakpoint at the address. *BR* (with no argument) displays all breakpoints currently set. *NOBR* clears all breakpoints; *NOBR address* clears a breakpoint at an address.

Continuing from a Breakpoint: Type *G* to continue from the current address. *GT address* will set a temporary breakpoint and go until the address. You must set the user PC unless it is already pointing to the user program (such as just after a breakpoint). GT does not install other breakpoints.

Tracing a Program: The *T* command traces one program step at a time. *T n* traces *n* instructions at a time.

Displaying and Modifying Registers: Type *RM* to see the complete register set.

Modifying Individual Registers: Type the register name (A, B, CCR, X, Y, SP, or PC) and a value to change and display the contents of the register.

Displaying Memory: Type *MD address*.

TABLE 5–5 Summary of D-Bug12 Commands and Utility Routines

D-Bug12 Command	Function	Monitor Routine	M68HC12A4EVB Ver 1.xxxx Address	M68EVB912B32 Ver 2.xxx Address
ASM	Assemble programs	EraseEE	$FE1E	$F69E
BAUD	Set SCI Baud rate	getchar	$FE02	$F682
BF	Block fill memory	GetCmdLine	$FE08	$F688
BR	Breakpoint set	isalpha	$FE10	$F690
BULK	Bulk erase EEPROM	isxdigit	$FE0C	$F68C
G	Go run user program	main	$FE00	$F680
GT	Go till a breakpoint	out2hex	$FE16	$F696
HELP	Help	out4hex	$FE18	$F698
LOAD	Load program down to EVB	printf	$FE06	$F686
MD	Memory display-byte	putchar	$FE04	$F684
MDW	Memory display-word	SetUserVector	$FE1A	$F69A
MM	Memory modify-byte	sscanhex	$FE0A	$F68A
MMW	Memory modify-word	strcpy	$FE14	$F694
MOVE	Move memory	toupper	$FE0E	$F68E
NOBR	Clear breakpoint	WriteEEByte	$FE1C	$F69C
RD	Register display			
RM	Register modify			
T	Trace program			
UPLOAD	Upload from EVB			
VERIFY	Verify downloaded program			

Modifying Memory: *MM address* displays and allows you to enter new data.

Assembling Small Test Programs: *ASM address*. Enter the opcode mnemonics and hexadecimal operands. Conclude by typing period (.).

5.6 Problems

5.1   You downloaded an S-record file to the EVB and the D-Bug12 Monitor responds with the message "Invalid Command." What went wrong?

5.2   What sequence of keystrokes would you use to put the hexadecimal data 11, 22, 33, 44 into memory locations $5000–$5003?

5.3   Write a short D-Bug12 assembler (ASM) code segment showing how to use the D-Bug12 Monitor utility routine putchar to print the letter A on the terminal.

5.4   Write a short CASM12 code segment showing how to use the D-Bug12 Monitor utility routine putchar to print a $ on the terminal.

5.5   Write a short D-Bug12 assembler (ASM) code segment showing how to use the D-Bug12 Monitor utility routine printf to print a string starting at $5000.

5.6   Write a short CASM12 code segment showing how to use the D-Bug12 Monitor utility routine printf.

5.7   How does the D-Bug12 Monitor know when to stop printing characters in the printf routines?

5.8   Write a short CASM12 code segment showing how to use the D-Bug12 Monitor utility routine out4hex assuming the data to be printed are at $5000.

5.9   What command is used to set a breakpoint at $4016?

5.10   What command is used to clear all breakpoints?

5.11   What command is used to display what breakpoints are currently set?

5.12   What command is used to set register A to $AA?

5.13   What command is used to display memory locations $5000 to $502F?

Chapter 6

Programs for the M68HC12

OBJECTIVES

This chapter will show programming techniques and suggest an assembly language programming style. Examples of programs using the CASM12 assembler are given and explained. We will also show how to write structured assembly language programs that meet the goals of top-down software design.[1]

6.1 Assembly Language Programming Style

We discussed the syntax requirements of the CASM12 assembler in Chapter 3 and, like most assemblers, each program line must have its fields separated by white spaces. In addition to the syntactical requirements of each line, a standard format or style should be adopted when writing programs. This will make programs more readable for colleagues who may have to modify your code or collaborate on a software engineering project.

Source Code Style

A consistent style can make your programs easier to read.

Any program is a sequence of program elements, from the top to the bottom, and these elements should be organized in a readable and consistent style. Adopt a standard format and use it for all assembly language programs. Table 6–1 shows a format that can serve as an outline for your programs.

---

[1] Chapter 6 in *Microcontrollers and Microcomputers: Principles of Software and Hardware Engineering* shows how to design software using the top-down design method and structured pseudocode design tools. Modular software design and the problems of module coupling are discussed also.

TABLE 6–1 Assembly Language Program Elements

Program Element	Purpose
Program Header	Briefly describes the purpose of the program
Assembler Equates	Definition of constants used in the program
Program Location	Locates the program in ROM
Program Initialization	Initializes the stack pointer and other variables
Main Program Body	This contains the main program
Program End	Either return to the monitor or start the main program again
Program Subroutines	Location of subroutines and functions used in the main program
Constant Data Definitions	Definitions of constants in ROM
Variable Data Location	Locates variable data elements in RAM
Variable Data Allocation	Allocation of space for variable data elements

Program Header

After reading the header, you should know what the program does, not in any great detail, but at least in general. The author's name should be here so praise (or blame) can be apportioned correctly. The date of original code release and modification record is good information too. The modification record should indicate what has been done to the original code, when it was done, and by whom.

Program Element	Program Example
Program Header	; MC68HC12 Assembler Example
	;
	; This program is to demonstrate a
	; readable programming style.
	; It counts the number of characters
	; in a buffer and stores the result in
	; a data location. It then prints
	; the number of characters using
	; D-Bug12 Monitor routines.
	; Source File: M6812EX1.ASM
	; Author: F. M. Cady
	; Created: 5/15/97
	; Modifications: None

Assembler Equates

Equates are often found at the beginning of the program.

Some programmers put equates at the bottom of the program and some argue that it is more useful to put a constant definition right where it is used. We suggest that all equates be in one area in the program before they are used. The assembler always assumes a referenced label refers to a 16-bit address unless it already knows it is in direct address space (the first 256 memory locations). It is always better to let the assembler know the values of labels before they are used.

There are three general types of equates, as shown in the following table. *System equates* define labels for monitor subroutines and the locations of I/O registers. *Constant equates* define constants to be used in the program. The *memory map equates* define the location of various program elements.

Program Element	Program Example
| System Equates. | ```
;     Monitor Equates
out2hex:EQU     $FE16   ; Output 2 hex nibbles
putchar:EQU     $FE04   ; Print a character
;     I/O Ports
PORTH:  EQU     $24     ; Port H address
PORTJ:  EQU     $28     ; Port J address
``` |
| Constant Equates | ```
;     Constant Equates
CR:     EQU     $0d     ; CR code
LF:     EQU     $0a     ; LF code
NULL:   EQU     $00     ; End of ASCII string
NIL:    EQU     0       ; Initial data value
``` |
| Memory Map Equates | ```
;     Memory Map Equates
PROG:   EQU     $4000   ; Locate the program
DATA:   EQU     $6000   ; Variable data areas
STACK:  EQU     $8000   ; Top of Stack
``` |

Program Location

In an absolute assembler such as CASM12, you must *locate* the program. When using an evaluation board for developing programs, code usually is downloaded into RAM. Later, when the code is assembled for use in ROM, the equate defining the value of the symbol PROG can be easily changed.

Program Element	Program Example
Program Code Origination	`ORG     PROG     ; Locate the program`

Program Initialization

The *stack pointer* must be initialized before it is used for subroutine calls, interrupts, and data storage. Do it as the first instruction in the program. *Variables* must be initialized at run time. Put the section of code to do this here.

Program Element	Program Example
Stack Pointer Initialization	`lds     #STACK      ; Initialize stack pointer`
| Variable Data Initialization | ```
; Initialize the data area to zero
clr     Counter
``` |

Main Program Body

The main program starts here. Typically it will be short and consist of several subroutine calls.

Program Element	Program Example
| Main Program Body | ```
; Count the characters in the string
        ldd      #STRING
        jsr      count_em
; Output the result string
        ldd      #RESULT; Point to the string
        jsr      outstr
; Output the counter
        ldab     counter
        jsr      [out2hex,PCR]
; Now output a CRLF
        jsr      CRLF
``` |

Program End

When developing software on an evaluation system such as the EVB, you must return control to the monitor at the end of your program. This is often done with a *Software Interrupt* (SWI) instruction. In programs that run continuously with no need to return to the debugging monitor, a jump back to the beginning of the process loop is made.

Program Element	Program Example
Return to the Monitor	`swi    ; Return to the monitor`

Program Subroutines

It is good programming practice to make the main program a sequence of calls to subroutines. Most assemblers operate in two passes, so a subroutine's code can follow its call.

Program Element	Program Example
| Subroutines and Functions | ```
; Subroutine "count_em( char *StringP )"
; This routine counts the characters in a string
; until the NULL character is found.
; Entry:     D register pointing to the start
; Exit:      None
; Reg Mod:   CCR
; Data Mod:  Data location Counter contains the
;            number of characters
;
count_em
; Save the registers
        pshx
        tfr     d,x      ; Put the address in X
; WHILE the char is not ZERO
while_do:
        tst     0,x
        beq     found_eot
; DO count the chars
``` |

```
                inc      Counter
                inx
                bra      while_do
;  ENDO
found_eot:
;  ENDWHILE the char is not NULL
;  Restore the registers
                pulx
                rts
;  END subroutine "count_em()"
```

Constant Data Definitions

Constants are located in ROM. Usually it is best to have constants at the end of all code sections to decrease the danger of executing data. However, some programmers group constants with the section of code that uses them, i.e., constants used in a subroutine directly following the subroutine code.

Program Element	Program Example
Main Program Constants and Strings	; Constant data area in ROM STRING: DB "This is a string",NULL RESULT: DB "The number of characters is $",NULL

Variable Data Location

Variables are located in RAM. In a dedicated application system, the RAM memory is located at a different address than the ROM. Thus, another ORG is needed.

Program Element	Program Example
Variable Data Area Origination	; Variable data area in RAM ORG DATA

Variable Data Allocation

Use the DS to allocate all variable data elements.

Program Element	Program Example
Allocation of Data Areas	Counter: DS 1

Example 6–1 shows this program as a complete assembler list file.

EXAMPLE 6–1

```
m6812ex1.asm          Assembled with CASM  12/08/1998  02:38  PAGE 1

                   1  ; MC68HC12 Assembler Example
                   2  ;
                   3  ; This program is to demonstrate a
                   4  ; readable programming style.
                   5  ; It counts the number of characters
                   6  ; in a buffer and stores the result in
                   7  ; a data location.    It then prints
                   8  ; the number of characters using
                   9  ; D-Bug12  monitor routines.
                  10  ; Source File:   M6812EX1.ASM
                  11  ; Author:  F. M. Cady
                  12  ; Created: 5/15/97
                  13  ; Modifications: None
                  14  ;
                  15  ; Monitor Equates
0000              16  out2hex:  EQU   $FE16   ; Output 2 hex nibbles
0000              17  putchar:  EQU   $FE04   ; Print a character
                  18  ; I/O Ports
0000              19  PORTH:    EQU   $24     ; Port H address
0000              20  PORTJ:    EQU   $28     ; Port J address
                  21  ; Constant Equates
0000              22  CR:       EQU   $0d     ; CR code
0000              23  LF:       EQU   $0a     ; LF code
0000              24  NULL:     EQU   $00     ; End of ASCII string
                  25  ; Memory Map Equates
0000              26  PROG:     EQU   $4000   ; Locate the program
0000              27  DATA:     EQU   $6000   ; Variable data areas
0000              28  STACK:    EQU   $8000   ; To of stack
                  29
4000              30            ORG   PROG    ; Locate the program
4000 CF8000       31            lds   #STACK  ; Initialize stack pointer
                  32  ; Initialize the data area to zero
4003 796000       33            clr   Counter
                  34  ; Count the characters in the string
4006 CC4052       35            ldd   #STRING
4009 16401D       36            jsr   count_em
                  37  ; Output the result string
400C CC4063       38            ldd   #RESULT ; Point to the string
400F 16402C       39            jsr   outstr
                  40  ; Output the counter
4012 F66000       41            ldab  Counter
4015 15FBBDFD     42            jsr   [out2hex,PCR]
                  43  ; Now output a CRLF
4019 164041       44            jsr   crlf
```

EXAMPLE 6–1   Continued

```
401C 3F        45  swi                      ; Return to the monitor
               46
               47  ; Subroutine "count_em( char *StringP )"
               48  ; This routine counts the characters in a string
               49  ; until the NULL terminating character is found.
               50  ; Entry:    D register pointing to the start
               51  ; Exit:     None
               52  ; Reg Mod:  CCR
               53  ; Data Mod: Data location Counter contains the
               54  ;           number of characters
               55  count_em:
               56  ; Save the registers
401D 34        57          pshx
401E B745      58          tfr    d,x     ; put the address in X
               59  ; WHILE the char is not NULL
               60  while_do:
4020 E700      61          tst    0,x
4022 2706      62          beq    found_end
               63  ; DO count the chars
4024 726000    64          inc    Counter
4027 08        65          inx    ;         Increment pointer to next
4028 20F6      66          bra    while_do
               67  ; ENDO
               68  found_end:
               69  ; ENDWHILE the char is not NULL
               70  ; Restore the registers
402A 30        71          pulx
402B 3D        72          rts
               73  ; END subroutine "count_em()"
               74
               75  ; Subroutine outstr( char *StringP )
               76  ; Output a NULL terminated ASCII string
               77  ; Entry:  D points to the string to be printed
               78  ; Exit: None
               79  ; Reg Mod: CCR
               80  ; Data Mod: None
               81  outstr:
               82  ; Save the registers
402C 3B        83          pshd
402D 34        84          pshx
402E 35        85          pshy
402F B745      86          tfr    d,x     ; put the address in X
               87  ; WHILE the char is not NULL
               88  while_do_2:
4031 E700      89          tst    0,x
4033 2708      90          beq    found_end_2
               91  ; DO Output the character
```

EXAMPLE 6–1 Continued

```
4035  E630        92              ldab    1,x+    ; Get char and incr pointer
4037  15FBBDC9    93              jsr     [putchar,PCR]
403B  20F4        94              bra     while_do_2
                  95  ; ENDO
                  96  found_end_2:
                  97  ; ENDWHILE the char is not NULL
                  98  ; Restore the registers
403D  31          99              puly
403E  30         100              pulx
403F  3A         101              puld
4040  3D         102              rts
                 103  ; END subroutine "outstr()"
                 104
                 105  ; Subroutine "crlf( void )"
                 106  ; Output a CRLF sequence
                 107  ; Input: None
                 108  ; Output: None
                 109  ; Reg Mod: CCR
                 110  ; Data Mod: None
                 111  crlf:
4041  3B         112              pshd
4042  34         113              pshx
4043  C60D       114              ldab    #CR     ; Print the CR
4045  15FBBDBB   115              jsr     [putchar,PCR]
4049  C60A       116              ldab    #LF     ; Print the LF
404B  15FBBDB5   117              jsr     [putchar,PCR]
404F  30         118              pulx
4050  3A         119              puld
4051  3D         120              rts
                 121  ; End subroutine "crlf()"
                 122  ; Constant data area in ROM
4052  54686973   123  STRING:     DB      "This is a string",NULL
      20697320
      61207374
      72696E67
      00
4063  54686520   124  RESULT:     DB      "The number of characters is $",NULL
      6E756D62
      6572206F
      66206368
      61726163
      74657273
      20697320
      2400
                 125  ; Variable data area in RAM
6000             126              ORG     DATA
6000             127  Counter:    DS      1
```

To Indent or Not to Indent

Indentation is not used
very often in assembly
language programming.

In high-level languages, indentation shows lower levels of the design and makes the code more readable. Indentation is generally not used in assembly language programming. Historically, assemblers were used long before high-level language compilers that allowed indentation were developed. Also, an assembler's syntax is generally fixed. Often, labels must start in the first space on the line and there must be white space between labels, mnemonics, operands, and comments. Assembly language programmers are used to seeing the program with the fields all nicely lined up because it is easier to see the operations and operands. However, you may want to try a few programs with indented code to see how you like it.

Upper and Lower Case

Using *upper- and lower-
case* letters can make
your programs more
readable.

Upper- and lower-case letters can make your code more readable. The goal is to be able to look at a name or label and tell what it is without looking further. For example, upper-case labels can be used for constants and lower-case labels for variables. Mixed case used for multiple-word labels can make the label easier to read. Table 6–2 shows upper-, lower-, and mixed-case examples.

Use Equates, Not Magic Numbers

Equates make programs
easier to read and easier
to change in the future.

A number that appears in the code is called a magic number. For example, if the program statement

```
ldab   #8
```

TABLE 6–2 Examples of Upper, Lower, and Mixed Case

Case	Examples
Upper	
Constants defined by EQU	`NULL:    EQU   $0`
	`PORT_H:  EQU   $24`
Constants defined by DB, DW	`STRING:  DB    "This is a string."`
	`CRLF:    DW    $0D0A`
Assembler directives	`ORG, EQU, RMB`
Lower	
Instruction mnemonics	`ldaa, jsr, bne`
Labels	`loop: . . .`
	`         bne   loop`
Variables	`data:    DS    10`
Mixed	
Multiword variables and labels	`PrintData:`
	`NumChars:`
	`InputDataBuffer:`
Multiword subroutine names	`        jsr   PrintData`
Comments	`; Write sentences for comments.`

appeared in a program, you would have to ask, "What significance does the 8 have in the program?" Is it used as a counter or as an output value? You do not know. However, the following code,

```
COUNTER:    EQU    8
            ldab   #COUNTER
```

is much clearer. Further, if the counter is used in several places in the program and needs to be changed, it is easier to change the equate than to search for and change all places it is used. Always use the EQU directive to define constants in your program.

Using Include Files

An *include file* can contain frequently used symbols and definition.

Assembly language programs often use the same equates in each program. To reduce the amount of typing, use your text editor's facility to import another file into the source code. This technique is similar to the use of #include in C programs. More powerful assemblers such as CASM12 allow include files to be used as shown in Example 6–2.

EXAMPLE 6–2

include.asm Assembled with CASM 05/23/1998 18:55 PAGE 1

```
            1  ; include.asm
            2  ; Demonstration of the use of include files
            3  ;
0000        4  include "y:\hc12\casm\include1.h"
            5  ; This is the include1.h file
            6  ; A useful include file is one which defines
            7  ; commonly used constants
0000        8  EOT:   EQU    04     ; End of transmission
0000        9  CR:    EQU    $0d    ; Carriage-return
0000       10  LF:    EQU    $0a    ; Line-feed
0000       11  include "y:\hc12\casm\include2.asm"
           12  ; include2.asm
           13  ; This is the second include file
           14  ; You can have source code and macro
           15  ; definitions.
           16  ; Here is a macro definition
0000       17  MU100: EQU    !199   ; Delay loop counter
0000       18  $MACRO  Delay_100
           19  ; Macro to delay 100 microseconds for the A/D start up
           20          psha           ; save the A reg
           21          ldaa    #MU100
           22  loop:   deca
           23          bne    \@loop
           24          pula           ; restore the A reg
0000       25  $MACROEND
           26
```

Using Monitor Routines

Program development boards, such as the MC68HC12EVB, usually have a debugging monitor with input and output routines. A vector table in the monitor provides access to these I/O routines. To use them, equate a label to the address in the jump table and then use an indirect or indexed jump to subroutine (JSR). Chapter 5 shows examples for the D-Bug12 monitor; see also Example 6–3.

Commenting Style

There are various commenting styles. Some programmers would have a comment on each program line. Another style is to place comments in blocks that explain what the following section of code is to do, i.e., on the design or function of each block. Then, within the block of code, place comments on lines in which further explanations may be required. Using high-level, pseudocode design statements as comments in the program is very effective also.

Subroutine or Function Headers

Table 6–3 shows useful information that can be included as comments in each subroutine's header.

6.2 Structured Assembly Language Programming

Programs are often designed using pseudocode as a design tool.[2] After we have completed our design, we must write the assembly language code for it. There are two parts of the assembly language code to do structured programming. The first is a comment. This normally can be taken from the

---

EXAMPLE 6–3

Show how to use an EQU to define the vector for the putchar(int) D-Bug12 monitor subroutine.

Solution:

```
setvect2.asm      Assembled with CASM  06/26/1998  02:26  PAGE 1

0000             1  putchar:  EQU   $FE04   ;   Set vector location
                 2  ;
                 3  ; Print a character
0000 C621        4            ldab  #"!"
0002 15FBFDFE    5            jsr   [putchar,PCR]
```

---

[2] The pseudocode design tool is discussed in Chapter 6 of *Microcontrollers and Microcomputers: Principles of Software and Hardware Engineering.*

TABLE 6-3   Subroutine or Function Headers
;   Subroutine calling sequence or invocation
;   Subroutine name
;   Purpose of subroutine
;   Name of file containing the source
;   Author
;   Date of creation or release
;   Input and output variables
;   Registers modified
;   Global data elements modified
;   Local data elements modified
;   Brief description of the algorithm
;   Functions or subroutines called

pseudocode design document. The second part is the code that implements the comment. Let us look at the three structured programming elements as they might appear in assembly language.

Sequence

The sequence is straightforward. There should be a block of comments describing what the next section of assembly code is to do. Remember that the flow of the program is in at the top and out at the bottom. We must not enter or exit the code between BEGIN A and END A except to call and return from a subroutine. Do not jump into or out of the middle of a sequence block. See Example 6–4.

IF-THEN-ELSE Decision

A pseudocode design using the decision element and the associated assembly language code is shown in Example 6–5. See also Examples 6–6 and 6–7.

The IF-THEN-ELSE code always has the same form. The **bold** lines in Example 6–5 will appear in every decision structure.

> *Lines* 9, *11, 14, 18, and 23:* These lines contain the pseudocode design as comments in the source code.
> *Line 12:* Following the IF statement is code to set the condition code register for the conditional branch in *line 13* to the ELSE part.

EXAMPLE 6–4   Assembly Language for a Sequence Block

```
;* BEGIN A
;* Comments describing the function of this sequence block
.... (assembly language code to do the function)
;* END A
```

EXAMPLE 6–5   Decision Element Assembly Language Program

Pseudocode design

```
Get Temperature
IF Temperature > Allowed Maximum
THEN
    Turn the water valve off
ELSE
    Turn the water valve on
ENDIF Temperature > Allowed Maximum
```

Structured assembly code

```
decisn1c.asm       Assembled with CASM  05/23/1998  19:09  PAGE 1

                1 ; 68HC12 Structured assembly code
                2 ; IF-THEN-ELSE example
                3 ; Equates define constants need by the code
0000            4 AD_PORT:      EQU     $20   ; A/D Data port
0000            5 MAX_ALLOWED:  EQU     !128  ; Maximum Temp
0000            6 VALVE_OFF:    EQU     0     ; Bits for valve off
0000            7 VALVE_ON:     EQU     1     ; Bits for valve on
0000            8 VALVE_PORT:   EQU     $24   ; Port H
                9 ; Get Temperature
0000 9620      10        ldaa    AD_PORT
               11 ; IF Temperature > Allowed Maximum
0002 8180      12        cmpa    #MAX_ALLOWED
0004 2F06      13        bls     ELSE_PART
               14 ; THEN Turn the water valve off
0006 9600      15        ldaa    VALVE_OFF
0008 5A24      16        staa    VALVE_PORT
000A 2004      17        bra     END_IF
               18 ; ELSE Turn the water valve on
               19 ELSE_PART:
000C 9601      20        ldaa    VALVE_ON
000E 5A24      21        staa    VALVE_PORT
               22 END_IF:
               23 ; END IF Temperature > Allowed Maximum
```

Line 13: There will always be a conditional branch to the ELSE part, as shown here, or the THEN part. When branching to the ELSE part, the conditional branch instruction is the complement of the logic in the IF statement. In this example, the ELSE part is to be executed if the temperature is lower or the same as the allowed maximum because the THEN part is done when the temperature is greater.

Lines 15 and 16: This is the code for the THEN part.

Line 17: The THEN part ALWAYS ends with a branch-always or jump to the END_IF label. This branches around the ELSE part code.

Line 19: The label for the ELSE part conditional branch is always here.

Lines 20 and 21: This is the code for the ELSE part.

Line 22: The IF-THEN-ELSE always ends with an END-IF label.

WHILE-DO Repetition

The WHILE-DO structure is shown in Example 6–8. The elements common to all WHILE-DOs are shown in **bold**.

Lines 11, 13, 17, 18, 25, 26, 28, and 31: The pseudocode design appears as comments in the code.

EXAMPLE 6–6

For each of the logic statements, give the appropriate M68HC12 code to set the condition code register and to branch to the ELSE part of an IF-THEN-ELSE. Assume P and Q are 8-bit, signed numbers in memory locations P and Q.

A.   IF $P \geq Q$
B.   IF $Q > P$
C.   IF $P = Q$

Solution:

```
A.    ; IF   P>=Q
                ldaa      P
                cmpa      Q
                blt       ELSE_PART
B.    ; IF   Q > P
                ldaa      Q
                cmpa      P
                ble       ELSE_PART
C.    ; IF   P = Q
                ldaa      P
                cmpa      Q
                bne       ELSE_PART
```

Lines 15 and 16: A WHILE-DO tests the condition at the top of the code to be repeated. Thus, the conditional branch in *line 16* must be preceded by code that initializes the variable to be tested. The A register is initialized with the A/D value in *line 12*.

Line 14: There must be a label at the start of the conditional test code. This is the address for the BRA in *line 29*.

Line 15: Following the WHILE statement is code to set the condition code register for the subsequent conditional branch to the end of the WHILE-DO.

Line 16: A conditional branch allows us to exit this structure.

Lines 18–27: This is the code for the DO part.

Line 27: A special requirement of the WHILE-DO structure is code that changes whatever is being tested. If this were not here, the program would never leave the loop.

Line 29: The code block always ends with a branch back to the start.

As an assembly language programmer you might be smarter than the average compiler and realize that *line 27* could be eliminated if the code to initialize the A register with the A/D value (*line 12*) is moved below the label WHILE_START.

EXAMPLE 6–7

For each of the logic statements, give the appropriate M68HC12 code to set the condition code register and to branch to the THEN part of an IF-THEN-ELSE. Assume P and Q are 8-bit, signed numbers in memory locations P and Q.

A.   IF $P \geq Q$
B.   IF $Q > P$
C.   IF $P = Q$

Solution:

```
A.   ; IF   P>=Q
               ldaa      P
               cmpa      Q
               bge       THEN_PART
B.   ; IF   Q > P
               ldaa      Q
               cmpa      P
               bgt       THEN_PART
C.   ; IF   P = Q
               ldaa      P
               cmpa      Q
               beq       THEN_PART
```

EXAMPLE 6–8   Assembly Code for a WHILE-DO

Pseudocode design

```
Get the temperature from the A/D
WHILE the temperature > maximum allowed
    DO
        Flash light 0.5 sec on, 0.5 sec off
        Get the temperature from the A/D
    END_DO
END_WHILE the temperature > maximum allowed
```

Structured assembly code

```
while1c.asm        Assembled with CASM 05/23/1998 19:19 PAGE 1

                1  ; while1.asm
                2  ; 68HC12 Structured assembly code
                3  ; WHILE - DO Example
                4  ; Equates needed
0000            5  AD_PORT:     EQU     $70    ; A/D Data port
0000            6  MAX_ALLOWED: EQU     !128   ; Maximum Temp
0000            7  LIGHT_ON:    EQU     1
0000            8  LIGHT_OFF:   EQU     0
0000            9  LIGHT_PORT:  EQU     $24    ; Port H
               10  ;    - - -
               11  ; Get the temperature from the A/D
0000 9670      12       ldaa    AD_PORT
               13  ; WHILE the temperature > maximum allowed
               14  WHILE_START:
0002 8180      15       cmpa    #MAX_ALLOWED
0004 2312      16       bls     END_WHILE
               17  ; DO
               18  ; Flash light 0.5 sec on, 0.5 sec off
0006 9601      19       ldaa    LIGHT_ON
0008 5A24      20       staa    LIGHT_PORT   ; Turn the light
000A 160018    21       jsr     delay        ; 0.5 sec delay
000D 9600      22       ldaa    LIGHT_OFF
000F 5A24      23       staa    LIGHT_PORT   ; Turn the light off
0011 160018    24       jsr     delay
               25  ; End flashing the light
               26  ; Get the temperature from the A/D
0014 9670      27       ldaa    AD_PORT
               28  ; END_DO
0016 20EA      29       bra     WHILE_START
               30  END_WHILE:
               31  ; END_WHILE the temperature > maximum allowed
               32
               33  ; Dummy subroutine
0018 3D        34  delay:       rts
```

DO-WHILE Repetition

Another useful repetition is the DO-WHILE. In this structure, the DO part is executed at least once because the test is at the bottom of the loop. An example of the DO-WHILE is shown in Example 6–9 where, again, the parts common to all DO-WHILEs are shown in **bold**. See also Example 6–10.

Lines 7, 9, 11, 13 and 14: The pseudocode appears as comments.
Line 8: The start of the DO block has a label for the conditional branch instruction in *line 16.*
Line 9–12: These are the code lines for the DO part.
Lines 15 and 16: The DO-WHILE always ends with a test and a conditional branch back to the beginning of the DO block.
Line 17: A comment marks the end of the WHILE test code.

EXAMPLE 6–9   DO-WHILE Assembly Language Code

Pseudocode design

```
DO
    Get data from the switches
    Output the value to the LEDs
ENDO
WHILE Any switch is set
```

Structured assembly code

```
dowhl1c.asm    Assembled with CASM 05/23/1998  19:46  PAGE 1

            1  ; 68HC12 Structured assembly code
            2  ; DO-WHILE example
            3  ; Equates needed for this example
0000        4  SW_PORT:  EQU  $28   ; The switches are on Port J
0000        5  LEDS:     EQU  $24   ; The LEDs are on Port H
            6  ;         - - -
            7  ; DO
            8  DO_BEGIN:
            9  ; Get data from the switches
0000 9628  10          ldaa SW_PORT
           11  ; Output the data to the LEDs
0002 5A24  12          staa LEDS
           13  ; END_DO
           14  ; WHILE Any switch is set
0004 F70028 15          tst  SW_PORT
0007 26F7  16          bne  DO_BEGIN
           17  ; END_WHILE
```

6.3 Example Programs

Example programs are shown in Examples 6–11 to 6–13.

EXAMPLE 6–10

One of the most common structures found in assembly language programming is a loop controlled by a counter. Show the pseudocode and the structured assembly code to do this.

Solution:

Pseudocode design

```
Initialize the counter for 26 repetitions
DO
    The things that need to be done
ENDO
WHILE the counter is not equal to zero
```

Structured assembly code

```
dowhl2c.asm        Assembled with CASM  05/23/1998  19:56  PAGE 1

                1  ; dowhl2.asm
                2  ; Equates needed for this example
0000            3  COUNT: EQU   !26     ; Need to do loop 26 times
                4
                5  ; Initialize the counter for 26 repetitions
0000 C61A       6         ldab  #COUNT
                7  ; DO
                8  DO_BEGIN:
                9  ; The things that need to be done
               10  ;      - - -
               11  ; END_DO
               12  ; WHILE the counter is not equal to zero
0002 0431FD    13         dbne  b,DO_BEGIN ; Decrement the counter
               14                          ; and branch if not zero
               15  ; END_WHILE
```

Explanation of Example 6–11

Lines 0–8: The header information briefly explains the purpose of the program.

Lines 10 and 11: These equates define the locations of D-Bug12 Monitor subroutines.

Lines 13 and 14: These equates define the location of the code and stack.

Lines 16 and 17: Constant definitions are conveniently made at the top of the program.

Line 19: The ORG directive locates the program in memory.

Line 21: The stack pointer register must be initialized before using it.

Line 22: Indexed addressing will be used to access the data. This immediate addressing instruction loads the X register with the *address* of the first byte of data in the buffer.

Line 24: The number of bytes in the buffer is loaded using this assembler expression. The assembler evaluates the expression by subtracting DATA1 from DATA2. You can see the result by looking at the code bytes.

EXAMPLE 6–11

m6812ex2.asm   Assembled with CASM 06/26/1998 02:30 PAGE 1

```
                       0  ; MC68HC12 Assembler Example
                       1  ;
                       2  ; This program uses various D-Bug12 Monitor
                       3  ; routines to output the characters in the
                       4  ; DATA1 buffer to the terminal.
                       5  ; Source File: M6812EX2.ASM
                       6  ; Author: F. M. Cady
                       7  ; Created: 5/11/97
                       8  ; Modifications: None
                       9  ;
                      10  ; Monitor Equates
0000                  11  putchar:   EQU      $FE04   ; Print a char
                      12  ; Memory Map Equates
0000                  13  PROG:      EQU      $4000   ; Locate the program
0000                  14  STACK:     EQU      $8000   ; Stack
                      15  ; Constant Equates
0000                  16  CR:        EQU      $0d     ; CR character
0000                  17  LF:        EQU      $0a     ; LF character
                      18
4000                  19             ORG      PROG    ; Locate the program
                      20  ; BEGIN Initialization
4000 CF8000           21             lds      #STACK  ; Initialize stack pointer
4003 CE4023           22             ldx      #DATA1  ; Point to the characters
                      23  ; Initialize a counter
4006 CD0004           24             ldy      #DATA2-DATA1    ; Count the chars
                      25  ; END Initialization
                      26  ; DO
                      27  ; Output the characters that have been stored
                      28  ; as constant data in ROM.
4009 E630             29  loop:      ldab     1,x+    ; Get a character
400B 34               30             pshx             ; Save x and y reg
400C 35               31             pshy
400D 15FBBDF3         32             jsr      [putchar,PCR]
4011 31               33             puly
4012 30               34             pulx
                      35  ; END_DO
                      36  ; WHILE the counter is not zero
4013 0436F3           37             dbne     y,loop  ; Loop until done
                      38  ; END_WHILE
                      39  ; Now output a CRLF
4016 C60D             40             ldab     #CR
4018 15FBBDE8         41             jsr      [putchar,PCR]
401C C60A             42             ldab     #LF
401E 15FBBDE2         43             jsr      [putchar,PCR]
```

EXAMPLE 6–11   Continued

```
4022 3F               44                swi      ; Return to the monitor
                      45   ; Constant data area in ROM
4023 53544161         46   DATA1:    DB        $53,$54,'A','a'
4027                  47   DATA2:    EQU       *
                      48   ; DATA2 is a marker label for the next
                      49   ; location after the data.
```

Line 29: The character pointed to by the X register is loaded into B and the X register is postincremented to point to the next data byte.

Lines 30, 31, 33, 34: X and Y are first pushed onto the stack before calling the subroutine and then restored by pulling them afterward.

Line 32: Program counter relative indirect-indexed addressing is used to jump to the subroutine.

Line 37: The counter is decremented and a branch is taken to the start of the DO block if the counter is not zero.

Lines 40–43: A carriage-return, line-feed is output.

Line 44: A software interrupt (SWI) instruction returns control to the D-Bug12 Monitor at the end of the program.

Line 46: The assembler DB directive is used to define data in four memory locations starting at DATA1. You can see how the assembler evaluated these bytes by looking at the code bytes.

Line 47: DATA2 EQU * uses the assembler's ability to assign the value of the current memory location to a label. This gives a label that is used in the expression in *line 24* to calculate how many bytes are in the data buffer.

Explanation of Example 6–12

This program shows how to use and allocate both constant and variable data areas.

Lines 23–25: The memory map equates in this example include the locations for ROM and RAM memory.

Line 31: The counter in this example is initialized with a constant whose value has been defined in the equate on *line 21*.

Line 33–36: These lines show how to put the data on the stack and to initialize the D register before using the D-Bug12 printf routine.

Line 82: Constant data, like the string defined on this line, can be located in the ROM with the program code. The DB directive converts the characters in the string to ASCII code for each character in successive memory locations starting at PROMPT.

Line 84: The location of RAM for variable data is specified by this ORG statement.

Line 85: Enough storage for the program data is allocated by the reserve memory byte (DS) directive. An assembler expression is used.

Explanation of Example 6–13

This example program shows how structured assembly language programs can be written. This program has WHILE-DO, DO-WHILE, and IF-THEN-ELSE structures. It has a subroutine and both constant and variable data. We have pointed out similar features in the previous two examples, and here are some things to look for in this example.

EXAMPLE 6–12

```
m6812ex3.asm              Assembled with CASM 06/26/1998 02:32  PAGE 1
                    1 ; MC68HC12 Example
                    2 ;
                    3 ; This program prints a prompt, inputs three
                    4 ; characters, subtracts one from each and
                    5 ; displays the result on the screen.
                    6 ; It assumes an EVB with a D-Bug12 Monitor for
                    7 ; terminal I/O.
                    8 ; Source File: M6812EX3.ASM
                    9 ; Created: 5/11/97
                   10 ; Author: F. M. Cady
                   11 ; Modifications: None
                   12 ;
                   13 ; Monitor Equates
0000               14 putchar:  EQU     $FE04     ; Print a character
0000               15 getchar:  EQU     $FE02     ; Input a character
0000               16 printf:   EQU     $FE06     ; Output string term by NULL
                   17 ; Constant Equates
0000               18 NULL:     EQU     $0        ; End of string char
0000               19 CR:       EQU     !13       ; ASCII for carriage-return
0000               20 LF:       EQU     $0A       ; ASCII for line-feed
0000               21 NUMCHR:   EQU     3         ; Number of chars to I/O
                   22 ; Memory Map Equates
0000               23 PROG:     EQU     $4000     ; Pseudo ROM location
0000               24 DATA:     EQU     $6000     ; RAM data area
0000               25 STACK:    EQU     $8000     ; Stack location
                   26
4000               27           ORG     PROG      ; Locate program code
                   28 ; BEGIN Initialization
4000 CF8000        29           lds     #STACK    ; Initialize stack pointer
                   30 ; Initialize a counter
4003 CD0003        31           ldy     #NUMCHR   ; Use Y reg as a counter
                   32 ; Output a prompt for the user
4006 35            33           pshy              ; Save Y
4007 CC0003        34           ldd     #NUMCHR
400A 3B            35           pshd              ; The data for printf
400B CC4049        36           ldd     #PROMPT
400E 15FBBDF4      37           jsr     [printf,PCR]
4012 3A            38           puld              ; Clean up the stack
4013 31            39           puly
4014 CE6000        40           ldx     #data1    ; X points to the RAM
                   41 ; END Initialization
                   42 ; DO
                   43 ; Get a char from the terminal
4017 34            44 loop:     pshx              ; Save registers
4018 35            45           pshy
4019 15FBBDE5      46           jsr     [getchar,PCR]
401D 15FBBDE3      47           jsr     [putchar,PCR]    ; Echo the character
4021 31            48           puly
4022 30            49           pulx
```

EXAMPLE 6–12 Continued

```
4023 53        50              decb              ; Subtract one from it
4024 6B30      51              stab    1,X+      ; Store it in the data buff
               52                                ; Increment the pointer
               53  ; END_DO
               54  ; WHILE the counter is not zero
4026 0436EE    55              dbne    y,loop    ; Decrement the counter
               56                                ; Do it NUMCHR times
               57  ; END_WHILE
               58  ; BEGIN to fill in the string
               59  ; Now the input cycle is over, fill the rest
               60  ; of the output string with return, line-feed,
               61  ; and the NULL character.
4029 860D      62              ldaa    #CR
402B 6A30      63              staa    1,x+
402D 860A      64              ldaa    #LF
402F 6A30      65              staa    1,x+
4031 8600      66              ldaa    #NULL
4033 6A00      67              staa    0,x
               68  ; END filling in the string
               69  ; BEGIN output cycle
               70  ; Start the output cycle with CRLF
4035 C60D      71              ldab    #CR
4037 15FBBDC9  72              jsr     [putchar,PCR]
403B C60A      73              ldab    #LF
403D 15FBBDC3  74              jsr     [putchar,PCR]
               75  ; Now use the printf monitor routine for
               76  ; the message
4041 CC6000    77              ldd     #data1    ; Adr of the data -> D
4044 15FBBDBE  78              jsr     [printf,PCR]
               79  ; END the output cycle
4048 3F        80              swi       ; Return to the monitor
               81  ; Initialize constant string
4049 496E7075  82  PROMPT:     DB        "Input %d characters -> ",NULL
     74202564
     20636861
     72616374
     65727320
     2D3E2000
               83  ; Set up a data buffer plus CR, LF and NULL in RAM
6000           84              ORG     DATA
6000           85  data1:      DS      NUMCHR+3
```

The code in *lines 30–34* is a sequence block that initializes the stack pointer and variables. *Lines 34–85* are a WHILE-DO. Within this block, at *line 55*, is a jump to subroutine. The flow of the program is from this line, to *line 99*, through the subroutine to *line 124* where the return from subroutine instruction, RTS, transfers us back to *line 58*. Notice that the subroutine code simply follows after the main program. There is no need to locate the subroutine at any particular place in memory or to use an equate for the jsr hex_to_bin, as is done for the D-Bug12 subroutines.

EXAMPLE 6–13

ascchk12.asm   Assembled with CASM 12/08/1998 21:07 PAGE 1

```
                 1  ;    MC68HC12 Example
                 2  ;
                 3  ;    This program prompts for and accepts 2 ASCII hex
                 4  ;    digits. It then converts the hex digits to an 8-bit
                 5  ;    ASCII character and prints the character
                 6  ;    if it is printable, otherwise
                 7  ;    it prints "*" on the PC.  It continues
                 8  ;    until the user enters "00".
                 9  ;    Source File: ASCCHK12.ASM
                10  ;    Author: F. M. Cady
                11  ;    Created: 5/17/97
                12  ;    Modifications: None
                13  ;
                14  ;    Monitor Equates
0000            15  printf:   EQU    $FE06 ; Output string
0000            16  getchar:  EQU    $FE02 ; Get char from term
0000            17  putchar:  EQU    $FE04 ; Output char
                18  ;    Constant equates
0000            19  ALLBITS:  EQU    %11111111
0000            20  NULL:     EQU    $0    ; End of string
0000            21  NUMDIGS:  EQU    2     ; Number of hex digits
0000            22  CR:       EQU    $0d   ; Carriage-return
0000            23  LF:       EQU    $0a   ; Line-feed
                24  ;    Memory map equates
0000            25  PROG:     EQU    $4000
0000            26  DATA:     EQU    $6000
0000            27  STACK:    EQU    $8000
                28
4000            29            ORG    PROG
                30  ; BEGIN Initialize the machine state and input ASC_Char
4000 CF8000     31            lds    #STACK ;       Init stack pointer
                32  ;    Initialize ASC_Char to nonzero
4003 1C6002FF   33            bset   ASC_Char,ALLBITS
                34  ; END initialization
                35  ; WHILE ASC_Char != 0
                36  while_do_1:
4007 F76002     37            tst    ASC_Char          ; Check ASC_Char=0
400A 274E       38            beq    end_do_while_1    ; if=0, branch
                39  ; DO Print the prompt, get characters,
                40  ;    convert to ASCII, and print if
                41  ;    possible.
400C CC4079     42            ldd    #PROMPT
400F 15FBBDF3   43            jsr    [printf,PCR]
                44  ;    Get 2 ASCII Hex characters
4013 15FBBDEB   45            jsr    [getchar,PCR]
4017 15FBBDE9   46            jsr    [putchar,PCR]     ; Echo the char
```

EXAMPLE 6–13   Continued

```
401B  CD6000   47              ldy     #hex_dig          ;  Point to data area
401E  6B40     48              stab    0,y               ;  Put it in hex_dig
4020  35       49              pshy
4021  15FBBDDD 50              jsr     [getchar,PCR]     ;  Process second char
4025  15FBBDDB 51              jsr     [putchar,PCR]
4029  31       52              puly
402A  6B41     53              stab    1,y               ;  Put 2nd in hex_dig+1
               54  ;    Convert these bytes to one binary byte
               55  ;            jsr    hex_to_bin
               56  ;    The result returns in the A register
               57  ;    Save the result in ASC_Char
402C  7A6002   58              staa    ASC_Char
               59  ;    IF the result is printable
               60  ;            (it must be >$1f and <$7F)
402F  8120     61              cmpa    #' '              ;  Check for space
4031  2513     62              blo     not_printable
4033  817E     63              cmpa    #'~'              ;  Check for ~
4035  220F     64              bhi     not_printable
               65  ;    THEN print = and the char
4037  C63D     66              ldab    #'='
4039  15FBBDC7 67              jsr     [putchar,PCR]
403D  F66002   68              ldab    ASC_Char          ;  Get the ASC_Char back
4040  15FBBDC0 69              jsr     [putchar,PCR]     ;  Print the ASC_Char
4044  2006     70              bra     end_if_1
               71  ;    ELSE print a *
               72  not_printable:
4046  C62A     73              ldab    #"*"
4048  15FBBDB8 74              jsr     [putchar,PCR]
               75  end_if_1:
               76  ; Print CR, LF
404C  C60D     77              ldab    #CR
404E  15FBBDB2 78              jsr     [putchar,PCR]     ;  Print CR
4052  C60A     79              ldab    #LF
4054  15FBBDAC 80              jsr     [putchar,PCR]     ;  Print LF
               81  ;    ENDIF result printable
               82  ;    ENDO the main body
4058  20AD     83              bra     while_do_1        ;  Go back to top
               84  end_do_while_1:
               85  ; END_WHILE Input ASC_Char !=0
               86  ; Now done
405A  3F       87              swi
               88
               89  ; Subroutine to convert two ASCII hex bytes to
               90  ; one byte.
               91  ; Entry:   Y pointing to most significant byte
               92  ; Exit:    A = binary equivalent
```

EXAMPLE 6–13   Continued

```
                    93  ; Regs Mod: CCR, A
                    94  ; Data Mod: Two bytes pointed to by Y
                    95  ; Algorithm: Assumes (does not check) a valid
                    96  ;            hex digit. Subtracts $30. If
                    97  ;            result > 9, subtracts 7
                    98  hex_to_bin:
405B 35             99              pshy        ; Save registers
405C 37            100              pshb
405D C602         101              ldab    #NUMDIGS
                  102  ; DO convert digits from ASCII hex to binary
                  103  do_while_1:
405F A640         104              ldaa    0,y   ; Get most sig digit
4061 8030         105              suba    #'0'  ; Take away $30
4063 8109         106              cmpa    #9
4065 2302         107              bls     digit_ok
4067 8007         108              suba    #7
                  109  digit_ok:
4069 6A70         110              staa    1,y+  ; Store and point to next
                  111  ;  WHILE haven't done 2 bytes
406B 0431F1       112              dbne    b,do_while_1
                  113  ;  END_DO_WHILE
                  114  ;  DO get nibbles from memory and put into A
406E A65E         115              ldaa    −2,y
4070 48           116              lsla          ; Shift to ms nibble
4071 48           117              lsla
4072 48           118              lsla
4073 48           119              lsla
4074 AA5F         120              oraa    −1,y  ; OR in ls nibble
                  121  ;  ENDO getting nibbles into ACCA
4076 33           122              pulb          ; Restore registers
4077 31           123              puly
4078 3D           124              rts
                  125
                  126  ;  Constant data in ROM
4079 496E7075     127  PROMPT:     DB      "Input two hex digits -> ",NULL
     74207477
     6F206865
     78206469
     67697473
     202D3E20
     00
                  128
                  129  ;  Data storage area in RAM
6000              130              ORG     DATA
6000              131  hex_dig:    DS      NUMDIGS
6002              132  ASC_Char:   DS      {NUMDIGS/2}
```

6.4 Conclusion and Chapter Summary Points

Learning to write an effective and well-organized assembly language programs takes time. The essential elements are (1) it does what it is supposed to do, (2) it is written so it can be understood by another assembly language programmer, and (3) it makes use of assembler directives and the ability of the assembler to evaluate expressions.

- An effective assembly language programming style can consist of the following sections:
    A program header with a short description of the program.
    Assembler equates defining the system information, constants, and the memory map.
    An ORG directive to locate the code in ROM.
    A section of code to initialize the stack pointer and other variable data.
    The main body of the program consisting mainly of subroutine calls.
    The program subroutines.
    Definitions for constants used in the program.
    An ORG directive to locate the variable data in RAM.
    DS directives to allocate memory for variables.

- Although indentation is used for high-level languages to show structure in the design, it is not used very often in assembly language programming.

- Using upper- and lower-case letters can make your program more readable.

- Avoid magic numbers in your code by using the EQU directive to define constants.

- Frequently used definitions and text can be kept in include files.

- Include files can be imported into your source code file to reduce the amount of typing needed.

- An effective commenting style makes use of pseudocode design comments.

- Structured assembly language programming should be used to convert your pseudocode design to a program.

6.5 Bibliography and Further Reading

Cady, F. M., *Microcontrollers and Microcomputers*, Oxford University Press, New York, 1997.

68HC12 CPU12 Reference Manual, Motorola, 1996.

MC68HC12A4EVB Evaluation Board User's Manual, Motorola, 1996.

Transporting M68HC11 Code to M68HC12 Devices, AN1284/D, Motorola, 1996.

Using and Extending D-Debug12 Routines, AN1280/D, Motorola, Inc., 1996.

6.6 Problems

6.1   For each of the logic statements, give the appropriate M68HC12 code to set the condition code register and to branch to the ELSE part of an IF-THEN-ELSE. Assume P and Q are 8-bit, unsigned numbers in memory locations P and Q.
        a.   IF $P \geq Q$

      b. IF Q > P

      c. IF P = Q

6.2   For each of the logic statements, give the appropriate M68HC12 code to set the condition code register and to branch to the ELSE part of an IF-THEN-ELSE. Assume P and Q are 8-bit, signed numbers in memory locations P and Q.

      a. IF P ≥ Q

      b. IF Q > P

      c. IF P = Q

6.3   For each of the logic statements, give the appropriate M68HC12 code to set the condition code register and to branch to the ELSE part of an IF-THEN-ELSE. Assume P, Q, and R are 8-bit, signed numbers in memory locations P, Q, and R.

      a. IF P + Q ≥ 1

      b. IF Q > P − R

      c. IF (P > R) OR (Q < R)

      d. IF (P > R) AND (Q < R)

6.4   Write M68HC12 assembly language code for the following pseudocode design assuming K1, K2, and K3 are 8-bit, signed or unsigned, numbers in memory locations K1, K2, and K3. Assume memory has been allocated for these data.

```
WHILE K1 does not equal $0d
      DO
            IF K2 = K3
            THEN
                  K1 = K1 + 1
                  K2 = K2 − 1
            ELSE
                  K1 = K1 − 1
            ENDIF K2 = K3
      ENDO
ENDWHILE
```

6.5   Write a section of M68HC12 code to implement the design given below in which K1 and K2 are unsigned 8-bit numbers in memory locations K1 and K2.

```
IF K1 < K2
      THEN K2 = K1
      ELSE K1 = 64
ENDIF K1 < K2
```

6.6   Write a section of M68HC12 code to implement the design below in which K1, K2, and K3 are signed 8-bit integer numbers stored at memory locations K1, K2, and K3.

```
WHILE K1 < K2
      DO
            IF K3 > K2
                  THEN K2 = K1
                  ELSE K2 = K3
            ENDIF K3 > K2
            K1 = K1 + 1
      ENDO
ENDWHILE K1 < K2
```

6.7   For Problem 6.6, assume K1=1, K2=3, and K3=−2. How many times should the code pass through the loop and what final values do you expect for K1, K2, and K3?

6.8   Write structured M68HC12 code for the following design:

```
IF  A1 = B1
    THEN
          WHILE  C1 < D1
              DO
                    Decrement  D1
                    A1 = 2  *  A1
              ENDO
          ENDWHILE  C1 < D1
    ELSE
          A1 = 2  *  B1
ENDIF  A1 = B1
```

Assume that A1, B1, C1, and D1 are 16-bit, unsigned binary numbers and that memory has been allocated in the program by the following code:

```
A1:    DS    2
B1:    DS    2
C1:    DS    2
D1:    DS    2
```

Assume A1, B1, C1, and D1 are initialized to some value in some other part of the program.

6.9   For Problem 6.8, assume A1 = 2, B1 = 2, C1 = 3, and D1 = 6. What final values do you expect after the code has been executed?

6.10   For the program in Example 6–11, how does the assembler evaluate the expression DATA2 − DATA1. What is its value. Why use an expression here instead of just putting in a defined (equated) constant value?

6.11   For the program in Example 6–11, what is printed on the screen when the program is executed?

6.12   Why are JSR instructions used to branch to the D-Bug12 Monitor subroutines rather than BSR instructions?

6.13   For the program in Example 6–12, how many bytes are reserved for "data" in the RAM.

6.14   How does the D-Bug12 Monitor know when to stop printing characters in the printf() routines?

6.15   Write a routine using the putchar() monitor subroutine to output characters to the terminal. Assume the register X points to the start of the string to be output and the string is terminated by the ASCII EOT character.

6.16   Write a routine that outputs the character in A. The routine is to check for unprintable ASCII characters (codes $00–$1F, $7F–$FF). If one of these characters occurs, print the "#" character.

6.17   A 16-bit number is in sequential memory positions DATA1 and DATA1+1 with the most significant byte in DATA1. Write an M68HC12 code segment to store the negative of this 16-bit number in DATA2 and DATA2+1.

Chapter *7*

M68HC12 Parallel I/O

OBJECTIVES

This chapter describes the parallel I/O capabilities of the M68HC12. You will find that almost all I/O features must be programmed or initialized before use by setting and resetting bits in control registers. Examples show how this is done.

7.1 Introduction

An input interface, when connected to a computer bus, consists of a three-state driver to allow multiple sources to exist on the bus, and three-state control signals derived from address and timing information. An output interface is a latch whose clock signal is derived from similar address and timing information.[1] These general principles can be used when the M68HC12 is operating in *expanded mode*. There is also a *single-chip mode* in which all I/O interfaces are contained within the chip itself. External interfaces do not have to be designed when the M68HC12 is operating in single-chip mode.

7.2 MC68HC812A4 and MC68HC912B32

The two versions of the M68HC12 differ in their I/O capability. Table 7–1 summarizes these differences; we will discuss them in more detail in the following sections in this chapter.

7.3 Operating Modes

The M68HC12 offers four more operating modes than the M68HC11. Each mode is selected by the BKGD, MODA, and MODB pins when the external $\overline{\text{RESET}}$ is applied. Table 7–2 shows there are eight modes. The three of interest to us now are the *Normal Single-Chip* mode and the *Normal*

---

[1] Chapter 7 in *Microcontrollers and Microcomputers: Principles of Software and Hardware Engineering* discusses I/O concepts including addressing, I/O synchronization and timing, and computer buses. It also describes programmable I/O devices with features similar to the I/O capabilities of the M68HC12.

163

TABLE 7-1 M68HC12 Parallel I/O Comparison

Port	MC68HC812A4	MC68HC912B32
A	General-purpose I/O; multiplexed address/data buses	General-purpose I/O; multiplexed address/data buses
B	General-purpose I/O; multiplexed address/data buses	General-purpose I/O with key wakeup; multiplexed address/data buses
C	General-purpose I/O; multiplexed address/data buses	None
D	General-purpose I/O with key wakeup; multiplexed address/data buses	None
DLC	None	General-purpose I/O and byte data link communications (BDLC)
E	General-purpose I/O and bus control signals	General-purpose I/O and bus control signals
F	General-purpose I/O and chip selects	None
G	General-purpose I/O and memory expansion addresses	None
H	General-purpose I/O and key wakeup	None
J	General-purpose I/O and key wakeup	None
P	None	General-purpose I/O and pulse-width modulator output
S	General-purpose I/O and serial communications	General-purpose I/O and serial communications
T	General-purpose I/O and timer system signals	General-purpose I/O and timer system signals
AD	General-purpose input and analog-to-digital converter	General-purpose input and analog-to-digital converter

Expanded-Narrow and *Normal Expanded-Wide* modes. The *Special* modes shown in Table 7–2 allow greater access to protected control registers and bits for special testing.

Normal Single-Chip Mode

In *single-chip mode*, all I/O and memory are contained within the microcontroller.

In the single-chip mode, the microcontroller is totally self-contained, except for an external clock source (an internal one is also available) and a reset circuit. A basic single-chip system is shown in Figure 7–1.

TABLE 7-2 Comparison of M68HC12 and M68HC11 Operating Modes

M68HC12 Mode	B K G D	M O D B	M O D A	M68HC11 Mode	M O D B	M O D A
Special Single-Chip (BDM active)	0	0	0	Special Bootstrap	0	0
Special Expanded-Narrow	0	0	1			
Special Peripheral	0	1	0			
Special Expanded-Wide	0	1	1	Special Test	0	1
Normal Single-Chip	1	0	0	Normal Single-Chip	1	0
Normal Expanded-Narrow	1	0	1			
Reserved	1	1	0			
Normal Expanded-Wide	1	1	1	Normal Expanded	1	1

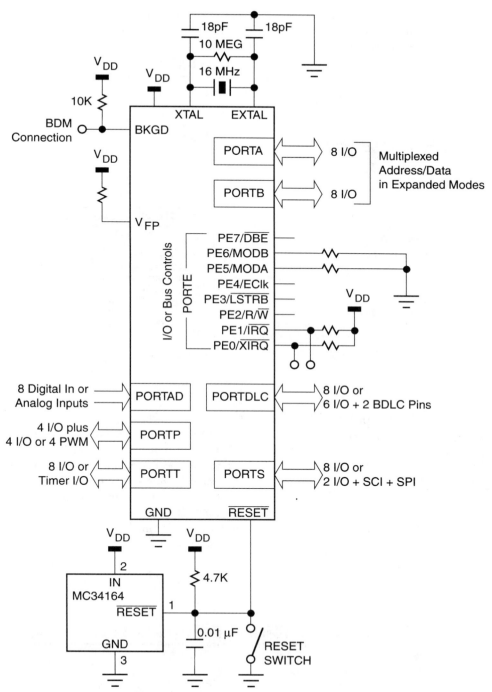

Figure 7–1 MC68HC912B32 single-chip mode.

The single-chip mode, with only a few parts, is ideally suited for many systems. All input/output and memory reside on the microcontroller chip, and only specialized I/O circuitry needed for the particular application must be designed.

The MC68HC912B32 is most suited for single-chip systems. As we will see in Chapter 9, it contains 32 Kbytes of EEPROM, enough program memory space for many applications. It also has 1 Kbyte of RAM for variable data storage.

Normal Expanded Mode

Comparison of M68HC12 and M68HC11 Normal Expanded Modes	
M68HC12	**M68HC11**
Expanded-Narrow Ports A and B provide a nonmultiplexed, 16-bit address bus; Port C is a bidirectional, multiplexed, 8-bit data bus	**Expanded** Port B is the high byte of the 16-bit multiplexed address bus; Port C provides the low byte of the address bus multiplexed with the 8-bit data bus
Expanded-Wide Ports A and B provide a nonmultiplexed, 16-bit address bus; Ports C and D are a bidirectional, nonmultiplexed, 16-bit data bus	

In *expanded mode*, the MC68HC812A4 gives up the normal use of I/O Ports A, B, C (and D in expanded-wide mode) to create address and data buses. Parts of Port E are used for bus control signals. All other I/O features remain in the microcontroller.

An MC68HC912B32 operating in single-chip mode may not have enough resources in some applications. This is particularly true when more memory, especially RAM, is needed. The MC68HC812A4 is well suited for expanded mode operation. The expanded mode provides address, data, and control buses at the expense of Ports A, B, C, and D (for expanded-wide mode), and some pins in Port E. Ports A and B give a full 16-bit expansion address bus. In *expanded-narrow* mode, Port C is a bidirectional 8-bit data bus. Port D is used in *expanded-wide* mode for the high byte of a 16-bit, nonmultiplexed data bus. In the expanded modes, Port E, bit 2 provides the R/$\overline{\text{W}}$ control signal. A basic expanded-mode system is shown in Figure 7–2.

Comparison of M68HC12 and M68HC11 Expanded Mode Control Bits	
M68HC12	**M68HC11**
Port E gives R/$\overline{\text{W}}$ the E-clock and a low-byte strobe signal $\overline{\text{LSTRB}}$	STRB functions as R/$\overline{\text{W}}$ with STRA acting as an address strobe AS; the E-clock is available

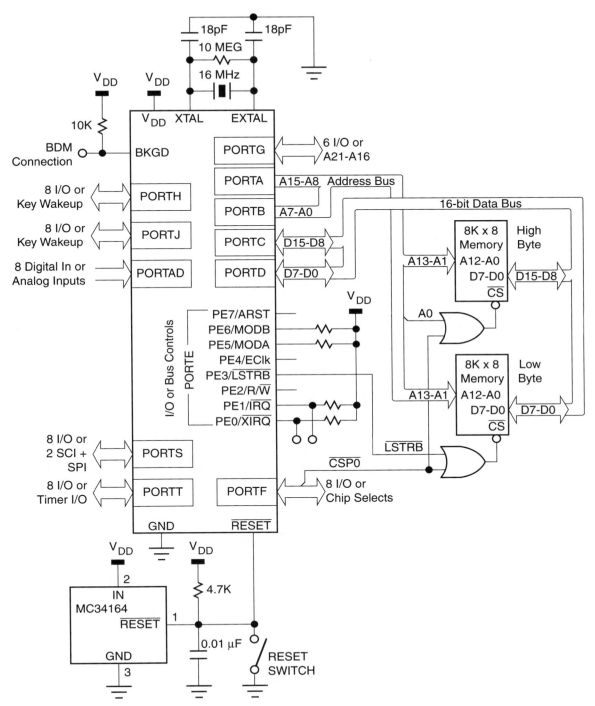

Figure 7-2 MC68HC812A4 expanded mode.

Mode Register

A *Mode* register controls the operating modes and various configuration options.

MODE—$000B—Mode Register

	Bit 7	6	5	4	3	2	1	0
Reset	SMODN	MODB	MODA	ESTR	IVIS	0	EMD	EME
Single-Chip	1	0	0	1	0	0	0	0
Exp-Nar	1	0	1	1	0	0	0	0
Exp-Wide	1	1	1	1	0	0	0	0

SMODN, MODB, MODA

Mode Select Special, B and A.
These bits show the current operating mode by reflecting the status of BKGD, MODB, and MODA input pins captured at reset. See Table 7–2.

ESTR

E-Clock Stretch Enable.
   0 = E never stretches (always free running).
   1 = E stretches high during external access cycles, and low during nonvisible accesses (default).
The bit determines if the E-clock behaves as a simple free-running clock or as a bus control signal that is active only for external bus cycles. See Chapter 9.

IVIS

Internal Visibility.
   0 = no visibility of internal bus operations on external bus (default).
   1 = internal bus operations are visible on the external bus.
This bit allows internal address, data, R/$\overline{\text{W}}$ and $\overline{\text{LSTRB}}$ signals to be seen externally during internal operations. This feature is used to allow hardware debuggers to monitor internal operations.

EME, EMD

Emulate Port D and E bits. See Chapter 15.

7.4 The Programmer's I/O Model

512 registers contain bits to control all aspects of the M68HC12 I/O.

The M68HC12 has a particularly rich, fully integrated, suite of I/O capabilities, including parallel and serial I/O, analog input, and timer functions. Many of the I/O pins have shared or dual-purpose functions. All I/O, and control of I/O, is done using a set of 512 *control registers*, which are initially located at memory locations $0000–$01FF.[2]

In the following sections we will describe the parallel I/O features of the M68HC12. Except for very few cases, most of the I/O ports require initialization before use. This is done by programming bits in the control registers.

7.5 M68HC12 Parallel I/O Ports

Ports A and B

Ports A and B may be used for I/O in single-chip mode but are used for the external address and data buses in expanded modes.

These ports are available as general purpose I/O ports only in single-chip mode. When in this mode, a data direction register for each, *DDRA* and *DDRB* control the direction, input or output, of each bit in each register. When reading from or writing to these registers any of the M68HC12 memory addressing modes may be used. Example 7–1 illustrates the various addressing modes.

When the M68HC12 is in expanded mode, Ports A and B are used for the external address and data buses as shown in Table 7–3.

PORTA—$0000—Port A Data

Bit 7	6	5	4	3	2	1	Bit 0
PA7	PA6	PA5	PA4	PA3	PA2	PA1	PA0

PORTB—$0001—Port B Data

Bit 7	6	5	4	3	2	1	Bit 0
PB7	PB6	PB5	PB4	PB3	PB2	PB1	PB0

Port C

Port C is available only in the MC68HC812A4. It provides an 8-bit general-purpose I/O port in single-chip mode and the data bus in expanded modes as shown in Table 7–4.

---

[2] The location of these registers may be changed by writing to the INITRG register. See Chapter 9.

EXAMPLE 7–1   Indexed Addressing Used to Access Port B in Single-Chip Mode

```
portb12c.asm          Assembled with CASM 12/08/1998  21:32  PAGE 1

0000 A6E30000    1  REGS:    EQU    $0000   ; Register Base address
0000             2  PORTB:   EQU    $01     ; Offset to PORTB
                 3  ;            - - -
0000 CE0000      4           ldx    #REGS   ; Initialize X register
                 5  ;            - - -
                 6  ; Read Port B
0003 9601        7           ldaa   PORTB   ; Direct Addressing
0005 A601        8           ldaa   PORTB,x ; Indexed
0007 FE000E      9           ldx    VECTOR
000A A6E30000   10           ldaa   [0,x]   ; Indexed-Indirect
                11  ;
000E 0001       12  VECTOR:  DW     PORTB   ; Address of PORTB
```

PORTC—$0004—Port C Data

	Bit 7	6	5	4	3	2	1	Bit 0
Reset	PC7	PC6	PC5	PC4	PC3	PC2	PC1	PC0
Single-Chip	0	0	0	0	0	0	0	0
Exp-Wide	DB15	DB14	DB13	DB12	DB11	DB10	DB9	DB8
Exp-Nar	DB15/7	DB14/6	DB13/5	DB12/4	DB1/3	DB10/2	DB9/1	DB8/0

TABLE 7–3   Port A and Port B Expansion Mode Use

Port	Mode	MC68HC812A4	MC68HC912B32
A	Expanded-narrow	ADDR[15:8]	Multiplexed ADDR[15:8]/DATA[7:0]
	Expanded-wide	ADDR[15:8]	Multiplexed ADDR[15:8]/DATA[15:8]
B	Expanded-narrow	ADDR[7:0]	ADDR[7:0]
	Expanded-wide	ADDR[7:0]	Multiplexed ADDR[7:0]/DATA[7:0]

TABLE 7–4   Port C Expansion Mode Use

Port	Mode	MC68HC812A4	MC68HC912B32
C	Expanded-narrow	Multiplexed DATA[15:8]/DATA[7:0]	Port C not available
	Expanded-wide	DATA[15:8]	

Port D

Comparison of M68HC12 and M68HC11 Port D		
MC68HC812A4	**MC68HC912B32**	**M68HC11**
8-bit general-purpose I/O with *key wakeup* inputs or data bus in expanded-wide mode	Not available	6-bit general-purpose I/O or used for the serial communications or serial peripheral interfaces SCI or SPI

Port D is available only in the MC68HC812A4 where it is used for the low byte of the 16-bit data bus in expanded-wide mode and is available for general purpose I/O in the other modes (Table 7–5). A feature of Port D (and Ports H and J) is that any of the pins can be used as *key wakeup* inputs. When the key wakeup feature is enabled, by setting bits in a control register called *Key Wakeup Port D Interrupt Enable Register (KWIED)*, an interrupt can be generated on falling signal edge. We will discuss these features in more detail in Chapter 8.

PORTD—$0005—Port D Data

	Bit 7	6	5	4	3	2	1	Bit 0
Reset	PD7	PD6	PD5	PD4	PD3	PD2	PD1	PD0
Single-Chip Exp-Nar	0	0	0	0	0	0	0	0
Exp-Wide	DB7	DB6	DB5	DB4	DB3	DB2	DB1	DB0
Alt. Pin	KWD7	KWD6	KWD5	KWD4	KWD3	KWD2	KWD1	KWD0

TABLE 7–5 Port D Expansion Mode Use			
Port	**Mode**	**MC68HC812A4**	**MC68HC912B32**
D	Expanded-narrow Expanded-wide	I/O DATA[7:0]	Port D not available

Port E

Comparison of M68HC12 and M68HC11 Port E	
M68HC12	**M68HC11**
6-bit general-purpose I/O plus $\overline{IRQ}$ and $\overline{XIRQ}$ in single-chip mode; control signals in expanded modes	8-bit general-purpose digital input or 8 analog inputs to A/D converter

Port E is the first of the M68HC12 registers in which the bits have a variety of functions in any of the expanded modes. In single-chip mode, bits 2–7 are I/O and controlled by the data direction register DDRE. Bits 0 and 1 are associated with interrupt inputs and when used for general purpose I/O are input only. The *Port E Assignment Register (PEAR)* is used to enable control signals when in expanded modes.

PORTE—$0008—Port E Register

	Bit 7	6	5	4	3	2	1	Bit 0
Reset	PE7	PE6	PE5	PE4	PE3	PE2	PE1	PE0
Single-Chip	0	0	0	0	0	0	0	0
Exp-Nar	0	0	0	0	0	0	0	0
Alt. Pin	ARST	IPIPE1	IPIPE0	ECLK	$\overline{LSTRB}$	R/$\overline{W}$	$\overline{IRQ}$	$\overline{XIRQ}$

or

$\overline{DBE}$

ARST

(MC68HC812A4) Auxiliary Reset Input.
　　When PEAR[ARSIE] = 1, ARST is an active-high reset.

$\overline{DBE}$

(MC68HC912B32)—Data Bus Enable.
　　When PEAR[NDBE] = 0, $\overline{DBE}$ is used for external data bus control on memories.

PIPE1:PIPE0

Pipe Status Signals.
　　When PEAR[PIPOE] = 1, these bits are output and indicate the status of the instruction queue.

ECLK

E-clock.
　　When PEAR[NECLK] = 0, PE4 is the external E-clock pin.

LSTRB

Least Significant Byte Strobe.
When PEAR[LSTRE] = 1, $\overline{\text{LSTRB}}$ is used during external data writes.

RW

Read/Write.
When PEAR[RDWE] = 1, PE2 is configured as the R/$\overline{\text{W}}$ used in expanded modes.

IRQ

Interrupt Request.

XIRQ

Nonmaskable Interrupt Request.

PEAR—$000A—Port E Assignment Register

	Bit 7	6	5	4	3	2	1	0
Reset	ARSIE NDBE	CDLTE	PIPOE	NECLK	LSTRE	RDWE	0	0
Single-Chip	0	0	0	1	0	0	0	0
Expanded	0	0	0	0	0	0	0	0

ARSIE

(MC68HC812A4) Auxiliary Reset Input Enable.
0 = PE7 is general-purpose I/O (default).
1 = PE7 is an active-high reset input.

NDBE

(MC68HC912B32) No Data Bus Enable.
0 = PE7 is used for external control of data enables on memories (default).
1 = PE7 is used for general-purpose I/O.

CDLTE

CDL Testing Enable.
Not used in normal single-chip or expanded modes; used only for factory testing.

PIPOE

Pipe Status Signal Output Enable.
    0 = PE[6:5] are general-purpose I/O (default).
    1 = PE[6:5] are used to indicate the state of the instruction pipeline queue (in expanded
        mode only).

NECLK

No External E-clock.
    0 = PE4 is the internal E-clock. In single-chip modes, to see the E-clock, NECLK must be
        zero and either IVIS = 1 or ESTR = 0. These latter bits are in the MODE register.
    1 = PE4 is general-purpose I/O.

LSTRE

Low Strobe $\overline{\text{LSTRB}}$) Enable.
    0 = PE3 is general-purpose I/O (default).
    1 = Enable the low-byte strobe output. This is used to detect bus access type in external
        modes. See Chapter 15.

RDWE

Read/Write Enable.
    0 = PE2 is general-purpose I/O (default).
    1 = PE2 is configured as the R/$\overline{\text{W}}$ pin used in expanded modes. In single-chip modes, PE2
        is always I/O.
R/$\overline{\text{W}}$ is disabled at RESET. If an expanded system uses external memory into which the processor is to write, RDWE should be set to one to enable R/$\overline{\text{W}}$.

Port F

Comparison of M68HC12 and M68HC11 Port F		
MC68HC812A4	**MC68HC912B32**	**M68HC11**
7-bit general-purpose I/O or memory expansion chip selects	Not available	No equivalent register

Port F is not available in the MC68HC912B32. There are seven bits in Port F that may be used for general-purpose I/O or for memory expansion chip select signals. *Chip Select Control Register 0 (CSCTL0)* controls which bits are used for I/O and which for chip selects. *Port F Data Direction Register (DDRF)* is used to control the direction of I/O.

PORTF—$0030—Port F Register

Bit 7	6	5	4	3	2	1	0
	PF6	PF5	PF4	PF3	PF2	PF1	PF0

Reset	0	0	0	0	0	0	0	0
Alt. Pin	0	CSP1	CSP0	CSD	CS3	CS2	CS1	CS0

CSCTL0—$003C—Chip Select Control Register 0

Bit 7	6	5	4	3	2	1	0
0	CSP1E	CSP0E	CSDE	CS3E	CS2E	CSIE	CS0E

Reset	0	0	1	0	0	0	0	0

When in any of the expanded modes, setting these bits enables the corresponding chip select bit in Port F. Expanded memory details are covered in Chapter 9.

Port G

Comparison of M68HC12 and M68HC11 Port G		
MC68HC812A4	**MC68HC912B32**	**M68HC11**
6-bit general-purpose I/O or memory expansion address bits	Not available	No equivalent register

Port G is not available in the MC68HC912B32. Port G has six bits that may be used as general-purpose I/O or for memory expansion as shown in Chapter 9. As we have seen with other registers, there is a data register, *PORTG*, a data direction register, *DDRG*, and a control register, *MXAR*, involved.

PORTG—$0031—Port G Register

Bit 7	6	5	4	3	2	1	0
		PG5	PG4	PG3	PG2	PG1	PG0

Reset   0   0   0   0   0   0   0   0

Alt. Pin   ADR21 ADR20 ADR19 ADR18 ADR17 ADR16

MXAR—$0038—Memory Expansion Assignment Register

Bit 7	6	5	4	3	2	1	Bit 0
		A21E	A20E	A19E	A18E	A17E	A16E

Reset   0   0   0   0   0   0   0   0

A21E:A16E

Select the memory expansion pins PG[5:0] [ADR21:ADR16].
   0 = Select general-purpose I/O (default).
   1 = Select memory expansion. See Chapter 9.

Port H and Port J

Comparison of M68HC12 and M68HC11 Port H and J		
MC68HC812A4	**MC68HC912B32**	**M68HC11**
8-bit general-purpose I/O ports with key wakeup inputs	Not available	No equivalent registers

Ports H and J are general purpose I/O ports, but they are not available in the MC68HC912B32. An additional feature of these (and Port D) is that any of the pins can be used as *key wakeup* inputs. When the key wakeup feature is enabled, by setting bits in a control register called *Key Wakeup Port H,J Interrupt Enable Register [KWIE(H,J)],* an interrupt can be generated on the falling signal edge for Port H and either the rising or falling edge for Port J. We will discuss these features in more detail in Chapter 8.

PORTH—$0024—Port H Data

Bit 7	6	5	4	3	2	1	Bit 0
PH7	PH6	PH5	PH4	PH3	PH2	PH1	PH0

	Bit 7	6	5	4	3	2	1	Bit 0
Reset	0	0	0	0	0	0	0	0
Alt. Pin	KWH7	KWH6	KWH5	KWH4	KWH3	KWH2	KWH1	KWH0

PORTJ—$0028—Port J Data

Bit 7	6	5	4	3	2	1	Bit 0
PJ7	PJ6	PJ5	PJ4	PJ3	PJ2	PJ1	PJ0

	Bit 7	6	5	4	3	2	1	Bit 0
Reset	0	0	0	0	0	0	0	0
Alt. Pin	KWJ7	KWJ6	KWJ5	KWJ4	KWJ3	KWJ2	KWJ1	KWJ0

Port S

Comparison of M68HC12 and M68HC11 Serial I/O	
MC68HC812A4	**M68HC11**
Port S, 8-bit general-purpose I/O or two SCI and SPI	Port D, 6-bit general-purpose I/O or one SCI and one SPI
MC68HC912B32	
Port S, 8-bit general-purpose I/O, or one SCI, one SPI, and two general-purpose I/O	

Port S has eight bidirectional bits that can be used for digital I/O or for serial communications.

Eight, bidirectional Port S pins are shared with the serial communication interfaces (*SCIs*) (two on the MC68HC812A4 and one on the MC68HC912B32) and one serial peripheral interface (*SPI*). If any of these devices are enabled, the corresponding Port S bits are used for serial I/O and may not be used for parallel I/O.

On reset, Port S is available for use as a general-purpose, 8-bit I/O register. If you wish to use any of the serial I/O features of Port S, you must enable them by setting bits in control registers. We will discuss the serial peripheral and serial communication interfaces in Chapter 11.

PORTS—$00D6—Port S Data Register

Bit 7	6	5	4	3	2	1	Bit 0
PS7	PS6	PS5	PS4	PS3	PS2	PS1	PS0

Serial Function	$\overline{SS}$ $\overline{CS}$	SCK0	MOSI MOMI	MISO SISO	TXD1	RXD1	TXD0	RXD0

Port T

Comparison of M68HC12 and M68HC11 Timer	
M68HC12	**M68HC11**
Port T, 8-bit general-purpose I/O or eight timer bits, any of which may provide the output compare or input capture functions; one bit may be used as a pulse accumulator input	Port A, 8-bit general-purpose I/O or five output compare, three input capture, and one pulse accumulator

The timer port on the M68HC12 can be configured to provide a mixture of output compare and input capture functions. We will cover each of these in Chapter 10. Any of the eight bits in Port T can be used for general-purpose I/O. Each bit's function, I/O or timer, is controlled by the *Timer Input Capture/Output Compare Select* (*TIOS*) register. Any of the bits *IOS7–IOS0* set to zero allow the corresponding Port T bit to be used for I/O. The I/O direction is controlled by the *Data Direction Register for Timer Port (DDRT)*.

PORTT—$00AE—Timer Port Data Register

Bit 7	6	5	4	3	2	1	0
PT7	PT6	PT5	PT4	PT3	PT2	PT1	PT0

Timer Pulse Acc	I/OC7 PAI	I/OC6	I/OC5	I/OC4	I/OC3	I/OC2	I/OC1	I/OC0

TIOS—$0080—Timer Input Capture/Output Compare Select

Bit 7	6	5	4	3	2	1	Bit 0
IOS7	IOS6	IOS5	IOS4	IOS3	IOS2	IOS1	IOS0

Reset	0	0	0	0	0	0	0	0

IOS[7:0]

Input Capture or Output Compare Channel Designator.
  0 = The corresponding channel acts as input capture or an I/O bit (default).
  1 = The channel acts as an output compare.
When IOS[7:0] is zero, the Port T bit can act as an I/O pin whose direction is controlled by the data direction register DDRT. See Chapter 10.

Port AD

Comparison of M68HC12 and M68HC11 A/D	
M68HC12	**M68HC11**
Port AD, 8-bit digital or analog input	Port E, 8-bit digital or analog input

Port AD may be an 8-bit input port or used for eight analog inputs to the on-board A/D converter.

Port AD is another port that has two functions. In one case, the eight bits may be used as a general purpose input port. Alternatively, Port AD is used for the eight analog inputs for the A/D converter system.

All bits in Port AD may be read for their digital values by reading memory location $006F. The A/D converter operation is covered fully in Chapter 12.

PORTAD—$006F—Port AD Data Input Register

Bit 7	6	5	4	3	2	1	Bit 0
PAD7	PAD6	PAD5	PDA4	PAD3	PAD2	PAD1	PAD0

7.6 Data Direction Registers

Comparison of M68HC12 and M68HC11 Data Direction Register	
M68HC12	**M68HC11**
Data direction registers for Ports A, B, C, D, E, F, G, H, J, S and T	Data direction control only for the bidirectional bits PA-7, Port D and Port C

All bidirectional data registers may be programmed to be either input or output. When the CPU is reset, all registers (with the exception of a few bits such as Port E, bit 3) are placed in the input mode. Setting the direction of any bit in any register is done with the *Data Direction Registers*. Each has the format shown below where x is A, B, C, D, E, F, G, H, J, S, or T; the addresses for each are given in Table 7–6. Example 7–2 shows how to initialize the most significant nibble in Port D for output. If a port has a mixture of input and output bits, writing to the port affects only those

TABLE 7-6 Data Direction Register Addresses

Data Direction Register	Address
DDRA	$02
DDRB	$03
DDRC	$06
DDRD	$07
DDRE	$09
DDRF	$32
DDRG	$33
DDRH	$25
DDRJ	$29
DDRS	$D7
DDRT	$AF

EXAMPLE 7-2   Initializing Port D for Use

```
port12dc.asm          Assembled with CASM 05/24/1998  20:29  PAGE 1

0000               1  PORTD:   EQU    5             ; PORTD address
0000               2  DDRD:    EQU    7             ; Data Direction Reg
0000               3  OBITS:   EQU    %11110000     ; Bits to be output
                   4  ;            - - -
0000 4C07F0        5           bset   DDRD,OBITS    ; Set direction register
                   6  ;            - - -
                   7  ; Output data to bits 7-4
0003 86F0          8           ldaa   #%11110000
0005 5A05          9           staa   PORTD
                  10  ; Read data on bits 3-0
0007 9605         11           ldaa   PORTD
```

bits that are outputs. Reading the port returns the values on the input bits as well as the last values output to the output bits.

DDRx—$00yy—Port x Data Direction Register

Bit 7	6	5	4	3	2	1	Bit 0
Bit 7	6	5	4	3	2	1	Bit 0

Reset   0   0   0   0   0   0   0   0

DDRX7:DDRX0

Data Direction Control Bits.
    0 = Associated pin is a high-impedance input (default).
    1 = Associated pin is an output.
Data direction register bits determine the direction of the corresponding data register.

7.7 Input and Output Pin Electronics

Comparison of M68HC12 and M68HC11 I/O Pin Electronics	
M68HC12	**M68HC11**
Pull-up control for Ports A, B, C, D, E, F, G, and H Reduced drive control for Ports B, C, D, E, F, G, H, and J	No equivalent features

Pull-up Control

It is a good electronic design practice to tie unused input pins to either a high or low logic level. In CMOS devices this reduces the chance for a potentially destructive condition called *latch-up* to occur. The M68HC12 provides a *Pull-up Control Register* (*PUCR*) to enable pull-up resistors on any of the ports that are configured as inputs. On reset, all pull-up resistors are enabled. You may disable them selectively for ports where you wish. This might be done to improve speed performance and to reduce power consumption.

PUCR—$000C—Pull-Up Control Register

	Bit 7	6	5	4	3	2	1	Bit 0
	PUPH	PUPG	PUPF	PUPE	PUPD	PUPC	PUPB	PUPA
Reset	1	1	1	1	1	1	1	1

PUPH, PUPG, PUPF
Pull-up Port H, G, F Enable.   0 = Port pull-ups are disabled.   1 = Port pull-ups are enabled (default).

PUPE
Pull-up Port E Enable.   0 = Port E pin PE3, PE2, and PE0 are disabled.   1 = Enable PE3, PE2, and PE0 pull-ups (default).

PUPD, PUPC, PUPB, PUPA

Pull-up Port D, C, B, A Enable.
  0 = Port pull-ups are disabled.
  1 = Port pull-ups are enabled (default).
These bits have no effect if the port is being used in expanded mode for a data or address bus.

Reduced Drive

Drive refers to the amount of current available at an output pin to be sourced to whatever is connected to the pin. High drive current is an advantage when the output must drive a capacitive load. High drive current results in higher speed switching between logic levels. Unfortunately, high drive current means higher power consumption and the increased likelihood of radio frequency interference (RFI). The *Reduced Drive of I/O Lines (RDRIV)* allows you to reduce the drive level to reduce power consumption and RFI emissions.

RDRIV—$000D—Reduced Drive of I/O Lines

Bit 7	6	5	4	3	2	1	Bit 0
RDPJ	RDPH	RDPG	RDPF	RDPE	RDPD	RDPC	RDPB

RESET   0   0   0   0   0   0   0   0

RDPJ, RDPH, RDPG, RDPF, RDPE, RDPD, RDPC, RDPB

Reduced Drive Enable for Ports J, H, G, F, D, C, and B.
  0 = All port pins have full drive enabled (default).
  1 = All port pins have reduced drive capability.

7.8 I/O Software

> I/O software has an *initialization* part, a data *input/output* part, and must be *synchronized* with the I/O device.

There are three major elements in I/O software. First, as shown in the examples above, is an *initialization* part to set up the function of the ports and the direction of data flow. Second, there is a *data input and output* section that simply reads from or writes to the appropriate register in the control register stack. There is a third element, namely *software synchronization*, which must be considered as well. I/O software must synchronize the reading and writing of the data with the timing requirements of the I/O device. Typically, microprocessors are much faster than the I/O devices they serve and must be synchronized using software and hardware techniques. Hardware handshaking techniques for the M68HC12 are discussed in Section 9, and there are two software I/O synchronization methods. Interrupts are used also for I/O synchronization, and we discuss those in Chapter 8.

Real-Time Synchronization

Real-time synchronization uses a software delay to match the timing requirements of the software and hardware. For example, consider outputting characters to a parallel port (say Port H) at a rate no faster than 10 characters per second. If we assume negligible time is spent in getting and outputting each character, a delay of 100 msec is required between each output operation. This could be done with a pair of subroutines; one gets and outputs the characters, and another delays 100 msec before returning.

Real-time synchronization has its problems. It is dependent upon the CPU's clock frequency and it usually has some overhead cycles that cause errors so the timing is not exact. Thus software timing loops may not be accurate enough, depending on the requirements of the application. In Chapter 10 we will see how to generate highly accurate timing delays using the M68HC12 timer system.

Polled I/O

Polled I/O software use I/O bits as status bits for external I/O devices. For example, an external device receiving data from the M68HC12 via Port H could use PJ0 as a status bit. PJ0 will be asserted by the external device when it is ready for new data and deasserted when it is not. Obviously, hardware logic is required in the external device to assert and deassert this bit. The polling software monitors the status bit and outputs data only when the external device is ready. Example 7–3 shows a program that polls Port J, bit 0 to determine when it is safe to output more data to bits 3–0 of Port H. See Figure 7–3a for the hardware used.

Polled input software (and hardware) is similar. Now, a data input port receives data from the external device and another bit, say PJ1, is asserted by the external device when it has new data ready to be input. The polling software can be doing other things while it is waiting for the external device to supply new data. Figure 7–3b shows the direction flow and hardware needed for input and output polling and Example 7–3 shows a sample of program code.

A question you might reasonably ask at this point is, "In the polled input scenario, how does the external device know when the CPU has taken its data?" The NEW_DATA_READY bit is information *from* the external device *to* the M68HC12. There is no corresponding timing information going the other direction to let the external device know that the M68HC12 has taken the current data and that it is safe to supply new data. The solution to this problem may have two forms. First, NEW_DATA_READY could activate a *key wakeup* bit in Port J and generate an interrupt to ensure the CPU takes the data in a timely fashion. We will discuss this procedure more completely in Chapter 8. Second, *handshaking I/O* can be used as discussed in the next section.

7.9 Hardware Handshaking I/O

Comparison of M68HC12 and M68HC11 Hardware Handshaking	
M68HC12	**M68HC11**
No dedicated hardware for handshaking I/O; general-purpose I/O pins and software can be used	Has several handshaking I/O modes using the STRA and STRB signals

---

EXAMPLE 7–3   Using a Status Bit for I/O Polling

```
statio12.asm          Assembled with CASM  12/08/1998  22:13  PAGE 1

0000              1  PORTJ:   EQU    $28    ; Port J address
0000              2  PORTH:   EQU    $24    ; Port H address
0000              3  DDRH:    EQU    $25    ; Data direction Port H
0000              4  BIT0:    EQU    %00000001
0000              5  BIT1:    EQU    %00000010
0000              6  O_BITS:  EQU    %00001111
                  7  ;        - - -
                  8  ; Initialization
                  9  ; Set up PORTH[3:0] to be output
0000 4C250F      10           bset   DDRH,O_BITS  ; Port H output
                 11  ;        - - -
                 12  ; Output data to Port H
                 13  ; Wait until the status bit, Port J, Bit 0 is 1
0003 4F2801FC    14  SPIN1:  brclr  PORTJ,BIT0,SPIN1
                 15  ; Now can output the data
0007 B60015      16           ldaa   data1
000A 5A24        17           staa   PORTH
                 18  ;        - - -
                 19  ; Input data from Port H
                 20  ; Wait until the status bit, Port J, Bit 1 is 1
000C 4F2802FC    21  SPIN2:  brclr  PORTJ,BIT1,SPIN2
                 22  ; Now can input the data
0010 9624        23           ldaa   PORTH
0012 7A0016      24           staa   data2
                 25  ;        - - -
0015             26  data1:   DS     1
0016             27  data2:   DS     1
```

The M68HC12 does not have dedicated hardware circuitry for handshaking I/O like the M68HC11.[3] Instead, general-purpose I/O bits plus software similar to polling are used. Figure 7–4 shows the general hardware picture for output and input handshaking. Figure 7–4a and Example 7–4 show output handshaking. The initialization code must set the data direction register for Port H and Port J-1 and -3 to enable the output direction. It then clears the NEW_DATA_READY and READY_FOR_NEW_DATA (*lines 12–15*). The M68HC12 starts the output process by polling the READY_FOR_NEW_DATA bit on Port J, bit 0 (*line 19*).

---

[3]   *Microcontrollers and Microcomputers: Principle of Software and Hardware Engineering*, Chapter 7 describes handshaking I/O. These features available in the M68HC11 are covered in Chapter 7 of *Software and Hardware Engineering: Motorola M68HC11.*

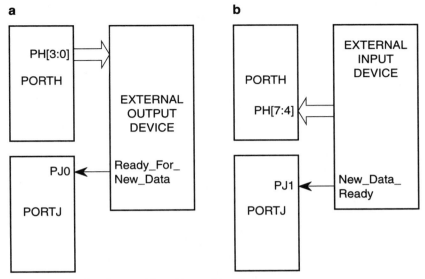

Figure 7-3   Output (a) and input (b) polling.

When it is asserted (there must be hardware in the external output device that asserts this signal), the program knows that the external device has processed the last data and is ready for new data. It then outputs the new data to Port H (*line 22*) and pulses (usually) the NEW_DATA_READY bit (*lines 24 and 25*).

Input handshaking shown in Figure 7–4b is very similar with the polling software asserting

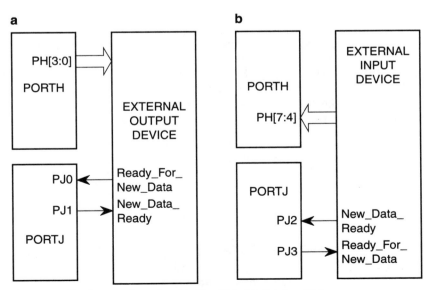

Figure 7-4   Hardware handshaking I/O. (a) Output; (b) input.

EXAMPLE 7-4   Handshaking I/O Software

hskio1c.asm   Assembled with CASM 05/24/1998 23:35 PAGE 1

```
0000                   1  PORTJ:  EQU   $28      ; Port J address
0000                   2  DDRJ:   EQU   $29      ; Data direction Port J
0000                   3  PORTH:  EQU   $24      ; Port H address
0000                   4  DDRH:   EQU   $25      ; Data direction Port H
0000                   5  BIT0:   EQU   %00000001
0000                   6  BIT1:   EQU   %00000010
0000                   7  BIT2:   EQU   %00000100
0000                   8  BIT3:   EQU   %00001000
0000                   9  O_BITS: EQU   %00001111
                      10  ;       - - -
                      11  ; Initialization
0000 4C250F           12          bset   DDRH,O_BITS      ; Port H output
0003 4C290A           13          bset   DDRJ,BIT1|BIT3   ; Port J-1,3 output
0006 4D280A           14          bclr   PORTJ,BIT1|BIT3  ; Reset NEW_DATA_READY
0009 4D2808           15          bclr   PORTJ,BIT3       ; READY_FOR_NEW_DATA
                      16  ;       - - -
                      17  ; Handshaking output data to Port H
                      18  ; Wait until the status bit, Port J, Bit-0 is 1
000C 4F2801FC         19  SPIN1:  brclr  PORTJ,BIT0,SPIN1
                      20  ; Now can output the data
0010 B6002A           21          ldaa   data1
0013 5A24             22          staa   PORTH
                      23  ; and can strobe the handshaking bit
0015 4C2802           24          bset   PORTJ,BIT1
0018 4D2802           25          bclr   PORTJ,BIT1
                      26  ;       - - -
                      27  ; Handshaking input data from Port H
                      28  ; Set READY_FOR_NEW_DATA on Port J, Bit-3
001B 4C2808           29          bset   PORTJ,BIT3
                      30  ; Wait until the status bit, Port J, Bit-2 is 1
001E 4F2804FC         31  SPIN2:  brclr  PORTJ,BIT2,SPIN2
                      32  ; Now can input the data
0022 9624             33          ldaa   PORTH
0024 7A002B           34          staa   data2
                      35  ; and reset the READY_FOR_NEW_DATA
0027 4D2808           36          bclr   PORTJ,BIT3
                      37  ;       - - -
002A                  38  data1:  DS     1
002B                  39  data2:  DS     1
```

READY_FOR_NEW_DATA (*line 29*), waiting until NEW_DATA_READY is asserted (*line 31*), reading the data (*line 33*), and then resetting the READY_FOR_NEW_DATA signal (*line 36*). A common variation on both input and output handshaking themes is that the READY_FOR_NEW_DATA and NEW_DATA_READY status bits can generate key wakeup interrupts on Port J.

7.10 Chapter Summary Points

This chapter has covered the parallel I/O capabilities of the M68HC12 microcontroller. The following points are summarized:

- The MC68HC812A4 and MC68HC912B32 versions have differing I/O capabilities.
- When ports are not being used for expanded mode or other I/O they may be used for general-purpose parallel I/O.
- Ports A, B, C, and sometimes D may not be used for I/O when in expanded modes.
- All I/O ports have programmable functions.
- Bidirectional ports have Data Direction Registers to specify the data flow direction.
- Port S shares functions with parallel I/O and the serial I/O.
- Port AD shares functions with parallel I/O and the A/D converter system.

7.11 Bibliography and Further Reading

Cady, F. M., *Microcontrollers and Microcomputers*, Oxford University Press, New York, 1997.

Cady, F. M., *Software and Hardware Engineering: Motorola M68HC11*, Oxford University Press, New York, 1997.

MC68HC812A4 Technical Summary, MC68HC812A4TS/D, Motorola, 1996.

MC68HC912B32 Technical Summary, MC68HC912B32TS/D, Motorola, 1997.

7.12 Problems

7.1 What levels must be on the BKGD, MODA, and MODB pins at $\overline{\text{RESET}}$ to place the M68HC12 into normal-expanded mode? Into normal single-chip mode?

7.2 Give the data register addresses for Ports A, B, C, H, and J.

7.3 How do you control the direction of the bidirectional bits in the M68HC12 I/O ports?

7.4 Design an output circuit with 8 LEDs connected to Port B. The LEDs are to be on when bits in a byte stored in location DATA1 are 1s. Show the hardware and software required.

7.5 Design an input circuit to input the states of eight switches to the M68HC12.

Chapter <u>8</u>

M68HC12 Interrupts

OBJECTIVES

This chapter covers the interrupt system of the M68HC12. You will learn about the vectors and the hardware prioritization that can be modified dynamically by a program. Nonmaskable interrupts are covered. Examples are given for interrupt service routines used in dedicated applications and when operating in debugging environments such as the HC12A4EVB and M68EVB912B32 evaluation boards. The discussion of the interrupts of the parallel I/O system started in Chapter 7 is continued here.

8.1 Introduction

The interrupts in the M68HC12 are vectored, although polling is used when multiple external sources are on the external IRQ line.

The M68HC12 microcontroller contains vectored interrupts with hardware priority resolution that can be customized with software. It has two, dedicated, external interrupt inputs. These are $\overline{\text{IRQ}}$, a maskable, general purpose, external interrupt request, and $\overline{\text{XIRQ}}$, a nonmaskable (after the programmer enables it) interrupt. Twelve other signals associated with the timer subsystem (a Real Time Interrupt, eight Timer Channels, a Timer Overflow, and two Pulse Accumulator signals) generate interrupts, and we will discuss these in Chapter 10. The serial interface is allocated three interrupts and the analog-to-digital converter is allocated one. The serial interface and its interrupts are covered in Chapter 11 and the A/D in Chapter 12. In addition to external interrupts $\overline{\text{IRQ}}$ and $\overline{\text{XIRQ}}$, three I/O ports with key wakeup capability, Ports D, H, and J, are important sources of interrupts when using the MC68HC812A4, and we discuss these later in this chapter. There are four other special interrupts including a software interrupt, unimplemented opcode trap, and a watchdog timer and clock failure interrupt.[1]

---

[1] Chapter 8 of *Microcontrollers and Microcomputers: Principles of Software and Hardware Engineering* describes the interrupt process and how an interrupt system must resolve which of several interrupting devices needs service. Guidelines for interrupt service routines are given there also.

8.2 M68HC12 and M68HC11 Interrupt Comparison

Interrupts in these two microcontrollers are very similar. The M68HC12 has a few more timer channel interrupts. It also has an interrupt for the analog-to-digital converter to signal when the conversion is complete; the M68HC11 does not have this useful feature. The M68HC12 does not have the Strobe A/Strobe B (STRA/STRB) signals for handshaking and interrupt I/O. Instead, in the MC68HC812A4 version of the M68HC12, there are three, 8-bit I/O ports with interrupting capabilities called *key wakeups*. These may be used for I/O interrupts. The MC68HC912B32 chips do not have the key wakeup feature.

8.3 The Interrupt Process

The Interrupt Enable

M68HC12 and M68HC11 Interrupt Enable and Disable	
M68HC12	**M68HC11**
SEI replaced by ORCC #%00010000[a]	Set interrupt mask—SEI
CLI replaced by ANDCC #%11101111	Clear interrupt mask—CLI

[a]*Many M68HC12 assemblers accept the M68HC11 instructions SEI and CLI to set and clear the interrupt mask. We will adopt that practice in our examples.*

> The condition code register contains bits to globally *mask* and *unmask* interrupts.

Two bits in the condition code register give overall control of the interrupt system. The *I* and *X* bits are *mask* bits that, when set, disable the interrupt system. The I bit is controlled by the instructions ORCC #%00010000 (SEI) to set the interrupt mask ANDCC #%11101111 (CLI) to clear it. The I bit can be thought of as a shade in a window that looks out on the interrupting world. If the blind is pulled, I=1 and interrupt requests cannot get through. An open window, I=0, lets the CPU "see" the interrupts. As we discovered in Chapter 2, the I and X bits are set when the CPU is reset so that interrupts will not be acted on until the program is ready for them.

The I bit acts *globally* and allows or disallows *all* interrupts except for a few that are *unmaskable*. We will discuss these exceptions in Section 8.6. A second level of interrupt control is available. Each interrupt source may be enabled or disabled individually by setting a bit in a control register. As we will see in more detail later, when the I/O device's enable bit is set and an interrupt is to be generated, a flag is set in the I/O device triggering the interrupt request. In most of the I/O devices in the M68HC12, this flag bit must be reset in the interrupt service routine before subsequent interrupt requests can be generated.

The Interrupt Disable

> Further interrupts are masked when the interrupt service routine is entered.

When an interrupt occurs the I bit is automatically set, masking further interrupts. Nested interrupts, which should be avoided, are allowed if the I bit is cleared in the interrupt service routine. Before doing this, you must disable the interrupting source or clear its interrupting flag so that it does not immediately generate another interrupt, resulting in an infinite loop and a locked-up program.

All interrupts are disabled when the M68HC12 is reset. Interrupts may be globally disabled in your program any time by setting the interrupt mask with the ORCC #%00010000 (SEI) instruction. Individual interrupts are disabled by clearing the enable bit associated with the device.

The Interrupt Request

The M68HC12 has both internal and external sources of interrupts. The internal requests come from the internal I/O systems and from exceptional or error conditions. Each interrupt is serviced through its own vector as described in Section 8.4. The two external interrupt request signals, $\overline{\text{IRQ}}$ and $\overline{\text{XIRQ}}$, are active-low, edge- or level-sensing. Figure 8–1 shows how to interface these signals to the M68HC12. Multiple interrupting devices may pull the request line low using wired OR, open-collector gates. The M68HC12 must poll the devices to determine which generated the interrupt because there is only one vector associated with $\overline{\text{IRQ}}$.

The Interrupt Sequence

> All registers, including the *condition code register*, are pushed onto the stack at the start of the interrupt service sequence.

When interrupts have been unmasked and enabled, and a request has been generated, the following events take place:

1. Generally, the CPU waits until the currently executing instruction finishes before servicing the interrupt. This component of interrupt latency will depend on the instruction being executed. Most instructions are two to four cycles, but the EDIVS instruction takes 12 clock cycles. Some of the longer M68HC12 instructions can be interrupted before they complete.

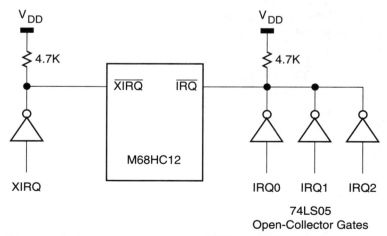

F i g u r e 8 – 1   Hardware interface for $\overline{\text{IRQ}}$ and $\overline{\text{XIRQ}}$ signals.

2. The CPU then determines the address of the interrupt service routine to be executed through a vectoring system.[2]

3. The return address is pushed onto the stack.

4. All CPU registers, including X, Y, A, B, and CCR, are pushed onto the stack.

5. After the CCR is pushed onto the stack, the I bit is set, masking further interrupts.

6. The CPU branches to the interrupt service routine.

The Interrupt Return

> If an interrupt is generated by an internal source, the *flag* causing the interrupt must be *reset* in the interrupt service routine.

> The *RTI* instruction is used at the end of the interrupt service routine.

Before returning to the interrupted program, you must *reenable the interrupting device's interrupt capability.* This is usually done by *resetting the flag* that caused the interrupt. If this is not done correctly, another interrupt will immediately occur. The RTI—return from interrupt instruction is used to return to the interrupted program.

You do not have to, and in general you should not, unmask global interrupts in the interrupt service routine.[3] The RTI pulls all registers that were pushed onto the stack at the start of the interrupt service routine, including the CCR, which had the mask bit cleared. Beginning programmers often put a redundant CLI instruction in their interrupt service routines.

8.4 Interrupt Vectors

In any interrupt driven system, the CPU must somehow branch to and start executing the correct interrupt service routine for that request. The M68HC12 uses *vectored* interrupts. Each interrupt source has its own vector in memory. This vector is simply the *address* of the interrupt service routine to be executed.

M68HC12 System Vectors

> An *interrupt vector* is the address of the start of the interrupt service routine.

There are 19 hardware interrupts that are enabled by bits locally within the particular I/O system generating the interrupt. Each of these interrupting sources has a dedicated vector location as shown in Table 8–1 for the MC68HC812A4 and Table 8–2 for the MC68HC912B32. When an interrupt request is generated, the CPU fetches the address of the interrupt service routine from the vector location. Tables 8–1 and 8–2 also show the vector locations for the nonmaskable interrupt $\overline{\text{XIRQ}}$, a software interrupt, SWI, an unimplemented opcode trap interrupt, interrupts associated with the Computer Operating Properly (COP) timer and the Clock Monitor Circuit, and the hardware $\overline{\text{RESET}}$.

---

[2] The M68HC12 chooses the interrupt source and fetches the vector at the start of the interrupt sequence. This allows it to interleave three program word fetches in the interrupt sequence to refill the instruction queue.

[3] Exception: You will have to unmask interrupts if you need to allow nested interrupts or if there is a higher priority device that may need service.

TABLE 8-1 Interrupt Vector Assignments MC68HC812A4

Vector Address	Interrupt Source	Local Enable Bit	See Register	See Chapter
$FF80:FFCD	Reserved	—		
$FFCE:FFCF	Key Wakeup H	KWIEH[7:0]	KWIEH	8
$FFD0:FFD1	Key Wakeup J	KWIEJ[7:0]	KWIEJ	8
$FFD2:FFD3	A/D Converter	ASCIE	ATDCTL	12
$FFD4:FFD5	SCI-1 Serial System	See Chapter 11		11
$FFD6:FFD7	SCI-0 Serial System	See Chapter 11		11
$FFD8:FFD9	SPI Serial Transfer Complete	SPIE	SP0CR1	11
$FFDA:FFDB	Pulse Accumulator Input Edge	PAI	PACTL	10
$FFDC:FFDD	Pulse Accumulator Overview	PAOVI	PACTL	10
$FFDE:FFDF	Timer Overflow	TOI	TMSK2	10
$FFE0:FFE1	Timer Channel 7	C7I	TMSK1	10
$FFE2:FFE3	Timer Channel 6	C6I	TMSK1	10
$FFE4:FFE5	Timer Channel 5	C5I	TMSK1	10
$FFE6:FFE7	Timer Channel 4	C4I	TMSK1	10
$FFE8:FFE9	Timer Channel 3	C3I	TMSK1	10
$FFEA:FFEB	Timer Channel 2	C2I	TMSK1	10
$FFEC:FFED	Timer Channel 1	C1I	TMSK1	10
$FFEE:FFEF	Timer Channel 0	C0I	TMSK1	10
$FFF0:FFF1	Real Time Interrupt	RTIE	RTICTL	10
$FFF2:FFF3	$\overline{IRQ}$ pin or Key Wakeup D	IRQEN,KWIED[7:0]	INTCR	8
$FFF4:FFF5	$\overline{XIRQ}$ pin	X	CCR	8
$FFF6:FFF7	SWI	None		8
$FFF8:FFF9	Unimplemented Opcode Trap	None		8
$FFFA:FFFB	COP Failure (Reset)	None		8
$FFFC:FFFD	Clock Monitor Fail (Reset)	None		8
$FFFE:FFFF	$\overline{RESET}$	None		8

TABLE 8-2 Interrupt Vector Assignments MC68HC912B32

Vector Address	Interrupt Source	Local Enable Bit	See Register	See Chapter
$FF8O:FFCF	Reserved	—		
$FFD0:FFD1	BDLC	IE	BCR1	15
$FFD2:FFD3	A/D Converter	ASCIE	ATDCTL	12
$FFD4:FFD5	Reserved	—		
$FFD6:FFD7	SCI-0 Serial System	See Chapter 11.		11
$FFD8:FFD9	SPI Serial Transfer Complete	SPIE	SP0CR1	11
$FFDA:FFDB	Pulse Accumulator Input Edge	PAI	PACTL	10
$FFDC:FFDD	Pulse Accumulator Overflow	PAOVI	PACTL	10
$FFDE:FFDF	Timer Overflow	TOI	TMSK2	10
$FFE0:FFE1	Timer Channel 7	C7I	TMSK1	10
$FFE2:FFE3	Timer Channel 6	C6I	TMSK1	10
$FFE4:FFE5	Timer Channel 5	C5I	TMSK1	10
$FFE6:FFE7	Timer Channel 4	C4I	TMSK1	10
$FFE8:FFE9	Timer Channel 3	C3I	TMSK1	10
$FFEA:FFEB	Timer Channel 2	C2I	TMSK1	10
$FFEC:FFED	Timer Channel 1	C1I	TMSK1	10
$FFEE:FFEF	Timer Channel 0	C0I	TMSK1	10
$FFF0:FFF1	Real Time Interrupt	RTIE	RTICTL	10
$FFF2:FFF3	$\overline{IRQ}$ pin	IRQEN	INTCR	8
$FFF4:FFF5	$\overline{XIRQ}$ pin	X	CCR	8
$FFF6:FFF7	SWI	None		8
$FFF8:FFF9	Unimplemented Opcode Trap	None		8
$FFFA:FFFB	COP Failure (Reset)	None		8
$FFFC:FFFD	Clock Monitor Fail (Reset)	None		8
$FFFE:FFFF	$\overline{RESET}$	None		8

Initializing the Interrupt Vectors

In a dedicated system,[4] the interrupt vector locations shown in Tables 8–1 and 8–2 must be initialized to the start of the interrupt service routine. This is easy to do in assembly language, and Example 8–1 shows a short example. The EQU at *line 3 locates* where the address of the interrupt service routine is to be placed. On *line 20* the assembler evaluates the label TC0ISR, which is the label on the interrupt service routine, as the address to be placed in the vector location. Examples 8–8 and 8–9 show how to do this in more complete examples.

D-Bug12 Monitor Interrupt Vector Jump Table

When developing a system using interrupts with the D-Bug12 Monitor, an *interrupt vector jump table* must be used.

A special problem exists when using a development or evaluation board such as the HC12A4EVB with the D-Bug12 Monitor. The memory locations reserved for the vectors in Tables 8–1 and 8–2 are in ROM and are *preprogrammed.* You cannot initialize them to point to the interrupt service routine you are developing. Thus, an indirect method must be used. The D-Bug12 vector for each interrupt points to an area of RAM dedicated to D-

---

EXAMPLE 8–1   Initializing the M68HC12 Interrupt Vector

```
invect1c.asm      Assembled with CASM  05/28/1998  01:33  PAGE 1

               1  ; Initializing M68HC12 interrupt vectors
               2  ; Initialize Timer Channel 0 Interrupt vector
0000           3  TC0:     EQU   $FFEE    ; Address of the vector
0000           4  PROG:    EQU   $E000    ; Program location
               5  ; . . .
E000           6           org   PROG
               7  ; Main program
E000 A7        8           nop
               9  ; . . .
              10  ; The interrupt service routine starts with a label
              11  ; at the first opcode to be executed.
              12  TC0ISR:
E001 A7       13           nop
              14  ; . . .
              15  ; The isr ends with a RTI
E002 0B       16           rti
              17  ; . . .
              18  ; Locate the vector
FFEE          19           ORG   TC0
FFEE E001     20           DW    TC0ISR   ; The label is the address
              21                          ; of the isr
```

---

[4] We define a dedicated system as one that does not have a debugging monitor such as D-Bug12.

Bug12. This area is called the *Interrupt Vector Jump Table* and you must initialize this to point to your interrupt service routine. Use the D-Bug12 *SetUserVector* routine that was discussed briefly in Chapter 5. Table 8–3 shows the vector number passed as a parameter to SetUserVector for all interrupts. Examples 8–2 and 8–10 show how to use SetUserVector to initialize the jump table in your programs.

Explanation of Example 8–2

The skeletal code in Example 8–2 shows how to initialize the interrupt vector in D-Bug12 systems. In *lines 4–10* a *conditional assembly* construct is used to equate SetVect to the proper value for the version of D-Bug12 being used. There are two versions—1.xxx for systems using the MC68HC812A4 and 2.xxx for the MC68HC912B32. If Ver1, defined TRUE by the $SET in *line 4* is TRUE, then the SetVect location $FE1A is used (*line 26*). If Ver1 were to be FALSE, $F69A will be used. *Line 5* shows how to set Ver1 FALSE. The D-Bug12 vector is initialized in *lines 23–27*. *Lines 28–35* enable the timer, reset any pending interrupts, enable the timer overflow, and unmask the I bit.

8.5 Interrupt Priorities

> The hardware prioritization order can be modified by the program.

Hardware must be used to resolve simultaneous interrupts in a vectored system. The priorities in the M68HC12 are fixed in hardware as shown in Table 8–4 but can be dynamically changed by the programmer. Any single interrupting source can be elevated to the highest priority position. The rest of the order remains fixed as given in Table 8–4.

TABLE 8–3 D-Bug12 Monitor Interrupts

Number$_{10}$	MC68HC812A4 Interrupt D-Bug12 Version 1.xxx	MC68HC912B32 Interrupt D-Bug12 Version 2.xxx
7	Port H Key Wakeup	Reserved
8	Port J Key Wakeup	BDLC
9	Analog-to-Digital Converter	Analog-to-Digital Converter
10	Serial Communications Interface 1 (SCI1)	Reserved
11	Serial Communications Interface 0 (SCI0)	Serial Communications Interface 0 (SCI0)
12	Serial Peripheral Interface 0 (SPI0)	Serial Peripheral Interface 0 (SPI0)
23	Timer Channel 0	Timer Channel 0
22	Timer Channel 1	Timer Channel 1
21	Timer Channel 2	Timer Channel 2
20	Timer Channel 3	Timer Channel 3
19	Timer Channel 4	Timer Channel 4
18	Timer Channel 5	Timer Channel 5
17	Timer Channel 6	Timer Channel 6
16	Timer Channel 7	Timer Channel 7
14	Pulse Accumulator Overflow	Pulse Accumulator Overflow
13	Pulse Accumulator Input Edge	Pulse Accumulator Input Edge
15	Timer Overflow	Timer Overflow
24	Real Time Interrupt	Real Time Interrupt
25	IRQ and Key wakeup D	IRQ
26	XIRQ	XIRQ
27	Software Interrupt (SWI)	Software Interrupt (SWI)
28	Unimplemented Opcode Trap	Unimplemented Opcode Trap
−1	Return to starting address of the RAM vector table	Return the starting address of the RAM vector table

EXAMPLE 8–2 Setting an Interrupt Vector with the D-Bug12 Monitor

```
invect2c.asm            Assembled with CASM 12/08/1998 22:53 PAGE 1

                    1  ; Initializing D Bug12 interrupt vectors jump table.
                    2  ; Initialize Timer Overflow Interrupt vector
0000                3  TOVF:     EQU     !15       ; D-Bug12 number
0000                4  $SET      Ver1              ; Using D-Bug12 version 1.xxx
                    5  ;$SETNOT  Ver1              ; Using D-Bug12 version 2.xxx
0000                6  $IF       Ver1
0000                7  SetVect:  EQU     $FE1A     ; D Bug12 routine in Ver 1
0000                8  $ELSEIF
                    9  SetVect:  EQU     $F69A     ; D Bug12 routine in Ver 2
0000               10  $ENDIF
0000               11  TOF:      EQU     %10000000 ; Timer Overflow Flag
0000               12  TOI:      EQU     %10000000 ; Timer Overflow Interrupt
0000               13  TFLG2:    EQU     $8f       ; TFLG2 register
0000               14  TMSK2:    EQU     $8d       ; TMSK2 register
0000               15  TSCR:     EQU     $86       ; Timer system control
0000               16  TEN:      EQU     %10000000 ; Timer enable bit
                   17  ; . . .
                   18  ; Main program
                   19
                   20  ; . . .
                   21  ; The vector is initialized before interrupts are
                   22  ; enabled.
0000 CC0017        23            ldd     #TOVISR   ; Get the address of the isr
0003 3B            24            pshd              ; Put it on the stack
0004 CC000F        25            ldd     #TOVF     ; Get the number for overflow
0007 15FBFE0F      26            jsr     [SetVect,PCR]
000B 3A            27            puld              ; Clean up the stack
                   28  ; Enable the timer
000C 4C8680        29            bset    TSCR,TEN
                   30  ; Reset any pending interrupts
000F 8680          31            ldaa    #TOF
0011 5A8F          32            staa    TFLG2
                   33  ; Enable the interrupts
0013 5A8D          34            staa    TMSK2     ; Enable timer overflow
0015 10EF          35            cli               ; Unmask interrupts
                   36  ; . . .
                   37  ; . . .
                   38  ; The interrupt service routine starts with a label
                   39  ; at the first opcode to be executed.
                   40  TOVISR:
                   41  ; . . .
                   42  ; Reset the overflow flag in the ISR
0017 8680          43            ldaa    #TOF
0019 5A8F          44            staa    TFLG2
                   45  ; The isr ends with a RTI
001B 0B            46            rti
                   47  ; . . .
```

TABLE 8–4 Interrupt Priorities

Priority	MC68HC812A4 Maskable Interrupt Source	MC68HC912B32 Maskable Interrupt Source	HPRIO Value to Promote
1	Highest according to HPRIO	Highest according to HPRIO	
2	IRQ or Key Wakeup D	IRQ	$F2
3	Real Time Interrupt	Real Time Interrupt	$F0
4	Timer Channel 0	Timer Channel 0	$EE
5	Timer Channel 1	Timer Channel 1	$EC
6	Timer Channel 2	Timer Channel 2	$EA
7	Timer Channel 3	Timer Channel 3	$E8
8	Timer Channel 4	Timer Channel 4	$E6
9	Timer Channel 5	Timer Channel 5	$E4
10	Timer Channel 6	Timer Channel 6	$E2
11	Timer Channel 7	Timer Channel 7	$E0
12	Timer Overflow	Timer Overflow	$DE
13	Pulse Accumulator Overflow	Pulse Accumulator Overflow	$DC
14	Pulse Accumulator Input Edge	Pulse Accumulator Input Edge	$DA
15	SPI Serial Transfer Complete	SPI Serial Transfer Complete	$D8
16	SCI-0 Serial System	SCI-0 Serial System	$D6
17	SCI-1 Serial System	Reserved	$D4
18	Analog-to-Digital Converter	Analog-to-Digital Converter	$D2
19	Key Wakeup J	BDLC	$D0
20	Key Wakeup H	Reserved	$CE

The *HPRIO—Highest Priority Interrupt Register* contains bits *PSEL5–PSEL1* to select which device has the highest priority as shown in Table 8–4. To promote any of the interrupts to the highest priority, write the low byte of its vector to HPRIO. Do this only when interrupts are masked with the I bit set. When the CPU is reset, HPRIO = $F2 giving IRQ the highest priority. See Example 8–3.

HPRIO—$001F—Highest Priority I Interrupt Register

Bit 7	6	5	4	3	2	1	Bit 0
1	1	PSEL5	PSEL4	PSEL3	PSEL2	PSEL1	0
Reset 1	1	1	1	0	0	1	0

Write the value shown in Table 8–4 to promote a particular interrupt to the highest priority.

8.6 Nonmaskable Interrupts

In any system there are events that are so important that they should never be masked. These are sometimes called *exceptions* and a good example is the RESET signal. When this is asserted, everything stops and the processor is reset. These very important events are called *nonmaskable interrupts*.

EXAMPLE 8–3

Write a small segment of code to raise Timer Channel 2 to the highest priority position.

Solution:

```
hprio1c.asm        Assembled with CASM  05/28/1998  02:20  PAGE 1

0000          1 HPRIO:     EQU    $1F      ; HPRIO address
0000          2 TC2VECT:   EQU    $FFEA    ; Channel 2 Vector
              3 ;  . . .
              4 ; Mask interrupts while setting HPRIO
0000 1410     5            sei             ; Set I bit
              6 ; Raise Timer Channel 2 to the highest priority
0002 CCFFEA   7            ldd    #TC2VECT
0005 5B1F     8            stab   HPRIO
0007 10EF     9            cli             ; Clear interrupt mask
```

Table 8–5 shows six nonmaskable interrupt sources. These can always interrupt the CPU and thus have higher priority than any of the maskable interrupts.

RESET

This is the hardware reset normally done when powering up the M68HC12. It can be accomplished also by a pushbutton switch and has the highest priority of all. Hardware for $\overline{\text{RESET}}$ is shown in Chapter 2. The MC68HC812A4 has an alternate reset pin (PE7/ARST). When bit 7 of the *Port E Assignment Register (PEAR)* is set, Port E, bit 7 operates as an active high reset input. It uses the same vector and accomplishes everything the $\overline{\text{RESET}}$ does.

When the CPU detects either of the external reset signals, or the internally generated Clock Monitor, or COP Failure reset, the $\overline{\text{RESET}}$ pin is driven low. This helps the CPU determine if the reset action was caused by the external reset pins or an internal source. To properly apply an external reset signal, ensure your reset circuitry asserts $\overline{\text{RESET}}$ or ARST for more than 32 E-clock cycles.

TABLE 8–5   M68HC12 Nonmaskable Interrupt Priorities

Priority	Nonmaskable Interrupt Source	Vector Address	Enable Bit	See Register
1	RESET	$FFFE:FFFF	None	
2	Clock Monitor Fail	$FFFC:FFFD	CME, DISR	COPCTL
3	COP Failure	$FFFA:FFFB	DISR	COPCTL
4	Unimplemented Opcode Trap	$FFF8:FFF9	None	
5	Software Interrupt SWI	$FFF6:FFF7	None	
6	$\overline{\text{XIRQ}}$	$FFF4:FFF5	X	CCR

The M68HC12 also has a *Power-On Reset.* A positive transition on the positive power supply, V_{DD}, initializes internal CPU circuitry. It does not provide an external reset signal, however.

Clock Monitor Failure

If the CPU's clock signals slow down or fail, and the *Clock Monitor Enable* (*CME*) bit in the *COPCTL* register is set and the *Force Clock Monitor Enable* (*FCME*) is reset, the clock monitor will detect the problem and issue a CME reset signal. A vector at $FFFC:FFFD is available in case something special should be done if this occurs. Note that the M68HC12 cannot complete the reset sequence, including the low drive on $\overline{RESET}$ and fetching the vector until clocks resume.

COPCTL—$0016—COP Control Register

	Bit 7	6	5	4	3	2	1	Bit 0
	CME	FCME	FCM	FCOP	DISR	CR2	CR1	CR0
Normal	0	0	0	0	0	1	1	1
Special	0	0	0	0	1	1	1	1

(Reset label appears at left of register row)

CME

Clock Monitor Enable.
  0 = Clock monitor is disabled. Slow clocks and the STOP instruction can be used (default).
  1 = Slow or stopped clocks (including the STOP instruction) will cause a system reset.
If the FCME bit is set, CME has no meaning or effect. To use both the STOP and the Clock Monitor, CME should be cleared before executing the STOP instruction and set again after recovery from the stopped state.

FCME

Force Clock Monitor Enable.
  0 = The CME bit controls the Clock Monitor (default).
  1 = Slow or stopped clocks will cause the Clock Monitor reset.
FCME can be written only once in normal modes and at anytime in special modes.
If you plan on using the STOP instruction, keep FCME = 0 and clear CME before the STOP and set it after.

FCM

Force Clock Monitor Reset.
  0 = Normal operation (default).
  1 = Force a clock monitor reset if CME = 1.
FCM can be written at anytime in special modes and not at all in normal modes.

DISR

Disable Resets from COP Watchdog and Clock Monitor.
    0 = Normal operation (default).
    1 = COP and Clock Monitor cannot generate a system reset.
This bit can be written only in special modes.

FCOP, CR2:CR0

Force COP Watchdog Reset and COP Watchdog Timer Rate Select Bits.

Computer Operating Properly (COP)

Comparison of M68HC12 and M68HC11 COP	
M68HC12	**M68HC11**
COP is enabled in normal modes at reset; it may be disabled by writing to the COPCTL register	COP is disabled at reset; it must be enabled by programming the EEPROM CONFIG register

> The *Computer Operating Properly* function is a *watchdog timer.* It can reset the M68HC12 if the program gets lost.

A COP, or watchdog, system is a vital part of computers used in dedicated applications. The system must have some way to recover from unexpected errors that may occur. Power surges or programming errors may cause the program "to get lost" and thus to lose control of the system. This could be disastrous and so the watchdog timer is included to help the program recover. When in operation, the program is responsible for pulsing the COP at specific intervals. This is accomplished by choosing a place in the program to pulse the watchdog timer regularly. Then, if the program fails to do this, the COP automatically provides a hardware reset to begin the processing again.

For the M68HC12 operating in normal modes, the COP is enabled when the CPU is reset. The COP timeout period is controlled by the *CR2:CR1:CR0* bits in the *COPCTL* control register. These bits may be programmed to give a COP time-out period ranging from 1.024 msec to 1.049 sec, and the default established by $\overline{\text{RESET}}$ is 1.049 sec when the M-clock is 8 MHz.[5] After the COP timer has started, the program must write first $55 followed by $AA to the *Arm/Reset COP Timer Register (CO-PRST)* before the COP times out. During each COP time-out period, this sequence ($55 followed by $AA) must be written. Other instructions can be executed between the $55 and the $AA, but both must be completed in the time-out period to avoid a COP reset. When a COP timeout occurs, or if the program writes anything other than $55 or $AA to the COPRST register, a COP reset is generated and the program restarts at the program location given by the COP failure vector. See Table 8–6.

---

[5] If you are using a system with the D-Bug12 monitor, you will find that CR2:CR1:CR0 = 000, which turns the COP system off.

You may disable the COP timer by writing bits CR2:CR1:CR0 equal to zero.

TABLE 8–6 COP Failure Interrupt Vectors

Interrupt	Vector	D-Bug12 SetUserVect Number$_{10}$
COP Failure (Timeout)	$FFFA:FFFB	29

COPCTL—$0016—COP Control Register

	Bit 7	6	5	4	3	2	1	Bit 0
Reset	CME	FCME	FCM	FCOP	DISR	CR2	CR1	CR0
Normal	0	0	0	0	0	1	1	1
Special	0				1	1	1	1

CME
Clock Monitor Enable.

FCME
Force Clock Monitor Enable.

FCM
Force Clock Monitor Reset.

FCOP

Force COP Watchdog Reset.
    0 = Normal operation (default).
    1 = Force a COP reset if DISR = 0.

DISR

Disable Resets from COP Watchdog and Clock Monitor.
    0 = Normal operation (default).
    1 = Clock Monitor and COP Watchdog will not generate reset interrupts.
This bit can be written only in special modes.

CR2, CR1, CR0					
COP Watchdog Timer Rate select bits.					
CR2	CR1	CR0	Divide M by:	Interrupt Time: M = 4.0 MHz	Interrupt Time: M = 8.0 MHz
0	0	0	Off	Off	Off
0	0	1	2^{13}	2.048 msec	1.024 msec
0	1	0	2^{15}	8.192 msec	4.096 msec
0	1	1	2^{17}	32.768 msec	16.384 msec
1	0	0	2^{19}	131.072 msec	65.536 msec
1	0	1	2^{21}	524.288 msec	262.144 msec
1	1	0	2^{22}	1.048 sec	424.288 msec
1	1	1	2^{23}	2.097 sec	1.049 sec

COPRST—$0017—Arm/Reset COP Timer Circuitry

Bit 7	6	5	4	3	2	1	Bit 0
7	6	5	4	3	2	1	0

Reset 0   0   0   0   0   0   0   0

Write $55 followed by $AA to this register to reset the COP timer.

Unimplemented Instruction Opcode Trap

If the program somehow gets lost and starts executing data, it is likely to encounter an unimplemented opcode. Executing data is a disaster and executing an illegal opcode even more of a disaster. The CPU can detect an unimplemented opcode and will vector itself to the address in $FFF8:FFF9.

Software Interrupt (SWI)

The software interrupt is, in effect, a 1-byte, indirect branch to a subroutine whose address is at the vector location $FFF6:FFF7. The SWI instruction is frequently used in debugging monitors, such as the D-Bug12 Monitor in the HC12A4EVB, to implement a 1-byte breakpoint instruction. It operates like the rest of the interrupt system in that all registers are pushed onto the stack, making it ideal for debugging. When you are using a Version 2.xxx D-Bug12 and operating through the background debugging mode to a target system, a BGND instruction is used instead of SWI.

Nonmaskable Interrupt Request $\overline{XIRQ}$

Once the $\overline{XIRQ}$ interrupt is unmasked, it cannot be masked again, unless the M68HC12 is reset.

$\overline{XIRQ}$ is an external, nonmaskable interrupt input. The system designers have included the X bit in the condition code register to mask interrupts on this pin until the program has initialized the stack pointer (and the vector jump table, if required). The X bit is similar to the I bit in that it masks when set and unmasks when cleared. A programmer has control over when the X bit is cleared and thus can set up the stack pointer and other critical program elements beforehand. The ANDCC #%10111111 instruction is used to reset the X bit and to unmask the interrupt.

Once the X-bit is reset, the program *absolutely cannot* mask it again. However, when an $\overline{XIRQ}$ occurs, the X bit is set, just like the I bit, so that nested $\overline{XIRQ}$s cannot occur. On leaving the interrupt service routine, the bit is reset, and further $\overline{XIRQ}$ interrupts can then occur. Figure 8–1 shows how $\overline{XIRQ}$ is to be interfaced to the M68HC12.

8.7 External Interrupt Sources

Comparison of M68HC12 and M68HC11 External Interrupt	
M68HC12	**M68HC11**
$\overline{IRQ}$, $\overline{XIRQ}$	$\overline{IRQ}$, $\overline{XIRQ}$, STRA
Three, 8-bit Key Wakeup Ports in the MC68HC812A4	
Both can use timer inputs for external interrupt sources	

The interrupts of the parallel I/O system were not covered in Chapter 7. Now that we know more about the interrupt system, let us look at the details we postponed.

$\overline{IRQ}$

$\overline{IRQ}$ is an interrupt request that is generated by some external device. For example, you may have a sensor that generates an interrupt every time a vehicle passes a traffic counter. $\overline{IRQ}$ is an *active-low* signal and you may choose a level-activate (the default) or a negative-edge-sensitive response. The *Interrupt Control Register* (*INTCR*) contains a bit to select which of these responses is needed and to enable/disable the $\overline{IRQ}$ signal.

INTCR—$001E—Interrupt Control Register

Bit 7	6	5	4	3	2	1	Bit 0
IRQE	IRQEN	DLY	0	0	0	0	0

Reset 0	1	1	0	0	0	0	0

IRQE

$\overline{IRQ}$ Select Edge Sensitivity.

        0 = $\overline{IRQ}$ generates an interrupt when it is low level (default).

        1 = $\overline{IRQ}$ generates an interrupt on the falling edge.

IRQEN

$\overline{IRQ}$ Enable.

        0 = External $\overline{IRQ}$ (and Key Wakeup D signals) are disabled.

        1 = External $\overline{IRQ}$ (and key Wakeup D signals) are enabled (default).

DLY

This bit controls the startup of the processor after a STOP instruction. See Chapter 15.

The interrupt vector $FFF2:FFF3 is shared between the $\overline{IRQ}$ input and the parallel I/O system. We will discuss how to distinguish between these two sources of interrupts in Section 8.10.

Key Wakeups

The MC68HC812A4 version of the M68HC12 has three key wakeup ports (Ports D, H, and J) designed to issue interrupts to wake up the CPU when it has gone to sleep following a STOP instruction.[6] Each port has a *Data Register* for I/O (*PORTx*[7]) and a *Data Direction Register* (*DDRx*) to select input or output for each bit. There is a *Key Wakeup Interrupt Enable Register* (*KWIEx*) and a *Key Wakeup Flag Register* (*KWIFx*) to enable interrupts and to show which bit generated the interrupt. Port J also has a register to select the edge that activates the interrupt, *Key Wakeup Port J Polarity Register* (*KPOLJ*), and two registers to enable and select pull-up and pull-down resistors. Table 8–7 show a summary of the registers used for each port.

Interrupt Enable and Flags Registers

We saw how to use the data and data direction registers in Chapter 7. The additional registers used with the key wakeup feature are the *Interrupt Enable* and *Interrupt Flag* registers.

    Each of the key wakeup register bits can be individually allowed (or disallowed) to generate interrupts. The KWIEx register provides this control. Setting a bit in one of these registers enables

---

[6] The STOP instruction stops the CPU clocks to reduce power consumption. The processor does not execute any instructions when put to sleep like this and requires an interrupt to wake up. See Chapter 15.

[7] x = D, H, or J.

TABLE 8-7 M68HC11 Key Wakeup Registers

Port	Registers	Register Name	Address	Interrupt Vector	Assertion Level
D	PORTD	Port D Data	$0005	$FFF2:FFF3	Falling edge;
	DDRD	Data Direction D	$0007	shared with	INTCR[IRQEN]
	KWIED	Key Wakeup Interrupt Enable D	$0020	$\overline{\text{IRQ}}$	must be set
	KWIFD	Key Wakeup Interrupt Flag D	$0021		
	INTCR	Interrupt Control	$001E		
H	PORTH	Port H Data	$0024	$FFCE:FFCF	Falling edge
	DDRH	Data Direction H	$0025		
	KWIEH	Key Wakeup Interrupt Enable H	$0026		
	KWIFH	Key Wakeup Interrupt Flag H	$0027		
J	PORTJ	Port J Data	$0028	$FFD0:FFD1	Falling or rising
	DDRJ	Data Direction J	$0029		edge selected by
	KWIEJ	Key Wakeup Interrupt J	$002A		KPOLJ
	KWIFJ	Key Wakeup Interrupt Flag J	$002B		
	KPOLJ	Key Wakeup Polarity J	$002C		
	PUPSJ	Key Wakeup Pull-up Select J	$002D		
	PULEJ	Key Wakeup Pull-up Enable J	$002E		

the corresponding key wakeup bit to generate an interrupt request. (Remember that you must initialize the vector and unmask the I bit before the interrupt can be acknowledged.) When the key wakeup input is asserted (falling edge on D and H, either falling or rising on J), the corresponding bit in the KWIFx register is set. When more than one key wakeup bit is active, the interrupt service routine must check the flag register to see which bit did the deed. Before leaving the ISR, the flag must be reset. This is done by *writing a one* to the bit. See Examples 8–4 and 8–5.

KWIED—KWIEJ—Key Wakeup Port Interrupt Enable Registers

KWIED—$0020—Key Wakeup Port D Interrupt Enable Register
KWIEH—$0026—Key Wakeup Port H Interrupt Enable Register
KWIEJ—$002A—Key Wakeup Port J Interrupt Enable Register

Bit 7	6	5	4	3	2	1	Bit 0
7	6	5	4	3	2	1	0

Reset 0 0 0 0 0 0 0 0

KWIEX[7:0]
Key Wakeup Port x Interrupt Enable.
0 = Interrupt for the bit is disabled (default).
1 = Interrupt for the bit is enabled.

KWIFD—KWIFJ—Key Wakeup Port Interrupt Flag Registers

KWIFD—$0021—Key Wakeup Port D Interrupt Flag Register
KWIFH—$0027—Key Wakeup Port H Interrupt Flag Register
KWIFJ—$002B—Key Wakeup Port J Interrupt Flag Register

Bit 7	6	5	4	3	2	1	Bit 0
7	6	5	4	3	2	1	0

Reset 0   0   0   0   0   0   0   0

KWIFX[7:0]

Key Wakeup Port x Interrupt Flag.
     0 = Interrupt signal on this bit has not occurred (default).
     1 = Interrupt for the bit has occurred.

Port J Rising and Falling Edge Selection

The interrupt flags for Port D (KWIFD[7:]) and Port H (KWIFH[7:0]) are set on the falling edge. For Port J, KWIFJ[7:0] are set on either the rising or falling edge as determined by the bits in *Key Wakeup Port J Polarity Register (KPOLJ)*.

KPOLJ—$002C—Key Wakeup Port J Polarity Register

Bit 7	6	5	4	3	2	1	Bit 0
7	6	5	4	3	2	1	0

Reset 0   0   0   0   0   0   0   0

KPOLJ[7:0]

Key Wakeup Port J Polarity Select.
     0 = Falling edge on the corresponding pin sets the flag in KWIFJ (default).
     1 = Rising edge sets the flag.

Port J Pull-up/Pull-down Selection

We discussed the importance of pull-up and pull-down resistors in Chapter 7. You may choose pull-up or pull-down resistors for any of the bits in Port J by programming *PUPSJ* and *PULEJ*.

PUPSJ—$002D—Key Wakeup Port J Pull-up/ Pull-down Select Register

Bit 7	6	5	4	3	2	1	Bit 0
7	6	5	4	3	2	1	0

Reset 0   0   0   0   0   0   0   0

PUPSJ[7:0]
Key Wakeup Port J Pull-up/Pull-down Select.
0 = Associated Port J pin has a pull-down device (default).
1 = The Port J pins have pull-ups selected.
PUPSJ should be initialized before enabling pull-ups or pull-downs in PULEJ.

PULEJ—$002E—Key Wakeup Port J Pull-up/Pull-down Enable Register

Bit 7	6	5	4	3	2	1	Bit 0
7	6	5	4	3	2	1	0

Reset 0   0   0   0   0   0   0   0

PULEJ[7:0]
Key Wakeup Port J Pull-up/Pull-down Enable.
0 = Associated Port J pin has no pull-up or pull-down device (default).
1 = The Port J pin has a pull-up or pull-down (selected by PUPSJ) if the pin is an input.

Key Wakeup Initialization

You should initialize key wakeup features in the order shown in Table 8–8. Example 8–4 shows how to use the key wakeup features of Port J.

TABLE 8-8 Initializing Key Wakeup Registers

Step	Port	Procedure
1	D	Make sure the IRQ enable bit in the INTCR register (INTCR[IRQEN]) is set to enable the interrupt
2	All	Set the direction of the key wakeup bits to input by writing zeros in the data direction register
3	J	Select the bits for which pull-up or pull-down resistors are needed by writing ones and zeros to the Pull-up/Pull-down Select Register PUPSJ
4	J	Enable the bits that have pull-up or pull-down resistors by writing ones to the Pull-up/Pull-down Enable Register PULEJ
5	J	Select rising or falling edges for each of the key wakeup bits by writing ones and zeros into the Key Wakeup Polarity Register KPOLJ
6	All	Initialize the Key Wakeup interrupt vector
7	All	Clear any flags that have been set in the Key Wakeup Flag Register KWIFx
8	All	Enable the key wakeup bit by writing ones into the Key Wakeup Interrupt Enable Register KWIEx
9	All	Make sure all other interrupt vectors have been initialized
10	All	Finally, clear the global interrupt mask (after all interrupt processes have been initialized properly)

Explanation of Example 8–4

The data direction register bits 7–4 are set and 3–0 reset to make output and input bits, respectively, in *lines 37 and 38*. We enable pull-up resistors for bits 3–0 in *lines 39–42*, falling edge interrupts for bits 3 and 2 in *line 44*, and rising edge interrupts for bits 1 and 0 in *line 45*. The interrupt vector is initialized in *lines 46–51* and any flags that are currently set are cleared and interrupts enabled in *lines 53–56*. Finally, the mask is cleared and, in this simple example, a WAI instruction executed to wait for the interrupt.

The interrupt service routine starts at *line 65*. Because only one vector is used for the four possible interrupts, the flags are polled to see which one interrupted.

8.8 Interrupt Flags

Comparison of Clearing M68HC11 and M68HC12 Interrupt Flags

Both the M68HC11 and M68HC12 reset interrupt flags by writing a one to the flag

Multiple Key Wakeup Interrupts

All key wakeup bits set *flags* in registers when the key wakeup signal is asserted. As there is only one vector for each key wakeup port, and therefore only one interrupt service routine, the flags can be used to determine which of several key wakeup interrupts have occurred. Example 8–4 shows how this can be done in the interrupt service routine. *Lines 67–70, 78–79, 87–88,* and *96–97* check each wakeup flag until a flag that has been set is found. Note that this code will service only one interrupt each time the ISR is entered. If multiple key wakeup interrupts occur simultaneously, the

EXAMPLE 8–4   Initializing Port J Key Wakeup Pins

portj1c.asm   Assembled with CASM   08/09/1998   00:23 PAGE 1

```
                   1  ; Initialize Port J for I/O and key wakeups
                   2  ; Use bits 3-0 for inputs/key wakeups and
                   3  ; bits 7-4 for output.
0000               4  ALLBITS:   EQU     %11111111
0000               5  IN_BITS:   EQU     %00001111         ; Bits 3-0
0000               6  O_BITS:    EQU     %11110000         ; Bits 7-4
0000               7  BIT3:      EQU     %00001000         ; Bit-3
0000               8  BIT2:      EQU     %00000100         ; Bit-2
0000               9  BIT1:      EQU     %00000010         ; Bit-1
0000              10  BIT0:      EQU     %00000001         ; Bit-0
                  11  ; Choose bits 3 and 2 for falling edge interrupts
0000              12  FALLING:   EQU     %00001100
                  13  ; Choose bits 1 and 0 for rising edge interrupts
0000              14  RISING:    EQU     %00000011
0000              15  DDRJ:      EQU     $29       ; Data direction register
0000              16  PORTJ:     EQU     $28       ; Data register
0000              17  KWIEJ:     EQU     $2A       ; Interrupt enable register
0000              18  KWIFJ:     EQU     $2B       ; Flags register
0000              19  KPOLJ:     EQU     $2C       ; Polarity register
0000              20  PUPSJ:     EQU     $2D       ; Pull-up select
0000              21  PULEJ:     EQU     $2E       ; Enable pull-ups
0000              22  KWJNUM:    EQU     8         ; D-Bug12 number
0000              23  $SET       Ver1              ; D-Bug12 version
0000              24  $IF        Ver1
0000              25  SetVect:   EQU     $FE1A     ; D-Bug12 routine in Ver 1
0000              26  $ELSEIF
                  27  SetVect:   EQU     $F69A     ; D-Bug12 routine in Ver 2
0000              28  $ENDIF
                  29  ; Memory map equates
0000              30  PROG:      EQU     $0800     ; ROM location
0000              31  DATA:      EQU     $0900     ; RAM location
0000              32  STACK:     EQU     $0a00     ; Stack location
                  33
0800              34             ORG     PROG
0800 CF0A00       35             lds     #STACK
                  36  ; Initialize data direction register
0803 4C29F0       37             bset    DDRJ,O_BITS
0806 4D290F       38             bclr    DDRJ,IN_BITS
                  39  ; Select pull-ups for bits 3-0
0809 4C2D0F       40             bset    PUPSJ,IN_BITS
                  41  ; Enable pull-ups
080C 4C2E0F       42             bset    PULEJ,IN_BITS
                  43  ; Set polarity bits 3-2 falling, bits 1-0 rising
080F 4D2C0C       44             bclr    KPOLJ,FALLING
0812 4C2C03       45             bset    KPOLJ,RISING
                  46  ; Initialize the interrupt vector in D-Bug12
```

EXAMPLE 8–4   Continued

```
0815  CC082C      47                  ldd     #ISR        ; Address of the ISR
0818  3B          48                  pshd
0819  CC0008      49                  ldd     #KWJNUM    ; D-Bug12 number
081C  15FBF5FA    50                  jsr     [SetVect,PCR]
0820  3A          51                  puld                ; Clean up stack
                  52  ; Clear the flags register of any pending interrupt
0821  860F        53                  ldaa    #IN_BITS
0823  5A2B        54                  staa    KWIFJ
                  55  ; Now it is safe to enable the interrupts
0825  4C2A0F      56                  bset    KWIEJ,IN_BITS
                  57  ; Unmask I bit
0828  10EF        58                  cli
                  59  ; Do the foreground job
082A  3E          60                  wai                 ; Wait
082B  3F          61                  swi                 ; Back to monitor
                  62  ; . . .
                  63  ; . . .
                  64  ; Interrupt Service routine
                  65  ISR:
                  66  ; Find out which Key Wakeup set the flag
082C  962B        67                  ldaa    KWIFJ       ; Get the flags
                  68  ; IF bit 0
082E  8501        69                  bita    #BIT0
0830  2706        70                  beq     Chk_1
                  71  ; THEN DO the bit 0 ISR
                  72  ; . . .
                  73  ; Reset KWIFJ interrupt flag
0832  8601        74                  ldaa    #BIT0
0834  5A2B        75                  staa    KWIFJ
0836  201C        76                  bra     Done
                  77  ; ELSE IF bit 1
0838  8502        78  Chk_1:          bita    #BIT1
083A  2706        79                  beq     Chk_2
                  80  ; THEN DO the bit 1 ISR
                  81  ; . . .
                  82  ; Reset KWIFJ interrupt flag
083C  8602        83                  ldaa    #BIT1
083E  5A2B        84                  staa    KWIFJ
0840  2012        85                  bra     Done
                  86  ; ELSE IF bit 2
0842  8504        87  Chk_2:          bita    #BIT2
0844  2706        88                  beq     Chk_3
                  89  ; THEN DO the bit 2 ISR
                  90  ; . . .
                  91  ; Reset KWIFJ interrupt flag
0846  8604        92                  ldaa    #BIT2
0848  5A2B        93                  staa    KWIFJ
084A  2008        94                  bra     Done
```

EXAMPLE 8–4   Continued

```
               95  ; ELSE IF bit 3
084C  8508     96  Chk_3:       bita    #BIT3
084E  2704     97               beq     Done
               98  ; THEN DO the bit 3 ISR
               99  ;  . . .
              100  ; Reset KWIFJ interrupt flag
0850  8608    101               ldaa    #BIT3
0852  5A2B    102               staa    KWIFJ
              103  ;
              104  Done:
0854  0B      105               rti     ; Return to interrupted prog
```

other flag(s) will still be set when the RTI instruction on *line 105* is executed and thus a new interrupt request will be generated immediately. See Problem 8.21.

Resetting Interrupt Flags

> All interrupt flags are reset by *writing a one* to the flag register bit.

The flags must be reset, or cleared, in the interrupt service routine before interrupts are reenabled. Flags are cleared *by writing a one* to the flag that is set. For example, resetting the key wakeup Port H, bit 0 flag can be done with the following code sequences:

```
ldaa    #%00000001
staa    KWIFH
```

An alternative is

```
bclr    KWIFH,#%11111110
```

The bit clear (BCLR) instruction has a mask byte with ones in the bit positions where zeros are to be written (bits cleared). Here is how this instruction works:

> The data byte is read from KWIFH, say %00000011 (bit 1 and bit 0 flags both set).
> The mask byte is complemented %11111110 → %0000001.
> The complemented mask byte is ANDed with the data and written back to KWIFH, i.e., KWIFH is written with %000000001, resetting bit 0 *and leaving bit 1 flag set.*

Perversely, the bit set instruction (BSET) *will not work.* The instruction

```
bset    KWIFH,#000000001
```

operates in this way:

> The data byte, say %00000011 (bit 1 and bit 0 flags both set), is read from KWIFH.
> The mask byte is ORed with the data byte and written back to KWIFH, i.e., KWIFH is written with %00000011! This resets *both* bit 1 and bit 0 bits.

Example 8–5 shows how to initialize the key wakeup bits in Port D and to clear the interrupt flags.

EXAMPLE 8-5   Port D Key Wakeup Interrupt Service Routine

keywd1c.asm   Assembled with CASM   12/08/1998   23:03 PAGE 1

```
                   1  ; Use bit-0 on Port D as a key wakeup
0000               2  BIT0:    EQU    %00000001
0000               3  BIT6:    EQU    %01000000
0000               4  PORTD:   EQU    $05      ; Data register
0000               5  DDRD:    EQU    $07      ; Data direction register
0000               6  KWIED:   EQU    $20      ; Key wakeup interrupt enable
0000               7  KWIFD:   EQU    $21      ; Key wakeup interrupt flags
0000               8  PDVECT:  EQU    $FFF2    ; Vector for Port D
0000               9  PDNUM:   EQU    !25      ; Number for D-Bug12
0000              10  INTCR:   EQU    $1E      ; Interrupt control register
0000              11  IRQEN:   EQU    BIT6     ; IRQ Enable
0000              12  $SET     Ver1            ; D-Bug12 version
0000              13  $IF      Ver1
0000              14  SetVect: EQU    $FE1A    ; D-Bug12 routine in Ver 1
0000              15  $ELSEIF
                  16  SetVect: EQU    $F69A    ; D-Bug12 routine in Ver 2
0000              17  $ENDIF
                  18  ; Memory map equates
0000              19  PROG:    EQU    $0800    ; ROM location
0000              20  DATA:    EQU    $0900    ; RAM location
0000              21  STACK:   EQU    $0a00    ; Stack location
                  22
0800              23           ORG    PROG
0800 CF0A00       24           lds    #STACK
                  25  ; Enable IRQEN in case it was disabled
0803 4C1E40       26           bset   INTCR,IRQEN
                  27  ; Set Port D bit 0 to input
0806 4D0701       28           bclr   DDRD,BIT0
                  29  ; Initialize the vector
0809 CC0820       30           ldd    #PDISR
080C 3B           31           pshd
080D CC0019       32           ldd    #PDNUM
0810 15FBF606     33           jsr    [SetVect,PCR]
0814 3A           34           puld
                  35  ; Clear key wakeup flag
0815 8601         36           ldaa   #BIT0
0817 5A21         37           staa   KWIFD
                  38  ; Enable key wakeup bit
0819 4C2001       39           bset   KWIED,BIT0
                  40  ; Unmask interrupts
081C 10EF         41           cli
081E 3E           42           wai
081F 3F           43           swi
                  44  ; . . .
                  45  ; The Interrupt service routine
```

EXAMPLE 8–5   Continued

```
                46  PDISR:
                47  ; . . .
                48  ; Clear interrupt flag
0820 8601       49          ldaa    #BIT0
0822 5A21       50          staa    KWIFD
                51  ; Return to the regularly scheduled program
0824 0B         52          rti
```

Explanation of Example 8–5

This example is very similar to Example 8–4. The new code to notice is at *line 26* where the IRQEN bit is set to enable Port D key wakeup interrupts. This has to be done because Port D and the external $\overline{\text{IRQ}}$ interrupts share the vector. The key wakeup flag is cleared before interrupts are enabled (*lines 36–37*) and during the interrupt service routine (*lines 49–50*).

8.9 Internal Interrupt Sources

Most internal interrupts are generated by a flag that must be reset in the ISR.

Table 8–1 shows several other internal interrupt sources, such as timer channels, that are generated within the M68HC12. These all operate like external I/O interrupts. An enable bit must be set, and when an interrupt occurs, a flag is set in a flags register. The flag must be reset in the interrupt service routine before the return from interrupt instruction is executed. We will see examples of these other interrupts when we study the devices generating them.

8.10 Advanced Interrupts

Shared $\overline{\text{IRQ}}$ and Parallel I/O Interrupt Vector

The vector at $FFF2:FFF3 must accommodate both the interrupt requested by $\overline{\text{IRQ}}$ and the Port D key wakeup interrupts in the MC68HC812A4. If both interrupt sources are active, a polling process can find out which of the two is requesting service. The flags in the KWIFD register can be used in the following logic in the interrupt service routine to determine if the device needing service is the external device activating $\overline{\text{IRQ}}$ or something asserting one of the Port D key wakeup bits.

The polling algorithm shown in Figure 8–2 shows that if a KWIFD bit is set, the key wakeup system must have generated the interrupt request. If it is not, then an external $\overline{\text{IRQ}}$ must be serviced. Notice that at the end of a service routine the key wakeup bit or the external hardware that generated the $\overline{\text{IRQ}}$ is reset. This is done to keep from generating another interrupt. This algorithm also solves the problem of simultaneous key wakeup and external $\overline{\text{IRQ}}$ interrupts. The key wakeup interrupt will be serviced first and the flag cleared. If external $\overline{\text{IRQ}}$ is still asserted, it will generate another interrupt and be recognized and serviced next.

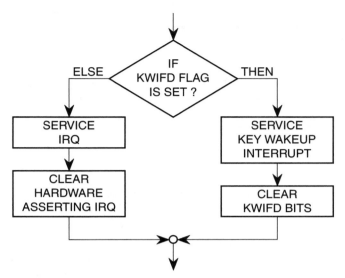

Figure 8–2   Polling algorithm used to determine the source of an interrupt.

Polling for Multiple External Devices

Polling is used when
multiple devices share
the IRQ line.

Polling methods can be used when there are multiple devices interrupting on the $\overline{\text{IRQ}}$ line. Each device must have a status register and an "I did it" bit. The M68HC12 does not have an interrupt acknowledge control signal to reset the interrupt request. If one is needed for the external application, an output bit from a port may be used.

Selecting Edge or Level Triggering

The external $\overline{\text{IRQ}}$ interrupt is normally a low-level sensitive input. This is suitable for use in a system with several devices whose interrupt request lines may be tied in a wired-OR configuration. You may choose to have a negative-edge sensitive interrupt request by programming the IRQE bit in the INTCR register. An edge sensitive interrupt is appropriate only if there is just one interrupt source connected to $\overline{\text{IRQ}}$.

What to Do While Waiting for an Interrupt

There are three ways to make the M68HC12 spin its wheels while waiting for an interrupt to occur. These are *spin loops*, and the WAI, *wait for interrupt*, and STOP, *stop clocks*, instructions.

   Spin Loop: The simplest way to make the CPU wait is the spin loop. You make the processor branch to itself with the code shown in Example 8–6.

   When an interrupt occurs, the CPU will finish executing the instruction, which is, of course, a branch to the same instruction. Before executing it again the interrupt will be acknowledged and

---

EXAMPLE 8–6   Using a Spin Loop to Wait for an Interrupt

```
spin1c.asm      Assembled with CASM  05/28/1998  02:18  PAGE  1

0000 20FE    1  spin:       bra     spin    ; Wait for interrupt
             2  ; An equivalent instruction is
0002 20FE    3              bra     *
             4  ; The * stands for the current PC location.
```

---

the interrupt service routine executed. The program will fall back into the spin loop when it returns. When using the spin loop all processing is done in the interrupt service routine.

WAI—Wait for Interrupt: The WAI instruction performs two functions. First, it pushes all the registers onto the stack in preparation for a subsequent interrupt. This reduces the delay (the *latency*) in executing the interrupt service routine. This could be important in time-critical applications. Second, the WAI places the CPU into the WAIT mode. This is a reduced power-consumption, standby state that will be discussed further in Chapter 15. See Example 8–7.

STOP—Stop Clocks: The STOP instruction stops all M68HC12 clocks, thus dramatically reducing the power consumption. The S bit in the condition code register must be zero for the instruction to operate. See Chapter 15.

EXAMPLE 8–7

Show a short code example how to use the WAI instruction to wait for an interrupt after doing what needs to be done in a foreground job.

Solution:

```
waiex1c.asm     Assembled with CASM  05/28/1998  02:20  PAGE  1

             1  ; Example of the WAI instruction in
             2  ; a foreground job.
             3  ;
             4  foreground:
             5  ; Here is the code to be done in the
             6  ; foreground. When all is complete,
             7  ; wait for the next interrupt.
             8  ; . . .
0000 3E      9      wai
            10  ; When come out of the interrupt branch
            11  ; back to the foreground job.
0001 20FD   12      bra     foreground
```

8.11 The Interrupt Service Routine

The interrupt service
routine is called an *ISR*.

The interrupt service routine (*ISR*) is executed when the vector has been initialized properly, interrupts have been unmasked and enabled, an interrupt has occurred, the CPU registers have been pushed onto the stack, and the vector has been fetched. Here are some hints for M68HC12 interrupt service routines.

Interrupt Service Routine Hints

Reenable Interrupts in the ISR Only If You Need To: If there are higher priority interrupts that must be serviced, you must unmask interrupts by clearing the I bit.

Do Not Use Nested Interrupts: Unless you have to.

Reset Any Interrupt Generating Flags in I/O Devices: Each device is different and requires somewhat different procedures. If you do not reset the flag, interrupts will be generated continuously.

Do Not Worry About Using Registers in the ISR: The M68HC12 automatically pushes all registers and the CCR onto the stack before entering the ISR. Remember to use the RTI instruction to restore them at the end of the ISR.

Do Not Assume Any Register Contents: Never assume the registers contain a value needed in the interrupt service routine unless you have full control over the whole program and can guarantee that the contents of a register never change in the program that is interrupted.

Keep It Simple to Start: Learning how to use an interrupt can be frustrating if you try to do too much in the ISR. The first step should be to see if the interrupts are occurring and if the interrupt service routine is being entered properly. After that is working, you can make the ISR do what it is supposed to do.

Keep It Short: Do as little as possible in the ISR. This reduces the latency in servicing other interrupts should they occur while in the current ISR.

M68HC12 Dedicated Application System ISR Examples

Example 8–8—Port H Key Wakeup—Explanation

Example 8–8 shows how to initialize the interrupt vectors in a dedicated application in which the program and the interrupt vectors are in read only memory. The code is located in ROM memory at *line 40* and the interrupt system is enabled by clearing any pending flags (*lines 50–51*) and enabling the key wakeup bits (*line 53*). The global I bit is unmasked in *line 55*. The interrupt service routine has a label, KWisr, at *line 67*, memory location $E017. This is the address that must be stored in the vector location $FFCE. This is done in *lines 110* and *111*. ORG KWHVEC sets the location counter to $FFCE and the assembler evaluates DW KWisr as a 16-bit constant equal to $E017. Another vector initialized is the reset vector; this is done in *lines 112* and *113*.

EXAMPLE 8–8   Interrupt Service Routine for an M68HC12 Dedicated System

int12x1c.asm   Assembled with CASM 12/08/1998 23:05 PAGE 1

```
             1  ; MC68HC12 Example
             2  ;
             3  ; This is a test program showing how to use
             4  ; the key wakeup I/O interrupts in
             5  ; a dedicated system without
             6  ; using the D-Bug12 Monitor.
             7  ; The program does nothing but spin while
             8  ; waiting for an interrupt on Port H.
             9  ; Source File: INT12EX1.ASM
            10  ; Author: F. M. Cady
            11  ; Created: 6/27/97
            12  ; Modifications: None
            13  ;
            14  ; Constant Equates
0000        15  MAX:       EQU    !30    ; Number times to interrupt
0000        16  ALLBITS:   EQU    %11111111
0000        17  BIT0:      EQU    %00000001
0000        18  BIT1:      EQU    %00000010
            19  ; System Register Equates
0000        20  PORTH:     EQU    $24    ; Data register
0000        21  DDRH:      EQU    $25    ; Data direction
0000        22  KWIEH:     EQU    $26    ; Key wakeup interrupt enable
0000        23  KWIFH:     EQU    $27    ; Interrupt flags
0000        24  PORTJ:     EQU    $28    ; Data register
0000        25  DDRJ:      EQU    $29    ; Data direction
0000        26  KWIEJ:     EQU    $2A    ; Key wakeup interrupt enable
0000        27  KWIFJ:     EQU    $2B    ; Interrupt flags
0000        28  KPOLJ:     EQU    $2C    ; Polarity register
0000        29  PUPSJ:     EQU    $2D    ; Pull-up select
0000        30  PULEJ:     EQU    $2E    ; Pull-up enable
            31  ; Memory Map Equates
0000        32  PROG:      EQU    $E000  ; PROG location
0000        33  DATA:      EQU    $0800  ; DATA location
0000        34  STACK:     EQU    $0A00  ; Stack pointer location
0000        35  KWJVEC:    EQU    $FFD0  ; Vector for key wakeup J
0000        36  KWHVEC:    EQU    $FFCE  ; Vector for key wakeup H
0000        37  RSTVEC:    EQU    $FFFE  ; Vector for reset
            38
            39
E000        40             ORG    PROG
            41  prog_start:
E000 CF0A00 42             lds    #STACK
            43  ; Initialize counter to zero
E003 790800 44             clr    count
            45  ; Set PORTJ all bits to output
```

EXAMPLE 8–8 Continued

```
E006  4C29FF     46                  bset    DDRJ,ALLBITS
                 47  ; Enable interrupt system
                 48  ; Set Port H bits 0,1 for key wakeup interrupts
E009  4D2503     49                  bclr    DDRH,BIT1|BIT0      ; Make the bits input
E00C  8603       50                  ldaa    #BIT1|BIT0
E00E  5A27       51                  staa    KWIFH              ; Clear pending flags
                 52  ; Enable key wakeup bits
E010  4C2603     53                  bset    KWIEH,BIT1|BIT0
                 54  ; Unmask the HC12 interrupts
E013  10EF       55                  cli
                 56
                 57  ; DO Forever
E015  20FE       58  start:     bra     start
                 59  ; End DO forever
                 60
                 61  ; Key wakeup ISR
                 62  ; This ISR increments a count value on each
                 63  ; interrupt from key wakeup[0] and decrements
                 64  ; for each key wakeup[1].   When it reaches a maximum
                 65  ; given by MAX, it strobes all bits on PORTJ high
                 66  ; and then low and resets the counter to zero.
                 67  KWisr:
                 68  ; Find out which key wakeup was activated.
                 69  ; Check the flags register.
                 70  ; IF bit-0 generated the interrupt
E017  9627       71                  ldaa    KWIFH
E019  44         72                  lsra             ; Shift bit 0 to carry
E01A  2409       73                  bcc     bit_1_did_it
                 74  ; THEN increment the counter and reset the flag
E01C  720800     75                  inc     count
E01F  8601       76                  ldaa    #BIT0
E021  5A27       77                  staa    KWIFH
E023  200A       78                  bra     endif_1
                 79  ; ELSE IF bit-1 generated the interrupt
                 80  bit_1_did_it:
                 81  ; Double check for a flag in case got here
                 82  ; by some other interrupt.
E025  44         83                  lsra             ; Shift bit-1 into carry
E026  2407       84                  bcc     endif_1
                 85  ; Decrement the counter and reset the flag
E028  730800     86                  dec     count
E02B  8602       87                  ldaa    #BIT1
E02D  5A27       88                  staa    KWIFH
                 89  endif_1:
                 90  ; IF count = maximum
E02F  B60800     91                  ldaa    count
E032  811E       92                  cmpa    #MAX
```

EXAMPLE 8–8   Continued

```
E034  2609        93                bne      endif_2
                  94  ; THEN strobe PORTJ
E036  4C28FF      95                bset     PORTJ,ALLBITS    ; Set PORTJ high
E039  4D28FF      96                bclr     PORTJ,ALLBITS    ; Set PORTJ low
                  97  ; and reset the count
E03C  790800      98                clr      count
                  99  ; ENDIF count=maximum
                 100  endif_2:
                 101
                 102  ; And play it again Sam
E03F  0B         103                rti      ; Return to main prog
                 104
                 105  ; Set up a count buffer
0800             106                ORG      DATA
0800  01         107  count:        DB       1
                 108
                 109  ; Initialize the interrupt vectors in top memory
FFCE             110                ORG      KWHVEC
FFCE  E017       111                DW       KWisr         ; Point to the isr
FFFE             112                ORG      RSTVEC
FFFE  E000       113                DW       prog_start    ; RESET vector
```

Example 8–9—Unused Interrupt Initialization— Explanation

All unused interrupt vectors should be initialized.

Example 8–8 shows how to initialize the vector for the Port H Key Wakeup interrupt and the reset vector. It is good programming practice to initialize all unused interrupts as well, just in case an unexpected interrupt occurs due to a bug in the program, or hardware, or some other fault. The code segment in 8–9 shows how to do this. A *dummy interrupt service routine* is shown in *lines 21–24*. It simply is an RTI instruction. Thus if an unwanted and unplanned interrupt occurs, the program can resume at the point it was interrupted. *Lines 28–51* initialize all the vectors pointing to this dummy ISR.

D-Bug12 Monitor ISR Examples

Example 8–8 shows how to use the assembler to initialize the vector locations in high memory. When a system is using a D-Bug12 Monitor, the *interrupt vector jump table* must be initialized using the D-Bug12 SetUserVect routine. Table 8–9 shows the SetUserVector parameters and Example 8–10 shows a program initializing the vector jump table address and doing the minimum necessary in the main program. The ISR tests a data value incremented for each interrupt. When the value reaches a maximum set by the constant MAX, the terminal bell is beeped.

EXAMPLE 8–9   Code to Initialize All Unused Interrupt Vectors

```
inivectc.asm      Assembled with CASM  05/28/1998  02:24  PAGE 1

                1  ; Initialization code for unused interrupt
                2  ; vectors
0000            3  IVECT:    EQU    $FFCE        ; Start of vector table
0000            4  KWIFH:    EQU    $27
0000            5  ROM:      EQU    $E000        ; Start of ROM
E000            6            ORG    ROM
                7  ;*************************************
                8  prog_start:
                9  ; This is the main program
               10  ; . . .
               11  ;*************************************
               12  KWHisr:
               13  ; This is the isr for Key wakeup H
               14  ; . . .
               15  ; Reset the key wakeup flags
E000 9627      16            ldaa   KWIFH
E002 5A27      17            staa   KWIFH
               18  ; Return to main program
E004 0B        19            rti
               20  ;*************************************
               21  ; Dummy isr for unused interrupts
               22  dummy_isr:
E005 0B        23            rti
               24  ;*************************************
               25  ; Initialize the HC12 vector table
FFCE           26            ORG    IVECT
               27  ; Make all but key wakeup H point to the dummy
FFCE E000      28            DW     KWHisr       ; Key wakeup H
FFD0 E005      29            DW     dummy_isr    ; Key wakeup J
FFD2 E005      30            DW     dummy_isr    ; A/D
FFD4 E005      31            DW     dummy_isr    ; SCI-1
FFD6 E005      32            DW     dummy_isr    ; SCI-0
FFD8 E005      33            DW     dummy_isr    ; SPI
FFDA E005      34            DW     dummy_isr    ; Pulse accum edge
FFDC E005      35            DW     dummy_isr    ; Pulse accum overflow
FFDE E005      36            DW     dummy_isr    ; Timer overflow
FFE0 E005      37            DW     dummy_isr    ; Timer Channel 7
FFE2 E005      38            DW     dummy_isr    ; Timer Channel 6
FFE4 E005      39            DW     dummy_isr    ; Timer Channel 5
FFE6 E005      40            DW     dummy_isr    ; Timer Channel 4
FFE8 E005      41            DW     dummy_isr    ; Timer Channel 3
FFEA E005      42            DW     dummy_isr    ; Timer Channel 2
FFEC E005      43            DW     dummy_isr    ; Timer Channel 1
FFEE E005      44            DW     dummy_isr    ; Timer Channel 0
FFF0 E005      45            DW     dummy_isr    ; Real time interrupt
```

EXAMPLE 8–9   Continued

```
FFF2  E005    46            DW      dummy_isr    ; IRQ or key wakeup D
FFF4  E005    47            DW      dummy_isr    ; XIRQ
FFF6  E005    48            DW      dummy_isr    ; SWI
FFF8  E005    49            DW      dummy_isr    ; Op Code trap
FFFA  E005    50            DW      dummy_isr    ; COP failure
FFFC  E005    51            DW      dummy_isr    ; Clock failure
              52  ; Initialize the RESET vector
FFFE  E000    53            DW      prog_start   ; RESET Vector
```

Example 8–10 Explanation

Example 8–10 is very similar to Example 8–8 except we see that the program is located in the EVB's RAM (at *line 38*) and that the D-Bug12 vector table is initialized in *lines 45–50*. We use the conditional assembly feature of the assembler in *lines 29–36* to define the correct addresses for the D-Bug12 Monitor version. In this case version 1 is in use (as defined by $SET Ver1 in *line 29*). If you wish to try this program on a system using D-Bug12 version 2.xxx, you simply use $SETNOT Ver1 and reassemble the program.

TABLE 8–9 D-Bug12 Monitor Interrupts

Number$_{10}$	MC68HC812A4 Interrupt (Ver 1.xxx)	MC68HC912B32 Interrupt (Ver 2.xxx)
7	Port H Key Wakeup	Reserved
8	Port J Key Wakeup	BDLC
9	Analog-to-Digital Converter	Analog-to-Digital Converter
10	Serial Communications Interface 1 (SC11)	Reserved
11	Serial Communications Interface 0 (SCI0)	Serial Communications Interface 0 (SCI0)
12	Serial Peripheral Interface 0 (SPI0)	Serial Peripheral Interface 0 (SPI0)
23	Timer Channel 0	Timer Channel 0
22	Timer Channel 1	Timer Channel 1
21	Timer Channel 2	Timer Channel 2
20	Timer Channel 3	Timer Channel 3
19	Timer Channel 4	Timer Channel 4
18	Timer Channel 5	Timer Channel 5
17	Timer Channel 6	Timer Channel 6
16	Timer Channel 7	Timer Channel 7
14	Pulse Accumulator Overflow	Pulse Accumulator Overflow
13	Pulse Accumulator Input Edge	Pulse Accumulator Input Edge
15	Timer Overflow	Timer Overflow
24	Real Time Interrupt	Real Time Interrupt
25	IRQ and Key Wakeup D	IRQ
26	XIRQ	XIRQ
27	Software Interrupt (SWI)	Software Interrupt (SWI)
28	Unimplemented Opcode Trap	Unimplemented Opcode Trap
−1	Return the starting address of the RAM vector table	Return the starting address of the RAM vector table

EXAMPLE 8–10   Interrupt Service Routine for the D-Bug12 Monitor

```
int12x2c.asm            Assembled with CASM 08/09/1998 00:27 PAGE 1
                 1  ; MC68HC12 Example
                 2  ;
                 3  ; This is a test program showing how to use
                 4  ; the key wakeup I/O interrupts in
                 5  ; a system with the D-Bug12 monitor.
                 6  ; The program does nothing but spin while
                 7  ; waiting for an interrupt.
                 8  ; Source File: INT12X2C.ASM
                 9  ; Author: F. M. Cady
                10  ; Created: 6/27/97
                11  ; Modifications: None
                12  ;
                13  ; Constant Equates
0000            14  MAX:      EQU    30         ; Number times to interrupt
0000            15  ALLBITS:  EQU    %11111111
0000            16  BIT0:     EQU    %00000001
0000            17  BIT1:     EQU    %00000010
0000            18  BELL:     EQU    $07        ; Bell character
                19  ; System Register Equates
0000            20  PORTH:    EQU    $24        ; Data register
0000            21  DDRH:     EQU    $25        ; Data direction
0000            22  KWIEH:    EQU    $26        ; Key wakeup interrupt enable
0000            23  KWIFH:    EQU    $27        ; Interrupt flags
                24  ; Memory Map Equates
0000            25  PROG:     EQU    $0800      ; PROG location
0000            26  DATA:     EQU    $0900      ; DATA location
0000            27  STACK:    EQU    $0A00
                28  ; D-Bug I/O Equates
0000            29  $SET      Ver1       ; D-Bug12 version
0000            30  $IF       Ver1
0000            31  SetVect:  EQU    $FE1A      ; D-Bug12 routine in Ver 1
0000            32  putchar:  EQU    $FE04      ; Putchar to terminal
0000            33  $ELSEIF
                34  SetVect:  EQU    $F69A      ; D-Bug12 routine in Ver 2
                35  putchar:  EQU    $F684      ; Putchar to terminal
0000            36  $ENDIF
0000            37  KWHNUM:   EQU    7          ; Number of key wakeup H
0800            38            ORG    PROG
                39  prog_start:
0800 CF0A00     40            lds    #STACK
                41  ; Initialize counter to zero
0803 790900     42            clr    count
                43  ; Set Port H bits 0 for key wakeup interrupt
0806 4D2501     44            bclr   DDRH,BIT0   ; Make the bits input
                45  ; Set up the D-Bug12 vector table
0809 CC0820     46            ldd    #KWisr
```

EXAMPLE 8–10   Continued

```
080C  3B          47                pshd
080D  CC0007      48                ldd     #KWHNUM
0810  15FBF606    49                jsr     [SetVect,PCR]
0814  3A          50                puld                    ; Clean up the stack
                  51    ; Clear any pending interrupts
0815  8601        52                ldaa    #BIT0
0817  5A27        53                staa    KWIFH
                  54    ; Enable key wakeup bits
0819  4C2601      55                bset    KWIEH,BIT0
                  56    ; Unmask the HC12 interrupts
081C  10EF        57                cli
                  58
                  59    ; DO Forever
081E  20FE        60    start:      bra     start
                  61    ; End DO forever
                  62
                  63    ; Key wakeup ISR
                  64    ; This ISR increments a count value on each
                  65    ; interrupt from key wakeup[0]. When it reaches a
                  66    ; maximum given by MAX, it rings the bell on the
                  67    ; terminal.
                  68
                  69    KWisr:
                  70    ; Increment the counter
0820  720900      71                inc     count
                  72    ; IF count = maximum
0823  B60900      73                ldaa    count
0826  8130        74                cmpa    #MAX
0828  2609        75                bne     endif
                  76    ; THEN Ring the bell
082A  C607        77                ldab    #BELL
082C  15FBF5D4    78                jsr     [putchar,PCR]
                  79    ; and reset the counter
0830  790900      80                clr     count
                  81    endif:
                  82    ; Clear the key wakeup flag
0833  8601        83                ldaa    #BIT0
0835  5A27        84                staa    KWIFH
                  85    ; And play it again Sam
0837  0B          86                rti     ; Return to main prog
                  87    ; Set up a count buffer
0900              88                ORG     DATA
0900  01          89    count:      DB      1
```

8.12 Conclusion and Chapter Summary Points

The M68HC12 has a variety of interrupting sources within the microcontroller itself and these systems will be covered in following chapters. Each interrupt source has its own vector with a limited, programmable hardware prioritization. To activate and use the interrupt system, the programmer must be sure to do the following:

- Initialize the stack pointer before unmasking interrupts.
- Initialize the user vector jump table if using a development environment such as the EVB evaluation board.
- Initialize the interrupt vector location(s) if not working in a development environment.
- Reset any interrupt-causing bits in the I/O devices to be used.
- Enable the I/O device's interrupt capability by setting the appropriate bit in a control register.
- Unmask global interrupts by clearing the I-bit in the condition code register.

The interrupt service routine is entered after the processor finishes the current instruction, pushes the registers and program counter onto the stack, and masks further interrupts. During the interrupt service routine, the programmer must do the following:

- Use global data for interprocess communications.
- Keep the interrupt service routine short.
- Reset any flags that caused the interrupts.
- Use the RTI instruction to return to the interrupted program.

8.13 Bibliography and Further Reading

Cady, F. M., *Microcontrollers and Microcomputers*, Oxford University Press, New York, 1997.

Cady, F. M., *Software and Hardware Engineering: Motorola M68HC11*, Oxford University Press, New York, 1997.

68HC12 CPU12 Reference Manual, CPU12RM/AD, Motorola, 1996.

Using The Callable Routines in D-Bug12, Motorola Semiconductor Application Note AN1280a/D, Motorola, 1997.

8.14 Problems

8.1   When the I bit in the condition code register is set to 1, interrupts are
a. enabled
b. disabled
c. The I bit does not affect interrupts

8.2   Interrupts are masked when you get to the interrupt service routine—true or false?

8.3   In the M68HC12 interrupt service routine, you MUST unmask interrupts with the CLI instruction before returning—true or false?

8.4   How are interrupts unmasked if the CLI instruction is not executed in the interrupt service routine?

8.5   How many bytes are pushed onto the stack when the M68HC12 processes an interrupt request?

8.6   Which instruction is used to globally unmask interrupts?

8.7   Which instruction is used to globally mask interrupts?

8.8   What address does the M68HC12 use to find the address of an interrupt service routine for a timer overflow?

8.9   Assume a dedicated application system (no D-Bug12 monitor) with ROM at $E000–$FFFF and RAM at $0800–$0BFF. Show how to initialize the interrupt vectors for the $\overline{IRQ}$ and Timer Channel 1 interrupts. Assume IRQISR and TC1ISR are labels on the respective interrupt service routines.

8.10   Repeat Problem 8.9 but assume your code is to be run on a system with a D-Bug12 monitor. Show the code that is necessary to vector the M68HC12 to the correct interrupt service routines.

8.11   For the interrupt service routine in Example 8–10, where would you put a breakpoint to find out if you are getting to the interrupt service routine?

8.12   Assume you have written a program similar to Example 8–10 in which the bell is to beep whenever you assert Port H, bit 0. When you run the program, instead of beeping once, the bell beeps continuously, much to the annoyance of your laboratory partners and supervisor. What has gone wrong?

8.13   Write a complete M68HC12 program in assembly language for an interrupt occurring on the external IRQ source. The interrupt vector is to be at $FFF2:FFF3. When the interrupt occurs, the ISR is to increment an 8-bit memory location "COUNT" starting from $00. The foreground job is to be a spin loop "SPIN BRASPIN". Assume
    a. The D-Bug12 monitor is *not* installed.
    b. Code is to be located in ROM at $E000.
    3. RAM is available between $0800 and $0BFF

8.14   What is the priority order of interrupts in the M68HC12?

8.15   How can the priority order of interrupts be changed?

8.16   The Timer Channel 3 interrupt and the Real Time Interrupt happen to occur simultaneously. Which is serviced first?

8.17   What is the SWI instruction and what does it do?

8.18   What instructions can be used to reduce power consumption when waiting for an interrupt to occur?

8.19   Define interrupt latency.

8.20   What are the components of interrupt latency?

8.21   Show how to modify the code in Example 8–4 to have the ISR service all interrupts generated by any of the four key wakeup bits.

Chapter 9

M68HC12 Memories

OBJECTIVES

This chapter describes the types of memories in the M68HC12. The amount and the memory maps differ for different versions of the processor, and memory map examples are given for the MC68HC812A4 and the MC68HC912B32. Examples showing how to program the EEPROM are given. We also discuss the memory expansion capability of the MC68HC812A4.

		Comparison of M68HC12 and M68HC11 Memory		
	M68HC12	Initial Location	**M68HC11**	Initial Location
RAM	1 Kbyte	$0800–$0BFF	256 to 1 Kbytes	$0000–$00FF
Registers	512	$0000–$01FF	64	$1000–$103F
ROM	None		Various, up to 12 Kbytes	
EEPROM	MC68HC812A4 4 Kbytes	$F000–$FFFF or $1000–$1FFF	512 bytes	$B600–$B7FF
	MC68HC912B32 768 bytes	$0D00–$0FFF		
Flash EEPROM	MC68HC912B32 32 Kybtes	$0000–$7FFF or $8000–$FFFF	None	
Mapping	RAM and registers mappable to any 2-Kbyte boundary; can be mapped at any time but only once in a program EEPROM can be mapped to any 4-Kbyte boundary		RAM and registers mappable to any 4-Kbyte boundary within 64 cycles after reset	

9.1 Introduction

The M68HC12 contains *RAM* and one or two types of *EEPROM*.

The M68HC12 includes on-chip static *RAM* for program variables and the stack and electrically erasable *EEPROM* memory for program code.[1] The amount of each depends on the family member.

9.2 M68HC12 Memory Map

In *expanded mode*, unused internal address space is mapped to the external address bus for memory and I/O expansion.

The amount of memory and its location in the memory map depend on the version of the chip chosen and on the mode of operation. The memory maps for an MC68HC812A4 are shown in Figure 9–1 and for an MC68HC912B32 in Figure 9–2. We can see that each version of the microcontroller has RAM, for use in registers and read/write memory, and ROM, for program and constant data storage. Table 9–1 compares the memory in the two microcontrollers.

MC68HC812A4 Memory

We see in the single-chip mode map in Figure 9–1 that the 512-byte control register block is initially located at $0000–$01FF and 1 Kbyte of RAM is at $0800–$0BFF. There are 4096 bytes (4 Kbytes) of EEPROM at $F000–$FFFF. These locations are the default established when the CPU is reset but they can be changed by programming the *INITRG*, *INITRM*, and *INITEE* registers as described in Section 9.3. In the expanded modes, the EEPROM is initially located at $1000–$1FFF, the registers and RAM remain the same, and any unused memory addresses are mapped to the external address bus. This allows external memory and I/O to be added. Chapter 14 will discuss the single-chip special mode used in background debugging.

MC68HC912B32 Memory

The MC68HC912B32 memory map is shown in Figure 9–2. The 512-byte control register block is initially located at $0000–$01FF. Like the MC68HC812A4, there is 1 Kbyte of RAM located at $0800–$0BFF. These register and RAM locations are the default when the CPU is reset but they can be changed by programming the *INITRG* and *INITRM* registers as described in Section 9.3. The ROM memory in the MC68HC912B32 is significantly different than the MC68HC812A4. There are only 768 bytes of EEPROM. These are initially located at $0D00–$0FFF and can be

---

[1] Chapter 9 in *Microcontrollers and Microcomputers: Principles of Software and Hardware Engineering* covers the basic principles of memory elements and the design of memory systems. Different types of memory and the timing of memory read and write operations are explained, and the interaction of memory with the CPU is covered.

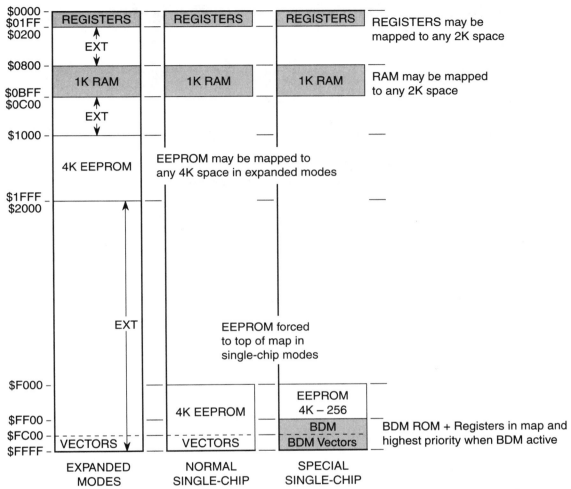

Figure 9-1 MC68HC812A4 memory maps. In expanded modes, any space not occupied by internal memory resources is available as external memory space.

remapped into any 4K address space by programming the *INITEE* register. EEPROM will normally be used in your programs to store nonvolatile variable data. To compensate for the lack of nonvolatile program storage, the MC68HC912B32 chip has a full 32 Kbytes of *Flash EEPROM*. In the single-chip mode, the Flash EEPROM is located in the upper half of memory, $8000–$FFFF. In the expanded modes, the Flash memory is disabled initially but can be located in either half of memory. If it is located in the lower half, memory accesses to the registers, RAM, and EEPROM take precedence over the Flash memory.

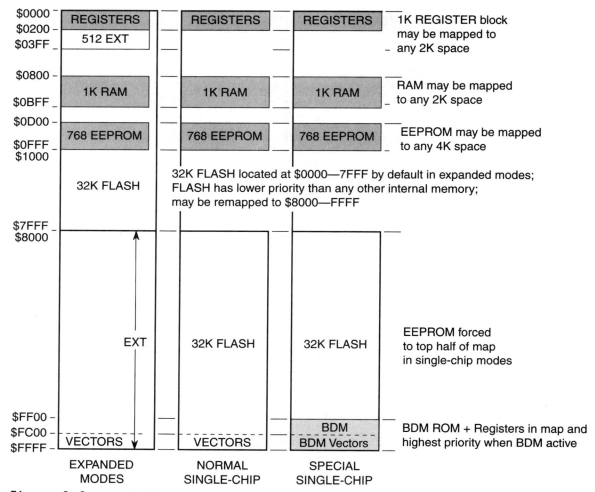

Figure 9-2   MC68HC912B32 memory maps. In expanded modes, any space not occupied by internal memory resources is available as external memory space. The 512 bytes following the REGISTERS is external space that has lower priority than the 32K internal flash.

9.3 M68HC12 RAM

Data RAM and the I/O register locations can be *remapped* (but only once) in your program.

The memory maps in Figures 9–1 and 9–2 show two sections of internal RAM in each microcontroller. The 512-byte register block is initially at address $0000. When the registers are located here, you can use direct addressing for faster access to data variables than extended addressing. Another 1K block of RAM is available in each processor for data and stack storage. At reset, this RAM is initially at $0800–$0BFF. The registers and RAM may be relocated on any 2-Kbyte boundary in the memory space by writing to

TABLE 9-1 Comparison of MC68HC821A4 and M68HC912B32 Memory

Memory	MC68HC821A4		MC68HC912B32	
	Single-Chip	Expanded	Single-Chip	Expanded
Registers	512 bytes; initially at $0000; mappable to any 2K space			
RAM	1 Kbyte; initially at $0800–$0BFF; mappable to any 2K space			
EEPROM	4 Kbyte; initially at $F000–$FFFF; mappable to any 4K space	4 Kbyte; initially at $1000–$1FFF; mappable to any 4K space	768 bytes; initially at $0D00–$0FFF; mappable to any 4K space	
Flash EEPROM	None	None	32 Kbytes; initially at $8000–$FFFF; mappable to $0000–$7FFF	32 Kbytes initially disabled can be mapped to $0000–$7FFF or $8000–$FFFF

the *Register* and *RAM Initial Position Registers (INITRG* and *INITRM)*. These registers can be written *once only* in your program. It is a good practice to do so during the initialization phase early in your program to avoid unintended modification later. The remapping takes place directly after the register modification has been written. To avoid any unintended operations, follow the remapping with an NOP instruction. See Example 9–1.

Either of these RAM areas could be remapped into an area occupied by internal ROM or by external memory. When addresses conflict like this, the M68HC12 resolves the conflict by giving the register block priority. Any conflicting ROM or external addresses are not accessed and no harmful conflicts occur. Table 9–2 shows the precedence of resource mapping.

INITRG—$0011—Initialization of Internal Register Position Register

Bit 7	6	5	4	3	2	1	Bit 0
REG15	REG14	REG13	REG12	REG11	0	0	MMSWAI

Reset 0   0   0   0   0   0   0   0

REG[15:11]
Internal register map position. These bits specify the upper 5 bits of the 16-bit address.

MMSWAI

Memory Mapping Interface Stop in Wait Control (MC68HC912B32 only). This bit controls access to the memory mapping interface when in Wait mode.
    0 = Memory mapping interface continues to function in Wait mode (default).
    1 = Memory mapping interface is shut down during Wait mode.

EXAMPLE 9–1   Remapping the RAM and I/O Register Locations

rammap1c.asm   Assembled with CASM 05/28/1998 21:09 PAGE 1

```
                  1  ; Code example to swap the RAM and
                  2  ; I/O register memory map locations
                  3  ;
0000              4  RAMLOC:    EQU    $0000     ; Locate RAM at $0000 and
0000              5  REGLOC:    EQU    $1000     ; I/O Regs at $1000
0000              6  ROMLOC:    EQU    $F000     ; Keep EEPROM at $F000
0000              7  INITRG:    EQU    $11       ; Initialize Register
0000              8  INITRM:    EQU    $10       ; Initialize RAM
0000              9  INITEE:    EQU    $12       ; Initialize EEPROM
F000             10             ORG    ROMLOC
                 11  ; . . .
                 12  ; Initialization of the machine state.
                 13  ; Remapping code can be executed only once.
                 14  ; First, program the EEPROM location so it doesn't
                 15  ; accidently change later.
F000 180BF000    16             movb   #{ROMLOC>8},INITEE   ; Fix EEPROM
     12
F005 A7          17             nop
                 18  ; Now move the internal RAM and registers
                 19  ; Do the RAM
F006 180B0000    20             movb   #{RAMLOC>8},INITRM
     10
F00B A7          21             nop
                 22  ; Do the registers
F00C 180B1000    23             movb   #{REGLOC>8},INITRG
     11
F011 A7          24             nop
                 25  ; . . .
```

INITRM—$0010—Initialization of Internal RAM Position Register

Bit 7	6	5	4	3	2	1	Bit 0
RAM15	RAM14	RAM13	RAM12	RAM11	0	0	0
Reset 0	0	0	0	1	0	0	0

RAM[15:11]
Internal RAM map position. These bits specify the upper 5 bits of the 16-bit address.

TABLE 9-2 Register, RAM and EEPROM Mapping

Precedence	Resource
1	Background Debugging Module ROM (if active; see Chapter 14)
2	Control register block
3	Internal 1 Kbyte RAM
4	Internal 4 Kbytes EEPROM in the MC68HC812A4 and 768 bytes in the MC68HC912B32
5	External memory

Explanation of Example 9–1

In addition to showing how to remap the registers, EEPROM and RAM by using the MOVB instruction, this example shows a useful assembler expression evaluation. Each position register, INITRG, INITRM, and INITEE, is 8 bits. *Lines 4–6* define the location of the RAM, registers, and EEPROM as 16-bit addresses, which is a good documentation technique. In *line 16* the assembler evaluates the immediate operand in MOVB #{ROMLOC>8},INITEE by *logical right shifting* the 16-bit ROMLOC value 8 bits. This becomes the 8-bit operand needed for the INITEE register. Motorola recommends that a NOP follow each instruction that remaps these registers and memory (*lines 17, 21, and 24*).

9.4 M68HC12 EEPROM

> The EEPROM can be programmed without an additional power supply because a charge pump has been included to develop the programming voltage.

The initial locations for the EEPROM in each microcontroller are given in Table 9–1. The location of the EEPROM can be remapped to any 4-Kbyte block, similar to the RAM remapping by writing to the *INITEE* register. See Example 9–1. The EEPROM can be disabled by clearing the EEON bit in the *INITEE* register.

When the EEPROM is enabled and located in memory according to the INITEE register, you may *read* it, *erase* it, or *program* it.

The EEPROM has a minimum program/erase life of 10,000 cycles over its complete operating temperature range.

INITEE—$0012—Initialization of Internal EEPROM Position Register

	Bit 7	6	5	4	3	2	1	Bit 0
Reset	EE15	EE14	EE13	EE12	0	0	0	EEON
Single-chip (A4)	1	1	1	1	0	0	0	1
Expanded (A4)	0	0	0	1	0	0	0	1
Both modes (B32)	0	0	0	0	0	0	0	1

EE[15:12]

Internal EEPROM map position. These bits specify the upper 4 bits of the 16-bit address.

EEON
Internal EEPROM enabled.
      0 = Remove (disable) the EEPROM from the memory map.
      1 = Place the EEPROM in the memory map at the address selected by EE15:EE12
         (default).

EEPROM Reading

To read the EEPROM, the EELAT bit in EEPROG must be zero. This is the default when the CPU is reset. When it is zero, the rest of the bits in EEPROG have no meaning, and EEPROM operates like ROM. The other bits in EEPROG are used to control the programming operation.

EEPROG—$00F3—EEPROM Control

Bit 7	6	5	4	3	2	1	Bit 0
BULKP	0	0	BYTE	ROW	ERASE	EELAT	EEPGM

Reset 1   0   0   0   0   0   0   0

BULKP

Bulk Erase Protection.
      0 = EEPROM can be bulk erased.
      1 = EEPROM protected from being bulk or row erased (default).
BULKP can be changed if EEPGM=0 and PROTLCK=0.

BYTE

Byte and Aligned Word Erase.
      0 = Bulk or row erase is enabled (default).
      1 = One byte or one aligned word erase only.
An aligned word is 16 bits with the most significant byte at an even and the least significant byte at an odd address. See Figure 9–4. BYTE can be written if EEPGM=0.

ROW

Row or Bulk Erase (if BYTE=0).
   0 = Erase entire EEPROM array (bulk erase) (default).
   1 = Erase only one 32-byte row.
ROW can be written if EEPGM=0.

ERASE

Erase Control.
   0 = EEPROM configured for programming (default).
   1 = EEPROM configured for erasing.
ERASE can be written if EEPGM=0.

EELAT

EEPROM Latch Control.
   0 = EEPROM configured for normal reading (default).
   1 = EEPROM address and data latches set up for programming or erasing.
EELAT can be written if EEPGM=0. BYTE, ROW, ERASE, and EELAT can be written simultaneously or in sequence.

EEPGM

Program and Erase Enable.
   0 = Disables program/erase voltage to EEPROM (default).
   1 = Applies program/erase voltage to EEPROM.
EEPGM can be set only if EELAT is previously set.

EEPROM Control

The EEPROM erasing and programming are controlled by three registers—*EEPROM Programming Register* (*EEPROG*), *EEPROM Module Configuration* (*EEMCR*), and *EEPROM Block Protect* (*EEPROT*). A fourth register, *EEPROM TEST* (*EETST*), is used for testing in special modes. The erased state of an EEPROM byte is $FF and bits are changed to zero during programming. If any bit in a byte needs to be changed from a zero to a one, the entire byte must be erased and then programmed. However, individual bits can be changed from a one to a zero without erasing the entire byte.

The main control register for programming is the EEPROG register. In it are bits to control both erasing and programming one or more EEPROM locations. In addition to these bits is *Block*

Protect Write Lock (PROTLCK) in the *EEMCR* register and the *EEPROM Block Protect (BPROT6:BPROT0)* bits in the *EEPROT* register.

PROTLCK must be zero to allow any of the EEPROT bits or the BULKP bit in the EEPROG register to be erased or written. The seven block protect bits in EEPROT divide the 4-Kbyte EEPROM into seven blocks. Each of these can be individually protected from being programmed or erased. Table 9–3 and Figure 9–3 show how you can use this to protect program code or other data stored in the EEPROM from accidently being erased or modified. This is especially important in single-chip mode for the MC68HC812A4 when the interrupt and reset vectors are stored in $FFC0–$FFFF. Protecting these locations by setting BPROT0=1 ensures that an unintentional bulk or row erase will not disturb these critical vectors.

PROTLCK is a *write-once* control bit and any changes from its reset state (zero) should be considered carefully. If you write PROTLCK to zero you can make changes to the block protect bits or BULKP later in your code but you cannot subsequently write PROTLCK to a one to keep block protect bits from changing. Conversely, if you write PROTLCK to one, the block protect and BULKP bits are frozen until the next reset when PROTLCK is reset.

EEMCR—$00F0—EEPROM Module Configuration

Bit 7	6	5	4	3	2	1	Bit 0
1	1	1	1	1	EESWAI	PROTLCK	EERC

Reset 1   1   1   1   1   1   0   0

EESWAI

(MC68HC912B32) EEPROM Stops in Wait Mode.
    0 = EEPROM is not affected during wait mode.
    1 = EEPROM is not clocked during wait mode.
This bit should be cleared if the wait mode vectors are mapped in the EEPROM array.

PROTLCK

Block Protect Write Lock.
    0 = Allow the block protect bits (BPROT[6:0] in EEPROT) and the bulk erase protection bit (BULKP in EEPROG) to be written (default).
    1 = Block protect bits are locked.
This bit can be written only once (to a zero or a one) in normal modes. In special modes it can be written at any time.

EERC
EEPROM Charge Pump Clock.
0 = System clock is used as clock source for the internal charge pump and the internal RC oscillator is stopped.
1 = Internal RC oscillator drives the charge pump. The RC oscillator is needed when the system clock is lower than f_{PROG}.

EEPROT—$00F1—EEPROM Block Protect Register

Bit 7	6	5	4	3	2	1	Bit 0
1	BPROT6	BPROT5	BPROT4	BPROT3	BPROT2	BPROT1	BPROT0

Reset 1   1   1   1   1   1   1   1

BPROT[6:0]
EEPROM Block Protect.
0 = Associated EEPROM block can be programmed and erased.
1 = Associated EEPROM block is protected from being programmed and erased (default).[2]
These bits protect the EEPROM blocks shown in Table 9–3 from accidental programming or erasing.

EEPROM Erasing

There are three ways to erase the EEPROM. You may *bulk erase* all the EEPROM memory, *row erase* 32 bytes (for example $1000–$101F, $1020–$103F, etc.), or *byte erase* a single byte or aligned word. The erased state of an EEPROM cell is $FF. Subroutines for each of these procedures are shown in Examples 9–2 to 9–4.

Explanation of Example 9–2

The bulk erase subroutine shown in Example 9–2 erases the entire EEPROM. First, the current values of the EEPROT and EEPROG registers are saved (on the stack and in the A register *lines 22–24*) to be restored at the end of the subroutine. The BPROT bits are cleared in *line 26*. In your

---

[2] The reset (default) state of each BPROT bit is 1, protecting the blocks from programming and erasing. In systems with the D-Bug12 Monitor you will find the bits are reset, allowing you to program the EEPROM without first changing them.

TABLE 9-3 EEPROM Block Protection

Bit	MC68HC812A4 Block Protected		Block Size	MC68HC912B32 Block Protected Both Modes	Block Size
	Expanded Mode	**Single-Chip Mode**			
BPROT6	$1000–$17FF	$F000–$F7FF	2 Kbytes		
BPROT5	$1800–$1BFF	$F800–$FBFF	1 Kbyte		
BPROT4	$1C00–$1DFF	$FC00–$FDFF	512 bytes	$0D00–$0DFF	256 bytes
BPROT3	$1E00–$1EFF	$FE00–$FEFF	256 bytes	$0E00–$0EFF	256 bytes
BPROT2	$1F00–$1F7F	$FF00–$FF7F	128 bytes	$0F00–$0F7F	128 bytes
BPROT1	$1F80–$1FBF	$FF80–$FFBF	64 bytes	$0F80–$0FBF	64 bytes
BPROT0	$1FC0–$1FFF	$FFC0–$FFFF	64 bytes	$0FC0–$0FFF	64 bytes

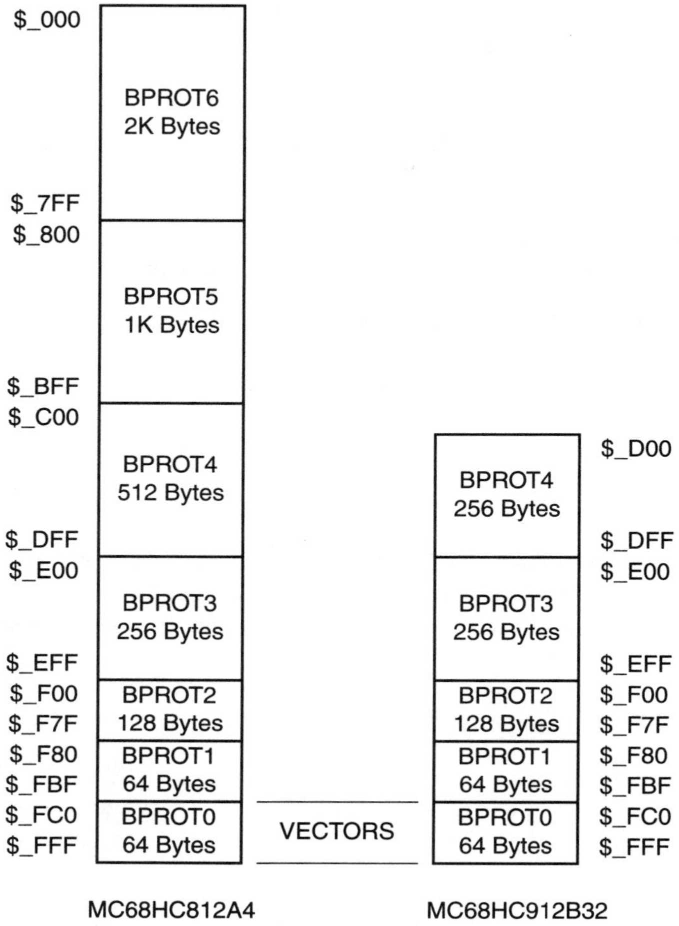

Figure 9-3 EEPROM block protection.

EXAMPLE 9–2 Bulk Erasing the EEPROM

```
eebulk1c.asm        Assembled with CASM 12/09/1998 03:24 PAGE 1

                 1  ; EEPROM bulk erase subroutine
                 2  ; Entry:   Assume:EEPROM is in normal reading mode
                 3  ;                  PROTLCK=0, EELAT=0, EEPGM=0
                 4  ; Exit:    Nothing
                 5  ; Registers Modified: CCR
0000             6  BULKP:    EQU    %10000000        ; BULKP bit
0000             7  BYTEB:    EQU    %00010000        ; BYTE bit
0000             8  ROW:      EQU    %00001000        ; ROW bit
0000             9  ERASE:    EQU    %00000100        ; ERASE bit
0000            10  EELAT:    EQU    %00000010        ; EELAT Bit
0000            11  EEPGM:    EQU    %00000001        ; EEPGM bit
0000            12  LOC4K:    EQU    %01111111        ; All 4K locations
0000            13  REGLOC:   EQU    $0
0000            14  EEPROT:   EQU    REGLOC+$F1       ; EEPROT register
0000            15  EEPROG:   EQU    REGLOC+$F3       ; EEPROG register loc
0000            16  EEPROM:   EQU    $1000            ; EEPROM location
0000            17  tERASE:   EQU    !10              ; msec for tERASE
                18
                19  ee_bulk_erase:
0000 3B         20            pshd                 ; Save the A & B regs
                21  ; Get and save the current values of EEPROT and EEPROG
0001 96F1       22            ldaa     EEPROT
0003 36         23            psha                 ; Save on the stack
0004 96F3       24            ldaa     EEPROG    ; Save it in A register
                25  ; Allow all 4K locations to be erased
0006 4DF17F     26            bclr     EEPROT,LOC4K
                27  ; Assume EEPGM=0, otherwise you need to clear it here
                28  ; Clear BULKP, ROW, BYTE
0009 4DF398     29            bclr     EEPROG,BULKP|BYTEB|ROW
                30  ; Set ERASE and EELAT
000C 4CF306     31            bset     EEPROG,ERASE|EELAT
                32  ; Write any data to any EEPROM location to set the
                33  ; address latch properly
000F 7A1000     34            staa     EEPROM        ; Just dummy data
0012 4CF301     35            bset     EEPROG,EEPGM  ; Turn on high voltage
0015 C60A       36            ldab     #tERASE
0017 160027     37            jsr      DlyNms        ; Delay tERASE msec
001A 4DF301     38            bclr     EEPROG,EEPGM  ; Turn off prog voltage
                39  ; Reset EELAT
001D 4DF302     40            bclr     EEPROG,EELAT
                41  ; Return the EEPROT and EEPROG registers to original
0020 5AF3       42            staa     EEPROG
0022 32         43            pula
0023 5AF1       44            staa     EEPROT
0025 3A         45            puld                 ; Restore A & B reg
```

EXAMPLE 9–2   Continued

```
0026 3D           46              rts
                  47
                  48  ; Delay N milliseconds
                  49  ; Entry: B register with the number of milliseconds
                  50  ; Uses: Timer Output Compare Channel 6
                  51  ; Exit: Nothing
                  52  ; Registers Modified: None
                  53  ; Constant Equates
0027              54  ONE_MS:     EQU     !8000      ; Clocks per msec
                  55  ; I/O Register Equates
0027              56  TIOS:       EQU     $80        ; Input Capt/Out Compare Select
0027              57  TSCR:       EQU     $86        ; Timer System Control
0027              58  TCNT:       EQU     $84        ; TCNT register
0027              59  TFLG1:      EQU     $8E        ; TFLG1 register
0027              60  TC6:        EQU     $9C        ; Timer channel 6
0027              61  C6F:        EQU     %01000000  ; Output compare 6 Flag
0027              62  TEN:        EQU     %10000000  ; Timer Enable
                  63
                  64  DlyNms:
0027 3B           65              pshd
                  66  ; Enable the timer hardware
0028 4C8680       67              bset    TSCR,TEN
                  68  ; Enable Output Compare Channel 6
002B 4C8040       69              bset    TIOS,C6F
                  70  ; Grab the value of the TCNT register
002E DC84         71              ldd     TCNT
                  72  ; Set up the channel for 1 msec
0030 C31F40       73              addd    #ONE_MS
0033 5C9C         74              std     TC6
                  75  ; Now reset the flag and wait until it is set
0035 8640         76              ldaa    #C6F
0037 5A8E         77              staa    TFLG1
                  78  ; Wait until the flag is set
0039 4F8E40FC     79  spin:       brclr   TFLG1,C6F,spin
                  80  ; Now reset the flag
003D 8640         81              ldaa    #C6F
003F 5A8E         82              staa    TFLG1
0041 DC9C         83              ldd     TC6
0043 C31F40       84              addd    #ONE_MS
0046 5C9C         85              std     TC6
0048 3A           86              puld                    ; Get the counter back
                  87  ; WHILE the msec counter is not 0
0049 53           88              decb
004A 3B           89              pshd                    ; Save the counter
004B 26EC         90              bne     spin
004D 3A           91              puld                    ; Restore regs
004E 3D           92              rts
```

eerow1c.asm   Assembled with CASM 05/28/1998 21:59 PAGE 1

```
                 1  ; EEPROM row erase subroutine
                 2  ; Entry: x = Row address to be erased
                 3  ; Assume:  EEPROM is in normal reading mode
                 4  ;          PROTLCK=0, EELAT=0, EEPGM=0
                 5  ; Exit:    Nothing
                 6  ; Registers Modified: CCR
0000             7  BULKP:      EQU     %10000000     ; BULKP bit
0000             8  BYTEB:      EQU     %00010000     ; BYTE bit
0000             9  ROW:        EQU     %00001000     ; ROW bit
0000            10  ERASE:      EQU     %00000100     ; ERASE bit
0000            11  EELAT:      EQU     %00000010     ; EELAT Bit
0000            12  EEPGM:      EQU     %00000001     ; EEPGM bit
0000            13  LOC4K:      EQU     %01111111     ; All 4K locations
0000            14  REGLOC:     EQU     $0
0000            15  EEPROT:     EQU     REGLOC+$F1    ; EEPROT register
0000            16  EEPROG:     EQU     REGLOC+$F3    ; EEPROG register loc
0000            17  tERASE:     EQU     !10           ; msec delay for tERASE
                18
0000 3B         19  ee_row_erase:       pshd          ; Save the A & B regs
                20  ; Get and save the current values of EEPROT and EEPROG
0001 96F1       21              ldaa    EEPROT
0003 36         22              psha                  ; Save on the stack
0004 96F3       23              ldaa    EEPROG        ; Save in A reg
                24  ; Allow any row in the 4K locations to be erased
0006 4DF17F     25              bclr    EEPROT,LOC4K
                26  ; Assume EEPGM=0, otherwise you need to clear it here
                27  ; Clear BULKP, BYTE
0009 4DF390     28              bclr    EEPROG,BULKP|BYTEB
                29  ; Set ROW, ERASE, EELAT
000C 4CF30E     30              bset    EEPROG,ROW|ERASE|EELAT
                31  ; Erase a row
000F 6A00       32              staa    0,X           ; Set adr latch
0011 4CF301     33              bset    EEPROG,EEPGM  ; Turn on high voltage
0014 C60A       34              ldab    #tERASE
0016 160026     35              jsr     DlyNms        ; Delay tERASE
0019 4DF301     36              bclr    EEPROG,EEPGM  ; Turn off prog voltage
                37  ; Reset EELAT
001C 4DF302     38              bclr    EEPROG,EELAT
                39  ; Return the EEPROT and EEPROG registers to original
001F 5AF3       40              staa    EEPROG
0021 32         41              pula
0022 5AF1       42              staa    EEPROT
0024 3A         43              puld                  ; Restore regs
0025 3D         44              rts
                45  DlyNms:
                46  ; See the bulk erase example for the delay code.
0026 3D         47              rts
```

EXAMPLE 9–4   EEPROM Byte Erase

eebyte1c.asm   Assembled with CASM 05/28/1998 22:13 PAGE 1

```
                    1  ; EEPROM byte erase subroutine
                    2  ; Entry: X = address to erase
                    3  ;        Assume:  EEPROM is in normal reading mode
                    4  ;                 PROTLCK=0, EELAT=0, EEPGM=0
                    5  ; Exit: C=0 if byte erased OK, C=1 if not
                    6  ; Registers Modified: CCR
0000                7  BY_B:      EQU      %00010000    ; BYTE bit
0000                8  ROW:       EQU      %00001000    ; ROW bit
0000                9  ERASE:     EQU      %00000100    ; ERASE bit
0000               10  EELAT:     EQU      %00000010    ; EELAT Bit
0000               11  EEPGM:     EQU      %00000001    ; EEPGM bit
0000               12  ERASED:    EQU      %11111111    ; Erased state
0000               13  LOC4K:     EQU      %01111111    ; All 4K locations
0000               14  REGLOC:    EQU      $0
0000               15  EEPROT:    EQU      REGLOC+$F1   ; EEPROT register
0000               16  EEPROG:    EQU      REGLOC+$F3   ; EEPROG register loc
0000               17  tERASE:    EQU      !10          ; ms delay for tERASE
                   18
                   19  ee_byte_erase:
0000 3B            20          pshd                ; Save the regs
                   21  ; Get and save the current values of EEPROT and EEPROG
0001 96F1          22          ldaa     EEPROT
0003 36            23          psha                ; Save on stack
0004 96F3          24          ldaa     EEPROG  ; Save in A reg
                   25  ; Allow any byte in the 4K locations to be erased
0006 4DF17F        26          bclr     EEPROT,LOC4K
                   27  ; Assume EEPGM=0, otherwise you need to clear it here
                   28  ; Set BYTE, ERASE, and EELAT
0009 4CF316        29          bset     EEPROG,BY_B|ERASE|EELAT
000C 6A00          30          staa     0,x         ; Set adr latch to byte
000E 4CF301        31          bset     EEPROG,EEPGM ; Turn on high voltage
0011 C60A          32          ldab     #tERASE
0013 16002F        33          jsr      DlyNms      ; Delay tERASE msec
0016 4DF301        34          bclr     EEPROG,EEPGM ; Turn off prog voltage
0019 4DF302        35          bclr     EEPROG,EELAT ; Reset EELAT
                   36  ; Return the EERC, BPROT and EEPROG bits to orig values
001C 5AF3          37          staa     EEPROG
001E 32            38          pula
001F 5AF1          39          staa     EEPROT
                   40  ; Check to see if the location was erased
                   41  ; IF the memory location is erased
0021 A600          42          ldaa     0,x
0023 81FF          43          cmpa     #ERASED
0025 2604          44          bne      error
                   45  ; THEN return with carry clear
```

EXAMPLE 9–4   Continued

```
0027  10FE    46              clc
0029  2002    47              bra     endif
              48  ; ELSE return with carry set
002B  1401    49  error:      sec
002D  3A      50  endif:      puld                ; Restore regs
002E  3D      51              rts
              52  ;
              53  DlyNms:
              54  ; See the bulk erase example for the delay code.
002F  3D      55              rts
```

program you may wish to unprotect only some of these EEPROM blocks. At *line 27* we assume the EEPGM bit in EEPROG is cleared. This bit must be zero to allow the other bits in EEPROG to be written. The BYTE, ROW, and BULKP bits are cleared in *line 29* and the ERASE and EELAT bits are set (*line 31*). This enables the bulk erase and sets up the EEPROM for erasing. This process is started in *line 34* by writing any data to any EEPROM location. This arms the latches associated with the EEPROM. The programming voltage is then turned on in *line 35* and a delay of t_{ERASE} (nominally 10 msec, see Table 9–5) is entered. After this delay the program voltage is turned off (*line 38*), EELAT is returned to its normal setting (*line 40*), and the EEPROG and EEPROT registers are restored.

Lines 48–92 show a delay subroutine using the timer output compare. This subroutine is entered with the B register containing the number of milliseconds of delay needed. We will discuss the operation of the timer in detail in Chapter 10.

Example 9–2 shows a trick that makes your program more portable for systems that may remap the register locations as described in Example 9–1. *Line 13* defines the 16-bit memory location where the registers are located and *lines 14–15* identify the locations of the EEPROM registers *relative* to this. If you choose to remap the register locations as shown in Example 9–1, the new value of REGLOC will automatically be added to define the correct locations of the registers when you assemble this program.

Explanation of Example 9–3

The row erase in Example 9–3 erases just one 32-byte "row" of the EEPROM and is similar to the bulk erase subroutine in Example 9–2 except that the ROW bit is set in *line 30* instead of cleared.

Explanation of Example 9–4

The byte erase procedure is similar to row erase except that the BYTE bit is set instead of cleared in *line 29*. Note that we have added a section of code (*lines 40–50*) to verify if the EEPROM location has been erased properly. If it has, the carry bit is returned reset (0); if any error has occurred and the byte has not been erased, the carry is set. The program that calls this subroutine will have to handle any error conditions.

EEPROM Programming

As discussed in *Microcontrollers and Microcomputers: Principles of Software and Hardware Engineering*, a significant advantage of EEPROM over EPROM is that it can be programmed when it is in the circuit. Before programming a location in EEPROM, check to see if it can be programmed (all bits in their erased state—$FF). If not, you must first erase it. Programming is similar to erasing in that the control register bits are set in the proper sequence and then a programming voltage is applied. After a delay, the programming voltage is turned off. Well-designed software should then check that the EEPROM location has been programmed correctly and take some action if it has not.

EEPROM Programming Voltage

A high voltage (higher than the normal 5-V operating voltage) is required to program and erase EEPROM memory. For the M68HC12, a 19-V programming voltage must be supplied. The Motorola designers have added a charge pump circuit to generate this voltage on the chip without the need of an external source. The system clock is used as an oscillator to pump V_{DD} up to the 19 V required by the EEPROM. If the system clock frequency is less than f_{PROG},[3] an internal RC oscillator must be turned on by setting EERC = 1 (bit 0 in the EEMCR register).

EEPROM Programming Software

Table 9–4 shows the various EEPROM control bit combinations for reading, erasing, and programming. The sequence in which these bits are set or reset is important, and a program or erase operation should follow these steps:

1. Ensure PROTLCK = 0 to allow the block protect bits and BULKP to be written, or make sure block protect bits and BULKP are already in the desired states.

2. Reset block protect bits BPROT6:BPROT0 so that the address to be erased or programmed is not protected.

TABLE 9–4			**EEPROM Programming Control Bits**			
BULKP	**BYTE**	**ROW**	**ERASE**	**EELAT**	**EEPGM**[a]	**Programming**
1	x	x	x	x	x	Cannot be bulk or row erased
x	x	x	x	x	0	Erase/programming voltage is not applied
x	x	x	x	0	0	Normal reading
x	x	x	0	1	1	Set up for programming
0	0	0	1	1	1	Bulk erase
0	0	1	1	1	1	32-byte row erase
x	1	x	1	1	1	Byte or aligned word erase

[a]*EEPGM must be written to 1 after EELAT is already 1.*

---

[3] f_{PROG} is the minimum bus frequency required to drive the EEPROM charge pump and t_{ERASE} is the time delay required to erase the EEPROM. These are nominally 1 MHz and 10 msec, but may change in different versions of the M68HC12 CPUs. See Table 9–5.

EXAMPLE 9–5   EEPROM Program Example

eeprog1c.asm   Assembled with CASM 05/30/1998 16:29 PAGE 1

```
                    1  ; EEPROM programming subroutine
                    2  ; Entry: A = data, X = address
                    3  ; Assume: EEPROM is in normal reading mode
                    4  ;          PROTLCK=1, ERASE=0, EELAT=0, EEPGM=0
                    5  ; Exit: Nothing
                    6  ; Registers Modified: CCR
                    7  ;                    EEPROG: BYTE and ROW cleared
0000                8  EELAT:    EQU    %00000010   ; EELAT Bit
0000                9  EEPGM:    EQU    %00000001   ; EEPGM bit
0000               10  LOC4K:    EQU    %01111111   ; All 4K locations
0000               11  REGLOC:   EQU    $0
0000               12  EEPROT:   EQU    REGLOC+$F1  ; EEPROT register
0000               13  EEPROG:   EQU    REGLOC+$F3  ; EEPROG register loc
0000               14  tPROG:    EQU    !10         ; Delay for programming
                   15
                   16  ee_prog:
0000 37            17            pshb               ; Save the B reg
                   18  ; Get and save the current values of EEPROT, and EEPROG
0001 D6F1          19            ldab   EEPROT
0003 37            20            pshb
0004 D6F3          21            ldab   EEPROG
0006 37            22            pshb
                   23  ; Allow any byte in the 4K locations to be programmed
0007 4DF17F        24            bclr   EEPROT,LOC4K
                   25  ; Assume EEPGM and ERASE = 0, otherwise you
                   26  ; need to clear them
000A 4CF302        27            bset   EEPROG,EELAT ; EELAT=1
000D 6A00          28            staa   0,x          ; Store data
000F 4CF301        29            bset   EEPROG,EEPGM ; Turn on prog voltage
0012 C60A          30            ldab   #tPROG
0014 160025        31            jsr    DlyNms       ; Delay tPROG msec
0017 4DF301        32            bclr   EEPROG,EEPGM ; Turn off prog voltage
001A 4DF302        33            bclr   EEPROG,EELAT ; Reset EELAT
                   34  ; Return EEPROT and EEPROG to original values
001D 33            35            pulb
001E 5BF3          36            stab   EEPROG
0020 33            37            pulb
0021 5BF1          38            stab   EEPROT
0023 33            39            pulb                ; Restore B reg
0024 3D            40            rts
                   41  ;
                   42  DlyNms:
                   43  ; See the bulk erase example for the delay code.
0025 3D            44            rts
```

3. Ensure EEPGM = 0. BULKP, BYTE, ROW, ERASE, and EELAT cannot be changed when EEPGM = 1.

4. Write BULKP, BYTE, ROW, and ERASE to the desired values.

5. Set EELAT = 1.

6. Write data to the address in EEPROM. This loads the EEPROM address and data latches with the data to be programmed. This has to be done even when you are bulk erasing.

7. Set EEPGM = 1. EEPGM must be set *after* EELAT is set.

8. Wait for the programming (t_{PROG}) or erase (t_{ERASE}) delay time.

9. Clear EEPGM to zero to turn off the programming voltage.

10. Return BYTE, ROW, and ERASE to the reset state (cleared).

11. Set the block protect bits back to one if block protection is needed.

12. Clear EELAT to zero to return to reading mode.

A subroutine to program a single EEPROM location is shown in Example 9–5.

Explanation of Example 9–5

This subroutine, like the preceding examples, saves and restores the EEPROT and EEPROG registers. You may choose to eliminate these steps if there are no other places in your program that control the EEPROM. Setting the EELAT bit (*line 27*) enables the data to be latched for the EEPROM (*line 28*). After this is done, the program bit, EEPGM, is set to one (*line 29*) to enable the high programming voltage and a delay routine is entered for t_{PROG} msec. After returning from the delay, EEPGM (*line 32*) is cleared before the EELAT bit (*line 33*) is reset to return the EEPROM to read mode.

Programming EEPROM from EEPROM

You *cannot* program EEPROM if your programming code is in EEPROM.

When EELAT is set, the entire EEPROM is *not available for reading*. This means that any programs residing in the EEPROM cannot be executed when trying to program any unused EEPROM locations. This is a problem especially when operating in single-chip mode where your program and any interrupt vectors are in EEPROM. If this is the case, you should turn interrupts off, and any timing or serial communications must be done with polling during programming. A solution to this problem can be engineered by moving the code that needs to be executed while EELAT = 1 to RAM memory where it can be executed safely. See Example 9–6.

Explanation of Example 9–6

The programming code in this example is the same as that shown in Example 9–5 except that the code for the t_{PROG} delay is "in-line" instead of a subroutine that is called. The critical code be-

EXAMPLE 9–6   Transferring EEPROM Programming Code to RAM

eprog3c.asm   Assembled with CASM 12/09/1998 03:28 PAGE 1

```
                 1  ; EEPROM programming subroutine with EEPROM programming
                 2  ; portion moved to RAM
                 3  ; Entry: A = data, X = address
                 4  ; Assume:  EEPROM is in normal reading mode
                 5  ;          PROTLCK=0, ERASE=0, EELAT=0, EEPGM=0
                 6  ; Exit: Nothing
                 7  ; Registers Modified: CCR, EEPROG: BYTE and ROW cleared
0000             8  EELAT:    EQU    %00000010   ; EELAT Bit
0000             9  EEPGM:    EQU    %00000001   ; EEPGM bit
0000            10  LOC4K:    EQU    %01111111   ; All 4K locations
0000            11  REGLOC:   EQU    $0
0000            12  EEPROT:   EQU    REGLOC+$F1  ; EEPROT register
0000            13  EEPROG:   EQU    REGLOC+$F3  ; EEPROG register loc
0000            14  tPROG:    EQU    !10         ; msec delay for prog
                15  ; Constant and I/O Equates for the timer delay
0000            16  ONE_MS:   EQU    !8000    ; Clocks per msec
0000            17  TIOS:     EQU    $80      ; Input Cap/Out Compare Select
0000            18  TSCR:     EQU    $86      ; Timer System Control
0000            19  TCNT:     EQU    $84      ; TCNT register
0000            20  TFLG1:    EQU    $8E      ; TFLG1 register
0000            21  TC6:      EQU    $9C      ; Timer channel 6
0000            22  C6F:      EQU    %01000000 ; Output compare 6 Flag
0000            23  TEN:      EQU    %10000000 ; Timer Enable
                24
0000 3B         25  ee_prog:  pshd                    ; Save the regs
0001 35         26            pshy
0002 34         27            pshx
                28  ; Get and save the current values of EEPROT and EEPROG
0003 D6F1       29            ldab   EEPROT
0005 37         30            pshb
0006 D6F3       31            ldab   EEPROG
0008 37         32            pshb
                33  ; Allow any byte in the 4K locations to be programmed
0009 4DF17F     34            bclr   EEPROT,LOC4K
                35  ; Assume EEPGM and ERASE = 0, otherwise
                36  ; you need to clear them
                37  ; Transfer the code bytes to RAM to execute them
000C CE0023     38            ldx    #ram_code   ; Source address
000F CD0065     39            ldy    #ram_prog   ; Destination address
                40  ; DO transfer the bytes
0012 180A3070   41  loop:     movb   1,x+,1,y+
                42  ; WHILE X < rom_code address
0016 8E005B     43            cpx    #rom_code
0019 26F7       44            bne    loop
                45  ; ENDDO
```

EXAMPLE 9–6   Continued

```
001B EE82      46          ldx    2,sp      ; Restore the EEPROM address
               47 ; Now do the EEPROM programming code in RAM
001D 160065    48          jsr    ram_prog
               49 ; Jump over the programming code to complete the program
0020 06005B    50          jmp    rom_code
               51 ; ******************
               52 ; The following code is transferred to the RAM and
               53 ; treated as a subroutine
               54 ram_code:
0023 4CF302    55          bset   EEPROG,EELAT  ; EELAT=1
0026 6A00      56          staa   0,x           ; Store data
0028 4CF301    57          bset   EEPROG,EEPGM  ; Turn on prog voltage
               58 ; Use the timer for a tPROG delay
               59 ; Enable the timer hardware
002B 4C8680    60          bset   TSCR,TEN
               61 ; Grab the value of the TCNT register
002E DC84      62          ldd    TCNT
               63 ; Enable Output Compare Channel 6
0030 4C8040    64          bset   TIOS,C6F
               65 ; Set up the channel for 1 msec
0033 C31F40    66          addd   #ONE_MS
0036 5C9C      67          std    TC6
               68 ; Now reset the flag and wait until it is set
0038 8640      69          ldaa   #C6F
003A 5A8E      70          staa   TFLG1
003C C60A      71          ldab   #tPROG        ; Number of msec to delay
003E 37        72          pshb                 ; Need to save it
               73 ; DO wait until the timer flag is set
003F 4F8E40FC  74 spin:    brclr  TFLG1,C6F,spin
               75 ; Now reset the flag
0043 8640      76          ldaa   #C6F
0045 5A8E      77          staa   TFLG1
0047 DC9C      78          ldd    TC6
0049 C31F40    79          addd   #ONE_MS
004C 5C9C      80          std    TC6
               81 ; WHILE the msec counter is not 0
004E 33        82          pulb                 ; Retrieve the counter
004F 53        83          decb
0050 37        84          pshb
0051 26EC      85          bne    spin
0053 33        86          pulb                 ; Clean up stack ptr
               87 ; Now the delay is done
0054 4DF301    88          bclr   EEPROG,EEPGM  ; Turn off prog voltage
0057 4DF302    89          bclr   EEPROG,EELAT  ; Reset EELAT
005A 3D        90          rts
               91 ; ******************
               92 rom_code:
               93 ; Restore the EEPROG and EEPROT registers
```

EXAMPLE 9–6   Continued

```
005B 33        94              pulb
005C 5BF3      95              stab    EEPROG
005E 33        96              pulb
005F 5BF1      97              stab    EEPROT
0061 30        98              pulx                    ; Restore the regs
0062 31        99              puly
0063 3A        100             puld
0064 3D        101             rts
               102
               103  ; The following memory buffer must be located in RAM
               104  ram_prog:
               105  ; Reserve enough bytes to store the program
0065           106             DS      {rom_code-ram_code+1}
```

tween *line 55* and *line 90* is transferred to a RAM area by the code in *lines 41–46*. Enough storage for the program in RAM is allocated at *line 106*. An assembler expression is evaluated to automatically set aside the correct storage.

EEPROM Warnings and Cautions

Byte and Word Alignment

The EEPROM is organized as a 16-bit memory as shown in Figure 9–4. The EEPROM can be read as either bytes, aligned words, or misaligned words. Aligned words are 16 bits with the most significant byte at an even address. A misaligned word will be 16 bits with the most significant byte at an odd address. See Example 9–7.

Programming must be done as either byte or aligned words. Erasing must be either byte, aligned word, row, or bulk modes. When programming or erasing, a byte or aligned word operation will be done depending on the size of the data written to the EEPROM. If you attempt to program a misaligned word, only the lower byte will be latched and programmed. Example 9–8 shows how to check that a programming address is word aligned and to program a word aligned 16-bit location.

Explanation of Example 9–8

Compare *line 43* in this example with *line 28* in Example 9–5. Here, a word is written by the STD 0,X instruction. Additional code in Example 9–8 protects against ill-advised attempts to write to a misaligned word. For aligned words, the address must be an even number. The code in *lines 24–28*

High Byte	Low Byte
$1000	$1001
$1002	$1003
$1004	$1005

F i g u r e   9 – 4   16-bit EEPROM byte alignment.

EXAMPLE 9–7   Reading Aligned and Misaligned Words

Using the EEPROM locations given in Figure 9–4, give examples of instructions that do
(1) byte, (2) aligned word, and (3) misaligned word read operations.

Solution

(1) Byte
```
    ldaa    $1000    ; ($1000) → A
    ldaa    $1001    ; ($1001) → A
```
(2) Aligned word
```
    ldd     $1000    ; ($1000) → A, ($1001) → B
    ldd     $1002    ; ($1002) → A, ($1003) → B
```
(3) Misaligned word
```
    ldd     $1001    ; ($1001) → A, ($1002) → B
```

---

checks to see if the address in the X register is even or odd. If it is odd, an error has occurred and
the subroutine returns with the carry bit set. An even address can be programmed successfully and
the routine returns with the carry bit clear. The calling program can take some action based on the
carry bit to recover from the error.

EEPROM Programming When in Wait and Stop Modes

In Chapter 4 we described the WAI and STOP instructions. These are designed to reduce power
consumption by shutting the CPU down when waiting for an interrupt to occur. When in the
WAIT mode (a WAI instruction has been executed), EEPROM programming can continue.

If the STOP mode is entered, programming or erasing is stopped. When an interrupt occurs
and the CPU exits from the stopped state, programming is automatically turned back on. Motorola
engineers recommend that you do not do this. You should complete the programming cycle before
entering stop mode.

EEPROM Test Register

The EETST register can be used in the special operating modes (special single-chip, special expanded-narrow and expanded-wide, and special peripheral).

EETST—$00F2—EEPROM Test

Bit 7	6	5	4	3	2	1	Bit 0
EEODD	EEVEN	MARG	EECPD	EECPRD	0	EECPM	0
Reset 0	0	0	0	0	0	0	0

EEODD

Odd Row Programming.
  0 = Odd row bulk programming/erasing is disabled (default).
  1 = Bulk program/erase all odd rows.

EEVEN

Even Row Programming.
  0 = Even row bulk programming/erasing is disabled (default).
  1 = Bulk program/erase all even rows.

MARG

Program and Erase Voltage Margin Test Enable.
  0 = Normal operation (default).
  1 = Program and erase margin test.

EECPD

Charge Pump Disable.
  0 = Charge pump is on during program/erase (default).
  1 = Disable charge pump.

EECPRD

Charge Pump Ramp Disable.
  0 = Charge pump is turned on progressively during program/erase (default).
  1 = Disable charge pump controlled ramp up.

EECPM

Charge Pump Monitor Enable.
  0 = Normal output (default).
  1 = Output the charge pump voltage on the $\overline{\text{IRQ}}/V_{\text{PP}}$ pin.

EEPROM Programming Characteristics

The timing characteristics for the M68HC12 EEPROM are given in Table 9–5. The minimum clock frequency, f_{PROG}, must be maintained to allow the charge pump to operate correctly. If the system clock is less than this, the EEPROM module's RC oscillator must be enabled by setting the

---

EXAMPLE 9–8   Word-Aligned EEPROM Programming

```
eeprog2c.asm              Assembled with CASM  05/30/1998  17:31  PAGE 1
                    1  ; EEPROM programming aligned word subroutine
                    2  ; Entry: D = data, X = address
                    3  ;    Assume:  EEPROM is in normal reading mode
                    4  ;             PROTLCK=0, ERASE=0, EELAT=0, EEPGM=0
                    5  ; Exit:    Carry=1 if error, otherwise Carry=0
                    6  ; Registers Modified:  CCR
                    7  ;                      EEPROG: BYTE and ROW cleared
0000                8  EELAT:    EQU    %00000010    ; EELAT Bit
0000                9  EEPGM:    EQU    %00000001    ; EEPGM bit
0000               10  ERASE:    EQU    %00000100    ; ERASE bit
0000               11  LOC4K:    EQU    %01111111    ; All 4K locations
0000               12  REGLOC:   EQU    $0
0000               13  EEMCR:    EQU    REGLOC+$F0   ; EEMCR register
0000               14  EEPROT:   EQU    REGLOC+$F1   ; EEPROT register
0000               15  EEPROG:   EQU    REGLOC+$F3   ; EEPROG register loc
0000               16  tPROG:    EQU    !10          ; tPROG delay in msec
                   17
                   18  ee_prog_2:
0000 3B            19          pshd
0001 34            20          pshx
                   21  ; Now check to see if the address is word aligned
                   22  ; X must be an even number
                   23  ; IF X is an even number
0002 B7C5          24          exg    d,x
0004 56            25          rorb                 ; rotate lsb into carry
0005 30            26          pulx                 ; restore original contents
0006 3A            27          puld
0007 252A          28          bcs    error         ; X was odd
                   29  ; THEN go ahead and program it
                   30  ; Get and save the current values of EEPROT, and EEPROG
0009 3B            31          pshd
000A D6F1          32          ldab   EEPROT        ; Read EEPROT and EEPROG
000C 3B            33          pshd
000D D6F3          34          ldab   EEPROG
000F 37            35          pshb
                   36  ; Allow any 2 bytes in the 4K to be programmed
0010 4DF17F        37          bclr   EEPROT,LOC4K
                   38  ; Assume EEPGM and ERASE = 0, otherwise you need to
                   39  ; clear them
0013 4CF302        40          bset   EEPROG,EELAT  ; EELAT = 1
                   41  ; Get the data off the stack
0016 EC82          42          ldd    2,sp
0018 6C00          43          std    0,x           ; Store data
001A 4CF301        44          bset   EEPROG,EEPGM  ; Turn on prog voltage
001D C60A          45          ldab   #tPROG
001F 160036        46          jsr    DlyNms        ; Delay tPROG msec
```

EXAMPLE 9–8   Continued

```
0022 4DF301    47              bclr    EEPROG,EEPGM  ; Turn off prog voltage
0025 4DF302    48              bclr    EEPROG,EELAT  ; Reset EELAT
               49  ; Clean up the stack and restore the registers
0028 33        50              pulb
0029 5BF3      51              stab    EEPROG
002B 33        52              pulb
002C 5BF1      53              stab    EEPROT
002E 3A        54              puld                  ; Restore original D
002F 10FE      55              clc                   ; Clear carry, no error
0031 2002      56              bra     endif
               57  ; ELSE process any error actions
0033 1401      58  error:      sec                   ; Error, set carry
               59  endif:
0035 3D        60              rts
               61  ;
               62  DlyNms:
               63  ; See the bulk erase example for the delay code.
0036 3D        64              rts
```

EERC bit in the EEMCR register. The EEPROM can be erased and programmed (*program/erase endurance*) at least 10,000 times. If the average maximum operating temperature is below 85°C, the write/erase endurance can be 30,000 cycles.

9.5 MC68HC912B32 Flash EEPROM

Flash EEPROM is faster and has more storage than standard EEPROM.

The MC68HC912B32 version of the M68HC12 has 32 Kbytes of *Flash EEPROM*. This EEPROM design is similar to "standard" EEPROM in that it is nonvolatile and can be programmed and erased electrically. It offers the advantages of faster programming and erasing but can be bulk erased only. Also, it does not have a charge pump so an external programming voltage must be supplied. Flash EEPROM cells are smaller than EEPROM cells and can thus provide more storage per unit area.

The Flash EEPROM is configured as 16-bit words and can be read as either bytes, aligned words, or misaligned words. It can be programmed *only* in byte or aligned words.

TABLE 9–5   EEPROM Programming Characteristics

	Symbol	Min	Typical	Max	Units
Minimum programming clock frequency	f_{PROG}	10			MHz
Programming time	t_{PROG}			10	msec
Clock recovery following STOP	t_{CRSTOP}			10	msec
Erase time	t_{ERASE}			10	msec
Program/erase endurance		10,000	30,000		Cycles
Data retention		10			Years

The initial location for the Flash EEPROM depends on the operating mode. In single-chip mode the memory resides at $8000–$FFFF on reset. For the expanded modes the Flash EEPROM is located from $0000–$7FFF but is disabled initially, and locations $8000–$FFFF are mapped to be used with external memory. The location and whether or not the Flash EEPROM are enabled are controlled by the *MAPROM* and *ROMON* bits in the *Miscellaneous Mapping Control Register* (*MISC*). If the Flash EEPROM is mapped into an area in which either RAM or the registers reside, the RAM or registers have higher priority, blocking access to those Flash locations.

MISC—$0013—Miscellaneous Mapping Control Register

	Bit 7	6	5	4	3	2	1	Bit 0
Reset	EWDIR	NDRC NDRF	RFSTR1	RFSTR0	EXSTR1	EXSTR0	MAPROM	ROMON
Single-Chip	0	0	0	0	0	0	1	1
Expanded	0	0	0	0	0	0	0	0

EWDIR
Extra Window Positioned in Direct Space. See Section 9.6.

NDRC
Narrow Data Bus for Register Chip Select Space (MC68HC812A4).

NDRF
Narrow Data Bus for Register-Following Map (MC68HC912B32).

RFSTR1:RFSTR0
Register-Following Stretch Bit 1 and 0 (MC68HC912B32). See Section 9.8.

EXSTR1:EXSTR0
External Access Stretch Bits 1 and 0 (MC68HC912B32). See section 9.8.

MAPROM

Map Location of Flash EEPROM.
　　　0 = Flash EEPROM located from $0000 to $7FFF (default expanded modes).
　　　1 = Flash EEPROM located from $8000 to $FFFF (default single-chip modes).
This bit locates the Flash EEPROM but does not have any effect if ROMON is zero.

ROMON

Enable Flash EEPROM.
　　　0 = Disables Flash EEPROM in the memory map (default expanded modes).
　　　1 = Enables Flash EEPROM (default single-chip modes).

Flash EEPROM Hardware Interlocks

The Flash EEPROM module has a comprehensive set of interlocks to protect its contents from accidental corruption or programming and erasing.

Boot Block

A *boot block* is a section of code that is used to *bootstrap*, or start-up, the microcontroller at reset.

The *boot block* can be used to provide *bootstrap* or *startup* code when the microcontroller is reset. Once the bootstrap code has been programmed into the Flash EEPROM, it should be protected from erasures or other modifications. Two bits in two different registers, *BOOTP* in the *FEEMCR* register and *LOCK* in the *FEELCK* register, provide protection for the boot block.

FEELCK—$00F4—Flash EEPROM Lock Control Register

Bit 7	6	5	4	3	2	1	Bit 0
0	0	0	0	0	0	0	LOCK

Reset 0　　　0　　　0　　　0　　　0　　　0　　　0　　　0

LOCK

Lock Register Bit.
　　　0 = Enable the BOOTP bit in FEEMCR to be written (default).
　　　1 = Disable write to the FEEMCR register.
In normal modes, LOCK can be written *only once* after reset.

FEEMCR—$00F5—Flash EEPROM Module Configuration Register

	Bit 7	6	5	4	3	2	1	Bit 0
	0	0	0	0	0	0	0	BOOTP
Reset	0	0	0	0	0	0	0	1

BOOTP
Boot Protect Bit.
0 = Enable erase and program of the boot block.
1 = Boot block is protected against erasing and programming (default).
BOOTP can be changed *only* if LOCK is reset and ENPE in the FEECTL register is reset.

Flash EEPROM Control

There are three bits, *ERAS, LAT,* and *ENPE,* in the *Flash EEPROM Control Register* (*FEECTL*) that control the operation of the Flash EEPROM. Not only are the states of these bits important, but the sequence in which they are set and reset are important, too, for proper programming. Table 9–6 summarizes how these bits should be set for various memory operations.

FEECTL—$00F7—Flash EEPROM Control Register

	Bit 7	6	5	4	3	2	1	Bit 0
	0	0	0	FEESWAI	SVFP	ERAS	LAT	ENPE
Reset	0	0	0	0	0	0	0	0

FEESWAI
Flash EEPROM Stop in Wait Control.
0 = Do not halt Flash EEPROM clock when the MCU is in Wait mode (default).
1 = Halt the clock when in Wait mode.

SVFP
Status V_{FP} Voltage.
0 = Voltage of V_{FP} is below normal programming voltage levels (default).
1 = Voltage of V_{FP} is above the V_{DD} voltage level.
SVFP can be used by the programmer to verify that V_{FP} is above its normal level V_{DD}. It is the responsibility of external circuitry to ensure that V_{FP} is within specified limits.

TABLE 9-6 Flash EEPROM Programming Bits

FEELCK LOCK	FEEMCR BOOTP	ERAS	FEECTL LAT	ENPE	Operation
x	x	x	0	0	Normal reading of the Flash EEPROM
0	0 ↔ 1	x	x	0	BOOTP in FEEMCR can be written
1	x	x	x	0	Disable write to FEEMCR; BOOTP cannot be written; LOCK can be written only once after reset
0	1	x	x	0	Protects the boot block; ENPE and LOCK must be zero to set or reset BOOTP; BOOTP=1 is the default reset state
0	0	x	x	0	Boot block can be erased or programmed; ENPE and LOCK must be zero to reset BOOTP
x	x	0	1	0	EEPROM configured for programming; when reading, the location being programmed is read
x	x	1	1	0	EEPROM configured for erasing; when reading, normal reading is allowed
x	x	x	1	1	Programming voltage is applied; *before* ENPE can be set, LAT must be set and a write to the data and address latches *must* have occurred

---

ERAS

Erase Control.

      0 = Flash EEPROM configured for programming (default).

      1 = Flash EEPROM can be erased.

ERAS can be read at anytime but can be written only when ENPE = 0. When ERAS is set, all locations in the array will be erased except for the boot block when BOOTP = 1.

LAT

Latch Control.

      0 = Normal read mode. Programming latches disabled (default).

      1 = Programming latches enabled.

LAT can be read at anytime but can be written only when ENPE = 0.

ENPE

Enable Programming/Erase.

      0 = Programming/erase voltage disabled (default).

      1 = Programming/erase voltage applied to the Flash EEPROM.

ENPE can be set *only after* LAT has been set and *after* data has been written to a valid Flash EEPROM address.

Flash EEPROM Programming Voltage

W A R N I N G

V_{FP} must be kept higher than $V_{DD} - 0.5$ V at all times or the Flash EEPROM array can be damaged.

Unlike the EEPROM, the programming voltage for the Flash EEPROM must be supplied from an external source. The programming voltage, V_{FP}, is nominally $+12$ volts[4] for programming. When the chip is in read mode, V_{FP} must be equal to V_{DD} (± 0.5 V). You can control this voltage in two ways. A microcontroller output bit can be used to raise the voltage from V_{DD} to V_{FP} (requires external circuitry) when programming or an external supply can be attached.

Flash EEPROM Programming

Program and erase operations are very similar. The Flash EEPROM has various hardware interlocks to prevent the corruption or programming of memory cells unless the programmer takes specific steps. To begin either sequence, the V_{FP} voltage must be applied and stabilized. The programming control bits are set to their required values and data are written to a valid Flash EEPROM address. The ENPE bit is set to apply the programming voltage for the duration of the programming pulse (t_{PPULSE}) and then reset. Another delay (t_{VPROG}) is entered to wait for the programming voltage to be turned off. You then read the data to *verify* that they have been programmed correctly. If they have not, you repeat the program pulse and verify steps, counting the number of cycles it takes to program the cell correctly. At this point you repeat the number of program pulses to give a 100% *program margin*. The control bits are then returned to their normal, read state. The steps required to program a location can be summarized as follows:

1. If the location to be programmed is in the boot block, BOOTP = 0, otherwise set BOOTP = 1 to protect the block.

2. Turn on the V_{FP}.

3. Clear ERAS to enter programming mode and set LAT to enable the programming latches.

4. Write data to a valid Flash EEPROM address. If the address is in the boot block and BOOTP = 1, the attempt to program the boot block will be ignored.

5. Set ENPE to enable the programming voltage.

6. Wait for one program pulse (t_{PPULSE}).

---

[4] V_{FP} is defined as minimum = 11.0, typical = 11.4, and maximum = 11.8 during programming and between $V_{DD} - 0.35$ and $V_{DD} + 0.5$ when reading. These are preliminary electrical specifications from *Technical Supplement MC68HC912B32 Electrical Specifications,* 9/09/97, Motorola, 1997. You should contact Motorola for up-to-date specifications if you program the Flash EEPROM on any system. See Motorola's web page http://www.mcu.motsps.com/ for the latest technical specifications for all M68HC12 versions.

7. Clear ENPE.

8. Wait for programming voltage to be turned off (t_{VPROG}).

9. Read the address that was programmed.

   a. If the location is not programmed, repeat Steps 5–8 until the location is programmed or until the number of times the programming pulse is applied is equal to the maximum allowed (n_{PP}).

   b. If the location is programmed, repeat the same number of programming pulses to give a 100% programming margin.

10. Read the location one more time to make sure it is programmed correctly.

11. Clear LAT.

12. If there are more locations to program, repeat Steps 3–11.

13. Return V_{FP} to V_{DD}.

The flow chart in Figure 9–5 and the pseudocode design in Example 9–9 show the recommended programming sequence.

Flash EEPROM Erasing

The erased state of any Flash EEPROM cell is a logic one and a bit must be programmed to change it to logic zero. Erasing restores the bit to logic one. The erasing process erases *all* cells in a bulk erase, except for the boot block area, which may be protected against erasure by the BOOTP bit.

1. If the boot block is to be erased, set BOOTP = 0, otherwise set BOOTP = 1.

2. Turn on the V_{FP}.

3. Set ERAS to enter erase mode and set LAT to enable the programming latches.

4. Write data to any valid Flash EEPROM address.

5. Set ENPE to enable the programming voltage.

6. Wait for one erase pulse (t_{EPULSE}).

7. Clear ENPE.

8. Wait for programming voltage to be turned off (t_{VERASE}).

9. Read the entire array to ensure all Flash EEPROM addresses are erased.

   a. If all locations are not erased, repeat Steps 5–8 until all locations are erased or until the number of times the erase is applied is equal to the maximum allowed (n_{EP}).

   b. If all of the Flash EEPROM is erased, repeat the same number of erase pulses to give a 100% erase margin.

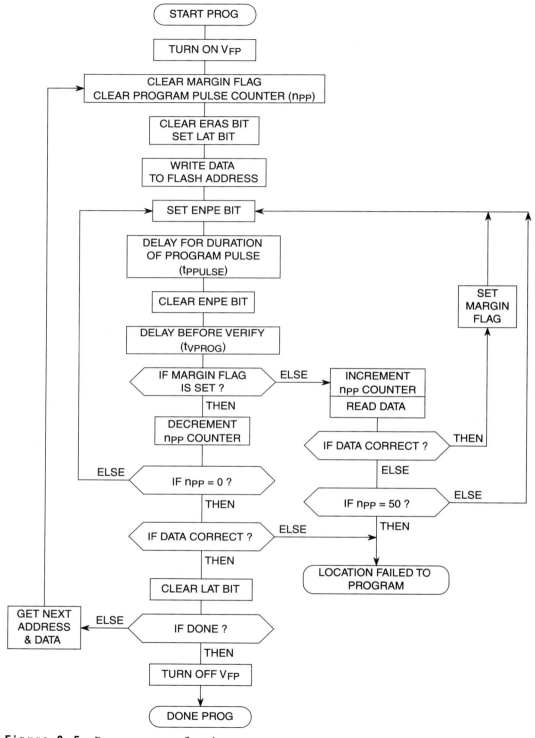

Figure 9-5 Program sequence flow chart.

EXAMPLE 9–9   Flash EEPROM Programming Pseudocode Design

```
; Turn on the programming voltage
; DO
;   Get next data and address
;   Clear Data_OK_Flag
;   Initialize Prog_Pulse_Counter=0
;   Clear ERAS and Set LAT
;   Write data to the address
;   DO
;     Set ENPE
;     Delay for tPPULSE
;     Clear ENPE
;     Delay for tVPROG
;     IF Data_OK_Flag is set
;       THEN
;         Decrement Prog_Pulse_Counter
;       ELSE
;         Increment Prog_Pulse_Counter
;         Read the data
;         IF Data is correct
;           THEN
;             Set Data_OK_Flag
;         ENDIF Data is correct
;       ENDIF Data_Ok_Flag is set
;   ENDO WHILE (Prog_Pulse_Counter > 0) and (Prog_Pulse_Counter < nPP)
;   Clear LAT
;   Read the data
;   IF Data is not correct
;       THEN
;         Clear Data_OK_Flag
;     ENDIF Data is not correct
; ENDO WHILE (More data to program) and (Data_OK_Flag = 1)
; Turn off the programming voltage
; IF Data_OK_Flag is not set
;   THEN
;     Process the error condition
; ENDIF Data_OK_Flag is not set
```

10. Read the entire array one more time to make sure it is erased correctly.

11. Clear LAT.

12. Return V_{FP} to V_{DD}.

The flow chart in Figure 9–6 and the pseudocode design in Example 9–10 show the recommended programming sequence.

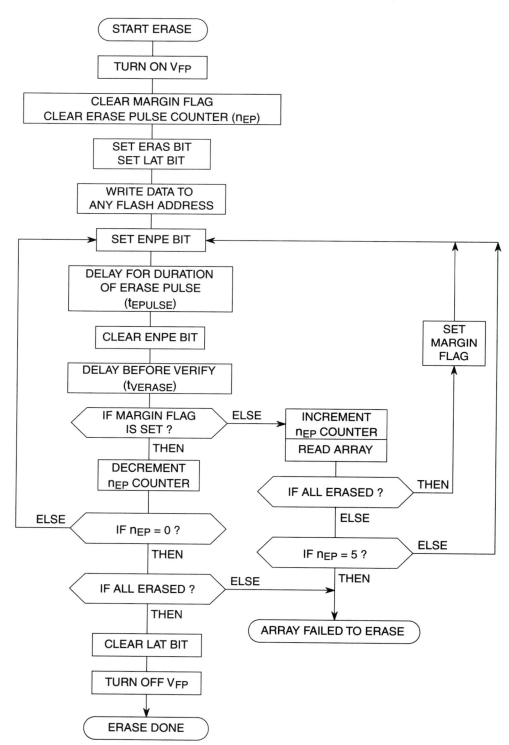

Figure 9-6 Erase sequence flow chart.

EXAMPLE 9-10   Flash EEPROM Erase Pseudocode Design

```
; Turn on the programming voltage
; Get a valid array address
; Clear Erased_OK_Flag
; Initialize Erase_Pulse_Counter=0
; Set ERAS and Set LAT
; Write any data to the address
; DO
;   Set ENPE
;   Delay for tEPULSE
;   Clear ENPE
;   Delay for tVPROG
;   IF Erased_OK_Flag is set
;     THEN
;       Decrement Erase_Pulse_Counter
;     ELSE
;       Increment Erase_Pulse_Counter
;       Read the whole array
;       IF the entire array is erased
;         THEN
;           Set Erased_OK_Flag
;       ENDIF the entire array is erased
;   ENDIF Erased_OK_Flag is set
; ENDO WHILE (Erase_Pulse_Counter > 0) and (Erase_Pulse_Counter < nEP)
; Clear LAT
; Read the whole array
; IF the entire array is not erased
;   THEN
;     Process the error condition
; ENDIF the entire array is not erased
; Turn off the programming voltage
```

Flash EEPROM Programming Characteristics

> Flash EEPROM may be erased and programmed only 100 times compared to 10,000 or more for standard EEPROM.

The timing characteristics of the Flash EEPROM are shown in Table 9–7. If we compare Table 9–7 with Table 9–5 we can see some of the major differences between EEPROM and the Flash EEPROM. Each Flash cell can be programmed faster than the EEPROM cell even if the maximum number of pulses is required. The erase time for the Flash EEPROM is at least a factor of 10 longer than the EEPROM. The data retention, 10 years, is the same for both types of memory. The number of program and erase cycles (program/erase endurance) for the Flash EEPROM is much less than the standard EEPROM (100 vs. 10,000–30,000).[5]

---

[5] The number of program and erase cycles given is what the manufacturer guarantees over the full temperature range of the device (up to 85°C). Typically, for lower temperatures, the number of times you can program and erase the Flash EEPROM is many more.

TABLE 9-7 Flash EEPROM Programming Characteristics

	Symbol	Min	Typical	Max	Units
Number of programming pulses	n_{PP}			50	Pulses
Programming pulse width	t_{PPULSE}	20		25	μsec
Time delay after programming	t_{VPROG}	10			μsec
Programming margin		100			%
Number of erase pulses	n_{EP}			5	Pulses
Erase pulse width	t_{EPULSE}	90	100	110	msec
Time delay after erasing	t_{VERASE}	1			msec
Erase margin		100			%
Program/erase endurance		100			Cycles
Data retention		10			Years

9.6 MC68HC812A4 Expansion Memory

The MC68HC812A4 can address up to 4 Mbytes in external, paged, program memory plus 1.25 Mbyte for data storage.

Many microcontroller applications need more than 64 Kbytes of memory for their programs and data. Although the MC68HC812A4 has a 64-Kbyte address space, it can access over 4 Mbytes of memory through three *memory expansion windows*. To use the expansion memory, the MC68HC812A4 must be operated in one of the expanded modes. Let us clearly define these two terms. An *expanded mode* (as opposed to single-chip mode) allows memory that is *external* to the microcontroller. In expanded mode the A, B, C, and D ports are used for the external 16-bit address and 8- or 16-bit data buses. *External memory* is within the 64-Kbyte memory space but physically *external* to the M68HC12. Figure 9–7a shows the expanded mode memory map. Any part of the memory map not internal (registers, RAM, and EEPROM) can be external memory. *Expansion memory* refers to memory that goes beyond the standard 64-Kbyte memory address space.

Figure 9–7b shows expansion memory windows in the external memory space. There are three windows including a 16-Kbyte program space window ($8000–$BFFF), a 4-Kbyte data window ($7000–$7FFF), and a 1-Kbyte extra window (which may be located at $0000–$03FF or $0400–$07FF). Each of these windows allow access to 256 pages of expansion memory. Figure 9–8 shows the ports used to create the expansion, and expanded, address, data, and control buses.

Before we look at each of these windows in detail, let us consider how expansion memory operates. Figure 9–9 shows a 32-Kbyte nonvolatile RAM with a real-time clock. The chip must be supplied with 15 address bits for addresses ranging between $0000 and $7FFF. There is also a chip enable, $\overline{CE}$ and other control signals such as $\overline{W}$ and $\overline{OE}$. For this to be used in any of the expansion windows, the MC68HC812A4 must provide the 15-bit physical address and the chip enable. Each address in the expansion memory consists of two parts. There is a *page address* and an *offset address* within the page.[6] For example, if this memory is used in the data window, there are eight 4-Kbyte pages. The 15-bit physical address consists of three bits for the page address and 12 bits for the offset within each 4-Kbyte page.

Let us use this RAM chip in the data window $7000–$7FFF. The complete expansion memory address is generated in two parts as shown in Figure 9–10. The three least-significant bits in

---

[6] Chapter 9 in *Microcontrollers and Microcomputers: Principles of Software and Hardware Engineering*, discusses paged memory architectures.

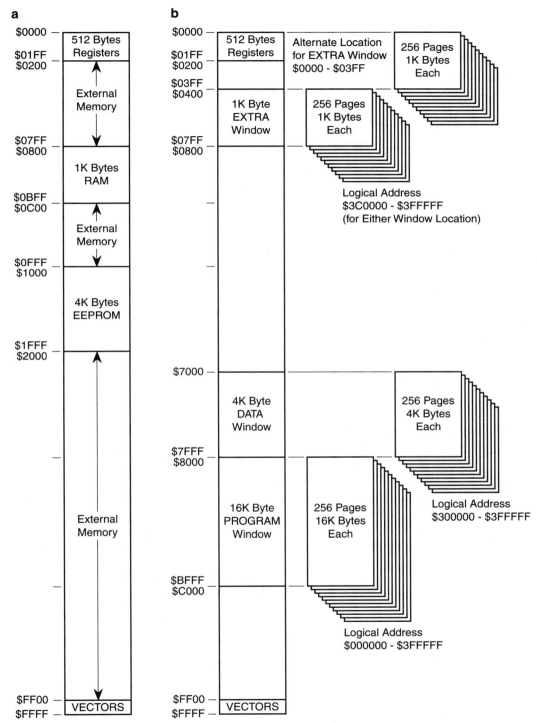

Figure 9-7 MC68HC812A4 expansion memory. (a) Expanded mode memory map. (b) Expansion memory windows.

263

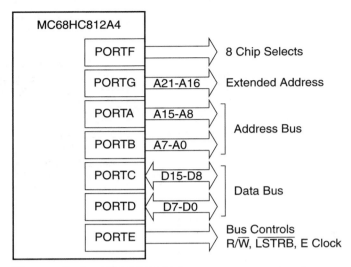

Figure 9-8   MC68HC812A4 expansion memory interface.

the 8-bit DPAGE register holds the page address %xxxxx000 to %xxxxx111 and the M68HC12 generates the 12-bit offset address. These 15 bits are transferred to the external address bus when an address in the data window is generated. The *CSD chip select*, in bit 5 of the PORTF register, is asserted automatically by the MC68HC812A4 during this time. See Figure 9–10.

Expansion Address Mapping

> The programmer must initialize a page register before using memory in an expansion page.

Addresses in the expansion memory must be mapped, or translated, to associated addresses in the expansion window. An example of an address translation table is shown in Table 9–8. Note that each address within the window can access different locations in the memory, depending on the DPAGE register. It is the programmer's responsibility to program the page registers with the correct value to be able to access the cor-

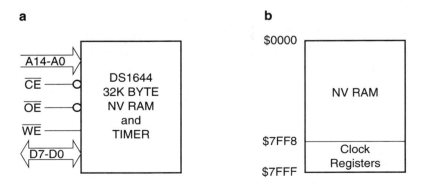

Figure 9-9   Dallas Semiconductor nonvolatile RAM (NVRAM) with real-time clock. (a) Address and control. (b) Memory map.

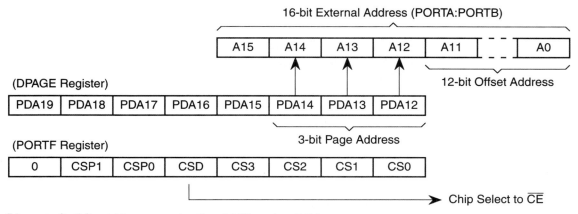

Figure 9-10 Address generation for a 32-Kbyte data RAM.

rect page. See Example 9–11. We will discuss the software issues for the extra, data, and program windows in Section 9.6.

Memory Expansion Control Registers

The Port G and Port F registers connect the expansion address and chip select bits to the external world.

PORTG and *PORTF* are registers that may be used for general-purpose I/O or memory expansion. PORTG provides up to six expansion address bits and PORTF contains seven chip select signals. A *Memory Expansion Assignment Register (MXAR)* can enable the PORTG address bits. Each window has a page register with an 8-bit page address. These are the *Data Page Register (DPAGE)*, the *Program Page Register (PPAGE)*, and the *Extra Page Register (EPAGE)*. When any of the windows are enabled, by setting the *DWEN, PWEN,* or *EWEN* bits in the *Window Definition Register (WINDEF)*, the page address in the appropriate page register is automatically multiplexed onto address lines when the MC68HC812A4 accesses memory in the window. Also at this time, depending on the state of the control bits in the *Chip Select Control Register 0* and *1*, chip select bits in PORTF will be asserted automatically.

TABLE 9-8 Expansion Memory Address Table for DS1644 32-Kbyte Memory

15-bit Expansion Address	DPAGE Register	Internal Window Address	Comment
$0000	$00	$7000	Page 0, offset 0
$0001	$00	$7001	Page 0, offset 1
$1000	$01	$7000	Page 1, offset 0
$7000	$07	$7000	Page 7, offset 0
$7F00	$07	$7F00	Page 7, offset F00

EXAMPLE 9–11

The nonvolatile RAM shown in Figure 9–9 maintains its clock functions in an 8-byte block from $7FF8 to $7FFF. Give the page, offset, and the expansion addresses used to read the first clock register.

Solution

Page $07, offset $FF8, expansion address $7FF8

Memory Expansion Addresses

The expansion memory page addresses are held internally in the page registers and transferred to the external world's address bus. The MXAR register enables which PORTG bits are used for expansion addresses and the WINDEF register enables which windows are active.

PORTG—$0031—Port G Register

Bit 7	6	5	4	3	2	1	Bit 0
0	0	ADDR21	ADDR20	ADDR19	ADDR18	ADDR17	ADDR16
Reset 0	0	0	0	0	0	0	0

ADDR21:ADDR16
Address Bits for Memory Expansion. The Port G address bits that are enabled by MXAR for expansion use are copied from the DPAGE, PPAGE, or EPAGE register when the MC68HC812A4 addresses one of these windows. At all other times these bits are set to one. Any Port G bits not enabled for memory expansion by MXAR may be used for general-purpose I/O. The direction of these is controlled by Data Direction Register G (DDRG).

MXAR—$0038—Memory Expansion Assignment Register

Bit 7	6	5	4	3	2	1	Bit 0
0	0	A21E	A20E	A19E	A18E	A17E	A16E
Reset 0	0	0	0	0	0	0	0

A21E:A16E

Select memory expansion pins ADDR21:ADDR16 on Port G.
> 0 = Selects general-purpose I/O (default).
> 1 = Selects memory expansion. Overrides DDRG.

WINDEF—$0037—Window Definition Register

Bit 7	6	5	4	3	2	1	Bit 0
DWEN	PWEN	EWEN	0	0	0	0	0

Reset 0　　　　0　　　　0　　　　0　　　　0　　　　0　　　　0　　　　0

DWEN

Data Window Enable.
> 0 = Disables DPAGE (default).
> 1 = Enables data space window (4 Kbytes at $7000–$7FFF).

PWEN

Program Window Enable.
> 0 = Disables PPAGE (default).
> 1 = Enables program space window (16 Kbytes at $8000–$BFFF).

EWEN

Extra Window Enable.
> 0 = Disables EPAGE (default).
> 1 = Enables the extra space window (1 Kbyte at either $0000–$03FF or
> $0400–$03FF; see the EWDIR bit).

DPAGE—$0034—Data Page Register

Bit 7	6	5	4	3	2	1	Bit 0
PDA19	PDA18	PDA17	PDA16	PDA15	PDA14	PDA13	PDA12

Reset 0　　　　0　　　　0　　　　0　　　　0　　　　0　　　　0　　　　0

PDA19:PDA12

Data Page Address.
When enabled by DWEN = 1, this address determines which of the 256 4-Kbyte data pages is in the window. An access to the window forces PDA19:PDA16 to the expansion address register PORTG and PDA15:PDA12 to the address bus ADR15:ADR12. If PORTG[ADDR21:ADDR20] are enabled by MXAR, they are forced to one.

PPAGE—$0035—Program Page Register

Bit 7	6	5	4	3	2	1	Bit 0
PPA21	PPA20	PPA19	PPA18	PPA17	PPA16	PPA15	PPA14

Reset 0   0   0   0   0   0   0   0

PPA21:PPA14

Program Page Address.
When enabled by PWEN = 1, this address determines which of the 256 16-Kbyte program pages is in the window. An access to the window forces PPA21:PPA16 to the expansion address register PORTG and PPA15:PDA14 to the address bus ADR15:ADR14.

EPAGE—$0036—Extra Page Register

Bit 7	6	5	4	3	2	1	Bit 0
PEA17	PEA16	PEA15	PEA14	PEA13	PEA12	PEA11	PEA10

Reset 0   0   0   0   0   0   0   0

PEA17:PEA10

Extra Page Address.
When enabled by EWEN = 1, this address determines which of the 256 1-Kbyte extra pages is in the window. An access to the window forces PEA17:PDA16 to the expansion address register PORTG and PDA15:PDA10 to the address bus ADR15:ADR10. If PORTG[ADDR21:ADDR18] are enabled by MXAR, they are forced to one.

Memory Address Conflicts

Note in Figure 9–7b that the expansion extra memory window can be mapped into the range $0000–$03FF. This overlaps the default location of the internal registers. The registers can be moved, as showed in Example 9–1, but if they are not, any register access will take priority over the expansion memory. All internal and expansion memory modules have a priority of access as shown in Table 9–9.

Expansion Memory Chip Select

The designers of the MC68HC812A4 have included chip select signals that make it easy to interface external memory and I/O. The chip select signals are enabled by bits in Chip Select Control Registers 0 and 1 and appear on Port F.

PORTF—$0030—Port F Register

Bit 7	6	5	4	3	2	1	Bit 0
0	CSP1	CSP0	CSD	CS3	CS2	CS1	CS0

Reset 0   0   0   0   0   0   0   0

CSP1:CSP0
Chip Select Program 1 and 0. When enabled by CSP1E:CSP0E, these bits are asserted (low) for program expansion memory.

CSD
Chip Select Data. When enabled by CSDE, asserted (low) for data expansion memory.

CS3
Chip Select 3. When enabled by CS3E, asserted (low) for extra expansion memory.

TABLE 9–9 Expansion and Internal Memory Priority

Priority	Memory
1	512 byte on-chip register space
2	Internal, 256-byte background debug module memory ($FF00–$FFFF)
3	Internal on-chip RAM
4	Internal on-chip EEPROM
5	Extra expansion memory
6	512 bytes following the internal register space
7	Program expansion memory
8	Data expansion memory
9	All other memory

CS3:CS0

Chip Select 3–0.
When enabled by CS3E:CS0E, these are asserted (low) for various combinations of address in the 512 bytes following the internal registers.

Any of these bits that are not enabled for chip select use (by CSCTL0) may be used for general-purpose I/O. The direction is controlled by Data Direction Register F (DDRF).

CSCTL0—$003C—Chip Select Control Register 0

Bit 7	6	5	4	3	2	1	Bit 0
0	CSP1E	CSP0E	CSDE	CS3E	CS2E	CS1E	CS0E

Reset 0   0   1   0   0   0   0   0

CSP1E:CSP0E

Chip Select Program 1 and 0 Enable.
    0 = Chip selects for program expansion memory disabled.
    1 = Chip selects are enabled.
CSP0 is enabled by default out of reset in case it is needed to fetch an external reset vector. All other chip selects default to the disabled condition.

CSDE

Chip Select Data Enable.
    0 = Disable the chip select for data expansion memory (default).
    1 = Enable.

CS3E:CS0E

Chip Select 3–0 Enable.
    0 = Disable the chip select (default).
    1 = Enable.
These four chip selects are associated with the 512-byte space that follows the on-chip register space. CS3 can optionally be associated with the extra expansion memory.

CSCTL1—$003D—Chip Select Control Register 1

Bit 7	6	5	4	3	2	1	Bit 0
0	CSP1FL	CSPA21	CSDHF	CS3EP	0	0	0

Reset 0   0   0   0   0   0   0   0

CSP1FL

Program Chip Select 1 Covers Full Map.
       0 = CSP1 covers half the map ($8000–$FFFF) (default).
       1 = CSP1 covers the full map ($0000–$FFFF).
If CSPA21 is set, this bit has no meaning or effect.

CSPA21

Program Chip Select Based on ADDR21.
       0 = CSP0 and CSP1 do not rely on ADDR21 (default).
       1 = CSP0 and CSP1 are a function of ADDR21.
See Table 9–16.

CSDHF

Data Chip Select Covers Half the Map.
       0 = Data Chip Select (CSD) covers $7000–$7FFF (default).
       1 = CSD covers $0000–$7FFF.

CS3EP

Chip Select 3 Follows the Extra Page.
       0 = Chip Select 3 only accesses a 128-byte space in the register following memory (default). See Table 9–19.
       1 = Chip Select 3 is used for the extra memory space. See Table 9–18.

Chip Select Priorities

The control registers for the chip select signals allow a variety of hardware designs. A chip select priority scheme has been included to eliminate potential memory access conflicts. These priorities are shown in Table 9–10.

TABLE 9–10 Chip Select Priorities

Highest						Lowest
CS3	CS2	CS1	CS0	CSP0	CSD	CSP1

Data Memory Expansion Window

There may be 1 Mbyte of expansion memory for data.

The details of the data memory expansion address and chip select generation are shown in Figure 9–11 and Table 9–11. Any of the 256 4-Kbyte pages can be mapped by a combination of addresses and a chip select into the window address $7000–$7FFF. Ports G, A, and B supply the external address bus. When the MC68HC812A4 generates a window access, 8 bits in the DPAGE register and the 12-bit offset address are asserted on the external address bus as follows:

PDA19–PDA16 (bits 7–4 of DPAGE) are transferred to Port G as address bits A19–A16.
PDA15–PDA12 (bits 3–0 of DPAGE) are transferred to Port A as address bits A15–A12.
The 12-bit offset address is output on PORTA[3:0] and PORTB[7:0].

PORTG[ADDR21:ADDR20] are forced to one if they are enabled for use as expansion addresses. PORTF[CSD] should be enabled by setting CSTL0[CSDE] = 1. See Table 9–11.

Another control bit, *Data Chip Select Covers Half the Map* (CSCTL1[CSDHF]) can enable CSD to be asserted for addresses $0000–$7FFF (half the map) or for the 4-Kbyte window $7000–$7FFF only. This could be used to add a large, say 64-Kbyte, memory that can be used as both external and expansion data storage. The first $7000 locations (28 Kbytes) would be used as normal external memory with any internal resources taking priority over the external memory. The remaining memory can be accessed as nine 4-Kbyte pages through the data expansion window.

Program Memory Expansion Window

Up to 4 Mbytes may be added for program expansion.

The details of the program memory expansion address and chip select generation are shown in Figure 9–12. This window and the associated chip select signals are designed to allow external and expansion memory to be added with a minimum of extra "glue" logic. There are a variety of scenarios and design cases that can be made, and we will discuss a few to help you design your own system.

Figure 9–12 shows the full expansion address PPAGE register and the chip select signals CSP1 and CSP0. There are two additional bits, CSCTL1[CSPA21] and CSCTL1[CSP1FL], that control the operation of these registers and two additional facts to remember. First, CSP0 has priority over CSP1. In any range of addresses in which both could be asserted, only CSP0 will be. Second, when addresses outside the window are generated ($0000–$7FFF and $C000–$FFFF, called *unpaged addresses*) expansion address bits ADDR21–ADDR16 are set to one. The chip selects may or may not be asserted depending on their control bits.

Let us now consider two memory expansion designs and control bit choices.

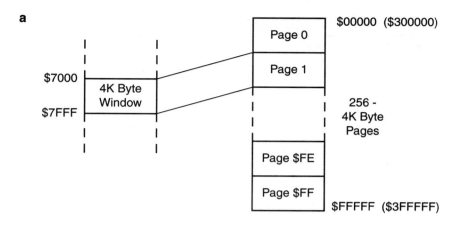

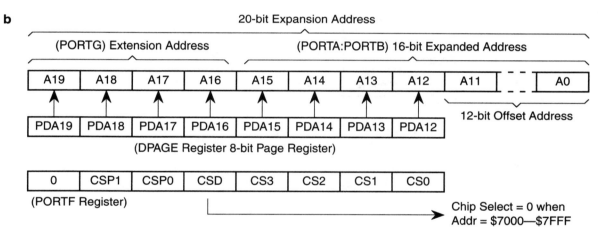

Figure 9-11   Data expansion memory. (a) Data memory expansion window. (b) Data memory expansion addresses and chip selects.

One-Megabyte Program Memory Expansion

A 1-Mbyte memory, such as that shown in Figure 9–13a, is to be added. It requires a 20-bit physical address and is viewed through the program expansion window as 63 16-Kbyte pages plus one more 16-Kbyte page for vectors and other startup code at $C000–$FFFF. The expansion window control bits are set up as shown in Table 9–12.

Any memory access within the range of $8000–$BFFF such as

```
LDAA       $8000
```

causes the current contents of the PPAGE register to be transferred to PORTG and the two most significant bits of the expanded mode address bus A15:A14. If a memory access in the range of

TABLE 9–11 Active-Low Chip Select for the Data Window[a]

CSDHF=1 CSD	CSDHF=0 CSD	Memory Block	Address
0	1	28 Kbytes	$000–$6FFF
0	0	4 Kbytes	$7000–$7FFF (default)
1	1	All other addresses	

[a]*CSCTL0[CSDE] = 1 to enable PORTF[CSD]; CSCTL1[CSDHF] = 1 to select half the map.*

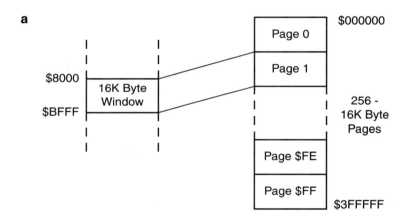

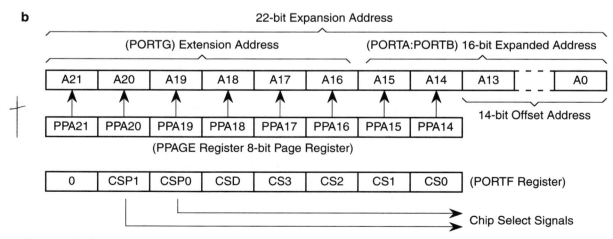

Figure 9–12 Program memory expansion. (a) Program memory expansion window. (b) Program memory expansion addresses and chip selects.

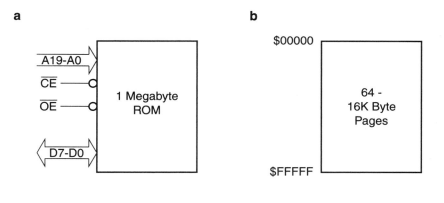

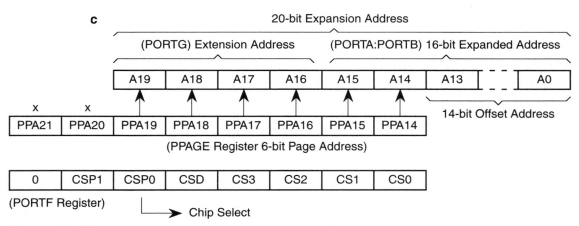

Figure 9-13 One-megabyte program memory expansion. (a) Address and control. (b) Memory map. (c) One-megabyte expansion window addresses and chip select.

TABLE 9-12 One-Megabyte Expansion Memory Control Bits

Control Bit	Value	Comment
CSCTL1[CSPA21] Program Chip Selects Based on A21	0	CSP1 and CSP0 are independent of address bit A21; our next example will show a case where they follow A21
CSCTL1[CSP1FL] CSP1 Covers the Full Map	x	Chip select one is not used
CSCTL0[CSP1E] CSP1 Enable	0	Chip select one is not used in this example; the bit could be used for I/O
CSCTL0[CSP0E] CSP0 Enable	1	Chip select zero is enabled
WINDEF[PWEN] Program Window or Enable	1	Enable the program memory expansion window

$C000–$FFFF occurs, all bits in PORTG that are enabled for expansion memory use[7] are forced to one and the expansion memory "sees" addresses $FC000–$FFFFF. The address translation table in Table 9–13 helps us understand how the address translation is done and Table 9–14 shows us how the chip select signal is asserted. Figure 9–14 shows how easy it is to connect the expansion memory to the MC68HC812A4.

Four-Megabyte Program Memory Expansion

The program chip selects are designed to allow two 2-Mbyte memories to be easily added as expansion memory. Two of these chips are shown in Figure 9–15 and the control bits for this design are shown in Table 9–15. CSPA21 is set and both CSP1 and CSP0 are enabled. Table 9–16 shows us that when in the window and when A21 is low, CSP1 is asserted. When A21 is high, CSP0 is asserted. Outside the window in the range $C000–$FFFF CSP0 is asserted to allow the highest 16 Kbytes to be used as external memory for startup code and vectors. Table 9–17 show how various addresses are translated.

Extra Memory Expansion Window

256 Kbytes of extra expansion memory may be added.

The details of the extra memory expansion window are shown in Figure 9–16 and Table 9–18. Depending on the state of MISC[EWDIR], the 256 1-Kbyte pages can be mapped into either $0000–$03FF (EWDIR = 1) or $0400–$07FF (EWDIR = 0, the default). Chip select 3 is used with the extra window. It is asserted when addresses

TABLE 9–13 One Megabyte Expansion Memory Address Translation Table

16-bit External Address A15–A0	PPA19– PPA14	14-bit Offset Address A13–A0	20-bit Expansion Physical Address A19–A0	Comment
$000–$7FFF	xx	xxxx	$Fxxxx	CSP0 = 1, expansion memory is not selected; A19–A16 forced to one
$8000–$BFFF	00	$0000–$3FFF	$00000–$03FFF	CSP0 = 0, page 0 expansion memory
$8000–$BFFF	01	$0000–$3FFF	$04000–$07FFF	CSP0 = 0, page 1
$8000–$BFFF	3E	$0000–$3FFF	$F8000–$FBFFF	CSP0 = 0, page 62
$C000–$FFFF	xx	$C000–$FFFF (16-bit external address)	$FC000–$FFFFF	CSP0 = 0, expansion memory page 63 used for external address $C000–$FFFF because A19–A16 forced to one.

20-bit Physical Expansion Memory Address

19	18	17	16	15	14	13	12	11	10	9	8	7	6	5	4	3	2	1	0
6-bit PPAGE Address						14-bit Page Offset Address													

---

[7] In this case we would enable only bits 0–3 and we could use PORTG[5:4] for general-purpose I/O.

TABLE 9-14 **Chip Select Program 0**

Internal Address	CSP0	Comment
$0000–$7FFF	1	CSP0 not asserted for addresses below the window
$8000–$BFFF	0	CSP0 asserted by all expansion memory in the window
$C000–$FFFF	0	CPS0 asserted for the unpaged (but external) memory from $C000 to $FFF

are in the range of the window providing CSCTL1[CS3EP] = 1 and CSCTL0[CS3E] = 1. When an address in the extra window is generated by the MC68HC812A4, the EPAGE[PEA17:PEA16] bits are copied to PORTG[17:16] and EPAGE[PEA15:PEA10] to the address bus [15:10] as shown in Figure 9–16.

If EWDIR = 1, the extra window space conflicts with the internal registers if they have not been moved to another location as showed in Example 9–1. If this is the case any access to the registers will take priority over the extra page memory as shown in Table 9–9.

Register-Following Memory Space

The 512 bytes immediately following the internal registers (wherever the registers are mapped) is called the *register-following memory*. CS[3:0] can be used for either memory or I/O devices in blocks as shown in Table 9–19.

Programming for Expansion Memory

Using expansion memory in our programs can be broken into the techniques needed for accessing data in the extra or data windows and those needed for executing code in the program expansion window.

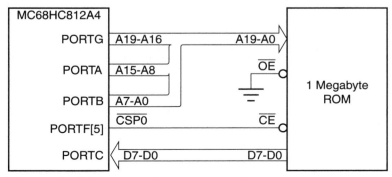

Figure 9-14 One-megabyte memory interface.

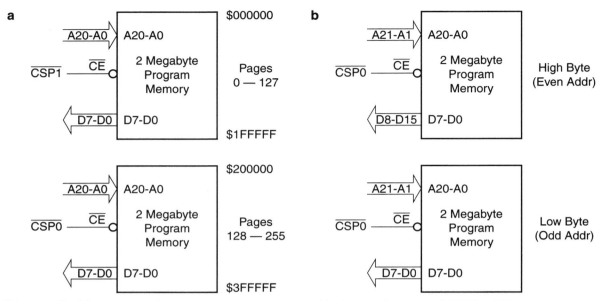

Figure 9–15   Four-megabyte expansion program memory. (a) Narrow 8-bit system. (b) Wide 16-bit system.

Extra and Data Expansion Windows

The data in either of the extra or data expansion windows may be accessed by first writing a page address in the page register (having first enabled the appropriate chip select bits as shown in our previous examples) and then simply writing program code to store or load data to or from the memory in the window.

You must manage the pages in the data memory in your programs and it is wise to keep individual data blocks to less than 1 or 16 Kbytes to avoid having to manipulate the page register in mid-data. Example 9–12 shows a short program segment to transfer data from one 2-Kbyte block in page 10 to page 62 of a 256-Kbyte expansion memory.

TABLE 9–15   Four-Megabyte Expansion Memory Control Bits

Control Bit	Value	Comment
CSCTL1[CSPA21] Program Chip Selects Based on A21	1	CSP1 and CSP0 follow the state of expansion address bit A21 (and the chip priority shown in Table 9–10)
CSCTL1[CSP1FL] CSP1 Covers the Full Map	x	CSPA21 takes priority over CSP1FL
CSCTL0[CSP1E] CSP1 Enable	1	Chip select one is enabled
CSCTL0[CSP0E] CSP0 Enable	1	Chip select zero is enabled
WINDEF[PWEN] Program Window Enable	1	Enable the program memory expansion window

16-bit External Address A15–A0	A21	CSP1	CSP0	Comment
				TABLE 9–16 Program Chip Selects for 4-Mbyte Memory
$0000–$7FFF	1	1	1	Outside the program expansion window A21–A16 are forced high and neither CSP1 nor CSP0 is asserted
$8000–$BFFF	0	0	1	In the expansion window, when A21 = 1, the low (first 2-Mbyte chip) is enabled by CSP1
$8000–$BFFF	1	1	0	The high 2-Mbyte chip is enabled by CSP0
$C000–$FFFF	1	1	0	Outside the program expansion window A21–A16 are forced high and CSP0 is asserted; the highest 16-Kbyte page is used for program code and vectors in $C000–$FFFF

Explanation of Example 9–12

This program segment moves 2048 bytes from the source page S_Page (*line 2*) to the destination page D_Page (*line 3*). This code works for buffers located at any arbitrary location in either page. *Lines 27–31* show how to define different buffers for each of the pages. We can see that the source buffer starts at the beginning of the page (*line 28*) and the destination buffer does not start at the beginning of the page (*line 31*). In *line 16* the DPAGE register is initialized to the source page and the data byte is loaded into the A register in *line 17*. *Line 18* shifts DPAGE to the destination page and the data are stored in *line 19*.

TABLE 9–17 Four-Megabyte Memory Address Translation Table

16-bit External Address A15–A0	PPA21–PPA14	14-bit Offset Address A13–A0	21-bit Expansion Physical Address A21–A0	Comments
$0000–$7FFF	xx	xxxx	$3Fxxxx	CSP1=1, CSP0=1, expansion memory is not selected, A21–A16 are forced to one
$8000–$BFFF	$00	$0000–$3FFF	$000000–$003FFF	CSP1=0, CSP0=1, expansion memory page 0
$8000–$BFFF	$7F	$0000–$3FFF	$1FC000–$1FFFFF	CSP1=0, CSP0=1, expansion memory page 127
$8000–$BFFF	$80	$0000–$3FFF	$200000–$203FFF	CSP1=1, CSP0=0, expansion memory page 128
$8000–$BFFF	$FE	$0000–$3FFF	$3F8000–$3FBFFF	CSP1=1, CSP0=0, expansion memory page 254
$C000–$FFFF	xx	$C000–$FFFF (16-bit address A15–A0)	$3FC000–$3FFFFF	CSP1=1, CSP0=0, expansion memory page 255 used for external memory $C000-$FFFF because A21–A16 are forced to one

22-bit Physical Expansion Memory Address

21	20	19	18	17	16	15	14	13	12	11	10	9	8	7	6	5	4	3	2	1	0

8-bit PPAGE Address	14-bit Page Offset Address

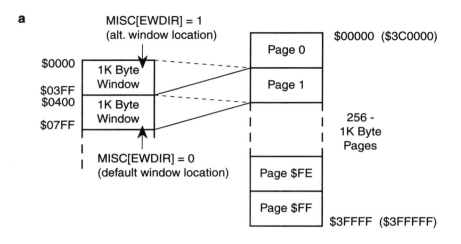

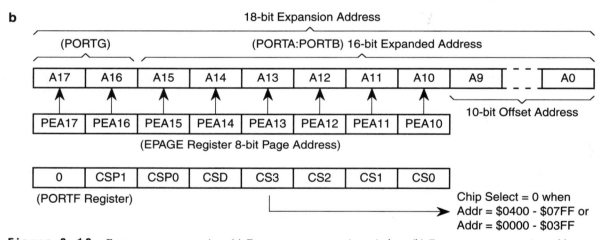

Figure 9-16 Extra memory expansion. (a) Extra memory expansion window. (b) Extra memory expansion addresses and chip select.

TABLE 9-18 Active-Low Extra Memory Chip Selects[a]

CS3	EWDIR	Memory	Address
0	1	1 Kbyte	$0000–$03FF
0	0	1 Kbyte	$0400–$07FF (default)
1	1	63 Kybtes	$0400–$FFFF
1	0	63 Kbytes	$0000–$03FF, $0800–$FFFF

[a]*CSCTL1[CS3EP] = 1 to enable CS3 for the extra page.*

TABLE 9-19 Active-Low Register-Following Memory Chip Select[a]

CS3	CS2	CS1	CS0	Memory	Address
1	1	1	0	128 bytes	REGLOC+$0200–REGLOC+$027F
0	1	1	0	128 bytes	REGLOC+$0280–REGLOC+$02FF
1	1	0	0	128 bytes	REGLOC+$0300–REGLOC+$037F
1	0	0	0	128 bytes	REGLOC+$0380–REGLOC+$03FF
1	1	1	1	All other memory	

Chip Select				Memory	Address
CS0				512 bytes	REGLOC+$0200–REGLOC+$03FF
CS1				256 bytes	REGLOC+$0300–REGLOC+$03FF
CS2				128 bytes	REGLOC+$0380–REGLOC+$03FF
CS3				128 bytes	REGLOC+$0280–REGLOC+$02FF

[a]CSCTL1[CSEP]= 0 to allow CS3 to be asserted for 128 bytes. CSCTL0[CS3E:CS0E]= 1 to be enable PORTF[CS3:CS0].
REGLOC is the base address of the registers.

EXAMPLE 9-12   Interpage Data Transfer

pgblock1.asm   Assembled with CASM 12/10/1998 21:18 PAGE 1

```
               1   ; Transfer 2 Kbytes from page 10 to page 62
0000           2   S_Page:   EQU    !10        ; Source block page
0000           3   D_Page:   EQU    !62        ; Destination block page
0000           4   N_Bytes:  EQU    !2048      ; Size of the block
0000           5   DPAGE:    EQU    $34        ; Data expansion page register
0000           6   D_WIN:    EQU    $7000      ; Start of data window
0000           7   CODE:     EQU    $C000      ; Code location
0000           8   STACK:    EQU    $0A00      ; Stack location
C000           9             ORG    CODE
C000 CF0A00   10             lds    #STACK
              11   ; DO move bytes
C003 CE7000   12             ldx    #Source    ; Start of source
C006 CD7002   13             ldy    #Dest      ; Start of dest
C009 CC0800   14             ldd    #N_Bytes   ; Loop counter
C00C 3B       15   loop:     pshd              ; Save counter
C00D 180B0A00 16             movb   #S_Page,DPAGE  ; Initialize page reg
     34
C012 A600     17             ldaa   0,x        ; Get the data
C014 180B3E00 18             movb   #D_Page,DPAGE  ; Set the dest page
     34
C019 6A40     19             staa   0,y        ; Store the data
C01B 08       20             inx               ; Point to next bytes
C01C 02       21             iny
              22   ; UNTIL the last byte is transferred
C01D 3A       23             puld              ; Restore the counter
C01E 0434EB   24             dbne   d,loop     ; Go until last byte
C021 3F       25             swi
              26   ; Define the buffers
7000          27             ORG    D_WIN
7000          28   Source:   DS     N_Bytes    ; Source buffer
7000          29             ORG    D_WIN
7000          30   Temp:     DS     2
7002          31   Dest:     DS     N_Bytes    ; Destination buffer
```

Programs in Expansion Memory

When using paged memory for programs we normally avoid changing from one page to another. For example, the following code segment will not work:

```
pgchgc1.asm               Assembled with CASM  05/31/1998  14:55  PAGE 1

0000                   0  Page_0:   EQU    0         ; Page 0 in the window
0000                   1  Page_1:   EQU    1         ; The next page of code
0000                   2  PPAGE:    EQU    $35       ; Memory expansion page reg
0000                   3  P_WIN:    EQU    $8000     ; Start of program window
0000                   4  CODE:     EQU    $C000     ; Code location
                       5  ; Define the addresses for each page in expansion memory
0000                   6  PG_0:     EQU    0         ; Page 0
0000                   7  PG_1:     EQU    $4000     ; Page 1
C000                   8            ORG    CODE
                       9  ; This code is located in unpaged memory and we want
                      10  ; to transfer to code in the window on page 0
                      11  ; Set the PPAGE register
C000 180B0000         12            movb   #Page_0,PPAGE
     35
C005 068000           13            jmp    P_WIN     ; Go to the page
                      14  ; Define the code on page 0
0000                  15            ORG    PG_0
0000 A7               16            nop
                      17  ; After about 16 Kbytes of code on page 0 we need to
                      18  ; transfer to the next page.
                      19  ; Now jump to page 1
0001 180B0100         20            movb   #Page_1,PPAGE
     35
0006 068000           21            jmp    P_WIN
                      22  ; Define the code on page 1
4000                  23            ORG    PG_1
4000 A7               24            nop
```

There are two page jumps in this code. The first works but the second does not. The code in *lines 12–13* is located on *unpaged* memory $C000–$FFFF. For memory accesses in unpaged memory, including all instruction fetch operations, the PPAGE register is not transferred to the external address bus. Thus, after the PPAGE register is changed on *line 12* the fetch of the JMP instruction on *line 13* works properly and we would find ourselves executing the code at *line 16*. However, the next page jump, *lines 20–21*, does not work. The PPAGE register is changed on *line 20* but because the JMP opcode at *line 21* is located in the window (on page 0) it will never be fetched.

It is possible, although not the easiest way, to transfer to another page by locating any page switching code in unpaged memory. Example 9–13 shows how to do this.

EXAMPLE 9–13   Page Changing Code

```
pgswchc1.asm           Assembled with CASM  05/31/1998  15:02  PAGE 1

0000              1  PPAGE:    EQU   $35      ; Memory expansion page reg
0000              2  P_WIN:    EQU   $8000    ; Start of program window
0000              3  CODE:     EQU   $C000    ; Code location
                  4  ; Define the addresses for each page in expansion memory
0000              5  PG_0:     EQU   0        ; Page 0
0000              6  PG_1:     EQU   $4000    ; Page 1
0000              7            ORG   PG_0
                  8  ; . . .
                  9  ; This code is located paged memory and we want
                 10  ; to transfer to code in the next window
0000 06C000      11            jmp   next_page
                 12  ;
4000             13            ORG   PG_1
                 14  ; This is the next code page
4000 A7          15            nop
                 16  ; . . .
                 17  ; . . .
C000             18            ORG   CODE
                 19  ;
                 20  ; This code to change the PPAGE register must
                 21  ; be somewhere in unpaged memory
                 22  next_page:
C000 720035      23            inc   PPAGE    ; Point to next page
C003 068000      24            jmp   P_WIN    ; Go to the page
                 25  ; . . .
```

Explanation of Example 9–13

Any code located in a window page (*lines 9–11*) must jump first to unpaged memory (*lines 22–24*) where the PPAGE register can be safely changed. This is the method used in traditional banked systems that do not have the benefit of CALL and RTC instructions like the M68HC12.

The CALL and RTC Instructions

The M68HC12 includes two instructions that make accessing code segments in the expansion memory much simpler than trying to jump from one page to another. These are the *CALL* and *RTC* (*Return from Call*) instructions. The CALL syntax is

> The CALL instruction pushes the current PPAGE register on the stack and RTC restores it.

```
CALL dest_adr,dest_page
```

where *dest_adr* is the subroutine address and *dest_page* is the page on which the subroutine is located.

CALL is similar to JSR (jump to subroutine) in that the return address is placed on the stack. In addition, the current PPAGE register is stacked. The RTC instruction is to be used to return from the subroutine because it restores the PPAGE register. You **must not** use RTS to return from a subroutine that has been CALLed.

The CALL and RTC instructions can be used to go from unpaged memory to paged and from one page to another. Nested CALLs can be used. Example 9–14 shows various combinations of the CALL, RTC, JSR, and RTS instructions.

EXAMPLE 9–14   CALL and RTC Instructions

```
pgcallc1.asm           Assembled with CASM  05/31/1998  15:09  PAGE 1

0000                1  PPAGE:    EQU   $35      ; Memory expansion page reg
0000                2  P_WIN:    EQU   $8000    ; Start of program window
0000                3  Page_1:   EQU   1        ; Pages for code
0000                4  Page_2:   EQU   2
                    5  ; Define the addresses for each page in expansion memory
0000                6  PG_0:     EQU   0        ; Page 0
0000                7  PG_1:     EQU   $4000    ; Page 1
0000                8  PG_2:     EQU   $8000    ; Page 2
                    9  ;*********************************************
                   10  ; Page 0 code
0000               11            ORG   PG_0
                   12  ; Call a subroutine on page 1
0000 4A400001      13            call  sub1,Page_1
                   14  ; Call a subroutine on page 2
0004 4A800002      15            call  sub2,Page_2
                   16  ; Jump to a local subroutine located on this page
0008 16000C        17            jsr   local_sub
000B 3F            18            swi
                   19  ; This is a subroutine on the local page.
                   20  ; It can ONLY be accessed from this page
000C A7            21  local_sub:      nop
                   22  ; Use an RTS to return
000D 3D            23            rts
                   24  ;*********************************************
                   25  ; Page 1 code
4000               26            ORG   PG_1
                   27  ; Subroutine 1
4000 A7            28  sub1:     nop
                   29  ; Call a subroutine on page 2
4001 4A800002      30            call  sub2,Page_2
                   31  ; Use the RTC to return
4005 0A            32            rtc
                   33  ;*********************************************
                   34  ; Page 2 code
8000               35            ORG   PG_2
                   36  ; Subroutine 2
8000 A7            37  sub2:     nop
                   38  ; Use RTC to return
8001 0A            39            rtc
```

Explanation of Example 9–14

Three code segments are defined for page 0 (*lines 10–23*), page 1 (*lines 24–32*), and page 2 (*lines 33–39*). The page 0 code calls subroutines on page 1 (*line 13*) and page 2 (*line 15*) and also jumps to the local subroutine (*line 17*). The JSR is shorter and quicker than the CALL and can be used if you guarantee that the subroutine is on the current page and the PPAGE register does not have to be changed. A nested subroutine call is seen in the page 1 code at *line 30* where the subroutine on page 2 is called.

Hints for Using Expansion Memory

Enable the Chip Selects Used by the Hardware: Chip selects are used by the hardware to reduce the external logic required to enable the memory. Chip selects are enabled in the CSCTL0 and CSCTL1 registers.

Enable Port G Register Bits for Memory Expansion: The MXAR register enables which of the Port G bits are used for memory expansion. Any unused Port G bits can be used for general-purpose I/O.

Enable the Expansion Window: PWEN, DWEN, and EWEN in the WINDEF register must be written.

Initialize the Page Registers: The PPAGE, DPAGE, and EPAGE registers have to be initialized with the page number before accessing the page.

The Program Must Manage the Contents of the Windows: The program examples in this section show that any page is *located* by an ORG at the start of the window. Each page must have its own ORG.

Keep Data Structures Less Than or Equal to the Page Size: This will eliminate messy page changes when accessing data.

Avoid Jumping between Pages: Code to change to a new page must be located in unpaged memory to accomplish this. It is OK to jump between pages using the CALL and RTC instructions.

Use Program Pages to Hold Subroutines: Use the CALL and RTC instructions.

Do Not Locate Interrupt Service Routines in Paged Memory: The interrupt vector is the address of the start of the service routine and has no knowledge of a page register. Subroutines executed as part of an interrupt service routine can be located in paged memory, however.

Do Not Locate the Stack in Paged Memory: If the stack is in paged memory and the page register is changed, the old page register must be saved to be able to return to the paged stack.

9.7 Expanded-Narrow and Expanded-Wide Memory Designs

> Commonly available 8-bit-wide memories can be used in the expanded-wide mode.

The M68HC12 is a 16-bit microcontroller and it achieves its speed performance by using a full, 16-bit data bus in expanded-wide mode. The system designers have given us an expanded-narrow mode to allow less performance-minded systems to use a simpler, more cost-effective 8-bit-wide data bus. They have also provided a control signal called *Low Byte Strobe* ($\overline{LSTRB}$) for external glue logic when using 8-bit memories in expanded-wide mode. Here is the design problem. In expanded-wide mode, two 8-bit memories can be accessed in 16-bit-wide mode by connecting the external address bus bit A1 to the memory address line A0. There are four memory access scenarios to be considered.

1. Read or write an aligned word (16 bits).

   ```
   LDD  $7000   or   STD  $7002
   ```

2. Read or write a misaligned word.

   ```
   LDD  $7005   or   STD  $7005
   ```

3. Read or write a byte from or to an even memory address.

   ```
   LDAA  $7000   or   STAA  $7000
   ```

4. Read or write a byte from or to an odd memory address.

   ```
   LDAA  $7001   or   STAA  $7001
   ```

Figure 9–17 shows how memory is aligned. In an aligned word the high byte is at an even address. Reading or writing an aligned word is done in one memory cycle. The address is supplied to the bus and both memory chips respond if both chip enables are asserted. Reading or writing a misaligned word requires two memory cycles consisting of an odd and an even memory access. Figure 9–18 shows an expanded-mode memory design using 8-bit-wide memory chips. Table 9–20 shows the control signals that can be used in the design.

When an aligned word is read, say by LDD $7002, A0 is low and $\overline{\text{LSTRB}}$ is asserted to enable both chips. An even byte may be read by LDAA $7000. In this case A0 is low but $\overline{\text{LSTRB}}$ is high and only $\overline{\text{CEH}}$ is asserted. When an odd byte is read, A1 = 1 and $\overline{\text{LSTRB}}$ = 0 and $\overline{\text{CEL}}$ enables the low byte. A misaligned word read, for example LDD $7005, requires both odd and even read cycles.

The *Low Byte Strobe* ($\overline{\text{LSTRB}}$) is in bit 3 in the PORTE register and it is enabled by setting the *LSTRE* enable bit in the *Port E Assignment Register* (PEAR).

9.8 Clock Stretch Bits

The E-clock output on Port E bit 4 is used for the external bus clock when operating the M68HC12 in expanded mode. The MCU expects to be able to complete a full bus cycle, say reading or writing, in one E-clock cycle. The seven chip select bits in Port F are used for expansion memory and are normally asserted in one E-clock cycle as shown in Figure 9–19a. In a system with a 16-MHz

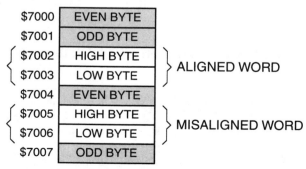

Figure 9–17 Expanded-wide mode memory alignment.

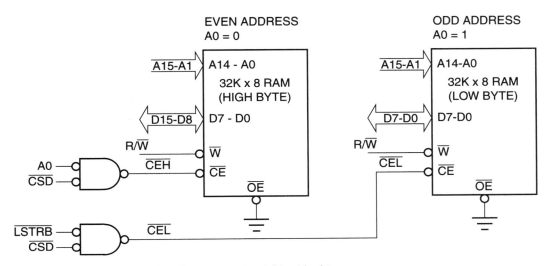

Figure 9-18   Expanded-mode memory using 8-bit-wide chips.

external oscillator, the E-clock is one-half this frequency and so the bus cycle lasts only 125 nsec. This may be too short for some external memory or I/O devices and so the MC68HC812A4 has the ability to stretch the chip select (and the E-clock on Port E, bit 4) zero, one, two, or three cycles as shown in Figure 9–18. *Chip Select Stretch Registers 0* and *1* (*CSSTR0* and *CSSTR1*) control the amount of stretch for each of the seven chip selects. The *MODE* register *E-clock Stretch Enable* (*ESTR*) bit must be set to allow the E-clock to stretch.

CSSTR0—$003E—Chip Select Stretch Register 0

Bit 7	6	5	4	3	2	1	Bit 0
7	6	STRP1A	STRP1B	STRP0A	STRP0B	STRDA	STRDB

Reset 0   0   1   1   1   1   1   1

TABLE 9-20   Chip Select Logic for Expanded-Wide Mode

Memory Access Type	$\overline{CSD}$	R/$\overline{W}$	A0	$\overline{LSTRB}$	CEH	CEL
Read aligned word	0	1	0	0	0	0
Read even byte	0	1	0	1	0	1[a]
Read odd byte	0	1	1	0	1[a]	0
Write aligned word	0	0	0	0	0	0
Write even byte	0	0	0	1	0	1[b]
Write odd byte	0	0	1	0	1[b]	0

[a]*The chip enable could be low when reading because the CPU will read only the half of the data bus it needs.*
[b]*This chip enable cannot be asserted because only the odd or even byte should be written.*

STRP1A:STRP1B
Stretch CSP1 as shown in Table 9–21.

STRP0A:STRP0B
Stretch CSP0.

STRDA:STRDB
Stretch CSD.

CSSTR1—$003F—Chip Select Stretch Register 1

Bit 7	6	5	4	3	2	1	Bit 0
STR3A	STR3B	STR2A	STR2B	STR1A	STR1B	STR0A	STR0B
Reset 1	1	1	1	1	1	1	1

STR3A:STR3B
Stretch CS3.

STR2A:STR2B
Stretch CS2.

STR1A:STR1B
Stretch CS1.

STR0A:STR0B
Stretch CS0.

TABLE 9–21 **Clock Stretch Bit Definition**

STRxxA	STRxxB	Number E-clocks Stretched
0	0	0
0	1	1
1	0	2
1	1	3 (default)

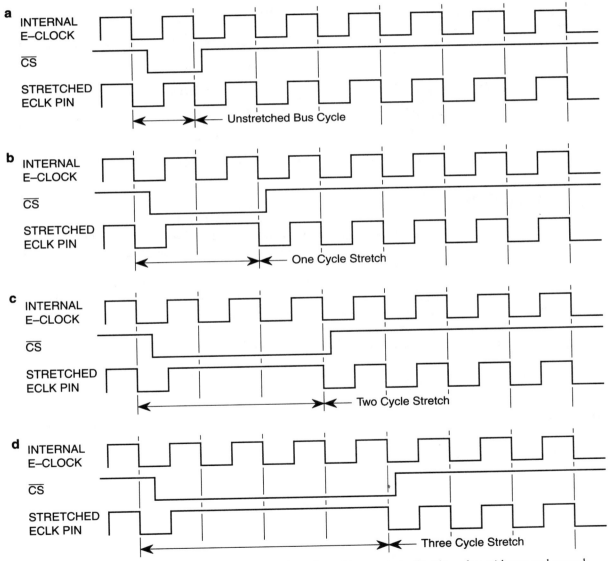

Figure 9–19 Chip selects with clock stretch. (a) Chip select with no stretch. (b) Chip select with one cycle stretch. (c) Chip select with two cycle stretch. (d) Chip select with three cycle stretch.

9.9 Conclusion and Chapter Summary Points

The M68HC12 contains on-chip RAM and EEPROM. The amount of each depends on the version of the chip. The MC68HC912B32 has 32 Kbytes of Flash EEPROM. New versions of the M68HC12 are being released by Motorola regularly so contact a chip supplier for the latest information on available devices.

9.10 Bibliography and Further Reading

Cady, F. M., *Microcontrollers and Microcomputers*, Oxford University Press, New York, 1997.

68HC12 CPU12 Reference Manual, CPU12RM/AD, Motorola, 1996.

MC68HC812A4 Technical Summary, MC68HC812A4TS/D, Rev 1., Motorola, 1997.

MC68HC912B32 Technical Summary, MC68HC912B32TS/D, Motorola, 1997.

Technical Supplement MC68HC812A4 Electrical Characteristics, 1/16/97, Motorola, 1997.

Technical Supplement MC68HC912B32 Electrical Characteristics, 9/09/97, Motorola 1997.

9.11 Problems

9.1   On reset, the RAM in the MC68HC812A4 is mapped to $0800 and the 512-byte register block to $0000. The locations of these can be changed. Describe how this is done.

9.2   What registers are used to remap the data RAM, EEPROM, and control registers?

9.3   What is the default memory location of EEPROM in the MC68HC812A4?

9.4   What is the default memory location of the Flash EEPROM in the MC68HC912B32 in single-chip mode? In expanded mode?

9.5   What are the three methods that can erase EEPROM?

9.6   How does the M68HC12 generate the 19 V needed to program the EEPROM?

Chapter 10

M68HC12 Timer

O B J E C T I V E S

This chapter describes the M68HC12 timer system and we compare the MC68HC812A4 and MC68HC912B32 versions. The timer system in both includes a *free running counter* and eight timer channels. These channels may be configured in any combination of timer comparison channels, called *output compares*, or *input capture* channels, which capture the time when an external event occurs. There is a *real-time periodic interrupt* and a counter for external events called the *pulse accumulator*. The interrupting capabilities of the timer are covered and programming examples are given. We also describe the *pulse width modulated* waveform generator available in the MC68HC912B32.

10.1 Introduction

Comparison of M68HC12 and M68HC11 Timer	
M68HC12	**M68HC11**
Eight timer channels; each may be configured as an output compare or input capture; one 16-bit pulse accumulator; real-time interrupt; computer operating properly watchdog timer	Five output compare channels; three input capture channels; one 8-bit pulse accumulator; real-time interrupt; computer operating properly watchdog timer

The timer section in the M68HC12 is based on a 16-bit counter operating from a system clock called the *M-clock*. At this point we will delay our discussion of how this clock is generated until Chapter 15 and concentrate now on learning about the timer capabilities. The 16-bit counter provides basic, real-time functions with the following features:

- A *timer overflow* to extend the 16-bit capability of the timer section counter.

- Up to eight *output compare functions* that can generate a variety of output waveforms by comparing the 16-bit timer counter with the contents of a programmable register.

- Up to eight *input capture functions* that can latch the value of the 16-bit counter on selected edges of eight timer input pins.

- A programmable, periodic interrupt generator called the *real-time interrupt.*

- A 16-bit *pulse accumulator* to count external events or act as a gated timer counting internal clock pulses.

The timer system is by far the most complex subsystem in the M68HC12. It uses many I/O control registers and many control bits. All timer functions have interrupt controls and separate interrupt vectors. Figure 10–1 shows the timer subsystem block diagram.

All timer functions have similar programming and operational characteristics. They all have flags in a control register that are set when some programmable condition is satisfied and that must be reset by the program. They all have interrupts that are enabled or disabled by a bit in a control register. Thus, when the operation of one timer function has been learned, the procedures are easily transferred to the others.

10.2 Basic Timer

The key to the operation of the M68HC12 timer is the 16-bit, free-running counter called *TCNT* shown in Figure 10–1. Its input clock is from the system M-clock, which may be prescaled by dividing it by 1, 2, 4, 8, 16, or 32. Typical M-clock frequencies are 4 and 8 MHz. The counter starts at 0000 when the microcontroller is reset and runs continuously after that unless you turn it off or cause it to stop in WAIT or background debug mode. The counter cannot be set to a particular value by the program when the CPU is operating in a normal mode, but it can be written in special modes. It can also be reset when a successful output compare occurs on timer channel seven. The TCNT register's current value can be read anytime. Every 65,536 pulses the counter reaches a maximum and overflows. When this occurs, the counter is reset to $0000 and a *Timer Overflow Flag* is set. This flag can extend the counter's range.

Prescaler

Comparison of M68HC12 and M68HC11 Prescaler	
M68HC12	**M68HC11**
Divides M-clock by a factor of 1, 2, 4, 8, 16, or 32; may be changed at any time	Divides E-clock by a factor of 1, 4, 8, or 16, but only if initialized in the first 64 E-clock cycles after reset

The clock source for the TCNT counter is the system M-clock, which can be prescaled by a programmable divider. The prescaler shown in Figure 10–1 is controlled by the three PR2:PR0 bits in the *Timer Interrupt Mask Register 2.*

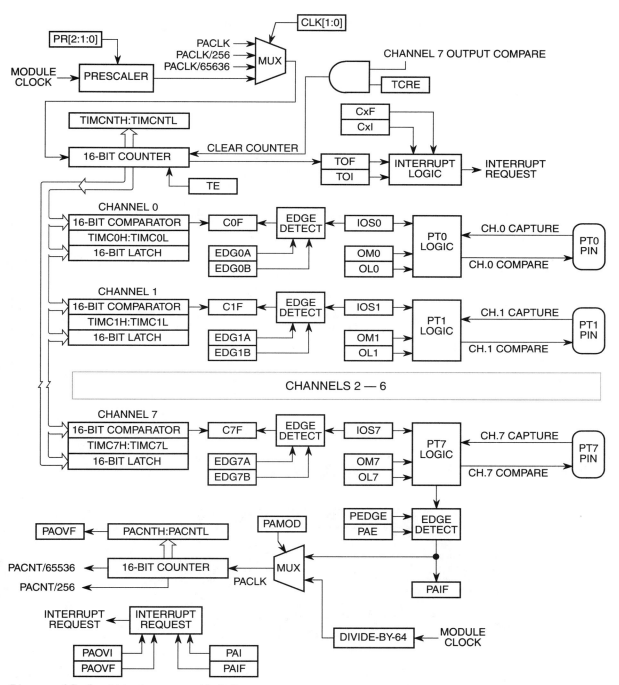

Figure 10-1 Main timer system block diagram.

TMSK2—$008D—Timer Interrupt Mask Register 2

Bit 7	6	5	4	3	2	1	Bit 0
TOI	0	TPU	TDRB	TCRE	PR2	PR1	PR0

Reset 0   0   1   1   0   0   0   0

TOI
Timer Overflow Interrupt Enable.
TPU
Timer Pull-up Resistor Enable.
TDRB
Timer Drive Reduction.
TCRE
Timer Counter Reset Enable.

Prescale Factor	PR2	PR1	PR0
1	0	0	0
2	0	0	1
4	0	1	0
8	0	1	1
16	1	0	0
32	1	0	1
Reserved	1	1	x

Sixteen-Bit Free-Running TCNT Register

Comparison of M68HC12 and M68HC11 TCNT	
M68HC12	**M68HC11**
16-bit, free running counter; starts at $0000 at reset; can be written to in special operating modes; can be reset when an output comparison is made on timer channel seven; TCNT can be stopped by disabling it or when in WAIT or in background debug mode	16-bit, free running counter; starts at $0000 at reset; continues to count forever; cannot be reset or written to at any time

The *TCNT* free-running counter is the heart of the timer system.

The *TCNT* register starts at $0000 when the processor is reset and counts continuously until it reaches the maximum count of $FFFF. On the next pulse, the counter rolls over to $0000, sets the *Timer Overflow Flag* (*TOF*), and continues to count.

The timer counter is designed to be read with a 16-bit read instruction such as LDD $84 or LDX $84. If you were to do two, 8-bit read instructions, for example,

```
LDAA    $84    ; Get the high 8 bits
LDAB    $85    ; Get the low 8 bits
```

the low 8 bits of the counter will be incremented and will be different by the time the second load instruction is executed.

TCNT—$0084:0085—Timer Count Register

Bit 7	6	5	4	3	2	1	Bit 0
15	14	13	12	11	10	9	8
7	6	5	4	3	2	1	0

Reset 0   0   0   0   0   0   0   0

TCNT Control Registers

Two registers allow some program control over the TCNT registers. These are the *Timer System Control Register* (*TSCR*) and the *TCRE* bit in the *Timer Interrupt Mask 2* (*TMSK2*) register.

TSCR—$0086—Timer System Control Register

Bit 7	6	5	4	3	2	1	Bit 0
TEN	TSWAI	TSBCK	TFFCA	0	0	0	0

Reset 0   0   0   0   0   0   0   0

TEN
Timer Enable. 0 = Disables the timer, including TCNT (default). 1 = Enables the timer. The timer can be disabled to reduce power consumption.

TSWAI
Timer Stops While in Wait. 0 = Allows timer to continue running during wait (default). 1 = Stops the timer while in the wait mode. This can be used to reduce power consumption but timer interrupts cannot be used to get out of the wait mode.

TSBCK

Timer Stops While in Background Mode.
      0 = Allows the timer to continue running while in background debugging mode (default).
      1 = Stops the timer when in background mode. This is useful for emulation. See Chapter 14 for more information on background debugging.

TFFCA

Timer Fast Flag Clear All. See Section 10.10 for more information about clearing the timer flags.

TMSK2—$008D—Timer Interrupt Mask Register 2

Bit 7	6	5	4	3	2	1	Bit 0
TOI	0	TPU	TDRB	TCRE	PR2	PR1	PR0

Reset 0   0   1   1   0   0   0   0

TCRE

Timer Counter Reset Enable.
      0 = Counter reset inhibited and TCNT free runs (default).
      1 = TCNT is reset to $0000 when a successful output compare occurs on timer channel 7.

TOI

Timer Overflow Interrupt Enable.

TPU

Timer Pull-up Resistor Enable.

TDRB

Timer Drive Reduction.

PR2:PR0

Timer Prescaler Selects.

Timer Overflow Flag

The timer overflow flag (*TOF*), is set when the timer rolls over from $FFFF to $0000. The programmer can extend the range of the count by detecting the overflow and incrementing another counter in the program. The timer overflow flag is in the *TFLG2* register. Figure 10–2 shows the timer overflow hardware in the M68HC12.

The TOF can be used in two ways—polling or interrupting. In polling, the program is responsible for watching the TOF flag (by reading bit 7 in the TFLG2 register). When the flag is set, the program can increment its local counter. The TOF <u>must</u> be reset by the program each time it is set by the counter. This is done by <u>writing</u> a <u>one</u> to bit-7 in the TFLG2 register. Example 10–1 shows how to use the timer overflow bit to generate a delay in increments of 8.192 msec when using an 8 MHz M-clock.

TFLG2—$008F—Timer Interrupt Flag 2

Bit 7	6	5	4	3	2	1	Bit 0
TOF	0	0	0	0	0	0	0

Reset 0   0   0   0   0   0   0   0

TOF
Timer Overflow Flag
This bit is set when the TCNT register count goes from $FFFF to $0000. The timer overflow bit is reset *by writing a one* to bit-7 of TFLG2. See Section 10.10.

F i g u r e 1 0 – 2   Timer overflow hardware.

EXAMPLE 10–1   Polling the Timer Overflow Flag

tofpol1c.asm   Assembled with CASM 12/11/1998 14:51 PAGE 1

```
                    1  ; MC68HC12 Assembler Example
                    2  ; This is an example of using the timer
                    3  ; overflow flag to generate a delay of
                    4  ; approximately 1 sec. (The delay
                    5  ; will be 122 timer overflow flags which is
                    6  ; equal to 0.999 sec with a 8 MHz M-clock.
                    7  ; Monitor Equates
0000                8  putchar:EQU     $FE04
                    9  ; Constant Equates
0000               10  BELL:    EQU    $07        ; BELL character
0000               11  NTIMES:  EQU    !122       ; Number of TOF's
                   12  ; I/O Register Equates
0000               13  TFLG2:   EQU    $8F        ; TFLG2 register
0000               14  TSCR:    EQU    $86        ; Timer system control reg
0000               15  TOF:     EQU    %10000000  ; Timer overflow flag
0000               16  TEN:     EQU    %10000000  ; Timer enable
                   17  ; Memory Map Equates
0000               18  PROG:    EQU    $0800      ; Locate the program
0000               19  DATA:    EQU    $0900      ; Variable data areas
0000               20  STACK:   EQU    $0a00      ; Stack
                   21  ; Source File:  TOFPOL1.ASM
0800               22           ORG    PROG       ; Locate the program
0800 CF0A00        23           lds    #STACK     ; Init stack pointer
                   24  ; Clear the TOF first
0803 8680          25           ldaa   #TOF
0805 5A8F          26           staa   TFLG2
                   27  ; Enable the timer
0807 4C8680        28           bset   TSCR,TEN
                   29  ; Initialize the counter and wait for NTIMES
080A 867A          30  repeat:  ldaa   #NTIMES
080C 7A0900        31           staa   counter
                   32  ; spin WHILE TOF is not set
080F F7008F        33  spin1:   tst    TFLG2
0812 2AFB          34           bpl    spin1      ; Branch if TOF=0
                   35  ; After the TOF=1, reset TOF
0814 8680          36           ldaa   #TOF
0816 5A8F          37           staa   TFLG2
                   38  ; and decrement the counter
0818 730900        39           dec    counter
                   40  ; IF counter != 0 spin
081B 26F2          41           bne    spin1
                   42  ; ELSE ring the BELL and reinitialize
081D C607          43           ldab   #BELL
081F 15FBF5E1      44           jsr    [putchar,PCR]
0823 20E5          45           bra    repeat
```

EXAMPLE 10–1   Continued

```
            46  ; RAM data area
0900        47            ORG    DATA
0900        48  counter: DS     1
```

Explanation of Example 10–1

This example shows how to use the timer overflow occurring at intervals of 8.192 msec to delay for longer periods. The TOF bit is reset in *line 26*, the timer is enabled in *line 28*, and a counter is initialized in *line 31*. *Lines 33 and 34* are a spin loop waiting for the TOF bit to be set. When it is, the flag is reset in *lines 36 and 37* and the counter is decremented (*line 39*). If the counter is not zero, the spin loop is reentered, otherwise the terminal bell is rung.

The delay in Example 10–1 has a resolution one-half of the period of the timer overflow, ± 4.096 msec. To generate an exact delay, to the resolution of the M-clock (125 nsec), count the extra clock cycles needed to make up the delay. A better and easier way is to use the *output compare* function discussed in Section 10.3.

Timer Overflow Interrupts

Timer interrupts allow your program to do other things while waiting for a timing event to occur.

A disadvantage of the program in Example 10–1 is that the TOF bit must be polled until 122 overflows have occurred. During this time the program could be doing other things but an overflow might be missed. An interrupt can allow the program to go about some other business while waiting for an event, the timer overflow for example, to occur. To use the timer overflow interrupt, the *TOI* bit in *TMSK2* must be enabled, the vector (or interrupt vector jump table) must be initialized, and the I-bit in the condition code register must be unmasked.

TMSK2—$008D—Timer Interrupt Mask Register 2

Bit 7	6	5	4	3	2	1	Bit 0
TOI	0	TPU	TDRB	TCRE	PR2	PR1	PR0

Reset 0   0   1   1   0   0   0   0

TOI
Timer Overflow Interrupt Enable.
0 = Interrupt inhibited (default).
1 = Interrupt requested when the TOF flag is set.

TPU
Timer Pull-up Resistor Enable.
TDRB
Timer Drive Reduction.
TCRE
Timer Counter Reset Enable.
PR2:PR0
Timer Prescaler Selects.

> The *timer overflow interrupt enable* bit must be set to allow the interrupt request to be generated.

The timer overflow flag (TOF) is ANDed with the timer overflow interrupt (TOI) enable bit to generate the interrupt request as shown in Figure 10–2. This request is further qualified by the interrupt mask bit (I-bit) in the condition code register as discussed in Chapter 8. Either the timer overflow interrupt vector or the D-Bug12 monitor SetUserVect number must be initialized properly to be able to transfer to the interrupt service routine (Table 10–1). An interrupt service routine using the timer overflow flag is given in Example 10–2.

Explanation of Example 10–2

In *lines 8–15* a conditional assembly construct is used to equate SetVect to the proper value for the version of D-Bug12 being used. There are two versions—1.xxx for systems using the MC68HC812A4 and 2.xxx for the MC68HC912B32. If Ver1, defined TRUE by the $SET in *line 8* is TRUE, the SetVect location $FE1A defined in *line 10* is used in *line 43*. If Ver1 is defined FALSE by changing *line 8* to $SETNOT Ver1, $F69A will be used. The correct vector location for the D-Bug12 Monitor routine putchar is defined also.

The timer overflow interrupt vector jump table is initialized in *lines 39–44*, just like the parallel I/O examples in Chapter 8. The interrupt system is unmasked by the CLI in *line 51*. The interrupt service routine resets the TOF bit in *lines 77* and *78* before returning to the interrupted program. See Example 10–3.

10.3 Output Compare

> The *output compare* allows more accurate timing delays than the timer overflow flag.

The timer overflow flag and interrupt discussed in the last section is suitable for timing to a resolution of $\pm 2^{15}$ clock cycles (± 4.096 msec for an 8-MHz clock). This may be sufficiently accurate for many applications, but when more precise timing is needed, the *output compare* features of the M68HC12 timer can be used.

TABLE 10–1 **Timer Overflow Interrupt Vectors**

Interrupt	Vector	D-Bug12 SetUserVect Number$_{10}$
Timer Overflow Interrupt	$FFDE:FFDF	15

EXAMPLE 10–2   Timer Overflow Interrupts

tofint1c.asm   Assembled with CASM 12/11/1998 14:52 PAGE 1

```
                    1  ; This is a test program showing the use
                    2  ; of the Timer Overflow Interrupts
                    3  ; using the D-Bug12 monitor.
                    4  ; The program uses the WAI
                    5  ; instruction while waiting for an interrupt.
                    6  ; After a second has elapsed, the bell is rung.
                    7  ; Monitor Equates
0000                8  $SET       Ver1                ; D-Bug12 version
0000                9  $IF        Ver1
0000               10  SetVect:   EQU    $FE1A        ; D-Bug12 routine in Ver 1
0000               11  putchar:   EQU    $FE04        ; Putchar to terminal
0000               12  $ELSEIF
                   13  SetVect:   EQU    $F69A        ; D-Bug12 routine in Ver 2
                   14  putchar:   EQU    $F684        ; Putchar to terminal
0000               15  $ENDIF
0000               16  TOFNUM:    EQU    !15
                   17  ;              Constant Equates
0000               18  NTIMES:    EQU    !122         ; Number times to interrupt
0000               19  BELL:      EQU    $07          ; BELL character
                   20  ; I/O Register Equates
0000               21  TOF:       EQU    %10000000        ; Timer Overflow Flag
0000               22  TOI:       EQU    %10000000        ; Timer Overflow Int
0000               23  TEN:       EQU    %10000000        ; Timer enable
0000               24  TSCR:      EQU    $86              ; Timer control reg
0000               25  TFLG2:     EQU    $8F              ; TFLG2
0000               26  TMSK2:     EQU    $8D              ; TMSK2 offset
                   27  ; Memory Map Equates
0000               28  PROG:      EQU    $0800        ; ROM location
0000               29  DATA:      EQU    $0900        ; RAM location
0000               30  STACK:     EQU    $0a00        ; Stack pointer location
                   31
                   32  ; Now do the program
0800               33            ORG     PROG
                   34  prog_start:
0800 CF0A00        35            lds     #STACK
                   36  ; Initialize the Counter
0803 790900        37            clr     Counter
                   38  ; Initialize the vector
0806 CC0832        39            ldd     #isr
0809 3B            40            pshd
080A CC000F        41            ldd     #TOFNUM
080D 15FBF609      42            jsr     [SetVect,PCR]
0811 3A            43            puld                ; Clean up stack
                   44  ; Enable the timer
0812 4C8680        45            bset    TSCR,TEN
```

EXAMPLE 10–2   Continued

```
                      46  ; Clear the TOF
0815  8680            47              ldaa    #TOF
0817  5A8F            48              staa    TFLG2
                      49  ; Enable the interrupt system
0819  4C8D80          50              bset    TMSK2,TOI ; Enable timer overflow
081C  10EF            51              cli         ; Unmask hc12 interrupts
                      52  ; Do Forever
081E  3E             53  start:       wai         ; Wait for the interrupt
                      54  ; When the counter incremented by the ISR
                      55  ; reaches a maximum given
                      56  ; by NTIMES, ring the bell on the
                      57  ; terminal and reset the Counter value.
                      58  ; IF Counter = maximum
081F  B60900          59              ldaa    Counter
0822  817A            60              cmpa    #NTIMES
0824  260A            61              bne     endif
                      62  ; THEN ring the BELL
0826  C607            63              ldab    #BELL
0828  15FBF5D8        64              jsr     [putchar,PCR]
                      65  ; and reset the Counter
082C  87             66              clra
082D  7A0900          67              staa    Counter
                      68  ; ENDIF Counter=maximum
                      69  endif:
0830  20EC            70              bra     start
                      71  ; End do forever
                      72  ; Timer Overflow ISR
                      73  ; This ISR increments a Counter value on each
                      74  ; interrupt.
0832  720900          75  isr:         inc     Counter
                      76  ; Clear the TOF bit
0835  8680            77              ldaa    #TOF
0837  5A8F            78              staa    TFLG2
                      79  ; And play it again Sam
0839  0B             80              rti         ; Return to main prog
                      81  ; Set up a Counter buffer
0900                  82              ORG     DATA
0900                  83  Counter:DS          1
```

The output compare hardware is shown in Figure 10–3. The 16-bit TCNT register is clocked by the M-clock that is *prescaled* by the PR2:PR1:PR0 prescaler. A 16-bit *Timer Input Capture/Output Compare* register, *TCn*,[1] may be loaded by the program with a 16-bit load instruction. This register is compared with the current value of the TCNT register at every M-clock cycle, and when

---

[1] *n* is 0–7 for each of the timer channels. Any of the channels can be input capture or output compare.

EXAMPLE 10-3

Why is the TOF bit cleared in *line 48* in Example 10–2?

Solution:

If the TOF bit is set when the timer interrupts are enabled and interrupts ummasked, an interrupt will occur immediately. This may upset the required timing for the first iteration of the program.

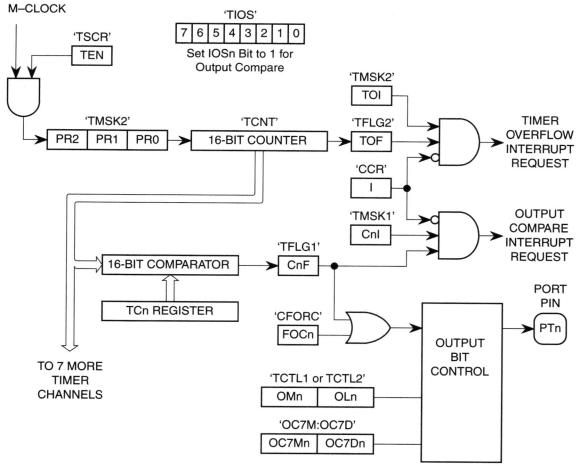

Figure 10-3   Timer output compare hardware.

the TCn is identical to TCNT, the *Input Capture/Output Compare Channel n Flag, CnF,* is set. Tracing through Figure 10–3, you can see that CnF is ANDed with a *Timer Interrupt Enable* bit (*CnI*) to generate an interrupt when both the flag and the enable bit are set and interrupts are unmasked. CnF is also ORed with a bit called *Timer Compare Force* bit *n* (*FOCn*) and routed to the output bit control logic. Two bits, *OMn* and *OLn,* control the action on the Port T output bit when a successful output compare occurs.

Each of the timer channels may be configured to give an input capture or an output compare function. Port T bits can be controlled by the output compare functions or can serve as the input signals for the input captures. As shown in Chapter 7, Port T can be used for general-purpose I/O if the timer functions are not being used. The choice is made by programming the *Timer Input Capture/Output Compare Select* (*TIOS*) register. When bits in TIOS are set, the output compare bit is controlled by the OMn:OLn bits in TCTL1 and TCTL2. When bits in TIOS are zero, the associated Port T bits can be an input capture or an I/O bit whose direction is controlled by DDRT.

After you have initialized the TIOS register to select which channel is to be an Output Compare, and have initialized the corresponding Timer Input/Output Compare (TCn) register with a 16-bit value, and have reset the Input Capture/Output Compare Channel Flag (CnF), you may start to generate very accurate timing signals. When the TCNT and TCn register are identical, the CnF flag is set. You can use this event in one of two ways. You can *poll* the flag and when it is set accomplish the timing that you want, or you can use an *interrupt* that can be generated. You can use the timing information in your program, say for generating a time delay for some purpose, or you can allow the flag to generate an action on the associated Port T output bit.

TIOS—$0080—Timer Input Capture/Output Compare Select

Bit 7	6	5	4	3	2	1	Bit 0
IOS7	IOS6	IOS5	IOS4	IOS3	IOS2	IOS1	IOS0

Reset 0   0   0   0   0   0   0   0

IOS[7:0]

Input Capture or Output Compare Channel Designator.
    0 = The corresponding channel acts as input capture or an I/O bit (default).
    1 = The channel acts as an output compare.
When IOS[7:0] is zero, the Port T bit can act as an I/O pin whose direction is controlled by the state of the data direction register DDRT.

TC0–TC7—Timer Input Capture/Output Compare Registers

TC0—$0090:0091—Timer Input Capture/Output Compare Register 0

TC1—$0092:0093—Timer Input Capture/Output Compare Register 1

TC2—$0094:0095—Timer Input Capture/Output Compare Register 2

TC3—$0096:0097—Timer Input Capture/Output Compare Register 3

TC4—$0098:0099—Timer Input Capture/Output Compare Register 4

TC5—$009A:009B—Timer Input Capture/Output Compare Register 5

TC6—$009C:009D—Timer Input Capture/Output Compare Register 6

TC7—$009E:009F—Timer Input Capture/Output Compare Register 7

Bit 7	6	5	4	3	2	1	Bit 0
15	14	13	12	11	10	9	8
7	6	5	4	3	2	1	0

These eight, 16-bit registers hold the value for comparison with the TCNT register.

TFLG1—$008E—Timer Interrupt Flag 1

Bit 7	6	5	4	3	2	1	Bit 0
C7F	C6F	C5F	C4F	C3F	C2F	C1F	C0F

Reset 0   0   0   0   0   0   0   0

C7F:C0F
Timer interrupt flags. When the corresponding timer channel is configured for output compare, the flag is set when the TCNT and TCn register contents are identical. When the corresponding timer channel is configured for input capture, the flag is set when a selected edge is detected at the timer input pin. See Section 10.4. The flag is reset by writing a one to the register. See Section 10.10.

Output Compare Time Delays

The output compare can generate timing delays with much higher accuracy than the timer over-flow flag. Consider generating a delay that is less than 8.192 msec, for example, 1 msec. In a system with an 8-MHz M-clock, a 1 msec delay is 8000 M-clock cycles. In Example 10–4, a 1 msec delay is generated by reading the current contents of the TCNT register (*line 35*), adding 8000 cycles to it (*line 36*), and storing this value into the TC1 register (*line 37*). The C1F bit is reset in *lines 39* and *40* by writing a one to the register. The program then waits for C1F to be set in a spin loop at *line 42*. One millisecond after the TCNT register was read in *line 35* the C1F bit is set and the program will drop out of the spin loop.

EXAMPLE 10–4 1 msec Delay Program Using the Output Compare

tocdly1c.asm   Assembled with CASM 02/16/1998 00:37 PAGE 1

```
                1 ; This is a test program showing the use
                2 ; of the Output Compare to generate time
                3 ; delays. It outputs a 1 msec wide pulse
                4 ; on Port J-7
                5 ; Constant Equates
0000            6 ONE_MS:   EQU     !8000     ; Clocks per msec
                7 ; I/O Register Equates
0000            8 TIOS:     EQU     $80       ; Input Cap/Out Compare Select
0000            9 TSCR:     EQU     $86       ; Timer System Control
0000           10 TCNT:     EQU     $84       ; TCNT register
0000           11 TFLG1:    EQU     $8E       ; TFLG1 register
0000           12 TC1:      EQU     $92       ; Timer channel 1
0000           13 PORTJ:    EQU     $28       ; Data reg Port J
0000           14 DDRJ:     EQU     $29       ; Port J data direction reg
0000           15 BIT7:     EQU     %10000000
0000           16 C1F:      EQU     %00000010  ; Output compare 1 Flag
0000           17 TEN:      EQU     %10000000  ; Timer Enable
               18 ; Memory Map Equates
0000           19 PROG:     EQU     $0800     ; ROM location
0000           20 DATA:     EQU     $0900     ; RAM location
0000           21 STACK:    EQU     $0a00     ; Stack pointer location
0800           22           ORG     PROG
               23 prog_start:
0800 CF0A00    24           lds     #STACK
               25 ; Enable the timer hardware
0803 4C8680    26           bset    TSCR,TEN
               27 ; Enable Output Compare Channel 1
0806 4C8002    28           bset    TIOS,C1F
               29 ; Set Port J bit 7 to output
0809 4C2980    30           bset    DDRJ,BIT7
               31 ; Set the bit high
080C 4C2880    32           bset    PORTJ,BIT7
               33 ; Just generate a 1 msec delay here
               34 ; Grab the value of the TCNT register
080F DC84      35           ldd     TCNT
0811 C31F40    36           addd    #ONE_MS
0814 5C92      37           std     TC1
               38 ; Now reset the flag and wait until it is set
0816 8602      39           ldaa    #C1F
0818 5A8E      40           staa    TFLG1
               41 ; Wait until the flag is set
081A 4F8E02FC  42           spin:   brclr    TFLG1,C1F,spin
               43 ; Reset Port J bit 7
081E 4D2880    44           bclr    PORTJ,BIT7
0821 3F        45           swi
```

Example 10–4 shows an output compare time delay that can have at most an 8.192 msec delay when the default 8-MHz M-clock is used. Figure 10–3 shows that the TMSK2 register has three prescaler bits PR2:PR1:PR0. These can be changed to select a prescaler of 1, 2, 4, 5, 16, or 32. Example 10–5 shows a program to generate a 10 msec delay. In *lines 33* and *34* the current value in the TMSK2 register is saved on the stack so it can be restored later (in *lines 59 and 60*). Lines *36* and *37* set the prescaler bits to 010 to divide by four. Now, each clock pulse is at 0.5 μsec and a 10 msec delay is represented by 20,000 counts.

If you use this technique to generate longer time delays, remember that any changes you make will affect all timing being done by the timer system in other parts of the program.

Output Compare Interrupts

An interrupt can be generated by the output compare flag if, like the timer overflow flag, the *Timer Interrupt* enable bit (*CnI*) is set. The enable bits for all timer functions are in *TMSK1*.

TMSK1—$008C—Timer Interrupt Mask 1

Bit 7	6	5	4	3	2	1	Bit 0
C7I	C6I	C5I	C4I	C3I	C2I	C1I	C0I

Reset 0   0   0   0   0   0   0   0

C7I:C0I

Timer Interrupt Enable.
    0 = The corresponding bit in TFLG1 is disabled from generating interrupts (default).
    1 = The corresponding bit in TFLG1 may generate an interrupt.

Delays longer than 8.192 msec can be generated by changing the prescaler as shown in Example 10–5 or by waiting for more output comparisons to be made. Example 10–6 shows how to generate a 1 sec delay using the output compare flag to generate an interrupt. The delay is achieved by waiting for 250 complete 4 msec delay times generated by the output compare. This is done by reading the TNCT register in *line 51* and then generating an interrupt every 4 msec after that. After 250 interrupts, the terminal will beep. A counter for this is initialized in *lines 48* and *49*. After the C2F flag is cleared and interrupts enabled and unmasked (*lines 55–58*), the processor waits for the interrupt to occur (*line 60*). When it does, the counter is checked to see if it is zero. After the counter reaches zero, it is reinitialized to NTIMES and the terminal is beeped. The interrupt service routine decrements the counter in *line 76*. With an M-clock of 8 MHz, each time an interrupt occurs D_4MS (32,000 M-clock cycles) is added to the TC2 register in *lines 77–80*. Finally the flag is cleared in *lines 82* and *83*. See Example 10–7 also. As shown in Chapter 8, the timer interrupt vectors must be initialized. These vectors are shown in Table 10–2.

EXAMPLE 10–5   Changing the Timer Prescaler

tocdly2c.asm   Assembled with CASM 02/16/1998 00:34 PAGE 1

```
                      1  ; This is a test program showing the use
                      2  ; of the Output Compare to generate time
                      3  ; delays that are longer than 8.192 msec by
                      4  ; changing the TCNT register prescaler.
                      5  ; It outputs a 10-msec-wide pulse
                      6  ; on Port J-7
                      7  ; Constant Equates
0000                  8  TEN_MS:   EQU      !20000    ; Clocks per 10 msec
                      9  ; I/O Register Equates
0000                 10  TIOS:     EQU      $80       ; Input Capt/Out Compare Select
0000                 11  TSCR:     EQU      $86       ; Timer System Control
0000                 12  TCNT:     EQU      $84       ; TCNT register
0000                 13  TFLG1:    EQU      $8E       ; TFLG1 register
0000                 14  TC1:      EQU      $92       ; Timer channel 1
0000                 15  TMSK2:    EQU      $8D       ; Timer mask 2
0000                 16  PR2:      EQU      %00000100  ; Prescale bit 2
0000                 17  PR1:      EQU      %00000010  ; Prescale bit 1
0000                 18  PR0:      EQU      %00000001  ; Prescale bit 0
0000                 19  PORTJ:    EQU      $28       ; Data reg Port J
0000                 20  DDRJ:     EQU      $29       ; Port J data direction reg
0000                 21  BIT7:     EQU      %10000000
0000                 22  C1F:      EQU      %00000010  ; Output compare 1 Flag
0000                 23  TEN:      EQU      %10000000  ; Timer Enable
                     24  ; Memory Map Equates
0000                 25  PROG:     EQU      $0800     ; ROM location
0000                 26  DATA:     EQU      $0900     ; RAM location
0000                 27  STACK:    EQU      $0a00     ; Stack pointer location
0800                 28            ORG      PROG
                     29  prog_start:
0800 CF0A00          30            lds      #STACK
                     31  ; Get the current prescaler value and save it
                     32  ; to be restored later
0803 D68D            33            ldab     TMSK2
0805 37              34            pshb
                     35  ; Set the prescaler to divide by 4
0806 4D8D05          36            bclr     TMSK2,PR2|PR0
0809 4C8D02          37            bset     TMSK2,PR1
                     38  ; Enable the timer hardware
080C 4C8680          39            bset     TSCR,TEN
                     40  ; Enable Output Compare Channel 1
080F 4C8002          41            bset     TIOS,C1F
                     42  ; Set Port J bit 7 to output
0812 4C2980          43            bset     DDRJ,BIT7
                     44  ; Set the bit high
0815 4C2880          45            bset     PORTJ,BIT7
```

EXAMPLE 10–5   Continued

```
                46  ; Just generate a 10 msec delay here
                47  ; Grab the value of the TCNT register
0818 DC84       48          ldd     TCNT
081A C34E20     49          addd    #TEN_MS
081D 5C92       50          std     TC1
                51  ; Now reset the flag and wait until it is set
081F 8602       52          ldaa    #C1F
0821 5A8E       53          staa    TFLG1
                54  ; Wait until the flag is set
0823 4F8E02FC   55  spin:   brclr   TFLG1,C1F,spin
                56  ; Reset Port J bit 7
0827 4D2880     57          bclr    PORTJ,BIT7
                58  ; Now restore the original prescaler values
082A 33         59          pulb
082B 5B8D       60          stab    TMSK2
082D 3F         61          swi
```

EXAMPLE 10–6   1 sec Delay Using Output Compare Interrupts

```
tocint1c.asm           Assembled with CASM 12/11/1998 15:02 PAGE 1

                1  ; Test program showing a 1 sec
                2  ; delay using output compare and interrupts.
                3  ; Monitor Equates
0000            4  $SET      Ver1              ; D-Bug12 version
0000            5  $IF       Ver1
0000            6  SetVect:  EQU     $FE1A     ; D-Bug12 routine in Ver 1
0000            7  putchar:  EQU     $FE04     ; Putchar to terminal
0000            8  $ELSEIF
                9  SetVect:  EQU     $F69A     ; D-Bug12 routine in Ver 2
               10  putchar:  EQU     $F684     ; Putchar to terminal
0000           11  $ENDIF
0000           12  OC2VEC:   EQU     !21       ; Timer channel 2 interrupt
               13  ; Constant Equates
0000           14  NTIMES:   EQU     !250      ; Number of 4 msec delays
0000           15  D_4MS:    EQU     !32000    ; Num clocks for 4 msec
0000           16  BELL:     EQU     7         ; Bell character
               17  ; I/O Register Equates
0000           18  TIOS:     EQU     $80       ; In capt/out compare select
0000           19  TCNT:     EQU     $84       ; TCNT register
0000           20  TSCR:     EQU     $86       ; Timer control register
0000           21  TMSK1:    EQU     $8C       ; Timer mask reg
0000           22  TFLG1:    EQU     $8E       ; TFLG1 offset
0000           23  TC2:      EQU     $94       ; Timer register 2
```

EXAMPLE 10–6 Continued

```
0000              24 TEN:      EQU   %10000000  ; Timer enable bit
0000              25 C2F:      EQU   %00000100  ; Output compare 2 Flag
0000              26 C2I:      EQU   C2F        ; Interrupt enable
0000              27 IOS2:     EQU   C2F        ; Select OC2
                  28 ; Memory Map Equates
0000              29 PROG:     EQU   $0800      ; ROM location
0000              30 DATA:     EQU   $0900      ; RAM location
0000              31 STACK:    EQU   $0a00      ; Stack pointer location
                  32 ;
0800              33           ORG   PROG
                  34 prog_start:
0800 CF0A00       35           lds   #STACK
                  36 ; Set up the interrupt vector
0803 CC0836       37           ldd   #isr       ; ISR address
0806 3B           38           pshd
0807 CC0015       39           ldd   #OC2VEC
                  40 ;         jsr   [SetVect,PCR]
080A 3A           41           puld             ; Clean up stack
                  42 ; Enable the timer system
080B 4C8680       43           bset  TSCR,TEN
                  44 ; Enable output compare channel 2
080E 4C8004       45           bset  TIOS,IOS2
                  46 ; Generate a 1 sec delay
                  47 ; Need NTIMES interrupts
0811 86FA         48           ldaa  #NTIMES
0813 7A0900       49           staa  counter
                  50 ; Grab the value of the TCNT register
0816 DC84         51           ldd   TCNT
0818 5C94         52           std   TC2
                  53 ; Now have 8 msec to set up the system
                  54 ; Set up interrupts
081A 8604         55           ldaa  #C2F
081C 5A8E         56           staa  TFLG1      ; Clear C2F
081E 4C8C04       57           bset  TMSK1,C2I  ; Enable TC2 Interrupt
0821 10EF         58           cli              ; Unmask global interrupts
                  59 ; Wait until the counter is 0
0823 3E           60 spin:     wai              ; Wait for interrupt
0824 F70900       61           tst   counter
0827 26FA         62           bne   spin
                  63 ; When out of the spin loop
                  64 ; Reinitialize the counter
0829 86FA         65           ldaa  #NTIMES
082B 7A0900       66           staa  counter
                  67 ; And beep the bell
082E C607         68           ldab  #BELL
0830 15FBF5D0     69           jsr   [putchar,PCR]
```

EXAMPLE 10–6   Continued

```
              70  ; Return to wait for the next interrupt
0834  20ED    71          bra       spin
              72
              73  ; Interrupt Service Routine
              74  ; Decrement the counter
0836  730900  75  isr:     dec       counter
              76  ; Set up TC2 for the next interrupt
0839  DC94    77          ldd       TC2
              78  ; Add the clock pulses
083B  C37D00  79          addd      #D_4MS
083E  5C94    80          std       TC2
              81  ; And clear the C2F
0840  8604    82          ldaa      #C2F
0842  5A8E    83          staa      TFLG1
0844  0B      84          rti
0900          85          ORG       DATA
0900          86  counter: DS        1
```

Output Compare Bit Operation

The output compare flags can automatically set or reset Port T bits when the flag is set.

Look again at Figure 10–3 and see that the output compare flags pass through an OR gate to a block called *Output Bit Control* and then to Port T. The Port T pins are multipurpose and may be programmed to be simple I/O pins as shown in Chapter 7, or for use by the output compare functions. Let us first look at how C0F to C7F can be used as output compare pins. The registers that control this function are the *Timer Control Register 1 and 2*. When a successful output comparison is made, one of four actions may occur at the output pin in Port T. It can either be disconnected, toggled, cleared, or set. Two bits for each Port T output, *OMn* and *OLn*, are programmed to make this selection. OM7:OL7–OM0:OL0 are in the *Timer Control Registers 1* and 2. Example 10–8 shows how to set bits OM2:OL2 to automatically toggle the Port T-2 when output compares occur every 4 msec. See also Example 10–9.

TCTL1—$0088—Timer Control Register 1

TCTL2—$0089—Timer Control Register 2

	Bit 7	6	5	4	3	2	1	Bit 0
TCTL1	OM7	OL7	OM6	OL6	OM5	OL5	OM4	OL4
TCTL2	OM3	OL3	OM2	OL2	OM1	OL1	OM0	OL0
Reset	0	0	0	0	0	0	0	0

EXAMPLE 10–7

In Example 10–6 the programmer calculates the count for the next interrupt by adding 32,000 clock cycles to the current value of the TC2 register (*lines 78–81*). Why didn't the programmer first read the TCNT register and then add 32,000 to find the time for the next interrupt?

Solution:

Interrupts are required every 4 msec in this example. If the TCNT register is used every time to calculate the time for the next interrupt, the time interval will be longer than 4 msec because the TCNT register increments with every clock cycle.

OM7:OM0
Output Mode Select.
OL7:OL0
Output Level Select.

OMn	OLn	Output Action at Successful Compare
0	0	Timer disconnected from output pin logic. No action (default).
0	1	Toggle PTn output line.
1	0	Clear PTn output line to zero.
1	1	Set PTn output line to one.

When either OMn or OLn is set, the corresponding output capture pin (on Port T) becomes an output regardless of the state of the associated DDRT bit.

TABLE 10–2 Vectors for the Output Compare Interrupts

Interrupt	Vector	D-Bug12 SetUserVect Number$_{10}$
Timer Channel 0	$FFEE:FFEF	23
Timer Channel 1	$FFEC:FFED	22
Timer Channel 2	$FFEA:FFEB	21
Timer Channel 3	$FFE8:FFE9	20
Timer Channel 4	$FFE6:FFE7	19
Timer Channel 5	$FFE4:FFE5	18
Timer Channel 6	$FFE2:FFE3	17
Timer Channel 7	$FFE0:FFE1	16

EXAMPLE 10-8   Output Compare Bit Operation

```
tocint2c.asm                Assembled with CASM 12/11/1998  15:06  PAGE 1

                     1  ; Test program showing a 4 msec
                     2  ; delay using output compare and interrupts.
                     3  ; When the output compare occurs, PT-2
                     4  ; is toggled.
                     5  ; Monitor Equates
0000                 6  $SET       Ver1              ; D-Bug12 version
0000                 7  $IF        Ver1
0000                 8  SetVect:   EQU    $FE1A      ; D-Bug12 routine in Ver 1
0000                 9  putchar:   EQU    $FE04      ; Putchar to terminal
0000                10  $ELSEIF
                    11  SetVect:   EQU    $F69A      ; D-Bug12 routine in Ver 2
                    12  putchar:   EQU    $F684      ; Putchar to terminal
0000                13  $ENDIF
0000                14  OC2VEC:    EQU    !21        ; Timer channel 2 interrupt
                    15  ; Constant Equates
0000                16  D_4MS:     EQU    !32000     ; Num clocks for 4 msec
                    17  ; I/O Register Equates
0000                18  TIOS:      EQU    $80        ; In capt/out compare select
0000                19  TCNT:      EQU    $84        ; TCNT register
0000                20  TSCR:      EQU    $86        ; Timer control register
0000                21  TMSK1:     EQU    $8C        ; Timer mask reg
0000                22  TFLG1:     EQU    $8E        ; TFLG1 offset
0000                23  TC2:       EQU    $94        ; Timer register 2
0000                24  TCTL2:     EQU    $89
0000                25  OM2:       EQU    %00100000
0000                26  OL2:       EQU    %00010000
0000                27  TEN:       EQU    %10000000  ; Timer enable bit
0000                28  C2F:       EQU    %00000100  ; Output compare 2 Flag
0000                29  C2I:       EQU    C2F        ; Interrupt enable
0000                30  IOS2:      EQU    C2F        ; Select OC2
                    31  ; Memory Map Equates
0000                32  PROG:      EQU    $0800      ; ROM location
0000                33  DATA:      EQU    $0900      ; RAM location
0000                34  STACK:     EQU    $0a00      ; Stack pointer location
                    35  ;
0800                36             ORG    PROG
                    37  prog_start:
0800 CF0A00         38             lds    #STACK
                    39  ; Set up the interrupt vector
0803 CC082B         40             ldd    #isr       ; ISR address
0806 3B             41             pshd
0807 CC0015         42             ldd    #OC2VEC
080A 15FBF60C       43             jsr    [SetVect,PCR]
080E 3A             44             puld              ; Clean up stack
                    45  ; Enable the timer system
```

EXAMPLE 10–8   Continued

```
080F  4C8680     46              bset    TSCR,TEN
                 47  ; Enable output capture channel 2
0812  4C8004     48              bset    TIOS,IOS2
                 49  ; Set up Output capture action to toggle the bit-2
0815  4D8920     50              bclr    TCTL2,OM2
0818  4C8910     51              bset    TCTL2,OL2
                 52  ; Grab the value of the TCNT register
081B  DC84       53              ldd     TCNT
081D  5C94       54              std     TC2
                 55  ; Now have 32 msec to set up the system
                 56  ; Set up interrupts
081F  8604       57              ldaa    #C2F
0821  5A8E       58              staa    TFLG1      ; Clear C2F
0823  4C8C04     59              bset    TMSK1,C2I  ; Enable TC2 Interrupt
0826  10EF       60              cli                ; Unmask global interrupts
                 61  ; Wait until the counter is 0
0828  3E         62  spin:       wai                ; Wait for interrupt
0829  26FD       63              bne     spin
                 64  ; Interrupt Service Routine
                 65  isr:
                 66  ; Set up TOC2 for the next interrupt
082B  DC94       67              ldd     TC2
                 68  ; Add the clock pulses
082D  C37D00     69              addd    #D_4MS
0830  5C94       70              std     TC2
                 71  ; And clear the C2F
0832  8604       72              ldaa    #C2F
0834  5A8E       73              staa    TFLG1
0836  0B         74              rti
```

EXAMPLE 10–9

Write a short section of code to cause Port T, bit-5 to clear the bit when an output comparison is made.

Solution:

Port T, bit 5 is connected to Output Compare 5. Therefore, use the code

```
: Set OM5, OL5 in TCTL1 to 1 0
     bset    $88, %00001000
     bclr    $88, %00000100
```

One Output Compare Controlling up to Eight Outputs

Output Compare 7 can simultaneously switch up to eight outputs.

The Output Compare 7 channel has special features that are controlled by the *OC7M* and *OC7D* registers. OC7M and OC7D work together to define the action taken on Port T, bits 7–0. OC7D is a data register and its contents are transferred to the output bits on Port T when a successful output comparison is made on channel 7. OC7M is a mask register and a 1 in a bit position in the mask means that the corresponding data bit in the data register, OC7D, is transferred to the output bit in Port T. Thus, up to eight bits can be simultaneously changed by one output comparison. This is useful in applications where bit streams are controlling devices that must be changed in synchronism. Any change designated by a bit in OC7D overrides any action from the other output compare channels. See Example 10–10.

OC7M—$0082—Output Compare 7 Mask Register

Bit 7	6	5	4	3	2	1	Bit 0
OC7M7	OC7M6	OC7M5	OC7M4	OC7M3	OC7M2	OC7M1	OC7M0

Reset 0   0   0   0   0   0   0   0

Setting any bit in OC7M enables the corresponding bit in OC7D to be output to the corresponding pin in Port T. Setting OC7Mn sets the Port T bit to be an output regardless of the state of bits in DDRT.

OC7D—$0083—Output Compare 7 Data Register

Bit 7	6	5	4	3	2	1	Bit 0
OC7D7	OC7D6	OC7D5	OC7D4	OC7D3	OC7D2	OC7D1	OC7D0

Reset 0   0   0   0   0   0   0   0

When a bit in OC7M is set, the data value in the corresponding bit in OC7D is output to the corresponding pin in Port T when the output compare in channel 7 is made.

Explanation of Example 10–10

Example 10–10 illustrates how to toggle five bits simultaneously using one output compare. PT7–PT3, defined by BITS_5 in *line 17*, are to be toggled. The initial data state for these bits is %10101 as defined in *line 16* by BITS. Output compare channels 7–3 are initialized for use in *lines 25–38* and the initial data are stored in OC7D in *line 40*. The mask register, OC7M, is set

---

EXAMPLE 10–10   Toggle Five Bits with One Output Compare

toc5bitc.asm   Assembled with CASM 02/16/1998 02:56 PAGE 1

```
                    1  ; Test program showing five bits toggling
                    2  ; every 1 msec using the Output Compare 7
                    3  ; Constant Equates
0000                4  D_1MS:    EQU        !8000      ; Num clocks for 1 msec
                    5  ; I/O Register Equates
0000                6  TIOS:     EQU        $80        ; Timer IO Select
0000                7  OC7M:     EQU        $82        ; Output compare 1 mask
0000                8  OC7D:     EQU        $83        ; Output compare 1 data
0000                9  TCNT:     EQU        $84        ; TCNT register
0000               10  TSCR:     EQU        $86        ; Timer System Control
0000               11  TFLG1:    EQU        $8E        ; TFLG1 register
0000               12  TC7:      EQU        $9E
0000               13  DDRT:     EQU        $AF        ; Data Direction Port T
0000               14  TEN:      EQU        %10000000  ; Timer Enable
0000               15  C7F:      EQU        %10000000  ; Output compare 1 Flag
0000               16  BITS:     EQU        %10101000  ; Bit pattern to output
0000               17  BITS_5:   EQU        %11111000  ; Five bits output
                   18  ; Memory Map Equates
0000               19  PROG:     EQU        $0800      ; ROM location
0000               20  DATA:     EQU        $0900      ; RAM location
0000               21  STACK:    EQU        $0A00      ; Stack pointer location
0800               22            ORG        PROG
                   23  prog_start:
0800 CF0A00        24            lds        #STACK
                   25  ; Enable the timer
0803 4C8680        26            bset       TSCR,TEN
                   27  ; Enable the output compare channels 7-3
0806 4C80F8        28            bset       TIOS,BITS_5
                   29  ; Grab the value of the TCNT register
0809 DC84          30            ldd        TCNT
080B 5C9E          31            std        TC7
                   32  ; Reset output compare flag
080D 8680          33            ldaa       #C7F
080F 5A8E          34            staa       TFLG1
                   35  ; Initialize the mask register
0811 86F8          36            ldaa       #BITS_5
0813 5A82          37            staa       OC7M
                   38  ; Initialize the data register
0815 86A8          39            ldaa       #BITS
0817 5A83          40            staa       OC7D
                   41  ; Wait until the C7F is set
0819 4F8E80FC      42  spin:     brclr      TFLG1,C7F,spin
                   43  ; Now set up for the next 1 msec interval
081D DC9E          44            ldd        TC7
081F C31F40        45            addd       #D_1MS
```

```
0822  5C9E        46              std       TC7
                  47   ; Reset the C7F
0824  8680        48              ldaa      #C7F
0826  5A8E        49              staa      TFLG1
                  50   ; Toggle the bits in OC7D
0828  9683        51              ldaa      OC7D
082A  88F8        52              eora      #BITS_5
082C  5A83        53              staa      OC7D
                  54   ; Return to spin
082E  20E9        55              bra       spin
```

up in *line 37* and a spin loop is entered at *line 42* to wait for the output compare to be made. When it does, the data in OC7D are transferred to the output pins automatically. *Lines 44–49* set up for the next output compare time and reset the C7F flag. *Lines 51–53* then complement the data bits in the OC7D data register.

Very Short Duration Pulses

Pulses as short as one M-clock period can be generated.

Output Compare 7 can be used with another Output Compare channel to produce very short duration pulses. In Example 10–11 a 2-μsec pulse is generated using Output Compare 7 and 6. Output Compare 7 can control the normal Output Compare 6 output bit by using OC7M6 and OC7D6. In this example, Output Compare 7 is set to output a 1 on Port T, bit-6. Sixteen clock cycles later Output Compare 6 will reset the bit to zero. See also Example 10–12.

Explanation of Example 10–11

To create a very short pulse we first set up output compare channel 7 to successfully compare at some time in the future (*line 36*) and then set output compare channel 6 to compare 2 μsec later by initializing TC6 in *line 39*. OC7M and OC7D are set to output a one on Port T-6 when output compare 7 is made (*lines 43–47*) and output compare 6 to reset the bit (*lines 50–51*). The two spin loops at *line 53* and *line 55* wait until OC7 and then OC6 are made.

Forced Output Compares

An output comparison can be forced by the program writing to the CFORC register.

The final feature of the timer output comparison section is the *Forced Output Compare*. Figure 10–3 shows that the *CFORC* register bit (*FOCn*) is ORed with the output compare flag. Writing a one to this register forces a comparison action to occur at the output pins. This forced comparison does not set the output compare flag and therefore no interrupt will be generated.

EXAMPLE 10–11   A Very Short Duration Pulse

tocshrtc.asm   Assembled with CASM 02/16/1998 23:22 PAGE 1

```
                    1  ; Test program showing how to use Output
                    2  ; Compare 1 and 2 to generate a 2 usec
                    3  ; pulse on port T, bit-6
                    4  ; Constant Equates
0000                5  DELAY:    EQU      !16      ; Number for 2 usec
                    6  ; I/O Register Equates
0000                7  TIOS:     EQU      $80      ; Timer IO Select
0000                8  OC7M:     EQU      $82      ; Output compare 7 mask
0000                9  OC7D:     EQU      $83      ; Output compare 7 data
0000               10  TCNT:     EQU      $84      ; TCNT register
0000               11  TSCR:     EQU      $86      ; Timer System Control
0000               12  TCTL1:    EQU      $88      ; Timer Control 1
0000               13  TFLG1:    EQU      $8E      ; TFLG1 register
0000               14  TC6:      EQU      $9C      ; Timer 6 register
0000               15  TC7:      EQU      $9E      ; Timer 7 register
0000               16  TEN:      EQU      %10000000 ; Timer Enable
0000               17  C7F:      EQU      %10000000 ; Output compare 7 Flag
0000               18  C6F:      EQU      %01000000 ; Output compare 2 flag
0000               19  OM6:      EQU      %00100000 ; OM6 Bit
0000               20  OL6:      EQU      %00010000 ; OL6 Bit
0000               21  BITS:     EQU      %01000000 ; Bit pattern to output
0000               22  BIT6:     EQU      %01000000 ; Output bit-6
                   23  ; Memory Map Equates
0000               24  PROG:     EQU      $0800    ; ROM location
0000               25  DATA:     EQU      $0900    ; RAM location
0000               26  STACK:    EQU      $0a00    ; Stack pointer location
0800               27            ORG      PROG
                   28  prog_start:
0800 CF0A00        29            lds      #STACK
                   30  ; Enable the timer
0803 4C8680        31            bset     TSCR,TEN
                   32  ; Select the output compare bits 7 and 6
0806 4C80C0        33            bset     TIOS,C7F|C6F
                   34  ; Grab the value of the TCNT register
0809 DC84          35            ldd      TCNT
080B 5C9E          36            std      TC7
                   37  ; Set TC6 to compare DELAY cycles later
080D C30010        38            addd     #DELAY
0810 5C9C          39            std      TC6
                   40  ; Reset output compare flags
0812 86C0          41            ldaa     #C7F|C6F
0814 5A8E          42            staa     TFLG1
                   43  ; Initialize the mask register
0816 8640          44            ldaa     #BIT6
0818 5A82          45            staa     OC7M
                   46  ; Initialize the data register
```

EXAMPLE 10–11   Continued

```
081A 5A83       47              staa      OC7D
                48  ; Set up OC6 to reset the bit
                49  ; Set OM6=1, OL6=0
081C 4C8820     50              bset      TCTL1,OM6
081F 4D8810     51              bclr      TCTL1,OL6
                52  ; Wait until the OC7F is set
0822 4F8E80FC   53  spin7:      brclr     TFLG1,C7F,spin7
                54  ; Wait until the OC6F is set
0826 4F8E40FC   55  spin6:      brclr     TFLG1,C6F,spin6
                56  ; Reset the OC7F, OC6F
082A 86C0       57              ldaa      #C7F|C6F
082C 5A8E       58              staa      TFLG1
                59  ; Return to spin
082E 20F2       60              bra       spin7
```

EXAMPLE 10–12

Example 10–11 shows a program to output a 2-μsec pulse on Port T, bit-6. What is the period of this pulse?

Solution:

The output compare registers are not changed after their initialization. Therefore the period of the pulse is 8.192 msec.

CFORC—$0081—Timer Compare Force Register

Bit 7	6	5	4	3	2	1	Bit 0
7	6	5	4	3	2	1	0

Reset 0   0   0   0   0   0   0   0

FOC7:FOC0
Force Output Compare Action for Channels 7–0. Writing a one to any of these bits causes the action programmed by OMn:OLn bits to occur.

Output Compare Software Checklist

Here are the steps to check when writing your software for timer output compares:

1. Initialize the interrupt vector(s) for the timer channel(s) if interrupts are to be used.

2. Set bit-7 (TEN) in TSCR to enable the timer.

3. Set bits in TIOS to enable the Output Compare channels.

4. Initialize the OMn and OLn bits in TCTL1 and TCTL2 if the timer output pins are to be activated.

5. Set the bits in OC7M and OC7D if any timer channel 7 override is to be done.

6. Load the current value for TCNT and add the required delay to it.

7. Store the (TCNT+delay) value into the TCn register to be used.

8. Reset the flag(s) in TFLG1.

9. Enable any required interrupts in TMSK1.

10. Unmask interrupts by clearing the I-bit in the condition code register.

11. Wait for the output compare to set the flag by either polling the flag or waiting for the interrupt.

12. After the output compare action occurs, reinitialize the TCn register with the new delay value by adding the delay to the current TCn value.

13. Reset the CnF flag bit to prepare for the next output compare.

10.4 Input Capture

Input capture allows the TCNT register value to be latched when an external event occurs.

The input capture hardware is shown in Figure 10–4. Again, the 16-bit free-running TCNT register is the heart of the system, and the same eight, 16-bit *Timer Input Capture/Output Compare* registers, *TC7–TC0*, used for the output capture function, latch the value of the free-running counter in response to a program-selected, external signal coming from Port T. For example, the period of a pulse train can be found by capturing the TCNT at the start of the period, signified by a rising or falling edge, and storing it. The next rising or falling edge will capture the count at the end of the period. The difference in the two counts, taking into account timer overflows, will be the period in M-clock cycles. The length of the positive pulse can be measured by capturing the time at the rising edge and then again at the falling edge.

Two bits for each Input Capture channel, *EDGnB* and *EDGnA* in *Timer Control Registers 3* and *4*, control when the signal on Port T causes the capture event to occur. You may select rising, falling, or both edges to be active.

The input capture interrupts operate just like output compare interrupts. The interrupt enable bits in TMSK1 must be set. Then, when the flag in TFLG1 is set by the selected input capture edge, the interrupt request is forwarded to the CPU. The interrupt vectors or the D-Bug12 interrupt vector jump table must be initialized before the interrupt is allowed to occur.

Example 10–13 shows a subroutine that measures the period of a waveform, so long as it is less than 8.192 msec. Input capture one is to be used; it is enabled in *line 22*, and a rising edge is selected in *lines 24* and *25*. The IC1 flag is reset in *lines 27* and *28*. The program then waits until the first positive edge appears on Input Capture 1 in *line 31*. When this happens, the contents of the TCNT register are latched into the TC1 register and the program leaves the *line 31* spin loop.

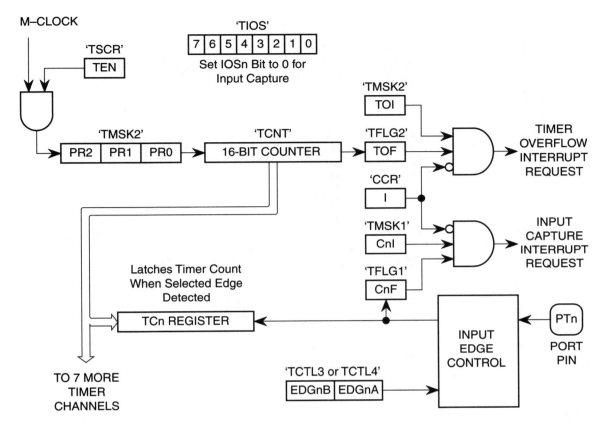

Figure 10-4   Input capture hardware.

The first count is saved in a buffer in *line 34*, the IC1 flag is reset, and the second spin loop (*line 39*) is entered. After the second rising edge, the duration of the pulse is calculated by subtracting the second TCNT value from the first.

TCTL3—$008A—Timer Control Register 3

TCTL4—$008B—Timer Control Register 4

	Bit 7	6	5	4	3	2	1	Bit 0
TCTL3	EDG7B	EDG7A	EDG6B	EDG6A	EDG5B	EDG5A	EDG4B	EDG4A
TCTL4	EDG3B	EDG3A	EDG2B	EDG2A	EDG1B	EDG1A	EDG0B	EDG0A
Reset	0	0	0	0	0	0	0	0

EXAMPLE 10–13   A Subroutine to Measure the Period of a Waveform

icper1c.asm   Assembled with CASM 02/16/1998 23:46 PAGE 1

```
                  1  ; Subroutine GET_PERIOD
                  2  ; Subroutine to measure the period of a wave.
                  3  ; Source File: ICPER1.ASM
                  4  ; Input parameters:  None
                  5  ; Output parameters: D register contains the
                  6  ;                      period in clock cycles
                  7  ; Registers Modified: A, B, CCR
                  8  ; I/O Register Equates
0000              9  TIOS:      EQU      $80          ; Timer I/O select
0000             10  TSCR:      EQU      $86          ; Timer Control
0000             11  TFLG1:     EQU      $8E          ; Timer flag 1
0000             12  TC1:       EQU      $92          ; Input Capture 1
0000             13  TEN:       EQU      %10000000    ; Timer enable bit
0000 4F8E02FC    14  C1F:ff     EQUU     %00000010    ; Input Capt 1 Flag
0000             15  EDG1R:     EQU      %00000100    ; Edge 1 Rising
0000             16  TCTL4:     EQU      $8B          ; Timer Control 4
                 17  GET_PERIOD:
0000 34          18             pshx                  ; Save reg
                 19  ; Enable the timer system
0001 4C8680      20             bset     TSCR,TEN
                 21  ; Reset TIOS bit to enable input capture
0004 4D8002      22             bclr     TIOS,C1F
                 23  ; Initialize IC1 for rising edge
0007 8604        24             ldaa     #EDG1R
0009 5A8B        25             staa     TCTL4
                 26  ; Reset IC1 Flag
000B 8602        27             ldaa     #C1F
000D 5A8E        28             staa     TFLG1
                 29  ; Wait for the first rising edge
                 30  ; by waiting for the IC1 Flag
000F 4F8E02FC    31  spin1:     brclr    TFLG1,C1F,spin1
                 32  ; Now get the count that was latched
0013 DC92        33             ldd      TC1
0015 7C0027      34             std      First        ;Save it
                 35  ; Reset the IC1 Flag
0018 8602        36             ldaa     #C1F
001A 5A8E        37             staa     TFLG1
                 38  ; Wait for the next rising edge
001C 4F8E02FC    39  spin2:     brclr    TFLG1,C1F,spin2
                 40  ; Get the ending count
0020 DC92        41             ldd      TC1
                 42  ; Calculate the period
0022 B30027      43             subd     First
                 44  ; Return with the value in D
0025 30          45             pulx                  ; Restore reg
0026 3D          46             rts
                 47  ; Data storage needed
0027             48  First:     DS       2
```

EDGNB:EDGNA		
Input Capture Edge Control.		
EDGnB	**EDGnA**	**Input Capture Edge Configuration**
0	0	Input capture disabled (default).
0	1	Capture on rising edges only.
1	0	Capture on falling edges only.
1	1	Capture on rising or falling edges.

Input Capture Software Checklist

Here is a list of the steps to check when writing your software for input captures:

1. Initialize the interrupt vector(s) for the timer channel(s) if interrupts are to be used.

2. Set bit-7 (TEN) in TSCR to enable the timer.

3. Reset bits in TIOS to disable the Output Compare channels.

4. Initialize the EDGnB and EDGnA bits in TCTL3 and TCTL4 to select the active edge for the input capture trigger signal.

5. Reset the flag(s) in TFLG1.

6. Enable any required interrupts in TMSK1.

7. Unmask interrupts by clearing the I-bit in the condition code register.

8. Wait for the input capture to set the flag by either polling the flag or waiting for the interrupt.

9. After the input capture event occurs, use the data in the TCn register.

10. Reset the CnF flag bit to prepare for the next input capture.

10.5 Pulse Accumulator

Comparison of M68HC12 and M68HC11 Pulse Accumulator	
M68HC12	**M68HC11**
16-bit accumulator	8-bit accumulator

The *pulse accumulator* can be used to count external events.

The pulse accumulator is a 16-bit counter that can operate as an *event counter*, counting external clock pulses, or a *gated time accumulator*. In gated time operation, the M-clock is divided by 64 and gated by the pulse accumulator input into the accumulator. These operating modes are shown in Figure 10–5. Timer channel 7 (Port T-7) is used as the input for the pulse accumulator. You may select the edge (positive or negative) for event counting or the level (high or low) for gated time accumulation. There are three registers to be programmed when using the pulse accumulator. The *PACTL* register enables the system, selects the mode of operation, enables a prescaler for the clock, and enables pulse accumulator interrupts. The *PAFLG* register contains the interrupt flags and the 16-bit *PACNT* register records the accumulated input pulses.

PACTL—$00A0—Pulse Accumulator Control Register

Bit 7	6	5	4	3	2	1	Bit 0
	PAEN	PAMOD	PEDGE	CLK1	CLK0	PAOVI	PAI

Reset 0   0   0   0   0   0   0   0

PAEN

Pulse Accumulator System Enable.
      0 = Pulse accumulator system disabled (default).
      1 = Enabled.
PAEN is independent of the timer system enable bit TEN; both must be set for pulse accumulator operation.

PAMOD

Pulse Accumulator Mode.
      0 = Event counter mode (default).
      1 = Gated time accumulation mode.

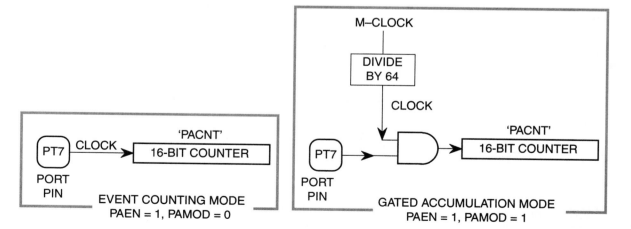

Figure 10–5 Pulse accumulator operating modes.

PEDGE

Pulse Accumulator Edge Control.

For PAMOD = 0 (event counter mode).

    0 = Falling edges on PT7 cause the count to be increased (default).

    1 = Rising edges are counted.

For PAMOD = 1 (gated time accumulation mode).

    0 = PT7 going high enables the M-clock/64 to pulse the accumulator. The subsequent falling edge of PT7 sets the *Pulse Accumulator Input Edge* (*PAIF*) flag.

    1 = PT7 going low enables the clock to the accumulator. The subsequent rising edge of PT7 sets the PAIF flag.

CLK1:CLK0

Clock Select Register.

PAOVI

Pulse Accumulator Overflow Interrupt Enable.

    0 = Interrupt inhibited (default).

    1 = Interrupt requested when the PAOVF bit is set.

PAI

Pulse Accumulator Input Interrupt Enable.

    0 = Interrupt enabled (default).

    1 = Interrupt requested if the PAIF bit is set.

PACNT—$00A2:00A3—16-bit Pulse Accumulator Count Register

Bit 7	6	5	4	3	2	1	Bit 0
15	14	13	12	11	10	9	8
7	6	5	4	3	2	1	0

This 16-bit register holds the number of accumulated input pulses. You may write it at any time and you should use a 16-bit read to simultaneously read the high and low bytes.

Pulse Accumulator Interrupts

The pulse accumulator interrupts operate like the other functions in the timer section. A flag is set by the hardware when the appropriate condition is true, and if an interrupt enable is set, the interrupt request is generated. There are two flags and two interrupts that can be generated; these are controlled by the *PAOVI* and *PAI* bits in the *PACTL* register. When the pulse accumulator overflows, the PAOVF flag bit in the PAFLG register is set. PAOVI enables this flag to generate an interrupt request. *PAI* is the *Pulse Accumulator Input Edge* interrupt enable. When the selected input edge occurs (chosen by PEDGE in PACTL), the *Pulse Accumulator Input Edge Flag* (*PAIF*) in the PAFLG is set. If PAI is set, an interrupt is generated. These interrupts are enabled by following the procedures outlined in the previous sections.

The pulse accumulator can interrupt the processor after a number of external events have occurred. Let us say that a sensor on a conveyor belt is detecting a product passing by and a crate is to be filled after 24 counts. Example 10–14 shows pseudocode to initialize the interrupt and to do the interrupt service routine. Table 10–3 shows the interrupt vector location.

PAFLG—$00A1—Pulse Accumulator Flag Register

Bit 7	6	5	4	3	2	1	Bit 0
0	0	0	0	0	0	PAOVF	PAIF

Reset 0   0   0   0   0   0   0   0

PAOVF
Pulse Accumulator Overflow Flag. This bit is set when the pulse accumulator overflows from $FFFF to $0000. You reset the flag in the normal way by writing a one to PAFLG bit-1.

PAIF
Pulse Accumulator Input Edge Flag. Set when the selected edge is detected at the pulse accumulator input. In the event mode, the selected event sets PAIF. In gated time accumulation mode, the trailing edge of the gate signal sets the bit and triggers the interrupt.

10.6 Plain and Fancy Timing

The Pulse Accumulator Control Register (PACTL) has two clock select bits (CLK1:CLK0) that can select the clock source for the TCNT register. Normally, when the Pulse Accumulator enable bit (PAEN) is zero, the M-clock is prescaled by the PR2:PR1:PR0 bits (in TMSK2) giving us a

---

EXAMPLE 10–14   Pulse Accumulator Overflow Interrupt Pseudocode Design

An interrupt service routine will be used. The pulse accumulator is initialized with −24 and is incremented with each external event. After 24 counts, the pulse accumulator overflows and generates an interrupt. The pseudocode design is as follows:

```
INITIALIZE the D-Bug12 Monitor interrupt vector jump table.
ENABLE the pulse accumulator in event counter mode and select
      the correct input edge in PACTL.
CLEAR the pulse accumulator overflow flag PAOVF in PAFLG.
SET the PAOVI bit in PACTL to enable pulse accumulator overflow
interrupts.
INITIALIZE the pulse accumulator register (PACNT) to −24.
CLEAR the interrupt mask in the condition code register.
DO Foreground Job
```

The Interrupt service routine pseudocode is as follows:

```
DO Whatever is needed at the 24th count.
INITIALIZE the pulse accumulator register (PACNT) to −24.
CLEAR the pulse accumulator overflow flag PAOVF in PAFLG.
RETURN from interrupt.
```

---

counter clock frequency ranging from 8 MHz to 250 kHz. However, as shown in Table 10–4 and Figure 10–6, when the pulse accumulator is enabled (PAEN = 1), the TCNT clock source can be derived from either the event signal on PT-7 in event counting mode (PAMOD = 0) or the M-clock (or P-clock in the MC68HC912B32) further divided. PAEN:CLK1:CLK0 are the select inputs for the TCNT clock multiplexer. For 000–100, the TCNT register receives the normal M-

TABLE 10–3   Pulse Accumulator Interrupt Vectors

Interrupt	Vector	D-Bug12 SetUserVect Number$_{10}$
Pulse Accumulator Overflow	$FFDC:FFDD	14
Pulse Accumulator Input Edge	$FFDA:FFDB	13

TABLE 10–4   TCNT Counter Clock Selection

PAMOD	PAEN	CLK1	CLK0	Clock Used the TCNT
x	0	x	x	The normal prescaled M-clock is used when the pulse accumulator is disabled
x	1	0	0	Normal prescaled M-clock
0	1	0	1	Pulse accumulator input (PT7) when in event counter mode
0	1	1	0	PT7 divided by 256
0	1	1	1	PT7 divided by 65,536
1	1	0	1	M-clock divided by 64 when in gated time accumulation mode (125 kHz for 8 MHz M-clock)
1	1	1	0	M-clock/(64 × 256) (488.28 Hz for 8 MHz M-clock)
1	1	1	1	M-clock/(64 × 65,536) (1.9 Hz for 8 MHz M-clock)

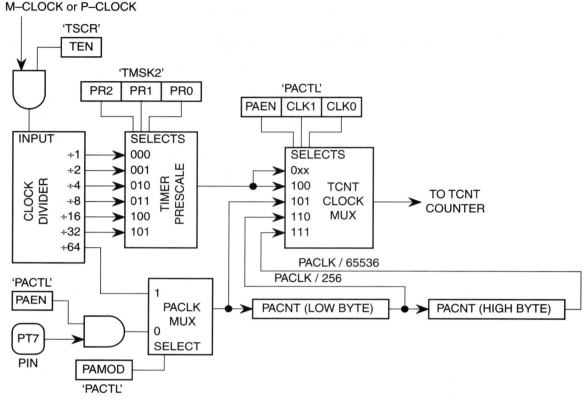

Figure 10–6   TCNT clock generator

clock divided by the PR2:PR1:PR0 prescaler. If PAMOD = 0, TCNT is clocked by a signal supplied at Port T-7 (PAEN:CLK1:CLK0 = 101) or the Port T-7 input divided by 256 or 65,536 for PAEN:CLK1:CLK0 = 110 and 111, respectively. If PAMOD = 1, TCNT is clocked by the normal M-clock, M-clock/256, or M-clock/65,536 (PAEN:CLK1:CLK0 = 101, 110, and 111). Special counting and timing requirements, such as counting long pulse streams or long periods, can use these special features of the M68HC12 timer.

10.7 Real-Time Interrupt

The *real-time interrupt* can generate periodic interrupts at various rates.

The real-time interrupt (RTI) operates like the timer overflow interrupt except that the rate at which interrupts are generated can be selected. See Figure 10–7. The real-time interrupt rate is generated by a 13-bit counter that divides the system M-clock (P-clock in the MC68HC912B32) by 8192. The clock can be divided further by a programmable prescaler such as the prescaler used for the TCNT register. The control bits for this are in the *Real-Time Interrupt Control Register (RTICTL)*.

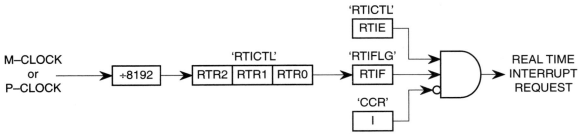

Figure 10-7 Real-time interrupt hardware.

Real-time interrupts are controlled by the RTIE enable bit in the *RTICTL* register. The real-time interrupt flag (*RTIF*) is in the *Real-Time Interrupt Flag Register* (*RTIFLG*).

The interrupt vector or the D-Bug12 SetUserVect number must be initialized before using the real-time interrupt. Table 10–5 gives the vectors and the D-Bug12 interrupt number for using SetUserVect.

RTICTL—$0014—Real-Time Interrupt Control Register

Bit 7	6	5	4	3	2	1	Bit 0
RTIE	RSWAI	RSBCK	0	RTBYP	RTR2	RTR1	RTR0

Reset 0   0   0   0   0   0   0   0

RTIE
Real-Time Interrupt Enable.   0 = Interrupt requests from RTI are disabled (default).   1 = Enable RTI interrupts.

RSWAI
RTI and COP Stop While in Wait.   0 = RTI and COP continue to run if the CPU is in a WAIT mode (default).   1 = RTI and COP stop when in a WAIT.

TABLE 10-5 Vectors for the Real-Time Interrupt

Interrupt	Vector	D-Bug12 SetUserVect Number$_{10}$
Real-Time Interrupt	$FFF0:FFF1	24

RSBCK
___

RTI and COP Stop While in Background Debug Mode.
 0 = RTI and COP continue to run when in Background Debug Mode (default).
 1 = RTI and COP stop when in Background Debug Mode.

RTBYP
___

Real-Time Interrupt Divide Chain Bypass.
This bit can be written only in special modes and bypasses the 2^{13} divider chain.

RTR2:RTR0
___

Real-time Interrupt Rate Select.

RTR2	RTR1	RTR0	Divide M by:	Interrupt Time: M = 4.0 MHZ (msec)	Interrupt Time: M = 8.0 MHz (msec)
0	0	0	Off	Off	Off
0	0	1	2^{13}	2.048	1.024
0	1	0	2^{14}	4.096	2.048
0	1	1	2^{15}	8.192	4.096
1	0	0	2^{16}	16.384	8.192
1	0	1	2^{17}	32.768	16.384
1	1	0	2^{18}	65.536	32.768
1	1	1	2^{19}	131.072	65.536

RTIFLG—$0015—Real-Time Interrupt Register

Bit 7	6	5	4	3	2	1	Bit 0
RTIF	6	0	0	0	0	0	0

Reset 0   0   0   0   0   0   0   0

RTIF
___

Real-Time Interrupt Flag.
The flag is set by real-time interrupt circuitry timing out at the intervals given above. The flag is reset by writing a one to bit-7 of RTIFLG.

10.8 Timer Input and Output Electronics

We discussed the merits of using pull-up resistors on inputs and of controlling the drive capabilities of an output in Chapter 7. All Port T bits can be controlled by the *TPU* and *TDRB* bits in *TMSK2*.

TMSK2—$008D—Timer Interrupt Mask Register 2

Bit 7	6	5	4	3	2	1	Bit 0
TOI	0	TPU	TDRB	TCRE	PR2	PR1	PR0

Reset 0   0   1   1   0   0   0   0

TPU

Timer Pull-up Resistor Enable.
    0 = Disable pull-up resistor function.
    1 = Enable pull-up resistor function (default).

TDRB

Timer Drive Reduction.
    0 = Normal output drive capability (default).
    1 = Enable output drive reduction capability.

10.9 External Interrupts Using Timer Interrupts

The external timer inputs that generate interrupts may be used as general-purpose, vectored, external interrupts if the pins are not otherwise being used for I/O or timer functions. Table 10–6 shows the pins that may be used. You can program positive or negative edges, or *either edge*, to generate the interrupt for each of the input capture signals (see Section 10.4). Allowing interrupts to occur on either rising or falling edges cannot be done with any of the other interrupt sources.

10.10 Clearing Timer Flags

Comparison of M68HC12 and M68HC11 Flag Clearing	
M68HC12	**M68HC11**
Flags are cleared by writing a one to the bit or a fast clearing mechanism may be used	Flags cleared by writing a one to the bit; there is no fast clearing mechanism.

TABLE 10-6   Timer External Interrupt Inputs

Function	Port T Bit	I-Bit	Flag	Vector	D-Bug12 SetUserVect Number$_{10}$
Pulse Accumulator Input Edge	7	PACTL[PAI]	PAFLG[PAIF]	$FFDA:FFDB	13
Input Capture 0	0	TMSK1[C0I]	TFLG1[C0F]	$FFEE:FFEF	23
Input Capture 1	1	TMSK1[C1I]	TFLG1[C1F]	$FFEC:FFED	23
Input Capture 2	2	TMSK1[C2I]	TFLG1[C2F]	$FFEA:FFEB	21
Input Capture 3	3	TMSK1[C3I]	TFLG1[C3F]	$FFE8:FFE9	20
Input Capture 4	4	TMSK1[C4I]	TFLG1[C4F]	$FFE6:FFE7	19
Input Capture 5	5	TMSK1[C5I]	TFLG1[C5F]	$FFE4:FFE5	18
Input Capture 6	6	TMSK1[C6I]	TFLG1[C6F]	$FFE2:FFE3	17
Input Capture 7	7	TMSK1[C7I]	TFLG1[C7F]	$FFE0:FFE1	16

> **All timer flags are cleared by *writing a one* to the bit.**

A common theme for all elements of the timer is the setting and resetting of various flags. The hardware, such as the timer overflow, sets the flag and the software you write must reset it. When interrupts are enabled, the setting of the flag also generates the interrupt (if the I-bit is clear). The flag must always be reset, either in the interrupt service routine or in the polling software. In all cases, the flag is reset by *writing a one* to the flag. For example, resetting the timer channel 7 interrupt flag can be done with the following code sequences:

```
LDAA    #%10000000
STAA    TFLG1
```

An alternative is:

```
BCLR    TFLG1,#%01111111
```

The bit clear (BCLR) instruction has a mask byte with ones in the bit positions where zeros are to be written (bits cleared). The way this instruction works is as follows:

The data byte is read from TFLG1, say %11000000 (timer channels 7 and 6 flags both set). The mask byte is complemented %01111111 → %1000000.
The complemented mask byte is ANDed with the register value and this result is written back to the register, i.e., TFLG1 is written with %10000000.

Perversely, the bit set instruction (BSET) <u>will not work</u>. The instruction

```
BSET    TFLG1,#%10000000
```

operates like this:

The data byte is read from TFLG1, say %11000000 (timer channels 7 and 6 flags are both set). The mask byte is ORed with the data byte and written back to TFLG1, i.e., TFLG1 is written with %11000000! This resets <u>both</u> the channel 7 and 6 flags.

Fast Timer Flag Clearing

Each of the methods for clearing flags shown above incurs some software overhead. The *Timer System Control Register* (*TSCR*) has the *Timer Fast Flag Clear All* (*TFFCA*) bit that operates as follows when TFFCA = 1:

TFLG1 contains the flags for all seven timer channels; TFLG2 has the timer overflow flag and PAFLG has the pulse accumulator overflow and input edge flags.

A read from an input capture or output compare channel (TC0–TC7) causes the corresponding channel flag, CnF in TFLG1, to be reset automatically.

Any access to the TCNT register (reading it for example) clears the TOF flag in TFLG2.

Any access to the pulse accumulator count register (PACNT) clears both the PAOVF and PAIF flags in the PAFLG register.

This method eliminates software overhead associated with clearing the flag, but the programmer must be wary of accidental flag clearing if an unintended access to the registers occurs.

10.11 MC68HC912B32 Pulse-Width Modulator

> The MC68HC912B32 can output *pulse-modulated waveforms* continuously without causing program overhead.

The MC68HC912B32 has a *pulse-width modulation* (*PWM*) module giving up to four pulse-width modulated waveforms. After the PWM module has been initialized and enabled, PWM waveforms will be output automatically with no further action required by the program. This is very useful in applications such as controlling stepper motors.

Figure 10–8 shows a pulse-width modulated waveform. There are two times that must be specified and controlled. These are the period (t_{PERIOD}) and the time the output is high (t_{DUTY}). A term used to describe a pulse-width modulated waveform is *duty cycle*. Duty cycle is defined as the ratio of t_{DUTY} to t_{PERIOD} and is usually given as a percent.

$$\text{Duty Cycle} = \frac{t_{DUTY}}{t_{PERIOD}} \times 100\% \qquad (10–1)$$

A simplified block diagram of the pulse-width modulator in the MC68HC912B32 is shown in Figure 10–9. An 8-bit (or 16-bit) counter, *PWCNTn*,[2] is clocked by the signal *CNTn*. This clock

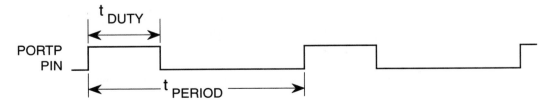

Figure 10–8 Pulse-width modulation waveform.

---

[2] *n* is 0, 1, 2, or 3. A 16-bit counter may be contrived by combining two PWCNTn registers.

is derived by dividing the system P-clock[3] by a prescaler and other division logic. There are two registers that control the period and the duty cycle, *PWDTYn* and *PWPERn*. The system must be initialized with values in these two registers and a clock frequency must be selected. When PWCNTn is reset, the pulse-width modulator output, *PWn*, is set high (or low, depending on the *PPOLn* polarity control bit). PWCNTn counts up and when it matches the value in PWDTYn, the *8-bit Duty Cycle Comparator* causes the output to go low (or high). As PWCNTn continues to count, it ultimately matches the value in the *8-bit Period Comparator*, which sets the output high (or low) again and resets PWCNTn to start the process over.

The hardware shown in Figure 10–9 gives a *left-aligned* pulse as shown in Figure 10–10a. Figure 10–10b shows a *center-aligned* pulse. Figure 10–11 shows the slightly different hardware used for this waveform. When PWCNTn reaches the value set in PWDTYn, the output T flip-flop toggles, making the output high (or low, depending again on PPOLn). PWCNTn continues to count and when it reaches the value in PWPERn the comparator changes the $\overline{\text{UP}}$/DOWN control signal and PWCNTn then counts down. When it matches PWDTYn again, the flip-flop is toggled and PWCNTn continues down to zero where its direction changes to UP and the cycle repeats.

Figure 10–12 shows three pulse-width modulated waves with 25, 50, and 75% duty cycle signals running simultaneously. Figure 10–12a illustrates left-aligned pulses and Figure 10–12b illus-

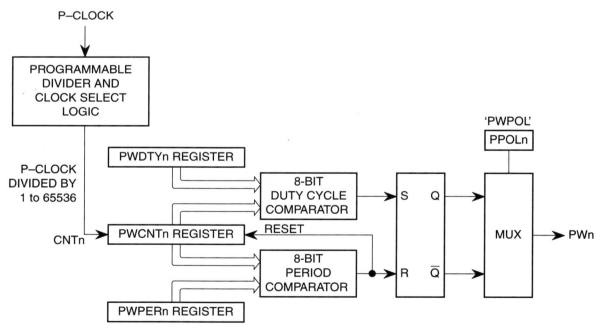

Figure 10–9 Simplified block diagram of the pulse-width modulator for left-aligned pulses.

---

[3] P-clock is normally (the default) one-half the frequency of the external system clock oscillator. It may be changed, however. See Chapter 15 for further discussion of the M68HC12 clock signals.

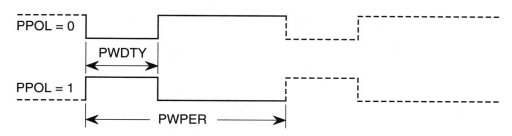

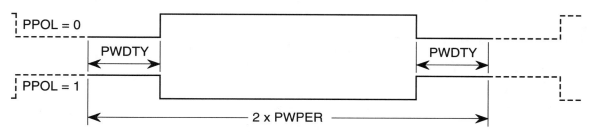

Figure 10-10 Left-aligned (a) and center-aligned (b) pulse-width modulator waveforms.

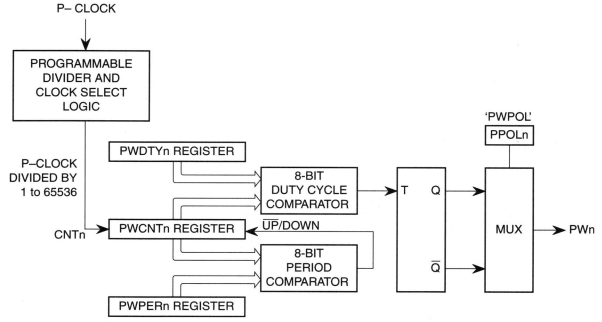

Figure 10-11 Center-aligned pulse-width modulator.

trates center-aligned pulses. If it is not necessary for the signals to be aligned as shown in Figure 10–12a, the center-aligned pulses will result in less system noise because all outputs are not switching at the same time.

The pulse-width modulation registers and the counter may be concatenated in pairs to give 16-bit timing resolution. For example, PWCNT3 and PWCNT2 or PWCNT1 and PWCNT0 can be concatenated. This gives a longer period and higher duty cycle resolution than can be achieved with the normal 8-bit operation. A control bit in one of the registers can be set to enable 16-bit operation. You may have four 8-bit, two 16-bit, or one 16-bit and two 8-bit PWM registers.

Pulse-Width Modulator Clock Control

> You must calculate values for the PWPER and PWDTY registers and select a clock frequency when initializing the pulse-width modulator.

Initializing the PWM module selects the clock rate, the polarity of the output, left- or center-aligned pulses, and which of the PWM outputs are enabled. Figure 10–13 shows the clock control circuitry.

There are four clock sources derived from the system P-clock. These are *Clock A*, *Clock B*, *Clock S0*, and *Clock S1*. Bits in the *PWCLK* register control the divider stages for Clock A and Clock B. These two independent clocks may be slower than the P-clock by a factor of 1, 2, 4, 8, 16, 32, 64, or 128. Clocks S0 and S1 are produced by further dividing Clock A and Clock B by **twice** the value in *PWSCAL0* (for Clock A) and *PWSCAL1* (for Clock B). Clocks S0 and S1 may be anywhere from 1/2 to 1/512th the frequency of Clock A and Clock B. Any of these clocks may be selected by the clock select logic to be used by PWM channels 0 through 3. As shown in Figure 10–13, channels 0 and 1 may use Clock A or Clock S0 and channels 2 and 3 may use Clock B or Clock S1. The PCLK0–PCLK3 bits in the PWPOL register select which of the clock signals is used on each channel. PWM channel enable bits PWEN0–PWEN3 allow the selected clock signal to be gated to the PWM. If all four channels are disabled, the clock prescaler shuts off to reduce power consumption.

The *PWEN* register is used to enable the four channels with PWEN3–PWEN0. The *PWPOL* register has the clock select bits PCLK3–PCLK0 plus bits to control the polarity of each output.

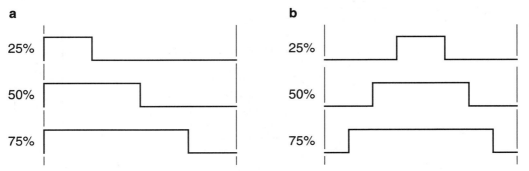

Figure 10–12   25%, 50% and 75% duty cycle pulses. (a) Left-aligned pulses. (b) Center-aligned pulses.

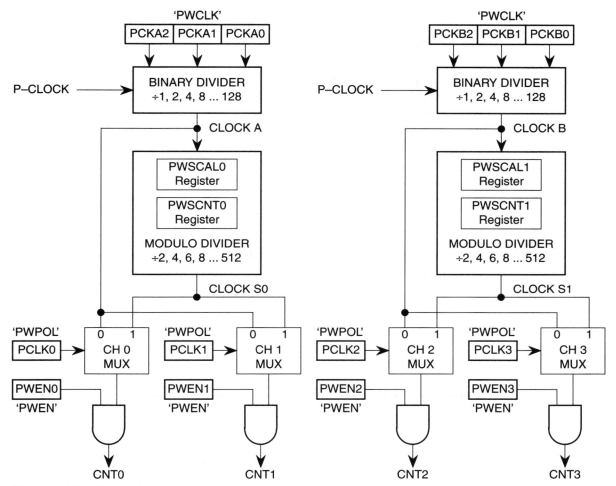

Figure 10-13 PWM clock circuit.

Pulse-Width Modulation Control Registers

There are a number of registers that control the pulse-width modulator module. Table 10–7 summarizes and provides detailed information for each register.

PWCLK—$0040—PWM Clocks and Concatenate

Bit 7	6	5	4	3	2	1	Bit 0
CON23	CON01	PCKA2	PCKA1	PCKA0	PCKB2	PCKB1	PCKB0

Reset 0   0   0   0   0   0   0   0

CON23

Concatenate PWM Channels 2 and 3.

CON01

Concatenate PWM Channels 0 and 1.

        0 = Channels are separate 8-bit PWMs (default).

        1 = Concatenate channels to make a 16-bit PWM.

Channels 3 and 2 and/or 1 and 0 can be concatenated to create 16-bit PWMs. When channels 2 and 3 are concatenated, channel 2 is the high-order byte and channel 3 controls the output bit. Channel 3 clock-select control bits determine the clock source. When channels 0 and 1 are concatenated, channel 0 is the high-order byte and channel 1 controls the output. Channel 1 clock-select bits determine the clock source.

PCKA2:PCKA0

Prescaler for Clock A.

PCKB2:PCKB0

Prescaler for Clock B.

TABLE 10-7 PWM Control Registers

Register	Name	Adr	Function
PWCLK	PWM Clocks and Concatenate	$40	Concatenate PWM counters and clock prescaler control bits
PWPOL	PWM Clock Select and Polarity	$41	Clock select bits for each channel and polarity select bits
PWEN	PWM Enable	$42	PWM channel enable bits
PWPRES	PWM Prescaler Counter	$43	Prescaler register—read only
PWSCAL0	PWM Scale Register 0	$44	Divider register Clock A → Clock S0
PWSCNT0	PWM Scale Counter 0	$45	Down counter for Clock A scaler—read only
PWSCAL1	PWM Scale Register 1	$46	Divider register Clock B → Clock S1
PWSCNT1	PWM Scale Counter 1	$47	Down counter for Clock B scaler—read only
PWCNT0	PWM Channel Counters	$48	PWM counter registers
PWCNT1		$49	
PWCNT2		$4A	
PWCNT3		$4B	
PWPER0	PWM Channel Period Registers	$4C	Select the period for each channel
PWPER1		$4D	
PWPER2		$4E	
PWPER3		$4F	
PWDTY0	PWM Channel Duty Registers	$50	Select the duty cycle time
PWDTY1		$51	
PWDTY2		$52	
PWDTY3		$53	
PWCTL	PWM Control Register	$54	PWM control bits
PORTP	Port P Data Register	$56	PWM output bits
DDRP	Port P Data Direction Register	$57	Data direction bits

PCKA2 PCKB2	PCKA1 PCKB1	PCKA0 PCKB0	Value of Clock A Value of Clock B
0	0	0	P-clock
0	0	1	P-clock/2
0	1	0	P-clock/4
0	1	1	P-clock/8
1	0	0	P-clock/16
1	0	1	P-clock/32
1	1	0	P-clock/64
1	1	1	P-clock/128

PWPOL—$0041—PWM Clock Select and Polarity

Bit 7	6	5	4	3	2	1	Bit 0
PCLK3	PCLK2	PCLK1	PCLK0	PPOL3	PPOL2	PPOL1	PPOL0

Reset 0　　　0　　　0　　　0　　　0　　　0　　　0　　　0

PCLK3 (PCLK2)
PWM Channel 3 (2) Clock Selects. 　　0 = Clock B is the clock source for channel 3 (2). 　　1 = Clock S1 is the clock source for channel 3 (2).

PCLK1 (PCLK0)
PWM Channel 1 (0) Clock Selects. 　　0 = Clock A is the clock source for channel 1 (0). 　　1 = Clock S0 is the clock source for channel 1 (0).

PPOL3–PPOL0
PWM Channel 3–0 Polarity. 　　0 = Channel output is low at the beginning of the PWM cycle and high when the duty count is reached. 　　1 = Channel output is high at the beginning of the PWM cycle and low when the duty count is reached. If the polarity bit is zero, and left alignment is selected, the duty registers contain a count of the low time. If the polarity bit is one, the duty registers contain a count of the high time. For center-aligned operation, the high or low time is twice the count.

PWEN—$0042—PWM Enable

Bit 7	6	5	4	3	2	1	Bit 0
0	0	0	0	PWEN3	PWEN2	PWEN1	PWEN0

Reset   0   0   0   0   0   0   0   0

PWEN3—PWEN0

PWM Channel 3–0 Enable.
    0 = Channel is disabled (default).
    1 = Channel is enabled.
The PWM signal will be available at its Port P bit when its clock source begins the next cycle. Setting any of the PWENn bits causes the Port P line to become an output regardless of the data direction register (DDRP). When the PWENn bits are set, the PWM clock is enabled to the PWEN circuit. If all four channels are disabled, the prescaler counter shuts off to save power.

PWSCAL0—$0044—PWM Scaler Counter for Clock S0

PWSCAL1—$0046—PWM Scaler Counter for Clock S1

Bit 7	6	5	4	3	2	1	Bit 0
7	6	5	4	3	2	1	0

Reset   0   0   0   0   0   0   0   0

Clock S0 can be used by PWM channels 0 and 1 and Clock S1 by channels 2 and 3. Both clocks are generated by dividing Clock A (for S0) and Clock B (for S1) by the value in PWSCAL0 and PWSCAL1 and then dividing again by two. If PWSCAL0 or PWSCAL1 is $00, Clock A or Clock B is divided by 256 and then by two.

PWCNT0–PWCNT3—PWM Channel Counters

PWCNT0—$0048—PWM Channel 0 Counter

PWCNT1—$0049—PWM Channel 1 Counter

PWCNT2—$004A—PWM Channel 2 Counter

PWCNT3—$004B—PWM Channel 3 Counter

Bit 7	6	5	4	3	2	1	Bit 0
7	6	5	4	3	2	1	0

Reset 0   0   0   0   0   0   0   0

> The channel counters contain the current count against which the channel period registers (PWPERn) and the duty cycle registers (PWDTYn) are compared.
> A counter is reset to $00 anytime it is written.
> To avoid a truncated period, write to the PWCNTn register when the counter is disabled.
> If you stop a PWM counter and then enable it again, the PWM channel counter starts at the count in the PWCNTn register.
> The counter may be read at any time without affecting the value of the counter.

PWPER0–PWPER3—PWM Channel Period Registers

PWPER0—$004C—PWM Channel 0 Period Register

PWPER1—$004D—PWM Channel 1 Period Register

PWPER2—$004E—PWM Channel 2 Period Register

PWPER3—$004F—PWM Channel 3 Period Register

Bit 7	6	5	4	3	2	1	Bit 0
7	6	5	4	3	2	1	0

Reset 0   0   0   0   0   0   0   0

> The channel period registers contain the count specifying the end of the period.
> If a PWPERn register is written while the PWM is enabled, the new value will not take effect until the existing period terminates.
> To start a new period immediately, write the PWPERn register and then write to the PWCNTn register to reset it to $00.
> PWPERn can be read at any time to find the most recent value written.
> The PWM period is as follows:
> Left-Aligned Waveform:
> $$\text{Period} = \text{Channel\_Clock\_Period}/(\text{PWPERn}+1)$$
> Center-Aligned Waveform:
> $$\text{Period} = \text{Channel\_Clock\_Period}/[2 \times (\text{PWPER}+1)]$$

PWDTY0–PWDTY3—PWM Channel Duty Registers

PWDTY0—$0050—PWM Channel 0 Duty Register

PWDTY1—$0051—PWM Channel 1 Duty Register

PWDTY2—$0052—PWM Channel 2 Duty Register

PWDTY3—$0053—PWM Channel 3 Duty Register

Bit 7	6	5	4	3	2	1	Bit 0
7	6	5	4	3	2	1	0

Reset 0   0   0   0   0   0   0   0

The channel duty registers contain the count specifying the end of the present high (or low) duty time.

If a PWDTYn register is written while the PWM is enabled, the new value will not take effect until the existing period terminates.

If PWDTYn is greater than or equal to the period register PWPERn, there will be no PWM pulse.

If PWDTYn is $FF, the output is equal to the complement of the PPOLn polarity bit.

PWPERn can be read at any time to find the most recent value written.

The duty cycle can be calculated as follows:

Left-Aligned Waveform:

$$\text{Duty Cycle} = [(PWDTYn+1)/PWPERn+1)] \times 100\% \qquad (PPOLn = 1)$$
$$\text{Duty Cycle} = [(PWPERn-PWDTYn)/(PWPERn+1)] \times 100\% \qquad (PPOLn = 0)$$

Center-Aligned Waveform:

$$\text{Duty Cycle} = [(PWDTYn+1)/(PWPERn+1)] \times 100\% \qquad (PPOLn = 1)$$
$$\text{Duty Cycle} = [(PWPERn-PWDTYn)/(PWPERn+1)] \times 100\% \qquad (PPOLn = 0)$$

PWCTL—$0054—PWM Control Register

Bit 7	6	5	4	3	2	1	Bit 0
0	0	0	PSWAI	CENTR	RDPP	PUPP	PSBCK

Reset 0   0   0   0   0   0   0   0

PSWAI
PWM Halts While in Wait Mode.

0 = PWM clock generator continues to operate in wait mode (default).

1 = PWM clock generator halted when in wait mode.

CENTR

Center-Aligned Output Mode.
>   0 = Operate in left-aligned output mode (default).
>   1 = Operate in center-aligned output mode.

RDPP

Reduced Drive of Port P.
>   0 = All Port P pins have normal drive capability (default).
>   1 = All Port P pins have reduced drive capability.

PUPP

Pull-up Port P Enable.
>   0 = All Port P pins have an active pull-up device disabled (default).
>   1 = Port P pins active pull-ups are enabled.

PSBCK

PWM Stops While in Background Mode.
>   0 = Allows PWM to continue while in background debug mode (default).
>   1 = Disable PWM input clock while in background debug mode.

PORTP—$0056—Port P Data Register

Bit 7	6	5	4	3	2	1	Bit 0
PP7	PP6	PP5	PP4	PP3 PWM3	PP2 PWM2	PP1 PWM1	PP0 PWM0

Reset -   -   -   -   -   -   -   -

PP7–PP0

Port P Data.
General-purpose I/O whose direction is controlled by DDRP.

PWM3–PWM0

PWM Outputs.
Enabled PWM outputs take precedence over general-purpose pins. After reset all pins are general-purpose, high-impedance inputs.

DDRP—$0057—Data Direction Register

Bit 7	6	5	4	3	2	1	Bit 0
DDP7	DDP6	DDP5	DDP4	DDP3	DDP2	DDP1	DDP0

Reset 0   0   0   0   0   0   0   0

DDP7—DDP0

Data Direction Port P.
    0 = Corresponding Port P bit is an input (default).
    1 = Port P bit is an output.

Other Pulse-Width Modulation Registers

PWPRES—$0043—PWM Prescaler Counter

	6	5	4	3	2	1	Bit 0
	6	5	4	3	2	1	0

Reset   0   0   0   0   0   0   0

This 7-bit counter serves as the prescaler for the PWM clock. It can be read at any time but cannot be written. Clock A is selected by PCKA2:PCKA0 and Clock B by PCKB2:PCKB0.

PWSCNT0—$0045—PWM Scaler Counter for S0

PWSCNT1—$0047—PWM Scaler Counter for S1

Bit 7	6	5	4	3	2	1	Bit 0
7	6	5	4	3	2	1	0

Reset 0   0   0   0   0   0   0   0

These counters count down to $00 and then are loaded with the PWSCALn value. They may be read at any time.

PWTST—$0055—PWM Special Mode Register

Bit 7	6	5	4	3	2	1	Bit 0
DISCR	DISCP	DISCAL					

Reset 0   0   0   0   0   0   0   0

DISCR

Disable Reset of Channel Counter on Write to Channel Counter.
   0 = Normal operation. Writing to the PWM channel counter will reset the channel
       counter (default).
   1 = Writing the PWM channel counter does not reset it.

DISCP

Disable Compare Count Period.
   0 = Normal operation (default).
   1 = Match of period (PWPERn = PWCNTn) does not reset or change the
       PWCNTn direction.

DISCAL

Disable Load of Scale Counters on Write to the Associated Scale Registers.
   0 = Normal operation (default).
   1 = Write to PWSCALn does not load scale counters.

These bits may be written only in special mode (SMODN = 0).

Choosing Pulse-Width Modulation Counter Prescaler Values

> Finding values for PW-
> PER, PWDTY, and the
> clock is sometimes an
> iterative process.

Figures 10–9 and 10–13 show several clock dividers and counter registers that must be initialized before using the pulse-width modulators. When PWMs drive motors or other mechanical systems, the PWM frequency (if too low) can cause objectionable audible noise. For this reason, it is important to be able to get the PWM frequency above 20 kHz (not easy or practical in software). If the frequency is too high, though, some components may not be able to follow the rate of change. Another common use of the PWM is to use it to drive an R-C low pass filter to get a crude digital-to-analog converter. In this case the PWM frequency needs to be high enough to be able to choose reasonable resistors and capacitors. Here

---

EXAMPLE 10–15

Choose values for the PWDTY1, PWPER1, and PWSCAL0 registers and the PCKA2:PCKA0, PCKB3:PCKB0, PPOL1, CENTR, and CON01 control bits to generate a pulse-width modulated waveform on PWM channel 1 with a frequency of 20 kHz and a high duty cycle time of 10 μsec. Assume the P-clock is 8 MHz.

Solution:

1. The t_{period} is 50 μsec.

2. Calculate the period of CNT1:

3. T_{CNT1} = 50 μsec/256 = 0.1953 μsec.
   Calculate the total divisor required:
   Total divisor = 0.193 μsec/0.125 μsec = 1.56.
   Not an integer, so choose total divisor = 2.
   Recalculate T_{CNT1}:
   T_{CNT1} = 2 × 0.125 μsec = 0.25 μsec.
   Recalculate PWPER+1:
   PWPER+1 = 50 μsec/0.25 μsec = 200.

4. Calculate the number of counts required in PWDTY1 for 10 μsec.
   PWDTY1+1 = 10 μsec/0.25 μsec = 40

5. Choose a divisor combination to achieve a total divisor = 2. This can be done by choosing Clock A.
   Clock A = P-clock/Prescaler
   For a total divisor of 2, choose the prescaler = 2.

The control bits are as follows:
PCKA2:PCKA0 = %001, PWSCAL0 = don't care or whatever might be required for Clock S0, PCKB2:PCKB0 are don't cares or whatever might be needed for Clock S1, PCKL1 = 0, CON01 = 0, CENTR = 0, and PPOL1 = 1.

---

is a strategy to pick appropriate values for the PWM registers based on the period and duty cycle of the pulse-width modulated waveform. See Example 10–15.

1. Choose PWPERn = 255. This gives the best resolution when choosing the duty cycle count for PWDTYn.

2. Divide t_{PERIOD} by 256. This establishes the period of the CNT clock.

$$T_{CNT} = \frac{t_{PERIOD}}{256} \tag{10–2}$$

3. Divide the CNT period by the P-clock period. This gives the total divisor needed.

$$Total\ Divisor = \frac{T_{CNT}}{P\text{-}clock_{PERIOD}} \tag{10–3}$$

If the total divisor is greater than 65,536—[(128 in the PWPRES prescaler) × (256 in the PWSCNTn down counter) × (2)]—16-bit concatenated registers are needed.

If the total divisor is not an integer, choose the next higher integer value and recalculate the CNT period.

$$T_{CNT} = \textit{Total Divisor} \times \textit{P-clock}_{PERIOD} \qquad (10\text{--}4)$$

Recalculate PWPERn+1.

$$PWPER + 1 = \frac{t_{PERIOD}}{T_{CNT}} \qquad (10\text{--}5)$$

4. Calculate the number of counts needed in the PWDTYn register based on the CNT period.

$$PWDTY + 1 = \frac{t_{DUTY}}{T_{CNT}} \qquad (10\text{--}6)$$

If PWDTYn is not an integer, round up or down to the nearest integer value. Make sure PWDTYn ≤ 255 (or 65535).

5. Select an appropriate divider combination to give the total divisor and a clock source to give CNT. If the total divisor is not a power of two, you will have to use a combination of Clock A or Clock B and PWSCALn to achieve an exact period and duty cycle. If the total divisor is not an integer, round down to the nearest integer and recalculate PWPERn and PWD-TYn register values. Again, be sure PWPERn does not exceed the maximum.

6. If you are using Clock A or Clock B and the total divisor is not a power of 2, choose the nearest value and recalculate PWPERn and PWDTYn registers values.

Another strategy to select appropriate values for each register is based on the *duty cycle resolution* required by the application. See Examples 10–16 to 10–19.

Duty cycle resolution is the smallest unit of time by which t_{DUTY} (Figure 10–8) may change. This may be given as the actual time or as a percentage of the full PWM period. Duty cycle resolution determines the minimum count value for the PWPERn register.

$$\textit{Duty Cycle Resolution \%} = \frac{\Delta t_{DUTY}}{t_{PERIOD}} \times 100\% = \frac{1}{PWPER + 1} \times 100\% \qquad (10\text{--}7)$$

Here is a method to choose PWPERn, PWDTYn, and the clock frequency.

1. Find the minimum value for the PWPERn register based on Equation Equation 10–7. Choose any value greater than this but less than 256 (or 65,536 in a 16-bit system).

2. Divide t_{PERIOD} by the value chosen for PWPERn + 1. This establishes the period of the CNT clock.

$$T_{CNT} = \frac{t_{PERIOD}}{PWPER + 1} \qquad (10\text{--}8)$$

EXAMPLE 10–16

Choose values for the PWDTY1, PWPER1, and PWSCAL0 registers and the PCKA2:PCKA0, PCKB3:PCKB0, PPOL1, CENTR, and CON01 control bits to generate a pulse-width modulated waveform on PWM channel 1 with a period of 20 msec and a high duty cycle time of 7 msec. The duty cycle resolution is to be 0.5%. Assume the P-clock is 8 MHz.

Solution:

1. The required duty cycle resolution is 0.5%. This tells us that the ratio of Δt_{DUTY} to t_{PERIOD} is 1:200 and that an 8-bit PWPER register should be sufficient. Choose a value of 200 for PWPER1+1.

2. Calculate the period of CNT1:
   T_{CNT1} = 20 msec/200 = 100 μsec.

3. Calculate the number of counts required in PWDTY1 for 7 msec.
   PWDTY1+1 = 7 msec/100 μsec = 70.

4. Calculate the total divisor required.
   Total divisor = 100 μsec/0.125 μsec = 800.

5. Choose a divisor combination to achieve 800. This can be done by choosing Clock S0.
   Clock S0 = P-clock/(Prescaler $\times$ PWSCAL0 $\times$ 2).
   For a total divisor of 800, choose the prescaler = 16 and PWSCAL0 = 25 (16 $\times$ 25 $\times$ 2 = 800).

The registers and control bits are as follows:
PCKA2:PCKA0 = %100, PWSCAL0 = $19, PCKB2:PCKB0 are don't cares or whatever might be needed for Clock S1, PCKL1 = 1, CON01 = 0, CENTR = 0, and PPOL1 = 1.

---

3. Calculate the number of counts needed in the PWDTY register based on the CNT period.

$$PWDTY + 1 = \frac{t_{DUTY}}{T_{CNT}} \tag{10–9}$$

If PWDTY is not an integer, choose the next higher value and recalculate the CNT period and a new PWPER value. Make sure PWPER $\leq$ 255 (or 65,535).

4. Divide the CNT period by the P-clock period. This gives the total divisor needed.

$$Total\ Divisor = \frac{T_{CNT}}{P\text{-}clock_{PERIOD}} \tag{10–10}$$

If the total divisor is greater than 65,536—[(128 in the PWPRES prescaler) $\times$ (256 in the PWSCNTn down counter) $\times$ (2)]—16-bit concatenated registers are needed.

EXAMPLE 10–17

Specify the divider value and PWPER3 and PWDTY3 register values for a pulse-width modulated waveform on PWM3 using Clock B. The period is to be 1.8 msec, $t_{DUTY} = 0.1$ msec, and the duty cycle resolution is to be less than (better than) 1%. Assume the P-clock is 8 MHz. State the final t_{DUTY}, t_{PERIOD} and duty cycle resolution achieved by your design. Calculate the percent error in t_{DUTY} and t_{PERIOD} if the design does not achieve exact timing.

Solution:

1. Duty cycle resolution is 1%. Therefore, PWPER3+1 must be ≥ 100. Choose PWPER3+1 = 200.

2. Calculate the period of CNT.
   T_{CNT} = 1.8 msec/200 = 9 μsec.

3. PWDTY3+1 = 0.1 msec/9 μsec = 11.1 .
   PWDTY3+1 is not an integer, so choose next higher PWDTY3+1 = 12.
   To achieve t_{DUTY} when PWDTY3+1 = 12, T_{CNT} = 0.1 msec/12 = 8.33 μsec.
   New PWPER3+1 = 1.8 msec/8.33 μsec = 216.

4. Total divisor = 8.33 μsec/0.125 μsec = 66.64.
   The next smaller Clock B divisor is 64, so choose that.

5. Recalculate the period of CNT and new values for PWPER3+1 and PWDTY3+1.
   T_{CNT} = 0.125 μs × 64 = 8 μsec.
   PWPER3+1 = 1.8 msec/8 μsec = 225.
   PWDTY3+1 = 0.1 msec/8 μsec = 12.5. Choose 12.

   Final t_{PERIOD} = 225 × 8 μs = 1.8 msec.
   Error = 0%.
   Final t_{DUTY} = 12 × 8 μsec = 0.096 msec.
   Error = (0.1 − 0.096)/0.1 = 4%.
   Duty cycle resolution = 1/225 = 0.4%.

EXAMPLE 10–18

What is the longest PWM period that can be obtained using a single 8-bit PWM register assuming an 8-MHz P-clock and left-aligned waveforms?

Solution:

The longest period is achieved using an 8-bit PWPER register and the slowest Clock S. The slowest Clock S0 or S1 is formed by dividing the P-clock by 128 to give Clock A or B and then by setting PWSCAL to $00, which divides Clock A or B by 512. The period is PWPER+1 times this clock period. Therefore, the longest period is

$$P\text{-}clock_{PERIOD} \times 128 \times 512 \times 256 = 2.09 \text{ sec}$$

EXAMPLE 10–19

What is the longest PWM period that can be obtained using concatenated PWM registers assuming an 8-MHz P-clock and left-aligned waveform?

Solution:

The longest period is achieved using a 16-bit PWPER register and the slowest Clock S. The slowest Clock S0 or S1 is formed by dividing the P-clock by 128 to give Clock A or B and then by setting PWSCAL to $00, which divides Clock A or B by 512. This clock drives the concatenated PWCNT1:PWCNT0 or PWCNT3:PWCNT2 channel counters and the period is found by concatenating PWPER1:PWPER0 or PWPER3:PWPER2. Therefore, the longest period is

$$P\text{-}clock_{\text{PERIOD}} \times 128 \times 512 \times 65{,}536 = 536.8 \text{ sec}$$

---

5. Select an appropriate divider combination to give the total divisor and a clock source to give CNT. If the total divisor is not a power of 2, you will have to use a combination of Clock A and PWSCAL to achieve an exact period and duty cycle. If the total divisor is not an integer, round down to the nearest integer and recalculate PWPER and PWDTY register values. Again, be sure PWPER does not exceed the maximum.

6. If you are using Clock A or Clock B and the total divisor is not a power of 2, choose the nearest value and recalculate PWPER and PWDTY registers values.

10.12 Conclusion and Chapter Summary Points

The timer features of the M68HC12 are useful in many applications. Although the programming and control of the elements seem complex, the operation of all functions is similar with similar control requirements. The common elements are as follows:

- Timing is derived from the M-clock.
- The M-clock may be prescaled (divided) by 1, 2, 4, 8, 16, or 32.
- A 16-bit free-running counter, TCNT, provides the basic counting functions in the system.
- TCNT generates a timer overflow every 65,536 clock cycles.
- Eight channels of output compare can set an output compare flag when the TCNT register is equal to the output compare register.
- Eight channels of input capture can latch the TCNT on an input signal.
- All timer functions set a flag to indicate when their particular event has occurred.

- Each timer flag can be ANDed with an interrupt enable bit to generate an interrupt when the particular event has occurred.

- In all events, the flag is reset by software writing a one to the flag.

- The MC68HC912B32 has a pulse-width modulator waveform generator.

10.13 Problems

10.1. What is wrong with the following code to get the 16-bit value of the TCNT register?

```
LDAA $84 Get the high byte
LDAB $85 Get the low byte
```

10.2 What is wrong with the following code to get the 16-bit value of the TCNT register?

```
LDAB $85 Get the low byte
LDAA $84 Get the high byte
```

10.3 How should you read the 16-bit TCNT value?

10.4 How is the TCNT clock prescaler programmed?

10.5 Give the name of the bit, the name of the register that it is in, the register's address, which bit, and the default or reset state of the bit for each of the following:
   a. What bit indicates that the timer has overflowed?
   b. What bit enables the timer overflow interrupts?
   c. What bits are used to prescale the timer clock?

10.6 When is the timer overflow flag set?

10.7 How is the timer overflow flag reset?

10.8 What timing resolution can be achieved with the output compare?

10.9 Give the name of the bit, the name of the register that it is in, the register's address, which bit, and the default or reset state of the bit for each of the following:
   a. What bit indicates that a comparison has been made on Output Compare 2?
   b. What bit enables the Output Compare 2 interrupt?
   c. What bits are used to set the Output Compare 3 I/O pin high on a successful comparison?

10.10 Write a small section of code to set the Output Compare 2 I/O pin to toggle on every comparison.

10.11 Write a small section of code to enable Output Compare 7 to set bits PT7, PT6, and PT5 to one on the next successful comparison.

10.12 What two registers control which data bits are output when the Output Compare 7 flag is set?

10.13 How does the programmer select the active edge for Input Capture 2?

10.14 Write a short section of code demonstrating how to reset the Input Capture 2 Flag C2F.

10.15 Write a short section of code demonstrating how to enable the Input Capture 1 interrupts.

10.16 Write a short section of code demonstrating how to enable the real-time interrupt and to set the nominal rate to 16.384 msec assuming an 8-MHz M-clock.

10.17   Write a short section of code demonstrating how to reset the COP timer.

10.18   Write a short section of code demonstrating how to enable the Pulse Accumulator as an event counter counting rising edges.

10.19   Write a short section of code demonstrating how to enable the Pulse Accumulator as a gated time accumulator with a high level enable accumulation.

10.20   What bits in what registers must be set to enable the Pulse Accumulator Input Edge interrupt.

Chapter *11*

MC68HC12 Serial I/O

O B J E C T I V E S

This chapter discusses the M68HC12 serial I/O capabilities. The Asynchronous Serial Communications Interfaces, SCI0 and SCI1, and the Synchronous Serial Peripheral Interface, SPI, are covered. We briefly describe the Byte Data Link Communications Module available in the MC68HC912B32.

11.1 Introduction

The M68HC12 contains three serial interfaces. The MC68HC812A4 has two *Asynchronous Serial Communications Interface*, (*SCIs*). These are universal asynchronous receiver-transmitters (UARTs) designed for serial communications to a terminal or other asynchronous serial devices such as personal computers. The MC68HC912B32 has one SCI plus a *Byte Data Link Communication* (*BDLC*), module. This provides an interface with the SAE J1850 serial data protocol commonly used in automotive electronics applications. Another interface in both M68HC12s is called the *Synchronous Serial Peripheral Interface* (*SPI*). This is a high-speed, synchronous serial interface used between an M68HC12 and a serial peripheral such as a Motorola MC68HC68A1 serial 10-bit A/D converter or between two M68HC12s. Figure 11–1 shows the two types of interfaces.

11.2 Port S Serial I/O

The SCIs and the SPI share serial input and output data pins with Port S. If any of these devices are enabled, the corresponding Port S bits are used for serial I/O and may not be used for parallel I/O. The function of these pins is configured by enabling the SCI and SPI functions (they are independent, and one may be enabled without the other) by setting bits in each system's control registers.

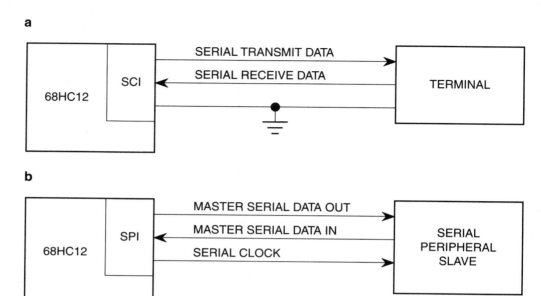

Figure 11–1   M68HC12 (a) asynchronous and (b) synchronous serial peripheral interfaces.

PORTS—$00D6—Port S Data Register

	Bit 7	6	5	4	3	2	1	Bit 0
	PS7	PS6	PS5	PS4	PS3	PS2	PS1	PS0
Serial Function	$\overline{SS}$ $\overline{CS}$	SCK	MOSI MOMI	MISO SISO	TxD1[1] I/O[2]	Rxd1[1] I/O[2]	TxD0	RxD0

$\overline{SS}$, $\overline{CS}$, SC, MOSI, MOMI, MISO, SISO
These bits are used in the SPI. See Section 11.4.

TxD0, RxD0, TxD1, RxD1
Transmit (output) and received (input) data bits for SCI0 and SCI1.

---

[1]   In the MC68HC812A4.

[2]   In the MC68HC912B32.

11.3 Asynchronous Serial Communications Interface (SCI)

Comparison of M68HC12 and M68HC11 SCI	
M68HC12	**M68HC11**
Two SCIs in the MC68HC812A4; one SCI in the MC68HC912B32; hardware parity generation; single-wire operation	One SCI; softare parity generation; two-wire operation only

The SCI is a *Universal Asynchronous Receiver-Transmitter (UART)*.

The SCIs are full duplex, asynchronous, serial interfaces. Each has an on-chip, independent, baud rate generator that can produce standard serial communication rates from normal M68HC12 M-clock frequencies. The receiver and transmitter are double buffered and although they operate independently, they use the same baud rate and data format. Each system can send and receive 8- or 9-bit data, has a variety of interrupts, and is fully programmable.

Using and programming each SCI can be broken into three parts. These are (1) initialization of the device's data rate, word length, parity, and interrupting capabilities, (2) writing to the SCI data register, taking care not to exceed the data transmission rate, and (3) reading data from the SCI data register making sure to read the incoming data before the next serial data arrives.

SCI Data

Serial data are read from and written to the SCDR register.

Two data registers, *SCnDRH* and *SCnDRL*,[3] shown in Figure 11–2, contain the 8- or 9-bit serial data received and to be transmitted for each SCI. Each SCnDRL register is two separate registers occupying the same memory address. Data to be transmitted serially are written to and serial data received are read from these registers.

SCnDRH and SCnDRL form the 9-bit data registers when sending and receiving 9-bit data. The ninth transmit bit (T8) does not have to be changed each time new serial data are sent. The same value will be transmitted until T8 is changed. If 9-bit data are to be used, the SCnDRH bit should be written before SCnDRL to ensure the correct data are transferred to the SCI transmit data register when SCnDRL is written. If an 8-bit data format is being used, only SCnDRL needs to be read or written.

SCnDRL contains the 8-bit serial transmitted and received data. *Reading* from SCnDRL reads the last *received* data and *writing* to it sends (transmits) the serial data. Writing to SCnDRL does not overwrite or destroy the contents of the data that have been received.

---

[3]   In these register discussions, *n* means 0 or 1, referring to SCI0 or SCI1 in the MC68HC812A4. For the MC68HC912B32 *n* is 0.

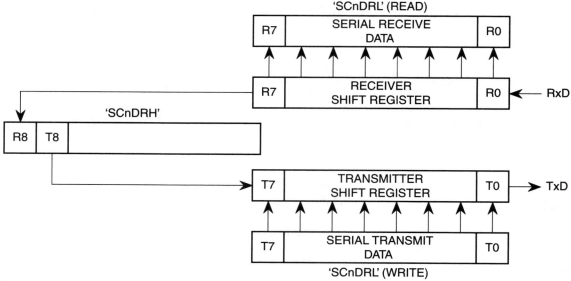

Figure 11–2   SCI data registers.

SC0DRH—$00C6—SCI0 Data Register High

SC1DRH—$00CE—SCI1 Data Register High

	Bit 7	6	5	4	3	2	1	Bit 0
	R8	T8	0	0	0	0	0	0
Reset	0	0	0	0	0	0	0	0

R8
Received bit 8.

T8
Transmit bit 8.
These are the ninth received and transmitted data bits when sending and receiving 9-bit serial data.

SC0DRL—$00C7—SCI0 Data Register Low

SC1DRL—$00CF—SCI1 Data Register Low

Bit 7	6	5	4	3	2	1	Bit 0
R7/T7	R6/T6	R5/T5	R4/T4	R3/T3	R2/T2	R1/T1	R0/T0

Reset 0   0   0   0   0   0   0   0

R7/T7:R0/T0
Received/transmit bits 7 to 0. Read operations access received data and writes access transmit data.

SCI Initialization

Receiver and Transmitter Enable

As with any programmable device, the SCI must be initialized before use and there are a variety of registers and bits to be programmed. First, each SCI channel's transmitter and receiver are enabled by setting *TE* and *RE* in the *SCI Control Register 2* (*SCnCR2*) for each SCI channel. SCnCR2 contains bits to enable various interrupts, the SCI wakeup control, and a break generation bit. These will be discussed in a later section.

SC0CR2—$00C3—SCI0 Control Register 2

SC1CR2—$00CB—SCI1 Control Register 2

Bit 7	6	5	4	3	2	1	Bit 0
TIE	TCIE	RIE	ILIE	TE	RE	RWU	SBK

Reset 0   0   0   0   0   0   0   0

TIE
Transmit Interrupt Enable.
TCIE
Transmit Complete Interrupt Enable.
RIE
Receiver Interrupt Enable.
ILIE
Idle Line Interrupt Enable.

TE
Transmitter Enable.
0 = Transmitter disabled (default).
1 = Transmitter enabled and the TxD pin on Port S is an output used for serial I/O.

RE
Receiver Enable.
0 = Receiver disabled (default).
1 = SCI receiver enabled.

RWU
Receiver Wakeup Control.

SBK
Send Break.

SCI Mode Control

Comparison of M68HC12 and M68HC11 SCI Mode	
M68HC12	**M68HC11**
Loop and single-wire modes; wired-OR mode; 8- or 9-bit data; wakeup mode; short or long idle line detection; hardware parity generation	8- or 9-bit data; wakeup mode; no hardware parity generation

In addition to enabling the receiver/transmitter, the SCI operation mode must be initialized. This is done in the *SCI Control Register 1 (SCnCR1)*.

SCI Wired-OR Mode

The wired-OR mode is one in which an output pin is an *open-drain* connection. This mode requires an external pull-up resistor to generate a logic-high level but allows several open-drain sources to be connected together. This is used in a single-wire system with several SCI devices connected together. The wired-OR mode is controlled by the *WOMS* bit in the SCnCR1 register.

SCI Loop Mode

The M68HC12 offers a loop mode useful for testing serial I/O software when the external serial device may not be available. In the loop mode, the receiver is connected directly to the transmitter and thus anything you send out comes straight back in. Loop mode is enabled by setting *LOOPS* to one. You have a choice of how the receiver is connected to the transmitter. If the *Receiver Source (RSRC)* bit is zero, the receiver is connected internally to the transmitter and the transmitter can be disconnected from the TxD pin [by letting the data direction register, DDRS bit-1 (or -3), for the TxD bit be zero]. See Figure 11–3.

SCI Single-Wire Mode

A new feature of the M68HC12 is the *single-wire mode*. When this mode is selected, the TxD output and RxD input is from Port S (bit-1 or -3) and the normal RxD pins (Port S bit-0 or -2) can be used for general-purpose I/O. In normal single-wire operation the TxD pin is an *open-drain* pin and can thus be active (when transmitting data) or can allow another SCI's transmitted data to be received. When RSRC is one, the receiver is connected to the TxD pin, which may or may not be active depending on the state of the data direction register DDRS-1 or -3. RSRC = 1 allows the single-wire mode to be used. Figure 11–4 shows the configuration of the M68HC12 in normal single-wire mode, and Table 11–1 gives a summary of the TxD activity for these modes.

8-Bit or 9-Bit Data

The number of data bits to be sent and received is controlled by the *M* bit in SCnCR1. M = 0 for one start, eight data, and one stop bit; M = 1 for one start, eight data, ninth data, one stop bit.

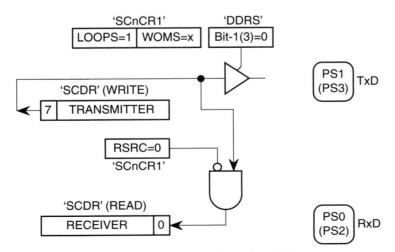

F i g u r e 1 1 – 3   Normal SCI loop mode without TXD output.

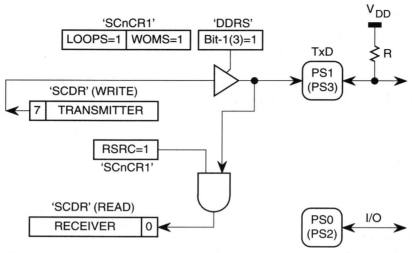

Figure 11–4 Normal single-wire mode.

Idle Line

An *idle* line is a line in which the receive line is in a mark[4] condition (logic high) for more than one character time. Idle line detect may be used in half-duplex systems in which the line needs to be "turned around" when the remote transmitter is done transmitting. The idle condition is detected when the RxD input remains in the mark (1) condition for a full character time. In long idle detect mode, the idle detect logic does not start counting logic 1-bit times until after a stop bit. In short idle detect mode, the idle detect logic starts counting logic 1s after a start bit so the stop bit time and any contiguous 1s at the end of a serial character can cause idle to be detected earlier than expected.

TABLE 11–1 Loop Mode Functions

TxD Function	TxD Logic Level	LOOPS	RSRC	DDRS1,3	WOMS
Normal operations with TxD output	CMOS	0	x	1	0
Normal operations with TxD output	Open-drain	0	x	1	1
LOOP mode without TxD output	High-impedance	1	0	0	0/1
LOOP mode with TxD output	CMOS logic levels	1	0	1	0
LOOP mode with TxD output	Open-drain	1	0	1	1
Single wire without TxD output; TxD used as receiver input only	High impedance	1	1	0	x
Single wire with TxD output; output fed back to the receiver	CMOS logic levels	1	1	1	0
Normal single wire for transmitting and receiving.	Open-drain	1	1	1	1

---

4 Mark and space are terms used in asynchronous serial communications to denote a logic one (mark) and zero (space). *Microcontrollers and Microcomputers: Principles of Software and Hardware Engineering* describes these and other terms in Chapter 10.

Parity

Unlike the M68HC11, the M68HC12 can generate a parity bit in hardware. Parity generation for transmitting and checking for receiving is enabled by setting the *PE* bit. The type of parity, even or odd, is selected by the *PT* bit. Both PE and PT are in the SCnCR1 register.

SC0CR1—$00C2—SCI0 Control Register 1

SC1CR1—$00CA—SCI1 Control Register 1

Bit 7	6	5	4	3	2	1	Bit 0
LOOPS	WOMS	RSRC	M	WAKE	ILT	PE	PT

Reset   0   0   0   0   0   0   0   0

LOOPS

SCI LOOP and Single-Wire Mode Enable.
        0 = Normal SCI operation (default).
        1 = SCI receive section is disconnected from the RxD pin. RxD is available for general-purpose I/O.
Both RE and TE must be set to enable the receiver and transmitter to use the LOOP mode.

RSRC

Receiver Source.
When LOOPS = 1, RSRC determines the internal feedback path to the receiver.
        0 = Receiver input is connected to the transmitter internally (not the TxD pin).
        1 = Receiver input is connected to the external TxD pin.
See Table 11–1 and Figures 11–3 and 11–4.

WOMS

Wired-OR Mode for Serial Pins.
        0 = Pins operate normally with high and low drive capability (default).
        1 = Each pin that is an output operates in wired-OR mode.

M

Character Format Select.
        0 = One start, eight data, one stop bit (default).
        1 = One start, eight data, plus ninth data, one stop bit.

WAKE

Wakeup Mode Select.

ILT

Idle Line Type.
    0 = Short idle detect (default).
    1 = Long idle detect.

PE

Parity Enable.
    0 = Parity is disabled (default).
    1 = Parity is enabled and inserted into the most significant bit on transmit. The most significant bit is checked on receive.

PT

Parity Type.
    0 = Even parity (default).
    1 = Odd parity.

SCI Baud Rate Selection

Comparison of M68HC12 and M68HC11 SCI Baud Rate Selection	
M68HC12	**M68HC11**
A single 13-bit register is programmed with a divider; standard Baud rates up to 38,400; nonstandard rates from 30 to 500,000 Baud	A prescaler and Baud rate generator bits to be initialized; standard rates up to 9600; nonstandard rates up to 125,000

The rate at which serial data are sent is called the Baud rate. Both the receiver and transmitter use the same rate and a 13-bit divider (one for each SCI channel) derives standard Baud rates from the M-clock in the MC68HC812A4 and the P-clock in the MC68HC912B32. These clocks are normally one-half the external oscillator frequency. Table 11–2 shows how the bits in the *SCI Baud Rate Control Registers* select standard rates. Nonstandard Baud rates can be chosen by initializing the Baud rate registers with other BR values. The value to choose is given by the following relationships:

TABLE 11–2 SBR12:SBR0 Decimal Values for Standard Baud Rates

Standard Baud Rate	M-clock = 4 MHz	M-clock = 8 MHz
110	2273	4545
300	833	1667
600	417	833
1200	208	417
2400	104	208
4800	52	104
9600	26	52
14,400	17	35
19,200	13	26
38,400	—	13

$$SCI\ Baud\ Rate = \frac{M\text{-}clock}{16 \times BR}$$

or

$$BR = \frac{M\text{-}clock}{16 \times SCI\ Baud\ Rate}$$

SC0BDH—$00C0—SCI0 Baud Rate Control Register High

SC1BDH—$00C8—SCI1 Baud Rate Control Register High

Bit 7	6	5	4	3	2	1	Bit 0
BTST	BSPL	BRLD	SBR12	SBR11	SBR10	SBR9	SBR8
Reset 0	0	0	0	0	0	0	0

SC0BDL—$00C1—SCI0 Baud Rate Control Register Low

SC1BDL—$00C9—SCI1 Baud Rate Control Register High

Bit 7	6	5	4	3	2	1	Bit 0
SBR7	SBR6	SBR5	SBR4	SBR3	SBR2	SBR1	SBR0
Reset 0	0	0	0	0	1	0	0

SBR12:SBR0
13-bit Baud rate select bits.

BTST, BSPL, BRLD
Reserved for test function.

SCI Status Flags

The SCI system has several status flags and interrupts to inform you of its progress and of error conditions that may occur. Your program may poll the flags or make use of the interrupts. The status flags are in the *SCI Status Register 1 and 2* and the interrupt enable bits are in the *SCI Control Register 2.*

SC0SR1—$00C4—SCI0 Status Register 1

SC1SR1—$00CC—SCI1 Status Register 1

Bit 7	6	5	4	3	2	1	Bit 0
TDRE	TC	RDRF	IDLE	OR	NF	FE	PF

Reset 1   1   0   0   0   0   0   0

TDRE

Transmit Data Register Empty Flag.
    0 = Not empty.
    1 = Empty (default).
This flag is set when the last character written to the SCI data register (SCnDRL) has been transferred to the output shift register. Normally the program should check this bit before writing the next character to the SCnDRL. The flag is reset (cleared) by reading the SCnSR1 register with TDRE set and then writing the next byte to the SCnDRL.

TC

Transmit Complete Flag.
        0 = Transmitter is busy sending a character.
        1 = Transmitter is done sending the last character (default).
This bit is different than the TDRE bit. It shows when the last character has been completely sent from the output shift register. The flag is reset (cleared) by reading the SCnSR1 register with TC set and then writing the next byte to the SCnDRL.

RDRF

Receive Data Register Full Flag.
  0 = Data register not full. Nothing has come in since the last data were read from the SCDR (default).
  1 = Data register has new data.
The flag is reset (cleared) by reading the SCnSR1 register with RDRF set and then reading SCnDRL.

IDLE

Idle Line Detected Flag.
  0 = The receive line is either active now or has never been active since IDLE was last reset (default).
  1 = The receive line has become idle.
The idle flag is cleared by reading SCnSR1 (while IDLE = 1) and then reading SCnDRL. After the IDLE flag has been reset, it will not be set again until the receive line becomes active and then idle again.

OR

Receiver Overrun Error Flag.
  0 = No overrun error (default).
  1 = An overrun has occurred.
Overrun occurs if a new character has been received before the old data have been read by the program. The new data are lost and the old data are preserved. The flag is cleared by reading SCnSR1 (with OR = 1) and then reading the SCnDRL.

NF

Noise Flag.
  0 = No noise detected during the last character (default).
  1 = Noise was detected.
The hardware takes three samples of the received signal near the middle of each data bit and the stop bit. Seven samples are taken during the start bit. If the samples in each bit do not agree, the noise flag is set. The flag may be reset by reading SCnSR1 (with NF=1) followed by a read of SCnDRL.

FE

Framing Error.
    0 = No framing error (default).
    1 = Framing error occurred.
A framing error occurs if the receiver detects a space during the stop bit time instead of a mark. This kind of error can occur if the receiver misses the start bit or if the sending and receiving data rates are not equal. It is possible to have bad framing or mismatched Baud rates but not get a framing error indication if a mark is detected where a stop bit was expected. The flag is reset by reading SCnSR1 (with FE = 1) and then reading the SCnDRL.

PF

Parity Error Flag.
    0 = Parity on the last received data is correct (default).
    1 = Parity incorrect.
PE is reset by reading ScnSR1 with PF set and then reading SCnDRL.

SC0SR2—$00C5—SCI0 Status Register 2

SC1SR2—$00CD—SCI1 Status Register 2

Bit 7	6	5	4	3	2	1	Bit 0
0	0	0	0	0	0	0	RAF

Reset 0   0   0   0   0   0   0   0

RAF

Receiver Active Flag.
    0 = A character is not being received (default).
    1 = A character is being received.
This bit is set when a received character's start bit arrives and is reset if the start bit is determined to be false or when an idle state is detected.

SCI Interrupts

The SCI interrupts are enabled by setting bits in the *SCnCR2 SCI Control Register 2*. Each SCI's interrupts are serviced by interrupt service routines whose vectors are shown in Table 11–3. There are five potential sources of interrupts shown in Table 11–4. When an SCI receiver interrupt oc-

TABLE 11-3 SCI Interrupt Vector Assignments

Vector Address	Interrupt Source	Local Enable Bit	D-Bug12 SetUser Vect Number$_{10}$
$FFD6:FFD7	SCI 0	See Table 11-4	11
$FFD4:FFD3	SCI 1	See Table 11-4	10

curs, the service routine must test the SCnSR1 status register to determine which condition caused the interrupt. As in the case of all other interrupting sources, the flag that caused the interrupt must be cleared in the interrupt service routine. This is done by reading the SCnSR1 register and then writing the next data byte to the SCnDRL.

SC0CR2—$00C3—SCI0 Control Register 2

SC1CR2—$00CB—SCI1 Control Register 2

Bit 7	6	5	4	3	2	1	Bit 0
TIE	TCIE	RIE	ILIE	TE	RE	RWU	SBK

Reset 0 0   0   0   0   0   0   0

TIE

Transmit Interrupt Enable.
   0 = TDRE interrupts disabled (default).
   1 = TDRE interrupts enabled.
An SCI interrupt is requested when the transmit data register is empty. If you have many characters in a buffer to be sent, using this interrupt is a good way to make sure you do not send the next character until the previous one has been transferred from the transmit data register to the output shift register.

TABLE 11-4 SCI Serial System Interrupts

Interrupt Cause	SCnCR2 Enable Bit	SCnSR1 Status Register Bit
Receive Data Register Full	RIE	RDRF
Receiver Overrun	RIE	OR
Idle Line Detect	ILIE	IDLE
Transmit Data Register Empty	TIE	TDRE
Transmit Complete	TCIE	TC

TCIE

Transmit Complete Interrupt Enable.
        0 = TC interrupts disabled (default).
        1 = TC interrupts enabled.
This is similar to the TIE but the interrupt is generated when the output shift register has finished sending the last character instead of when the transmit data register is emptied. You could use this in a single-wire system to disable the TxD output when the transmitter has completed sending the character.

RIE

Receive Interrupt Enable.
        0 = RDRF and OR interrupts are disabled (default).
        1 = An interrupt is generated when either RDRF <u>or</u> OR flags are set.
If this interrupt is used and occurs, the program must check the SCI status register (SCnSR1) to see which flag has generated the interrupt.

ILIE

Idle Line Interrupt Enable.
        0 = Idle interrupts are disabled (default).
        1 = An SCI interrupt request is generated when an idle line condition is detected.

SCI Wakeup

The SCI features a sleep and wakeup mode. This may be used in multidrop applications in which one M68HC12 is broadcasting data to many serial receivers in a network as shown in Figure 11–5. Software in each receiver puts it to sleep (by setting the *RWU* bit in the *SCnCR2* register) until the programmed wakeup sequence is received. At the start of a broadcast, each receiver automatically wakes up and software in all receivers decodes who the message is for. Only the addressed station stays awake to receive the message. Each of the others are put back to sleep until the start of the next broadcast. Receivers that are asleep do not respond to received data. However, only the SCI receiver is asleep and the CPU can continue to operate and do other chores. The CPU can wake up the SCI by resetting the RWU bit to zero, although the automatic hardware mechanism normally wakes up sleeping receivers. The wakeup mode and receiver wakeup enable are controlled by bits in SCnCR1 and SCnCR2.

When the program puts a receiver to sleep by writing a one to the RWU bit, all receiver interrupts are disabled until the receiver is awakened by one of two wakeup methods. If WAKE = 0, a full character of idle line (a mark) wakes up the receiver. If WAKE = 1, any byte with a one in the most significant bit wakes it up.

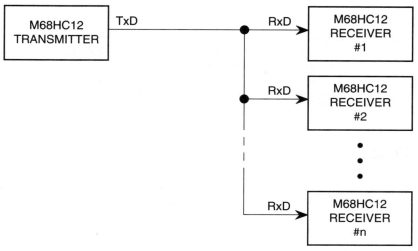

Figure 11–5   Multidrop serial I/O network.

SC0CR2—$00C3—SCI0 Control Register 2

SC1CR2—$00CB—SCI1 Control Register 2

Bit 7	6	5	4	3	2	1	Bit 0
TIE	TCIE	RIE	ILIE	TE	RE	RWU	SBK

Reset 0   0   0   0   0   0   0   0

RWU
Receiver Wakeup Control.   0 = Normal SCI receiver (default).   1 = Enables the wakeup function and inhibits further receiver interrupts.

SC0CR1—$00C2—SC0 Control Register 1

SC1CR1—$00CA—SC1 Control Register 1

Bit 7	6	5	4	3	2	1	Bit 0
LOOPS	WOMS	RSRC	M	WAKE	ILT	PE	PT

Reset 0   0   0   0   0   0   0   0

WAKE

Wake Up by Address Mark or Idle
    0 = Wake up by IDLE line recognition. At least one full character of idle line causes
      the receiver to wake up (default).
    1 = Wake up by address mark. A logic one in the most significant bit position or the
      received data causes the receiver to wake up.

SCI Break Character

The SCI can send a break character, 10 or 11 zeros, by the program writing a one into the SBK bit in the SCnCR2 register. Break characters are used in some systems to wake up the receiving end.

SC0CR2—$00C3—SCI0 Control Register 2

SC1CR2—$00CB—SCI1 Control Register 2

Bit 7	6	5	4	3	2	1	Bit 0
TIE	TCIE	RIE	ILIE	TE	RE	RWU	SBK

Reset 0   0   0   0   0   0   0   0

SBK

Send Break Character.
    0 = Break generator off (default).
    1 = Full character times of logic 0 are queued and transmitted as long as SBK = 1.

Port S SCI I/O

Port S provides the serial I/O data and control bits. For any serial function not enabled, the bits may be used for general-purpose I/O.

PORTS—$00D6—Port S Data Register

Bit 7	6	5	4	3	2	1	Bit 0
PS7	PS6	PS5	PS4	PS3	PS2	PS1	PS0

| Serial Function | $\overline{SS}$ $\overline{CS}$ | SCK | MOSI MOMI | MISO SISO | TxD1 I/O | RxD1 I/O | TxD0 | RxD0 |

DDRS—$00D7—Port S Data Direction Register

Bit 7	6	5	4	3	2	1	Bit 0
DDRS7	DDRS6	DDRS5	DDRS4	DDRS3	DDRS2	DDRS1	DDRS0

Reset 0   0   0   0   0   0   0   0

Data direction register bits determine the direction of the corresponding data register. When an SCI function is enabled, the corresponding DDRS bit has no meaning or effect.

    0 = Associated pin is a high-impedance input (default).
    1 = Associated pin is an output.

DDRS2, DDRS0

Data Direction for Port S, bit-2 and -0.
If the SCI receiver is configured for two-wire SCI operation (LOOPS=0), the Port S pins will be an input regardless of these bits. If LOOPS=1, a single-wire SCI is in operation and bit-2 and/or -0 are I/O whose direction is controlled by DDRS2 and DDRS0.

DDRS3, DDRS1

Data Direction for Port S, bit-3 and -1.
If the SCI transmitter is configured for two-wire operation (LOOPS=0), Port S bit-3 and -1 are outputs regardless of this bit. If LOOPS=1, Port S bits-3 and -1 are either high or high impedance depending on the state of RSRC. See Table 11–1.

DDRS7–DDRS4

See Section 11.4.

SCI Programming Example

Example 11–1 shows subroutines for initializing the SCI to operate at 9600 baud, one start and stop bit, and eight data bits including odd parity. The example shows initialization, data output, receiver status check, and data input subroutines.

EXAMPLE 11–1 Serial I/O Subroutines

ser12ex1.asm   Assembled with CASM 03/17/1998 02:39 PAGE 1

```
                    1 ;            MC68HC12 SCI I/O Example
                    2 ;            Source File: SER12EX1.ASM
                    3 ;            This file gives subroutines for SCI input
                    4 ;            and output.
                    5 ;
                    6 ; SCI Register Equates
0000                7 TE:       EQU      %00001000    ; Transmitter Enable
0000                8 RE:       EQU      %00000100    ; Receiver Enable
0000                9 TDRE:     EQU      %10000000    ; TX Data Reg Empty
0000               10 RDRF:     EQU      %00100000    ; Rx Data Reg Full
0000               11 MODE:     EQU      %00010000    ; Mode bit
0000               12 PE:       EQU      %00000010    ; Parity Enable
0000               13 ODD_P:    EQU      %00000001    ; Set odd parity
0000               14 B9600:    EQU      !52          ; Baud rate = 9600
0000               15 SC0BDH:   EQU      $C1          ; Baud rate register
0000               16 SC0CR1:   EQU      $C2          ; Control register 1
0000               17 SC0CR2:   EQU      $C3          ; Control register 2
0000               18 SC0SR1:   EQU      $C4          ; Status register
0000               19 SC0DRL:   EQU      $C7          ; Data register
                   20
                   21 ;****************************************
                   22 ; Subroutine init_sci
                   23 ; Initialize SCI to 1 start, 8 data and 1 stop
                   24 ; bit, odd parity and 9600 Baud.
                   25 ; Inputs: None
                   26 ; Outputs: None
                   27 ; Reg Mod: CCR
                   28 init_sci:
0000 3B            29         pshd                    ; Save D reg
                   30 ; Set 1 start, 8 data and 1 stop bit
0001 4DC210        31         bclr     SC0CR1,MODE
                   32 ; Choose odd parity and enable it
0004 4CC203        33         bset     SC0CR1,PE|ODD_P
                   34 ; Enable transmitter and receiver
0007 4CC30C        35         bset     SC0CR2,TE|RE
000A CC0034        36         ldd      #B9600
000D 5CC1          37         std      SC0BDH          ; Set Baud rate
000F 3A            38         puld                     ; Restore x
0010 3D            39         rts
                   40 ;****************************************
                   41 ; Subroutine sci_out
                   42 ; Send SCI data
                   43 ; Inputs: A register = data to send
                   44 ; Outputs: None
                   45 ; Reg Mod: CCR
                   46 sci_out:
                   47 ; Wait until the transmit data reg is empty
```

EXAMPLE 11-1 Continued

```
0011 4FC480FC     48    spin:       brclr    SC0SR1,TDRE,spin
                  49    ; Output the data and reset TDRE
0015 5AC7         50                staa     SC0DRL
0017 3D           51                rts
                  52    ;***************************************
                  53    ; Subroutine sci_char_ready
                  54    ; Check the RDRF flag
                  55    ; If a character is ready, returns with C=1
                  56    ; the character in the A register, and the
                  57    ; status information in the B register.
                  58    ; Otherwise, C=0 and the A and B regs are
                  59    ; unchanged
                  60    ; Inputs: None
                  61    ; Outputs: A = character, Carry bit T or F
                  62    ;          B = status information
                  63    ; Reg Mod:  A, CCR
                  64    sci_char_ready:
0018 10FE         65                clc                  ; Clear carry
                  66    ; IF RDRF is set
001A 4FC42006     67                brclr    SC0SR1,RDRF,exit
                  68    ; THEN the character is there
001E 96C7         69                ldaa     SC0DRL      ; Get the data
0020 D6C4         70                ldab     SC0SR1      ; Get the status
0022 1401         71                sec                  ; Set the carry
                  72    ; ENDIF
0024 3D           73    exit:       rts
                  74    ;***************************************
                  75    ; Subroutine sci_input
                  76    ; Get a character from SCI
                  77    ; Inputs: None
                  78    ; Outputs: A = character
                  79    ; Reg Mod:        A, CCR
                  80    sci_input:
0025 96C7         81                ldaa     SC0DRL
0027 3D           82                rts
                  83    ;***************************************
```

11.4 Synchronous Serial Peripheral Interface (SPI)

Comparison of M68HC12 and M68HC11 SPI	
M68HC12	**M68HC11**
Up to 4 Mbit/sec; LSB or MSB first; open-drain for wired-OR or CMOS for normal modes; input pull-up; output reduced drive capability	Up to 1 Mbit/sec; LSB first; CMOS output only

The SPI is designed to send high-speed serial data to peripherals and other SPI equipped MCUs and digital signal processors. Data rates up to 4 Mbit/sec can be achieved.

Interprocessor Serial Communications

> The SPI is a synchronous serial interface because the master provides a clock to shift data in and out.

Figure 11–6 shows a typical application of the SPI. Two M68HC12s are connected in a master/slave arrangement. The 8-bit shift registers in the master and slave make a circular 16-bit register. When data are to be transmitted from the master to the slave, a clock signal, *SCK* (Port S, bit-6), is generated by the master device to *synchronize* the transfer of each bit. Data are transferred out of each shift register simultaneously so that the master receives what was in the slave. The transmitted data are single buffered; this means that the program must wait until the last transmitted data bit is shifted out before writing new data to the register. A flag, *SPI Transfer Complete Flag* (*SPIF*), is available for polling or interrupts. Received data, on the other hand, are buffered and so the program has one character time to read the data before the next data overwrite it. The slave select, $\overline{SS}$, signal must be low to select an M68HC12 as a slave and high for the master.

SPI Data Register

The *SPI Data Register* (*SP0DR*) is similar to the SCI Data Register in that two registers occupy one memory location, $00D5. Data to be transmitted serially are written to this register and serial data received are read from it.

SP0DR—$00D5—SPI Data Register

Bit 7	6	5	4	3	2	1	Bit 0
7	6	5	4	3	2	1	0

Reset 0   0   0   0   0   0   0   0

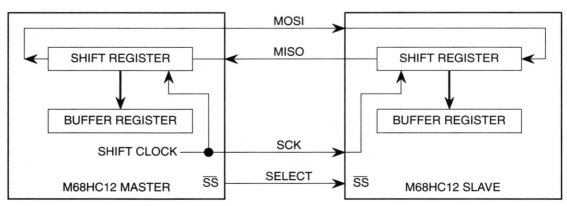

Figure 11–6   Master/slave serial peripheral interface.

SPI Initialization

The SPI is initialized by the *SPI Control Registers* (*SP0CR1* and *SP0CR2*) and the *Port S Data Direction Control Register* (*DDRS*).

SP0CR1—$00D0—SPI Control Register 1

Bit 7	6	5	4	3	2	1	Bit 0
SPIE	SPE	SWOM	MSTR	CPOL	CPHA	SSOE	LSBF

Reset 0   0   0   0   0   0   0   0

SPIE

SPI Interrupt Enable.
    0 = SPI interrupts are disabled (default).
    1 = Interrupts are enabled.
See *SPI Status Register and Interrupts.*

SPE

SPI System Enable.
    0 = SPI internal hardware is initialized and the SPI system is in a low-power disabled state (default).
    1 = SPI bits (Port S, bits 4–7] are dedicated to the SPI function.

SWOM

Port S Wired-OR Mode.
    0 = SPI and/or Port S, bits 4–7 output buffers operate normally (default).
    1 = SPI output bits behave as open-drain outputs.

MSTR

SPI Master/Slave Mode Select.
    0 = Slave mode (default).
    1 = Master mode.

CPOL, CPHA

SPI Clock Polarity and Clock Phase. See *SPI Data Rate and Clock Formats.*

SSOE

Slave Select Output Enable.
    0 = Slave select output is not enabled (default).
    1 = Slave select output can be asserted if SSOE = 1 and DDRS7 = 1.

LSBF

SPI Least Significant Bit First Enable.
    0 = Data are transferred most significant bit first (default).
    1 = Data are transferred least significant bit first.

SP0CR2—$00D1—SPI Control Register 2

Bit 7	6	5	4	3	2	1	Bit 0
0	0	0	0	PUPS	RDS	0	SPC0

Reset 0   0   0   0   1   0   0   0

PUPS

Pull-up Port S Enable.
    0 = No internal pull-ups on Port S (default).
    1 = All Port S input pins have active pull-up. If a pin is programmed as an output,
        the pull-up device becomes inactive.
See Chapter 7 for a further discussion of pull-ups and reduced drive capability.

RDS

Reduced Drive of Port S Output.
    0 = Port S drivers operate normally (default).
    1 = Port S output pins have reduced drive capability.

SPC0
Serial Pin Control 0.
0 = Normal two-wire mode (default).
1 = Bidirectional mode.
SPC0 controls the configuration of the SPI pins with MSTR. See Table 11–5.

SPI Master and Slave Modes

An SPI system consists of a master unit, which controls all timing and data transfer, and one, or more, slave units. The *MSTR* bit in the *SP0CR1* register chooses the master mode (MSTR=1) or the slave mode (MSTR=0). In addition, the *SPC0* bit in the *SP0CR2* register can select either a normal, two-wire mode or a single-wire, bidirectional mode. Figure 11–7 shows the normal mode where two wires, *MOSI* and *MISO*, are needed to transfer the data. Figure 11–8 shows the single-wire, bidirectional mode. DDRS4 (in the slave) and DDRS5 (in the master) must be controlled by

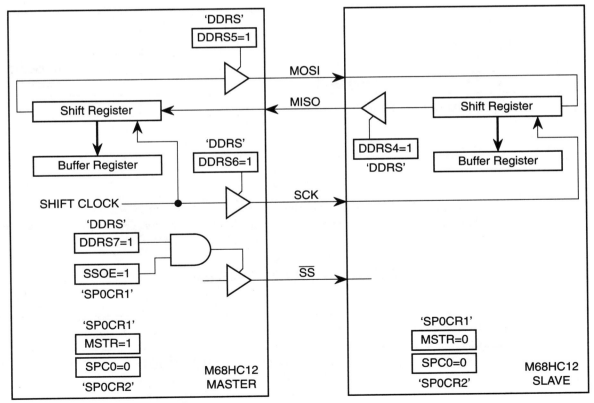

Figure 11–7 SPI Master/Slave normal two-wire operation.

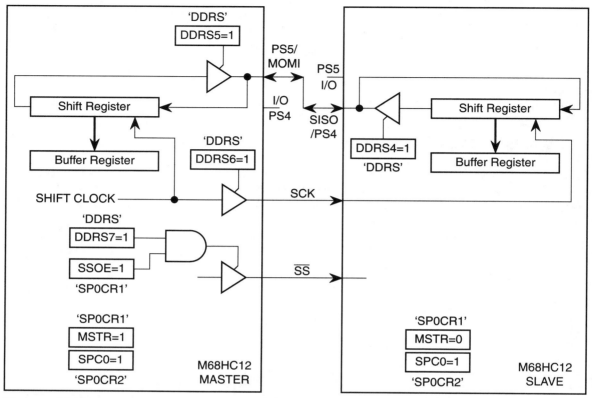

Figure 11-8   SPI Master/Slave bidirectional mode.

a program in each unit when transmitting and receiving. The bidirectional modes allow the un-used SPI bits (PS4 on the master and PS5 on the slave) to be used as general-purpose I/O. Table 11–5 shows the SPI pin names and their various functions under different operating modes.

PORTS—$00D6—Port S Data Register

Bit 7	6	5	4	3	2	1	Bit 0
PS7	PS6	PS5	PS4	PS3	PS2	PS1	PS0

	Bit 7	6	5	4	3	2	1	Bit 0
Normal SPI	$\overline{SS}$	SCK	MOSI	MISO	TxD1	RxD1	TxD0	RxD0
Bidirectional SPI	$\overline{CS}$		MOMI	SISO				

TABLE 11-5 SPI Pin Names and Functions[1]

Signal	Port S Bit	SPC0	DDRS Bit	MSTR	SSOE	Function
MISO	4	0	4=x	1	—	*Master-in*/(*Slave-out*) for the master in normal two-wire mode
MISO	4	0	4=1	0	—	(*Master-in*)/*Slave-out* for the slave in normal two-wire mode
I/O	4	1	4=0,1	1	—	General-purpose I/O for the master in bidirectional mode
SISO	4	1	4=0,1	0	—	*Slave-in/Slave-out* for the slave in bidirectional mode
MOSI	5	0	5=1	1	—	*Master-out*/(*Slave-in*) for the master in normal two-wire mode
MOSI	5	0	5=x	0	—	(*Master-out*)/*Slave-in* for the slave in normal two-wire mode
MOMI	5	1	5=0,1	1	—	*Master-out/Master-in* for the master in bidirectional mode
I/O	5	1	5=0,1	0	—	General-purpose I/O on the slave in bidirectional mode
SCK	6	x	6=1	1	—	SPI clock is output from the master
SCK	6	x	6=x	0	—	SPI clock is input to the slave
$\overline{SS}$	7	x	1	1	1	$\overline{SS}$ is output from the master
$\overline{SS}$	7	x	x	0	x	$\overline{SS}$ is input to the slave

[1] *SPC0, Serial Pin Control 0. 0 = 2-wire, 1 = bidirectional mode. DDRS Bits, Data Direction Register Port S. 0 = input, 1 = output. MSTR, Master/Slave Select. 0 = Slave, 1 = Master. SSOE, Slave Select Output Enable. 0 = not enabled, 1 = enabled.*

DDRS—$00D7—Port S Data Direction Register

Bit 7	6	5	4	3	2	1	Bit 0
DDRS7	DDRS6	DDRS5	DDRS4	DDRS3	DDRS2	DDRS1	DDRS0

Reset 0   0   0   0   0   0   0   0

Data direction register bits determine the direction of the corresponding data register.
  0 = Associated pin is a high-impedance input (default).
  1 = Associated pin is an output.

DDRS6–DDRS4

Data Direction for Port S, bit-6 to bit-4.
If the SPI is enabled and expects the corresponding bit to be an input, the states of these DDRS bits have no effect. If the Port S bit is an output, the corresponding DDRS bit MUST be set.

DDRS7

Data Direction for Port S, bit-7.
In SPI slave mode, Port S, bit-7 is the $\overline{SS}$ input regardless of DDRS7. When the SPI is enabled as a master (MSTR=1), the function of PS7/ $\overline{SS}$ depends on DDRS7 and Slave Select Output Enable (SSOE in SP0CR1).

DDRS7	SSOE	Master Mode	Slave Mode
0	0	$\overline{SS}$ input with MODF feature (see MODF explanation below)	$\overline{SS}$ input
0	1	Reserved	$\overline{SS}$ input
1	0	General-purpose output	$\overline{SS}$ input
1	1	$\overline{SS}$ Output	$\overline{SS}$ input

SPI Data Rate and Clock Formats

The rate at which data are transferred and the format of the clock to do the shifting are controlled by the *SPI Baud Rate Register (SP0BR)* and the *CPOL* and *CPHA* bits in the *SP0CR1* register. The *P-clock* (see Chapter 15) controls the basic clocking rate for the data in the SPI. It can be further divided by three bits, *SPR2, SPR1,* and *SPR0,* as shown in Table 11–6.

The SPI clock output from the master, *SCK* (Port S, bit-6), controls the rate at which data are transferred. In addition, both the master and the slave modes can be programmed to sample the data according to four modes controlled by the CPOL and CPHA bits in the SP0CR1 register. The four choices shown in Figure 11–9 allow a variety of SPI devices to be used.

SP0BR—$00D2—SPI Baud Rate Register

Bit 7	6	5	4	3	2	1	Bit 0
0	0	0	0	0	SPR2	SPR1	SPR0

Reset 0   0   0   0   0   0   0   0

TABLE 11–6   SPI Clock Rate Selection

SPR2	SPR1	SPR0	Divisor	P-clock=4 MHz	P-clock=8 MHz
0	0	0	2	2 MHz	4 MHz
0	0	1	4	1 MHz	2 MHz
0	1	0	8	500 kHz	1 MHz
0	1	1	16	250 kHz	500 kHz
1	0	0	32	125 kHz	250 kHz
1	0	1	64	62.5 kHz	125 kHz
1	1	0	128	31.25 kHz	62.5 kHz
1	1	1	256	15.625 kHz	31.25 kHz

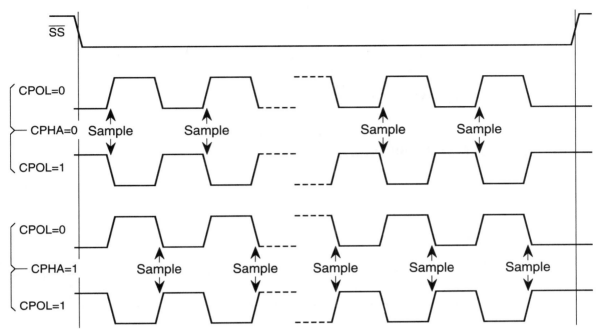

Figure 11-9   SPI clock phases.

SPR2:SPR1:SPR0
SPI Clock Rate Select Bits. See Table 11–6.

SP0CR1—$00D0—SPI Control Register 1

Bit 7	6	5	4	3	2	1	Bit 0
SPIE	SPE	SWOM	MSTR	CPOL	CPHA	SSOE	LSBF

Reset 0   0   0   0   0   0   0   0

CPOL

SPI Clock Polarity Select.
        0 = SCK is low when not shifting data (default).
        1 = SCK is high when not shifting data.

CPHA

SPI Clock Phase Select.

    0 = The serial data bit is sampled on the rising edge of SCK if CPOL=0 (default) and the falling edge of SCK if CPOL=1.

    1 = The serial data bit is sampled on the falling edge of SCK if CPOL=0 and the rising edge of SCK if CPOL=1.

SPI Status Register and Interrupts

The *SPI Status Register (SP0SR)* contains status and error bits. You may poll them or use them to generate interrupts.

SP0SR—$00D3—SPI Status Register

Bit 7	6	5	4	3	2	1	Bit 0
SPIF	WCOL	0	MODF	0	0	0	0
Reset 0	0	0	0	0	0	0	0

SPIF

SPI Interrupt Request Flag.
This flag is set at the end of an SPI transfer. It is cleared by reading the SP0SR with SPIF set, followed by an access (reading or writing) of the SPI data register, SP0DR. If the SPI interrupt enable bit (SPIE) is set, an SPI interrupt is generated.

WCOL

Write Collision Error Flag.
This flag is set if the SP0DR is written while a data transfer is taking place. The bit may be reset by reading SP0SR and then reading or writing SP0DR. This bit does not generate an interrupt.

MODF

Mode Error Flag.
A mode error occurs if $\overline{SS}$ is pulled low while the SPI is in master mode. This indicates that some other SPI device is trying to act as a master and a data collision may occur. An interrupt may be generated if SPIE is enabled. MODF may be reset by reading SP0SR and then writing to SP0DR.

TABLE 11-7 SPI Interrupt Vector Assignments			
Vector Address	Interrupt Source	Condition Code Register Mask	Local Enable Bit	D-Bug12 SetUser Vect Number$_{10}$
$FFD8:FFD9	SPI Serial System	I Bit	SPIE	12

SPI Interrupts

There are only two bits that can generate an interrupt. These are the *SPI Transfer Complete Flag* (*SPIF*) and the *Mode-Fault Error Flag* (*MODF*). The *SPI Interrupt Enable* (SPIE, in SP0CR1) must be set and when an interrupt occurs, SPIF and MODF must be polled to determine the source of the interrupt. The interrupt vector and the D-Bug12 SetUserVect number are shown in Table 11–7.

SPI Programming Example

A typical example of an SPI I/O device is the serial digital-to-analog (D/A) converter shown in Figure 11–10. Example 11–2 shows a short program that outputs a sawtooth wave to the SPI D/A.

Explanation of Example 11–2

The SPI outputs for master mode operation are set in *lines 39 and 40*. The SPI is enabled and set to master mode and its baud rate clock set to 4 MHz in *lines 41–46*. The Maxim MAX512 serial D/A used in this example requires that its $\overline{CS}$ input be driven low when it is to start receiving 2

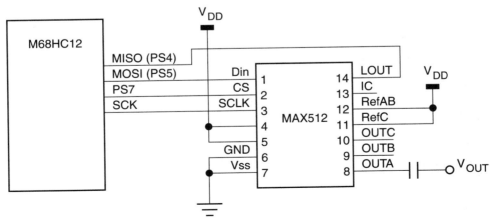

Figure 11-10   SPI serial D/A.

EXAMPLE 11–2   SPI Programming Example

spiex1a.asm   Assembled with CASM 12/18/1998 21:51 PAGE 1

```
              1  ;************************************************
              2  ; Serial Peripheral Interface Example
              3  ; spiex1a.asm
              4  ;
              5  ; This program continuously outputs a sawtooth
              6  ; wave to the SPI port.  This interface is
              7  ; connected to a Maxim MAX512 serial D/A converter.
              8  ;************************************************
              9  ; Variables and constants
             10  ; ------------------------
             11  ; Maxim D/A control byte (all outputs enabled)
0000         12  DASETUP:  EQU    %10000111
             13  ; SPI control bits
0000         14  SPIF:     EQU    %10000000           ; SPI Flag
0000         15  SPE:      EQU    %01000000           ; SPI enable
0000         16  MSTR:     EQU    %00010000           ; Master select
0000         17  SS:       EQU    %10000000           ; Slave Select
             18  ; Enable Port S bits 5,6, and 7 as outputs
0000         19  SMASK:    EQU    %11100000
             20  ; Enable the SPI as a master serial device
0000         21  SPISETUP: EQU    SPE|MSTR
             22  ; Ports and control registers
0000         23  PORTS:    EQU    $00D6     ; Port S
0000         24  DDRS:     EQU    $00D7     ; Data direction Port S
0000         25  SP0CR1:   EQU    $00D0     ; SPI control register
0000         26  SP0BR:    EQU    $00D2     ; SPI Baud rate register
0000         27  SP0SR:    EQU    $00D3     ; SPI Status Register
0000         28  SP0DR:    EQU    $00D5     ; SPI Data Register:in and out
             29  ; Memory Map Equates
             30  ; ------------------------
0000         31  PROG:     EQU    $4000
0000         32  STACK:    EQU    $8000
0000         33  DATA:     EQU    $6000
             34  ; ---------------------
4000         35            ORG    PROG
4000 CF8000  36            lds    #STACK
             38  ; Set Port S bit 7-5 output
4003 86E0    39            ldaa   #SMASK
4005 5AD7    40            staa   DDRS
             41  ; Enable the SPI in master mode
4007 8650    42            ldaa   #SPISETUP
4009 5AD0    43            staa   SP0CR1
             44  ; Set the SCLK to 4 MHz
400B 8600    45            ldaa   #$00
```

EXAMPLE 11-2   Continued

```
400D  5AD2        46            staa     SP0BR
                  47  ; Initialize the output data
400F  796000      48            clr      sawtooth
                  49  ; Main Loop
                  50  ; Continuously output a sawtooth wave
                  51  LOOP:
                  52  ; Set SS low to select the D/A
4012  4DD680      53            bclr     PORTS,SS
                  54  ; Write an 8 bit control word to the serial
                  55  ; D/A converter before writing the data
4015  8687        56            ldaa     #DASETUP      ; Write control to D/A
4017  5AD5        57            staa     SP0DR
                  58  ; Spin loop to do nothing until the data is shifted
                  59  ; out onto the serial line (MOSI). Wait for SPIF.
4019  4FD380FC    60  SPIN:     brclr    SP0SR,SPIF,SPIN
                  61  ; Clear the flag by reading the status register
                  62  ; and the data register
401D  96D3        63            ldaa     SP0SR      ; Status register
401F  96D5        64            ldaa     SP0DR      ; Data register
                  65  ; Get the current sawtooth data value
4021  F66000      66            ldab     sawtooth
                  67  ; and store it into the serial shift register
4024  5BD5        68            stab     SP0DR
                  69  ; Increment the sawtooth value for the next time
4026  726000      70            inc      sawtooth
                  71  ; Spin loop to do nothing until the data is shifted
                  72  ; out onto the serial line (MOSI)
4029  4FD380FC    73  SPIN2:    brclr    SP0SR,SPIF,SPIN2
402D  96D3        74            ldaa     SP0SR      ; Clear the SPIF flag
402F  96D5        75            ldaa     SP0DR
                  76  ; Raise the SS line to tell the D/A converter to
                  77  ; output the data
4031  4CD680      78            bset     PORTS,SS
4034  20DC        79            bra      LOOP       ; Continue forever
6000              80            ORG      DATA
6000              81  sawtooth: ds       1
```

bytes of data. This is done in *line 53*. The first byte, sent in *lines 56* and *57*, is a command byte that directs the D/A to output the data on all three of its output channels. The program then enters a spin loop at *line 60* to wait until the SPIF bit is set, indicating that the byte of data has been transferred out of the SPI data register. The SPIF bit is reset by a two-step process. First, the SP0SR status register is read (*line 63*) and then the SP0DR data register is read (*line 64*). The next byte sent to the SPI and the D/A is the current value of the sawtooth waveform (*line 68*). The spin loop in *line 73* waits until this transfer is complete before raising the D/A's $\overline{CS}$ signal in *line 78*.

11.5 MC68HC912B32 Byte Data Link Communications Module

The *Byte Data Link Communications (BDLC)* module provides access to an external serial communications multiplexed bus. It operates according to the Society of Automotive Engineers (SAE) J1850 protocol and offers the following features:

- SAE J1850 compatibility

- 10.4 kbps VPW bit format

- Digital noise filter

- Collision detection

- Hardware CRC generation and checking

- Two power saving modes with automatic wakeup on network activity

- Polling and CPU interrupts with vector lookup available

- Receive and transmit block mode supported

- Supports 4X receive mode (41.6 kbps)

- Digital loopback mode

- In-frame response (IFR) types 0, 1, 2, and 3 supported

- Dedicated register for symbol timing adjustments

- Digital module only, requires external analog transceiver

NOTE

A full explanation of the SAE J1850 protocol is outside the scope of this text. The reader should be familiar with the *SAE Standard J1850 Class B Data Communication Network Interface* specification before reading this chapter.[5]

BDLC Modes

The BDLC has several operating modes.

Power Off: Entered from the reset mode whenever the BDLC supply voltage V_{DD} drops below the minimum value for guaranteed operation.

Reset: Entered from the power off mode whenever the BDLC supply voltage V_{DD} rises above its minimum specified value and an M68HC12 reset source is asserted.

---

5   Available from Society of Automotive Engineers, Dept. 4195, SAE, 400 Commonwealth Drive, Warrendale, PA 15096. Order information can be found at http://www.sae.org/PRODSERV/STANDARD/gv/343.htm.

Run: Entered from the reset mode after all M68HC12 reset sources are no longer asserted. It is entered from the BDLC wait mode whenever activity is sensed on the J1850 bus. Run is entered from the BDLC stop mode whenever network activity is sensed, although messages will not be received properly until the clocks have stabilized and the M68HC12 is also in the run mode. Ensure that all BDLC transmissions cease before leaving the run mode.

BDLC Wait: This is a power-saving mode that is entered when the M68HC12 executes a WAIT instruction when the WCM bit in the BCR register is cleared. BDLC clocks continue to run and the first passive-to-active transition of the bus wakes up the BDLC and the CPU. If a valid byte is successfully received an interrupt request will be generated.

BDLC Stop: This is a power-saving mode that is entered when the M68HC12 executes a STOP instruction, or if the CPU executes a WAIT instruction with the WCM bit set. The BDLC clocks are stopped until network activity is sensed and an interrupt is generated.

BDLC Loopback Testing

The BDLC has two modes that allow testing to find the source of bus faults.

Digital Loopback: In this mode, the receiver is disconnected from the external world and connected internally to the transmitter. This allows you to see if a bus fault has been caused by a failure in the nodes's internal circuits or elsewhere in the network.

Analog Loopback: Analog loopback is used to determine if the fault is in the node's off-chip analog circuitry or elsewhere in the network. If the off-chip analog transceiver has a loopback mode, its receiver is connected to the transmitter for testing.

BDLC Control Registers

There are eight registers for controlling the operation of the BDLC and for communication data and status information.

BCR1—$00F8—BDLC Control Register 1

Bit 7	6	5	4	3	2	1	Bit 0
IMSG	CLCKS	R1	R0	0	0	IE	WCM

| Reset | 1 | 1 | 1 | 0 | 0 | 0 | 0 | 0 |

IMSG
Ignore Message.   0 = Enable receiver.   1 = Disable receiver (default). Disable the receiver until a new start-of-frame (SOF) is detected.

CLKS

Clock Select.
        0 = Integer frequency (1 MHz).
        1 = Binary frequency (1.048576 MHz) (default).
CLKS designates the nominal BDLC operating frequency (f_{BDLC}) for J1850 bus communication and automatic adjustment of symbol time.

R1, R0

Rate Select.
Determines the divisor of the system T-clock frequency to form the BDLC operating frequency f_{BDLC}. These bits may be written only once after reset. See Table 11–8.

IE

Interrupt Enable.
        0 = Disable interrupt request from BDLC (default).
        1 = Enable interrupt request.
Determines if the BDLC will generate interrupt requests in the run mode. It does not affect interrupt requests when exiting the BDLC stop or wait modes.

WCM

Wait Clock Mode.
        0 = Internal BDLC clocks run during CPU wait mode (default).
        1 = Stop BDLC clocks during wait mode.

TABLE 11–8 BDLC Rate Selection for Binary and Integer Frequencies

			External MCU Clock Frequency Required (MHz)	
R1	R0	Divisor	f_{BDLC} = 1.048576 MHz	f_{BDLC} = 1.000000 MHz
0	0	1	2.097152	2.000000
0	1	2	4.194304	4.000000
1	0	4	8.388608	8.000000
1	1	8	16.777216	16.000000

BCR2—$00FA—BDLC Control Register 2

Bit 7	6	5	4	3	2	1	Bit 0
ALOOP	DLOOP	RX4EX	NBFS	TEOD	TSIFR	TMIFR1	TMIFR0

Reset 1   1   0   0   0   0   0   0

ALOOP

Analog Loopback Status.
        0 = Off-chip analog transceiver has been taken out of the analog loopback mode.
        1 = Off-chip analog transceiver has been put into analog loopback mode (default).
This puts the BDLC state machine into a known state after the off-chip analog transceiver has been put into loopback mode.

DLOOP

Digital Loopback Mode.
        0 = RxPD is connected to the analog transceiver's receive output. The BDLC is taken out of digital loopback mode and can now drive and receive from the J1850 bus if ALOOP is not set.
        1 = RxPD is connected to TxPD. This is the BDLC digital loopback mode. The analog transceiver's transmit input is still driven by TxPD (default).

RX4XE

Receive 4X Enable.
        0 = BDLC transmits and receives at 10.4 kbps (default).
        1 = BDLC is in 4X receive-only operation.
Reception of a BREAK symbol automatically clears this bit and sets the BSVR register to $1C.

NBFS

Normalized Bit Format Select.
        0 = The normalization bit is zero when the response part of an in-frame response (IFR) does not end with a CRC byte. The normalization bit is a one when the in-frame response does end in a CRC byte (default).
        1 = The complement of above.

TEOD

Transmit End of Data.

0 = TEOD is automatically cleared at the rising edge of the first CRC bit or if an error is detected. When TEOD is used to end an in-frame response transmission, TEOD is cleared when the BDLC receives a valid EOD symbol back or when an error condition occurs.

1 = Transmit EOD symbol.

TEOD marks the end of a BDLC message by appending an 8-bit CRC after completing transmission of the current byte. This bit is also used to end an in-frame response transmission.

TSIFR

Transmit Single Byte IFR with no CRC.

0 = TSIFR will be cleared automatically once the BDLC has successfully transmitted the byte in the BDR onto the bus, or TEOD is set by the CPU, or an error is detected on the bus.

1 = If TSIFR is set prior to a valid EOD being received with no CRC error, once the EOD symbol has been received, the BDLC will attempt to transmit the appropriate normalization bit followed by the byte in the BDR.

TMIFR0

Transmit Multiple Byte IFR without CRC.

0 = TMIFR0 will be cleared automatically once the BDLC has successfully transmitted the EOD symbol, by the detection of an error on the multiplex bus, or by a transmitter underrun caused when the program does not write another byte to the BDR following the TDRE interrupt.

1 = If this bit is set prior to a valid EOD being received with no CRC error, once the EOD symbol has been received the BDLC will attempt to transmit the appropriate normalization bit followed by IFR bytes. The programmer should set TEOD after the last IFR byte has been written into the BDR register. After TEOD has been set, the last IFR byte to be transmitted will be the last byte that was written into the BDR register.

TMIFR1

Transmit Multiple Byte IFR with CRC.

0 = TMIFR1 will be cleared automatically once the BDLC has successfully transmitted the CRC byte and the EOD symbol, by the detection of an error on the multiplex bus, or by a transmitter underrun caused when the programmer does not write another byte to the BDR following the TDRE interrupt.

1 = If this bit is set prior to a valid EOD being received with no CRC error, once the EOD symbol has been received the BDLC will attempt to transmit the appropriate normalization bit followed by IFR bytes. After TEOD has been set by software and the last IFR byte has been transmitted, the CRC byte is transmitted.

BSVR—$00F9—BDLC State Vector Register

Bit 7	6	5	4	3	2	1	Bit 0
0	0	I3	I2	I1	I0	0	0

Reset 0   0   0   0   0   0   0   0

I3–I0

BDLC Interrupt Source Vector
These bits allow indexed addressing to be used to quickly access an interrupt routine for the eight interrupt sources in the BDLC. See Table 11–9 and Example 11–3.

The vector bits I3–I0 in the BSVR register can be cleared by reading the register except when the BDLC needs servicing, as shown in Table 11–9.

Explanation of Example 11–3

Example 11–3 shows how to use the vector in the BSVR register with indexed addressing to proceed directly to the interrupt service routine rather than polling the register to find which process needs servicing. When the BDLC requests an interrupt, the vector (*line 41*) directs the program to the interrupt service routine starting at *line 8*. The transfer to each interrupt service routine is done by reading the BSVR register (*line 12*) and then using the jump instruction with indexed addressing at *line 13*. The jump table starting at *line 15* contains jumps to each individual service routine and a nop. The nop is included to make each jump table entry start on a 4-byte boundary. For example, assume the RDRF interrupt request is generated. In this case, the BSVR register contains $0C. The JMP_TAB,X instruction of *line 13* jumps to the JMP SERVE_RDRF instruction on *line 22*, which continues to the service routine for the RDRF starting at *line 36*. Each interrupt service routine must end in the RTI instruction.

TABLE 11–9 BDLC Interrupt Sources

I3	I2	I1	I0	BSVR	Interrupt Source	Priority	Reset
0	0	0	0	$00	No interrupts pending	0 (lowest)	None
0	0	0	1	$04	Received EOF	1	Reading BSVR
0	0	1	0	$08	Received IFR byte (RXIFR)	2	Reading BSVR followed by reading BDR
0	0	1	1	$0C	Rx data register full (RDRF)	3	Reading BSVR followed by reading BDR
0	1	0	0	$10	Tx data register empty (TDRE)	4	Reading BSVR followed by writing BDR, or setting TEOD in BCR2
0	1	0	1	$14	Loss of arbitration	5	Reading BSVR
0	1	1	0	$18	CRC error	6	Reading BSVR
0	1	1	1	$1C	Symbol invalid or out of range	7	Reading BSVR
1	0	0	0	$20	Wakeup	8 (highest)	Reading BSVR

EXAMPLE 11-3   Using the BSVR State Vector Register

bdlcvec.asm   Assembled with CASM 03/18/1998 03:05 PAGE 1

```
                      1  ;   MC68HC912B32 BDLC Interrupt Service
                      2  ;   Vectors example
0000                  3  BSVR:      EQU     $F9       ; BDLC Vector Register
0000                  4  VECTOR:    EQU     $FFD0     ; BDLC Interrupt Vector
0000                  5  PROG:      EQU     $0800     ; Program location
0800                  6             ORG     PROG
                      7  ;          ***
                      8  BDLC_ISR:
                      9  ; The interrupt service routine can quickly access
                     10  ; the required interrupt by using the BSVR register
                     11  ; and indexed addressing
0800 DEF9            12             ldx     BSVR         ; Get the index
0802 05E20806        13             jmp     JMP_TAB,x    ; Go to ISR
                     14  ;
                     15  JMP_TAB:
0806 060815          16             jmp     no_service
0809 A7              17             nop
080A 060816          18             jmp     serve_EOF
080D A7              19             nop
080E 060817          20             jmp     serve_RXIFR
0811 A7              21             nop
0812 060818          22             jmp     serve_RDRF
                     23  ;          ***
                     24  ; Service routine dummy for No Interrupts Pending
                     25  no_service:
0815 0B              26             rti              ; Just a return
                     27  ;   Service routine for the Received EOF
                     28  serve_EOF:
                     29  ;          ***
0816 0B              30             rti
                     31  ;   Service routine for the RXIFR
                     32  serve_RXIFR:
                     33  ;          ***
0817 0B              34             rti
                     35  ;   Service routine for the RDRF
                     36  serve_RDRF:
                     37  ;          ***
0818 0B              38             rti
                     39  ; Initialize the BDLC vector
FFD0                 40             ORG     VECTOR
FFD0 0800            41             FDB     BDLC_ISR
```

BDR—$00FB—BDLC Data Register

Bit 7	6	5	4	3	2	1	Bit 0
D7	D6	D5	D4	D3	D2	D1	D0

Reset -   -   -   -   -   -   -   -

BDR[7:0]

BDLC input and output data.
Data should be written only after a transmit data register empty, TDRE, interrupt has occurred or the BSVR register has been polled indicating this condition.
Data should be read only after a received data register full, RDRF, or a received IFR byte, RX-IFR, interrupt has occurred, or the BSVR register has been polled indicating this condition.

BARD—$00FC—BDLC Analog Roundtrip Delay Register

Bit 7	6	5	4	3	2	1	Bit 0
ATE	RXPOL	0	0	BO3	BO2	BO1	BO0

Reset 1   1   0   0   0   1   1   1

ATE

Analog Transceiver Enable.
        0 = Select off-chip analog transceiver.
        1 = Select on-chip analog transceiver (default).
Note: The current version of the MC68HC912B32 *does not have* an on-board analog transceiver. This bit must be programmed to zero.

RXPOL

Receive Pin Polarity.
        0 = Select inverted polarity from the external transceiver.
        1 = Select normal/true polarity (default).

BO[3:0]

BARD Offset.
These bits compensate for the analog transceiver roundtrip delay. See Table 11–10.

TABLE 11-10 BARD Offset Bit Values and Transceiver Delay

BO[3:0]	Delay (μsec)
0000	9
0001	10
0010	11
0011	12
0100	13
0101	14
0110	15
0111	16
1000	17
1001	18
1010	19
1011	20
1100	21
1101	22
1110	23
1111	24

DLCSCR—$00FD—Port DLC Control Register

Bit 7	6	5	4	3	2	1	Bit 0
0	0	0	0	0	BDLCEN	PUPDLC	RDPDLC
Reset 0	0	0	0	0	0	0	0

BDLCEN

BDLC Enable.

  0 = Configure BDLC I/O pins as general-purpose I/O. BDLC is off.(default).
  1 = BDLC I/O pins function as BDLC. BDLC is on.

PUPDLC

BDLC Pull-up Enable.

  0 = Disable internal pull-ups from the PORTDLC I/O pins (default).
  1 = Connect internal pull-ups.

RDPDL

BDLC Reduced Drive.

  0 = Configure PORTDLC I/O pins for normal drive strength (default).
  1 = Configure the I/O pins for reduced drive.

PORTDLC—$00FE—Port DLC Data Register

Bit 7	6	5	4	3	2	1	Bit 0
0	6	5	4	3	2	1	0

Reset 0   -   -   -   -   -   -   -

PORTDLC[6:0]
Port DLC Data. These bits hold data to be driven out on Port DLC or data received from the Port DLC pins.

DDRDLC—$00FF—Port DLC Data Direction Register

Bit 7	6	5	4	3	2	1	Bit 0
0	DDDLC6	DDDLC5	DDDLC4	DDDLC3	DDDLC2	DDDLC1	DDDLC0

Reset 0   0   0   0   0   0   0   0

DDDLC[6:0]

Data Direction Port DLC
    0 = Configure I/O pin as input only (default).
    1 = Configure I/O pin as output.

BDLC J1850 Bus Errors

> The BDLC can detect several types of transmit and receive errors.

The BDLC can detect several transmit and receive errors. Transmit errors occur if the BDLC transmits a message containing invalid bits or framing symbols on nonbyte boundaries. When a transmission error occurs, the BDLC stops transmitting immediately. The error condition is reflected in the BSVR register and if the interrupt enable bit is set, an interrupt request is generated.

Receive errors include CRC errors, symbol errors, framing errors, and bus faults. See Table 11–11 for a summary of errors and how the BDLC handles them.

11.6 Conclusion and Chapter Summary Points

The serial interfaces in the M68HC12 support asynchronous data transfer between "normal" serial devices such as terminals, printers, and other computers. It also has a high-speed, synchronous data transfer mode for communications with other M68HC12s in a multiple-processor system.

TABLE 11-11 BDLC Error Summary

Error Condition	BDLC Action	Error Details
CRC Error	CRC error interrupt generated BDLC will wait for SOF	A CRC error occurs when the CRC calculation on the received data bytes and the received CRC byte is not equal to $C4; the CRC code should detect any single and 2-bit errors, all 8-bit burst errors, and almost all other types of errors
Symbol Error; BDLC receives invalid bits or noise	Transmission aborted immediately Invalid symbol interrupt generated	A symbol error occurs when an invalid symbol is detected in a message being received
Framing Error	Invalid symbol interrupt generated BDLC waits for SOF	A framing error occurs if an EOD or EOF symbol is detected on a nonbyte boundary
Bus shorted to V_{BATT}	BDLC will not transmit until the bus is idle	The BDLC waits until the bus falls to a passive state before transmitting any more data
Bus shorted to ground	Thermal overload will shut down the physical interface Invalid symbol error will be set in the BVSR	When the bus is shorted to ground, the BDLC attempts to transmit a message but will detect a transmission error because the bus cannot be driven to the active state; the BDLC will abort that transmission and wait until the CPU commands it to transmit again; if the bus short is temporary, the BDLC will resume normal operation as soon as the fault is cleared
BDLC receives a BREAK	BDLC waits for the next valid SOF Invalid symbol interrupt generated	Any BDLC transmitting when a BREAK is detected will treat the break as if a transmission error has occurred and halt the transmission If the BDLC is receiving and it receives a BREAK character, it treats it as a receiving error

- The SCIs give the M68HC12 UART capabilities.

- The SCIs can send and receive 8- or 9-bit data.

- There can be hardware parity generation.

- Each SCI has its own programmable Baud rate generator.

- The SCI status registers provides the following bits:

    TDRE—Transmit Data Register Empty
    TC—Transmission Complete
    RDRF—Receive Data Register Full
    IDLE—Idle Line Detect
    OR—Receiver Overrun Error
    NF—Noise Detected during Last Character
    FE—Framing Error
    PF—Parity Incorrect Flag
    RAF—Receiver Active Flag

- The SCI can generate interrupts for the following conditions:

    Transmit Data Register Empty
    Transmission Complete

Receiver Data Register Full and Receiver Overrun Error
Idle Line Detected

- The software must poll the status register to see which of the receiver interrupts has occurred.

- The SPI is a high-speed synchronous serial peripheral interface.

- The SPI can transfer serial data at up to 4 Mbit/sec.

- The SPI status register provides the following bits:

    SPIF—SPI Transfer Complete Flag
    WCOL—Write Collision Error Flag
    MODF—Mode-Fault Error Flag

- The SPI can generate interrupts for the following conditions:

    SPI Transfer Complete and Mode Fault Error

- The SPI status register must be checked to see which of the two interrupting sources has occurred.

- The MC68HC912B32 has a serial port that supports the SAE J1850 protocol.

11.7 Bibliography and Further Reading

AN991: Using the Serial Peripheral Interface to Communicate Between Multiple Microcomputers, Motorola Semiconductor Application Note, Phoenix, AZ, 1987.

Cady, F. M., *Microcontrollers and Microcomputers*, Oxford University Press, New York, 1997.

M68HC12 Reference Manual, Motorola, 1996.

MC68HC812A4 Technical Summary, MC68HC812A4TS/D, Motorola, 1997.

MC68HC912B32 Technical Summary, MC68HC912B32TS/D, Motorola, 1997.

11.8 Problems

11.1   For the SCI0, give the name of the bit, the name of the register it is in, the register's address, which bit, and the default or reset state of the bit for each of the following:
   a. What bit enables the SCI0 transmitter?
   b. What bit enables the SCI0 receiver?
   c. What bit determines how many data bits are sent?
   d. What bit can the user test to see if the last character has cleared the transmit data buffer?
   e. What bit can the user test to see if a new character has been received?
   f. What bit is used to indicate the software is not reading data from the SC0DRL fast enough?

g. What bit is an indication that the communication channel is noisy?

h. What bit is an indication that the sending and receiving Baud rates may not be identical?

11.2   For the SCI0, give the name of the bit, the name of the register it is in, the register's address, which bit, and the default or reset state of the bit for each of the following:

a. What bit enables an interrupt when the transmit buffer is empty?

b. What bit enables an interrupt when the transmitter has completely emptied its serial shift register?

c. What bit enables interrupts by the SCI0 receiver?

11.3   What SCI0 receiver conditions can generate an interrupt?

11.4   What different status information do the SCI0 status bits TDRE and TC give?

11.5   Give the meanings of the following mnemonics: TDRE, TC, RDRF, OR, and FE.

11.6   What is the M68HC12 I/O address for the SC0BDH register?

11.7   What is the value used to initialize the SCI0 for 4800 Baud assuming an E-clock of 8.0 MHz.

11.8   Which port and which bits are the serial communications interface (SCI0) transmitted and received data?

11.9   For the SPI, give the name of the bit, the name of the register it is in, the register's address, which bit, and the default or reset state of the bit for each of the following:

a. What bit enables the SPI?

b. What bit selects the master or slave mode?

c. What bits select the data transfer rate?

d. What bit is the Master Output/Slave Input?

e. What bit is the Master Input/Slave Output?

11.10   For the SPI, give the name of the bit, the name of the register it is in, the register's address, which bit, and the default or reset state of the bit for each of the following:

a. What bit indicates the SPI has completely sent the last data?

b. What bit indicates an error has occurred when new data have been written to the output register before the old data have cleared?

c. What bit is set to enable SPI interrupts?

11.11   How does the SPI differ from the SCI?

11.12   How does a slave station SPI send data to the master station?

11.13   What do the following mnemonics mean in the operation of the SPI: $\overline{SS}$, SCK, MOSI, MOMI, MISO, SISO, SPIE, SPE, and MSTR?

Chapter 12

M68HC12 Analog Input

O B J E C T I V E S

In this chapter we will learn how to initialize and use the M68HC12 A/D converter system.

12.1 Introduction

The M68HC12 contains an *eight-channel, multiplexed, 8-bit,*[1], *successive approximation* A/D converter with ± 1 *LSB accuracy.*[2] Its *charge redistribution* input circuit eliminates the need for an external sample-and-hold. The A/D is specified to be *linear to* ± 1 *LSB* over its full temperature range and there are *no missing codes.* Both the *conversion time* and the sample-and-hold *aperture time* are *programmable.*

12.2 M68HC12 A/D Converter

Comparison of M68HC12 and M68HC11 A/D Converter	
M68HC12	**M68HC11**
Programmable sample time; four or eight successive conversions; can generate conversion complete interrupts	Fixed sample time (32 E-clock cycles); can do four successive conversions; no interrupts on conversion complete

---

[1] In some future versions of the M68HC12 a 10-bit converter may be available.

[2] Chapter 11 in *Microcontrollers and Microcomputers: Principles of Software and Hardware Engineering,* explains many of the concepts and terms used in analog-to-digital conversion, including aliasing and aperture time. Errors associated with data conversion are described.

Figure 12–1 shows a block diagram of the M68HC12 analog-to-digital converter. Port AD bits PAD0–PAD7 are the analog input pins. These inputs may be used as general-purpose digital inputs when the A/D is not in use. An input multiplexer is controlled by a control register *A/D Control Register 5 (ATDCTL5)*. The resistive ladder/charge redistribution capacitors and sampling mechanism are modeled in Figure 12–1 by a switch and a single capacitor, C_D. The 8-bit successive approximation A/D uses two voltages, V_{RH} and V_{RL}, to optimize resolution over the input signal range. Normally, V_{RH} is set to the signal maximum and V_{RL} to the minimum. However, V_{RH} should not be higher than 6 V, V_{RL} should not be less than ground, and $V_{RH} - V_{RL}$ should be greater than 2.5 V. The 8-bit outputs from either four or eight successive conversions are placed into data registers ADR0H–ADR7H. ATDCTL5 bits *S8CM, SCAN, MULT,* and *CD–CA* select which channels are converted. See Example 12–1.

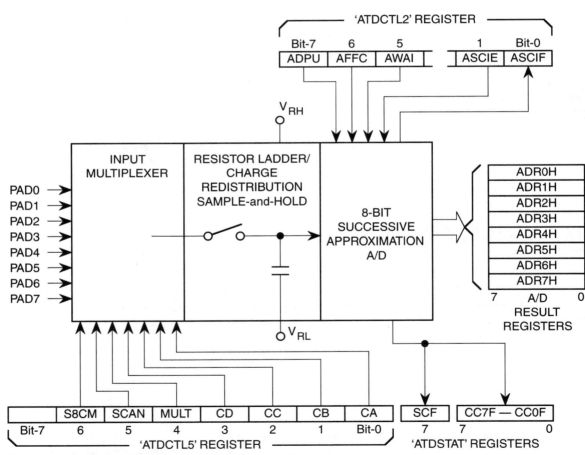

Figure 12–1   M68HC12 analog-to-digital converter block diagram.

EXAMPLE 12–1

The input signal to the A/D is unipolar and varies between 0 and 3 V. The system hardware designer has set V_{RH} = 5V and V_{RL} = 0. What is the resolution of the conversion?

Solution:

The resolution is $(V_{RH} - V_{RL})/256$ = 19.5 mV.

After reading the data book on the M68HC12 A/D, the system designer realizes that V_{RH} should be set to the maximum signal. After this is done, what is the resolution of the measurement.

Solution:

The resolution now is 3/256 = 11.7 mV.

A/D Initialization

A/D Power up

The A/D must be powered up before it is used. The *ATD power up bit* (*ADPU*) is in the *ATDCTL2* register. A short delay, of about 100 μsec, must be observed before using the A/D after it is powered up. You may choose to go about other tasks or enter a short delay program.

ATDCTL2—$0062—ATD Control Register 2

Bit 7	6	5	4	3	2	1	Bit 0
ADPU	AFFC	AWAI	0	0	0	ASCIE	ASCIF

Reset 0   0   0   0   0   0   0   0

ADPU

ATD Power Up.
    0 = Disables the A/D, including the analog circuitry for reduced power consumption (default).
    1 = Allows the A/D to function normally.
A short time delay of 100 μsec should be executed after powering up the A/D to allow all analog circuits to become stabilized.

AWAI

ATD Wait Mode.

AWAI = 0 ATD continues to run when the M68HC12 is in a wait mode.

AWAI = 1 ATD stops to save power when the M68HC12 is in a wait mode.

AFFC

ATD Fast Flag Clear All.

ASCIE

ATD Sequence Complete Interrupt Enable.

ASCIF

ATD Sequence Complete Interrupt Flag.

A/D Clock Selection and Sampling Time

Comparison of M68HC12 and M68HC11 A/D Converter Clock and Sampling	
M68HC12	**M68HC11**
The sampling time and A/D clock are programmable	Fixed sample time (32 E-clock cycles); if the E-clock is <750 kHz, an on-board RC oscillator should be used

Unlike the M68HC11, the sampling and conversion time for the M68HC12 A/D is programmable. The *ATD Control Register 4* controls the A/D timing. The total sample time can range from 2 to 16 and the total conversion time from 18 to 32 ATD clock periods.

The A/D derives its clock from the CPU's P-clock. Figure 12–2 shows how the ATDCTL4 prescaler select bits, PRS4–PRS0, and the sample time select bits, SMP1–SMP0 affect the timing.

The maximum and minimum conversion frequencies for the M68HC12 A/D are 2 MHz and 500 kHz, respectively, and so the P-clock, which is the basic system clock (see Chapter 10), must be scaled so that the A/D receives a clock frequency within this range. The prescaler bits, PRS4–PRS0, are chosen as shown in Table 12–1 and Figure 12–3 to generate an appropriate ATD clock frequency. See Example 12–2.

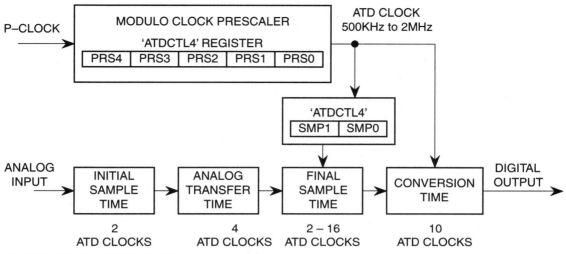

Figure 12-2   M68HC12 A/D sample and conversion timing.

ATDCTL4—$0064—ATD Control Register 4

Bit 7	6	5	4	3	2	1	Bit 0
0	SMP1	SMP0	PRS4	PRS3	PRS2	PRS1	PRS0

Reset 0   0   0   0   0   0   0   1

SMP1, SMP0
Sample Time Select Bits.

TABLE 12-1 ATD Clock Prescaler Selection

Prescaler Bits PRS4–PRS0	Total Divisor	Max P-clock	Max ATD Clock	Min P-clock	Min ATD Clock
00000	2	4 MHz	2 MHz	1 MHz	500 kHz
00001	4 (Default)	8 MHz	2 MHz	2 MHz	500 kHz
00010	6	8 MHz	1.33 MHz	3 MHz	500 kHz
00011	8	8 MHz	1 MHz	4 MHz	500 kHz
00100	10	8 MHz	800 kHz	5 MHz	500 kHz
00101	12	8 MHz	667 kHz	6 MHz	500 kHz
00110	14	8 MHz	571 kHz	7 MHz	500 kHz
00111	16	8 MHz	500 kHz	8 MHz	500 kHz
01xxx	Do not use				
11xxx	Do not use				

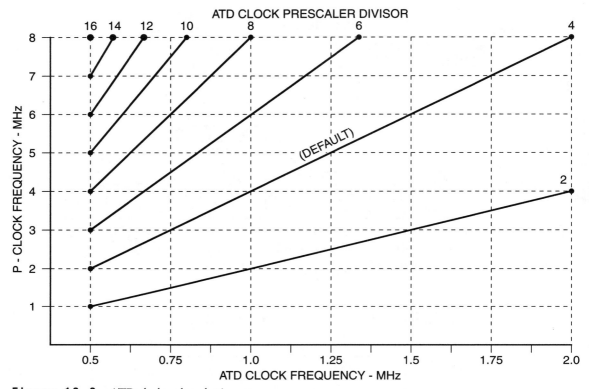

Figure 12-3   ATD clock scaler selection.

PRS4, PRS3, PRS2, PRS1, PRS0
ATD P-clock Prescaler Select Bits.

EXAMPLE 12–2   Selecting A/D Clock Prescaler Bits

The P-clock frequency in use is 3 MHz. Choose ATD clock prescaler bits PRS4–PRS0 so the A/D receives the highest possible clock frequency.

Solution:

Referring to Figure 12–3, for a P-clock of 3 MHz we would choose the total divisor of 2 to achieve an ATD clock of 1.5 MHz. PRS4:PRS0 = %00000.

Figure 12–2 shows that the A/D sampling process is divided into three subparts. The first is the *initial sample*, which occupies two ATD clocks. During this time the input is sampled by a small sample capacitor. The main sampling RC circuit is not connected to the input during this time. The second part is the *transfer time*. During this time the small input capacitor is disconnected from the input and connected to the main sampling RC circuit through a buffer amplifier to charge the RC network to the present input value. This occupies four more ATD clocks. Finally, during the *final sample period* the input pin is directly connected to the main sampling RC circuit, which is then charged to the final input value during the *final sample time* chosen by the SMP1–SMP0 bits. The optimal choice for the final sample time depends on the output impedance of the analog source. For high-impedance sources choose a longer final sample time. Finally, the successive approximation A/D converter then requires 10 ATD clocks to complete the 8-bit conversion.

Table 12–2 shows how the final sample time selection affects the total conversion time and thus the Nyquist and maximum analog input frequencies. The *Nyquist* frequency is the maximum frequency that can be sampled without aliasing and results from requiring two samples per period of the input signal. This is called the sampling criterion. See Example 12–3.

A/D Input Multiplexer and Input Scanning

The A/D has eight input channels that are selected by bits in the ATD Control Register 5. In addition to selecting which input signals are converted, you may control how and when conversions are done.

The A/D converter is started by writing to ATDCTL5. The A/D always completes a *sequence* of either four or eight conversions. The number of conversions in the sequence is selected by the Select 8 Channel Mode (S8CM) bit. The *SCAN* bit controls whether the A/D converts only one of these sequences or starts a continuous stream of conversion sequences. The MULT bit determines if the four or eight conversion sequences are done on a single channel or on sequential channels, and, finally, the channel select bits, CD–CA, choose which channel or channels are converted as shown in Table 12–3.

Single-Channel Operation: Single-channel mode can be selected by setting MULT = 0. When this is done, either four or eight (selected by S8CM = 0 or 1) successive A/D conversions of the selected channel, as shown in Table 12–3, will be placed into the A/D result registers.

Multiple-Channel Operation: In multiple channel operation, MULT = 1 and the four or eight A/D result registers contain the conversions from channels selected as shown in Table 12–3.

				Nyquist Frequency for 2-MHz ATD Clock (kHz)
SMP1	SMP0	Final Sample Time ATD Clock Periods	Total Conversion Time ATD Clock Periods	
0	0	2	18	55.5
0	1	4	20	50
1	0	8	24	41.7
1	1	16	32	31.25

TABLE 12–2 Final Sample Time Selection

EXAMPLE 12–3

Calculate the Nyquist frequency for a 1-MHz ATD clock and a final sample time of 4 ATD clock periods.

Solution:

The total conversion time is 20×1 μsec = 20 μsec
The maximum conversion frequency is 1/(20 μsec) = 50 kHz
The Nyquist frequency is 50 kHz/2 = 25 kHz

TABLE 12–3 Multichannel Mode Select and Result Register Assignment

S8CM	MULT	CD	CC	CB	CA	Channel(s) Converted	Result Registers	Comments
0	0	0	0	0	0	0	ADR0–ADR3	Sequence of four conversions
0	0	0	0	0	1	1	ADR0–ADR3	of a single channel
0	0	0	0	1	0	2	ADR0–ADR3	
0	0	0	0	1	1	3	ADR0–ADR3	
0	0	0	1	0	0	4	ADR0–ADR3	
0	0	0	1	0	1	5	ADR0–ADR3	
0	0	0	1	1	0	6	ADR0–ADR3	
0	0	0	1	1	1	7	ADR0–ADR3	
0	1	0	0	x	x	0–3	ADR0–ADR3	Sequence of four conversions
0	1	0	1	x	x	4–7	ADR0–ADR3	of four channels
0	x	1	0	x	x	Reserved		
0	0	1	1	0	0	V_{RH}	ADR0–ADR3	Four conversions of V_{RH}
0	0	1	1	0	1	V_{RL}	ADR0–ADR3	Four conversions of V_{RL}
0	0	1	1	1	0	$(V_{RH} - V_{RL})/2$	ADR0–ADR3	Four conversions of $(V_{RH} + V_{RL})/2$
0	0	1	1	1	1	Test/Reserved	—	—
1	0	0	0	0	0	0	ADR0–ADR7	Sequence of eight
1	0	0	0	0	1	1	ADR0–ADR7	conversions of a single
1	0	0	0	1	0	2	ADR0–ADR7	channel
1	0	0	0	1	1	3	ADR0–ADR7	
1	0	0	1	0	0	4	ADR0–ADR7	
1	0	0	1	0	1	5	ADR0–ADR7	
1	0	0	1	1	0	6	ADR0–ADR7	
1	0	0	1	1	1	7	ADR0–ADR7	
1	1	0	x	x	x	0–7	ADR0–ADR7	Sequence of eight conversions of eight channels
1	x	1	0	x	x	Reserved	—	—
1	0	1	1	0	0	V_{RH}	ADR0–ADR7	Eight convesions of V_{RH}
1	0	1	1	0	1	V_{RL}	ADR0–ADR7	Eight convesions of V_{RL}
1	0	1	1	1	0	$(V_{RH} + V_{RL})/2$	ADR0–ADR7	Eight conversions of $(V_{RH} + V_{RL})/2$
1	x	1	1	1	1	Test/Reserved	—	—
1	1	1	x	x	x	Reserved	—	—

ATDCTL5—$0065—ATD Control Register 5

Bit 7	6	5	4	3	2	1	Bit 0
0	S8CM	SCAN	MULT	CD	CC	CB	CA

Reset 0   0   0   0   0   0   0   0

S8CM

Select 8 Channel Mode.
        0 = Conversion sequence consists of four conversions (default).
        1 = Perform eight conversions in the conversion sequence.

SCAN

Enable Continuous Channel Scan.
        0 = Single conversion sequence each time ADTCTL5 is written (default).
        1 = Continuous conversion sequences.

MULT

Enable Multichannel Conversion.
        0 = All four or eight conversions are done on a single input channel selected by
            CD–CA (default).
        1 = Each of the four or eight conversions are done on sequential channels in groups
            selected by CD–CA. See Table 12–3.

CD–CA

Channel Select for Conversion. See Table 12–3.

A/D Operation

The A/D conversion is started by writing to the ATDCTL5 register; the A/D then does four or eight consecutive conversions. Each conversion requires the number of ATD clock cycles shown in Table 12–2. After the conversions are done, the A/D either waits for the program to write to the ATDCTL register again (when SCAN = 0) or starts another conversion cycle immediately (for SCAN = 1). See Examples 12–4 to 12–8.

EXAMPLE 12–4

The A/D is to be programmed to continuously convert a four conversion sequence of channel 3 in single channel mode. How must S8CM, SCAN, MULT, and the CD–CA bits be initialized?

Solution:

S8CM = 0, SCAN = 1, MULT = 0, and CD, CC, CB, CA = 0011.

EXAMPLE 12–5

After the A/D has been programmed as specified in Example 12–4, and assuming the ATD clock is 2 MHz and the final sample time is 2 ATD clocks, what is the maximum frequency that can be digitized on any channel without aliasing?

Solution:

Eighteen ATD clock cycles are required to complete each conversion and the next can start immediately in continuous scan, single-channel mode. Therefore the conversion time is 9 μsec and the Nyquist frequency is 55.5 kHz.

EXAMPLE 12–6

The A/D is to be programmed to continuously convert four channels (0–3). How must S8CM, SCAN, MULT, and the CD–CA bits be initialized?

Solution:

S8CM = 0, SCAN = 1, MULT = 1, CD, CC, CB, CA = 00xx.

EXAMPLE 12–7

After the A/D has been programmed as specified in Example 12–6, and assuming the ATD clock is 2 MHz and the final sample time is 2 ATD clocks, what is the maximum frequency that can be digitized on any channel without aliasing?

Solution:

Eighteen ATD clock cycles are required to complete each conversion. Therefore each signal will be sampled every 36 μsec giving a Nyquist frequency of 13.89 KHz.

EXAMPLE 12–8

The A/D is started by writing to ATDCTL5. What value must be written to convert all eight inputs in single conversion sequence mode?

Solution:

S8CM = 1, SCAN = 0, MULT = 1, CD–CA = 0xxx.
Write %01010000 to ATDCTL5.

Digital Results from the A/D

The M68HC12 A/D converter has eight, *16-bit, result registers.* These registers contain the *left-justified, unsigned* results from the A/D conversion. For versions of the M68HC12 with 8-bit resolution, only the high-order 8 bits of each result register are used. The channel from which the result is obtained is chosen by the mode and channel select bits in ATDCTL5 as described above.

The A/D channel input bits can be used for general-purpose digital inputs. Some Port AD pins may be used for digital inputs while others are being used as analog inputs (although Port AD digital reads are not recommended during the sample period.) For digital reads, data are read from the *PORTAD Data Input Register.*

ADR0H–ADR7H—A/D Converter Result Registers

ADR0H—$0070—A/D Converter Result Register 0

ADR1H—$0072—A/D Converter Result Register 1

ADR2H—$0074—A/D Converter Result Register 2

ADR3H—$0076—A/D Converter Result Register 3

ADR4H—$0078—A/D Converter Result Register 4

ADR5H—$007A—A/D Converter Result Register 5

ADR6H—$007C—A/D Converter Result Register 6

ADR7H—$007E—A/D Converter Result Register 7

Bit 7	6	5	4	3	2	1	Bit 0
7	6	5	4	3	2	1	0
Reset 0	0	0	0	0	0	0	0

ADRxH[7:0]
ATD Conversion Result. These bits are the left-justified, unsigned A/D conversion result. Although only 8 bits are shown here, future versions of the M68HC12 A/D converter may allow up to 10-bit accuracy and resolution. For these devices, a 16-bit read of a result register will return a left-justified, 10-bit result.

PORTAD—$006F—Port AD Data Input Register

Bit 7	6	5	4	3	2	1	Bit 0
PAD7	PAD6	PAD5	PAD4	PAD3	PAD2	PAD1	PAD0

Reset 0   0   0   0   0   0   0   0

PAD[7:0]
Port AD General-Purpose Digital Input Bits. Any bit not selected by the channel select bits CD–CA may be used as general-purpose inputs.

12.3 A/D Input Synchronization

Comparison of M68HC12 and M68HC11 A/D Synchronization	
M68HC12	**M68HC11**
Polling for the conversion sequence complete or for each individual channel conversion complete; interrupt on sequence conversion complete	Polling only on sequence conversion complete

Polling A/D Conversion Complete

The M68HC12 A/D can generate interrupts when the conversion is complete or the user may poll the conversion completion flag. There is a *Sequence Complete Flag* (*SCF*) that is set when the four or eight conversion sequence is completed, and there are eight *Conversion Complete Flags* (*CCF7–CCF0*) that are associated with each ATD result register. These flags are in the *ATDSTAT* register and are set when the current conversion writes into the associated result register.

ATDSTAT—$0066—ATD Status Register (high byte)

Bit 7	6	5	4	3	2	1	Bit 0
SCF	0	0	0	0	CC2	CC1	CC0

Reset 0   0   0   0   0   0   0   0

SCF
Sequence Complete Flag.   SCF is set at the end of each single conversion sequence (when SCAN=0 in ADTCTL5). When SCAN=1 giving continuous conversion sequences, SCF is set at the end of the first sequence. The SCF bit is cleared by one of two mechanisms as described below.

CC[2:0]
Conversion Counter for the Current Sequence.   These three bits give the binary code of the register that will be written next, indicating which channel is currently being converted.

ATDSTAT—$0067—ATD Status Register (low byte)

Bit 7	6	5	4	3	2	1	Bit 0
CCF7	CCF6	CCF5	CCF4	CCF3	CCF2	CCF1	CCF0

Reset 0   0   0   0   0   0   0   0

CCF[7:0]
Conversion Complete Flags.   These flags are associated with individual ATD result registers (ADR0H–ADR7H). Each bit is set at the end of the conversion for the associated channel. The bit remains set until cleared as discussed below.

Clearing Status Flags

The *ATD Fast Flag Clear All (AFFC)* bit in the *ATDCTL2* register controls how the status flags are reset.

ATDCTL2—$0062—ATD Control Register 2

Bit 7	6	5	4	3	2	1	Bit 0
ADPU	AFFC	AWAI	0	0	0	ASCIE	ASCIF
Reset 0	0	0	0	0	0	0	0

AFFC = 0:	The ATD Sequence Complete and Conversion Complete Flags are cleared in a two-step operation. First, the ATD Status Register is read. Then, when a Conversion Complete Flag = 1, reading the associated result register resets the flag. The Sequence Complete Flag is cleared when the ATDCTL5 is written to start a new conversion. AFFC = 0 is the normal operating mode and is used when polling either the SCF or the CCF bits while waiting for the conversion to be completed. (Default.)
AFFC = 1:	This changes the flag clearing mechanism to a *fast clear sequence.* The Conversion Complete Flags are cleared by reading the associated result register. The ATD Status Register does not need to be read beforehand. The Sequence Complete Flag is cleared when the first result register is read. This mode would normally be used when using the A/D interrupts to synchronize A/D input.

12.4 A/D Interrupts

Comparison of M68HC12 and M68HC11 A/D Converter Interrupt	
M68HC12	**M68HC11**
ATD Sequence Complete Interrupt	No interrupts available; polling must be used

The M68HC12 can generate an interrupt when the current four or eight conversion sequence is completed. The *ATD Sequence Complete Interrupt Enable (ASCIE)*, and the *ATD Sequence Complete Interrupt Flag (ASCIF)* in the ATDCTL2 register are used to enable and generate the interrupt. All normal interrupt service routine procedures (see Chapter 8) must be followed. Table 12–4 shows the interrupt vector location and the D-Bug12 SetUserVect number.

ATDCTL2—$0062—ATD Control Register 2

Bit 7	6	5	4	3	2	1	Bit 0
ADPU	AFFC	AWAI	0	0	0	ASCIE	ASCIF
Reset 0	0	0	0	0	0	0	0

TABLE 12-4 A/D Sequence Complete Interrupt Vector

Interrupt	Vector	D-Bug12 SetUserVect Number$_{10}$
ATD Sequence Complete	$FFD2:FFD3	9

ASCIE

ATD Sequence Complete Interrupt Enable.
       0 = Disable ATD interrupt (default).
       1 = Enable ATD interrupt on sequence complete.

ASCIF

ATD Sequence Complete Interrupt Flag.
       0 = No ATD interrupt occurred.
       1 = ATD sequence complete.
This flag is cleared by reading any result register when AFFC = 1.

ADPU

ATD Power Up.

AFFC

ATD Fast Flag Clear All.

AWAI

ATD Wait Mode.

12.5 Miscellaneous A/D Registers

There are several registers that normally are not used or used only in special circumstances.

ATDCTL3—$0063—ATD Control Register 3

	Bit 7	6	5	4	3	2	1	Bit 0
	0	0	0	0	0	0	FRZ1	FRZ0
Reset	0	0	0	0	0	0	0	0

FRZ1, FRZ0		

Background Debug Freeze Enable. When debugging an application using the background debugging mode, the A/D can be paused when a breakpoint is reached. See Chapter 14.

FRZ1	FRZ0	A/D Response
0	0	Continue conversions in active background mode (default).
0	1	Reserved.
1	0	Finish current conversion, then freeze.
1	1	Freeze when background debugging is active.

ATDCTL0—$0060—Reserved

ATDCTL1—$0061—Reserved

Bit 7	6	5	4	3	2	1	Bit 0
7	6	5	4	3	2	1	0

Reset 0   0   0   0   0   0   0   0

Both ATDCTL0 and ATDCTL1 are reserved for factory use and testing. You can write to ATDCTL0 to stop the current conversion sequence.

ATDTEST—$0068—ATD Test Register (high byte)

Bit 7	6	5	4	3	2	1	Bit 0
SAR9	SAR8	SAR7	SAR6	SAR5	SAR4	SAR3	SAR2

Reset 0   0   0   0   0   0   0   0

ATDTEST—$0069—ATD Test Register (low byte)

Bit 7	6	5	4	3	2	1	Bit 0
SAR1	SAR0	RST	TSTOUT	TST3	TST2	TST1	TST0

Reset 0   0   0   0   0   0   0   0

SAR[9;0]

Successive Approximation Register (SAR) Data.
Reading this register returns the current value of the successive approximation register. The register can be written to change the SAR value.

RST

ATD Module Reset.
        0 = No effect (default).
        1 = Causes all registers (except the ADPU bit in ATDCTL2) in the ATD to be reset to the power on state.

TSTOUT, TST[3:0]

Test bits reserved for factory testing.

12.6 A/D Control Register Summary

Table 12–5 summarizes the A/D control registers.

12.7 A/D Programming Summary

Although there are many registers that must be initialized to operate the M68HC12 A/D, the programming is straightforward. See Example 12–9.

1. Enable and power up the A/D by setting the ADPU bit in ATDCTL2.

2. Wait for 100 μsec to allow the analog circuitry to settle before attempting to use the A/D.

3. Choose the flag clearing mode (AFFC), the wait mode operation (AWAI), and enable the sequence complete interrupt (ASCIE) if desired and write these bits into ATDCTL2. If interrupts are to be used, remember to initialize the interrupt vector.

4. Initialize ATDCTL4 by choosing and writing the following bits:

   PRS[4:0] to keep the ATD clock in the range of 500 kHz to 2 MHz.

   SMP[1:0] to select the final sample time.

5. Choose the S8CM, SCAN, MULT, and CD–CA bits in ATDCTL5.

6. Write ATDCTL5 to start the conversion.

TABLE 12-5 A/D Control Register Summary

Register and Control Bit	Address and Bit	Register Name and Bit Summary
ATDCTL2	$0062	**ATD Control Register 2**
ADPU	7	Power Up A/D; set = 1 and then delay 100 μsec
AFFC	6	Fast Flag Clear All; flags cleared when one result register read
AWAI	5	Wait Mode stops A/D to save power in WAIT mode
ASCIE	1	Sequence Complete Interrupt Enable enables A/D interrupts
ASCIF	0	Sequence Complete Interrupt Flag is set when an interrupt occurs
ATDCTL3	$0063	**ATD Control Register 3**
FRZ1, FRZ0	1,0	Select A/D operation when in background debugging mode
ATDCTL4	$0064	**ATD Control Register 4**
SMP[1:0]	6,5	Select final sample time
PRS[4:0]	4–0	Select ATD clock prescaler
ATDCTL5	$0065	**ATD Control Register 5**
S8CM	6	Select 8 or 4 channel conversion sequence
SCAN	5	Enable continuous or single-channel scan
MULT	4	Enable multiple or single-channel conversions
CD-CA	3–0	Select conversion channels
ATDSTAT	$0066	**ATD Status Register**
SCF	7	Sequence complete flag set when the current conversion sequence is complete
CC[2:0]	2–0	Conversion counter bits point to the channel being converted
	$0067	
CCF[7:0]	7–0	Individual channel conversion complete flags
ADR0H–ADR7H	$0070–$007E	**A/D Converter Result Registers**
PORTAD	$006F	**Port AD Digital Input Register**
ATDCTL0	$0060	**A/D Test Registers**
ATDCTL1	$0061	These registers are used in special and factory testing
ATDTEST	$0068–$0069	

7. Wait for the conversion sequence to complete by polling the SCF bit in ATDSTAT or by using the sequence complete interrupt if it has been enabled.

8. Read the result in the ADR0H–ADR7H result registers.

12.8 A/D Programming Example

Example 12–9 shows how to initialize the A/D converter to convert channels 4–7 in single conversion mode.

Explanation of Example 12–9

The ATD is powered up by setting the ADPU bit in *line 47* followed by a 100 μsec delay in the delay loop *lines 48–51*. *Line 56* sets up the ATD Control Register 2 by choosing normal flag clearing, keep running in wait mode, and no interrupts. The P-clock is 8 MHz and the ATD clock

EXAMPLE 12–9 A/D Programming Example

ad12ex1c.asm   Assembled with CASM   08/09/1998   21:47 PAGE 1

```
            1  ;    This  is  a  test  program  showing  the  use
            2  ;    of  the  A/D  converter.
            3  ;    It  converts  the  data  on  Ch  4-7  and
            4  ;    shows  conversion  results  every  second
            5  ;    (approximately)
            6  ;
            7  ; Constant Equates
0000        8  N1:        EQU      !122           ; 122 times for 1 sec
0000        9  CR:        EQU      $0d
           10  ; Timer Equates
0000       11  TEN:       EQU      %10000000      ; Timer enable
0000       12  TSCR:      EQU      $86            ; Timer control reg
0000       13  TOF:       EQU      %10000000      ; Timer overflow flag
0000       14  TFLG2:     EQU      $8F            ; Timer flag reg 2
           15  ; A/D control registers
0000       16  ATDCTL2:   EQU      $62
0000       17  ATDCTL4:   EQU      $64
0000       18  ATDCTL5:   EQU      $65
0000       19  ADR0H:     EQU      $70            ; Results registers
0000       20  ADR1H:     EQU      $72
0000       21  ADR2H:     EQU      $74
0000       22  ADR3H:     EQU      $76
0000       23  ATDSTAT:   EQU      $66            ; A/D status register
0000       24  SCF:       EQU      %10000000      ; Seq complete flag
0000       25  AFFC:      EQU      %01000000      ; Fast clear
0000       26  AWAI:      EQU      %00100000      ; A/D wait mode
0000       27  ASCIE:     EQU      %00000010      ; SCF interrupt enable
0000       28  ADPU:      EQU      %10000000      ; A/D power up bit
0000       29  SMP:       EQU      %01100000      ; SMP0 and SMP1 bits
0000       30  PRS0:      EQU      %00000001      ; PRS0 bit
           31  ; AD Mode: S8CM=0  4 conversion sequence
           32  ;                  SCAN=0 Single conversion
           33  ;                     MULT=1  4 conversions on channels 4-7
           34  ; CD,CC,CB, CA=01xx Analog channel 4-7
0000       35  ADMODE:    EQU      %00010100
           36  ; Monitor Equates
0000       37  out2hex:   EQU      $FE16          ; Print 2 hex nibbles
0000       38  putchar:   EQU      $FE04          ; Put char to term
           39  ; Memory Map Equates
0000       40  CODE:      EQU      $0800
0000       41  DATA:      EQU      $0900
0000       42  STACK:     EQU      $0a00
           43
0800       44             ORG      CODE
0800 CF0A00 45            LDS      #STACK
```

EXAMPLE 12–9   Continued

```
               46  ;   Power up the A/D
0803 4C6280    47              bset    ATDCTL2,ADPU
               48  ;   Generate a "short" delay > 100 microsec
0806 86C8      49              ldaa    #!200        ; 200 loops for
0808 A7        50  delay:      nop                  ; 800 clock cycles
0809 0430FC    51              dbne    a,delay
               52  ;   Enable the timer
080C 4C8680    53              bset    TSCR,TEN
               54  ;   Now set up the A/D
               55  ;   Normal flag clearing, run in WAIT mode, no interrupts
080F 4D6262    56              bclr    ATDCTL2,AFFC|AWAI|ASCIE
               57  ;   Select 2 clock sample time and divide by 4 prescaler:
               58  ;   Assume P clock is 8 MHz
ad12ex1c.asm       Assembled with CASM 08/09/1998 21:47 PAGE 2
0812 4D6460    59              bclr    ATDCTL4,SMP  ; Select 2 sample time
0815 4C6401    60              bset    ATDCTL4,PRS0 ; 2 MHz conversion freq
               61  ;   Start the conversion by writing the scan select
               62  ;   information to ATDCTL5
0818 8614      63  loop:       ldaa    #ADMODE
081A 5A65      64              staa    ATDCTL5
               65  ;   And wait until conversion done
081C 4F6680FC  66  spin:       brclr   ATDSTAT,SCF,spin
               67  ;   Get the channel 4 value and print it
               68  ;   using the D-Bug12 Monitor
0820 87        69              clra                 ; set A=0
0821 D670      70              ldab    ADR0H        ; Channel 4 is here
0823 15FBF5EF  71              jsr     [out2hex,PCR]
               72  ;   Print a CR
0827 C60D      73              ldab    #CR
0829 15FBF5D7  74              jsr     [putchar,PCR]
               75  ;   Do the 1 (approx) sec delay
               76  ;   using the timer overflow
082D C67A      77              ldab    #N1
               78  ;   Clear the TOF to start the delay
082F 8680      79  delay1:     ldaa    #TOF
0831 5A8F      80              staa    TFLG2
               81  ;   and wait for N1 overflows
0833 F7008F    82  spin1:      tst     TFLG2
0836 2AFB      83              bpl     spin1
0838 0431F4    84              dbne    b,delay1
083B 20DB      85              bra     loop
```

maximum is 2 MHz. *Lines 57 and 60* choose to use a 2 clock sample time and the clock prescaler is set to divide P-clock by four. The ATD conversion mode is selected and the conversion is started by writing to the ATDCTL5 register in *line 64* and a spin loop is entered at *line 66* to wait until the conversion complete flag is set.

12.9 Chapter Summary Points

- The M68HC12 is an 8-bit successive approximation converter that may have 10-bit capability in the future.

- The A/D must be powered up by writing a one to the ADPU bit in the ATDCTL2 register.

- A 100 μsec delay must be observed after powering up the A/D before using it.

- There are eight input channels selected by an input multiplexer.

- The conversion time is programmable and can range from 18 to 32 ATD clock periods.

- The total sample-and-hold aperture time ranges from 4 to 18 ATD clock periods.

- Four or eight channels are converted in sequence with the results appearing in four or eight A/D results registers.

- Analog input synchronization may be done by polling the Sequence Complete Flag or any of the eight Conversion Complete Flags in the ATDSTAT registers.

- The A/D can generate a Sequence Complete interrupt.

12.10 Bibliography and Further Reading

AN1058: Reducing A/D Errors in Microcontroller Applications, Motorola Semiconductor Application Note, Phoenix, AZ, 1990.

Cady, F. M., *Microcontrollers and Microcomputers: Principles of Software and Hardware Engineering*, Oxford University Press, New York, 1997.

MC68HC812A4 Technical Summary, MC68HC812A4TS/D, Motorola, 1997.

M68HC12 Reference Manual, CPU12RM/AD, Motorola, 1996.

Zuch, E. L., ed., *Data Acquisition and Conversion Handbook, A Technical Guide to A/D and D/A Converters and Their Applications*, Datel Intersil, Mansfield, MA, 1979.

12.11 Problems

12.1   How is the A/D powered up?

12.2   How long must the program delay before using the A/D after powering it up?

12.3   The A/D is programmed to convert a sequence of four channels in continuous conversion mode. What is the maximum frequency signal on PAD0 that can be converted without aliasing (ignore aperture time effects, assume the final sample time is two ATD clocks and the ATD clock is 2 MHz).

12.4   The analog input ranges from 1 to 4 V.
    a. What should V_{RH} and V_{RL} be?
    b. What is the resolution?
    c. The analog result register shows $56. What is the analog voltage?

12.5   The analog input is 0 to 5 V and $V_{RH} = 5$, $V_{RL} = 0$. The A/D reading is \$24. What is the analog input voltage?

12.6   The following bytes are written to the ATDCTL5 to initiate the conversion. Give the channels expected in the A/D results registers ADR0H–ADR7H.

Byte	ADR0	ADR1	ADR2	ADR3	ADR4	ADR5	ADR6	ADR7
a. 00000000								
b. 00000100								
c. 00010000								
d. 00010100								
e. 01010000								
f. 01001100								

Chapter 13

Fuzzy Logic

OBJECTIVES

In this chapter we will investigate the fundamental principles of fuzzy logic and then see how to implement these ideas as microcontroller control programs.

13.1 Introduction

Control systems take inputs and produce outputs to control some process such as the fan speed of a furnace.

The goal of any control system is to provide appropriate output drive signals for every possible combination of input signals. In simple cases in which there are two inputs and one output, the system can be graphically represented by a three-dimensional *control surface* where the x- and y-axes represent the inputs and the z-axis represents the output.

An easy way to implement such a control system in a microcontroller is with a table look-up algorithm. For a one-input, one-output system you could simply build a two dimensional table in which the value stored at each address represents the desired output drive value. The "control surface" in this case is a line as shown in Figure 13–1. You can easily see there is one output for each input. If you tried to build such a table for a system with two 8 bit resolution inputs and one 8 bit output, you would quickly see the problem with using a table. Now the control surface is actually a surface as shown in Figure 13–2. Since each input has 256 possible values, the table would need to have 256 × 256 elements or 65,536 data points. Offsetting this size disadvantage, tables are computationally fast and simple. A 16 bit offset pointer can be created by using one input as the upper order 8 bits and the other input as the lower order 8 bits. For microcontrollers such as the MC68HC12, the CPU cannot handle such a large table directly. Over the years, programmers have found ways to compromise by reducing the input resolution or by limiting the range of interest to get tables that are more manageable.

In some systems, the input-to-output relationships can be expressed mathematically. Instead of building a very large table, you can compute the needed results for current values of system inputs. Proportional–Integral–Differential (PID) systems are an example of this technique. In a PID system the inputs are the error from the desired output (P), the integral of the error (I), and the first derivative of the error (D). Separate constant multipliers are provided for each of these terms, and

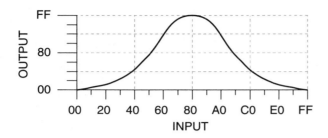

Figure 13-1   A one-input, one-output control "surface."

the output is computed as the sum of these three product terms. Control is achieved by adjusting the three constant multipliers and analyzing the resulting system behavior.

Control surfaces for PID controllers are planes because the equations are linear. Since there are three inputs, the control system is now a family of control surfaces rather than a single three-dimensional plot so it becomes more difficult to visualize the system. The linear nature of PID systems points to a significant limitation. Although many natural systems are fundamentally linear, they often involve secondary effects that interfere with ideal linear behavior. In these cases the resulting control system is only as good as the mathematical model. If you can develop a more accurate model to take into account additional factors, it will involve more complex computations to implement the control system.

13.2 Our Digital Heritage

Digital controllers are based on *Boolean* (binary) logic principles.

Modern microcontrollers are digital devices based on Boolean logic. This maps well onto traditional (western) ideas of logic dating back at least to Aristotle. In this Boolean world, everything is yes or no, true or false, black or white. For many practical applications this is fine. Very useful work is being done every day using these ideas. Fuzzy logic allows us to get beyond this binary limitation so we can deal effectively with problems that involve shades of gray.

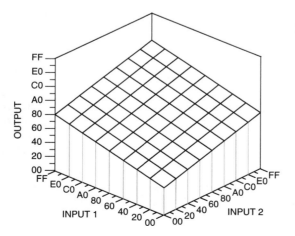

Figure 13-2   A two-input, one-output, linear control surface.

Although microcontrollers are fundamentally digital devices, we have learned to represent analog quantities to arbitrarily chosen levels of resolution using A/D converters. We also know how to use digital programs to perform floating point computations. We try to limit the use of floating point computations because they tend to be slow and expensive (in terms of time and computational resources).

> Fuzzy logic allows *subjective* concepts such as *"kind of warm"* to be used for control purposes.

Until now we have had relatively little success getting digital computers to understand abstract or subjective concepts such as "warm." You could select a range of actual temperatures and say that if temperature falls in that range it is "warm." Any temperature below this could be "cold" and any temperature above the range could be "hot" (see Figure 13–3). This still leaves a problem at the boundaries. If you said the lower bound of the warm range was 64°F, that implies that 63.5 is cold while 64.00 is warm. This is definitely not what humans think of when you say "warm."

As remarkable as human senses are, they do not resolve environmental temperatures to small parts of a degree (at least not consciously). In the decision process, people also do not perform complex mathematical computations to support their decisions. Yet ordinary humans routinely make complex decisions that cannot be made by traditional computing methods.

13.3 How Is Fuzzy Logic Different?

> Fuzzy logic does not mean imprecise logic.

Fuzzy logic introduces new concepts that allow a user to attach an unambiguous numerical meaning to linguistic terms such as "warm." In turn, this allows the programmer to carry out computations with these linguistic inputs to perform useful control and decision algorithms. Although the approach is quite different from traditional control methods, the result can still be mapped onto a control surface. For every possible set of input conditions there is a precise and repeatable control output. The common misconception, that the control output from a fuzzy logic system is approximate or imprecise, is simply incorrect.

Control programs usually start with an application expert. If you are trying to control a furnace in a steel plant you start by understanding what the furnace is supposed to do. With traditional methods you would try to model the operation of the furnace system. Since an expert furnace operator is not likely to be familiar with mathematical modeling techniques, there is a problem already. Either the operator has to explain what is being done to the model designer or the designer/programmer has to learn what the operator does. Often there is very little common ground for good communication.

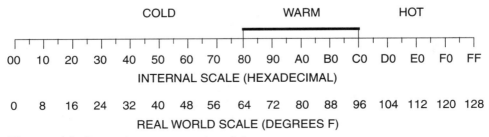

Figure 13–3   Tradition representation of abstract concepts.

In fuzzy logic systems, the control program is written in terms the application expert ur
stands rather than some abstract mathematical or programming language. When it comes tin
debug and fine tune the system, the human expert can actively participate.

13.4 What Is Fuzzy about Fuzzy Logic?

Since fuzzy logic involves new concepts, some new terminology is needed. Some of the terms s
so strange to traditional control system engineers that some have dismissed fuzzy logic as friv
nonsense. The following extreme example illustrates how this new terminology can cause prob
A major Japanese camera manufacturer introduced a new camera in the United States and desc
it with the phrase "fuzzy auto focus"! Would you buy a camera that automatically produced
pictures? Fuzzy just does not sound precise. It sounds too much like guessing or approxima
which a scientist or mathematician would not want to use in place of traditional control metl
The problem is that fuzzy refers to a way of describing sets and is not an adjective describin
quality of the control system outputs.

Traditional set theory is binary in that something either is or is not a member of a parti
set. There is no way to express "somewhat warm." The first powerful contribution from fuzzy
is the idea that this traditional view of sets is a very limited subset of what fuzzy logic calls "
sets." To understand this concept see Figure 13–4, which illustrates three different ways to ex
the meaning of cold, warm, and hot.

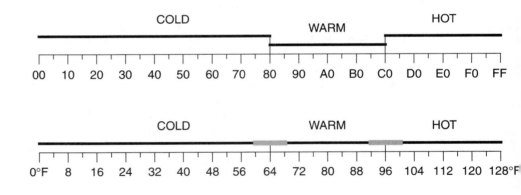

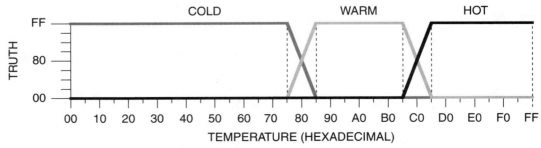

Figure 13–4   Different ways to represent abstract concepts.

Figure 13–4a shows how traditional digital computing methods might quantify the meaning of these three terms. The x-axis represents all possible values of temperature from some temperature sensor input. Any specific temperature either is or is not "warm."

Figure 13–4b tries to show what a human might mean by the terms cold, warm, and hot. In this case there are areas of uncertainty along the x-axis. It isn't that the human does not know what the temperature is, rather, the human isn't quite sure what to call these temperatures. In the band between warm and cold, you might say the temperature is somewhat cold and/or somewhat warm. There has been no good way to code this into traditional control programs.

Figure 13–4c shows how fuzzy logic deals with this problem. In this graphic representation, the x-axis still represents all possible values of the temperature input. The y-axis represents truth, where zero means completely false and $FF means completely true. (In fuzzy logic theory, the y-axis would range from zero to one. The zero to $FF range is just more convenient for small microcontrollers.) This is much closer to what a human means by the terms cold, warm, and hot. As the temperature changes from lower values within the cold range to higher values in the warm range, there is a gradual transition from cold to warm.

> Fuzzy logic allows unambiguous numerical meaning to be given to abstract concepts such as somewhat warm.

The ideas demonstrated in Figure 13–4c are so important that they deserve additional discussion. In a digital microcontroller you can now store an unambiguous numerical representation of the meaning of an abstract concept such as "warm." This graphic representation is called a "membership function" and in this figure trapezoids, which can easily be stored in a microcontroller as four 8-bit values (two points and two slopes), are used. This means a programmer can now write programs that perform mathematical computations with linguistic terms such as "warm."

Figure 13–4c also demonstrates that the boundaries of sets can be gradual or "fuzzy." This is a major improvement over the traditional methods in which a hundredth of a degree could mean the difference between cold and warm. It is also interesting that sets can (and almost always do) overlap. As the temperature rises from $78 to $88, cold gradually goes from completely true to false at the same time warm goes from false to completely true. In between you would say that it is both cold and warm at the same time (to different degrees of truth). It should be easy to imagine from this that a controller using this information would gradually change from doing what is expected when temperature is cold to doing what it should when temperature is warm.

13.5 Structure of a Fuzzy Logic Inference Program

> The three main operations in a fuzzy inference program are *fuzzifications, rule evaluation,* and *defuzzification.*

Figure 13–5 is a block diagram of a fuzzy logic inference program. System inputs enter from the left and outputs exit to the right. Major blocks in the diagram show the three main operations performed by the inference program. *Fuzzification* transforms digital input values into fuzzy truth values for linguistic labels such as cold, cool, warm, etc. The *rule evaluation* stage then uses these fuzzy input values to compute fuzzy output values for the fuzzy outputs. Similar to fuzzy input values, fuzzy output values represent the truth of linguistic output labels such as slow, mid, fast, etc. The final *defuzzification* block transforms the set of fuzzy outputs into a specific digital output value that is suitable to drive some output device.

In Figure 13–5, temperature and pressure are system inputs and each has a digital value between $00 and $FF when the fuzzy inference program starts to execute. Temperature has five labels in this example, COLD, COOL, NORMAL, WARM, and HOT. During the fuzzification step, a truth value is computed for each of these five labels. These results are called fuzzy inputs and each

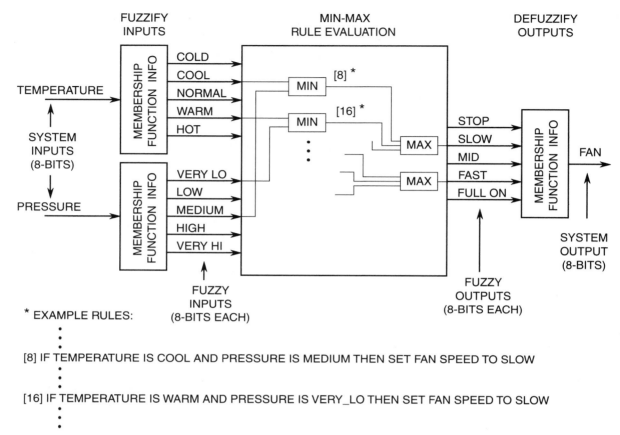

Figure 13-5 Fuzzy logic inference block diagram.

is represented by an 8-bit value in RAM. A $00 in the fuzzy input for cold means the linguistic expression "temperature is cold" is false. An $80 in the fuzzy input for warm means the expression "temperature is warm" is half true. We will see exactly how fuzzy inputs are computed a little later in this section, but for now you can see that subjective sounding linguistic expressions such as "temperature is warm" can be expressed as concrete values and further precise calculations are possible.

> Rule evaluation sets fuzzy output labels to a truth value.

In the *MIN-MAX rule evaluation* step, rules are processed using current input conditions (as represented by the current values in the fuzzy inputs) to produce fuzzy outputs. Like fuzzy inputs, fuzzy outputs are 8-bit values in RAM that represent the truth of a linguistic expression such as "set fan to medium." After rule evaluation, there can be more than one fuzzy output that is true to some degree. It would be ambiguous to attempt to drive a typical output device with these seemingly contradictory signals.

Rule evaluation consists of finding the smallest (minimum) fuzzy input associated with a rule and then applying that value to the associated fuzzy output, subject to a maximum computation. The maximum computation finds the rule that is most true associated with each fuzzy output and applies that truth value to the corresponding fuzzy output.

Defuzzification computes the final system output values.

The final step, called defuzzification, performs a weighted average computation to resolve the fuzzy outputs into a single specific output drive signal. Later in this section we will discuss differences between the kinds of membership functions used for inputs compared to those used for outputs.

Fuzzy logic is inherently a parallel computing technology because all fuzzy inputs could be computed simultaneously and independently if the hardware or computing resources were available. Similarly, all rules could be processed independently and simultaneously (rules are not considered to have any sequential importance). In practice, these tasks are performed sequentially because the CPU can do only one task at a time.

Figure 13–6 is another view of the fuzzy logic block diagram. In this figure, the system is broken into two sections, and each of these sections has a component associated with each of the three steps in the fuzzy inference process. The knowledge base is a set of data representing the knowledge that is specific to a particular application. This information is typically provided by an application expert. The fuzzy executable inference kernel is the processing portion of the fuzzy inference program. This section is somewhat independent of any specific application, and in fact may be used without modification to solve many different application problems simply by changing the information in the knowledge base.

Figure 13–6 is useful for discussing the memory and program requirements for the various parts of the fuzzy inference program. The following sections will discuss the fuzzification, rule evalua-

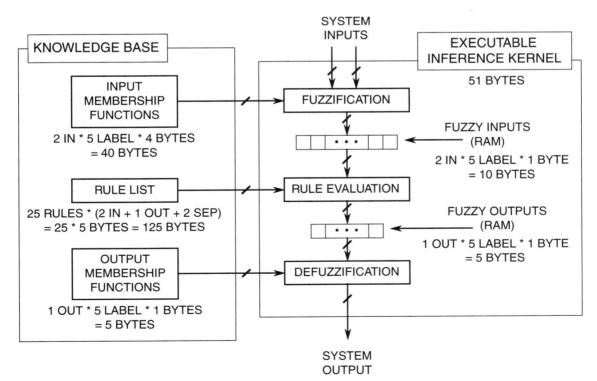

Figure 13–6 Fuzzy logic program structure.

tion, and defuzzification steps in greater detail. Along the way we will actually write a working fuzzy inference program in M68HC12 assembly language.

To explain the program and process, we will assume the specific example illustrated in the original fuzzy block diagram, Figure 13–5. There are two system inputs, Temperature and Pressure. Temperature has the labels Cold, Cool, Normal, Warm, and Hot. Pressure has the labels VeryLo, Low, Medium, High, and VeryHi. Each of these input labels corresponds to a fuzzy input in the system. There is one system output named Fan that has the labels Stop, Slow, Mid, Fast, and FullOn, each corresponding to one fuzzy output in the system.

13.6 Fuzzification

Membership functions to be evaluated by the MEM instruction are trapezoidal.

The inputs to the fuzzification step are the system inputs (8-bit data values indicating current system conditions), and input membership functions from the knowledge base. To be compatible with the membership function evaluation instruction (MEM) in the M68HC12, the input membership functions are *trapezoids*. These trapezoids are specified with the x-positions of the two endpoints of the base and the 8 bit values representing the slopes of the sides of the trapezoid.

Creation of membership functions is a job we tackle with the help of the application expert. For example, our expert might say that temperatures in the range of 44–56°F ($58–$70) are definitely Cool and temperatures below 32°F ($40) or above 68°F are definitely not Cool. The transition areas from 32 to 44°F and from 56 to 68°F are still considered part of the Cool set, but the degree of truth varies between $00 and $FF. (The hexadecimal values are what the A/D converter gives us when we read the temperature.) A trapezoidal membership function for Cool is shown in Figure 13–7 and is defined by the two x-values of the base ($40 and $88) and the slopes of the two sides [$FF/$18 = (255/25)$_{10}$ = 10.6$_{10}$ = $0B].[1]

Figure 13–8 illustrates what is done in the fuzzification step of the fuzzy inference program. The trapezoidal membership functions for each label of the temperature input and the pressure input

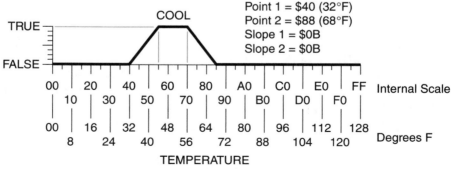

Figure 13–7   A trapezoidal membership function.

---

[1]   The magnitude of the slope is given. There are no negative values for the slope.

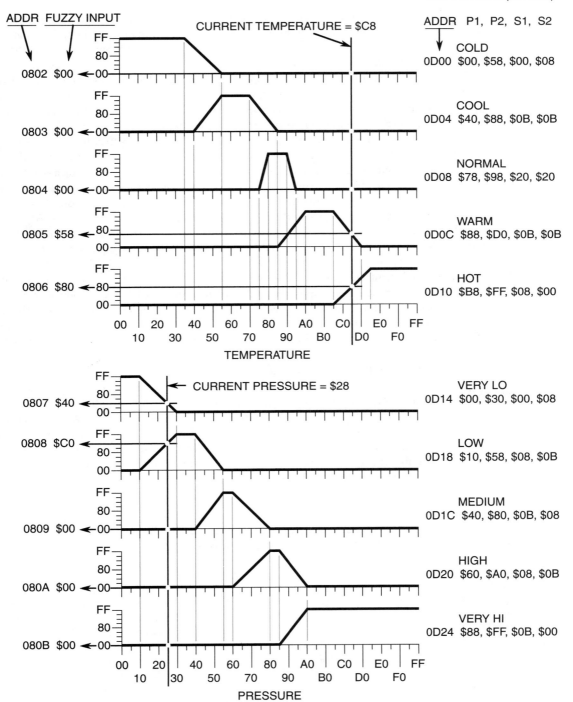

Figure 13-8 The fuzzification process.

429

are shown. All five membership functions for temperature share a common scale along their *x*-axis. Similarly, all five membership functions for pressure share a common scale along their *x*-axis. The vertical lines through all five temperature, and all five pressure, membership functions represent a current specific temperature and pressure.

To the right of each graphic membership function is the 4-byte representation of that membership function as it appears in the knowledge base memory. This memory would typically be ROM or some other nonvolatile memory because the membership functions would not usually change during normal operation of the application program.

During the fuzzification step, the program compares the current system input value (temperature or pressure) to each membership function and stores the resulting *y*-intercept into the corresponding fuzzy input location in RAM. These values are shown to the left of each graphic membership function. Note that these values would change if the temperature or pressure changed. These fuzzy input values represent an instantaneous snapshot of current input conditions.

In M68HC12 assembly language, the MEM instruction does most of this work for us. When a MEM instruction is executed, the X-index register points at a membership function data structure, the Y-index register points at the RAM location where the fuzzy input result will be stored, and the A accumulator holds the current value of the system input. The MEM instruction reads the 4-byte membership function definition from memory, computes the *y*-value corresponding to the current value of the system input, stores this result in the RAM location pointed to by Y, and updates X = X + 4 and Y = Y + 1 so the index pointers are ready for the next membership function computation. The contents of the A accumulator are not disturbed. By planning the arrangement of membership functions and fuzzy inputs in memory, the whole fuzzification step becomes a simple matter of setting up X and Y to initial positions and executing one MEM instruction for each label of each input (usually in a loop).

> A *crisp* input is a value from a sensor.

The assembly language code segment in Example 13–1 performs the entire fuzzification step for a system with two system inputs, each having five labels. For this example we will name the system inputs Temperature and Pressure. We will also assume any preprocessing of these inputs to adjust for gain or offset of the sensors was done prior to calling the fuzzy kernel program so the current (compensated) values of these inputs are simply stored in RAM locations named Temperature and Pressure. Because these system inputs are *real* values, not fuzzy, they are sometimes called *crisp* inputs.

EXAMPLE 13–1   Fuzzification Program Segment

```
8000  CE0D00   132   Fuzzify:    LDX   #Input_MFs    ;Point at MF definitions
8003  CD0802   133               LDY   #FuzzyIns     ;Point at fuzzy ins in RAM
8006  B60800   134               LDAA  Temperature   ;Get first system input
8009  C605     135               LDAB  #5            ;Temperature has 5 labels
800B  01       136   Fuz_loop:   MEM                 ;Evaluate one MF
800C  0431FC   137               DBNE  B,Fuz_loop    ;For 5 labels of 1 input
800F  B60801   138               LDAA  Pressure      ;Get second system input
8012  C605     139               LDAB  #5            ;Pressure has 5 labels
8014  01       140   Fuz_loop1:  MEM                 ;Evaluate one MF
8015  0431FC   141               DBNE  B,Fuz_loop1   ;For 5 labels of 1 input
```

13.7 Rule Evaluation

The REV or REVW instruction does the rule evaluation.

From the subjective sound of a rule such as "If temperature is warm and pressure is high then fan should be slow," you might think there could be an infinite number of rules, but this is not the case. The number of inputs and the number of labels per input force a limit to the maximum number of rules possible in a system. In our example, we have two inputs and each has five labels so there could not be more than 5 × 5 or 25 rules.

A common way to be sure you have specified a rule for all possible input combinations is to draw a rule matrix similar to Table 13–1 listing the labels for one input down the side and the labels for the other input across the bottom. If you have a third input, you would need as many of these matrices as there are labels for the third input. You can think of this rule matrix as a crude control surface viewed from above. This matrix shows only cases in which a single input label is

TABLE 13–1 Rule Matrix

Pressure

VeryHi	Stop	Slow	Mid	Fast	FullOn
	[5]	[10]	[15]	[20]	[25]
High	Stop	Slow	Mid	Fast	FullOn
	[4]	[9]	[14]	[19]	[24]
Med	Stop	Slow	Mid	Fast	Fast
	[3]	[8]	[13]	[18]	[23]
Low	Stop	Stop	Slow	Mid	Fast
	[2]	[7]	[12]	[17]	[22]
VeryLo	Stop	Stop	Slow	Slow	Mid
	[1]	[6]	[11]	[16]	[21]
	Cold	Cool	Normal	Warm	Hot

Temperature

[1] IF Temperature IS Cold AND Pressure IS VeryLo THEN SET Fan TO Stop

•

• OTHER RULES

•

[13] IF Temperature IS Normal AND Pressure IS Medium THEN SET Fan TO Mid

•

• OTHER RULES

•

[25] IF Temperature IS Hot AND Pressure IS VeryHi THEN SET Fan TO FullOn

true at a time. Later we will discuss what happens when the input falls in a range in which more than one label is partially true at the same time.

Next we need to code the rules into a compact form that can be processed by the REV or REVW instructions. The input expressions, such as "If temperature is warm," correspond to a fuzzy input so you can replace the subjective-sounding expression with a pointer to the fuzzy input. Each output expression, such as "fan should be fast," corresponds to a fuzzy output so you can replace the subjective-sounding expression with a pointer to the fuzzy output. Again, we call on our application expert to help us fill in the matrix and write the rules. The expert furnace operator can tell us, for example, that when the temperature is warm and the pressure is low the fan ought to be at its mid setting. For the M68HC12, the rule evaluation instructions use separator characters to tell when the rule input expressions stop and the rule output expressions start. This allows the instructions to work with rules that have a variable number of inputs and outputs.

All rules are in the following form:

IF *system_input_1* is [equal to] *fuzzy_input_label_m* AND *system_input_2* is [equal to] *fuzzy_input_label_n* AND ... THEN set *system_output_1* to *fuzzy_output_label_p*, *system_output_2* to *fuzzy_output_label_q*, . . .

For example, rule number [8] is

IF Temperature is COOL and Pressure is Medium then set Fan Speed to Slow.

Min-max rule evaluation uses the fuzzy AND operator to connect rule inputs and the (implied) fuzzy OR operator to connect successive rules. The fuzzy AND is equivalent to the mathematical MINIMUM operator and the fuzzy OR is equivalent to the mathematical MAXIMUM operator. Other types of rules and operators are possible in fuzzy logic but they are beyond the scope of this text.

In our example program, each rule has two inputs, a separator character, one output, and another separator before the next rule. A rule occupies 5 bytes in memory and is encoded as follows:

```
DB      Pointer_to_temperature_fuzzy_input_cool
DB      Pointer_to_pressure_fuzzy_input_medium
DB      $FE         ;Separates inputs from output
DB      Pointer_to_fan_fuzzy_output_slow
DB      $FE         ;Separates this rule from the next
```

The pointers to fuzzy inputs and fuzzy outputs are 8-bit offsets from a base address so a complete rule takes 5 bytes in the knowledge base. A special separator character is used to mark the end of the last rule.

During rule evaluation, the MCU simply looks up each fuzzy input and finds the smallest one (minimum). This value is the "truth value" for the rule. Before any rules are processed, all fuzzy outputs are set to zero (not true). As the rules are processed the truth value for a rule is compared against the referenced fuzzy output. If the fuzzy output is not already bigger (maximum), the truth value is stored to the fuzzy output location. After all rules are processed, each fuzzy output holds the truth value for the rule that was most true (and referenced this fuzzy output).

The M68HC12 has two rule evaluation instructions. REV is used for unweighted min/max rule evaluation and REVW is used for weighted min-max rule evaluation. In our example we will use the unweighted REV instruction. These are basically list-processing instructions that process a complete set of rules. In our example there are 25 rules.

Since the list of rules can be long, the REV and REVW instructions were designed so they can be interrupted and they will resume when you return from the interrupt. Everything the REV and REVW instructions need to resume is held in M68HC12 CPU registers so the normal stacking and unstacking for the interrupt takes care of the save and resume functions. Even the information about whether the instruction is currently processing inputs or outputs is held in the CCR V-bit so processing of rules can be interrupted anywhere in a rule without losing your place. The interrupt could even contain other REV or REVW instructions without interfering with the interrupted rule evaluation instruction.

The rule evaluation instruction does most of the work, but there is some setup before REV can start. First, all fuzzy outputs need to be cleared. This is part of the mechanism for doing the maximum computations. Say the first two rules, for example [1] and [2] in Table 13–1, both refer to the same fuzzy output (Stop). We clear all fuzzy outputs before starting the REV instruction. REV finds the truth for the first rule and compares this with the current contents of the fuzzy output (zero because it has not been changed since it was cleared before processing any rules). The truth value for the first rule is then written into the fuzzy output. The truth value for the second rule is now found, and this value is compared to the fuzzy output (which now holds the result of the first rule). The larger value (comparing the fuzzy output set by the previous rule and the truth value from the second) is now written to the fuzzy output. In this way the fuzzy output will eventually hold the truth value from the rule that was most true (and that referred to this fuzzy output). The assembly language code segment in Example 13–2 performs the entire rule evaluation step.

Figure 13–9 is similar to the rule matrix in Table 13–1, but it shows more detail so we can see what happens when more than one rule is active at the same time. The areas in which only one rule is active are marked by the number of the rule in square brackets. For example, in the rectangular area marked [1], only the rule that states "If Temperature is Cold and Pressure is VeryLo" will be active. For any other rule to become active, temperature would have to get higher than $40 and/or pressure would have to get higher than $10.

The five rules corresponding to "Temperature is Normal" ([11]–[15]) correspond to vertical lines at temperature $88 rather than rectangular areas because any temperature slightly above or below this value would cause "Temperature is Warm" or "Temperature is Cool" to be true to a small degree so other rules would become partially active.

In areas in which only one rule is active, the output drive level is simply the level stated in the corresponding rule because there is nothing to modify the conclusion proposed by that rule. Things get more interesting when more than one rule is active at the same time because the proposed output drive level from each of the active rules could be different (and somewhat contradictory). Lightly

---

EXAMPLE 13–2 Rule Evaluation Code Segment

```
               142    * Here X points at rule list, Y at fuzzy outputs
8018 C605      143            LDAB  #5           ;5 fuzzy outputs in RAM
801A 6970      144    Rule_eval:  CLR  1,Y+      ;Clr a fuz out & inc pntr
801C 0431FB    145            DBNE  B,Rule_eval  ;Loop to clr all fuz outs
801F CD0802    146            LDY   #FuzzyIns    ;Pointer to fuz ins & outs
               147    * X already pointing at top of rule list
8022 86FF      148            LDAA  #$FF         ;Init A & clears V-bit
8024 183A      149            REV                ;Process rule list
```

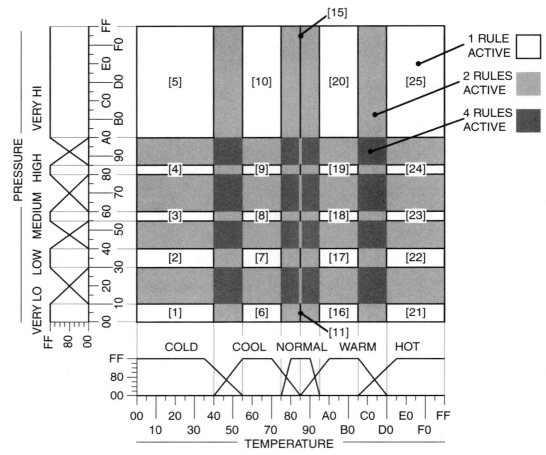

Figure 13-9   More detailed rule matrix.

shaded areas indicate areas in which two rules are active to some degree at the same time. Heavily shaded ares indicate four rules are active at the same time. The defuzzification step will resolve these apparent conflicts.

13.8 Defuzzification

The WAV instruction is used to defuzzify the output.

Control system output devices are typically things such as variable-speed motors or heating elements. Only one control value can drive such a device at a time but rule evaluation can result in more than one nonzero fuzzy output value. Defuzzification combines these fuzzy output values into a single value that is suitable to drive the control system output device. Although there are other methods of defuzzification, the most common is the weighted average method, which is supported directly by the WAV instruction.

Output membership functions are a little different than input membership functions. Both input and output membership functions provide the meaning of linguistic labels in an application system. We saw earlier how a trapezoidal membership function can be used to express the meaning of an input label such as "warm." For system outputs, we can use a simpler type of membership function called a singleton.

Singleton membership functions can be graphically represented as shown in Figure 13–10. In this figure, the x-axis represents all possible values of the output signal. Each singleton membership function is a vertical line of zero width whose height is equal to the fuzzy output (weight). The position of these membership functions is specified by a single 8-bit value in the knowledge base (the singleton position).

The fan speed is actually continuously variable. The five labels arise because these linguistic labels occur in the rules provided by the application expert. The fuzzy logic program needs to know what these linguistic terms mean in unambiguous numerical terms. You could ask the application expert to set the fan speed to "Fast" and then measure this speed. After discussing this with the expert you would add the output membership functions to the knowledge base.

```
DB      $00     ; MF for Fan  Stop
DB      $20     ; MF for Fan  Slow
DB      $50     ; MF for Fan  Mid
DB      $A0     ; MF for Fan  Fast
DB      $FF     ; MF for Fan  FullOn
```

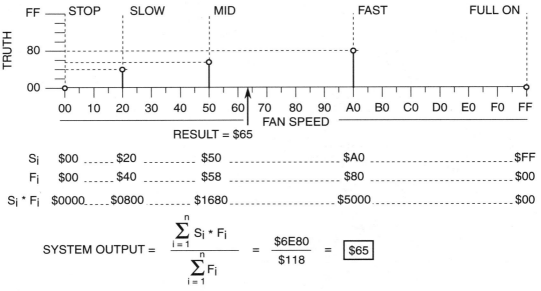

Figure 13-10 Singleton output membership function.

When more than one fuzzy output has a nonzero value, we compute a weighted average to combine these separate output instructions into a single output drive level. The formula used to compute the weighted average is

$$System\ Output = \frac{\sum_{i=1}^{n} S_i \times F_i}{\sum_{i=1}^{n} F_i} \qquad (13\text{--}1)$$

where n is the number of labels for this system output (five in our example system), S_i are the singleton positions from the knowledge base, and F_i are the corresponding fuzzy outputs that resulted from the rule evaluation step (weights).

The weighted average instruction (WAV) in the MC68HC12 computes the sum-of-products and the sum-of-weights. Before executing the WAV instruction, you must set the number of iterations, n, in the B accumulator. You also set index register X to point at the first element in the S_i list, and index register Y to point at the first element in the F_i list. Since this instruction could take more CPU cycles than normal instructions, it is designed so that it can be interrupted. When the WAV instruction is completed, the sum-of-products is returned in the 32-bit register pair Y:D and the sum-of-weights is returned in X. These are the correct registers so that the EDIV instruction can be used to complete the final division for the weighted average computation, returning the final result in the lower 8-bits of index register Y. The assembly language code segment in Example 13–3 performs the entire defuzzification step.

13.9 Putting It All Together

We now have all the information necessary to see how the fuzzy inference engine works. Before we look at a complete program, let us work through an example by hand to make sure we know what is going on. Figure 13–8 shows the membership functions for the temperature and pressure; let us assume the current temperature is $C8 and pressure is $28. The MEM instruction calculates the "truth" values for each of the fuzzy inputs. These are shown down the left side of Figure 13–8 and repeated here in Table 13–2. Table 13–3 shows the rule matrix of Table 13–1 with the truth values for each of the fuzzy inputs added.

EXAMPLE 13–3   Defuzzification Code Segment

```
                150   * Here X points at output MFs, Y at fuzzy inputs
8026 CD080C     151   Defuz:      LDY   #FuzzyOuts   ;Point at fuzzy outputs
                152   * X already pointing at singleton MFs
8029 C605       153               LDAB  #5           ;5 fuzzy outs per sys out
802B 183C       154               WAV                ;Calc sums for wtd ave
802D 11         155               EDIV               ;Final divide for wtd ave
802E B764       156               TFR   Y,D          ;Move result to A:B
8030 7B0811     157               STAB  FanSpeed     ;Store system output
```

The rule evaluation process (REV) takes each rule and, first, finds the minimum of the two fuzzy inputs associated with that rule. It then sets the specified fuzzy output to the maximum of this calculated minimum and the current fuzzy output. This is what is known as min-max rule evaluation. Table 13–4 shows this process for all 25 rules.

The rule evaluation step gives us the following fuzzy output (weights):

Stop = $00
Slow = $40
Mid = $58
Fast = $80
FullOn = $00

Figure 13–10 shows the singleton positions that we defined with our application expert (the S_i) and the weights assigned by the rule evaluation step (the F_i). The system output is calculated by Equation 13–1 and gives us the following:

$$Fan\ Speed = \frac{\$00 \times \$00 + \$20 \times \$40 + \$50 \times \$58 + \$A0 \times \$80 + \$FF \times \$00}{\$00 + \$40 + \$58 + \$80 + \$00}$$

$$Fan\ Speed = \frac{\$6E80}{\$118} = \$65$$

13.10 The Complete Fuzzy Inference System

Figure 13–11 shows a three-dimensional graphic representation of the entire process for our example system that has two system inputs and one system output. The fuzzy logic process is also applicable to much more complex systems, but it becomes very difficult to visualize what is happening when there are more than two inputs.

As in Table 13–1 and Figure 13–9, numbers in square brackets mark places at which a single rule is active. These areas correspond to flat areas on the control surface that are parallel to the base of the drawing and are located at a height (z) corresponding to a label of the system output. For example the area marked [10] corresponds to rule 10, "If Temperature is Cool and Pressure is VeryHi then Fan Speed should be Slow" so the flat area marked [10] is at height $20 which corresponds to slow on the z-axis.

TABLE 13–2 MEM Calculations

System Input	Fuzzy Input Label	Truth Value
Temperature	Cold	$00
	Cool	$00
	Normal	$00
	Warm	$58
	Hot	$80
Pressure	VeryLo	$40
	Low	$C0
	Med	$00
	High	$00
	VeryHi	$00

TABLE 13–3 Rule Matrix

Pressure

	Cold $00	Cool $00	Normal $00	Warm $58	Hot $80
VeryHi $00	Stop [5]	Slow [10]	Mid [15]	Fast [20]	FullOn [25]
High $00	Stop [4]	Slow [9]	Mid [14]	Fast [19]	FullOn [24]
Med $00	Stop [3]	Slow [8]	Mid [13]	Fast [18]	Fast [23]
Low $C0	Stop [2]	Stop [7]	Slow [12]	Mid [17]	Fast [22]
VeryLo $40	Stop [1]	Stop [6]	Slow [11]	Slow [16]	Mid [21]

Temperature

TABLE 13–4 Rule Evaluation

Rule	Fuzzy Input #1	Fuzzy Input #2	Min(#1:#2)	Current Fuzzy Output	New Fuzzy Output Max(Min:Current)
1	Cold = $00	VeryLo = $40	$00	Stop = $00	Stop = $00
2	Cold = $00	Low = $C0	$00	Stop = $00	Stop = $00
3	Cold = $00	Medium = $00	$00	Stop = $00	Stop = $00
4	Cold = $00	High = $00	$00	Stop = $00	Stop = $00
5	Cold = $00	VeryHi = $00	$00	Stop = $00	Stop = $00
6	Cool = $00	VeryLo = $40	$00	Stop = $00	Stop = $00
7	Cool = $00	Low = $C0	$00	Stop = $00	Stop = $00
8	Cool = $00	Medium = $00	$00	Slow = $00	Slow = $00
9	Cool = $00	High = $00	$00	Slow = $00	Slow = $00
10	Cool = $00	VeryHi = $00	$00	Slow = $00	Slow = $00
11	Normal = $00	VeryLo = $40	$00	Slow = $00	Slow = $00
12	Normal = $00	Low = $C0	$00	Slow = $00	Slow = $00
13	Normal = $00	Medium = $00	$00	Mid = $00	Mid = $00
14	Normal = $00	High = $00	$00	Mid = $00	Mid = $00
15	Normal = $00	VeryHi = $00	$00	Mid = $00	Mid = $00
16	Warm = $58	VeryLo = $40	$40	Slow = $00	Slow = $40
17	Warm = $58	Low = $C0	$58	Mid = $00	Mid = $58
18	Warm = $58	Medium = $00	$00	Fast = $00	Fast = $00
19	Warm = $58	High = $00	$00	Fast = $00	Fast = $00
20	Warm = $58	VeryHi = $00	$00	Fast = $00	Fast = $00
21	Hot = $80	VeryLo = $40	$40	Mid = $58	Mid = $58
22	Hot = $80	Low = $C0	$80	Fast = $00	Fast = $80
23	Hot = $80	Medium = $00	$00	Fast = $80	Fast = $80
24	Hot = $80	High = $00	$00	FullOn = $00	FullOn = $00
25	Hot = $80	VeryHi = $00	$00	FullOn = $00	FullOn = $00

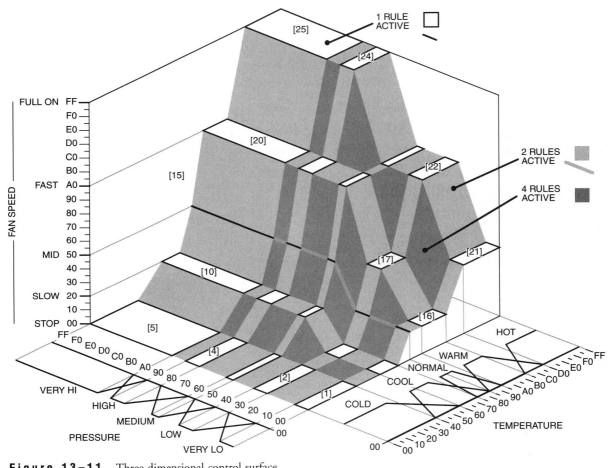

Figure 13-11   Three-dimensional control surface.

The sloping area between [5] and [10] corresponds to the range in which Cold and Cool overlap on the temperature scale and pressure is VeryHi. In this area both rules [5] and [10] are partially active at the same time. Defuzzification performs a surface interpolation to identify a point somewhere on the sloping surface.

In actual use, the fuzzy inference program needs to compute only one point on this control surface (the point corresponding to the current specific values of temperature and pressure at the time of the calculation). The complete control surface is shown here as a convenience to illustrate the input-to-output relationship for any combination of input values.

Although Figure 13-11 shows the transition from [5] to [10] as a sloping plane, this is not absolutely accurate because of the way the trapezoidal membership functions for Cold and Cool intersect. Usually adjacent membership functions would intersect like those for Pressure. For example, Low pressure starts to taper down from completely true at $40 just as Medium begins to rise from completely false. Low completes the transition to false at $58 just as Medium completes its transition to true. Cold and Cool do not quite follow this pattern. Cold begins its decent at $38 but Cool does not begin its rise until $40. Even though Cold is less than completely true in the range $38 to $40, it is the only label that is true at all so the sloping transition to [10] does not start until $40. Thus the nonsymmetrical overlap between the Cold and Cool membership functions causes a small amount of curvature in the sloping transition from [5] to [10].

Explanation of Example 13–4

Example 13–4 is a complete listing for the fuzzy logic system that was used as an example throughout this chapter. *Lines 12 and 13* allocate 1 byte of RAM each for the current system temperature and pressure input values. Five bytes are allocated for fuzzy inputs for the five labels of the input temperature (*lines 18–22*) and 5 bytes are allocated for the five labels for the input pressure (*lines 24–28*). Next, five locations are allocated for the five labels of the output fan speed (*lines 32–36*). Finally, 1 byte is allocated for the defuzzified output value FanSpeed (*line 39*).

The next section defines the knowledge base for the example problem. This knowledge base includes input membership functions for each label of each system input (*lines 47–58*), the list of control rules (*lines 89–118*), and output membership functions for each label of the system output (*lines 121–125*). *Lines 60–80* attached mnemonic names to offsets from a reference pointer at the start of the fuzzy inputs and outputs (FuzzyIns on *line 16*) to each fuzzy input and fuzzy output. These new program labels make the encoded rules in *lines 89–118* easier to read in the listing. Two special separator characters, Sep and Rule_end, used by the REV instruction for encoding rules, are defined in *lines 82 and 84*.

The actual executable fuzzy inference program is located in *lines 132–158. Lines 132–135* set up registers for the loop Fuz_loop. The two instruction loop in *lines 136–137* performs fuzzification of the five labels of the temperature input. *Lines 138 and 139* load the current pressure value and reset the loop counter. The two instruction loop in *lines 140–141* performs fuzzification of the five labels of the pressure input. At this point, the fuzzy inputs reflect current conditions of temperature and pressure in terms that can be used in the rule evaluation step to follow. Note that this program example does not show the steps that input the crisp values of temperature and pressure from the A/D converter. The two instruction loop in *lines 144–145* clears all fuzzy outputs in preparation for rule evaluation. *Lines 146 and 148* complete the setup for rule evaluation and the REV instruction in *line 149* processes the entire list of 25 rules. At this point, the values in the fuzzy outputs reflect the results of rule evaluation for current system conditions. *Lines 151 and 153* set up registers for the defuzzification step, and *lines 154 and 155* actually perform the defuzzification computation. Finally *lines 156 and 157* move the 8 bit result into the RAM location FanSpeed. The RTS in *line 158* makes it possible to call the executable fuzzy inference program as a subroutine.

Example 13–4 ORGs the variables in RAM, the knowledge base in EEPROM, and the executable portion in the FLASH (for an MC68HC912B32). For experimentation with this program in an EVB board, you may wish to changes these ORG statements (*lines 7, 41, and 128*) to other, more convenient locations.

13.11 Fuzzy Logic

Fuzzy Logic Instructions

The fuzzy logic instructions are the *Membership Function* (*MEM*), *Rule* and *Weighted Rule Evaluation* (REV and REVW), and *Weighted Average* (WAV).

EXAMPLE 13–4   Complete Fuzzy Inference Program

```
FUZYPROG.ASM          Assembled with CASMW     8/11/98      12:51:32 AM PAGE 1
                  1   **********
                  2   * Fuzzy Logic Inference Program
                  3   *   a small instructive example
                  4   *   2 system inputs with 5 labels
                  5   *   1 system output with 5 labels
                  6   **********
0800              7                 ORG    $800            ;Data memory start (RAM)
                  8   **********
                  9   * Following are the runtime RAM data storage locations
                 10   **********
                 11   * System inputs (1 byte each in RAM)
0800             12   Temperature   DS     1
0801             13   Pressure      DS     1
                 14
                 15   * Fuzzy Inputs (1 byte of RAM per label of a system
                                                                      input)
0802             16   FuzzyIns:     EQU    *     ;Used to ref fuz ins & outs
                 17   * Temperature
0802             18   Cold          DS     1
0803             19   Cool          DS     1
0804             20   Normal        DS     1
0805             21   Warm          DS     1
0806             22   Hot           DS     1
                 23   * Pressure
0807             24   VeryLo        DS     1
0808             25   Low           DS     1
0809             26   Medium        DS     1
080A             27   High          DS     1
080B             28   VeryHi        DS     1
                 29   * Fuzzy Outputs (1 byte of RAM per label of a system
                                                                      output)
080C             30   FuzzyOuts:    EQU    *
                 31   * Fan Speed
080C             32   Stop          DS     1
080D             33   Slow          DS     1
080E             34   Mid           DS     1
080F             35   Fast          DS     1
0810             36   FullOn        DS     1
                 37
                 38   * System output (1 byte of RAM)
0811             39   FanSpeed:     DS     1
                 40
0D00             41                 ORG    $D00            ;Knowledge base memory start
                 42   **********
                 43   * Following is the application specific knowledge base
                 44   **********
```

EXAMPLE 13–4   Continued

```
              45   Input_MFs:
              46   * Each trapezoidal MF defined by 4 bytes - pt1,pt2,slope1
                                                              ,slope2
              47   *  Temperature
0D00 00580008 48              DB     $00,$58,$00,$08    ;MF for temp Cold
0D04 40880B0B 49              DB     $40,$88,$0B,$0B    ;MF for temp Cool
0D08 78982020 50              DB     $78,$98,$20,$20    ;MF for temp Normal
0D0C 88D00B0B 51              DB     $88,$D0,$0B,$0B    ;MF for temp Warm
0D10 B8FF0800 52              DB     $B8,$FF,$08,$00    ;MF for temp Hot
              53   * Pressure
0D14 00300008 54              DB     $00,$30,$00,$08    ;MF for pressure VeryLo
0D18 1058080B 55              DB     $10,$58,$08,$0B    ;MF for pressure Low
0D1C 40800B08 56              DB     $40,$80,$0B,$08    ;MF for pressure Medium
0D20 60A0080B 57              DB     $60,$A0,$08,$0B    ;MF for pressure High
0D24 88FF0B00 58              DB     $88,$FF,$0B,$00    ;MF for pressure VeryHi
              59
              60   *****
              61   * Setup offsets so rules more understandable
              62   * all offsets relative to start of Fuzzy_ins
              63   *****
0D28          64   T_Cold    EQU    {Cold-FuzzyIns}    ;offset to fuzzy input
0D28          65   T_Cool    EQU    {Cool-FuzzyIns}
0D28          66   T_Normal  EQU    {Normal-FuzzyIns}
0D28          67   T_Warm    EQU    {Warm-FuzzyIns}
0D28          68   T_Hot     EQU    {Hot-FuzzyIns}
              69
0D28          70   P_VeryLo  EQU    {VeryLo-FuzzyIns}
0D28          71   P_Low     EQU    {Low-FuzzyIns}
0D28          72   P_Medium  EQU    {Medium-FuzzyIns}
0D28          73   P_High    EQU    {High-FuzzyIns}
0D28          74   P_VeryHi  EQU    {VeryHi-FuzzyIns}
              75
0D28          76   F_Stop    EQU    {Stop-FuzzyIns}
0D28          77   F_Slow    EQU    {Slow-FuzzyIns}
0D28          78   F_Mid     EQU    {Mid-FuzzyIns}
0D28          79   F_Fast    EQU    {Fast-FuzzyIns}
0D28          80   F_FullOn  EQU    {FullOn-FuzzyIns}
              81
0D28          82   Sep       EQU    $FE               ;Seperator between ins/outs
              83   * Same $FE is used to separate successive rules
0D28          84   Rule_end  EQU    $FF               ;Rule list terminator
              85
              86   Rule_list:
              87   * This comment shows the first rule as an example.
              88   * If Temp is Cold and Pressure is Very_lo then set Fan
                                                              to Stop.
0D28 0005FE0A 89              DB     T_Cold,P_VeryLo,Sep,F_Stop,Sep   ;Rule 1
     FE
```

EXAMPLE 13–4   Continued

0D2D	0006FE0A	90	DB	T_Cold,P_Low,Sep,F_Stop,Sep	;Rule 2
	FE				
0D32	0007FE0A	91	DB	T_Cold,P_Medium,Sep,F_Stop,Sep	;Rule 3
	FE				
0D37	0008FE0A	92	DB	T_Cold,P_High,Sep,F_Stop,Sep	;Rule 4
	FE				
0D3C	0009FE0A	93	DB	T_Cold,P_VeryHi,Sep,F_Stop,Sep	;Rule 5
	FE				
		94			
0D41	0105FE0A	95	DB	T_Cool,P_VeryLo,Sep,F_Stop,Sep	;Rule 6
	FE				
0D46	0106FE0A	96	DB	T_Cool,P_Low,Sep,F_Stop,Sep	;Rule 7
	FE				
0D4B	0107FE0B	97	DB	T_Cool,P_Medium,Sep,F_Slow,Sep	;Rule 8
	FE				
0D50	0108FE0B	98	DB	T_Cool,P_High,Sep,F_Slow,Sep	;Rule 9
	FE				
0D55	0109FE0B	99	DB	T_Cool,P_VeryHi,Sep,F_Slow,Sep	;Rule 10
	FE				
		100			
0D5A	0205FE0B	101	DB	T_Normal,P_VeryLo,Sep,F_Slow,Sep	;Rule 11
	FE				
0D5F	0206FE0B	102	DB	T_Normal,P_Low,Sep,F_Slow,Sep	;Rule 12
	FE				
0D64	0207FE0C	103	DB	T_Normal,P_Medium,Sep,F_Mid,Sep	;Rule 13
	FE				
0D69	0208FE0C	104	DB	T_Normal,P_High,Sep,F_Mid,Sep	;Rule 14
	FE				
0D6E	0209FE0C	105	DB	T_Normal,P_VeryHi,Sep,F_Mid,Sep	;Rule 15
	FE				
		106			
0D73	0305FE0B	107	DB	T_Warm,P_VeryLo,Sep,F_Slow,Sep	;Rule 16
	FE				
0D78	0306FE0C	108	DB	T_Warm,P_Low,Sep,F_Mid,Sep	;Rule 17
	FE				
0D7D	0307FE0D	109	DB	T_Warm,P_Medium,Sep,F_Fast,Sep	;Rule 18
	FE				
0D82	0308FE0D	110	DB	T_Warm,P_High,Sep,F_Fast,Sep	;Rule 19
	FE				
0D87	0309FE0D	111	DB	T_Warm,P_VeryHi,Sep,F_Fast,Sep	;Rule 20
	FE				
		112			
0D8C	0405FE0C	113	DB	T_Hot,P_VeryLo,Sep,F_Mid,Sep	;Rule 21
	FE				
0D91	0406FE0D	114	DB	T_Hot,P_Low,Sep,F_Fast,Sep	;Rule 22
	FE				
0D96	0407FE0D	115	DB	T_Hot,P_Medium,Sep,F_Fast,Sep	;Rule 23
	FE				

EXAMPLE 13–4 Continued

```
0D9B 0408FE0E  116           DB      T_Hot,P_High,Sep,F_FullOn,Sep      ;Rule 24
     FE
0DA0 0409FE0E  117           DB      T_Hot,P_VeryHi,Sep,F_FullOn        ;Rule 25
0DA4 FF        118           DB      Rule_end
               119
               120  Output_MFs:
0DA5 00        121           DB      $00      ;MF for Fan Stop
0DA6 20        122           DB      $20      ;MF for Fan Slow
0DA7 50        123           DB      $50      ;MF for Fan Mid
0DA8 A0        124           DB      $A0      ;MF for Fan Fast
0DA9 FF        125           DB      $FF      ;MF for Fan FullOn
               126  * End of Knowledge Base
               127
8000           128           ORG     $8000          ;Program memory start
               129  *********
               130  * Following is the executable part of the fuzzy program
               131  *********
8000 CE0D00    132  Fuzzify:   LDX     #Input_MFs    ;Point at MF definitions
8003 CD0802    133           LDY     #FuzzyIns     ;Point at fuzzy ins in RAM
8006 B60800    134           LDAA    Temperature   ;Get first system input
8009 C605      135           LDAB    #5            ;Temperature has 5 labels
800B 01        136  Fuz_loop:  MEM                   ;Evaluate one MF
800C 0431FC    137           DBNE    B,Fuz_loop    ;For 5 labels of 1 input
800F B60801    138           LDAA    Pressure      ;Get second system input
8012 C605      139           LDAB    #5            ;Pressure has 5 labels
8014 01        140  Fuz_loop1: MEM                   ;Evaluate one MF
8015 0431FC    141           DBNE    B,Fuz_loop1   ;For 5 labels of 1 input
               142  * Here X points at rule list, Y at fuzzy outputs
8018 C605      143           LDAB    #5            ;5 fuzzy outputs in RAM
801A 6970      144  Rule_eval: CLR     1,Y+          ;Clr a fuz out & inc pntr
801C 0431FB    145           DBNE    B,Rule_eval   ;Loop to clr all fuz outs
801F CD0802    146           LDY     #FuzzyIns     ;Pointer to fuz ins & outs
               147  * X already pointing at top of rule list
8022 86FF      148           LDAA    #$FF          ;Init A & clears V-bit
8024 183A      149           REV                   ;Process rule list
               150  * Here X points at output MFs, Y at fuzzy inputs
8026 CD080C    151  Defuz:     LDY     #FuzzyOuts    ;Point at fuzzy outputs
               152  * X already pointing at singleton MFs
8029 C605      153           LDAB    #5            ;5 fuzzy outs per sys out
802B 183C      154           WAV                   ;Calc sums for wtd ave
802D 11        155           EDIV                  ;Final divide for wtd ave
802E B764      156           TFR     Y,D           ;Move result to A:B
8030 7B0811    157           STAB    FanSpeed      ;Store system output
8033 3D        158           RTS
               159  *********
```

Membership Function

MEM fuzzifies the inputs. A current system input value is compared against a stored input membership function to determine the degree to which a label of the system input is true. MEM finds the y-value of the current input on a trapezoidal membership function. Before MEM is executed, the A, X, and Y registers must be set up as follows:

A must hold the current, 8-bit, crisp value of a system input variable.

X must point to a 4-byte data structure that describes the trapezoidal membership function for a system input label.

Y must point to the fuzzy input (RAM location) in which the resulting grade of membership (the truth value) is to be stored.

The data structure that describes the trapezoidal membership function is defined by the following 4 bytes, in order, starting at the address contained in X:

Point_1: The starting point for the leading edge of the trapezoid.

Point_2: The position for the rightmost point of the trapezoid.

Slope_1: The slope of the leading edge of the trapezoid.

Slope_2: The magnitude of the trailing edge slope.

A slope of $00 indicates a special case of infinite slope. Slope_1 = $00 indicates the membership function starts with a value of $FF at Point_1; Slope_2 = $00 is for a trapezoid whose ending value is $FF at Point_2.

After MEM is executed, A is unchanged, the memory location to which Y pointed contains the grade of membership calculated by MEM, Y is incremented (by one) to point to the next fuzzy input location, and X is incremented (by four) to point to the next membership function data structure. Example 13–4 shows the use of the membership functions and the MEM instruction. *Lines 48–58* show the trapezoidal membership functions for each of the five labels for the two input variables. The membership grade (the fuzzy input truth value) for each label is evaluated by the MEM instructions on *lines 136* and *140*.

Rule Evaluation

Rule Evaluation (REV) and *Weighted Rule Evaluation* (REVW) are similar and perform unweighted and weighted evaluation of a list of rules. They use fuzzy inputs (produced by MEM) to produce fuzzy outputs. REV and REVW can be interrupted so they do not adversely affect interrupt latency. The rule evaluation step first finds the minimum of the fuzzy inputs specified by the rule. It then sets the fuzzy output(s) to the maximum of this calculated minimum and the current fuzzy output.

Before executing the REV instruction, the following setup operations must be done:

X must point to the first 8-bit element in the rule list.

Y must point to the base address for fuzzy inputs and outputs.

A must contain the value $FF and the CCR V-bit must be 0. (LDAA #$FF places the correct value in A and clears V.)

All current fuzzy outputs must be set to zero.

Each rule in the knowledge base consists of a table of 8-bit offsets (from the base address of the table contained in the Y register) defining the fuzzy inputs associated with the rule. These are called the antecedent offsets. Terminating this list is the separator character $FE. Following the separator character is a list of 8-bit offsets pointing the fuzzy output(s) to be set. This is called the consequent list. Following this list is either a $FE separator or, if the rule is the last in the knowledge base, an end-of-list indicator $FF.

During execution X is incremented to point to the next rule element. When the rule evaluation is complete, X points to the address following the $FF and A contains the truth value for the last rule. The value in Y does not change.

In Example 13–4 the rule list is defined in *lines 89–118* and the rule setup and evaluation is carried out by the code in *lines 142–149*.

REVW is similar to REV except that the minimum calculated result can be multiplied by a weighting factor before finding the maximum for the fuzzy output. The knowledge base is similar also except the antecedent and consequent pointers are 16 bits each, $FFFE is the separator code, and $FFFF signifies the end of the list.

The multiplication by the weighting factor is optional and controlled by the state of the C (carry) bit in the CCR. Setting the C-bit enables weighted rule evaluation. The following setup operations must be done:

X must point to the first 16-bit element in the rule list.

A must contain the value $FF and the CCR V-bit must be 0. (LDAA #$FF places the correct value in A and clears V.)

All current fuzzy outputs must be set to zero.

Set or clear the carry bit (to enable or disable) weighted evaluation. When weighted evaluation is to be done, the Y register must point to the first item in a table of weighting factors. These factors are 8 bits each and there must be one for each rule to be evaluated.

Weighted Average

After the rule evaluation step gives us the fuzzy output values, the final step is to defuzzify the outputs to give a final value to each system output. The *Weighted Average* (WAV) does this. WAV computes a sum-of-products and a sum-of-weights that are needed to find a final weighted average. The knowledge base includes a list of singleton output membership functions (8-bit values relating each output label to a specific output value). Before WAV executes, the X register points to the first singleton membership function in the knowledge base, the Y register points to the fuzzy outputs, and the B register contains the number of elements to be included in the calculation. WAV calculates a 24-bit sum-of-products and returns it in Y:D. The sum-of-weights is calculated and returned in X. The final weighted average is calculated by following WAV with an EDIV instruction.

In Example 13–4 the output singleton membership functions are in *lines 121–125*. The defuzzification step is accomplished in *lines 151–157*.

Minimum and Maximum Instructions

The minimum and maximum instructions were implemented for general-purpose applications but they can be useful also for custom fuzzy logic programs. They are shown in Table 13–5 and find the minimum or maximum of two operands. The instructions perform an unsigned subtraction, setting the condition code register bits appropriately, and replacing the specified operand with the minimum (or maximum).

Table Look-up Instructions

The table look-up instructions, TBL and ETBL, linearly interpolate to one of 256 result values that fall between pairs of data entries in a look-up table stored in memory. TBL uses 8-bit table entries and returns an 8-bit result in A. ETBL uses 16-bit table entries and provides a 16-bit result in D.

TABLE 13–5 Fuzzy Logic and Maximum/Minimum Instructions

Function	Op Code	Symbolic Operation	Addressing Mode						Condition Codes			
			IMM	DIR	EXT	INDEX	INDIR	INH	N	Z	V	C
Membership Function	MEM								?	?	?	?
Rule Evaluation	REV								?	?	↕	?
Weighted Rule Evaluation	REVW[a]								?	?	↕	!
Weighted Average	WAV								?	↕	?	?
Minimum → D	EMIND	MIN(D,(M:M+1)) → D				x	x		↕	↕	↕	↕
Minimum → (M)	EMINM	MIN(D,(M:M+1)) → M				x	x		↕	↕	↕	↕
Minimum → A	MINA	MIN(A,(M)) → A				x	x		↕	↕	↕	↕
Minimum → (M)	MINM	MIN(A,(M)) → M				x	x		↕	↕	↕	↕
Maximum → D	EMAXD	MAX(D,(M:M+1)) → D				x	x		↕	↕	↕	↕
Maximum → (M)	EMAXM	MAX(D,(M:M+1)) → M				x	x		↕	↕	↕	↕
Maximum → A	MAXA	MAX(A,(M)) → A				x	x		↕	↕	↕	↕
Maximum → (M)	MAXM	MAX(A,(M)) → M				x	x		↕	↕	↕	↕
Table Look-up	ETBL					x			↕	↕	—	?
Table Look-up	TBL					x			↕	↕	—	?

[a]*If C = 1 when REVW is executed, weights are used; if C = 0, weights are not used.*

EXAMPLE 13–5

An 8-bit data table with two entries is defined by the following:

```
P1:     DB      2
P2:     DB      8
```

Show how to initialize the registers to use the TBL instruction and specify the result returned when you wish to find the data value midway between P1 and P2. Specify the result for three-quarters the way between P1 and P2.

Solution

```
; Initialize X and B
    ldx     #P1             ; Point to the first value
    ldab    #%10000000      ; Binary fraction for 0.5
    tbl     0,x
; On return, A contains the value 5
    ldab    #%11000000      ; Binary fraction for 0.75
    tbl     0,x
; On return, A contains the value 6
```

To use either instruction, initialize the X register pointing to the first data point (P1) and the B register with the binary fraction (radix point to the left of the most significant bit) representing the interpolation point for which a value is needed. The value returned in A or D is the unrounded result:

$$A \text{ (or } D) = P1 + [(B) * (P2 - P1)]$$

where P1 is the first data point and P2 is the second data point immediately following P1. See Example 13–5.

13.12 Conclusion and Chapter Summary Points

Like other control system methodologies, fuzzy logic produces a precise repeatable output for every combination of input conditions. Although the term "fuzzy" seems to suggest the control output is approximate, this is simply not true. Instead, fuzzy refers to a new way of representing sets that describe linguistic concepts such as warm. The boundaries of fuzzy sets are more like dimmer controls than digital on–off switches. As temperature decreases from a value we might agree is "warm," it eventually stops being warm and becomes cool or even cold. This transition is not sudden at some specific temperature—rather the degree to which we agree that the temperature is warm gradually decreases until we would no longer consider it to be warm. Since fuzzy logic offers a way to attach an unambiguous numerical meaning to these abstract concepts such as warm, we can now perform computations on these linguistic variables in order to design automatic control systems.

There are three processing steps in a fuzzy logic program:

- Fuzzification—compares the current value of a system input against the membership functions of each label of that input to determine fuzzy input values.

- Rule Evaluation—plugs fuzzy input values into control rules to determine fuzzy output values.

- Defuzzification—combines all fuzzy outputs into a single composite control output value.

The executable fuzzy logic program is generally not specific to any application.

For each of the three fuzzy program steps there is a data structure in the knowledge base that provides application-specific information. Input membership functions provide the meaning of each input label for the fuzzification step. A list of rules is encoded as a list of pointers to fuzzy inputs and fuzzy outputs. Output membership functions provide the meaning of each output label for the defuzzification step.

Although it seems as if there could be a large number of linguistic rules in a control system, the number of rules is actually limited to the product of the number of labels in each of the system inputs. For example, a system with two inputs with five labels each would have a maximum of 5×5 or 25 rules.

13.13 Bibliography and Further Reading

AN1295: Demonstration Model of fuzzyTECH® Implementation on M68HC12, Motorola Semiconductor Application Note, Austin, TX, 1996.

M68HC12 Reference Manual, Motorola, 1996.

von Altrock, C., *Fuzzy Logic & NeuroFuzzy Applications Explained*, Prentice Hall PTR, Englewood Cliffs, NJ, 1995.

13.14 Problems

13.1 Using table look-up (instead of a fuzzy logic system), how many bytes would be needed for the table in a system with three inputs with 8-bit resolution on each input and one output with 8-bits resolution?

13.2 Referring to Figure 13–4, for what temperature or temperatures are the expressions "temperature is cold" and "temperature is warm" true to the same degree?

13.3 Sketch graphic representations of the following input membership functions:
```
a. LOW   FCB   $20,$60,$08,$10   ;pt1,pt2,slope1,slope2
b. MID   FCB   $60,$A0,$10,$0B   ;pt1,pt2,slope1,slope2
c. HI    FCB   $A0,$E0,$0B,$08   ;pt1,pt2,slope1,slope2
```

13.4 What is the maximum number of rules that would be needed in a fuzzy logic system that has three inputs with three labels each? How many fuzzy inputs would there be in such a system and how many bytes of RAM would that require?

13.5 For the fuzzy logic system in Example 13–4, how many bytes of memory in the knowledge base did it take for all 25 rules?

13.6   In Figure 13–9, how many rules would be active if temperature was $C0 and pressure was $90? Which rule(s) would be active?

13.7   Using Figure 13–11, what value should be in FanSpeed if temperature is $B0 and pressure is $38?

13.8   Manually perform the defuzzification computation for the system in Example 13–4 if the temperature is $60 and pressure is $20.

13.9   How many bytes of program space are used for the executable portion of the fuzzy logic program in Example 13–4?

Chapter *14*

Debugging Systems

OBJECTIVES

In this chapter we investigate on-chip systems that support application development and debugging. The *Background Debug™ Module* (*BDM*) allows access to the internal operation of the MCU through a single interface pin. An *instruction tagging* mechanism allows external development hardware to stop the system on specific instruction boundaries.

The *on-chip breakpoint module* (found on some versions of the M68HC12) allows a user to debug systems even if the address and data bus are not available on external pins.

14.1 Introduction

As silicon technology has progressed, it has become possible to build more and more complex processing systems into a single chip. The rate of change has been so rapid that the tools engineers use to debug systems based on these microcontrollers have been unable to keep pace. In some cases, entirely new strategies have been developed to allow application development. The background debug system in the M68HC12 is an example of such a new strategy.

One of the most common development tools in the past was the *in-circuit emulator*. With such a system, you would remove the actual microcontroller chip from the target application and connect an emulator in its place. The emulator attempted to duplicate the functions of the original MCU while allowing direct access to internal data and control signals. This allowed the user to stop the system at any time and examine, or even modify, the contents of internal registers before continuing with the original program. The user could also establish complex sets of conditions and cause the system to stop (called "hitting a breakpoint") if or when these conditions ever occurred.

> It is difficult, if not impossible, to develop an in-circuit emulator for modern microcontrollers.

In-circuit emulator systems have run into two major problems. First, the newer microcontrollers have more pins and smaller pin spacing than older microcontrollers. Modern ball grid array (BGA) packages even place the connection points under the device to reduce the overall size of the package. This makes the mechanical connection of an in-circuit emulator much more difficult or even impossible. The second challenge is that modern microcontrollers have fast internal signals, internal pipelines, and multi-

451

ple data busses so there can be more activity going on within the MCU than you can report on the pins of the chip. Even the tiny propagation delays for signals through interface pin buffers can be so long, compared to signals inside the chip, that it is almost impossible to duplicate on-chip processes with external logic. Bundling dozens of such fast signals into an umbilical cable to connect the emulator to the target application can make the problem completely unsolvable.

> Background debugging systems build debugging hardware inside the microcontroller chip.

Background debugging systems build the debug logic inside the MCU with logic devices just as fast as the other parts of the system being debugged. Access to this internal debug logic is accomplished through a serial I/O interface. In the case of the MC68HC12, this serial interface is a single pin on the MCU. In the past, this would not have been practical because it would have increased the size (and therefore the cost) of the MCU. The size of individual transistors on a modern MCU has decreased so dramatically, and the total number of transistors has increased so much, that debug logic can now be included at negligible cost. As silicon technology continues to advance, this trend will continue until arbitrarily complex development logic can be included on the silicon die with the MCU.

Something else is happening in the semiconductor industry that may affect debug features of MCUs further into the future. So far, the cost and labor associated with developing a microcontroller have been so high that it was impractical to develop separate devices for development, and production. Although a few development devices were built in the earlier days of microprocessors, it is not considered practical at this time. Recent improvements in the software tools for chip design are making it possible to automatically generate logic and layouts for very complex integrated circuits from high-level software models. This may lead to separate devices for development, which include large amounts of specialized logic. For production quantities, the extra circuitry could be removed to make a smaller, less expensive MCU.

Some Debugging Definitions and Terms

Let us define some terms that are used in debugging systems.

Application System: The hardware and software dedicated to implementing some specific application or doing a particular job.

Target System: The target system is an application system being debugged.

Host System: Another computer system, often a PC, being used to debug a target system.

POD: Interface hardware between the host and target systems.

BDM: Background Debug Module. This is hardware specially added to the M68HC12 microcontroller for debugging.

Patch Code: Code that can be inserted into an application program to fix program bugs.

Breakpoint: A place at which the application program instruction execution flow is stopped and debugging mode is entered. A breakpoint may be specified by an address or a combination of address, data, and control signal states.

14.2 Development-Related Features of the M68HC12

There are three systems in the M68HC12 that support development and debugging of application programs and systems. After a brief introduction to these systems we will take a closer look at each one.

BDM: The background debug system is the most obvious debug feature in the M68HC12. Serial commands are sent to the target MCU and data are sent and received through a special single-wire interface. This system allows you to read or write any system memory location, read or write CPU registers, stop processing application programs, trace application program instructions one at a time, or go to any address to start application program execution.

Instruction Tagging: Instruction tagging is a way of making the CPU stop executing an application program when it reaches a specific instruction. In older microprocessor systems an interrupt could be used for this function, but the M68HC12 has an instruction queue (or pipe), which means instructions are not executed immediately after they are fetched from memory. In the case of jumps or branches, it is even possible that an instruction will be fetched but never executed. Instruction tags let a developer mark instructions as they are fetched from memory, and then if or when that instruction reaches the CPU, the background debug mode is entered rather than executing the tagged instruction.

Hardware Breakpoints: Some M68HC12 devices, such as the MC68HC912B32, have built-in hardware breakpoint logic that allows you to set two address breakpoints or one full address/data/control breakpoint. Although this system is primarily intended for debugging in a ROM MCU, it can be used to provide for a few patches to correct software errors in the mask-programmed ROM.

14.3 Hardware versus Software Breakpoints

We will compare and contrast three types of breakpoints that are useful in different situations. SWI-based, software breakpoints are created by replacing an instruction opcode in an application program with an SWI opcode. BGND-based, software breakpoints are used with a background debug pod and are similar to the SWI breakpoints except that a BGND opcode is used rather than the SWI opcode. Hardware breakpoints use comparator logic to detect specific address or data patterns and then to directly force the MCU to active background mode. Since hardware breakpoints do not require an SWI or BGND opcode to be written into the application program, they work in ROM and flash memory areas where software breakpoints cannot be used. Hardware breakpoints also work to stop a program when some data location is accessed rather than being limited to instruction opcode addresses.

SWI-Based Software Breakpoints

SWI-based breakpoints need to be placed in RAM (or EEPROM).

This type of breakpoint has been used in debug monitor programs, such as D-bug12, for many years. The user specifies the address(s) at which a breakpoint is needed. When a GO or CONTINUE command is entered to start execution of the application program, the monitor replaces the application opcode at each breakpoint address with an SWI opcode. The application opcodes are saved so they can be restored when the monitor program regains control. The application program executes normally until one of these SWI opcodes is encountered; then the user's CPU register values are saved on the application program's stack and the monitor regains control. The monitor then restores the original application opcodes at each breakpoint address. This allows the user to examine the application program opcodes while the monitor program is in control.

The monitor program can allow as many software breakpoints as needed, limited by how much monitor storage memory it wishes to dedicate for breakpoints. The monitor needs 3 bytes of RAM for each breakpoint, 2 bytes for the address, and another byte to save the original application opcode while the application program (as opposed to the monitor program) has control. The Buffalo monitor for the M68HC11 allowed four SWI-based breakpoints and the D-Bug12 monitor program for the M68HC12 allows 10 SWI-based breakpoints while it is configured for EVB mode.

Since SWI-based breakpoints execute an SWI instruction to save user registers when a breakpoint is encountered, 9 extra bytes are needed on the user's stack. Usually this is not a problem, but if the user's program causes the stack pointer to be corrupted, the monitor can lose track of the contents of user registers (they will be reported incorrectly after the breakpoint). There could also be unintended writes to unexpected application memory areas if the user program accidentally sets the stack pointer to point into a register or variable area of memory.

Since this breakpoint mechanism uses SWI, it interferes with any application use of SWI. There are techniques to allow both SWI breakpoints and user SWI instructions, but it causes significant complications and may have trouble in some unusual circumstances such as when a breakpoint is set at the address of a user SWI instruction.

BGND-Based Software Breakpoints

BGND-based breakpoints are placed in RAM (or EEPROM) also.

The D-Bug12 monitor program for the M68HC12 can operate in two distinct modes. In the EVB mode, it behaves as a traditional ROM monitor (like the Buffalo monitor for the M68HC11). In the POD mode, D-Bug12 uses a BDM interface to control a target M68HC12 so the monitor program is not using any memory resources in the target system. In EVB mode, software breakpoints use SWI opcodes as described above. In the POD mode, BGND opcodes are used instead of SWI opcodes. BGND can be used for breakpoints only when the monitor is controlling a target system through the background debug module.

The software that manages breakpoints is more or less the same for SWI-based or BGND-based breakpoints. You still need to store a 16-bit address and the user opcode from that address for each breakpoint. Since the monitor is not using memory from the user's memory map for this, it is less intrusive to add more breakpoints. Breakpoints are still entered into the application memory as control changes from the monitor to the user program (as in a GO command), and they are removed when control goes back to the monitor program (as in when a breakpoint is encountered).

When the user application is running and a BGND-based breakpoint is encountered, the BGND opcode causes the target MCU to enter active background mode, but registers are not pushed onto the user's stack as they were for SWI-based breakpoints. This is significantly less intrusive than the older SWI-based breakpoints. BGND-based breakpoints also work correctly even if the application program fails to maintain the stack pointer correctly because the BGND instruction saves the application's registers in special hardware instead of using the application's stack.

BGND-based software breakpoints do not interfere with any application use of the SWI instruction. There are no application uses for BGND instructions so there is no danger of any interference between monitor and application use of BGND instructions.

A complete description of the background debug module follows in Section 14.4.

Hardware Breakpoints

Hardware breakpoints are different than software breakpoints in several important ways. Hardware breakpoints do not write anything into application program memory so they can be used to set breakpoints in memory that cannot be modified during a debug session (such as ROM or flash memory). Since hardware breakpoints are based on real-time comparison against address and data busses rather than opcode substitution, hardware breakpoints are not limited to addresses that correspond to instruction opcodes. This means you can set a break to occur when a certain control register or memory location is read or written (something you cannot do with a software breakpoint).

Hardware breakpoints require comparators and control logic in the target system. Since this logic takes up valuable space on every MCU, there is a limit to the number of breakpoints you can allow. In the MC68HC912B32, the breakpoint module supports one full address and data breakpoint or two address breakpoints.

14.4 Background Debug Module

The M68HC12 BDM system uses a single wire (plus ground) for all debugging.

Compared to the bootstrap mode in the MC68HC11 family, the background debug system in the M68HC12 allows greater access to the internal operation of the target system and does not interfere with the application hardware or software. The M68HC11 bootstrap mode shared the target MCU's serial I/O subsystem and RAM, whereas the M68HC12 uses a separate serial I/O interface (BKGD pin) and no user memory. In the HC11 you had to plan ahead for bootstrap mode or it could not be used. With the M68HC12 BDM, you need only provide a way to connect to ground and the BKGD pin. There is no interference with user software. In fact, in the M68HC12 you can even read or write target system memory locations without stopping the running application program. The M68HC12 also includes logic for tracing a single instruction at a time in the target system.

As its name implies, the background debug system is primarily intended for system development and debug; however, the BDM system is also useful for other application purposes. It can be used to load or reload an application program into a target system after it has been completely assembled. It can be used also to calibrate finished systems or perform field upgrades of operation software. In a data logging application, the BDM could be used to retrieve logged data, thus making it unnecessary to add this function to the application software. We will explore some of these non-debug uses after a more detailed explanation of the BDM system.

As Figure 14–1 shows, a typical M68HC12 BDM system consists of a desktop PC, an intelligent interface pod, and the target M68HC12 system. The link from the PC to the intelligent pod is a simple RS232 asynchronous serial port. The link from the pod to the target system is a custom serial interface to the single-wire BDM system of the M68HC12.

A standard 6-pin debugging interface includes *BKGD*, V_{dd}, ground, RESET and the Flash memory programming voltage.

Motorola has defined a standard six-pin connector to allow a pod to be connected to any target M68HC12 system. The connection can be as simple as the BKGD and ground pins. It is common to include reset so the PC can remotely force a target system reset. A V_{dd} connection allows the pod to steal power from the target system. A fifth pin could be used to supply an 11.5-V Flash programming voltage to the target system although this pin is usually not used.

Single-Wire Physical Interface

The single background interface pin (BKGD) is used for three functions in the M68HC12 MCU. During reset, this pin is a mode select input that selects between normal (BKGD=1) and special

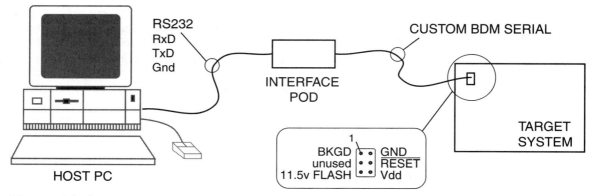

Figure 14-1 Typical M68HC12 BDM system.

(BKGD=0) modes of operation (see Chapter 15). After reset this pin becomes the dedicated serial interface pin for the background debug mode. If an appropriate serial command is received,
BKGD can be used to tag selected program instructions in the instruction queue.

Special-Mode Select Function

The background debug system is always available regardless of operating mode. Memory access does
not require background mode to be "active," so some debug commands may be used at any time
and in any operating mode. Other debug commands require the MCU to be in "active" background mode where the application program is stopped and BDM firmware is being executed instead. One way to get into active background mode is to reset the MCU into special single-chip
mode. This means you could design a system that operates in normal single-chip mode unless an
interface POD is connected to the BKGD pin. When the debug system is connected, it could hold
BKGD low (selecting special vs. normal mode) while providing an active-low reset signal.

This could be especially useful in a target system in which the main program is in a flash
EEPROM. An EEPROM programmer or debug system could be connected to the BKGD pin, and
the flash memory could be programmed before attempting to reset in normal mode. When the programmer is removed, the BKGD pin is pulled up through a simple pull-up resistor and the target
system will reset in normal single-chip mode.

Tagging Function

> Instruction tagging can
> generate a breakpoint
> when the instruction is
> about to be executed.

Because of the M68HC12s instruction queue (or pipe), instructions are fetched from
memory several cycles before they are executed. When jump and branch instructions
are executed, some instructions that were fetched into the pipe may be flushed from
the pipe without ever being executed. If you want the CPU to stop at a certain instruction, you can tag the instruction as it is fetched into the instruction queue. This
tag signal follows along with the opcode information in the instruction queue. If the tag is set when

the CPU is about to start an instruction, an exception (interrupt) causes the MCU to enter active background mode instead of executing the tagged instruction.

Tagging is enabled when a serial debug command (TAG_GO) is issued to start or resume an application program from active background mode. There are two tagging inputs so that you can tag the even byte, the odd byte, or both bytes of the program word as it is fetched into the instruction queue. The BKGD and low byte strobe ($\overline{\text{LSTRB}}$) pins are used to tag the even (high) byte or the odd (low) byte if tagging is enabled. Tag signals are captured at the falling edge on E-clock where the fetched program word is also valid.

While tagging is enabled, the BKGD pin cannot be used for serial debug commands because the interface would not be able to distinguish a serial command from a tag signal. If a debugger, connected to the BKGD pin, wanted to regain control, it could simply drive the BKGD pin low and hold it. Within a few instructions this would be seen as a tag request, and the MCU would enter active background mode. While in active background mode, tagging is disabled and the BKGD pin is dedicated for serial BDM communications. Tagging is described in greater detail later in Section 14.5.

Background Communication Function

The primary use of the BKGD pin is for bidirectional communications between an external host, such as a PC, and the target M68HC12 MCU. To keep this to a single pin (plus ground), a custom serial protocol was devised. This protocol is more tolerant of speed variations than other asynchronous protocols such as that used for ordinary RS232 terminals.

The asychronous serial protocol used by ordinary computer terminals assumes both the transmitting and receiving devices are using the same frequency for communication. Synchronization is achieved by recognizing the falling edge of a start bit, and no other synchronization takes place for the rest of a character (which is 10 bit-times long). If the transmitter or receiver is off frequency by more than about 3.5%, synchronization is lost and data may be received incorrectly.

The custom protocol used on the BKGD pin resynchronizes at the beginning of each bit so a much greater frequency tolerance, on the order of $\pm$ 20%, is allowed. All bits are started by a falling edge driven by the external host. When the target M68HC12 sees this edge, it waits nine E-clock cycles and samples the level on the BKGD pin.

There are four bit-time cases to consider as shown in Figure 14–2. All four cases begin when the host drives the BKGD pin low to generate a falling edge. Since the host and target are operating from separate clocks, it can take the target M68HC12 MCU anywhere from zero to one E-clock cycle to recognize this edge [1]. The target measures delays from this perceived start of the bit-time while the host measures delays from the point it actually drove BKGD low to start the bit (up to one target E-clock earlier). Synchronization between the host and target is established in this manner at the start of every bit-time.

> **Case 1:** Host transmits a logic 0. The host drives BKGD low for about 13 target E-clock cycles [2]. Nine E-clocks after the target recognized the start of the bit-time, the target senses the level on the BKGD pin and sees a zero [3]. The length (13 E-clocks) of this low time is not very critical. The bit will be sensed correctly as long as it is low when the target samples the level at cycle nine. The low can extend much longer without harm, as long as it goes high for at least one or two E-clocks before the falling edge that starts the next bit.
>
> The duration of one bit-time is nominally 16 target E-clocks [4], but the target actually starts looking for a new start edge just after the sample point. Command resynchronization is forced if

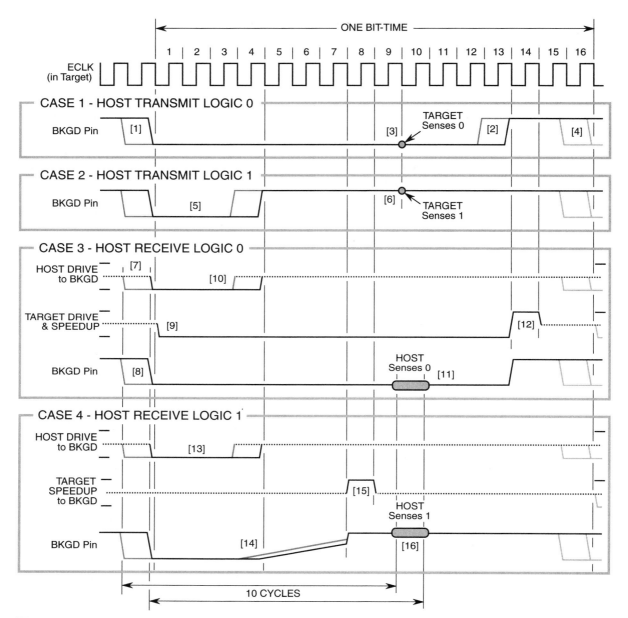

Figure 14-2   BDM serial communication timing details.

a new falling edge on BKGD is not found within 512 E-clock cycles. This is needed in case noise is incorrectly detected as the start of a new bit, which would confuse the receiver state machine.

Case 2: Host transmits a logic 1. The host drives BKGD low for about 4 target E-clock cycles [5]. Nine E-clocks after the target recognized the start of the bit-time, the target senses the level on the BKGD pin and sees a one [6]. The length of this low time (four E-clocks) is not very critical. It must be long enough to be detected as a low so the target can detect the falling edge at the start of the bit. The bit will be sensed correctly as long as it is high when the target samples the level at cycle nine.

Before describing the next two cases shown in Figure 14–2, we need to discuss a special timing concern. The BKGD pin is a pseudo-open-drain pin, which implies it has a pull-up and that drivers connected to BKGD do not typically drive the high level. But the RC rise time could be unacceptably long if we just relied on the pullup to get BKGD back to a logic one. The MCU overcomes this problem by providing brief, driven-high, speed-up pulses. The source of this speed-up pulse is the host for host-to-target cases and the target for target-to-host transmissions. Since the host drives these high, speed-up pulses in the first two cases, the rising edges just look like digitally driven signals. The receive cases below are more complicated.

Case 3: Host receives a logic 0. At [7] the host drives BKGD low to start the bit-time [8]. As soon as the target recognizes the bit start [9], it drives a low for 13 E-clocks to send a logic zero to the host. This low reinforces the low drive from the host that started the bit-time. The low drive from the host is released after about four E-clocks and the host's driver goes to a high-impedance state [10]. About 10 E-clocks after the host initiated the bit-time, it senses the level on BKGD [11]. This sense point appears in the figure to be spread over a whole E-clock because the position is measured by the host from the point it actually drove BKGD low. Because the target is driving BKGD low at this time, the host receives a logic zero for the bit. At the end of the 13 cycle low drive period, the target drives BKGD high for one E-clock cycle to force a rapid rising edge on BKGD, and then releases the pin to a high-impedance state. The BKGD pin itself stays high due to a weak on-chip pull-up resistor.[1]

Case 4: Host receives a logic 1. At [13] the host drives a low to start the bit-time. The target recognizes the bit start but because the target wants the host to receive a one, it does not drive the BKGD pin. When the host releases the bit start pulse at [14], the BKGD pin begins a relatively slow RC rise. During the eighth cycle after the target sensed the start of the bit, it drives a one-cycle high [15] to snap the BKGD pin to a valid high level. The target times this delay to allow the host to stop driving the low start pulse, but the speed-up pulse must occur before the host samples the pin level at [16]. Again, the sample point appears to be spread across a whole E-clock cycle because it is positioned relative to the point at which the host drove BKGD low.

Serial Commands

BDM hardware commands can be executed while the application program is running. Firmware commands require the CPU to be in active background debugging mode.

The BDM command set is broken into two groups of primitive debug commands. Hardware commands allow target system memory to be read or written. Target system memory includes all memory that is accessible by the CPU including on-chip RAM, EEPROM, etc., on-chip I/O and control registers, and external memory connected to the target M68HC12 MCU. As the name implies, hardware commands are implemented in hardware logic in the target MCU. These commands opportunistically watch the CPU buses to find a free bus cycle so the background access does not disturb running application programs. In the unlikely case in which no free cycle is found within 128 target E-clocks, the CPU is momentarily frozen so the BDM system can steal a cycle.

---

[1] A weak pull-up resistor is one with fairly high resistance, say 10 kΩ.

Table 14–1 shows the hardware debug commands. Any of these commands can be executed while the user program is running.

Commands in the second group of commands, shown in Table 14–2, are called firmware commands because they are implemented in a small ROM, which is part of the background debug module in the target MCU. Firmware commands are used for things that cannot be done while the application program is running. For example, it would not make sense to read and write CPU registers while a program was running because these values can change many times in the time it takes to execute a BDM serial command.

To use firmware commands, the MCU is first placed in "active" background mode. The usual way to get to active background mode is by the hardware command, BACKGROUND. As the MCU enters active background mode, a small ROM and a few BDM registers become visible in the on-chip memory map (at $FF00–$FFFF) and the CPU begins executing the BDM firmware. The BDM firmware watches for serial firmware commands and executes them as they are received. Hardware commands may be executed while the BDM is active, but they are still handled by hardware logic rather than the BDM firmware.

While BDM is active, the CPU registers are remembered so the application program can resume when BDM becomes inactive. The user can use firmware commands to read or modify the saved CPU registers before resuming the application program. One firmware command allows a user to trace the application program one instruction at a time, and the WRITE_PC command allows a user to return to (go to) a different address in the application program.

Table 14–3 lists all available BDM commands. Each command starts with an 8-bit command code. Depending on the command, a 16-bit address and/or a 16-bit data word is required. Hardware commands involve a delay where the BDM logic searches for a free cycle to allow an unobtrusive access. Since there is no practical way for the host to tell when the actual access has been

TABLE 14–1   BDM Commands Implemented in Hardware

Command	Code	Data	Description
BACKGROUND	$90	None	Enter active background mode.
READ_BYTE	$E0	16-bit address host → target 16-bit data target → host	Read a byte from user memory.
READ_BD_BYTE	$E4	16-bit address host → target 16-bit data target → host	Read a byte with BDM ROM and registers enabled in the memory map
READ_WORD	$E8	16-bit address host → target 16-bit data target → host	Read a word from user memory
READ_BD_WORD	$EC	16-bit address host → target 16-bit data target → host	Read a word with BDM ROM and registers enabled in the memory map
WRITE_BYTE	$C0	16-bit address host → target 16-bit data host → target	Write a byte to user memory
WRITE_BD_BYTE	$C4	16-bit address host → target 16-bit data host → target	Write a byte with BDM ROM and registers enabled in the memory map
WRITE_WORD	$C8	16-bit address host → target 16-bit data host → target	Write a word to user memory
WRITE_BD_WORD	$CC	16-bit address host → target 16-bit data host → target	Write a word with BDM ROM and registers enabled in the memory map

TABLE 14-2 BDM Commands Implemented in Firmware

Command	Code	Commands Executed When in Background Mode	
		16-bit Data	Description
READ_NEXT	$62	Target → host	X = X + 2; Read next word pointed-to by X
READ_PC	$63	Target → host	Read program counter
READ_D	$64	Target → host	Read D register
READ_X	$65	Target → host	Read X register
READ_Y	$66	Target → host	Read Y register
READ_SP	$67	Target → host	Read stack pointer
WRITE_NEXT	$42	Host → target	X = X + 2; write next word pointed-to by X
WRITE_PC	$43	Host → target	Write program counter
WRITE_D	$44	Host → target	Write D register
WRITE_X	$45	Host → target	Write X register
WRITE_Y	$46	Host → target	Write Y register
WRITE_SP	$47	Host → target	Write stack pointer
GO	$08	No data	Go to user program
TRACE1	$10	No data	Execute one user instruction and return to BDM
TAG_GO	$18	No data	Enable tagging and go to user program

completed, it must wait at least the worst-case, 128 cycles to be sure it was finished. Normally, a longer delay of 150 to 175 cycles is used in case the target was in the middle of a split and/or stretched memory access at the end of this 128-cycle delay, or the BDM requested access requires a split and/or stretched access, or in case the target is running a little slower than the pod thinks it is.

The command timing column approximates what would be seen on an oscilloscope if you captured the command. The command opcode blocks are a series of eight bit-times (MSB first) starting with a falling edge and having different low times for zeros and ones. The bar across the top of the blocks indicates that the BKGD line idles in the high state during a delay. The horizontal dimension is approximately to scale where 16-bit addresses take twice as long as the 8-bit command codes. The time for an 8-bit command is eight times 16 E-clocks or 16 μsec if the E-clock is 8 MHz.

The delay periods in the hardware memory access commands are required to account for the possible 128 cycle delay while the BDM logic looks for a free bus cycle. There is also a small amount of overhead since the request could involve an access that is split into two separate 8-bit accesses and each of these could be associated with a slow memory that is set for bus stretching. For this reason a delay of 150 target E-clock cycles is recommended, and extending the delay to 175 cycles would allow for a target that is about 20% slower than the host thinks it is. In the case of a read, the host must delay after sending the address but before initiating the data portion of the transfer. In the case of a write access, the host must delay after the data portion, before sending a new command, to be sure the write has finished. The overall time for a 16-bit word transfer using a hardware command is about 115 μsec.

The firmware commands READ_NEXT and WRITE_NEXT do not require an address for each transfer and they do not have such long delays as the hardware commands. These commands can transfer data at about 50–60 μsec per 16-bit word, which is comparable to an RS232 Baud rate of about 400 kBaud.

TABLE 14–3 BDM Commands and Command Timing

Command	Code	Command Timing
Hardware		
BACKGROUND	$90	Code | Dly
READ_BYTE	$E0	
READ_BD_BYTE	$E4	Code | Address | Dly_150 | Data: Target-to-host
READ_WORD	$E8	
READ_BD_WORD	$EC	
WRITE_BYTE	$C0	
WRITE_BD_BYTE	$C4	Code | Address | Data: Host-to-target | Dly_150
WRITE_WORD	$C8	
WRITE_BD_WORD	$CC	
Firmware		
READ_NEXT	$62	
READ_PC	$63	
READ_D	$64	Code | Dly | Data: Target-to-host
READ_X	$65	
READ_Y	$66	
READ_SP	$67	
WRITE_NEXT	$42	
WRITE_PC	$43	
WRITE_D	$44	Code | Data: Host-to-target | Dly
WRITE_X	$45	
WRITE_Y	$46	
WRITE_SP	$47	
GO	$08	
TRACE1	$10	Code | Dly
TAG_GO	$18	

BDM Registers

The BDM firmware ROM and BDM registers are not normally in the MCU memory map. Since these locations have the same addresses as some of the normal application memory map, there needs to be a way to decide which physical location is being accessed by the hardware BDM commands. This gives rise to separate memory access commands for the BDM locations as opposed to the normal application locations. In logic, this is accomplished by momentarily enabling the BDM memory resources, just for the access cycle of the READ_BD and WRITE_BD commands. This logic allows the debugging system to unobtrusively access the BDM locations even if the application program is running out of the same memory area in the normal application memory map.

There are seven BDM registers that are mapped into addresses $FF00–$FF06 when the BDM is active. Only two of these, the *BDM Status Register* at $FF01 and the *BDM CCR Holding Regis-*

ter at $FF06, are of interest to the programmer. The other registers are for use only by BDM firmware and logic.

STATUS—$FF01—BDM Status Register

Bit 7	6	5	4	3	2	1	Bit 0
ENBDM	BDMACT	ENTAG	SDV	TRACE	0	0	0

Reset   0   0   0   1   0   0   0   0

ENBDM
Enable BDM (permit active background debug mode).   0 = BDM cannot be made active (hardware commands still allowed)(default).   1 = BDM can be made active to allow firmware commands.

BDMACT
Background Mode Active Status.   0 = BDM not active (default).   1 = BDM active and waiting for serial commands.

ENTAG
Instruction Tagging Enable.   0 = Tagging not enabled or BDM active (default).   1 = Tagging active (BDM cannot process serial commands while tagging is active.) Set by TAG_GO instruction and cleared when BDM is entered.

SDV
Shifter Data Valid.   0 = No valid data.   1 = Valid data (default). Shows that valid data are in the serial interface shift register. Used by firmware-based instructions.

TRACE
Asserted by the TRACE1 instruction.

Other Registers

INSTRUCTION—$FF00—BDM Instruction Register

SHIFTER—$FF02:FF03—BDM Shift Register

ADDRESS—$FF04:FF05—BDM Address Register

CCRSAV—$FF06—BDM CCR Holding Register

It is recommended that the user not access these registers. In fact, you could interfere with proper BDM operation if you tried.

More Complex Commands

The primitive commands in the BDM command set provide everything needed for a full-featured debugging system. For example, a command to display all CPU registers could be made up of a series of separate primitive commands to read each CPU register. A command to read 8-bit accumulator A or B could be accomplished by doing a READ_D command and then using the appropriate half of the result.

The user CCR register is saved in a BDM register at $FF06 on entry into active BDM mode. There is no READ_CCR command because you can accomplish this with a "READ_BD_BYTE @ $FF06" command. Similarly you can write to the user CCR with a "WRITE_BD_BYTE @ $FF06" command.

Commands such as BDM_STATUS and ENABLE_FIRMWARE are sometimes considered part of the basic BDM command set, but like the commands to read or write the user CCR, these are also just special cases of the READ_BD_BYTE and WRITE_BD_BYTE commands. BDM status is read from a BDM register at $FF01 in the BDM memory map. BDM firmware commands are enabled by setting the MSB of the BDM STATUS register at $FF01 in the BDM memory map. To avoid disturbing the other bits in the BDM STATUS register, it is recommended that you read STATUS, OR in the ENBDM bit (in the MSB), and then write the result to the STATUS register. To disable BDM firmware commands you would read STATUS, AND it with $7F, and write the result back to STATUS.

Besides the BDM STATUS register at $FF01 and the CCRSAV register at $FF06 in the BDM map, there are 5 more bytes of registers to support the BDM system. The 8-bit BDM INSTRUCTION register, the 16-bit BDM SHIFTER, and the 16-bit BDM ADDRESS register are used only by BDM logic and the program in the BDM firmware ROM. You should have no reason to access these registers through serial BDM commands and in fact you could interfere with proper BDM operation if you tried.

Software breakpoints are typically implemented by placing a software interrupt (SWI) opcode in place of a user instruction opcode at the desired breakpoint address(es). This can create problems for a debug monitor if the normal application program also uses SWI instructions. In this new background debug system you use background (BGND) instructions instead of SWI instructions (provided the monitor is working through the BDM interface). After placing the breakpoints and GOing to the user program, the monitor program repeatedly checks the BDM STATUS register to see if the target MCU has executed the BGND and returned to active BDM. When a breakpoint address is reached, the target system goes to active background mode and waits for debug commands from the host. This is another example of how this background system is less intrusive than previous background debugging systems. These software breakpoints can be placed using BDM memory access commands. Some M68HC12s have a hardware breakpoint module, which we will study later in this chapter. Hardware breakpoints are used for cases in which the target memory cannot be modified to write software breakpoint codes, such as in ROM or flash memory.

Chip-Level BDM Details

The background debug module consists of a serial interface block, a state machine, a small set of BDM registers, and a small BDM firmware ROM. To avoid interference with the user system, the BDM registers and the BDM ROM are not part of the user's memory map. The BDM registers and ROM are switched into the memory map when the BDM is active (CPU is executing code in the BDM ROM rather than user application code). The only other time BDM memory resources are switched into the memory map is when you execute a hardware command to read or write to a BDM location. In these cases the switch puts the BDM resource into the map only during a free cycle in the user program or a stolen bus cycle (if no free cycle is available for the access).

> The background debug module is a serial interface, a state machine, and several registers.

While BDM is active, ordinary CPU instructions can access the BDM registers and firmware, but the BDM firmware cannot access the user memory at $FF00–FFFF. Conversely, user programs can never access the contents of the BDM firmware ROM or BDM registers. BDM hardware commands can always choose to access either user memory or BDM memory in the $FF00–FFFF space. However, typical monitor programs assume you want to look at user space and they do not directly allow you to read the BDM firmware ROM or registers.

The serial interface block handles communications through the BKGD pin, and serial timing is based on the E-clock. All timing is referenced to detection of falling edges on the BKGD pin (which is driven by the host pod at the start of each bit time). If no falling edge is detected within 512 E-clocks, the BDM logic is forced to reset which aborts any unfinished serial command. This provides a way to regain synchronization in the case of noise or a bad serial command.

The state machine shifts in an 8-bit serial command and stores it in the BDM instruction register to be decoded. The state machine proceeds then to one of several states based on this command. For a hardware write command the state machine shifts in a 16-bit address and a 16-bit data word, waits for a free CPU cycle, and performs the requested write operation. For a hardware read command, the state machine shifts in a 16-bit address, waits for a free cycle, performs the requested read operation, and stores the result to the BDM shifter so it can be shifted out to the host pod. After shifting the last data bit, the state machine returns to its starting point to await a new command.

For firmware write commands, the state machine shifts in a 16-bit data word and sets the shifter data valid (SDV) bit in the BDM STATUS register. BDM firmware performs the requested write operation. For firmware read commands, the BDM firmware performs the requested read and stores the value to the BDM SHIFTER so the host pod can shift it out. After the last bit of data is shifted out, the state machine returns to its starting point to await a new command.

The hardware BACKGROUND command is a special case that causes the MCU to enter active BDM mode. The three firmware commands GO, TRACE1, and TAG_GO are all associated with the active BDM exit sequence and they will be discussed later in this section.

Active BDM Entry Sequence Details

There are four ways to force entry into active BDM mode.

- The hardware BACKGROUND command,
- executing a BGND opcode,
- reset into special single chip mode, or
- a trigger signal from the hardware breakpoint module (not all M68HC12 derivatives have a hardware breakpoint module).

In the case of the hardware BACKGROUND command or a hardware breakpoint, a signal is sent to the CPU to force it to execute a BGND microcode sequence at the next instruction boundary (this is similar to what happens for ordinary interrupts). Unlike an interrupt, CPU registers are not stacked by the BGND microcode sequence because this would interfere with the user's application. Instead, the BGND microcode forces the user's return address to be saved in the TMP2 register in the CPU. The BDM ROM is then turned on and the CPU fetches the vector from $FFF6:FFF7, which points to the start of the BDM firmware program. $FFF6:FFF7 is where the SWI vector is located, but since the BDM ROM is enabled, the BDM vector is fetched rather than the user's SWI vector.

The first thing the BDM firmware does is to save the user's D register in another CPU temporary register (TMP3), and then it saves the user's CCR register in the CCRSAV register at $FF06. The TMP2 and TMP3 CPU registers are used for only a few of the most complex CPU12 instructions; as long as the BDM firmware avoids those instructions, the user program counter (PC) and D register values will not be disturbed. The user's X, Y, and SP registers are not changed by the BDM firmware so there is no need to stack or save these values while the BDM firmware is running. All interrupts are masked (prevented) while BDM is active so there is no danger that any user code can accidentally disturb the context before BDM firmware returns control to the user application program.

After saving the user context, BDM firmware checks the opcode at the return address (where the user PC is pointing). If it is a BGND opcode ($00), BDM firmware increments the return PC value to avoid the following infinite loop case. This preventative measure is required because the BDM firmware could have been entered due to the CPU encountering a BGND opcode. If the ENBDM bit in the BDM STATUS register is 0 (meaning active BDM mode is disabled), the BDM firmware tries to just return to the user program. If it were allowed to return to the same $00 opcode that got you into the BDM firmware in the first place, you would be stuck in an infinite loop. If the opcode at the user PC is not $00, it means you entered BDM by one of the other mechanisms and the user PC should not be changed. If you just happened to execute a BACKGROUND serial command just as the user program was about to execute a $00 opcode, this incrementing mechanism would cause you to skip over the $00 opcode, which is OK because you are already in active BDM mode.

Next the BDM firmware checks the ENBDM bit in STATUS to see if it is legal to be in active BDM. If not, the firmware exits to the user program. If the CPU encounters a request to enter BDM and the firmware is not enabled, it actually enters active BDM just long enough to find out it should not be there. In a real system this looks like a relatively long NOP instruction.

Finally the BDM firmware enters a loop waiting for a valid firmware command. When a firmware command is received, it is decoded and the requested task is completed before returning to the top of the program to wait for the next command. Once the BDM firmware is started (and provided it is allowed by ENBDM=1), it remains active until one of the three exit commands (GO, TRACE1, or TAG_GO) is received or the target MCU is reset.

When a BGND instruction ($00 opcode) causes you to enter the BDM firmware, the sequence is just like the serial BACKGROUND command or a hardware breakpoint except in this case the BDM firmware increments the user PC to point at the next opcode after the BGND instruction before entering the loop to wait for firmware BDM commands.

The last case is when the MCU is reset in special single-chip mode. In this case the BDM firmware ROM is already enabled before the reset vector is fetched. This means the BDM's reset vector is fetched rather than the user's. The only difference between this entry point and any other entry to active BDM mode is that a BSET instruction is executed to set the ENBDM bit in the BDM STATUS register before starting the rest of the BDM firmware program.

Active BDM Exit Sequence Details

There are three firmware commands (GO, TRACE1, and TAG_GO) that cause an exit from active BDM mode and resumption of a user program. In addition, BDM firmware exits to user code if the BDM was disabled (because ENBDM=0). During the exit sequence, user register values are restored, a value is stored to the BDM STATUS register, and a jump (indexed indirect) is executed to resume execution of the user program. These last two instructions and their cycle-by-cycle behavior are the key to the BDM exit sequence.

The last firmware instructions in the BDM exit sequence are as follows:

```
1   LDAB  CCRSAV             ;Reentry value for user CCR
2   STAA  CCRSAV             ;Use CCRSAV as temp, will move to STATUS
3   EXG   X,TMP2             ;Swap user X to TMP2 and user PC to X
4   STX   SHIFTER            ;Use SHIFTER as temp, will jmp indirect
5   EXG   X,TMP2             ;Swap user X back into X
6   TFR   B,CCR              ;Restore user CCR
7   EXG   TMP3,D             ;Restore user D value
8   MOVB  CCRSAV,STATUS  ;[OrPwPO] Write w/o changing CCR
9   JMP   [(SHIFTER - (*+4)),PC]   ;[fIfPPP] Go to user PC location
```

CCRSAV, SHIFTER, and STATUS are registers in the BDM map. TMP2 and TMP3 are CPU temporary storage registers. The user Y and SP values do not need to be restored because the BDM firmware does not disturb those registers. On entry into this sequence, accumulator A contains status information that must be written to the BDM STATUS register just as we are leaving the BDM firmware. *Line 1* retrieves the user's CCR information from CCRSAV and *line 2* saves the BDM status in CCRSAV as a temporary holding location so we can use a MOVB instruction to store to STATUS in *line 8*. This MOVB allows us to write without disturbing the user's CCR value, which was restored in *line 6* (the instructions in *lines 7, 8, and 9* must not alter the CCR value). We store the user's PC value in SHIFTER in *line 4* and use a PC-relative indexed-indirect JMP instruction in *line 9* to return to the user program without disturbing the user CCR value. The EXG instructions in *lines 5 and 7* could have been TFR instructions because we do not care what values are in TMP2 and TMP3 as we resume the user program.

The codes in the square brackets in the comment fields of *lines 8 and 9* describe the cycle-by-cycle operation of these instructions. The write to the BDM STATUS register (the w cycle) in *line 8* triggers the start of a series of timed events in the BDM logic. The I cycle in *line 9* is where the CPU is reading the user's return PC out of the BDM SHIFTER register. The PPP sequence at the end of *line 9* corresponds to the three program word fetches from the user program to fill the instruction queue (pipe). So that the user PC can be read from the BDM SHIFTER register and user program instructions can be read during the P cycle two cycles later, the BDM logic switches the BDM firmware ROM and registers out of the map between these two reads. If the exit was caused by a GO or because BDM firmware was not enabled, the exit sequence is finished. If a TAG_GO instruction caused the exit, the BDM logic must disconnect the BKGD pin from the BDM serial interface and connect it to the TAGHI input logic at the appropriate time so user instructions can be tagged. If a TRACE1 command caused the exit, the BDM logic must assert a signal to the CPU during the first cycle of the first user instruction such that you will return to active BDM after executing exactly one user program instruction.

If you want to go to a different user program address instead of just going back to where the program was executing when you entered active BDM, just use a WRITE_PC instruction to change the user PC before executing a GO command. The WRITE_PC instruction stores the supplied address to the TMP2 register so it will be used as the user PC during the exit sequence. Typically the monitor program in the host PC will allow you to type a command such as "G 0800" and the monitor will take care of executing a WRITE_PC command followed by a GO command.

Implementing a BDM POD

A debugging *POD* is connected between the target system and a host PC.

There are several ways to build a pod to interface to the BDM system. One company built a tiny pod that did little more than convert ASCII characters from a host PC into an equivalent bit pattern for the BDM interface. In that system, essentially all of the intelligence for the debug system was in the host PC. The Motorola SDI pod implemented a standard serial interface protocol that is used in a number of Motorola emulators. This made it possible for several third-party development tool vendors to design complex software debug tools including advanced features such as C source-level debugging. The M68EVB912B32 evaluation board includes a complete command-line-based monitor program in the pod so the host computer can be anything that can support a simple ASCII terminal (PC, Macintosh, UNIX workstation, etc.). The M68EVB912B32 can also act as a stand-alone evaluation system with a ROM monitor much like the M68HC11EVBU with its Buffalo monitor program. A jumper on the M68EVB912B32 selects EVB vs. POD mode. In POD mode, the EVB acts as a BDM pod and commands refer to a target M68HC12 connected through a six-pin cable.

Appendix A shows example M68HC12 routines that perform the lowest level single-wire BDM protocol that are essentially those used in the M68EVB912B32 evaluation board. These primitive communication routines can build the entire BDM command set shown in Table 14–3.

Application Uses for BDM

Nonvolatile Memory Programming

The BDM can program Flash, EPROM, and EEPROM memory in a target application.

One of the most valuable uses for the BDM system is to program system memory including internal flash and EEPROM memory as well as external nonvolatile memory from other manufacturers. This is possible because the BDM system can gain direct control of a target system through a simple BDM connector with only two to six pins and can access any location the CPU can access. This is independent of any user software in the target system so the user does not have to plan ahead for BDM access other than to provide the physical BDM connector. With so few connections needed it is often possible to tack wires into a system even if a BDM connector was not provided.

The BDM can transfer data at a rate approaching 50 μsec per word (using WRITE_NEXT word firmware commands) or about 40,000 bytes per second. Internal flash programming is likely to require about 90 to 130 μsec per word. This is slower than the BDM serial communication rate so serial BDM communications can take place in parallel with the flash programming algorithm. The speed of BDM communications should not be the limiting factor in flash programming.

EEPROM takes considerably longer to program (about 20 msec per byte/word) so you could also program on-chip EEPROM through BDM without being limited by the speed of serial BDM communications.

If the programming pod has to load an object file from a PC to the pod during programming, the speed of the PC-to-pod communications (typically 9600 or 19.2 kBaud) becomes the dominant factor in target system programming. To overcome this limitation you could equip the programming pod with a large nonvolatile memory so you can program it once from a PC and then the pod can program target systems at the fastest speed the programming algorithm allows.

Target System Calibration

Suppose you have a target system with sensors that need to be calibrated. Due to sensor-to-sensor variations and sensitive analog circuitry, it is best to perform calibration after final assembly of the application system so all parasitic effects can be taken into account. BDM allows access to the final system through a minimum two-wire interface. This is small enough for even the smallest embedded control application systems. As an added advantage, the calibration code can be downloaded into the application system through BDM at the time of calibration so it need not take up any memory space in the normal application program.

Field Diagnostics and Code Changes

> Debugging problems in the field can be done with the BDM.

It would be nice if you could write complex controller programs and just forget about them. Unfortunately, it is all too common to discover problems in the field after system delivery. Often, the problems disappear as soon as the controller is returned to a factory service center (because the subtle conditions that caused the problem are present only at the field location where it failed). The BDM system allows access to the internal operation of the product while it is executing the application program. If the problem can not be located unobtrusively, the BDM allows you to load pieces of diagnostic code to help isolate the application bugs. Once a bug is found, the BDM can be used to erase and reprogram the system Flash or EEPROM memory. The same technique can be used to load maintenance updates to products in the field without completely disassembling the product.

This technique was used at a major automotive manufacturer to locate a bug in the BDLC module of an early version of the MC68HC912B32. Because of the simplicity of a BDM connection, the debugging could be performed on the module without removing it from the vehicle. While looking for the bug, it was discovered that the BDLC communications system in the vehicle was experiencing thousands of corrupted bus communications (it was surprising the bus could even continue to function with so many errors). The silicon bug would not have been detected if it were not for the bus errors, but the bus errors were also a serious problem that needed to be solved. If the controller module had been removed from the vehicle to diagnose the errors, they would not have been found because the errors had to do with the interaction of the module with the noisy BDLC communication bus.

This debug session also relied heavily on the use of the on-chip hardware breakpoint module in the MC68HC912B32 that we discuss in Section 14.7. The system used the COP watchdog system and that interfered with debugging. Every time the debugger pod tried to gain control through BDM, a COP timeout would trigger, causing the system to reset. To get past this, a hardware breakpoint was inserted before the initialization code that enabled the COP. In response to this breakpoint, the debugger inserted a substitute initialization routine that left the COP disabled. This allowed the debug session to proceed.

Data Logger Applications

In a typical data logging application you would have a program to collect and record the desired data. You would also include some utility program to allow the collected data to be transferred from the data collection system into some other system for analysis and record keeping. The BDM system can eliminate the need for this extra utility program, leaving more memory space for the primary data collection software. After data have been collected, the BDM system can be used to read the recorded information out of the data collection system. BDM commands can then be used to erase the logging memory so the data collection system is ready for its next use.

14.5 Instruction Tagging

Instruction tagging makes use of an external logic analyzer to generate a breakpoint when a selected instruction is fetched into the instruction pipe. The M68HC12 uses an instruction queue to speed up program execution.

Instruction tagging is used in conjunction with external bus analysis logic to stop target application processing at selected instruction boundaries. This is most commonly used in larger emulation systems. To use tagging effectively you must understand all of the external bus signals and the instruction queue (or pipeline) mechanism. This is the same information you need if you are using a logic analyzer to debug an M68HC12 system. The next section covers this in detail.

Using the Tagging Function

The only mechanisms available to stop the M68HC12 CPU from executing an instruction when it would normally be executed are to either replace the selected instruction opcode with a BGND or SWI instruction opcode or use the tagging function. Of course the opcode replacement technique, which is used for traditional (software) breakpoints, cannot be used in nonvolatile memory such as ROM or flash memory. The tagging function causes an opcode to be "tagged" as it is fetched into the pipe. This tag follows the data in the pipe. If a tagged instruction reaches the head of the pipe, the CPU effectively executes a BGND opcode instead of the tagged instruction opcode so the MCU will go to active background mode.

There are separate tag inputs for the high and low bytes of the data entering the pipe so you can independently tag either byte or both. The $\overline{\text{TAGHI}}$ signal shares the BKGD/$\overline{\text{TAGHI}}$ pin and the $\overline{\text{TAGLO}}$ signal shares the $\overline{\text{LSTRB}}$/$\overline{\text{TAGLO}}$ pin. To tag a data value entering the pipe, you drive the $\overline{\text{TAGHI}}$ and/or $\overline{\text{TAGLO}}$ pin low before the falling edge of E. The tag signals and the data are captured at the falling edge of the E-clock signal. Since the $\overline{\text{TAGLO}}$ input signal shares the same pin as the $\overline{\text{LSTRB}}$ output, you must take care to avoid driving the pin with a tag signal for the quarter cycle before and after E-rise.

Tagging is not enabled normally. To turn on tagging, you must send a TAG_GO serial command into the BKGD pin while BDM is active. After enabling tagging, the BKGD pin switches from being the BDM communications signal to being the $\overline{\text{TAGHI}}$ input signal. The usual way to get back to active BDM and turn off tagging is to encounter a tagged instruction. If you want to regain control in active BDM without reaching a normal tagged location, you can simply drive the BKGD/$\overline{\text{TAGHI}}$ pin low for several cycles. This will be interpreted as tagging several instructions. As soon as one of these tagged instructions get to the end of the pipe, the MCU will enter active background mode and tagging is disabled.

From this description of the tagging function, it should be obvious that the tag signals must be associated with the opcode of an instruction (as opposed to an operand or memory access cycle). If you drive a tag signal into the pipe for an operand fetch, it will not cause the processor to stop.

Tags are somewhat like interrupts except they work regardless of whether interrupts are unmasked, and like BGND instructions, the CPU registers are not stacked (although they are remembered in CPU temporary registers and dedicated BDM registers).

To use tags, an emulator with circuitry that monitors the address bus in a target system is required. Registers in the emulation system hold addresses corresponding to instruction opcode locations where you would like to stop execution of the application program (breakpoints). Comparators constantly compare the address bus to the breakpoint register values and when there is a match, the emulator logic drives the appropriate $\overline{\text{TAGHI}}$ or $\overline{\text{TAGLO}}$ signal(s). If and when one of these tagged instructions reaches the head of the queue, the CPU will go to active BDM instead of executing the tagged instruction.

14.6 Capturing M68HC12 Bus Signals

State information for one M68HC12 bus cycle includes information captured at both the rising and falling edges of the E-clock. Because a bus cycle is actually a complex sequence of several other internal operations, and because the M68HC12 tries to interleave as many operations as possible between adjacent cycles, the boundaries of a bus cycle can be a bit fuzzy depending on your point of view. From the user's point of view a bus cycle starts at a falling edge of E and ends at a subsequent E falling edge. We will initially assume the most straightforward case in which there is no E-clock stretching, and later we can discuss stretching and special case cycles.

You can think of a bus cycle as beginning with an address portion, which roughly corresponds to the E-low period, and then a data portion corresponding to the E-high period. In a logic analyzer or emulator, you can capture address and R$\overline{\text{W}}$ at E-rise and data at E-fall. In the case of the MC68HC812A4, addresses include the memory expansion address lines ADDR21–ADDR16 that are optionally available at port G pins. In the MC68HC912B32, the 16-bit CPU address and the 16 bits of data are multiplexed on the same set of 16 pins, but are captured at different times within a cycle.

Since the M68HC12 can perform both 8-bit and 16-bit data accesses, another signal ($\overline{\text{LSTRB}}$) is needed to distinguish which of these is taking place. The $\overline{\text{LSTRB}}$ signal is captured at the rising edge of E along with address and R/$\overline{\text{W}}$. Table 14–4 shows how $\overline{\text{LSTRB}}$, R/$\overline{\text{W}}$, and address bit-0 (ADDR0) can be decoded to identify the type of memory access being performed in any cycle. To

TABLE 14-4   Decoding Bus Cycle Types

LSTRB	R/W̅	ADDR0	Cycle Type	Suggested Mnemonic
0	0	0	Write 16-bit word	W16
0	0	1	Write odd byte	W8L
0	1	0	Read 16-bit word	R16
0	1	1	Read odd byte	R8L
1	0	0	Write even byte	W8H
1	0	1	Write misaligned word	WLH
1	1	0	Read even byte	R8H
1	1	1	Read misaligned word	RLH

make it easier to discuss these cycle types, the table suggests a three-character mnemonic for each. Some logic analyzers, such as the HP16500 series, allow you to configure the display to show these symbolic substitutes for specific state patterns. W16 and R16 are self-explanatory. W8H and R8H identify 8-bit access cycles (write and read respectively) in which the data are on the high 8 bits of the 16-bit data bus. W8L and R8L identify 8-bit access cycles in which the data are on the low 8 bits of the 16-bit data bus. During 8-bit access cycles, data on the unused half of the data bus are not used and typically just stay at the value that was last present (because it would require a small amount of power supply current to change it to something else). For the nonmultiplexed MC68HC812A4, this would be the data from the previous cycle. For the multiplexed MC68HC912B32, the last value on those pins was a portion of the address for the same cycle. RLH and WLH cycles can occur only when there is a misaligned word access to the on-chip RAM and the cycle is visible on the external bus.

Typically, when the M68HC12 CPU makes a 16-bit access to an odd address (called a misaligned word access), the bus interface module splits the cycle into two successive 8-bit accesses. The CPU is momentarily frozen during the second 8-bit bus access. This split access is needed because typical 16-bit memories do not allow you to access portions of two separate 16-bit locations at the same time. The internal RAM in the M68HC12 is especially designed to allow misaligned word accesses in a single bus cycle. All even addresses are connected to the high-order 8 bits of the data bus while all odd addresses are connected to the low-order data bus. These sections have separate row decoders such that the high byte and low byte can come from adjacent 16-bit words. When the CPU accesses a 16-bit word at an odd address, the high byte of data comes from one address (row) in the RAM while the low byte comes from the next row. The high byte of data for the CPU is coming from a RAM location that is connected to the low half of the data bus and the low byte of data for the CPU is coming from a RAM location that is connected to the high half of the data bus. Internally, a bus swapper circuit exchanges the high and low bytes of data so they will be in the correct position for the CPU (the CPU is not aware of alignment and views memory as a linear array of 65,536 8-bit values). When these cycles are made visible on the external bus, the data appear in the incorrect order and the WLH and RLH cycle types instruct you to swap the data that were captured.

Because of the instruction queue in the M68HC12, we need to capture two more important pieces of information on each bus cycle. The IPIPE1 and IPIPE0 signals are optionally provided on the PE6/MODB and PE5/MODA pins, respectively. To see these signals, the PIPOE bit in the PEAR register must be set to 1. This is the default condition in special expanded mode. If the MCU is operating in normal modes, this bit must be set by the user in order to see the pipe status signals. At this time we are interested only in capturing this information. More detailed information about the operation of the pipe (or instruction queue) is provided in the next section.

The pipe status signals are time multiplexed to provide information about the movement of data into and through the pipe at E-rise (PER); the same two pins provide information about the start of execution of instructions and interrupts at E-fall (PEF). Table 14–5 provides mnemonic symbols and meanings for each state combination. The information in the upper half of the table allows you to reconstruct what is happening in the on-chip instruction queue. Once this information is known, the execution start information, captured at E-fall, can be used to tell what opcode is about to be executed. An interrupt is not an instruction in the user's program but it does correspond to execution of a specific sequence of microcode. The INT pipe status marks the start of the sequence of bus cycles associated with an interrupt.

Now that we know what signals need to be captured and which clock edges are used, we can show suggested logic analyzer setups for the MC68HC812A4 and the MC68HC912B32. The MC68HC812A4 has a nonmultiplexed address/data bus and can be configured for up to 22 bits of external address (A21–A0). Figure 14–3 shows a suggested setup for an HP16500 series analyzer. If you follow this and program the symbolic equivalents for the RW-TYP field from Table 14–4 and the PER and PEF fields from Table 14–5, you can get a useful listing display on the analyzer.

Explanation of Example 14–1

The analyzer labels allow you to group selected signals into a field where the label appears at the top of a column in the analyzer's state listing. You can choose to display each column in hexadecimal, binary, or as user-assigned symbols. We would choose to display the ADDR and DATA fields as hexadecimal values. We could display the R/$\overline{W}$ field as binary, but we do not need to display R/$\overline{W}$ in the listing because we have a more informative way to display that information (the RW-TYP field). The RW-TYP, PER, and PEF fields are displayed as symbols. Each line in the listing display will start with a state number (decimal) and show the information for one bus cycle.

If you would like to try to relate this logic analyzer state listing to a program, *lines 1–4* in the state listing of Example 14–1 correspond to a JSR WSerial_8 instruction. The WSerial_8 routine starts at *line 32* in Example A–1, Appendix A, and the cycle-by-cycle execution of the WSerial_8 program is shown in Figure A–2. Until we discuss the operation of the instruction pipe, it would be difficult for you to figure out the relationship of this analyzer listing to the WSerial_8 program unless you were told.

TABLE 14–5 Decoding Pipe Status Signals

IPIPE1:IPIPE0	Suggested Mnemonic	Meaning
E-Rise (PER)		
0:0	—	No data movement
0:1	LAT	Latch data from bus
1:0	ALD	Advance queue and load from data bus
1:1	ALL	Advance queue and load from latch
E-Fall (PEF)		
0:0	—	No start
0:1	INT	Start interrupt sequence
1:0	SEV	Start even instruction
1:1	SOD	Start odd instruction

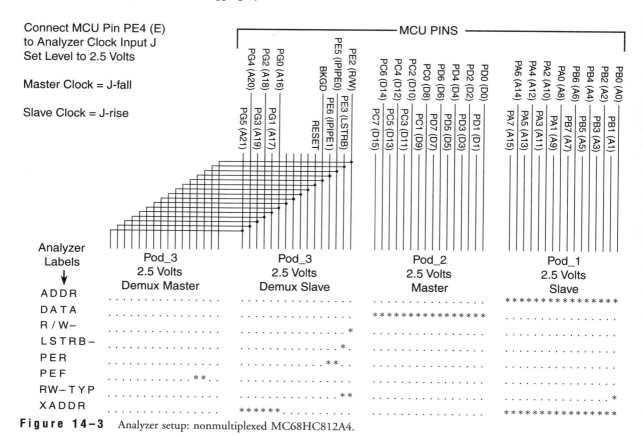

Figure 14-3   Analyzer setup: nonmultiplexed MC68HC812A4.

Figure 14–4 shows a suggested logic analyzer setup for the multiplexed MC68HC912B32. This is almost the same as for the MC68HC812A4 except Pod_1 is set up to capture both address and data (at different times within a bus cycle). The B32 also has no extra address lines. Once the bus state information is captured into records of one bus cycle each, it does not matter whether it came from a multiplexed or nonmultiplexed target MCU. The fields in the listing displays will be the same and the information will all be interpreted the same way. The only differences will be what is on the unused half of the data bus during 8-bit accesses and what is on the address and data lines during free (unused) bus cycles. Since these differences do not affect normal (intended) program operation, we will not explore them further.

The M68HC12 Instruction Queue (Pipeline)

> The M68HC12 uses an instruction queue to speed up program execution.

The M68HC12 includes a two- or three-word instruction queue to buffer program information into the CPU. Some documentation for this queue calls it a pipeline, but the term pipeline sometimes refers to the interleaving of operations from adjacent instructions. The M68HC12 always completes one instruction before starting the next so queue would be a more accurate term. It is OK to call the system a pipeline as long as you understand that this is an informal use of the term.

EXAMPLE 14–1   Sample Logic Analyzer Listing with Symbolic Fields

Label>	ADDR	DATA	RW_TYP	PER	PEF
Base >	Hex	Hex	Symbol	Symbol	Symbol
1	0E04	03CD	R16	ALD	
2	0E06	0008	R16	ALD	
3	0E08	CE40	R16	ALD	
4	09F8	0EBA	W16	LAT	sod
5	0E0A	C059	R16	ALL	
6	0E0C	B7C5	R16	ALD	sev
7	B7C5	B7C5	R8L	LAT	
8	0E0E	5BAE	R16	ALL	sod
9	0E10	5BAF	R16	ALD	sev
10	0E12	7A00	R16	ALD	sev
11	0E14	AE24	R16	ALD	
12	00AE	C0AE	W8H	LAT	sev
13	0E16	0E7B	R16	ALL	
14	00AF	00C0	W8L	LAT	sev
15	00AE	40AE	W8H	LAT	
16	40AE	40AE	R8H		
17	0E18	00AE	R16	ALL	sod
18	0E1A	B7C5	R16	ALD	sod
19	00AE	C0AE	W8H	ALD	
20	0E1C	59B7	R16		
21	0E1E	C503	R16	ALD	sev
22	0E20	2712	R16	ALD	sev
23	2712	2712	R16	LAT	sod
24	0E22	A720	R16	ALL	sod
25	0E24	EDB7	R16	ALD	sev
26	0E26	C559	R16	ALD	sev
27	C559	C559	R8L	LAT	sod
28	0E12	7A00	R16	ALL	
29	0E14	AE24	R16	ALD	
30	0E16	0E7B	R16	ALD	sev
31	00AE	40AE	W8H	LAT	
32	40AE	40AE	R8H		
33	0E18	00AE	R16	ALL	sod

The instruction queue greatly improves efficiency in two main ways. First, a queue acts as an elastic buffer for program information entering the CPU. Program words are always fetched as aligned 16-bit words and entered into the instruction queue. The CPU uses a 3-byte window into this queue and instructions may be from 1 to 6 bytes in length (note that this structure allows instructions to have an odd number of bytes unlike other 16-bit processors). In some 16-bit machines, instructions are required to be multiples of 16 bits. Since even the most simple instructions must use 16 bits of program memory, overall program size tends to be larger than it would be in the M68HC12.

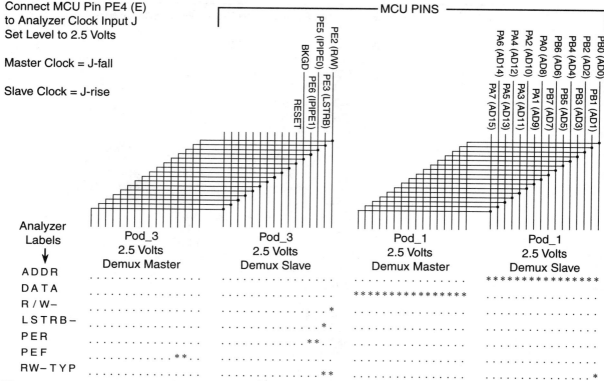

Figure 14-4   Analyzer setup: multiplexed MC68HC912B32.

The second way the instruction queue improves efficiency is by making three object code bytes available to the CPU at the start of each instruction. This allows the CPU to begin processing the instruction immediately rather than having to wait until the program information can be fetched into the CPU. There is a small penalty to refill the instruction queue whenever the processor executes a change-of-flow instruction such as a branch or jump. In these cases there is a three-cycle sequence to refill the instruction queue before starting to execute the new instruction. The ability to start all instructions earlier than if you had to wait for one or more bus accesses far outweighs the cost of refilling the queue on jumps and branches.

Each instruction is responsible for fetching enough 16-bit program information words to replace the number of bytes of object code in the instruction. The M68HC12 instruction set documentation includes single-letter codes for each type of bus cycle as shown in Table 14-6.[2] For example an LDAA #$55 instruction has two bytes of object code in the pipe (the opcode $86 and the operand $55). The cycle-by-cycle signature for this instruction is "P," which stands for a program word (16-bits) fetch. The load A extended version has 3 bytes, the opcode $B6 plus a 16-bit operand address. The cycle-by-cycle signature for this instruction is rOP. The r cycle is the read of a memory location into accumulator A. The P cycle is a program word fetch that replaces 2 of the 3 bytes

---

[2]   See the *CPU12 Reference Manual* (CPU12RM/AD) for information on complex sequences.

TABLE 14-6 CPU Cycle Access Details[a]

f		Free cycle; CPU doesn't use the bus
g		Read PPAGE internally
I		Read indirect pointer (indexed-indirect)
i		Read indirect PPAGE value (CALL indirect)
n		Write PPAGE internally
O		Optional program word fetch:
		P if the instruction is misaligned and has an odd number of object code bytes
		Otherwise a free cycle (f)
P		Program word fetch (always an aligned word)
r,	R	8- or 16-bit data read
s,	S	8- or 16-bit stack write
t,	T	8- or 16-bit conditional read (or free cycle)
u,	U	8- or 16-bit stack read
V		16-bit vector fetch
w,	W	8- or 16-bit data write
x		8-bit conditional write
PPP/P		Short branch, PPP if branch taken, P if not
OPPP/OP		Long branch, OPPP if branch taken, OPO if not

[a]*Each code letter equals one CPU cycle. Lower-case letters indicate 8-bit and upper-case letters indicate 16-bit operations.*

of object code for this instruction. The O cycle is an optional program word fetch. Remember that program information is always fetched as aligned 16-bit words. Instructions with an odd number of object code bytes will have an O cycle that counts as 1 byte of information to replenish the pipe. Each O cycle corresponds to either a free (f) bus cycle that fetches nothing or as a P cycle that fetches a 16-bit program information word. If an instruction has an odd number of bytes and the first byte of the instruction is misaligned, the O cycle will be treated as a program word fetch (P), otherwise the O cycle is treated as a free (f) cycle. The $18 prebyte for instructions on opcode map page 2 is treated by the CPU as a separate 1 byte instruction and always corresponds to an O cycle.

Figure 14–5 shows a functional block diagram of the instruction queue in the M68HC12. Program information is ALWAYS fetched into this queue as aligned 16-bit words. If the reset vector points to an odd address, information will be fetched into this queue starting at the even address just preceding the first instruction opcode at the odd reset vector. Similarly, when the CPU performs a branch or jump to an odd address, an extra byte of program information from the preceding even address is fetched.

The pipe is usually a two-word FIFO queue (when the latch stage is transparent), but occasionally a new word of information arrives before the other two stages are ready to advance and the latch acts as a third stage temporarily. There is a 4:3 byte multiplexer controlled by an alignment signal that selects Stage_2(even):Stage_2(odd):Stage_1(even) or Stage_2(odd):Stage_1(even):Stage_1(odd) to pass on to the CPU as the next 3 bytes of program information. When the CPU vectors, jumps, or branches to an even address, it sets the alignment signal. When the CPU vectors, jumps, or branches to an odd address it clears the alignment signal. Whenever the CPU executes an instruction with an odd number of object code bytes, it toggles the alignment signal. In this way, the alignment signal keeps track of whether the next instruction opcode is located at an even (aligned) or odd (misaligned) address. The pipe logic keeps track of this signal and the CPU is essentially unaware of alignment at any specific time.

Because of various propagation delays, there is a one cycle delay after the CPU fetches a piece of data before it can be used by the CPU. This delay is present regardless of whether the informa-

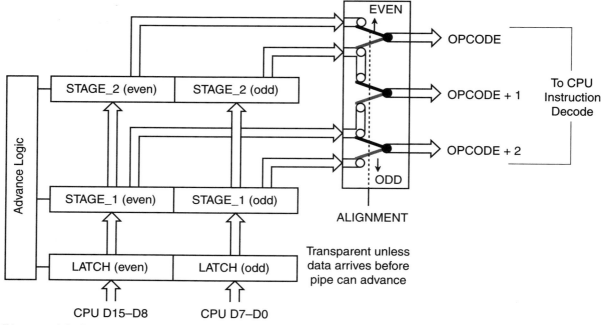

Figure 14–5 M68HC12 instruction queue (pipe).

tion is fetched from an internal or an external address. Consider the instruction "aaaa 9601 LDAA $01 ;read PORTB." The cycle-by-cycle signature for this instruction is rfP where the r stands for an 8-bit read (from PORTB at address $0001), the f is a free cycle because the CPU cannot see the data that were fetched by the r cycle yet, and the P cycle is a program word fetch to get another word of program information to replace the 9601 (LDAA opcode and direct address) that was in the pipe. Because the opcode (96) and operand address (01) were already in the instruction queue when the instruction started, it was able to perform the PORTB read in the first cycle of the instruction. If you think about this, you should realize that the CPU was already working on this instruction a little before the read-PORTB cycle because it had to build a 16-bit address out of the instruction-supplied 01 and a CPU-supplied upper byte of 00. Another way to think about this is that there is about one cycle of offset between what the CPU is working on and what we see on the external bus.

This apparent delay also means the CPU starts to fetch information into the pipe before it knows whether the pipe is ready to advance. Consider the case of an aligned single byte instruction such as a NOP. After this instruction is executed the high byte of the leading pipe stage is free to be pushed out of the pipe, but the low byte of the same word in the pipe is still needed (it is the opcode of the next instruction). If the cycle before this NOP was a program word fetch (P cycle), the data arrive at the input to the pipe before the pipe is ready to advance. In this case, the latch stage before Stage 1 of the pipe latches the information from the data bus but does not advance the pipe. As soon as the pipe is ready to advance, the Stage 1 information advances to Stage 2 and the information from the latch advances into Stage 1.

As Table 14–5 showed, there are four possible actions for the pipe in each bus cycle. PER (the status captured on IPIPE1:IPIPE0 at E-rise) pipe status 0:0 corresponds to no movement of information in the pipe. Pipe status 1:0 (ALD) means advance the pipe and load Stage 1 from the data bus (the latch stage is transparent at the time). Status 0:1 (LAT) means the pipe is not ready to advance so just latch the information from the data bus. Status 1:1 (ALL) means advance the pipe and load Stage 1 from the latch. It is possible to see more than one LAT cycle before you see an ALL cycle. In that case, the latch continues to hold the data that were present at the time of the first LAT cycle. The latch can become cleared (made transparent again) if a change of flow after a LAT cycle leads to an ALD cycle before an ALL cycle appeared.

The reason we need the information about movement of data through the pipe is that the execution status PEF (latched from IPIPE1:IPIPE0 at E-fall) refers to the information at the head (Stage 2) of the pipe. If you do not know what is in the pipe, you (or your logic analyzer) cannot tell which instruction is about to start executing.

Inside the M68HC12 only the data are captured and processed through the pipe. To reconstruct what instructions are executing, based on analysis of bus information, we will want to keep track of both data and address in the reconstructed pipe. The CPU does not need to do this because it has an elaborate block of logic to keep track of the program counter as instructions are executed.

Cycle-by-Cycle Mnemonic Codes

The M68HC12 instruction set documentation[3] includes single-letter codes for each type of bus cycle as shown in Table 14–6. We see these codes in Appendix A, Figures A–1 to A–6, where we document the relationship between the software BDM serial communication primitives and the signal at an MCU output pin. These code letters give us a good way to document logic analyzer listings but a few additions would help. O cycles can be executed as a free (f) cycle or as a program word fetch cycle (P). To clarify this in an analyzer listing we can use the mnemonics O-f and O-P. When the CPU performs a misaligned 16-bit memory access, or when the external data bus is 8 bits, the bus interface splits the CPU cycle into two 8-bit bus access cycles. We can use the mnemonics Wh, Wl, Rh, Rl, Sh, Sl, Uh, Ul, and in the case of an 8-bit external data bus Ph and Pl to document these cycles in an analyzer listing. For O-P cycles in a system with an 8-bit external data bus we can use the mnemonics OPh and OPl.

Working with Bus State Information

The pipe can be reconstructed manually or by software processing of captured bus state information. In an emulator, it is also possible to reconstruct the pipe in real time using hardware logic. However, you cannot stop the CPU by an interrupt before it executes a selected instruction because you cannot reconstruct the internal pipe activity quickly enough to realize an instruction has started until it is already being processed by the CPU. Manual reconstruction is straightforward though somewhat tedious. With a little practice, it is easy to reconstruct enough to establish a ref-

---

3 *CPU12 Reference Guide*, CPU12RG/AD, Motorola, 1998.

erence to a known instruction, and then you can write down the instructions with their cycle-by-cycle codes rather than continuing to rebuild the pipe. We will follow an example to show how this process works.

To reconstruct the pipe, we follow a small set of simple rules.

1. When we see an ALD cycle, we advance the information from Stage 1 of the pipe to Stage 2 and load the information from the data field of the PREVIOUS CYCLE into Stage 1.

2. When we see a LAT cycle, we copy the information from the data field of the previous cycle into the latch stage.

3. When we see an ALL cycle, we advance the information from Stage 1 of the pipe to Stage 2 and load the information from the latch into Stage 1.

Explanation of Example 14–2

Example 14–2 uses the same bus state information that was shown in Example 14–1 except we have added three columns corresponding to the Latch, Stage 1, and Stage 2 of the reconstructed pipe. Within each of these fields we list an address (four hex digits), a slash (/), and four hex digits of data. Initially we do not know what should be in any of these fields so we put question marks. At the first ALD or LAT cycle, we can begin to replace the question marks with known data. Since program information is always fetched as aligned 16-bit words, the addresses in these pipe reconstruction fields will always be even values.

The only reason we rebuild internal pipe activity is so we can tell what instruction is about to execute. Whenever we see an SEV or SOD cycle (start-even or start-odd), it means the next bus cycle will be the first cycle of the instruction whose opcode is in the even (odd) half of pipe Stage 2 during the corresponding SEV or SOD cycle. An INT cycle means the next bus cycle will be the first cycle of an interrupt response sequence. The interrupt response sequence has the same cycle signature as an SWI instruction.

In state 1 we see an ALD cycle, but since we cannot see the data from the previous cycle we cannot start to reconstruct the pipe yet. State 2 is another ALD cycle so we fill in the address and data from State 1 (0E04/03CD) into pipe Stage 1. Cycle 3 is an ALD cycle again so we move the 0E04/03CD from Stage 1 to Stage 2 and then fill in 0E06/0008 from address/data of state 2 into pipe Stage 1. Cycle 4 is a LAT cycle so we copy address/data (0E08/CE40 from state 3 to the latch stage of the pipe. We also see that state 4 is an SOD cycle, which means the instruction opcode in the odd (low) half of pipe Stage 2 will start to execute in the next cycle.

We reverse assemble the opcode $CD at 0E05 to get the following program instruction:

```
0E05 CD0008 LDY #$0008
```

The cycle signature for the LDY immediate instruction is OP and since the instruction is misaligned, the O cycle will be processed as a P cycle. Between the RW_TYPE and PER fields we write O-P in state 5 and P in state 6.

Since the LDY instruction is 3 bytes and it started at 0E05, the next instruction will start at 0E08 which is even. This agrees with the SEV in cycle 6. If we assume the CPU is working as it should, we do not have to keep track of the pipe anymore after we have established the relationship between a known instruction (LDY at 0E05 in this case) and the associated cycles in the state

EXAMPLE 14–2   Bus State Listing with Manual Pipe Reconstruction

Label>	ADDR	DATA	RW_TYP	PER	PEF	PT7	Pipe reconstruction and disassembly		
Base >	Hex	Hex	Symbol	Symbol	Symbol	Bin	Latch	Stage 1	Stage 2
1	0E04	03CD	R16	ALD		1	????/????	????/????	????/????
2	0E06	0008	R16	ALD		1	????/????	0E04/03CD	????/????
3	0E08	CE40	R16	ALD		1	????/????	0E06/0008	0E04/03CD
4	09F8	0EBA	W16_	_LAT	sod	1	0E08/CE40	0E06/0008	0E04/03CD
5	0E0A	C059	R16	O-P ALL		1	0E05	CD0008	LDY #8
6	0E0C	B7C5	R16_	P _ALD	sev	1			
7	B7C5	B7C5	R8L	O-f LAT		1	0E08	CE40C0	LDX #$40C0
8	0E0E	5BAE	R16_	P _ALL	sod	1			
9	0E10	5BAF	R16_	O-P _ALD	sev	1	0E0B	59	ASLD
10	0E12	7A00	R16_	P _ALD	sev	1	0E0C	B7C5	XGDX
11	0E14	AE24	R16	P ALD		1	0E0E	5BAE	STAB $AE
12	00AE	C0AE	W8H_	w _LAT	sev	1		(write $C0 to $00AE)	
13	0E16	0E7B	R16	P ALL		1	0E10	5BAF	STAB $AF
14	00AF	00C0	W8L_	w _LAT	sev	1		(write $C0 to $00AF)	
15	00AE	40AE	W8H	w LAT		0	0E12	7A00AE	STAA $00AE
16	40AE	40AE	R8H	O-f		0		(write $40 to $00AE)	
17	0E18	00AE	R16_	P _ALL	sod	0			
18	0E1A	B7C5	R16_	P _ALD	sod	0	0E15	200E	BRA $0E25
19	00AE	C0AE	W8H	w ALD		1	0E17	7B00AE	STAB $00AE
20	0E1C	59B7	R16	O-P		1		(write $C0 to $00AE)	
21	0E1E	C503	R16_	P _ALD	sev	1			
22	0E20	2712	R16_	P _ALD	sev	1	0E1A	B7C5	XGDX
23	2712	2712	R16_	O-f _LAT	sod	1	0E1C	59	ASLD
24	0E22	A720	R16_	P _ALL	sod	1	0E1D	B7C5	XGDX
25	0E24	EDB7	R16_	O-P _ALD	sev	1	0E1F	03	DEY
26	0E26	C559	R16_	P _ALD	sev	1	0E15	2712	BRA $0E34
27	C559	C559	R8L_	O-f _LAT	sod	1	0E22	A7	NOP
28	0E12	7A00	R16	P ALL		1	0E23	20ED	BRA $0E12
29	0E14	AE24	R16	P ALD		1			
30	0E16	0E7B	R16_	P _ALD	sev	1			
31	00AE	40AE	W8H	w LAT		0	0E12	7A00AE	STAA $00AE
32	40AE	40AE	R8H	O-f		0		(write $40 to $00AE)	
33	0E18	00AE	R16_	P _ALL	sod	0			

listing. From here we can simply follow and disassemble instructions, one after the other. If you ever get lost or just want to check, you can rebuild the pipe again for a few cycles and verify your relationship to the state listing again.

By keeping track of the cycle codes, we can determine what values are read or written during an instruction. For example, cycles 31–33 correspond to an STAA $00AE instruction whose signature is wOP. By looking at the CPU address and data, we see that $40 was written to $00AE in cycle 31.

EXAMPLE 14–3   Bus State Listing for a Narrow Bus MC68HC812A4 System

Label>	ADDR	DATA	RW_TYP	PER	PEF	Time	PT7	Latch	Stage 1	Stage 2
Base >	Hex	Hex	Symbol	Symbol	Symbol	Relative	Bin			
1	0E04	03FF	R8H	ALD		248 ns	1	????/????	????/????	????/????
2	0E05	CDFF	R8L			256 ns	1			
3	0E06	00FF	R8H	ALD		248 ns	1	????/????	0E04/03CD	????/????
4	0E07	08FF	R8L			248 ns	1			
5	0E08	CEFF	R8H	ALD		248 ns	1	????/????	0E06/0008	0E04/03CD
6	0E09	40FF	R8L			256 ns	1			
7	09F8	0EBA	W16	_LAT_	sod	120 ns	1	0E08/CE40	0E06/0008	0E04/03CD
8	0E0A	C0BA	R8H OPh	ALL		256 ns	1	0E05 CD0008	LDY	#8
9	0E0B	59BA	R8L OPl			248 ns	1			
10	0E0C	B7FF	R8H Ph	ALD		248 ns	1			
11	0E0D	C5FF	R8L Pl		sev	248 ns	1			
12	0E0D	C5FF	R8L O-f	LAT		128 ns	1	0E08 CE40C0	LDX	#$40C0
13	0E0E	5BFF	R8H Ph	ALL		248 ns	1			
14	0E0F	AEFF	R8L Pl		sod	256 ns	1			
15	0E10	5BFF	R8H Ph	ALD		248 ns	1	OEOB 59		ASLD
16	0E11	AFFF	R8L Pl		sev	248 ns	1			
17	0E12	7AFF	R8H Ph	ALD		248 ns	1	0E0C B7C5		XGDX
18	0E13	00FF	R8L Pl		sev	248 ns	1			
19	0E14	AEFF	R8H Ph	ALD		256 ns	1	0E0E 5BAE	STAB	$AE
20	0E15	24FF	R8L Pl			248 ns	1			
21	00AE	C0FF	W8H w	_LAT_	sev	128 ns	1	(write $C0 to $00AE)		
22	0E16	0EFF	R8H Ph	ALL		248 ns	1	0E10 5BAF	STAB	$AF
23	0E17	7BFF	R8L Pl			248 ns	1			
24	00AF	7BC0	W8L w	_LAT_	sev	128 ns	1	(write $C to $00AF)		
25	00AE	40C0	W8H w	LAT		120 ns	0	0E12 7A00AE	STAA	$00AE
26	00AE	40C0	R8H O-f			128 ns	0	(write $40 to $00AE)		
27	0E18	00DE	R8H Ph	ALL		248 ns	0			
28	0E19	AEFF	R8L Pl		sod	248 ns	0			
29	0E1A	B7FF	R8H Ph	ALD		256 ns	0	0E15 200E	BRA	$0E25
30	0E1B	C5FF	R8L Pl		sod	248 ns	0	(not taken)		
31	00AE	C0FF	W8H w	ALD		128 ns	1	0E17 7B00AE	STAB	$00AE
32	0E1C	59FF	R8H OPh			248 ns	1	(write $C0 to $00AE)		
33	0E1D	B7FF	R8L OPl			248 ns	1			
34	0E1E	C5FF	R8H Ph	ALD		248 ns	1			
35	0E1F	03FF	R8L Pl		sev	256 ns	1			
36	0E20	27FF	R8H Ph	ALD		248 ns	1	0E1A B7C5		XGDX
37	0E21	12FF	R8L Pl		sev	248 ns	1			
38	0E21	12FF	R8L O-f	_LAT_	sod	128 ns	1	0E1C 59		ASLD
39	0E22	A7FF	R8H Ph	ALL		248 ns	1	0E1D B7C5		XGDX
40	0E23	20FF	R8L Pl		sod	248 ns	1			
41	0E24	EDFF	R8H OPh	ALD		248 ns	1	0E1F 03		DEY
42	0E25	B7FF	R8L OPl		sev	256 ns	1			

EXAMPLE 14–3   Continued

43	0E26	C5FF	R8H	Ph	ALD		248	ns	1	0E15	2712	BRA	$0E34
44	0E27	59FF	R8L	Pl		sev	248	ns	1			(not taken)	
45	0E27	59FF	R8L	O-f	_LAT	sod	128	ns	1	0E22	A7		NOP
46	0E12	7AFF	R8H	Ph	ALL		248	ns	1	0E23	20ED	BRA	$0E12
47	0E13	00FF	R8L	Pl			248	ns	1			(taken)	
48	0E14	AEFF	R8H	Ph	ALD		256	ns	1				
49	0E15	24FF	R8L	Pl			248	ns	1				
50	0E16	0EFF	R8H	Ph	ALD		248	ns	1				
51	0E17	7BFF	R8L	Pl		sev	248	ns	1				
52	00AE	40FF	W8H	w	LAT		128	ns	0	0E12	7A00AE	STAA	$00AE
53	00AE	40FF	R8H	O-f			128	ns	0		(write $40 to $00AE)		
54	0E18	00FF	R8H	Ph	ALL		248	ns	0				
55	0E19	AEFF	R8L	Pl		sod	248	ns	0				

Explanation of Example 14–3

This example shows the state capture information for an MC68HC812A4 that is configured for expanded-narrow mode. The narrow expansion bus means the MCU can only fetch 8 bits of data at a time from external addresses. Internal addresses can still access 16-bit data and, if internal visibility is enabled, you will see all 16 bits of data in a single cycle. States 8 and 9 show an example of the CPU fetching a 16-bit word of program information as two 8-bit pieces. RW_TYP indicates R8L in cycle 9 even though the data are actually in the high half of the data field. This is because all data from external accesses use the high half of the data bus. In narrow modes, the low half of the data bus is used only for visibility of internal accesses. State 7 is an example of a 16-bit access to an internal memory location. The RW_TYP is W16 and the address is $09F8, which is in the internal RAM.

Example 14–3 is the same program sequence as Example 14–2 except it is running in a narrow MC68HC812A4 system instead of a wide MC68HC912B32. The same program instructions take 33 states (cycles) in the wide system and 55 states in the narrow system. Although there is a significant penalty for using a narrow system, it is not as bad as 2:1. The system in Example 14–3 also stretches accesses to external memory by a factor of one extra E-rate clock per external access. This is visible in the relative time column that was not included in the other examples. States 12 and 21 are examples of free or internal accesses and show a time of about 128 nsec each. States 8–11 are external accesses so they take about 256 nsec each.

The program shown in Examples 14–2 and 14–3 is the WSerial_8 program that is shown in Appendix A, Figure A–2. This program uses instruction timing to control the serial data stream to the BDM interface of a target MCU. This program should be run only from internal memory. The PT7 column in the bus state listings shows the state of the output pin that drives BKGD. We can clearly see by comparing states 15–18 of Example 14–2 to states 25–30 of Example 14–3 that the timing is significantly slower in the narrow system. This is because external accesses are stretched (slower) and 16-bit external accesses are split into two 8-bit accesses.

The pipe reconstruction is similar to Example 14–2 except we now need to look at the previous two cycles to get the data for the LAT and ALD cycles. In state 3 the ALD indicates we should copy the address and data from the previous CPU cycle into pipe Stage 1. But the previous CPU cycle was a 16-bit read from $0E04, which was split into two 8-bit reads in states 1 and 2. Otherwise the pipe reconstruction follows the same pattern as the previous example.

In state 7 we see an SOD cycle and we are able to disassemble the LDY #8 instruction at $0E05. The cycle signature is OP and the instruction is misaligned so the O cycle will be treated as a program fetch. Both the O-P and P cycles need to be split into successive 8-bit accesses so we fill in OPh, OPl, Ph, and Pl in states 8–11, respectively.

There is another complication in reading bus information in a narrow system. External accesses use only the high order data pins so an R8L cycle would still show the data in the high half of the data field. An 8-bit write to an odd address (W8L) in internal memory would show its data in the low half of the data field because the internal visibility cycles work just like cycles in a wide system. State 11 is an example of an R8L cycle to external memory and state 24 is an example of a W8L cycle to internal memory. Unlike the normal 16-bit data bus case, in a narrow system you need to be aware of the memory map (what is internal vs. external space).

If internal visibility is turned off, you do not even see the addresses and data during internal accesses. If E-clock stretching is also on to accommodate slow external memory, you do not even see the E-clock during internal accesses so no bus states are captured for internal accesses. For these reasons, it is strongly recommended that an analyzer or emulator should always enable internal visibility and connect leads to capture all 16 bits of data even in a narrow system.

Explanation of Example 14–4

This example shows the D-Bug12 monitor program responding to an interrupt. This provides a detailed view of the pseudovector mechanism that is implemented in D-Bug12. We will also see the details of the interrupt and RTI operations. Finally we will see how a bus trace can help you identify a bug in your program where usual debug monitor techniques might not let you zero in on the bug as quickly.

State 1 is an INT cycle, meaning the next bus cycle will be a vector fetch leading to interrupt processing. Since this interrupt vector fetch will tell us exactly where the next instruction is located, we do not need to go through the tedious process of reconstructing the pipe. Interrupt processing has the same cycle signature as an SWI instruction [VSPSSPSsP]. From the vector fetch in state 2 we see the vector $FF4E was fetched from $FFEC, which means the timer channel 1 caused this interrupt and the service routine starts at address $FF4E. We could even decipher what was in all of the CPU registers by taking note of what is pushed onto the stack. For example, in state 9 the CCR value $88 was pushed onto the stack at address $09F7. Watching bus activity during certain cycles in an instruction can tell us other things. State 12 is the I cycle in an indexed indirect jump. We see that the ultimate jump destination $DBDF is fetched from $F7EC.

Now let us look for our bug. States 11–40 correspond to the pseudovector function in the D-Bug12 monitor. Since a user cannot change the actual vector contents, which are part of D-Bug12 in the flash memory, D-Bug12 accesses a pseudovector from RAM that tells where it should go in response to an interrupt. This pseudovector is also checked so the monitor can warn a user if an interrupt arrives and the user has not set the pseudovector.

States 41–55 correspond to our interrupt service routine. If we look closely at the RTI instruction in states 46–55, we note that it follows the cycle sequence for a pending interrupt. Instead of returning to the user program that was originally interrupted, flow goes to the next pending interrupt. Even closer inspection reveals that the vector fetch is to $FFEC, which is another request from timer channel 1, which is the source we just serviced. We never cleared the TC1F flag before we returned so we are stuck in an infinite loop servicing a continuous interrupt from the timer. This sort of problem is easy to see on a logic analyzer, but it is more difficult to find with a debugging monitor.

EXAMPLE 14–4   Bus State Listing with Interrupt Bug

Label>Base>	ADDR Hex	DATA Hex	RW_TYP Symbol		PER Symbol	PEF Symbol	Pipe reconstruction and disassembly (interrupt so no need to reconstruct pipe)			
1	0830	CD61	R16		ALL	int				
2	FFEC	FF4E	R16	V	ALD		Begin interrupt response			
3	09FE	082D	W16	S	LAT		Vector was $FF4E at $FFEC			
4	FF4E	05FB	R16	P						
5	09FC	8602	W16	S	ALD					
6	09FA	9876	W16	S						
7	FF50	F89A	R16	P						
8	09F8	6402	W16	S	ALD					
9	09F7	0988	W8L	s						
10	FF52	05FB	R16	P		sev				
11	05FB	05FB	R8L	f	ALD		FF4E	05FBF89A	JMP	[F89A,PC]
12	F7EC	DBDF	R16	I			indirect fetch of $DBDF			
13	DBDF	DBDF	R8L	f						
14	DBDE	8FCD	R16	P						
15	DBE0	000F	R16	P	ALD					
16	DBE2	CCFF	R16	P	ALD	sod				
17	DBE4	EC20	R16	O-P	ALD		DBDF	CD000F	LDY	#$000F
18	DBE6	87CD	R16	P	ALD	sev				
19	87CD	87CD	R8L	O-f	LAT		DBE2	CCFFEC	LDD	#$FFEC
20	DBE8	0010	R16	P	ALL	sod				
20	DB6E	C43F	R16	P	ALD		DBE5	2087	BRA	$DB6E (taken)
22	DB70	CE0B	R16	P	ALD					
23	DB72	001A	R16	P	ALD	sev				
24	DB74	E5EC	R16	P	ALD	sev	DB6E	C43F	ANDB	#$3F
25	E5EC	E5EC	R16	O-f	LAT		DB70	CE0B00	LDX	#$0B00
26	DB76	0026	R16	P	ALL	sod				
27	DB78	057D	R16	P	ALD		DB73	1AE5	LEAX	B,X
28	DB78	057D	R16	P		sod				
29	0B2C	0900	R16	R	ALD		DB75	EC00	LDD	0,X
30	0900	0900	R16	f			(read $0900 from $0BC2)			
31	DB7A	0AC1	R16	P		sod				
32	DB7E	05E3	R16	P	ALD		DB77	2605	BRA	$DB7E (taken)
33	DB80	0000	R16	P	ALD					
34	DB82	CD00	R16	P	ALD	sev				
35	CD00	CD00	R16	f	ALD		DB7E	05E50000	JMP	[0000,X]
36	0B2C	0900	R16	I			indirect fetch of $0900			
37	0900	0900	R16	f						
38	0900	CE98	R16	P						
39	0902	767E	R16	P	ALD					
40	0904	6000	R16	P	ALD	sev				
41	6000	6000	R16	O-f	LAT		0900	CE9876	LDX	#$9876
42	0906	0B81	R16	P	ALL	sod				
43	6000	9876	W16	W	ALD		0903	7E6000	STX	$6000

EXAMPLE 14-4   Continued

```
44     0908  4D86  R16  O-P                              (write $9876 to $6000)
45_____090A  8062  R16  P____ALD____sev____
46     09F7  0988  R8L  u     LAT              0906   0B       RTI
47     09F8  6402  R16  U
48     09FA  9876  R16  U
49     09FE  082D  R16  U
50     09FC  8602  R16  U
51     FFEC  FF4E  R16  V    ←Interrupt was still pending
52     FF4E  FF4E  R16  f
53     FF4E  05FB  R16  P
54     FF50  F89A  R16  P     ALD
55_____FF52  05FB  R16  P____ALD____sev____
```

14.7 Hardware Breakpoints

Hardware breakpoints can be generated internally in the MC68HC912B32.

Hardware breakpoints provide a way to stop normal execution of an application program without adding external hardware. The MC68HC812A4 does not have a hardware breakpoint module, but the MC68HC912B32 does and we will study it in this section. Other newer derivatives in the M68HC12 family have slightly different breakpoint capabilities, but they use the same building blocks and functions as the breakpoint module described here. One of the new features on a newer breakpoint module is the addition of extra address bits so you can set breakpoints in paged expansion memory.

Successful breakpoint events can cause one of two actions depending on the selected breakpoint mode. A breakpoint can cause the MCU to go into active BDM mode, or it can cause the CPU to execute an SWI instruction instead of the opcode at the breakpoint address. There are two different mechanisms for handling a breakpoint. The first is similar to the tagging mechanism discussed in Section 14.5. A breakpoint register is set with the address of the opcode where a breakpoint is desired. The breakpoint tagging mechanism causes the CPU to execute a BGND or an SWI instruction rather than the opcode at the breakpoint address. The breakpoint must be set at the address of an instruction opcode and R/$\overline{W}$ and data are not used in the match comparison. In addition to this tagging mechanism, R/$\overline{W}$ and data can be included in the match comparisons and the breakpoint address can be set anywhere. This interrupt-like mechanism causes the CPU to enter active BDM mode at the next instruction boundary after the match event occurred. In all cases in which the breakpoint causes the MCU to enter active BDM mode, it is assumed that the ENBDM control bit in the BDM STATUS register has been previously set to allow active BDM mode (or the MCU will just return to the application program).

Breakpoint Module Registers and Control Bits

The heart of the breakpoint module is a 34-bit comparator that can be configured for various comparison modes. There are six, 8-bit registers associated with the breakpoint module. Breakpoint Control Registers 0 and 1 (BRKCT0 and BRKCT1) contain bits to set up conditions for the breakpoints and match bits for two R/$\overline{\text{W}}$ conditions. The remaining four registers (BRKAH, BRKAL, BRKDH, and BRKDL) provide match bits for the other 32 comparator bits. Control bits allow various parts of the comparator to be disabled so you can choose to ignore R/$\overline{\text{W}}$ or parts of the address or data.

Version 2.0.2 of the D-Bug12 monitor added a command (USEHBR) to support limited use of the hardware breakpoints in the MC68HC912B32. This function works in EVB or POD modes and allows one or two address breakpoints to be set. When the evaluation board is in POD mode, the dual address BDM mode of the breakpoint module (using the tagging mechanism) is used. When the evaluation board is in EVB mode, the dual address SWI mode of the breakpoint module (which also uses the tagging mechanism) is used. Since the tagging mechanism is used, the two breakpoints must be set to the addresses of instruction opcodes.

BRKCT0—$0020—Breakpoint Control Register 0

Bit 7	6	5	4	3	2	1	Bit 0
BRKEN1	BRKEN0	BKPM	0	BK1ALE	BK0ALE	0	0

Reset 0   0   0   0   0   0   0   0

BKEN1:BKEN0
Breakpoint Mode Enable Bits.
BKPM
Breakpoint on Program Address.

BRKEN1	BRKEN0	BKPM	Configuration
0	0	x	**Off**—no breakpoints enabled (default).
0	1	x	**Dual Address SWI** (tag)—two independent 16-bit breakpoints based on 16-bit addresses only will cause the MCU to execute an SWI instruction instead of executing the instruction at the break location (the tag mechanism is used).
1	0	x	**Full Address/Data Breakpoint** (int)—one 33-bit breakpoint based on a 16-bit address, 16-bit data, and R/$\overline{\text{W}}$ will cause the MCU to enter active BDM at the next instruction boundary after a match (the interrupt mechanism is used).
1	1	0	**Dual Address BDM** (int)—two independent 17-bit breakpoints based on 16-bit addresses and R/$\overline{\text{W}}$ will cause the MCU to enter active BDM at the next instruction boundary after a match (the interrupt mechanism is used).
1	1	1	**Dual Address BGND** (tag)—two independent 16-bit breakpoints based on 16-bit addresses only will cause the MCU to execute a BGND instruction instead of executing the instruction at the break location (the tag mechanism is used).

BK1ALE

Enable comparison of low order address with BRKDL match register.

    0 = Low order address ignored in comparison resulting in a match on any address in a 256-byte range set by the BRKDH match register (default).

    1 = Low order address must match BRKDL match register to trigger a breakpoint.

This bit is not used when the breakpoint is configured for full address/data operation.

BK0ALE

Enable comparison of low order address with BRKAL match register.

    0 = Low order address ignored in comparison resulting in a match on any address in a 256-byte range set by the BRKAH match register (default).

    1 = Low order address must match BRKAL match register to trigger a breakpoint.

BRKCT1—$0021—Breakpoint Control Register 1

Bit 7	6	5	4	3	2	1	Bit 0
0	BKDBE	BKMBH	BKMBL	BRK1RWE	BK1RW	BK0RWE1	BK0RW

Reset 0   0   0   0   0   0   0   0

BKDBE

Breakpoint Data Bus Enable.

    0 = BRKDH and BRKDL match registers are ignored (default).

    1 = BRKDH and BRKDL registers are used to compare address or data (depending on the mode selections BKEN1 and BKEN0; see Table 14–7).

BKMBH

Breakpoint Match High Byte.

    0 = High order data ignored in comparison (default).

    1 = High order data must match BRKDH match register to trigger a breakpoint.

Enable comparison of high order data with BRKDH match register. This bit is not used if any dual address comparison is specified, or if BKDBE = 0.

BKMBL

Breakpoint Match Low Byte.

  0 = Low order data ignored in comparison (default).

  1 = Low order data must match BRKDL match register to trigger a breakpoint.

This bit is not used if any dual address comparison is specified or if BKDBE = 0.

BK1RWE

Breakpoint 1 R/$\overline{W}$ Enable.

  0 = R/$\overline{W}$ ignored in comparison (default).

  1 = R/$\overline{W}$ must match BK1RW match bit to trigger a breakpoint.

This bit is ignored unless dual address BDM (int) comparison is specified with BKEN1:BKEN0:BKPM = 1:1:0.

BK1RW

Breakpoint 1 R/$\overline{W}$ Value.

  0 = Trigger breakpoint on a write cycle (default).

  1 = Trigger breakpoint on a read cycle.

Match bit for comparison with R/$\overline{W}$ when dual address BDM (int) comparison is specified with BKEN1:BKEN0:BKPM = 1:1:0 and BKDBE = BK1RWE = 1.

BK0RWE

Breakpoint 0 R/$\overline{W}$ Enable.

  0 = R/$\overline{W}$ ignored in comparison (default).

  1 = R/$\overline{W}$ must match BK0RW match bit to trigger a breakpoint.

This bit is ignored unless dual address BDM (int) or full address/data (int) comparison is specified with BKEN1:BKEN0:BKPM = 1:1:0 or 1:0:x.

BK0RW

Breakpoint 0 R/$\overline{W}$ Value.

  0 = Trigger breakpoint on a write cycle (default).

  1 = Trigger breakpoint on a read cycle.

Match bit for comparison with R/$\overline{W}$ when dual address BDM (int) or full address/data comparison is specified with BKEN1:BKEN0:BKPM = 1:1:0 or 1:0:x and BK0RWE = 1.

BRKAH—$0022—Breakpoint Match Register for High Order Address

Bit 7	6	5	4	3	2	1	Bit 0
15	14	13	12	11	10	9	8

Reset 0	0	0	0	0	0	0	0

These bits are compared against the most significant byte of the address bus. See Table 14–7.

BRKAL—$0023—Breakpoint Match Register for Low Order Address

Bit 7	6	5	4	3	2	1	Bit 0
7	6	5	4	3	2	1	0

Reset 0	0	0	0	0	0	0	0

These bits are compared against the least significant byte of the address bus. See Table 14–7.

BRKDH—$0024—Breakpoint Match Register for High Order Data

Bit 7	6	5	4	3	2	1	Bit 0
15	14	13	12	11	10	9	8

Reset 0	0	0	0	0	0	0	0

These bits are compared against the most significant byte of the data bus or the most significant byte of the address bus in dual address modes. See Table 14–7.

TABLE 14-7 Breakpoint Control Bits and Register Use

Breakpoints Disabled

BKEN1:BKEN0:BKPM	0:0:x

Dual Address SWI Breakpoint (tag instruction at breakpoint address and execute SWI)

BKEN1:BKEN0:BKPM	0:1:x
BRKAH	Breakpoint 0 high byte address
BRKAL	If BK0ALE = 1, breakpoint 0 low byte address
	If BK0ALE = 0, don't care; breakpoint anywhere in 256-byte block
BRKDH	Breakpoint 1 high byte address.
BRKDL	If BK1ALE = 1, breakpoint 1 low byte address
	If BK1ALE = 0, don't care; breakpoint anywhere in 256-byte block
BK0RWE	Don't care; R/$\overline{\text{W}}$ not used
BK0RW	Don't care
BK1RWE	Don't care; R/$\overline{\text{W}}$ not used
BK1RW	Don't care

Full Address/Data Breakpoint (interrupt when match and enter BDM)

BKEN1:BKEN0:BKPM	1:0:x	
BRKAH	Breakpoint high byte address	
BRKAL	If BK0ALE = 1, breakpoint low byte address	
	If BK0ALE = 0, don't care; breakpoint anywhere in 256-byte block	
BRKDH	If BKMBH = 1, breakpoint on high byte data	
	If BKMBH = 0, high data byte is don't care	
BRKDL	If BKMBL = 1, breakpoint on low byte data	
	If BKMBL = 0, low data byte is don't care	
BK1ALE	Don't care	
	BK0RWE = 1	**BK0RWE = 0**
BK0RW	0 = Read cycle	Don't care
	1 = Write cycle	
BK1RWE	Don't care	
BK1RW	Don't care	

Dual Address BDM Breakpoint (interrupt at breakpoint address and enter BDM)

BKEN1:BKEN0:BKPM	1:1:0	
BRKAH	Breakpoint 0 high byte address	
BRKAL	If BK0ALE = 1, breakpoint 0 low byte address	
	If BK0ALE = 0, don't care; breakpoint anywhere in 256-byte block	
BRKDH	Breakpoint 1 high byte address	
BRKDL	If BK1ALE = 1, breakpoint 1 low byte address	
	If BK1ALE = 0, don't care; breakpoint anywhere in 256 byte block	
	BK0RWE = 1	**BK0RWE = 0**
BK0RW	0 = Read cycle	Don't care
	1 = Write cycle	
	BK1RWE = 1	**BK1RWE = 0**
BK1RW	0 = Read cycle	Don't care
	1 = Write cycle	

Dual Address BGND Breakpoint (tag instruction when match and execute BGND)

BKEN1:BKEN0:BKPM	1:1:1
BRKAH	Breakpoint 0 high byte address
BRKAL	If BK0ALE = 1, breakpoint 0 low byte address
	If BK0ALE = 0, don't care; breakpoint anywhere in 256-byte block
BRKDH	Breakpoint 1 high byte address
BRKDL	If BK1ALE = 1, breakpoint 1 low byte address
	If BK1ALE = 0, don't care; breakpoint anywhere in 256-byte block
BK0RWE	Don't care; R/$\overline{\text{W}}$ not used
BK0RW	Don't care
BK1RWE	Don't care
BK1RW	Don't care

BRKDL—$0025—Breakpoint Match Register for Low Order Data

Bit 7	6	5	4	3	2	1	Bit 0
7	6	5	4	3	2	1	0

Reset 0   0   0   0   0   0   0   0

> These bits are compared against the least significant byte of the date bus or the least significant byte of the address bus in dual address modes. See Table 14–7.

Breakpoint Uses

The most obvious use of breakpoints is for development and debugging. The dual address BDM comparison mode using the tagging mechanism (BKEN1:BKEN0:BKPM = 1:1:1) is the most straightforward way to implement breakpoints if the debugger is operating through the BDM interface. This method offers up to two program instruction breakpoints, which force the target system to active background mode just before executing the user instruction at a breakpoint address. A slight twist is possible where you can elect to ignore the low order byte of the address for either breakpoint, which causes a break to occur if the target CPU attempts to execute any instruction within a 256-byte address range set by the trigger value in the high byte of address (these are referred to as range breakpoints).

If the debugger is operating as a ROM monitor within the same M68HC12 system as the application program, you can use the dual address SWI comparison mode, which uses the tagging mechanism (BKEN1:BKEN0 = 0:1). This method offers up to two program instruction breakpoints, which force the target system to execute an SWI instruction instead of executing the user instruction at a breakpoint address. This is very much like a traditional software breakpoint except you can set these breakpoints in a flash or ROM memory. This mode also supports range breakpoints that ignore the low half of the address bus. This type of hardware breakpoint is also useful if you are debugging a program in EEPROM. Although software breakpoints can be set in EEPROM, they use up limited program-erase cycles reducing the life expectancy of the EEPROM.

By configuring the breakpoint module for dual address BDM mode using the interrupt mechanism (BKEN1:BKEN0:BKPM = 1:1:0), you gain the ability to include an R/$\overline{\text{W}}$ value for each breakpoint. In addition, the breakpoint no longer has to be the address of an instruction opcode. Range breakpoints are still allowed and comparison of R/$\overline{\text{W}}$ is optional. This type of breakpoint causes the target system to enter active background mode at the next instruction boundary after the match occurs.

The fourth choice is to configure the breakpoint module for full address/data comparison using the interrupt mechanism (BKEN1:BKEN0 = 1:0). In this mode, 33 comparator bits are configured to establish one breakpoint based on a match against 16 address bits, 16 data bits, and R/$\overline{\text{W}}$. Control bits allow you to make the low half of the address, either half of the data bus, or R/$\overline{\text{W}}$ into don't cares. This type of breakpoint causes the target system to enter active background mode at the next instruction boundary after the match occurs.

ROM Patching

ROM patching allows bugs in ROM to be fixed.

A less obvious use of the hardware breakpoints is for patching programs in ROM, EEPROM, flash, or external nonvolatile memory (the MC68HC12BE32 is a ROM-based version of the MC68HC912B32). The ROM patching feature uses the dual address SWI mode of the breakpoint module and requires advance planning to accommodate ROM patches. Since you have no way to predict if or where a software error might be discovered in the ROM program, you need to leave a stub to a dummy program in volatile (RAM or EEPROM) memory during the initialization routine in your ROM program. It is better to place this stub at the beginning of your initialization or startup code because if you placed it at the end you could not use patching to correct errors in the initialization routine itself. You also need to set up the SWI vector (in ROM) to point at another stub routine in programmable memory so that when a hardware breakpoint generated SWI occurs, an SWI service routine can be executed to correct the problem and return to the ROM program somewhere after the bad ROM code.

Both stubs need to be designed so they do nothing if no patches are needed. When an error is discovered after the application program has been placed in ROM, you can modify the initialization stub to call a program in EEPROM or RAM with a routine that sets up the breakpoint module to trigger an SWI before executing the defective ROM program sequence. The dummy routine then jumps back to the initialization program and continues execution of the user program. The SWI stub would also be modified to call a program in EEPROM or RAM that corrects the ROM bug and returns to the ROM program at a point past the error. This structure can accommodate one or two patches. If there are two patches, the SWI response routine can check the return address that was stacked on execution of the patch SWI to see which patch to execute.

This patching mechanism can help during product debugging too. Suppose your product enables the COP watchdog timer. This can be a problem during debug because the watchdog continues to operate even when you have switched to active background mode. The result is that you get hit with a COP reset every time you try to gain control using BDM. You could reset the target system in special single-chip mode, disable the COP, and then resume the user code at a point after it enabled the COP, but this can be a nuisance if you have to do it very many times. If the application program is set up to allow patching, you can establish a patch before the COP is enabled and program the patch to skip that portion of the application program. Once the application starts up and the patch has executed, a debug pod can reconfigure the breakpoint module to use it for program debug. The next time the application system is reset, the patch code will reinitialize the patch breakpoint.

Examples 14–5 and 14–6 show one possible set of program additions you could use to support program patching. Many variations are possible such as changing the way you check for valid patch routines. In these examples, no ROM code bugs have been identified yet so there is no code to set up the breakpoint module. In the next example we will modify this code (without changing anything in the ROM) to correct a ROM software error.

Explanation of Examples 14–5 and 14–6

These examples include two separate pieces of code. The first (Example 14–5, *lines 1–22*) goes in the EEPROM, which is initially left in the erased state. If a ROM bug is discovered later, these EEPROM values can be modified to indicate the presence of a breakpoint initialization routine and one or two patches. The second piece of code (Example 14–6, *lines 1–70*) shows the small routines

---

EXAMPLE 14–5   ROM Patching Support Code

ROMPAT1.ASM   Assembled with CASMW 7/26/98 1:59:43 PM PAGE 1

```
                 1  ;**************************************************
                 2  ;This code section gets loaded into target system EEPROM
                 3
0FF8             4          ORG     $0FF8     ;In B32 EEPROM ($D00-FFF)
                 5  ;**************************************************
                 6  ; ROM patching setup. These locations are initially left
                 7  ; in the erased state ($FF). To activate patching, setup
                 8  ; as follows.
                 9  ; 0FF4,5 RST_CHK - 2's complement of RST_STUB = valid
                10  ; 0FF6,7 BUG1   - address of first ROM bug
                11  ; 0FF8,9 PATCH1 - address of first ROM patch
                12  ; 0FFA,B BUG2   - address of second ROM bug
                13  ; 0FFC,D PATCH2 - address of second ROM patch
                14  ; a value of $FFFF in BUG1(2) means disable patch1(2)
                15  ; 0FFE,F RST_STUB - address of RST service stub
                16  ;**************************************************
0FF4 FFFF       17  RST_CHK:    DW     $FFFF   ;2's complement of RST_STUB = valid
0FF6 FFFF       18  BUG1:       DW     $FFFF   ;1st ROM bug address (FFFF=off)
0FF8 FFFF       19  PATCH1:     DW     $FFFF   ;1st ROM patch address
0FFA FFFF       20  BUG2:       DW     $FFFF   ;2nd ROM bug address (FFFF=off)
0FFC FFFF       21  PATCH2:     DW     $FFFF   ;2nd ROM patch address
0FFE FFFF       22  RST_STUB:   DW     $FFFF   ;initialize ROM patches
```

that are incorporated in the user program so it will be capable of supporting ROM patches later if they are needed. Usually the correction routines would also be programmed into EEPROM so be sure to leave some room in case ROM bugs are detected later on.

Example 14–5 and *lines 5–10* of Example 14–6 define locations in EEPROM that support the ROM patching system. Until a problem is found in the ROM, these locations are erased to cause the patching stubs to fall through to normal user programs. When a ROM error is found, a new Example 14–5 program would be prepared with non-FF values in these locations and including any ROM bug correction code needed. Location RST_STUB would be set to the address of a new initialization routine that would set up the breakpoint module immediately after reset. As a safety check, location RST_CHK is programmed to the two's-complement of RST_STUB. This prevents the danger of misinterpreting a random value in the RST_STUB location and jumping to a nonexistent initialization routine. BUG1 and BUG2 get programmed to the addresses of errors (bugs) in the ROM program. PATCH1 and PATCH2 get programmed to the addresses of new correction routines. If PATCH2 is not needed, BUG2 can be left $FFFF so a second breakpoint will not be initialized.

The RST_PREP routine (starting at *line 30*) is the first code executed after a reset. *Lines 31–35* check for a valid patch initialization program by comparing RST_CHK against the two's-complement of RST_STUB. If these do not agree, the code branches to USER_RST, effectively skipping the RST_STUB routine that does not yet exist. If the check is successful, the indexed indirect jump

EXAMPLE 14–6   ROM Patching Support Code

ROMPAT2.ASM   Assembled with CASMW 7/26/98 3:13:51 PM PAGE 1

```
                  1   ;*******************************************************
                  2   ;This code section gets added to the user's program
                  3   ; NOTE: this code segment is not a stand alone program
                  4
0000              5   RST_CHK:   EQU   $0FF8     ;2's comp of RST_STUB = valid
0000              6   BUG1:      EQU   $0FF6     ;1st ROM bug address (FFFF=off)
0000              7   PATCH1:    EQU   $0FF8     ;1st ROM patch address
0000              8   BUG2:      EQU   $0FFA     ;2nd ROM bug address (FFFF=off)
0000              9   PATCH2:    EQU   $0FFC     ;2nd ROM patch address (FFFF=off)
0000             10   RST_STUB: EQU   $0FFE     ;initialize ROM patches
                 11
0000             12   STK_INIT: EQU   $0C00     ;stack at $0xxx - $0BFF
                 13
0000             14   SWIV:      EQU   $FFF6     ;SWI vector location
0000             15   RESETV:    EQU   $FFFE     ;Reset vector location
                 16
FF00             17              ORG   $FF00    ;In B32 flash ($8000-FFFF)
                 18   ;this ORG not required when adding code to a user prog
                 19   ;*******************************************************
                 20   ; Preparation code to allow for ROM patching.
                 21   ;   RST_PREP - allows for setup of the breakpoint module
                 22   ; if patching becomes necessary. If no patching needed,
                 23   ; this routine just continues with user initialization.
                 24   ;   SWI_PREP - if any patches are needed, this routine
                 25   ; jumps to the needed patch code.  If no patches are
                 26   ; needed, this routine continues to user SWI service
                 27   ; code (if any) or just returns.
                 28   ;*******************************************************
                 29
                 30   RST_PREP:
FF00 87          31          clra
FF01 C7          32          clrb            ;set D=0
FF02 B30FFE      33          subd  RST_STUB   ;2's comp RST_STUB → D
FF05 BC0FF8      34          cpd   RST_CHK    ;is there a valid RST_STUB?
FF08 2604        35          bne   USER_RST   ;if not skip to user init
FF0A 05FB10F0    36          jmp   [RST_STUB,pcr] ;if so go there
                 37   ;when done setting up breakpoint(s), jump back here
                 38   USER_RST:
FF0E CF0C00      39          lds   #STK_INIT ;initialize stack pointer
                 40   ;more user code goes here
                 41
                 42   SWI_PREP:
FF11 87          43          clra
FF12 C7          44          clrb  ;set D=0
FF13 B30FFE      45          subd  RST_STUB   ;2's comp RST_STUB → D
```

EXAMPLE 14–6   Continued

```
FF16  BC0FF8       46              cpd     RST_CHK   ;is there a valid RST_STUB?
FF19  261B         47              bne     USER_SWI  ;if not skip to user SWI
FF1B  EC87         48              ldd     7,sp      ;else check return address
FF1D  BC0FF6       49              cpd     BUG1      ;was this a patch break?
FF23  2606         50              bne     nxt_patch ;if not see if 2nd patch
FF25  1801870F     51              movw    PATCH1,7,sp ;make return addr=PATCH1
      F8
FF2A  0B           52              rti               ;restore regs and go patch
                   53      nxt_patch:
FF2B  BC0FFA       54              cpd     BUG2      ;was this 2nd patch break?
FF2E  2606         55              bne     USER_SWI  ;if not go to user code
FF30  1801850F     56              movw    PATCH2,7,sp ;make return addr=PATCH2
      FC
FF35  0B           57              rti               ;restore regs and go patch
                   58
                   59      ;when done servicing breakpoint,
                   60      ;and jump back to ROM past error
                   61
                   62      USER_SWI:
                   63      ;user's normal SWI service (if any) starts here
                   64      ;A, B, and CCR have been modified since the SWI
                   65
FFF6               66              ORG     SWIV
FFF6  FF11         67              DW      SWI_PREP  ;vector here on any SWI
                   68
FFFE               69              ORG     RESETV
FFFE  FF00         70              DW      RST_PREP  ;to prep immediately on reset
```

---

in *line 36* jumps to a new program that initializes the breakpoint module before continuing with the user's initialization.

SWI_PREP performs a similar check to be sure ROM patches are present before attempting to act on one. *Lines 43–47* compare RST_CHK against the two's-complement of RST_STUB, skipping to the user's SWI service routine if no valid patches are present. If patches are currently enabled, the routine continues to determine whether this SWI was caused by a valid patch breakpoint. *Line 48* reads the return address off the stack. If this address matches BUG1 (or BUG2), *line 51 (and 56)* moves the address of the patch routine onto the stack in the return address position. The RTI in *line 52 (and 57)* restores all registers including the CCR and the stack pointer to the values they had when the SWI arrived, and then execution picks up in the patch repair program. The patch program can now operate as though it was the next instruction in the user's main program even if the instruction at the break was a conditional branch. When the patch finishes, it should jump back to the user program at some point after the original error.

It is fairly uncommon for user's to use SWI instructions in their programs because SWI is used more often for software breakpoints during debugging. Still, the patch software in Example 14–5 allows user SWI routines to coexist with ROM patching. If there is no user SWI service routine,

EXAMPLE 14–7   ROM (or FLASH) Program with an Error

ROMERR.ASM   Assembled with CASMW 7/26/98 8:19:35 PM PAGE 1

```
                1   ;************************************************************
                2   ;This is a small user program which will be used to
                3   ;demonstrate ROM patching. There is an intentional error.
                4   ;This program will be loaded into the flash memory in
                5   ;an MC68HC912B32.
                6
0000            7   RST_CHK:      EQU      $0FF8     ;2's comp of RST_STUB = valid
0000            8   BUG1:         EQU      $0FF6     ;1st ROM bug address (FFFF=off)
0000            9   PATCH1:       EQU      $0FF8     ;1st ROM patch address
0000           10   BUG2:         EQU      $0FFA     ;2nd ROM bug address (FFFF=off)
0000           11   PATCH2:       EQU      $0FFC     ;2nd ROM patch address
0000           12   RST_STUB:     EQU      $0FFE     ;initialize ROM patches
               13
0000           14   PORTT:        EQU      $AE       ;address of port t
0000           15   DDRT:         EQU      $AF       ;address for port t direction
               16
0000           17   STK_INIT: EQU        $0C00      ;stack at $0xxx - $0BFF
               18
0000           19   SWIV:         EQU      $FFF6     ;SWI vector location
0000           20   RESETV:       EQU      $FFFE     ;Reset vector location
               21
F000           22                 ORG      $F000     ;In B32 flash ($8000-FFFF)
               23
               24   ;************************************************************
               25   ; Preparation code to allow for ROM patching.
               26   ;   RST_PREP - allows for setup of the breakpoint module
               27   ; if patching becomes necessary. If no patching needed,
               28   ; this routine just continues with user initialization.
               29   ;   SWI_PREP - if any patches are needed, this routine
               30   ; jumps to the needed patch code. If no patches are
               31   ; needed, this routine continues to user SWI service
               32   ; code (if any) or just returns.
               33   ;************************************************************
               34
               35   RST_PREP:
F000 87        36                 clra
F001 C7        37                 clrb                  ;set D=0
F002 B30FFE    38                 subd     RST_STUB     ;2's comp RST_STUB → D
F005 BC0FF8    39                 cpd      RST_CHK      ;is there a valid RST_STUB?
F008 2604      40                 bne      USER_RST     ;if not skip to user init
F00A 05FB1FF0  41                 jmp      [RST_STUB,pcr]     ;if so go there
               42   ;when done setting up breakpoint(s), jump back here
               43   USER_RST:
F00E CF0C00    44                 lds      #STK_INIT    ;initialize stack pointer
F011 8680      45                 ldaa     #$80
```

EXAMPLE 14-7 Continued

```
F013 5AAF      46                staa  DDRT          ;port t(7) to output
               47
               48  USER_MAIN:
F015 8680      49                ldaa  #$80
F017 5AAE      50                staa  PORTT         ;turn on MSB
F019 0707      51                bsr   dly_sub       ;leave on for 1 sec
F01B 87        52                clra
F01C 5AAE      53                staa  PORTT         ;turn off MSB
F01E 0702      54                bsr   dly_sub       ;leave off for 1 sec
F020 20F3      55                bra   USER_MAIN     ;continue forever
               56
               57  ;**************
               58  ;delay about 1 sec
               59  ;**************
               60  dly_sub:
F022 86FA      61                ldaa  #!250         ;delay constant
               62  dly_loop:
F024 CE1F40    63                ldx   #!8000        ;x_loop will delay 4 msec
               64  x_loop:
F027 09        65                dex                 ;[1] 8000*4cyc*125 nsec
F028 26FD      66                bne   x_loop        ;[3/1] = 4 msec
               67
F02A 43        68                deca                ;[1] 250*4 msec = 1 sec
F02B 2EF7      69                bgt   dly_loop      ;[3/1]loop till A =< 0
               70  ;branch should have been BHI or BNE
               71  ;BGT is a signed branch and fails on first loop
F02D 3D        72                rts                 ;return
               73
               74  SWI_PREP:
F02E 87        75                clra
F02F C7        76                clrb                ;set D=0
F030 B30FFE    77                subd  RST_STUB      ;2's comp RST_STUB → D
F033 BC0FF8    78                cpd   RST_CHK       ;is there a valid RST_STUB?
F036 261B      79                bne   USER_SWI      ;if not skip to user SWI
F038 EC87      80                ldd   7,sp          ;else check return address
F03D BC0FF6    81                cpd   BUG1          ;was this 1st patch break?
F040 2606      82                bne   nxt_patch     ;if not see if 2nd patch
F042 1801870F  83                movw  PATCH1,7,sp   ;make return addr=PATCH1
     FB
F047 0B        84                rti                 ;restore regs and go patch
               85  nxt_patch:
F048 BC0FFA    86                cpd   BUG2          ;was this 2nd patch break?
F04B 2606      87                bne   USER_SWI      ;if not go to user code
F04D 1801850F  88                movw  PATCH2,7,sp   ;make return addr=PATCH2
     FC
F052 0B        89                rti                 ;restore regs and go patch
               90
```

EXAMPLE 14–7   Continued

```
                91  ;when done servicing breakpoint,
                92  ;jump back to ROM past error
                93
                94  USER_SWI:
                95  ;no user SWI so jump to reset if you get here by mistake
F053  05FB0FA7  96          jmp    [RESETV,pcr] ;where you would on a reset
                97
FFF6            98          ORG    SWIV
FFF6  F02E      99          DW     SWI_PREP ;vector here on any SWI
                100
FFFE            101         ORG    RESETV
FFFE  F000      102         DW     RST_PREP ;to prep immediately on reset
```

you must decide what to do if you ever encounter an SWI that is not being used as a patch code. Most users would consider it a major error if they encountered an instruction that was not part of the intended program. One way to deal with such an incident is to jump to where the normal reset vector points.

In Example 14–7 we show a simple ROM program that includes a mistake. This program will be placed in the flash memory of an MC68HC912B32 so we can demonstrate ROM patching in the next example. The program in Example 14–7 has the additions that were recommended in Example 14–6.

Explanation of Example 14–7

Most of this example program consists of the code from Examples 14–5 and 14–6 to support later patching. The new user code includes the initialization of port T in *lines 44–46*, and the main program at *lines 48–72*. The program is intended to set port T bit 7 for about 1 sec and then to clear port T bit 7 for about 1 sec. The branch (BGT) at *line 69* is the wrong kind of branch. It is for signed numbers and since it interprets 250 ($FA) as a negative number, it fails on the first pass through the loop. This causes the delay to be about 4 msec rather than the intended 1 sec. In Example 14–8 we will repair this bug with a ROM patch that will change the branch to the unsigned branch BHI.

Explanation of Example 14–8

In this explanation you will be looking at the programs in both Examples 14–7 and 8. Any line number reference that is not specifically related to Example 14–7 refers to Example 14–8.

After discovering the error in our ROM program (Example 14–7, *line 69*) we write the program in Example 14–8 to correct the problem. This patch will be programmed into the EEPROM of the broken system. Because we had the foresight to prepare for such an emergency, our ROM program will now recognize the patch code is present. Now on reset, the original ROM program (see

EXAMPLE 14–8   Patching an Error in a ROM Program

```
ROMFIX1.ASM        Assembled with CASMW      7/26/98      10:14:57 PM  PAGE 1

                1   ;*********************************************************
                2   ;This code section gets loaded into target system EEPROM
                3   ;Set breakpoint at $F02B to replace defective branch
                4   ;no second breakpoint.
                5
                6   ;***Breakpoint control register equates***
0000            7   BRKCT0:  EQU  $20      ;breakpoint control register 0
                8   ;ROM patching always sets BRKCT0=%01001100
                9   ;dual addr SWI (tag) with low addresses set to care
               10
0000           11   BRKCT1:  EQU  $21      ;breakpoint control register 1
               12   ;0:BKDBE:BKMBH:BKMBL   : BK1RWE:BK1RW:BK0RWE:BK0RW
               13   ;for ROM patching all zero except
               14   ;BKDBE enables 2nd address (in BRKDH:BRKDL)
               15
0000           16   ADDRESS1 EQU  $22      ;BRKAH:BRKAL 1st patch address
0000           17   ADDRESS2 EQU  $24      ;BRKDH:BRKDL 2nd patch address
               18   ;***
               19
               20   ;***Addresses in ROM to be patched***
0000           21   USER_RST: EQU $F00E    ;address to enter user code
0000           22   P1_ADDR:  EQU $F02B    ;address of dly_loop in ROM
0000           23   P1_LOOP:  EQU $F024    ;address of dly_loop in ROM
0000           24   P1_THRU:  EQU $F02D    ;when BGT falls through
               25   ;***
               26
0FD8           27            ORG  $0FD8    ;In B32 EEPROM ($D00-FFF)
               28   ;***
               29   ;Run this code after reset but before
               30   ;running user initialization
               31   BRK_SET:
0FD8 864C      32            ldaa #%01001100
0FDA 5A20      33            staa BRKCT0 ;dual addr SWI (tag) no range
0FDC 8600      34            ldaa #%00000000
0FDE 5A21      35            staa BRKCT1 ;no second patch at this time
0FE0 CCF02B    36            ldd  #P1_ADDR ;address to patch
0FE3 5C22      37            std  ADDRESS1 ;set the address to match
0FE5 06F00E    38            jmp  USER_RST ;back to user ROM
               39   ;***
               40   ;BGT in user ROM should have been BHI
               41   REPAIR1:
0FE8 1822E038  42            lbhi P1_LOOP ;to jump back to user ROM
0FEC 06F02D    43            jmp  P1_THRU ;when loop count expired
               44
```

EXAMPLE 14-8 Continued

```
OFF4              45              ORG    $0FF4    ;In B32 EEPROM ($D00-FFF)
                  46  ;***********************************************************
                  47  ; ROM patching setup. These locations are initially left
                  48  ; in the erased state ($FF). To activate patching, set up
                  49  ; as follows.
                  50  ; OFF4,5 RST_CHK - 2's complement of RST_STUB = valid
                  51  ; OFF6,7 BUG1 - address of first ROM bug
                  52  ; OFF8,9 PATCH1 - address of first ROM patch
                  53  ; OFFA,B BUG2 - address of second ROM bug
                  54  ; OFFC,D PATCH2 - address of second ROM patch
                  55  ; a value of $FFFF in PATCH2 means to disable 2nd patch
                  56  ; OFFE,F RST_STUB - address of RST service stub
                  57  ;***********************************************************
OFF4  F028        58  RST_CHK: DW    {(BRK_SET ($FFFF))+1}
                  59  ;RST_CHK = 2's complement of value at RST_STUB
OFF6  F02B        60  BUG1:    DW    $F02B    ;1st ROM bug address
OFF8  OFE8        61  PATCH1:  DW    REPAIR1  ;1st ROM patch address
OFFA  FFFF        62  BUG2:    DW    $FFFF    ;2nd ROM bug address (FFFF=off)
OFFC  FFFF        63  PATCH2:  DW    $FFFF    ;2nd ROM patch address (FFFF=off)
OFFE  0FD8        64  RST_STUB: DW   BRK_SET  ;initialize ROM patches
```

Example 14–7, *line 41*) will jump to BRK_SET (*line 31* in this patch program). BRK_SET initializes the breakpoint module for dual address SWI (tag) mode and establishes a breakpoint at $F02B. Later when the ROM program reaches this address, the breakpoint will cause an SWI to execute instead of the defective instruction.

The SWI service routine in the ROM program (see Example 14–7, *lines 73–84*) will read the SWI return address from the stack and realize this is the address of a ROM program bug (BUG1). It then jumps to our patch code (REPAIR1 at *line 41*). As described previously in Example 14–7, all user registers, including the CCR, are just as they were when the ROM program was about to execute the instruction at the breakpoint. The patch consists of the proper branch (LBHI) and a jump back to the user ROM. A long branch was used because the destination is too far away to use a short branch. If the branch is taken, it returns to the user program to repeat the delay loop. If the branch falls through, the jump returns you to the instruction after the defective branch.

Once the ROM code has been patched as in Example 14–8, you can no longer use a BDM debug pod to set hardware breakpoints in the user program because the user's patch breakpoints need the breakpoint module. You can still use all other features of the BDM debug pod. In the earlier case in which we described using the patching mechanism to patch the user's initialization code, we know that the user's system is done with the patch mechanism shortly after the application is reset so in that case we are free to let the BDM debugger change the setup of the breakpoint module to use it for hardware breakpoints. If the application system resets for any reason, the breakpoint module gets reconfigured for the patch so it will work correctly.

14.8 Conclusion and Chapter Summary Points

There are three development-related systems in the M68HC12.

- Background Debug Module (BDM)

    The background debug module (BDM) uses a single-wire communication interface to allow nonintrusive access to target system memory and registers.

    Motorola has defined a standard six-pin header to allow BDM debug pods to connect to target systems. The minimum connection requires Gnd and the BKGD signal, but $\overline{RESET}$, V_{dd}, and an optional 11.5-V Flash programming power supply are included in the standard.

    In the single-wire BDM protocol, the host pod initiates all bit times by driving the BKGD pin low for about four target E-clock cycles.

    Serial hardware commands allow you to read or write bytes or 16-bit words without stopping execution of the application program.

    The BACKGROUND hardware command lets you stop the application program and enter active background mode where you can execute additional firmware commands.

    Firmware commands allow you to read or write CPU registers, GO, trace user instructions one at a time, or enable the tagging function.

    READ_NEXT_WORD and WRITE_NEXT_WORD firmware commands allow you to read or write target memory at about 50 μsec per 16-bit word.

    The BDM can be used to program flash and EEPROM memory in an application system after final assembly.

    The BDM can also be used to perform diagnostics and code upgrades in the field.

- Bus Analysis and Tagging

    An instruction tagging mechanism allows emulator systems to stop execution of the application program when a selected instruction is about to be executed.

    An emulator or logic analyzer is needed to monitor and reconstruct internal CPU activity to be able to tag selected instructions.

    The instruction pipe in the MC68HC12 complicates the problem of stopping an application program at a selected instruction.

    Tagged locations must correspond to the address of an instruction opcode.

- Hardware Breakpoint Module

    Some versions of the MC68HC12 include a hardware breakpoint module that allows a user to set various kinds of breakpoints even in ROM-based, single-chip applications where address and data busses are not visible on external pins.

    The hardware breakpoint module in the MC68HC912B32 includes 34 bits of comparator and match registers that can be configured in a variety of ways to trigger breakpoints.

    The tag mechanism (tag) works only for locations that correspond to instruction opcodes.

    The interrupt mechanism (int) can be used to detect any address, data, and R/$\overline{W}$ combination.

14.9 Bibliography and Further Reading

Cady, F. M., *Microcontrollers and Microcomputers: Principles of Software and Hardware Engineering*, Oxford University Press, New York, 1997.

CPU12 Reference Manual, CPU12RM/AD, Motorola, 1996.

CPU12 Reference Guide, CPU12RG/AD, Motorola, 1998.

Doughman, Gordon, *AN1718: A Serial Bootloader for Reprogramming the MC68HC912B32 Flash EEPROM*, AN1718/D, Motorola, 1997.

MC68HC812A4 Technical Summary, MC68HC812A4TS/D, Motorola, 1997.

MC68HC912B32 Technical Summary, MC68HC912B32TS/D, Motorola, 1997.

Ruff, Matt, *EB183: Erasing and Programming the FLASH EEPROM on the MC68HC912B32*, EB183/D, Motorola, 1997.

14.10 Problems

14.1 This is the waveform for one bit time in a BDM communication.

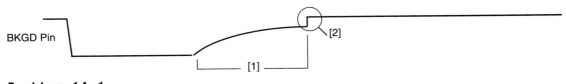

Problem 14-1

Which direction is data being transferred (host-to-target or target-to-host)?

14.2 Looking at the waveform in Problem 14.1, what causes the portion of the waveform labeled [1]? The portion labeled [2]?

14.3 This is the waveform for a BDM command. What is the command?

Problem 14-3

14.4 Looking at the waveform in Problem 14.3, what is the portion labeled [3] for?

14.5 Draw an approximate waveform for a BDM command to write $81 to address $08F1.

14.6 Where are each of the user registers CCR, D, X, Y, SP, and PC saved while the background debug mode is active?

14.7   Suppose a target application system is connected to a BDM pod. Which of the following types of memory could be programmed using the BDM interface?
   a. An external 256-Kbyte RAM (in an MC68HC812A4 based system).
   b. 32-Kbyte on-chip flash EEPROM (in an MC68HC912B32 based system).
   c. On-chip EEPROM.
   d. All of the above.
   e. b and c.

14.8   The following state information was captured in an MC68HC12 system.

```
**********************************************************
Label   >   ADDR    DATA    L̄S̄T̄R̄B̄   R/W̄
Base    >   Hex     Hex     Binary Binary
001         0801    55AA    1      0
**********************************************************
```

What took place during this cycle?

Use the following logic analyzer state listing to answer Problems 14.9 through 14.14.

```
***************************************************************
```

Label>	ADDR	DATA	RW_TYP	PER	PEF
Base >	Hex	Hex	Symbol	Symbol	Symbol
1	0822	7E09	R16	ALL	sev
2	7E09	7E09	R8L	LAT	sod
3	0824	01C6	R16	ALL	
4	0826	64FD	R16	ALD	sev
5	0901	7698	WLH	LAT	
6	7698	7698	R8H		
7	0828	0800	R16	ALL	sod
8	082A	7D19	R16	ALD	sod
9	0800	8602	R16	ALD	
10	082C	01CE	R16		
11	082E	6000	R16	ALD	sev
12	1901	1986	W8L	LAT	
13	1902	0202	W8H		
14	0202	0202	R8H		
15	0830	CD61	R16	ALL	int
16	FFEC	FF4E	R16	ALD	
17	09FE	082D	W16	LAT	
18	FF4E	05FB	R16		
19	09FC	8602	W16	ALD	
20	09FA	9876	W16		
21	FF50	F89A	R16		
22	09F8	6402	W16	ALD	
23	09F7	0988	W8L		
24	FF52	05FB	R16		sev

```
***************************************************************
```

14.9   Beginning from state 001, reconstruct the internal pipe activity until you reach the start of an identifiable instruction. What is the address, opcode, and disassembled instruction?

14.10   Which state numbers correspond to the execution of the disassembled instruction?

14.11   There is an STY $1901 instruction in states 12–15. The instruction set documentation says this instruction should take three cycles. Why did it take four cycles?

14.12   Which state corresponds to a misaligned write to the on-chip RAM? What value was written and to what address?

14.13   An interrupt is serviced after state 15, what caused this interrupt?

14.14   Find an O-f cycle and an O-P cycle in the state listing.

14.15   How is the tagging function enabled in the MC68HC12?

14.16   Which breakpoint mode would you set, using a BDM debug pod, for the following situations? State the 3-bit value you would write to BKEN1:BKEN0:BKPM for each case.
   a. To break upon any write to address $0945 or $0946.
   b. To break just before executing the instruction at $0822.
   c. To repair a program error at $8110 in on-chip ROM.
   d. To break if the value $55 is written to Port T.

14.17   What value would you write to BRKCT0:BRKCT1 to establish a breakpoint for a write of $80 to Port B (address $0001)?

14.18   Which breakpoint type(s) require a valid user stack?
   a. SWI-based software breakpoints.
   b. BGND-based software breakpoints.
   c. Hardware breakpoints.
   d. All of the above.
   e. None of the above.

14.19   What values would be written to all six registers in the breakpoint module to establish breakpoints for the instructions at $820 and $843?

14.20   What is the breakpoint condition that is set by writing the following values to the breakpoint registers?
   BRKCT0 = $80
   BRKCT1 = $72
   BRKAH = $09
   BRKAL = $FE
   BRKDH = $34
   BRKDL = $12

Chapter 15

Advanced M68HC12 Hardware

OBJECTIVES

In this chapter we finish our discussions of the M68HC12 by filling in some of the gaps left in previous chapters.

15.1 M68HC12 Clock Generators

Comparison of M68HC12 and M68HC11 Clock Generator	
M68HC12	**M68HC11**
Basic clock input frequency 16 MHz; E-clock frequency and other system clock frequencies are based on 8 MHz; timer clocks are programmable	Basic clock input frequency 8 MHz; E-clock frequency 2 MHz

The M68HC12 has more sophisticated and programmable features for its clock circuits than the M68HC11. Its external clock frequency is 16 MHz (16.8 MHz maximum). The MC68HC812A4 has a *Phase-Locked Loop* circuit that can provide other basic internal clock frequencies. System clocks are derived from either the external oscillator or the phase-locked loop circuit. There are also separate clock generator circuits for CPU clocks, the bus interface and background debugger, the Serial Peripheral Interface (SPI), analog-to-digital converter (ATD), the Serial Communication Interfaces (SCI), and the Timer.

Basic Clock Generators

The basic system clock, *SYSCLK*, shown in Figure 15–1a, is generated by the circuit shown in Figure 15–2 for the MC68HC812A4 and Figure 15–3 for the MC68HC912B32. Either a crystal or ceramic resonator between the EXTAL and XTAL or an external CMOS oscillator connected to

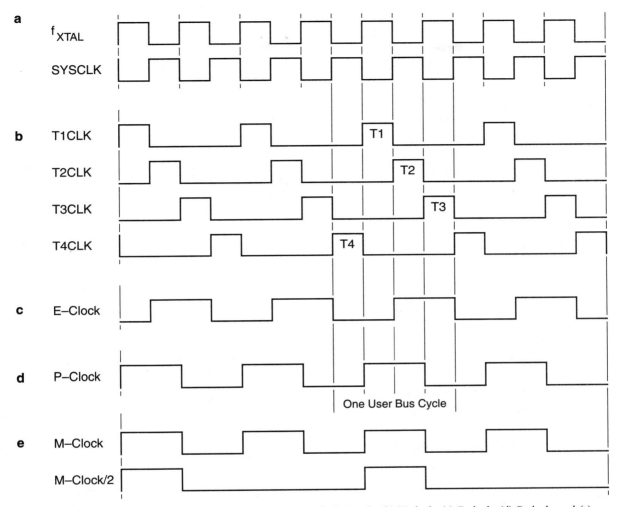

Figure 15–1   M68HC12 system clock signals. (a) Basic clock signals. (b) T-clock, (c) E-clock, (d) P-clock, and (e) M-clock generator signals.

EXTAL provides the system clock at frequency f_{XTAL}. All other clock signals shown in Figure 15–1 are derived from this basic clock. Table 15–1 summarizes the various system clocks found in both MCUs. A fundamental difference in the two systems is that the MC68HC812A4 contains a phase-locked loop that allows the SYSCLK to run at a different frequency than the external oscillator.

MC68HC812A4 Sysclk Generator

A *System Clock Multiplexer* (Figure 15–2) selects either the external oscillator or the output from the *Phase-Locked Loop*. A *System Clock Divider*, controlled by the bits BCSC:BCSB:BCSA in the *Clock Control Register*, (*CLKCTL*), can divide this frequency by factors ranging from 1 to 128. This

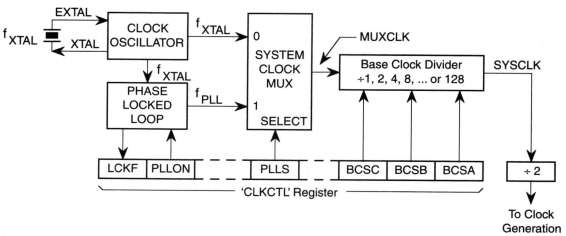

Figure 15-2   MC68HC812A4 basic clock circuit.

base clock is then divided by two again to become the SYSCLK and routed to the clock signal generators shown in Figure 15–4.

MC68HC912B32 Sysclk Generator

Figure 15–3 shows that the SYSCLK circuitry is much simpler in the MC68HC912B32 than the MC68HC812A4. The external clock oscillator is simply divided by two.

CLKCTL—$0047—Clock Control Register

	Bit 7	6	5	4	3	2	1	Bit 0
	LCKF	PLLON	PLLS	BCSC	BCSB	BCSA	MCSB	MCSA
Reset	0	0	0	0	0	0	0	0

LCKF
Phase-Locked Loop Circuit is locked,
PLLON
Phase-Locked Loop On.
PLLS
Phased-Locked Loop Select.

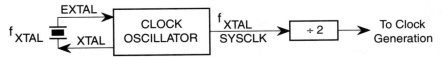

Figure 15-3   MC688HC912B32 basic clock circuit.

BCSC:BCSB:BCSA			
Base Clock Select.			
BCSC	**BCSB**	**BCSA**	**SYSCLK Rate**
0	0	0	SYSCLK = MUX Clock
0	0	1	Divide by 2
0	1	0	Divide by 4
0	1	1	Divide by 8
1	0	0	Divide by 16
1	0	1	Divide by 32
1	1	0	Divide by 64
1	1	1	Divide by 128

MCSB:MCSA		
Module Clock (M-clock) Select Bits.		
MCSB	**MCSA**	**M-clock Rate**
0	0	M-clock = P-clock
0	1	Divide by 2
1	0	Divide by 4
1	1	Divide by 8

Other System Clocks

Figure 15–4 shows how SYSCLK is used to generate other fundamental clock signals within the CPU.

T-clock Generator: The T-clock generator produces four clock signals, each delayed by one-quarter period, that are used by the CPU. These signals are shown in Figure 15–1b.

E-clock Generator: The E-clock generator produces the bus interface signals with which we are familiar in the M68HC11. It is used by external devices when the CPU is in one of its expanded modes. Figure 15–1c shows the timing relationship of E-clock with the other clock signals.

P-clock Generator: The P-clock, Figure 15–1d, is used by the Serial Peripheral Interface and the analog-to-digital converter (and the SCI and Timer in the MC68HC912B32). P-clock is also the input signal for the M-clock generator.

TABLE 15–1 Clock Circuit Summary

Signal	MC68HC812A4	MC68HC912B32
External Oscillator	Up to 16.8 MHz	Up to 16.8 MHz
Phase-Locked Loop clock	Provides a variable clock as a ratio of the external oscillator (Figure 15–7).	Not available
MUX Clock	The external oscillator or PLL clock selected by CLKCTL[PLLS] (Figure 15–2)	Not available
SYSCLK	MUX clock divided by CLKCTL ($\div 2$ to $\div 256$) (Figure 15–2)	External oscillator divided by 2 (Figure 15–3)
T-clocks	Frequency equal to SYSCLK$\div 2$; phased as shown in Figure 15–1 (Figure 15–4)	Frequency equal to SYSCLK$\div 2$; phased as shown in Figure 15–1 (Figure 15–4)
E-clock	Frequency equal to SYSCLK$\div 2$; used by BDM, external buses (Figure 15–4)	Frequency equal to SYSCLK$\div 2$; used by BDM, external buses (Figure 15–4)
P-clock	Frequency equal to SYSCLK$\div 2$; used by A/D, SPI (Figure 15–4)	Frequency equal to SYSCLK$\div 2$; used by SCI, BDLC, RTI, COP, A/D, timer, PWM (Figure 15–4)
M-clock	P-clock divided by CLKCTL ($\div 1$ to $\div 8$) (Figure 15–4)	None
SCI Baud Rate	M-clock divided by SCnBD ($\div 1$ to $\div 8192$) (Figure 15–5).	P-clock divided by SCnBD ($\div 1$ to $\div 8192$) (Figure 15–5)
RTI Clock	M-clock divided by RTICTL; total divisor 2^{13} to 2^{19} (Figure 10–7)	P-clock divided RTICTL; total divisor 2^{13} to 2^{19}, unless RTICTL[RTBYP]=1 and then the divisor is 2^4 to 2^8 (Figure 10–7)
COP Clock	M-clock divided by COPCTL[CR2:CR0]; total divisor = 2^{13} to 2^{23}	P-clock divided by COPCTL[CR2:CR0]; total divisor = 2^{13} to 2^{23}, unless RTICTL[RTBYP]=1 and then the divisor is 2^4 to 2^8
Timer Clock	M-clock enabled by TSCR[TEN] (Figure 10–6)	P-clock enabled by TSCR[TEN] (Figure 10–6)
A/D Clock	P-clock divided by ATDCTL4; total divisor = 2 to 16 (Figure 15–6)	P-clock divided by ATDCTL4; total divisor = 2 to 16 (Figure 15–6)
SPI Clock	P-clock divided by SP0BR; total divisor = 2 to 256 (Figure 15–6)	P-clock divided by SP0BR; total divisor = 2 to 256 (Figure 15–6)
BDM Clock	E-clock	E-clock
BDLC Clock	None	P-clock divided by BCR1 ($\div 1$ to $\div 8$)
PWM Clock	None	P-clock (Figure 10–13)

M-clock Generator: The M-clock, Figure 15–1e, is used by the Serial Communications Interfaces and the Timer in the MC68HC812A4. A divider circuit, controlled by *MCSB:MCSA*, allows the M-clock to be divided down from the P-clock.

SCI Clock Generator: Figure 15–5 shows the clock generator for the SCI. Either the M-clock or the P-clock is divided by SCnBDH:SCnBDL to produce standard Baud rates.

SPI and ATD Clock Generator: Figure 15–6 shows the SPI and ATD clock generator. Each clock circuit has a programmable divider to produce the desired subsystem clock rate.

Phase-Locked Loop

The phase-locked loop (PLL) is shown in Figure 15–7. There are two divider registers, the *Reference Divider* (*RDV*), which divides the crystal input frequency f_{XTAL}, and the *Loop Divider* (*LDV*), which divides the output frequency f_{PLL}. As you can see in Figure 15–2, the phase-locked loop is

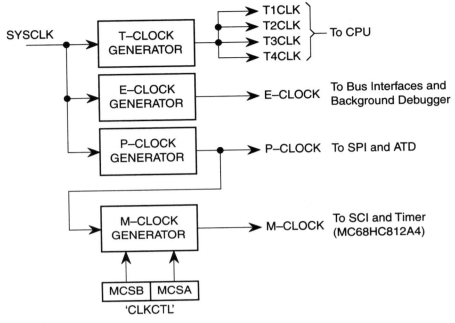

Figure 15-4   Clock signal generators.

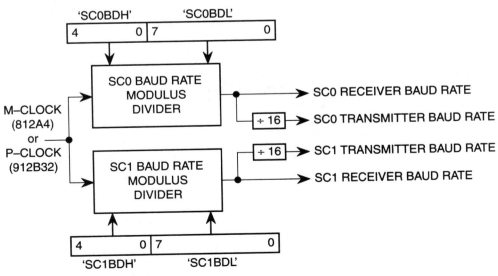

Figure 15-5   SCI clock generator.

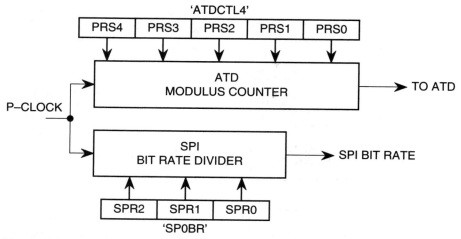

Figure 15-6   SPI and ATD clock generator.

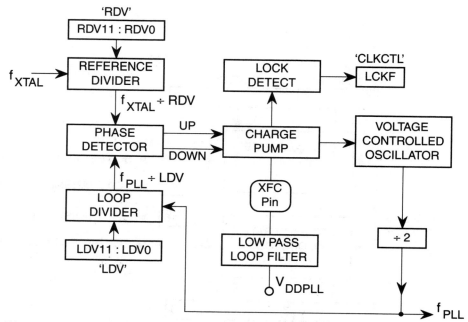

Figure 15-7   Phase-locked loop.

controlled by three bits in the *Clock Control Register* (*CLKCTL*). *PLLON* is set to enable the phase-locked loop oscillator; *PLLS* controls the System Clock Multiplexer to chose f_{PLL}; *LCKF* is set by the PLL when it is locked.

CLKCTL—$0047—Clock Control Register

Bit 7	6	5	4	3	2	1	Bit 0
LCKF	PLLON	PLLS	BCSC	BCSB	BCSA	MCSB	MCSA

Reset 0   0   0   0   0   0   0   0

LCKF

Phase-Locked Loop Circuit is Locked.
  0 = PLL is not on or not stable (default).
  1 = If the PLL is on (PLLON=1), indicates the PLL is at least half and no more than twice the target frequency.

PLLON

Phase-Locked Loop On.
  0 = Turns the PLL off (default).
  1 = Turns the PLL on.

PLLS

Phased-Locked Loop Select.
  0 = Select the crystal input frequency for MUXCLK (default).
  1 = After the PLL is locked, selects the PLL.

BCSC:BCSB:BCSA

Base Clock Select.

MCSB:MCSA

Module Clock (M-clock) Select Bits.

The PLL allows you to generate a different SYSCLK frequency than one-half f_{XTAL}. The *Reference Divider Register* (*RDV*) and the *Loop Divider Register* (*LDV*) control dividers for the f_{XTAL} and f_{PLL} frequencies producing f_{XTAL}/RDV and f_{PLL}/LDV, respectively. The *Phase Detector* compares these two signals and produces a current that, through the *Charge Pump*, drives the *Voltage Controlled Oscillator* to minimize the phase difference. The design procedure to use the PLL is as follows:

1. The maximum phase detector input frequency, f_{PDMAX}, must be no greater than 16 MHz. This establishes the minimum values of RDV and LDV:

$$RDV \geq \frac{f_{\text{XTAL}}}{f_{\text{PD}_{MAX}}}$$

and

$$LDV \geq \frac{f_{\text{PLL}}}{f_{\text{PD}_{MAX}}}$$

2. The maximum values for RDV and LDV are 2^{13}.

3. Choose values for RDV and LDV so the following equation holds:

$$\frac{f_{\text{PLL}}}{f_{\text{XTAL}}} \times \frac{RDV}{LDV} = 1$$

Choose the lowest values for RDV and LDV such that both are integers and are greater than the minimum and less than the maximum allowed. See Examples 15–1 and 15–2.

LDV—$0040:$0041—Loop Divider Registers

RDV—$0042:$0043—Reference Divider Registers

Bit 15	14	13	12	11	10	9	Bit 8
0	0	0	0	DV11	DV10	DV9	DV8
Reset 0	0	0	0	1	1	1	1

Bit 7	6	5	4	3	2	1	Bit 0
DV7	DV6	DV5	DV4	DV3	DV2	DV1	DV0
Reset 1	1	1	1	1	1	1	1

LDV11:LDV0, RDV11:RDV0

Loop and Reference Divider Values

In the reset state, the dividers are set to the maximum that produces an internal frequency of 3.907 kHz with $f_{XTAL} = 16.000$ MHz.

Any attempt to set LDV or RDV less than four results in the logic selecting a divide-by-two path.

Figure 15–7 shows a *Low Pass Loop Filter* that is connected to the MC68HC812A4 *XFC* pin. This second-order filter is designed so that its cutoff frequency is at most f_{XTAL}/RDV. The frequency response of $V(s)/I(s)$ for the circuit in Figure 15–8a is shown in Figure 15–8b, where the cutoff frequency is given by

$$\omega_c = \frac{1}{R_s \times (C_s\ C_p/C_s\ +\ C_p)}$$

Choosing a lower cutoff will give a more stable frequency reference but will give slower PLL-lock times. See Section 15.6 for more reference material on phase-locked loop design.

EXAMPLE 15–1   PLL Divider Registers

$f_{XTAL} = 16.000$ MHz and f_{PLL} is to be 11.26 MHz. Find appropriate values for RDV and LDV.

Solution:

Find the lowest integer values for RDV and LDV that satisfy the design criteria 1–3.

Hint:

Multiply by f_{XTAL} and f_{PLL} by 100 and then find the lowest common denominator. In this case, 1126/1600 = 563/800. Choose RDV = 800, LDV = 563.

EXAMPLE 15–2   PLL Resolution

If $f_{XTAL} = 16.000$ MHz, find the smallest increment in the output frequency that can be achieved.

Solution:

The smallest possible increment in the output frequency is found when using the largest divider for RDV. 16.000 MHz/4095 = 3.907 kHz.

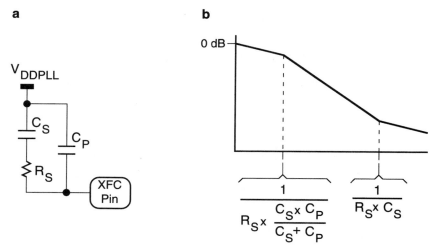

Figure 15-8   PLL loop filter. (a) Low pass loop filter. (b) Frequency response.

External Clock Oscillator

The M68HC12 needs an external oscillator for its clock circuits. EXTAL and XTAL are two pins used to supply this signal. An external crystal oscillator or ceramic resonator may be used or a CMOS-compatible clock signal may be applied. Figure 15–9a shows a commonly used crystal oscillator. The crystal frequency is chosen to be twice the SYSCLK frequency. The capacitors shown include stray capacitances and are normally about 22 pF. Care should be taken in circuit board layout around the crystal oscillator.

Figure 15–9b shows an external CMOS-compatible oscillator driving the EXTAL input pin. XTAL is normally left unconnected but could be used with a high-impedance buffer to drive other devices.

15.2 Hardware Mode Select

In Chapters 7 and 9 we discussed the single-chip and expanded modes. These are selected by the states of BKGD, MODB, and MODA when the M68HC12 is reset, as shown in Table 15–2.

Normal Operating Modes

There are three normal operating modes—*Single-Chip, Expanded-Narrow,* and *Expanded-Wide.*

Normal Single-Chip: There are no external address and data buses in this mode. The M68HC12 operates as a stand-alone device with all program, data, and I/O resources on-chip. External port pins (Ports A, B, C, and D) that are used for address and data in expanded modes are available for general-purpose I/O. The MC68HC912B32 is ideally suited for single-chip use.

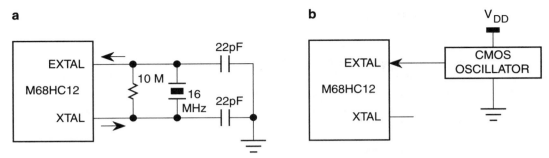

Figure 15-9   External oscillators. (a) Crystal oscillator. (b) CMOS oscillator.

Normal Expanded-Narrow: An expanded 16-bit address and 8-bit data bus are provided in this mode. Ports A and B provide the address bus and Port C the data bus. This mode is useful for smaller systems in which 8-bit memory devices may be in use. In this mode, 16-bit data are presented 1 byte at a time and the address is automatically incremented on the second bus cycle.

Normal Expanded-Wide: An expanded 16-bit address and 16-bit data bus is implemented. Ports A and B provide the address bus and Ports C and D are the data bus. The MC68HC812A4 is your best choice for this expanded mode.

Special Operating Modes

There are three special modes that correspond to the normal modes. These modes are commonly used in factory testing or system development. In addition, there is a *Special Peripheral* mode in which the CPU is not active. An external master, such as an integrated circuit tester, can control the on-chip peripherals for special, in-factory testing.

15.3 Expanded Mode Port E Emulation

Not all registers are visible in the memory map when the M68HC12 is operating in expanded modes. In the expanded-narrow modes, Ports A, B, and C are used for the 16-bit address and 8-bit data bus. In expanded-wide mode, Port D is also removed from the memory map because it is used for

			TABLE 15-2 Mode Selection			
BKGD	**MODB**	**MODA**	**Mode**	**Port A, Port B**	**Port C**	**Port D**
0	0	0	Special Single-Chip	G.P. I/O[a]	G.P. I/O	G.P. I/O
0	0	1	Special Expanded-Narrow	Address bus	Data bus	G.P. I/O
0	1	0	Special Peripheral	Address bus	Data bus	Data bus
0	1	1	Special Expanded-Wide	Address bus	Data bus	Data bus
1	0	0	Normal Single-Chip	G.P. I/O	G.P. I/O	G.P. I/O
1	0	1	Normal Expanded-Narrow	Address bus	Data bus	G.P. I/O
1	1	0	Reserved	—	—	—
1	1	1	Normal Expanded-Wide	Address bus	Data bus	Data bus

[a]*G.P., general purpose.*

the 16-bit data bus along with Port D. Port E may also be used for external control signals when operating in an expanded mode and is thus not able to be used for the general-purpose I/O features available in single-chip mode. Port E can be restored to the memory map and becomes available for use by *emulating* it. The *Emulate E (EME)* bit in the *Mode* register can be set when in one of the expanded modes. This allows both Port E ($0008) and DDRE ($0009) to be addressed. External hardware can be added to the external address and data bus to provide the Port E I/O functions.

The *Emulate D (EMD)* bit in the Mode register allows a similar emulation of Port D. However, this can be activated only when in the Special Expanded-Narrow mode.

15.4 Miscellaneous Registers

The MODE register controls the M68HC12 operating mode and various configuration options.

MODE—$000B—Mode Register

	Bit 7	6	5	4	3	2	1	Bit 0
Reset	SMODN	MODB	MODA	ESTR	IVIS	0	EMD	EME
Special Single-Chip	0	0	0	1	1	0	1	1
Special Exp-Narrow	0	0	1	1	1	0	1	1
Peripheral	0	1	0	1	1	0	1	1
Special Exp-Wide	0	1	1	1	1	0	1	1
Normal Single-Chip	1	0	0	1	0	0	0	0
Normal Exp-Narrow	1	0	1	1	0	0	0	0
Normal Exp-Wide	1	1	1	1	0	0	0	0

SMODN, MODB, MODA

Mode Select Special, A, and B.
These bits show the current operating mode and reflect the status of the BKGD, MODB, and MODA pins at the rising edge of RESET. They can be read anytime. SMODN can be written if SDMODN = 0 (in special modes) but the first write is ignored. MODB and MODA can be written once if SMODN = 1 (in normal modes) to change the operating mode; they can be written anytime if SMODN = 0 (in special modes).

ESTR

E-clock Stretch Enable.
    0 = E-clock never stretches and behaves as a free-running clock.
    1 = E-clock stretches high during external access cycles and low during nonvisible internal accesses.
In normal modes, ESTR may be written only once; in special modes, anytime.

IVIS

Internal Visibility.

This bit allows internal address, data, R/$\overline{W}$ and $\overline{LSTRB}$ signals to be seen on the external bus during accesses to internal locations. This is useful when using external debugging hardware such as an in-circuit emulator.

    0 = No visibility of internal bus operations on external bus.

    1 = Internal bus activity is visible externally.

In normal modes, IVIS can be written once; in special modes anytime except the first time.

EMD

Emulate Port D.

In expanded-wide mode, PORTD, DDRD, KWIED, KWIFD are removed from the map regardless of EMD. In single-chip modes and normal expanded-narrow modes, these ports are in the memory map regardless of EMD.

This bit has meaning only in special expanded-narrow mode.

    0 = PORTD, DDRD, KWIED, and KWIFD are in the memory map.

    1 = These registers are removed from the map. This allows the user to emulate their
        functions with external hardware.

EMD can be written once in normal modes; anytime in special modes except the first time.

EME

Emulate E.

In single-chip mode PORTE and DDRE are in the map regardless of EME.

In an expanded mode:

    0 = PORTE and DDRE are in the memory map.

    1 = The registers are removed from the internal memory map allowing the user to
        emulate their function with external hardware.

EME can be written once in normal modes; anytime in special modes except the first time.

15.5 Power-Saving Modes

The M68HC12 has a variety of power-saving features that you can use when minimum power consumption is a concern, such as applications that may be battery powered. The basic principle of power saving in CMOS circuits is to slow or stop any clocking operations.

Using a Slow Clock

It is worth analyzing the time required to accomplish the task needed in the application and then choosing the clock oscillator frequency to be just fast enough. As you can see in Figure 15–2, the MC68HC812A4 can divide the external oscillator of the phase-locked loop frequency by a factor ranging up to 128. One could adopt a strategy of programming the SYSCLK to be fast while doing processing and then slowing it down when not. You can also program the phase-locked loop to provide a lower frequency f_{PLL}.

Using the WAI and STOP Instructions

The STOP and WAIT modes are entered by executing either the STOP or WAI instructions. When in either of these modes, power consumption is reduced as shown in Table 15–3.

STOP Mode Operation

The STOP mode stops all clocks and places the M68HC12 into its lowest power consumption state. A key wakeup interrupt (from Port H or J), $\overline{IRQ}$, $\overline{XIRQ}$, or $\overline{RESET}$, is needed to exit STOP mode. On reset, the condition code register S bit is set, disabling the STOP instruction. STOP is treated as a NOP if the S bit is set. When coming out of STOP, the clocks must be restarted and you can enable a delay before resuming processing by setting the DLY bit in the INTCR register. When this bit is set, the program starts to execute 4096 clock cycles after coming out of STOP.

WAIT Mode Operation

WAIT mode shuts down some M68HC12 systems but leaves clocks running. This allows the program to restart faster than if it had been in a STOP state. An interrupt is needed to exit WAIT mode.

For lowest power consumption during WAIT, stop the EEPROM programming. It is recommended that you complete EEPROM programming before entering either WAIT or STOP modes. You can also set the EESWAI bit in EEMCR to stop clocking the EEPROM when in WAIT mode. You should not do this if the WAIT mode vectors are in EEPROM.

The real-time interrupt and COP can be stopped when in WAIT mode by setting the RSWAI bit in the RTICTL register.

You can choose to stop the timer while in WAIT mode by setting the TSWAI bit in the TSCR register. This does mean that timer interrupts cannot be used to exit the WAIT state.

TABLE 15–3   Maximum Total Supply Current for MC68HC812A4.

Characteristic	SYSCLK Frequency			
	2 MHz	4 MHz	8 MHz	Unit
RUN				
Single-Chip Mode	8	15	27	mA
Expanded Mode	14	27	35	mA
WAIT (all peripherals shut down)				
Single-Chip Mode	3	6	15	mA
Expanded Mode	5	10	20	mA
STOP (Single-Chip Mode, no clocks)				
−40 to +85°C	10	10	10	μA
+85 to +105°C	25	25	25	μA
+105 to +125°C	50	50	50	μA

Set AWAI in ATDCTL2 to stop the A/D in WAIT mode to reduce power consumption. This stops any A/D conversion that may be going on.

Disabling Unneeded Circuits

Reducing Drive of I/O Lines

The RDRIV register allows you to reduce the drive level for I/O lines on Ports B, C, D, E, F, G, H, and J. This can reduce total power consumption as well as reduce radio frequency interference.

Disable the Timer

The TEN bit in TSCR can be reset to 0 to disable the timer. There is also a bit, TDRB in TMSK2, that can reduce the output driver size for timer outputs. This, too, can reduce total power consumption.

Disable the SPI

When the SPE bit in SP0CR1 is reset, the SPI internal hardware is initialized, but the SPI system is in a low-power, disabled state. The RDS bit in SP0CR2 can be set to reduce the drive capability of Port S output bits.

Disable the A/D

The ADPU bit in ATDCTL2 is reset by default. This disables the A/D for reduced power consumption. Software can disable the A/D during operation and then turn it on again when it is needed. A stabilization time of about 100 μsec is needed after power up, though.

15.6 Bibliography and Further Reading

MC68HC812A4 Technical Summary, MC68HC812A4TS/D, Motorola, 1997.

MC68HC912B32 Technical Summary, MC68HC912B32TS/D, Motorola, 1997.

Technical Supplement MC68HC812A4 Electrical Characteristics, Motorola, 1997.

Technical Supplement MC68HC912B32 Electrical Characteristics, Motorola, 1997.

Appendix A

Debugging Systems POD Design

A.1 Implementing a BDM POD

Here we will discuss M68HC12 routines that perform the lowest level single-wire BDM protocol. These primitive communication routines can build the entire BDM command set shown in Chapter 14, Table 14–3. The routines shown in Example A–1 are essentially those used in the M68EVB912B32 evaluation board. We also include a few extra commands to check BDM status, enable BDM firmware, and read and write the user CCR. These last four commands are special cases of other BDM hardware commands so they are not shown in Table 14–3 as basic BDM commands.

These example routines were assembled so they can be loaded into the EEPROM of an EVB912B32 evaluation board for experimentation and study. They rely on cycle-by-cycle timing of instructions to generate timed waveforms so interrupts should not be allowed while using these routines. The routines do not block interrupts because the EVB does not have any interrupts enabled when it is operating in POD mode (for which the routines were originally written). If you have any interrupts enabled, you should set the I-bit in the CCR before calling any of the BDM routines. If you are working with the EVB for the MC68HC812A4, you can reassemble the program to locate these routines in the EEPROM of the 812A4. Do not try to run these routines out of external RAM or EPROM because that could affect the timing of some instructions and cause the routines to fail.

The complete listing for the BDM communication primitives and BDM commands is shown in Example A–1.

Explanation of Example A–1

To help orient you to the Example A–1 listing, let us go through the WRITE_WORD subroutine (*lines 215–237*). A gross picture of the structure of this command can be found in the third row of Table 14–3. We need to write an 8-bit command ($C8) followed by a 16-bit address and 16 bits of data (in the host-to-target direction). Finally we need a delay of at least 150 E-clocks to allow the BDM logic in the target MCU to complete the requested write before we send any other information to the target BKGD pin.

EXAMPLE A–1   BDM Communication Primitives and BDM Commands

```
BDMFAST.ASM           Assembled with CASMW 7/16/98

0000           1  $PAGELENGTH   73T        ;Set listing page to 73 lines/pg
0000           2  $BASE 10T                ;Change default base to decimal
0000           3  PORTT:    EQU    $00AE   ;Timer port data
0000           4  PORTTD:   EQU    $00AF   ;Timer port ddr
               5
0E00           6            ORG    $0E00   ;B3 EEPROM past Dbug12 pod use
               7  ;*****************************************************
               8  ; Serial BDM data writes. Alternate entry points for
               9  ; 8-bit and 16-bit values.
              10  ;
              11  ; WSerial_8 - Enter with data in A, D value lost.
              12  ; WSerial_16 - Enter with data in D, D value lost.
              13  ; X, Y, and D used in sub but not restored
              14  ;
              15  ; Port T bit-7 is tied to target BKGD for serial comm
              16  ; Port T bit-6 is tied to target RESET (=1 in this sub)
              17  ; This routine writes zero to bits 5-0 if GP output
              18  ;
              19  ; 16 clocks per bit time. Entry overhead to first
              20  ; falling edge is 11 cyc (8-bit) or 14 cyc (16-bit)
              21  ; Exit overhead from end of last bit time is 5 cyc if
              22  ; last bit=1, 7 cyc if last bit=0
              23  ; Total (+0/−2 cyc): 146 (8-bit) 277 (16-bit) cycles
              24  ;
              25  ;*** CAUTION: CRITICALLY TIMED ROUTINE ****************
              26  ;  assumes internal execution or no stretches
              27  ;*****************************************************
              28  WSerial_16:
0E00 CD0010   29      ldy      #16          ;[2] bit count = 16
0E03 2003     30      bra      Write_Fast   ;[3] Rest is same as Write8
              31
              32  WSerial_8:
0E05 CD0008   33      ldy      #8           ;[2] bit count = 8
              34
              35  Write_Fast:
0E08 CE40C0   36      ldx      #$40c0       ;[2] Patterns for BKGD low:hi
0E0B 59       37      asld                  ;[1] MSB of data to C-bit
0E0C B7C5     38      xgdx                  ;[1] data to X, $40c0 to D
0E0E 5BAE     39      stab     PORTT        ;[2] Pw Write BKGD output to 1
0E10 5BAF     40      stab     PORTTD       ;[2] Pw BKGD to active high
              41  Bit_Loop:
0E12 7A00AE   42      staa     ePORTT       ;[3] wOP BKGD output to 0
0E15 240E     43      bcc      Do_0         ;[1/3] Branch if bit is a 0
              44  Do_1:
0E17 7B00AE   45      stab     ePORTT       ;[3] wOP force BKGD back high
```

```
0E1A B7C5      46      xgdx                  ;[1] data to D, $40c0 to X
0E1C 59        47      asld                  ;[1] next data bit to C-bit
0E1D B7C5      48      xgdx                  ;[1] data to X, $40c0 to D
0E1F 03        49      dey                   ;[1] Update bit counter
0E20 2712      50      beq     Done_1F       ;[1/3] If last data bit sent
0E22 A7        51      nop                   ;[1] delay
0E23 20ED      52      bra     Bit_Loop      ;[3] Loop for next bit
               53  Do_0:
0E25 B7C5      54      xgdx                  ;[1] data to D, $40c0 to X
0E27 59        55      asld                  ;[1] next data bit to C-bit
0E28 B7C5      56      xgdx                  ;[1] data to X, $40c0 to D
0E2A 03        57      dey                   ;[1] Update bit counter
0E2B 2704      58      beq     Done_0F       ;[1/3] If last data bit sent
0E2D 5BAE      59      stab    PORTT         ;[2] Pw BKGD output to 1
0E2F 20E1      60      bra     Bit_Loop      ;[3] Loop for next bit
               61  Done_0F:
0E31 7B00AE    62      stab    ePORTT        ;[3] wOP force BKGD high
               63  Done_1F:
0E34 7900AF    64      clr     ePORTTD       ;[3] wOP force BKGD to hi-z
0E37 3D        65      rts                   ;[5] ** return **
               66
               67  ;*******************************************************
               68  ; Serial BDM data read. All background read operations
               69  ; involve 16-bit data even if only a byte is being read.
               70  ; Byte operations return data from odd addresses in B
               71  ; and data from even addresses in A. This routine always
               72  ; returns 16 bits of data in D (A:B).
               73  ;
               74  ; RSerial_16 - Returns data in D.
               75  ; X used in subroutine but not restored
               76  ;
               77  ; Port T bit-7 is tied to target BKGD for serial comm
               78  ; Port T bit-6 is tied to target RESET (=1 in this sub)
               79  ; This routine writes $C0 to DDRT
               80  ;
               81  ; 19 clocks per bit time. Entry overhead to first
               82  ; BKGD edge is 12 cycles. Exit overhead is 1 cycle.
               83  ; Total 317 cycles
               84  ;
               85  ;*** CAUTION: CRITICALLY TIMED ROUTINE *****************
               86  ;** assumes internal execution or no stretches
               87  ;*******************************************************
               88
               89  RSerial_16:
0E38 4DAF80    90      bclr    PORTTD,$80    ;[4] rPOw be sure BKGD is hi-z
0E3B 4DAE80    91      bclr    PORTT,$80     ;[4] rPOw write BKGD output to0
               92  ;BKGD will go to driven 0 when 1 written to PORTTD bit-7
```

```
0E3E  4CAF80   93        bset     PORTTD,$80   ;[4] rPOw BKGD low to start bit tim
0E41  4DAF80   94        bclr     PORTTD,$80   ;[4] rPOw return BKGD to hi-z
0E44           95        ldd      #$0003       ;[2] end when 1 shifts out MSB of D
0E47  2000     96        bra      Read_1F      ;[3] delay to match timing
               97 Read_1F:
0E49  DEAE     98        ldx      PORTT        ;[3] RfP read next data bit to MSB
0E4B  B7C5     99        xgdx                  ;[1] new bit to MSB of A, data to X
0E4D  48      100        asla                  ;[1] shift new data bit into Carry
0E4E  B7C5    101        xgdx                  ;[1] data to D, C not changed
0E50  4CAF80  102        bset     PORTTD,$80   ;[4] rPOw BKGD low to start bit tim
0E53  4DAF80  103        bclr     PORTTD,$80   ;[4] rPOw return BKGD to hi-z
0E56  55      104        rolb                  ;[1] shift new bit to LSB from rt
0E57  45      105        rola                  ;[1] 16-bit rotate
0E58  24EF    106        bcc      Read_1F      ;[1/3] bra=more bits, else done
              107 Read_done:
0E5A  B7C5    108        xgdx                  ;[1] data to X
0E5C  A7      109        nop                   ;[1] delay
0E5D  96AE    110        ldaa     PORTT        ;[3] rfP read last data bit to MSB
0E5F  48      111        asla                  ;[1] shift last data bit to carry
0E60  B7C5    112        xgdx                  ;[1] data to D, C not affected
0E62  55      113        rolb                  ;[1] shift new bit to LSB from rt
0E63  45      114        rola                  ;[1] 16-bit rotate
0E64  3D      115        rts                   ;[5] ** return **
              116
              117 ;PORT and ddr defined earlier, these EQUs force the
              118 ;assembler to use extended addressing rather than direct
0E65          119 ePORTT: EQU $00AE    ;Extended mode Timer port data
0E65          120 ePORTTD: EQU $00AF   ;Extended mode Timer port ddr
              121
              122 ;****************************************************
              123 ; Some BDM command subroutines end in a jmp to
              124 ; a primitive subroutine. The rts at the end of that
              125 ; routine returns to the program that called the
              126 ; command subroutine (double return).
              127 ;
              128 ; These routines require interrupts to be masked.
              129 ; If needed, mask interrupts before calling.
              130 ;****************************************************
              131 ; There are two groups of BDM commands. The first group
              132 ; consists of hardware commands which do not require
              133 ; the MCU to be in active BDM mode. The second group of
              134 ; commands are firmware commands which require that
              135 ; BDM is active.
              136 ;
              137 ; The hardware commands are...
              138 ;
              139 ; BACKGROUND - Go to active background mode
```

```
                  140  ; WRITE_BYTE - Write a byte with BDM not in map
                  141  ; WRITE_BD_BYTE - Write a byte with BDM in map
                  142  ; WRITE_WORD - Write a word with BDM not in map
                  143  ; WRITE_BD_WORD - Write a word with BDM in map
                  144  ; READ_BYTE - Read a byte with BDM not in map
                  145  ; READ_BD_BYTE - Read a byte with BDM in map
                  146  ; READ_WORD - Read a word with BDM not in map
                  147  ; READ_BD_WORD - Read a word with BDM in map
                  148  ;
                  149  ; Next four commands are not basic BDM commands,
                  150  ; they are built from basic BDM hardware commands.
                  151  ;
                  152  ; ENABLE_FIRM - Set ENBDM bit in BDM status reg
                  153  ;               Enables firmware command group
                  154  ;               and BGND instruction (opcode)
                  155  ; BDM_STATUS - Read BDM status register
                  156  ; WRITE_CCR - Write user CCR
                  157  ; READ_CCR - Read user CCR
                  158  ;*********************************************
                  159
                  160  ;*********************************************
                  161  ; BACKGROUND - $90 - Enter background mode
                  162  ;
                  163  ; skip if ENBDM bit not set - it would just return
                  164  ; to user code anyway
                  165  ;*********************************************
                  166  BACKGROUND:
0E65  160F03      167  jsr      BDM_STATUS   ;[4+958] read current status
0E68  D7          168  tstb                  ;[1] see if firmware enabled
0E69  2A08        169  bpl      Exit_BGND    ;[1/3] exit if not enabled
0E6B  8690        170  ldaa     #$90         ;[1] BACKGROUND command code
0E6D  160E05      171  jsr      WSerial_8    ;[4+146]
0E70  060F25      172  jmp      Dly_40       ;[3+45] delay then double return
                  173  Exit_BGND:
0E73  3D          174  rts                   ;[5] return
                  175
                  176  ;*********************************************
                  177  ; WRITE_BYTE - $C0 aaaa oooo
                  178  ;   Write byte - BDM out of map
                  179  ;
                  180  ; On entry D=addr to write,
                  181  ; data byte (dd) to write in low half of X (??:dd)
                  182  ;*********************************************
                  183  WRITE_BYTE:
0E74  34          184  pshx                  ;[2] save data
0E75  3B          185  pshd                  ;[2] save address
0E76  86C0        186  ldaa     #$c0         ;[1] WRITE_BYTE command code
```

```
              187
              188 WTb_com:
0E78 160E05   189     jsr     WSerial_8    ;[4+146] send command
0E7B EC80     190     ldd     0,sp         ;[3] address of byte to write
0E7D 160E00   191     jsr     WSerial_16   ;[4+277] send address
0E80 3A       192     puld                 ;[3] recover address and deallocate
0E81 C501     193     bitb    #$01         ;[1] test for odd/even address
0E83 3A       194     puld                 ;[3] recover data and deallocate
0E84 2602     195     bne     arn_swp0     ;[1/3] bra if addr odd (data in B)
0E86 B790     196     exg     b,a          ;[1] even addr so swap data to A
              197 arn_swp0:
0E88 160E00   198     jsr     WSerial_16   ;[4+277] send 16 bits of data
0E8B 060F15   199     jmp     Dly_175      ;[3+173] wait for free cycle
              200 ; NOTE: double return after Rd_Dly
              201
              202 ;*********************************************
              203 ; WRITE_BD_BYTE - $C4 aaaa oooo
              204 ;   Write a byte with BDM in map
              205 ;
              206 ; On entry D=addr to write,
              207 ; data byte (dd) to write in low half of X (??:dd)
              208 ;*********************************************
              209 WRITE_BD_BYTE:
0E8E 34       210     pshx                 ;[2] save data
0E8F 3B       211     pshd                 ;[2] save address
0E90 86C4     212     ldaa    #$c4         ;[1] WRITE_BD_BYTE command code
0E92 20E4     213     bra     WTb_com      ;[3] rest is same as WRITE_BYTE
              214
              215 ;*********************************************
              216 ; WRITE_WORD - $C8 aaaa oooo
              217 ;   Write word - BDM out of map
              218 ;
              219 ; On entry D=addr to write, data word to write in X
              220 ; Carry set on return if address was illegal (odd)
              221 ;*********************************************
              222 WRITE_WORD:
0E94 160F1C   223     jsr     Test4odd     ;[4]+10] proceed only if addr even
              224 ; NOTE: double returns if address was bad
0E97 34       225     pshx                 ;[2] save data
0E98 3B       226     pshd                 ;[2] save address
0E99 86C8     227     ldaa    #$c8         ;[1] WRITE_WORD command code
              228
              229 WTw_com:
0E9B 160E05   230     jsr     WSerial_8    ;[4+146] send command
0E9E 3A       231     puld                 ;[3] recover address and deallocate
0E9F 160E00   232     jsr     WSerial_16   ;[4+277] send address
0EA2 3A       233     puld                 ;[3] recover data and deallocate
```

```
OEA3  160E00    234    jsr     WSerial_16   ;[4+277] send data
OEA6  160F15    235    jsr     Dly_175      ;[4+173] wait for free cycle
OEA9  10FE      236    clc                  ;[1] indicate no error
OEAB  3D        237    rts                  ;[5] ** return **
                238
                239    ;*****************************************************
                240    ; WRITE_BD_WORD - $CC aaaa oooo
                241    ;   Write a word with BDM in map
                242    ;* NOTE: there are no writable words in BD space
                243    ;*       (so this command is not useful)
                244    ;
                245    ; On entry D=addr to write, data word to write in X
                246    ; Carry set on return if address was illegal (odd)
                247    ;*****************************************************
                248    WRITE_BD_WORD:
OEAC  076E      249    bsr     Test4odd     ;[4+10] proceed only if addr even
                250    ; NOTE: double returns if address was bad
OEAE  34        251    pshx                 ;[2] save data
OEAF  3B        252    pshd                 ;[2] save address
OEB0  86CC      253    ldaa    #$cc         ;[1] WRITE_BD_WORD command code
OEB2  20E7      254    bra     WTw_com      ;[3] rest is same as WRITE_WORD
                255
                256    ;*****************************************************
                257    ; READ_BYTE - $E0 aaaa iiii
                258    ; Read byte - BDM out of map
                259    ;
                260    ; On entry D=address to read,
                261    ; return data byte in D (00:B)
                262    ;*****************************************************
                263    READ_BYTE:
OEB4  3B        264    pshd                 ;[2] save address
OEB5  86E0      265    ldaa    #$e0         ;[1] command code for READ_BYTE
                266    RDb_com:
OEB7  160E05    267    jsr     WSerial_8    ;[4+146] send command
OEBA  EC80      268    ldd     0,sp         ;[3] address of byte to read
OEBC  160E00    269    jsr     WSerial_16   ;[4+277] send address
OEBF  0754      270    bsr     Dly_175      ;[4+173] wait for free cycle
OEC1  160E38    271    jsr     RSerial_16   ;[4+317] get 16 bits of data
OEC4  30        272    pulx                 ;[3] recover address and deallocate
OEC5  B7C5      273    xgdx                 ;[1] swap address to D for tests
OEC7  C501      274    bitb    #$01         ;[1] test for odd/even address
OEC9  B7C5      275    xgdx                 ;[1] swap address and data back
OECB  2602      276    bne     arn_tfr0     ;[1/3] bra if addr odd (data in B)
OECD  B701      277    tfr     a,b          ;[1] even addr so move data to B
                278    arn_tfr0:
OECF  87        279    clra                 ;[1] clear upper byte of returned D
OED0  3D        280    rts                  ;[5] ** return **
```

EXAMPLE A–1   Continued

```
      281
      282   ;****************************************************
      283   ; READ_BD_BYTE - $E4 aaaa iiii
      284   ;   Read a byte with BDM in map
      285   ;
      286   ; On entry D=address to read,
      287   ; return data byte in D (00:B)
      288   ;****************************************************
      289   READ_BD_BYTE:
0ED1 3B       290   pshd                       ;[2] save address
0ED2 86E4     291   ldaa     #$e4              ;[1] command code for READ_BD_BYTE
0ED4 20E1     292   bra      RDb_com           ;[3] rest is same as READ_BYTE
      293
      294   ;****************************************************
      295   ; READ_WORD - $E8 aaaa iiii
      296   ;   Read word - BDM out of map
      297   ;
      298   ; On entry D=address to read,
      299   ; return data word in D (A:B)
      300   ; Carry set on return if address was illegal (odd)
      301   ;****************************************************
      302   READ_WORD:
0ED6 0744     303   bsr      Test4odd          ;[4+10] cont. only if addr even
      304   ; NOTE: double returns if address was bad
0ED8 3B       305   pshd                       ;[2] save address
0ED9 86E8     306   ldaa     #$e8              ;[1] command code for READ_WORD
      307   RDw_com:
0EDB 160E05   308   jsr      WSerial_8         ;[4+146] send command
0EDE 3A       309   puld                       ;[3] recover address and deallocate
0EDF 160E00   310   jsr      WSerial_16        ;[4+277] send address
0EE2 0731     311   bsr      Dly_175           ;[4+173] wait for free cycle
0EE4 160E38   312   jsr      RSerial_16        ;[4+317] get 16 bits of data
0EE7 10FE     313   clc                        ;[1] indicate no error
0EE9 3D       314   rts                        ;[5] ** return **
      315
      316   ;****************************************************
      317   ; READ_BD_WORD - $Ec aaaa iiii
      318   ;   Read a word with BDM in map
      319   ;
      320   ; On entry D=address to read,
      321   ; return data word in D (A:B)
      322   ; Carry set on return if address was illegal (odd)
      323   ;****************************************************
      324   READ_BD_WORD:
0EEA 0730     325   bsr      Test4odd          ;[4+10] cont. only if addr even
      326   ; NOTE: double returns if address was bad
0EEC 3B       327   pshd                       ;[2] save address
```

EXAMPLE A-1   Continued

```
0EED 86EC     328  ldaa     #$ec          ;[1] command code for READ_BD_WORD
0EEF 20EA     329  bra      RDw_com       ;[3] rest is same as READ_WORD
              330
              331  ;*****************************************************
              332  ;  ENABLE_FIRM - $C4 $FF01 %1x000000
              333  ;
              334  ;  This command optionally writes $80 or $C0 to
              335  ;  BDM address $FF01 depending upon the current
              336  ;  value in BDM Status register $FF01.
              337  ;*****************************************************
              338  ENABLE_FIRM:
0EF1 0710     339  bsr      BDM_STATUS    ;[4+958] first read current status
0EF3 D7       340  tstb                   ;[1] See if ENBDM already enabled
0EF4 2B0C     341  bmi      Exit_EF       ;[1/3] exit if already enabled
0EF6 C440     342  andb     #$40          ;[1] keep current BDMACT status
0EF8 CA80     343  orab     #$80          ;[1] set FIRMware enable bit
0EFA 87       344  clra                   ;[1] clear other half of D
0EFB B745     345  tfr      d,x           ;[1] move data to X
0EFD CCFF01   346  ldd      #$ff01        ;[2] address of BDM status register
0F00 078C     347  bsr      WRITE_BD_BYTE ;[4+909] update STATUS register
              348  Exit_EF:
0F02 3D       349  rts                    ;[5] ** return **
              350
              351  ;*****************************************************
              352  ;  BDM_STATUS - $E4 FF01 iiii
              353  ;    Read BDM status register
              354  ;*****************************************************
              355  BDM_STATUS:
0F03 CCFF01   356  ldd      #$ff01        ;[2] addr of BDM status register
0F06 20C9     357  bra      READ_BD_BYTE ;[3+953] execute and double return
              358
              359  ;*****************************************************
              360  ;  WRITE_CCR - $c4 FF06 oooo
              361  ;    Write user CCR register, enter with data in A
              362  ;*****************************************************
              363  WRITE_CCR:
0F08 B745     364  tfr      d,x           ;[1] move data to X
0F0A CCFF06   365  ldd      #$ff06        ;[2] addr of CCRSAV register
0F0D 060E8E   366  jmp      WRITE_BD_BYTE ;[3+909] write & double return
              367
              368  ;*****************************************************
              369  ;  READ_CCR - $E4 FF06 iiii
              370  ;    Read user CCR register, data returned in A
              371  ;*****************************************************
              372  READ_CCR:
0F10 CCFF06   373  ldd      #$ff06        ;[2] addr of CCRSAV register
0F13 20BC     374  bra      READ_BD_BYTE ;[3+953] read and double return
```

```
                375
                376  ;** Local subroutine to delay about 175 target E cycles
                377  ;** to allow wait for dead cycle to complete access
                378  ;** overhead here is 9 cycles, n is 42, loop is 4(n-1)
                379  ;** total delay is 9+164=173 cycles (plus ext overhead)
                380  Dly_175:
0F15 CE002A     381  ldx     #!42         ;[2] initialize loop count
                382  dlydecx:
0F18 09         383  dex                  ;[1] update loop count=count-1
0F19 26FD       384  bne     dlydecx      ;[1/3] loop till X=0
0F1B 3D         385  rts                  ;[5] ** return **
                386
                387  ;** Local subroutine to check for illegal odd address
                388  ;** returns to calling routine or sets carry
                389  ;** (to indicate error) and double returns
                390  ;** to program that called calling routine
                391  Test4odd:
0F1C C501       392  bitb    #$01         ;[1] check for odd (illegal)
0F1E 2704       393  beq     notodd       ;[1/3] bra if addr was even
0F20 1401       394  sec                  ;[1] indicate error
0F22 1B82       395  leas    2,sp         ;[2] addr was odd so double return
                396  notodd:
0F24 3D         397  rts                  ;[5] ** return or double return **
                398
                399  ;** Local subroutine to delay about 40 target E cycles
                400  ;** to allow time for BDM to complete command or
                401  ;** to allow time for firmware to complete access
                402  ;** overhead here is 9 cycles, n is 10, loop is 4(n-1)
                403  ;** total delay is 9+36=45 cycles (plus ext overhead)
                404  Dly_40:
0F25 CE000A     405  ldx     #!10         ;[2] initialize loop count
                406  dly40decx:
0F2809          407  dex                  ;[1] update loop count=count-1
0F29 26FD       408  bne     dly40decx    ;[1/3] loop till X=0
0F2B 3D         409  rts                  ;[5] ** return **
                410
                411  ;***************************************************
                412  ; Firmware commands can only be executed while the
                413  ; background mode is active. If BDM is not active,
                414  ; these commands should not be issued.
                415  ; To find out if BDM is active, you can execute a
                416  ; BDM_STATUS command and check bit-6 of returned
                417  ; value in A (0=not active).
                418  ;
                419  ; The firmware commands are...
                420  ;
                421  ;   WRITE_NEXT - Pre-inc X by 2 and write word
```

EXAMPLE A-1 Continued

```
                       422  ;    WRITE_PC - Write user PC
                       423  ;    WRITE_D - Write user D accumulator
                       424  ;    WRITE_X - Write index register X
                       425  ;    WRITE_Y - Write index register Y
                       426  ;    WRITE_SP - Write stack pointer
                       427  ;    READ_NEXT - Pre-inc X by 2 and read word
                       428  ;    READ_PC - Read user PC
                       429  ;    READ_D - Read user D accumulator
                       430  ;    READ_X - Read index register X
                       431  ;    READ_Y - Read index register Y
                       432  ;    READ_SP - Read stack pointer
                       433  ;    BDM_GO - Resume user program from active BDM
                       434  ;    BDM_TRACE - Do 1 user inst. and return to BDM
                       435  ;    TAG_GO - Enable tagging and go to user program
                       436  ;**********************************************
                       437
                       438  ;**********************************************
                       439  ; WRITE_NEXT - $42 - Pre-inc X by 2 and write word
                       440  ;**********************************************
                       441  WRITE_NEXT:
0F2C 3B                442      pshd                   ;[2] save data
0F2D 8642              443      ldaa      #$42         ;[1] WRITE_NEXT command code
                       444
                       445  ;** Local common routine
                       446  Write_Firm:
0F2F 160E05            447      jsr       WSerial_8    ;[4+146] send command
0F32 3A                448      puld                   ;[3] recover data
0F33 160E00            449      jsr       WSerial_16   ;[4+277] send data
0F36 20ED              450      bra       Dly_40       ;[3+45] allow time to do write
                       451  ;double returns from end of delay routine
                       452
                       453  ;**********************************************
                       454  ; WRITE_PC - $43 - Write user PC
                       455  ;**********************************************
                       456  WRITE_PC:
0F38 3B                457      pshd                   ;[2] save data
0F39 8643              458      ldaa      #$43         ;[1] WRITE_PC command code
0F3B 20F2              459      bra       Write_Firm   ;[3+482] double return
                       460
                       461  ;**********************************************
                       462  ; WRITE_D - $44 - Write user D accumulator
                       463  ;**********************************************
                       464  WRITE_D:
0F3D 3B                465      pshd                   ;[2] save data
0F3E 8644              466      ldaa      #$44         ;[1] WRITE_D command code
0F40 20ED              467      bra       Write_Firm   ;[3+482] double return
                       468
                       469  ;**********************************************
```

EXAMPLE A-1   Continued

```
                470  ; WRITE_X - $45 - Write index register X
                471  ;*********************************************
                472  WRITE_X:
0F42  3B        473       pshd                   ;[2] save data
0F43  8645      474       ldaa      #$45         ;[1] WRITE_X command code
0F45  20E8      475       bra       Write_Firm   ;[3+482] double return
                476
                477  ;*********************************************
                478  ; WRITE_Y - $46 - Write index register Y
                479  ;*********************************************
                480  WRITE_Y:
0F47  3B        481       pshd                   ;[2] save data
0F48  8646      482       ldaa      #$46         ;[1] WRITE_Y command code
0F4A  20E3      483       bra       Write_Firm   ;[3+482] double return
                484
                485  ;*********************************************
                486  ; WRITE_SP - $47 - Write stack pointer
                487  ;*********************************************
                488  WRITE_SP:
0F4C  3B        489       pshd                   ;[2] save data
0F4D  8647      490       ldaa      #$47         ;[1] WRITE_SP command code
0F4F  20DE      491       bra       Write_Firm   ;[3+482] double return
                492
                493  ;*********************************************
                494  ; READ_NEXT - $62 - Pre-inc X by 2 and read word
                495  ;*********************************************
                496  READ_NEXT:
0F51  8662      497       ldaa      #$62         ;[1] READ_NEXT command code
                498
                499  ;** Local common routine
                500  Read_Firm:
0F53  160E05    501       jsr       WSerial_8    ;[4+146] send command
0F56  07CD      502       bsr       Dly_40       ;[4+45] allow firmware to do access
0F58060E38      503       jmp       RSerial_16   ;[3+317] read data & double return
                504
                505  ;*********************************************
                506  ; READ_PC - $63 - Read user PC
                507  ;*********************************************
                508  READ_PC:
0F5B  8663      509       ldaa      #$63         ;[1] READ_PC command code
0F5D  20F4      510       bra       Read_Firm    ;[3+519] double return
                511
                512  ;*********************************************
                513  ; READ_D - $64 - Read user D accumulator
                514  ;*********************************************
                515  READ_D:
0F5F  8664      516       ldaa      #$64         ;[1] READ_D command code
0F61  20F0      517       bra       Read_Firm    ;[3+519] double return
```

```
              518
              519   ;****************************************************
              520   ; READ_X - $65 - Read index register X
              521   ;****************************************************
              522   READ_X:
0F63 8665     523     ldaa    #$65        ;[1] READ_X command code
0F65 20EC     524     bra     Read_Firm   ;[3+519] double return
              525
              526   ;****************************************************
              527   ; READ_Y - $66 - Read index register Y
              528   ;****************************************************
              529   READ_Y:
0F67 8666     530     ldaa    #$66        ;[1] READ_Y command code
0F69 20E8     531     bra     Read_Firm   ;[3+519] double return
              532
              533   ;****************************************************
              534   ; READ_SP - $67 - Read stack pointer
              535   ;****************************************************
              536   READ_SP:
0F6B 8667     537     ldaa    #$67        ;[1] READ_SP command code
0F6D 20E4     538     bra     Read_Firm   ;[3+519] double return
              539
              540   ;****************************************************
              541   ; BDM_GO - $08
              542   ;   Resume user program from active BDM
              543   ;****************************************************
              544   BDM_GO:
0F6F 8608     545     ldaa    #$08        ;[1] BDM_GO command code
              546   Go_8:
0F71 160E05   547     jsr     WSerial_8   ;[4+146] send command
0F74 20AF     548     bra     Dly_40      ;[3+45] double return
              549
              550   ;****************************************************
              551   ; BDM_TRACE - $10
              552   ;   Do 1 user instruction and return to BDM
              553   ;****************************************************
              554   BDM_TRACE:
0F76 8610     555     ldaa    #$10        ;[1] BDM_TRACE command code
0F78 20F7     556     bra     Go_8        ;[3+198] send, dly & dbl return
              557
              558   ;****************************************************
              559   ; TAG_GO - $18
              560   ;   Enable tagging and go to user program
              561   ;****************************************************
              562   TAG_GO:
0F7A 8618     563     ldaa    #$18        ;[1] TAG_GO command code
0F7C 20F3     564     bra     Go_8        ;[3+198] send, dly & dbl return
```

The routine starts with a JSR to Test4odd. The Test4odd subroutine (*line 387*) checks to see if the supplied address is even (the BDM allows word writes only to an even address). To minimize the amount of stack space and program space used by these routines, an assembly language trick is used that may not be familiar to some readers. If the last instructions in a subroutine called Original_Sub are JSR Another_Sub followed by an RTS, you can substitute a BRA Another_Sub or a JMP Another_Sub instead of the JSR and RTS. This avoids a few bytes of object code and uses fewer bytes on the stack. At the end of the Another_Sub subroutine, the RTS returns you to the return address for Original_Sub. This is called a double-return and it can be useful if it is applied carefully and is well documented (otherwise there is a high risk of getting an unbalanced stack). When WRITE_WORD was originally called (from some higher-level monitor program), a return address was pushed onto the stack—we will call this "the original return address." When we execute the JSR to Test4odd, address $0E97 is also pushed onto the stack as a return address to the instruction after the JSR (*line 225*). Now go to the Test4odd subroutine in *lines 387–397*. Since the address to be written is in D, the BITB instruction in *line 392* is checking the LSB (it should be zero). The BEQ in *line 393* branches if the address is OK, otherwise you fall through to the SEC in *line 394* which sets the C bit in the CCR to indicate an error. The LEAS 2,sp instruction at *line 395* alters the stack pointer effectively removing the $0E97 that would take us back to the WRITE_WORD program. Now the stack pointer points to "the original return address." In the error case, this will cause a "double-return," which takes us back to the program that originally called WRITE_WORD. If the address is OK, the BEQ in *line 393* branches to *line 396* and returns to $0E97 (*line 225* in the WRITE_WORD routine). *Lines 225–227* push the 16-bit data and the 16-bit address that were brought into the WRITE_WORD routine in X and D, respectively, and loads accumulator A with $C8 (the code for the WRITE_WORD command). This brings us to WTw_com (a common entry point for write-word).

The JSR WSerial_8 (*line 230*) calls the low-level primitive communication subroutine to send the $C8 command to the target BKGD pin. *Line 231* recovers the address that was previously (*line 226*) saved on the stack. *Line 232* sends the 16-bit address to the target BKGD pin. *Lines 233* and *234* recover the 16-bit data word from the stack and send it to the target BKGD pin. *Line 235* calls the Dly_175 subroutine, which just delays about 175 E-clocks to allow the target enough time to find a free bus cycle to complete the requested write operation. We clear the C bit in the CCR as an indication everything went as planned, and then we return to whatever program originally called WRITE_WORD.

Most of the other routines in this program are easily understood from the comments in the listing; however, two more command subroutines may benefit from additional explanation. The BACKGROUND command (*lines 160–174*) first checks the BDM STATUS register in the target MCU. If the ENBDM bit is clear (BDM firmware disabled), there is no point in trying to execute the BACKGROUND command so the subroutine just returns. The ENABLE_FIRM command (*lines 331–349*) first executes a BDM_STATUS command to get the current value of the BDM STATUS register. If the ENBDM bit is already set, there is no need to do anything else and you take the BMI branch from *line 341* to Exit_EF and return. If ENBDM was not already set, *line 342* masks everything, except the BDMACT bit, to zero and then *line 343* ORs a one into the ENBDM bit. *Lines 344–347* set up and call WRITE_BD_BYTE to write this value into the STATUS register at $FF01 in the target MCU. The old value of BDMACT must be preserved because BDM may or may not be active at the time you try to set the ENBDM bit. If you change the BDMACT bit with a WRITE_BD_BYTE command, it can immediately enable or disable the BDM resources in the memory, which can cause unintended operation.

Critical Timing Elements

The primitive communication routines WSerial_16 (*line 28*), WSerial_8 (*line 32*), and RSerial_16 (*line 89*) are unusual in that they rely on instruction timing to implement the BDM serial protocol. By modifying a program listing to add extra lines (one for each cycle in each instruction), and writing down the cycle code letters from the CPU12 Reference Manual, we can document the relationship between the software routine and signal timing on the BKGD pin. The listing is turned sideways so the timing pattern can be drawn like an oscilloscope trace below this listing (see Figure A–1). This listing is not quite like an assembly listing because it shows instructions in execution order as opposed to source listing order. For example, in the case of a branch that is taken, this listing shows the next instruction that executes even though that would usually not be the next instruction in the assembly listing. Also, one instruction from the assembly listing can appear several times in these execution order listings.

Figure A–1 shows the entry overhead (the time delay from the WSerial_16 entry point until the first bit-time start), and the transition from a bit-time of logic zero to a bit-time of logic one. Before calling this routine, the Port T bit-7 pin was high-impedance. At [1], the pin changes to an actively driven logic one. The falling edge at [2] starts the bit-time. It can take the target up to a cycle to note the falling edge [3], so there is a one-cycle uncertainty about the sample point where the target senses the bit level [4]. Note that Figures A–1 to A–6 are drawn from the host's point of view while Figure 14–2 was drawn from the target's point of view. For reference, the WSerial_16 routine appears in *lines 28–65* of the Example A–1 listing.

If the target's E-clock is slower than 8 MHz, the sample point at which the BDM detects a one or a zero would appear to move to the right. The logic zero sample time is shown in the middle of Figure A–1. If the target's clock slowed below about 6.5 MHz and it took the target a whole

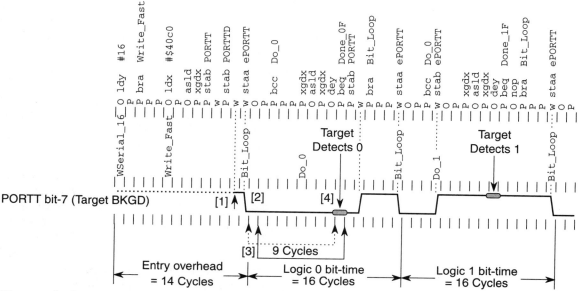

Figure A–1 Transmit 16 bit: entry and 0-to-1 transition.

cycle to detect the falling edge at the start, the sample point could move to the right past the next rising edge of BKGD, which would cause the bit level to be sensed incorrectly. The target's clock would need to be about 16 MHz before the sample point would move left into the logic one start pulse causing the bit to be sensed incorrectly. There are other areas in which a faster or slower target clock would cause the communications to fail so the overall tolerance is more like ±20%. This is still a much wider band of tolerance than an RS232 asynchronous serial interface allows.

Figure A–2 is very similar to Figure A–1 except it shows the entry overhead for the WSerial_8 entry point and it shows the transition from a logic one bit-time to a logic zero bit-time. Just before the falling edge that starts the first bit-time, there is a STAB PORTTD instruction that uses direct addressing mode. The STAA ePORTT instruction at Bit_Loop uses the extended version of the store accumulator instruction to get the write cycle (w) to occur in the first cycle of the instruction (the w cycle is the second cycle in the direct addressing mode version of the store accumulator instruction). To get the CASM assembler to choose extended addressing instead of direct, we added a second EQU statement for PORTT in *line 119* (we changed the label slightly to ePORTT to differentiate it from the equate at *line 3*). Since this equate appears after the instruction that accesses ePORTT (*line 42*), the assembler does not know that it could use direct addressing so it chooses extended. This is sometimes called a forward reference and it is usually considered bad form, but in this case we wanted to choose the extended mode to get a specific cycle-by-cycle sequence.

Figure A–3 shows the timing detail for a transition from a logic zero bit-time to a logic zero bit-time and the exit timing detail when the last bit is a logic zero. Figure A–4 shows the timing detail for a transition from a logic one bit-time to a logic one bit-time and the exit timing detail when the last bit is a logic one.

The instructions in the WSerial_16 and WSerial_8 primitive subroutines were carefully selected, the order of operations was carefully arranged, and delay padding (see the NOP instruction in *line 51*) was added in strategic places to cause all paths through the routine to match so each bit-time would be exactly 16 cycles long. This was accomplished through a combination of trial and error

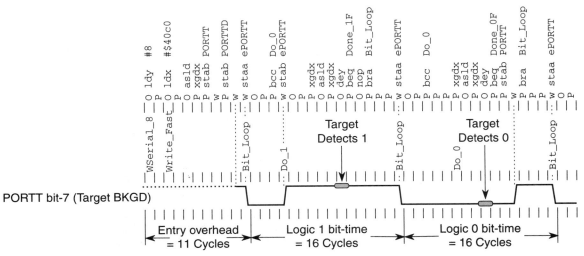

Figure A–2   Transmit 8 bit: entry and 1-to-0 transition.

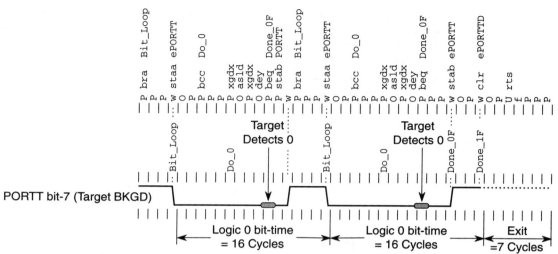

Figure A-3   Transmit: exit and 0-to-0 transition.

as well as using cycle-by-cycle timing diagrams such as Figures A–1 through A–4. Fortunately most assembly language programming does not require such extraordinary measures. With a little more effort, the entry and exit sequences could have been fine tuned to match as well but that was not important in this case. The bit-timing was worth a little extra effort so that the operation of the communication routines would not be data dependent (this simplifies testing of the finished routines).

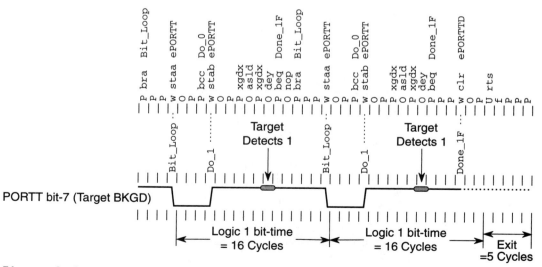

Figure A-4   Transmit: exit and 1-to-1 transition.

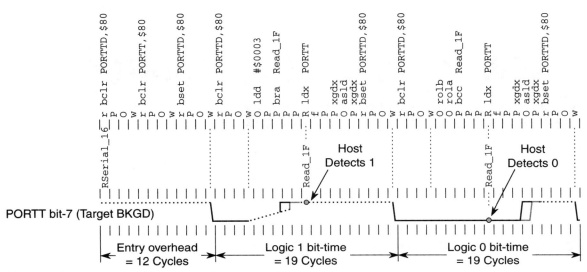

Figure A–5   Receive 16-bit: entry and 1-to-0 transition.

Refer to Figures A–5 and A–6 for an analysis of the timing for the RSerial_16 subroutine. This routine follows a single path through the code regardless of the data that are read. Figure A–5 shows the entry sequence to the start of the first data bit (falling edge on BKGD). Figure A–6 shows the exit overhead. For reference, the RSerial_16 routine appears in *lines 89–115* of the Example A–1 listing.

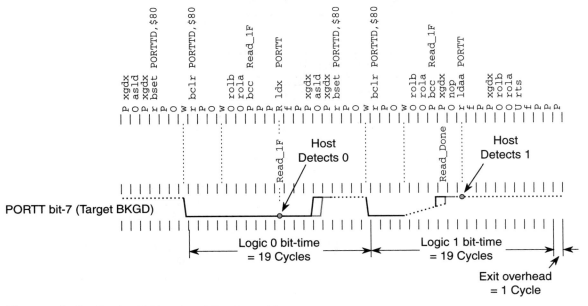

Figure A–6   Receive 16-bit: exit and 0-to-1 transition.

Answers to Odd-Numbered Chapter Problems

Solutions to Chapter 2 Problems

2.1   Which of the M68HC12 ports is used for the A/D converter inputs? Port AD.

2.3   Draw the programmer's model for the M68HC12.

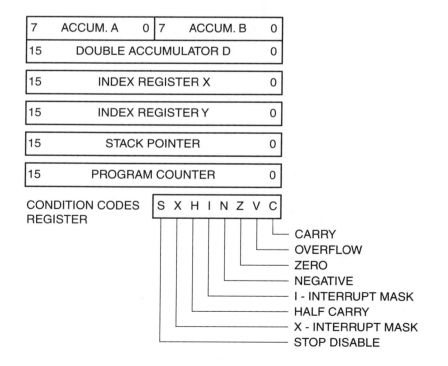

2.5   Calculate the effective address for each of the following examples of indexed addressing.

        a. X = $5000

           LDAA   0,X   EA = $5000

        b. Y = $5000

           STAA $10,Y   EA = $5010

        c. X = $500D

           LDAA $25,X   EA = $5032

2.7   Discuss the relative advantages and disadvantages of direct and extended addressing.

        Direct addressing uses only 8 bits to specify the address of the memory data and thus is faster and uses less memory than extended addressing. Its disadvantage is that only 256 memory locations can be addressed. Extended addressing requires 3 bytes for the instruction and address and thus takes longer to execute and requires more memory. Extended addressing can access the whole 64-Kbyte address space.

2.9   What is in the following CPU registers after a system reset?

        A, B, CCR, Stack Pointer.

        A, B = unknown. In the CCR, the I, X, and S bits are set and the rest of the bits are unknown. The stack pointer is unknown.

Solutions to Chapter 3 Problems

3.1   Give four ways to specify each of the following constants.

        a. The ASCII character X

           'X', "X", $58, 88, %01011000, @230

        b. The ASCII character x

           'x', "x", $78, 120, %01111000, @270

        c. 100_{10}

           100, $64, %01100100, @144

        d. 64_{16}

           100, $64, %01100100, @144

3.3   What assembler pseudooperation is used to allocate memory for data variables? DS

3.5   What assembler pseudooperation is used to define byte constants in ROM memory? DB

3.7   How are data storage areas located when using the CASM assembler?

By using ORG pseudooperations

3.9   Give the addressing mode and the effective address for each of the following instructions:

		Mode	Effective Address
a.	LDAA #5	Immediate	The contents of the program counter after the opcode has been fetched
b.	LDAA $5	Direct	$0005
c.	LDAA $5,X	Indexed	The contents of the X register plus 5
d.	STAA $081A	Extended	$081A

Solutions to Chapter 4 Problems

4.1   You be the assembler. Assemble the following source code just as the CASM12 assembler would do it.

```
cprb1ans.asm          Assembled with CASM  04/09/1998  21:12  PAGE  1
0000                1  COUNT:    EQU     !7
0000                2  MAX:      EQU     !10
0000                3  ROM:      EQU     $F000
0000                4  RAM:      EQU     $0800
F000                5            ORG     ROM
F000  8607          6            ldaa    #COUNT
F002  8B0A          7            adda    #MAX
F004  7A0800        8            staa    DATA
F007  3F            9            swi
0800               10            ORG     RAM
0800               11  DATA      DS      1
```

4.3   In the program above, what addressing mode is used for the STAA instruction? Extended

4.5   For each of the following questions, assume the memory display of the M68HC12 shows:

5000 B0 53 05 2B 36 89 00 FF FE 80 91 3E 77 AB 8F 7F

Give the results after each of the following instructions are executed.

a. LDAA $5000   A = $B0, NZVC = 100−

b. Assume X = $5000

LDAA   0,X   A = $B0, NZVC = 100−

c. Assume X = $5000

LDAA   6,X   A = $00, NZVC = 010−

4.7   Use the contents of memory shown in Problem 4.5 and give the results of the following instructions.

a. SP = $5005
   PULA   A = $89, SP = $5006

b. SP = $5005
   PULA   A = $89
   PULB   B = $00

c. SP = $5005
   PSHA
   PSHB   SP = $5003

d. SP = $500A
   PULA
   PSHB   A = $91, SP = $500A

4.9   Use the contents of memory shown in Problem 4.5 and give the results of the following instructions.

a. Assume X = $5000

   BSET   0,X,$0F   ($5000) = $BF

b. Assume X = $5000

   BSET   6,X,$AA   EA = $5006, (EA) = $AA

c. Assume X = $5007

   BCLR   0,X,$AA   ($5007) = $55

d. Assume Y = $5000

   BCLR   0,Y,$FF   ($5000) = $00

4.11   The ASLx instructions have the same operation codes as the LSLx instructions. Why?

   Both shift a 0 into the least significant bit and shift the most significant bit into the carry bit.

4.13   Use the contents of memory shown in Problem 4.5 and give the results of the following instructions.

a. LDAA $5006
   NEGA   A = $00, NZVC = 0100

b. LDAA $5007
   NEGA   A = $01, NZVC = 0001

c. NEG $5009   ($5009) = $80, NZVC = 1011

d. LDAA $5006
   COMA   A = $FF, NZVC = 1001

e. LDAA $5007
   COMA   A = $00, NZVC = 0101

f. COM $5009   ($5009) = $7F, NZVC = 0001

4.15   The following straight binary addition was done in the M68HC12. What is the binary result and what are the N, Z, V, and C flags?

01010111

01100110

10111101   N=1, Z=0, V=1, C=0

4.17   Use the contents of memory shown in problem 4.5 and give the results of the following instructions.

    LDAA $5002
    ADDA $5004   A = $3B
    DAA   A = $41

4.19   Use the contents of memory shown in Problem 4.5 and give the results of the following instructions.

a. LDAA $5000
   CMPA $5001   A = $B0, NZVC = 0010

b. TST $5006   NZVC = 0100

c. TST $5007   NZVC = 1000

4.21   Assume A = $05 and memory location DATA = $22. A CMPA DATA instruction is executed followed by a conditional branch. For each of the conditional branch instructions in the table, indicate by yes or no if you expect the branch to be taken.

BGE	BLE	BGT	BLT	BEQ	BNE
no	yes	no	yes	no	yes

BHS	BLS	BHI	BLO
no	yes	no	yes

4.23   Assume A = $22 and memory location DATA = $22. A CMPA DATA instruction is executed followed by a conditional branch. For each of the conditional branch instructions in the table, indicate by yes or no if you expect the branch to be taken.

BGE	BLE	BGT	BLT	BEQ	BNE
yes	yes	no	no	yes	no

BHS	BLS	BHI	BLO
yes	yes	no	no

4.25   Draw a memory map showing the contents of the stack expected after the program in Example 4–13 is executed. What value do you expect in the A register after the subroutine adds all the data?

9F4: 08 Return	9FA: 06 Data
9F5: 14 Address	9FB: 05 Data
9F6: 0A Data	9FC: 04 Data
9F7: 09 Data	9FD: 03 Data
9F8: 08 Data	9FE: 02 Data
9F9: 07 Data	9FF: 01 Data

A = $37

Solutions to Chapter 5 Problems

5.1 You downloaded an S-record file to the EVB and the D-Bug12 Monitor responds with the message "Invalid Command." What went wrong?

You probably forgot to start the download with the LOAD command.

5.3 Write a short D-Bug12 assembler (ASM) code segment showing how to use the D-Bug12 monitor utility routine putchar to print the letter A on the terminal.

```
ldab    #$41
ldx     $FE04
jsr     0,x
swi
```

5.5 Write a short D-Bug12 assembler (ASM) code segment showing how to use the D-Bug12 monitor utility routine printf to print a null-terminated string starting at $5000.

```
ldd     #$5000
ldx     $FE06
jsr     0,x
swi
```

5.7 How does the D-Bug12 monitor know when to stop printing characters in the printf routine?

The printf routine prints characters until it finds a null ($00) character.

5.9 What command is used to set a breakpoint at $4016?

BR 4016

5.11 What command is used to display what breakpoints are currently set?

BR

5.13 What command is used to display memory locations $5000 to $502F?

MD 5000 5020

Solutions to Chapter 6 Problems

6.1   For each of the logic statements, give the appropriate M68HC12 code to set the condition code register and to branch to the ELSE part of an IF-THEN-ELSE. Assume P and Q are 8-bit, unsigned numbers in memory locations P and Q.

a. IF P ≥ Q

```
;  IF  P ≥ Q
        ldaa    P
        cmpa    Q
        blo     ELSE_PART
```

b. IF Q > P

```
;  IF  Q > P
        ldaa    Q
        cmpa    P
        bls     ELSE_PART
```

c. IF P = Q

```
;  IF  P = Q
        ldaa    P
        cmpa    Q
        bne     ELSE_PART
```

6.3   For each of the logic statements, give the appropriate M68HC12 code to set the condition code register and to branch to the ELSE part of an IF-THEN-ELSE. Assume P, Q, and R are 8-bit, signed numbers in memory locations P, Q, and R.

a.
```
;  IF  P + Q ≥ 1
        ldaa    P
        adda    Q
        cmpa    #1
        blt     ELSE_PART
```

b.
```
;  IF  Q > P − R
        ldaa    Q
        adda    R
        cmpa    P       Q + R > P?
        ble     ELSE_PART
```

c.
```
;  IF  (P > R ) OR (Q < R)
        ldaa    P
        cmpa    R
        bgt     THEN_PART
        ldaa    Q
        cmpa    R
        bge     ELSE_PART
```

d.
```
;      (P > R) AND (Q < R)
        ldaa    P
```

```
cmpa      R
ble       ELSE_PART
ldaa      Q
cmpa      R
bge       ELSE_PART
```

6.5   Write a section of M68HC12 code to implement the design given below in which K1
        and K2 are unsigned 8-bit numbers in memory locations K1 and K2.

```
s6-5ansc.asm          Assembled with CASM 05/24/1998 02:14 PAGE 1
                      1  ; IF K1 < K2
0000 B60012           2       ldaa     K1
0003 B10013           3       cmpa     K2
0006 2405             4       bhs      Else_Part
                      5  ;   THEN K2=K1
0008 7A0013           6       staa     K2
000B 2005             7       bra      Endif
                      8  ;   ELSE K1=64
                      9  Else_Part:
000D 8664            10       ldaa     #!64
000F 7A0012          11       staa     K1
                     12  Endif:
                     13  ; ENDIF K1 < K2
0012                 14  K1:    DS      1
0013                 15  K2:    DS      1
```

6.7   For Problem 6.6, assume K1=1, K2=3, and K3=−2. How many times should the
        code pass through the loop and what are the final values of K1, K2, and K3?

        One pass through the loop; final values are K1=2, K2=−2, and K3=−2.

6.9   For Problem 6.8, assume A1=2, B1=2, C1=3, and D1=6. What final values do you
        expect after the code has been executed? A1=16, B1=2, C1=3, D1=3.

6.11   For the program in Example 6–11, what is printed on the screen when the program is
        executed?

        STAa carriage-return, line-feed.

6.13   For the program in Example 6–12, how many bytes are reserved for "data1" in the
        RAM. How many bytes of stack are used by the program?

        NUMCHR+3 = 6. The program uses 2 bytes of the stack each time it jumps to a
        monitor subroutine plus whatever the routine uses.

Solutions to Chapter 7 Problems

7.1   What levels must be on the BKGD, MODA, and MODB pins at $\overline{\text{RESET}}$ to place
        the M68HC12 into normal-expanded mode? (1 0 1) Into normal single-chip mode?
        (1 0 0)

7.3 How do you control the direction of the bidirectional bits in the M68HC12 I/O ports?

Each of the bidirectional data ports has a data direction register. Writing a one to a bit in the DDR enables that bit to be an output.

Solutions to Chapter 8 Problems

8.1 When the I bit in the condition code register is set to 1, interrupts are

b. disabled.

8.3 In the M68HC12 interrupt service routine, you MUST unmask interrupts with the CLI instruction before returning—false.

8.5 How many bytes are pushed onto the stack when the M68HC12 processes an interrupt request? 9

8.7 Which instruction is used to globally mask interrupts? SEI

8.9 Assume a dedicated application system (no D-Bug12 Monitor) with ROM at $E000–$FFFF and RAM at $0800–$0BFF. Show how to initialize the interrupt vectors for the $\overline{\text{IRQ}}$ and Timer Channel 1 interrupts. Assume IRQISR and TC1ISR are labels on the respective interrupt service routines.

```
prb8_9c.asm          Assembled with  CASM  01/25/1998  21:45  PAGE  1
0000              1  TC1VEC:  EQU   $FFEC   ; TC1 Vector location
0000              2  IRQVEC:  EQU   $FFF2   ; IRQ Vector location
0000              3  PROG:    EQU   $E000   ; Program location
                  4  ;
E000              5           ORG   PROG
                  6  ;
E000 A7           7  TC1ISR:  nop       ; TC1 ISR
E001 0B           8           rti
                  9  ;
E002 A7          10  IRQISR:  nop       ; IRQ ISR
E003 0B          11           rti
                 12  ; Locate the vectors
FFEC             13           ORG   TC1VEC
FFEC E000        14           DW    TC1ISR
FFF2             15           ORG   IRQVEC
FFF2 E002        16           DW    IRQISR
```

8.11 For the interrupt service routine in Example 8–10, where would you put a breakpoint to find out if you are getting to the interrupt service routine?

Set a breakpoint at the first instruction in the ISR.

8.13 Write a complete M68HC12 program in assembly language for an interrupt occurring on the external IRQ source. The interrupt vector is to be at $FFF2:FFF3. When the interrupt occurs the ISR is to increment an 8-bit memory location "COUNT" starting from $00. The foreground job is to be a spin loop "SPIN BRA SPIN". Assume

a. The D-Bug12 monitor is <u>not</u> installed.

b. Code is to be located in ROM at $E000.

c. RAM is available between $0800 and $0BFF

```
prb8_13c.asm    Assembled with CASM 01/25/1998 21:50 PAGE 1
0000            1 PROG:   EQU $E000 ; Program Location
0000            2 STACK:  EQU $0A00 ; Stack Location
0000            3 RAM:    EQU $0800 ; RAM Location
0000            4 IRQVEC: EQU $FFF2 ; IRQ Vector Location
0000            5 IRQEN:  EQU %01000000 ; IRQ Enable Bit
0000            6 INTCR:  EQU $1e   ; Interrupt Control Register
                7 ; Allocate Data Area
0800            8          ORG    RAM
0800 01         9 Count:  DB   1
               10 ;
E000           11          ORG PROG
E000 CF0A00    12          lds #STACK ; Initialize stack pointer
               13 ; Initialize memory counter = 0
E003 790800    14          clr Count
               15 ; Enable the IRQ interrupt
E006 4C1E40    16          bset INTCR,IRQEN
               17 ; Unmask interrupts
E009 10EF      18          cli
               19 ; Foreground job is a spin loop
E00B 20FE      20 spin:   bra spin
               21 ;
               22 ; Interrupt Service Routine
E00D 720800    23 ISR:    inc Count ; No overflow detection
E010 0B        24          rti
               25 ; Initialize the vector for IRQ
FFF2           26          ORG IRQVEC
FFF2 E00D      27          DW  ISR
```

8.15 How can the priority order of interrupts be changed?

The HPRIO register contains eight bits that can allow any of the interrupt sources to be promoted to the top of the hierarchical order. The priority can be changed only when the interrupts are masked (I-bit = 1).

8.17 What is the SWI instruction and what does it do?

SWI is a software interrupt instruction. It is a single byte and CPU treats it as if an interrupt has occurred. All registers are pushed onto the stack and the processor fetches a vector from $FFF6:FFF7.

8.19 Define interrupt latency.

Interrupt latency is the time delay between the interrupt request and when the interrupt service routine is entered.

8.21   Show how to modify the code in Example 8–4 to have the ISR service all interrupts generated by any of the four key wakeup bits.

```
; Interrupt Service routine
ISR:
; Service all interrupts that have been generated.
; Check each one in turn
        ldaa   KWIFJ       ; Get the flags
; IF bit 0
        bita   #BIT0
        beq    Chk_1
; THEN DO the bit 0 ISR
;            . . .
; IF bit 1
Chk_1:  ldaa   KWIFJ       ; Get the flags
        bita   #BIT1
        beq    Chk_2
; THEN DO the bit 1 ISR
;            . . .
; IF bit 2
Chk_2:  ldaa   KWIFJ       ; Get the flags
        bita   #BIT2
        beq    Chk_3
; THEN DO the bit 2 ISR
;            . . .
; IF bit 3
Chk_3:  ldaa   KWIFJ       ; Get the flags
        bita   #BIT3
        beq    Done
; THEN DO the bit 3 ISR
;            . . .
;
Done:
; Now reset all flags that have been set
        ldaa   KWIFJ
        staa   KWIFJ
        rti                ; Return to interrupted prog
```

Solutions to Chapter 9 Problems

9.1   On reset, the RAM in the MC68HC812A4 is mapped to $0800 and the 512-byte register block to $0000. The locations of these can be changed. Describe how this is done.

The INITRM ($0010) and INITRG ($0011) can be programmed with the most significant byte of the new address. This can be done only once in your program.

9.3   What is the default memory location of EEPROM in the MC68HC812A4?

$1000–$1FFF in expanded mode systems and $F000–$FFFF in single-chip systems.

9.5   What are the three methods that can erase EEPROM?

Byte erase, row erase, bulk erase.

Solutions to Chapter 10 Problems

10.1   What is wrong with the following code to get the 16-bit value of the TCNT register?

```
LDAA $84 ;Get the high byte
LDAB $85 ;Get the low byte
```

If the TCNT register is incrementing at each M-clock cycle, the low byte will have changed during the time the high byte is being read.

10.3   How should you read the 16-bit TCNT value?

```
LDD    $84
```
Latches the 16-bit data from the TCNT register so the value is stable.

10.5   Give the name of the bit, the name of the register that it is in, the register's address, which bit, and the default or reset state of the bit for each of the following:

a. What bit indicates that the timer has overflowed?

Timer overflow flag, TOF, in the TFLG2 register at $8F, bit-7; the reset state is 0.

b. What bit enables the timer overflow interrupts?

TOI in the TMSK2 register at $8D, bit-7. The default state is interrupts disabled.

c. What bits are used to prescale the timer clock?

PR2, PR1, and PR0, in the TMSK2 register at $8D, bits 2, 1, and 0. The default state is 000 to divide by 1.

10.7   How is the timer overflow flag reset?

By the software writing a one to bit-7 of TFLG2 register.

10.9   Give the name of the bit, the name of the register that it is in, the register's address, which bit, and the default or reset state of the bit for each of the following:

a. What bit indicates that a comparison has been made on Output Compare 2?

C2F, in the TFLG1 register at $8E, bit 2. The reset state is 0.

b. What bit enables the Output Compare 2 interrupt?

C2I, in the TMSK1 register at $8C, bit 2. The reset state is interrupts disabled.

c. What bits are used to set the Output Compare 3 I/O pin high on a successful comparison?

OM3 and OL3 in the TCTL2 register at $89, bits 7 and 6. The reset state is for the timer to be disconnected from the output pin.

10.11 Write a small section of code to enable Output Compare 1 to set bits PT7, PT6, and PT5 to one on the next successful comparison.

```
ldaa    #%11100000    ; Set bits 7, 6, 5 high
staa    $83           ; Write the Output Compare data
                        register OC7D
staa    $82           ; Enable bits 7, 6, and 5 in OC7M
                        mask register
```

10.13 How does the programmer select the active edge for Input Capture 2?

Timer Control Register 4 (TCTL4) at $8B contains bits to select the edge used for the input capture. Bits 5 and 4 control the edge for IC2 by the following truth table:

EDG2B	EDG2A	Edge
0	0	Capture Disabled
0	1	Capture on rising edges only
1	0	Capture on falling edges only
1	1	Capture on any edge, rising or falling

10.15 Write a short section of code demonstrating how to enable the Input Capture 1 interrupts.

```
ldaa    #%00000010    ; C1I position
staa    $8C           ;Write to TMSK1
```

10.17 Write a short section of code demonstrating how to reset the COP timer.

```
ldaa    #$55    ; Arm pattern
staa    $17     ; Write to COPRST register
ldaa    #$AA    ; Reset pattern
staa    $17     ; Write to COPRST register
```

10.19 Write a short section of code demonstrating how to enable the Pulse Accumulator as a gated time accumulator with a high level enable accumulation.

```
bset    $A0,x    %01100000    ; Set PAEN and PAMOD in PACTL
bclr    $A0,x    %00010000    ; Clear PEDGE in PACTL
```

Solutions to Chapter 11 Problems

11.1 For the SCI0, give the name of the bit, the name of the register it is in, the register's address, which bit, and the default or reset state of the bit for each of the following:

a. What bit enables the SCI0 transmitter?

TE, in the SC0CR2 register at $C3, bit-3; the transmitter is disabled on reset.

b. What bit enables the SCI0 receiver?

RE, in the SC0CR2 register at $C3, bit-2; the receiver is disabled on reset.

c. What bit determines how many data bits are sent?

M (mode), in SC0CR1 at $C2, bit-4; the default is 1 start, 8 data, and 1 stop bit.

d. What bit can the user test to see if the last character has cleared the transmit data buffer?

TDRE, in the SC0SR1 at $C4, bit-7; the default is that the buffer is empty.

e. What bit can the user test to see if a new character has been received?

RDRF, in the SC0SR1 at $C4, bit-5; the default is that the register is not full.

f. What bit is used to indicate the software is not reading data from the SC0DRL fast enough?

OR, in SC0SR1 at $C4, bit-3; no overrun by default.

g. What bit is an indication that the communication channel is noisy?

NF, in SC0SR1 at $C4, bit-2; default is no noise.

h. What bit is an indication that the sending and receiving Baud rates may not be identical?

FE, in SC0SR1 at $C4, bit-1; default to no framing error.

11.3   What SCI0 receiver conditions can generate an interrupt?

Receive data register full, receiver overrun, idle line detect.

11.5   Give the meanings of the following mnemonics.

TDRE—Transmit Data Register Empty

TC—Transmission Complete

RDRF—Receive Data Register Full

OR—(Receiver) OverRun

FE—Framing Error

11.7   What is the value used to initialize the SCI0 for 4800 Baud assuming an E-clock = 8.0 MHz? 104_{10}

11.9   For the SPI, give the name of the bit, the name of the register it is in, the register's address, which bit, and the default or reset state of the bit for each of the following:

a. What bit enables the SPI?

SPE, in the SP0CR1 register at $D0, bit-6; the default state is SPI disabled.

b. What bit selects the master or slave mode?

MSTR, in the SP0CR1 register at $D0, bit-4; SPI configured as a slave.

c. What bits select the data transfer rate?

SPR2, SPR1, SPR0, in the SP0BR register at $D2, bit-2, -1, -0; the reset state is 000.

      d. What bit is the Master Output/Slave Input?

         MOSI, Port S, $D6, bit 5; the default is to act as Port S, bit 5.

      e. What bit is the Master Input/Slave Output?

         MISO, Port S, $D6, bit 4; the default is to act as Port S, bit 4.

11.11   How does the SPI differ from the SCI?

         The SPI is a synchronous serial port. Data bits are transferred from a master to a slave when the master generates an SCK signal. Data rates can be much higher with this system than with the SCI.

11.13   What do the following mnemonics mean in the operation of the SPI?

         $\overline{SS}$—Slave select; SCK—SPI Clock; MOSI—Master Out, Slave In; MOMI—Master Out, Master IN; MISO—Master In, Slave Out; SISO—Slave In, Slave Out; SPIE—SPI Interrupt Enable; SPE—SPI System Enable; MSTR—Master/slave Mode Select

Solutions to Chapter 12 Problems

12.1   How is the A/D powered up?

         By writing a 1 to the ADPU bit in the ATDCTL2 register.

12.3   The A/D is programmed to convert a sequence of four channels in continuous conversion mode. What is the maximum frequency signal on PAD0 that can be converted without aliasing (ignore aperture time effects, assume the final sample time is two ATD clocks and the ATD clock is 2 MHz).

         The conversion time for any one channel is 18 ATD clock periods giving the total sequence conversion time of 72 clocks = 36 μsec. Thus the sampling frequency for any one channel is 27.78 kHz and the Nyquist frequency is 13.89 kHz.

12.5   The analog input is 0 to 5 V and $V_{RH} = 5$, $V_{RL} = 0$. The A/D reading is $24. What is the analog input voltage?

         $24 = 36_{10}$. The resolution is 5 V/256 = 19.5 mV, therefore the input voltage is 36 × 19.5 mV = 0.70 V.

Solutions to Chapter 13 Problems

13.1   Using table look-up (instead of a fuzzy logic system), how many bytes would be needed for the table in a system with three inputs with 8 bit resolution on each input and one output with 8 bits resolution?

         256 × 256 × 256 = 16,777,216

13.3   Sketch graphic representations of the following input membership functions:

    a. LOW   FCB $20,$60,$08,$10   ;pt1,pt2,slope1,slope2

    b. MID   FCB $60,$A0,$10,$0B   ;pt1,pt2,slope1,slope2

    c. HI   FCB $A0,$E0,$0B,$08   ;pt1,pt2,slope1,slope2

13.5   For the fuzzy logic system in Example 13–4, how many bytes of memory in the knowledge base did it take for all 25 rules?

    There are 5 bytes for each rule = 125 bytes.

13.7   Using Figure 13–11, what value should be in FanSpeed if temperature is $B0 and pressure is $38?

    $50

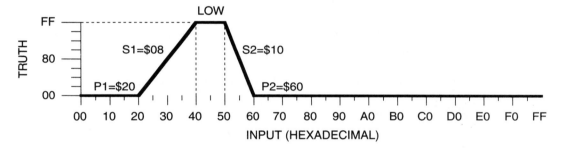

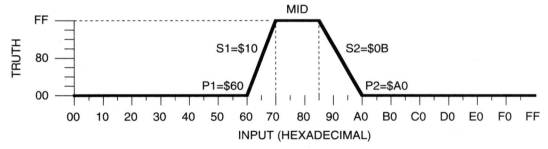

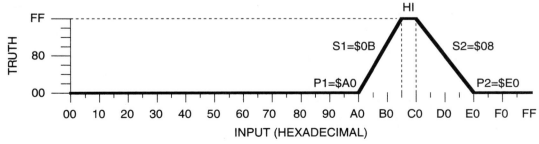

Problem 13–3

13.9   How many bytes of program space are used for the executable portion of the fuzzy logic program in Example 13–4?

!52

Solutions to Chapter 14 Problems

14.1   This is the waveform for one bit time in a BDM communication.

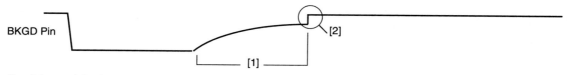

Problem 14-1

Which direction is data being transferred (host to target or target to host)?

From the target HC12 to the host pod.

14.3   This is the waveform for a BDM command. What is the command?

Problem 14-3

READ_BD_BYTE from address $FF01. The data value is $C0 (low half of $E4C0).

14.5   Draw an approximate waveform for a BDM command to write $81 to address $08F1.

Problem 14-5

14.7   Suppose a target application system is connected to a BDM pod. Which of the following types of memory could be programmed using the BDM interface?

a. An external 256-Kbyte RAM (in an MC68HC812A4 based system).

b. 32-Kbyte on chip flash EEPROM (in an MC68HC912B32 based system).

c. On chip EEPROM.

d. All of the above.

e. b and c.

d. All of the above. BDM can see any memory locations the CPU can see.

Use the following logic analyzer state listing to answer Problems 14.9 through 14.14.

```
* * * * * * * * * * * * * * * * * * * * * * * * * * * * * * * * * * * * *
Label>  ADDR  DATA  RW_TYP      PER      PEF
Base >  Hex   Hex   Symbol   Symbol   Symbol
   1    0822  7E09  R16         ALL      sev   ????/????  ????/????  ????/????
   2    7E09  7E09  R8L         LAT      sod   0822/7E09  ????/????  ????/????
   3    0824  01C6  R16         ALL            ????/????  0822/7E09  ????/????
   4____0826  64FD  R16_____ALD_____sev__????/????  0824/01C6  0822/7E09
   5    0901  7698  WLH  W      LAT            0822   7E0901   STX $0901
   6    7698  7698  R8H  O-f                   (write $9876 to $0901)
   7____0828  0800  R16_P___ALL____sod__
   8____082A  7D19  R16_P___ALD____sod__0825   C664     LDAB #$64  (100)
   9    0800  8602  R16  R      ALD            0827   FD0800   LDY $0800
  10    082C  01CE  R16  O-P                   (read $8602 from $0800)
  11____082E  6000  R16_P___ALD____sev__
  12    1901  1986  W8L  Wh     LAT            082A   7D1901   STY $1901
  13    1902  0202  W8H  Wl                    (write $8602 to $1901,1902)
  14    0202  0202  R8H  O-f
  15____0830  CD61  R16_P___ALL____int__
  16    FFEC  FF4E  R16  V      ALD            Begin processing interrupt
  17    09FE  082D  W16  S      LAT            (vector $FF4E fetched from $FFEC)
  18    FF4E  05FB  R16  P                     (this is the Timer Ch.1 vector)
  19    09FC  8602  W16  S      ALD
  20    09FA  9876  W16  S
  21    FF50  F89A  R16  P
  22    09F8  6402  W16  S      ALD
  23    09F7  0988  W8L  s
  24____FF52  05FB  R16_P_____sev__
* * * * * * * * * * * * * * * * * * * * * * * * * * * * * * * * * * * *
```

14.9   Beginning from state 001, reconstruct the internal pipe activity until you reach the start of an identifiable instruction. What is the address, opcode, and disassembled instruction?

Address=$0822, opcode=$7E, instruction=STX $0901.

14.11   There is an STY $1901 instruction in states 12–15. The instruction set documentation says this instruction should take three cycles. Why did it take four cycles?

The write was a misaligned write to an external address so it had to be split into two adjacent 8 bit writes.

14.13   An interrupt is serviced after state 15, what caused this interrupt?

The interrupt was caused by timer channel 1 because the vector address was $FFEC.

14.15   How is the tagging function enabled in the MC68HC12?

By the serial BDM command TAG_GO.

14.17   What value would you write to BRKCT0:BRKCT1 to establish a breakpoint for a write of $80 to PORTB (address $0001)?

   BKCTL0:BKCTL1 = $8452

14.19   What values would be written to all six registers in the breakpoint module to establish breakpoints for the instructions at $820 and $843?

BKCTL0:BKCTL1 = $EC40	or	BKCTL0:BKCTL1 = $EC40
BRKDH:BRKDL = $0843		BRKDH:BRKDL = $0820
BRKAH:BRKAL = $0820		BRKAH:BRKAL = $0843

INDEX